Alpha Five Desktop Applications Beyond The Basics

By Dr. Indera E. Murphy

Tolana Publishing
Teaneck, New Jersey

Published By:
Tolana Publishing
PO Box 719
Teaneck, NJ 07666 USA

Find us online at www.tolanapublishing.com
Inquiries may be sent to the publisher: tolanapub@yahoo.com

Our books are available online at www.barnesandnoble.com. They can also be ordered from Ingram.

Quantity discounts are available for corporations, non-profit organizations and educational institutions for educational purposes, fundraising or resale. www.tolana.com/wholesale.html

ISBN-13: 978-1-935208-24-2
ISBN-10: 1-935208-24-1

Library of Congress Control Number: 2013940469

Printed and bound in the United States Of America

Cover by Mary Kramer, owner of Milkweed Graphics, www.milkweedgraphics.com

v1.0

About The No Stress Tech Guide Series

Alpha Five Desktop Applications Beyond The Basics is part of a series of computer software books that are designed to be used as a self-paced learning tool. Our books can also be used in a classroom setting or in an online class. The books in this series contain an abundance of step-by-step instructions and screen shots to help reduce the "stress" often associated with learning new software. This book is geared towards the intermediate user. The other audience for this book is people that have already created basic desktop applications in Alpha Five and now want to take their skills to the next level.

Titles In The Series

Title	ISBN
ACT! 2007	978-0-9773912-5-7
ACT! 2009	978-1-935208-07-5
ACT! 2010	978-1-935208-09-9
ACT! Pro 2011	978-1-935208-13-6
ACT! Pro 2012	978-1-935208-17-4
Sage ACT! Pro 2013	978-1-935208-22-8
Using Crystal Reports 2008 With ACT! 2010 Databases	978-1-935208-10-5
Getting Started With Alpha Five Desktop Applications	978-1-935208-23-5
Alpha Five Desktop Applications Beyond The Basics	978-1-935208-24-2
Creating Reports & Charts For Alpha Five Desktop Applications Made Easy	978-1-935208-26-6
Using SAP Crystal Reports With Alpha Five Databases Made Easy	978-1-935208-25-9
Crystal Reports XI For Beginners (2nd Edition)	978-1-935208-00-6
What's New In Crystal Reports 2008	978-1-935208-01-3
Crystal Reports 2008 For Beginners	978-0-9773912-9-5
Crystal Reports 2011 For Beginners (2nd Edition)	978-1-935208-15-0
Crystal Reports Beyond The Basics	978-1-935208-18-1
Crystal Reports For Visual Studio 2005	978-0-9773912-6-4
Crystal Reports Basic For Visual Studio 2008	978-0-9773912-8-8
Crystal Reports For Visual Studio 2010	978-1-935208-12-9
Crystal Xcelsius 4.5	978-1-935208-02-0
Xcelsius 2008	978-1-935208-05-1
SAP Crystal Dashboard Design 2011 For Beginners	978-1-935208-11-2
OpenOffice.org 2 Writer	978-0-9773912-4-0
OpenOffice.org 3 Writer	978-1-935208-08-2
Microsoft Office Starter 2010 (Word & Excel)	978-1-935208-14-3
Microsoft PowerPivot For Excel 2010	978-1-935208-16-7
Microsoft Works 7	978-0-9773912-2-6
Microsoft Works 8 & 8.5	978-0-9773912-1-9
Microsoft Works 9	978-0-9773912-7-1
Windows XP	978-0-9773912-0-2

Why A Beyond The Basics Book For Alpha Five?

After receiving so much positive feedback from my first "Beyond" book (for a different software package), I came to the conclusion that there are a lot more non IT people using my books then I realized. I also realized that there are not a lot of books on Alpha Five.

The goal of my "Beyond" books is to provide coverage of topics that can help make the project that you are working on look as professional as possible. Many of the topics covered are often ones that have made me ask "How did they do that?"

About The Author

Dr. Indera Murphy is an author, educator and IT professional that has over 20 years of experience in the Information Technology field. She has held a variety of positions including technical writer, programmer, online adjunct professor, consultant, web designer, course developer and project leader. Indera has designed and developed software applications and websites, as well as, manage technology driven projects in several industries. In addition to being an Executive Director, she has taught courses in a variety of areas including project management, technical writing, Crystal Reports, information processing, Access, HTML, Windows, Excel, Dreamweaver and critical thinking.

Thank you for purchasing this book!

CONTENTS

COMMON TOOLBOX PANEL CONTROLS **6-1**

FORM TOOLBOX PANEL CONTROLS **7-1**

GETTING STARTED WITH ALPHA FIVE

This chapter provides a brief overview of what is covered in this book shows you how to download the files used in this book.

CHAPTER 1

Welcome To Alpha Five Desktop Applications Beyond The Basics!

This book picks up where my Getting Started With Alpha Five Desktop Applications book left off. The topics covered in this book will enhance basic applications. What is different in this book is that compared to the first book, which provides a lot of detailed information and steps, this book cuts to the chase. That is possible because this book is geared towards people that have already used the Desktop Edition of Alpha Five, version 11 or higher.

It is my sincere hope that whatever your current skill level is with Alpha Five, that you will learn more about features that you are already familiar with as you go through this book and that you learn about features that you did not know existed. Learning new tips and shortcuts will let you work faster and smarter. The more that you know about Alpha Five, the easier your day to day application design experiences will be.

So sit back, relax and lets get started!

How This Book Is Organized

Each chapter covers specific topics. This book is designed to be read from cover to cover. I do not advise skipping around in the book because some of the files needed in later chapters are created in earlier chapters. Below is an overview of what is covered in each chapter.

Chapter 1, Getting Started With Alpha Five covers background information, conventions that I use in this book and downloading the practice files.

Chapter 2, Tables And Sets covers the options on the Utilities submenu.

Chapter 3, Database Maintenance covers features that will help keep your applications running smoothly.

Chapter 4, View, Records And Tools Menu Options covers options on the View, Records and Tools menus that are for databases, tables and sets.

Chapter 5, Using Functions covers how to use some of the most popular functions in Alpha Five.

Chapter 6, Common Toolbox Panel Controls covers the controls that are available for several types of layouts.

Chapter 7, Form Toolbox Panel Controls covers the controls that are specifically for forms.

Chapter 8, Super Controls covers the controls in the Super Controls section of the Toolbox panel.

Chapter 9, Enhancing Forms covers features like Action Scripting and controls that you can use to make forms that you create look more professional.

Chapter 10, Enhancing A Browse covers features like Browse Controls that you can use to make browses that you create have more functionality.

Chapter 11, Sorting, Filtering And Querying Data covers different ways to search for records on a form or browse and using various tools to create queries.

Chapter 12, Importing Data covers tools and techniques used to import data into Alpha Five.

Chapter 13, Using Operations covers creating and using Ad-Hoc and other data manipulating operations.

Chapter 14, Exporting Data covers options to put data in an Alpha Five database into a different file format.

Chapter 15, Using Xdialog covers creating a dialog box that has prompts and displays data.

Chapter 16, Custom Menus And Toolbars covers creating menus and toolbars for forms, browses and reports.

Chapter 17, Customize An Application covers topics to finish an application, including startup forms, passwords and security.

Objectives Of This Book

The primary objective of this book is to introduce a variety of features in Alpha Five that can take the applications that you create to the next level. Because this is not a beginners book, you should know how to do the following in Alpha Five.

- ☑ Create and duplicate tables and sets
- ☑ Create forms from scratch
- ☑ Create basic reports

There seems to be a growing trend of Microsoft Access developers also using Alpha Five. As one that has used Access to develop applications, I understand. The good news is that there is a section in this book on importing data from Microsoft Access databases into Alpha Five.

This book is a visual guide that shows you how to use a large number of the features in Alpha Five. There are over 650 illustrations that practically eliminate the guess work and let you know that you are doing the steps correctly.

Step-by-step instructions are included throughout this book. This book takes a hands-on approach to teaching you how to use features in Alpha Five to provide the skills required to enhance desktop applications. After completing the exercises in this book, you will be able to perform the following tasks and more:

- ☑ Use the Toolbox controls to add functionality to forms
- ☑ Back up a database or specific objects in the database
- ☑ Use functions and create expressions
- ☑ Export Alpha Five data to other formats
- ☑ Enhance lookup lists
- ☑ Create operations

Conventions Used In This Book

I designed the following conventions to make it easier for you to follow the instructions in this book.

- ☑ The `Courier` font is used to indicate what you should type.
- ☑ **Drag** means to press and hold down the left mouse button while moving the mouse.
- ☑ **Right-click** means to press the right mouse button once, which will open a shortcut menu.

- ☑ **Click OK** means to click the OK button on the dialog box.
- ☑ **Press Enter** means to press the Enter key on your keyboard.
- ☑ **Press Next** means to click the Next button on the dialog box.
- ☑ **Click Finish** means to click the Finish button on the dialog box.
- ☑ **SMALL CAPS** are used to indicate an option to click on or to bring something to your attention.
- ☑ This icon indicates a shortcut or another way to complete the task that is being discussed. It can also indicate a tip or additional information about the topic that is being discussed. Some of this information comes from my experience in the IT field.
- ☑ This icon indicates a warning, like a feature that has been removed or information that you need to be aware of. This icon can also represent what I call a quirk, meaning a feature that did not work as I expected it to.
- ☑ This icon represents what I call an "Alpha Five-Ism". This means that the term or concept being presented is called something different in Alpha Five then it is commonly known as or called in many other software packages. Hopefully, this will help in the transition, if you have used other database or report design software.
- ☑ All of the files that you create and save will start with the letter "a". This will put them at the top of the list of file names on the Alpha Five Control Panel. This will make is easy to tell which files you create versus the practice files.
- ☑ [See Chapter 3, Database Concepts] refers to a section in a different chapter then the one you are currently viewing that you can use as a reference for the topic that is being discussed.
- ☑ [See Chapter 2, Figure 2-8] refers to an illustration (screen shot) in a different chapter then the one you are currently viewing that you can use as a reference for the topic that is being discussed.
- ☑ [See Show Break] or [See Figure 6-7] refers to a section or figure later in the chapter that you are currently in.
- ☑ When you see the instruction "Click the (field or option name) button", it means to click the button at the end of the field or option.
- ☑ Many of the dialog boxes in Alpha Five have OK, Cancel and Help buttons on the right side or bottom. Viewing these buttons on all of the screen shots adds no value, so they are not shown in the figures.
- ☑ When you see "**YOU SHOULD HAVE THE OPTIONS SHOWN IN FIGURE X-X**", or something similar in the exercises, check to make sure that your screen does look like the figure. If it does, continue with the next set of instructions. If your screen does not look like the figure, redo the steps that you just completed so that your screen does match the figure. Not doing so may cause you problems when trying to complete exercises later in the book.
- ☑ The section heading **EXERCISE X.Y:** (where X equals the chapter number and Y equals the exercise number) represents exercises that have step-by-step instructions that you should complete. You will also see sections that have step-by-step instructions that are not an exercise. Completing them as you go through the book is optional, but recommended.
- ☑ **TOOLS ⇒ FEATURE PACKS ⇒ INSTALL OPTIONAL FEATURE PACKS** means to open the **TOOLS** menu, select the option **FEATURE PACKS**, then select the **INSTALL OPTIONAL FEATURE PACKS** option, as shown in Figure 1-1.

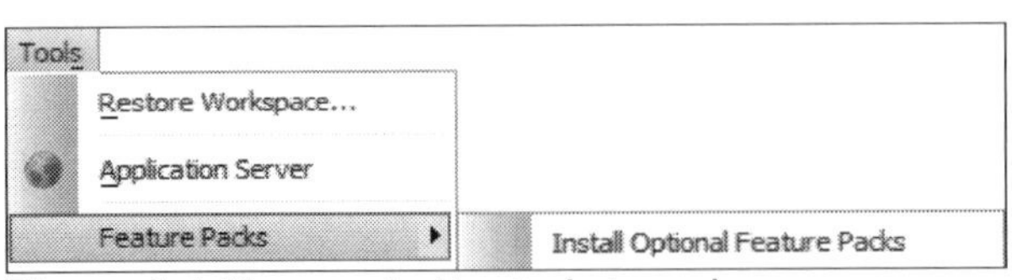

Figure 1-1 Menu navigation technique shown

Assumptions

Yes, I know one should never assume anything, but the following assumptions have been made. It is assumed that you . . . .

☑ Have Alpha Five version 11 or higher installed on your computer. If you are not sure what version you have installed, open Alpha Five, then select Help ⇒ About Alpha Five. You will see the version that is installed, at the top of the dialog box.

☑ Know that the version of Alpha Five used to write this book is Alpha Five, version 11.

☑ Know that you can select whether the term "Workspace" or "Database" is displayed in the software. For example, if Workspace is selected as the default option, when the Recent button on the Control Panel is clicked, the dialog box that opens will display "Select Workspace", as shown in the upper left corner of Figure 1-2, instead of "Select Databases". If you have Database selected as the default, keep this in mind when going through the book because your software will not look like some of the screen shots.

☑ Know that the operating system used to write this book is Windows 7. If you are using a different version of Windows, any or all of the following can apply:

① Some of the screen shots may have a slightly different look.

② Some of the instructions for Windows tasks may be different.

③ The path to folders and files on your computer may be different then the paths listed in this book.

☑ Understand that from time to time, I will point out functionality that may not work as expected. When I do this, I am not complaining, merely pointing out things that you should be aware of.

☑ Know that I am not perfect and sadly, you may find minor mistakes in this book. It is not intentional and I apologize for any inconvenience.

☑ Know that when you see <smile> in this book, it signifies my attempt of adding humor to the learning process.

☑ Understand that the term **OBJECT** refers to the tables, sets, browses, forms and reports that you create, as well as, items like buttons or images.

☑ Understand that most objects are saved as one word (for example, CustomerList) and are displayed that way on the Control Panel. In the instructions in this book, the object names are displayed with spaces between the words (for example Customer List) to make them easier to read.

☑ Have access to the Internet to download the practice files needed to complete the exercises in this book and to view some of the files that you will create.

☑ Understand that there will be options on dialog boxes that will not be referenced in the step-by-step instructions. When that is the case, accept the default value.

☑ That you know to click OK or the appropriate button to close a dialog box and know to save the changes.

☑ Optional: That you have Excel installed if you want to view any of the data that is exported to Excel.

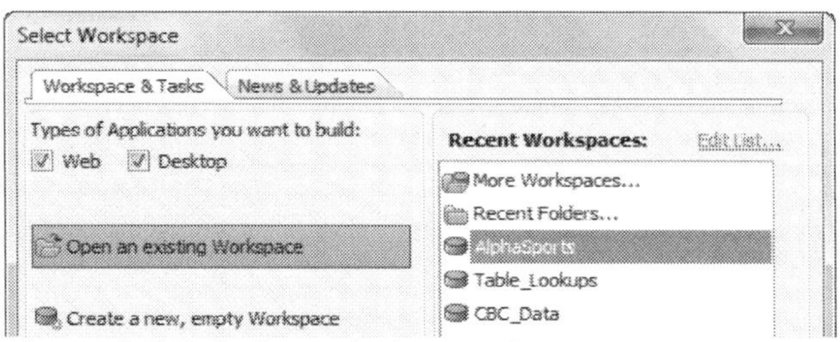

Figure 1-2 Default terminology setting

Exercise 1.1: Create A Folder For This Book And Download The Practice Files

In this book, you will learn how to perform tasks and create objects that would be used in a database application. It is a good idea to store all of the files in the same folder on your computers hard drive so that you can find them easily. I will refer to this folder as "your folder" throughout the book. The instructions below show you how to create the folder at the root of the C drive. If you want to create the folder in another location or under an existing folder, navigate to that location prior to starting step 2.

1. Open Windows Explorer, then click on the C drive.
2. File ⇒ New ⇒ Folder.
3. Type `A5 Beyond Book` as the folder name, then press Enter.
4. The practice files for this book are in a zip file named a5beyond.zip. To have the link for the zip file sent to you, send an email to a5beyond@tolanapublishing.com. If you do not receive an email in a few minutes with the subject line Alpha 5 Beyond The Basics Files, check the spam folder in your email software.
5. When you have the zip file, extract the files to your folder.
6. Open Alpha Five. On the Select Workspace dialog box shown above in Figure 1-2, click on the **MORE WORKSPACES** folder, then click OK. Navigate to your folder, then double-click on the a5beyond.dbf file.

Changing The Default Private Path Folder Location

By default, Alpha Five saves some files, like export files, to the Private Path folder illustrated in Figure 1-3.

View ⇒ Settings, opens this dialog box.

The default private path points to a temp folder on the computers hard drive.

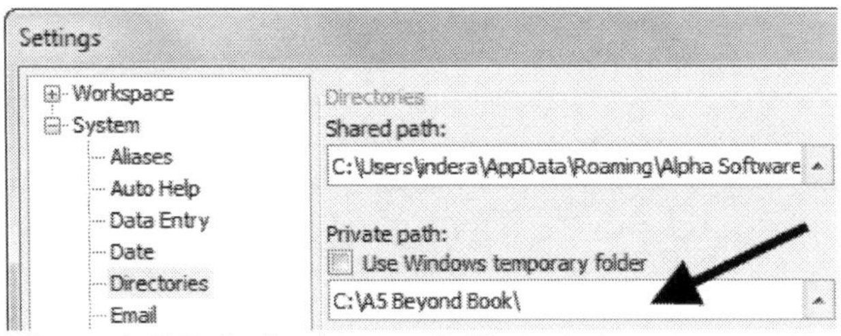

Figure 1-3 Default private path illustrated

If you want, you can change this folder to the folder that you created in Exercise 1-1, as shown in Figure 1-3, then change it back once you have completed this book. Doing this is optional, but it will make it easier to get to the files needed to complete the exercises in this book.

TABLES AND SETS

In this chapter you will learn about the following features that will enhance the functionality of tables and sets:

- ☑ Options on the selected table or set Utilities submenu
- ☑ Creating lookup lists
- ☑ Mapped tables

CHAPTER 2

Overview

Tables and sets are the foundation for creating forms, reports and other objects. Making sure that they are created properly will save you hours of headaches and time going forward. This chapter covers features that you can add to tables and sets so that additional functionality can be added to the forms, reports and other objects that are based on them.

> **Duplicating Objects**
> Many of the objects in the practice database will be used more than once. To preserve them, duplicate them and save them with a new name. The first step in most exercises will instruct you to save the object (table, form, etc.) with a new name. There are two options for saving an object with a new name, as explained below.
> ① Open the object in Design mode. File ⇒ Save As or click the Save As button, if available.
> ② Right-click on the object and select Duplicate, then type in the new name. For tables and sets, select Utilities, then select Duplicate.
>
> When prompted what to duplicate on the Duplicate Table (or Duplicate Set) dialog box, only duplicate the records and indexes, unless stated otherwise. When prompted to view the object, click No.

Modifying Lookup Lists

When you first create a lookup list, it may seem to be exactly what you need. While testing it, you may discover that some changes would make the lookup list look better. The next few exercises show you how to add more functionality to lookup lists by using options on the Field Rules dialog box.

Exercise 2.1: Modify The Simple List Lookup Style

In this exercise you will learn how to change the order of the entries in the list, add a column to the list and allow the user to add items to the lookup list.

Reorder The List

1. Save the Order lookup table as `aSimpleList`. Include the Dictionary and Field Rules.

2. On the Field Rules dialog box Lookups tab, select the How Shipped field.

   You should see the Simple list shown in Figure 2-1.

   As you can see, the entries are not in alphabetical order.

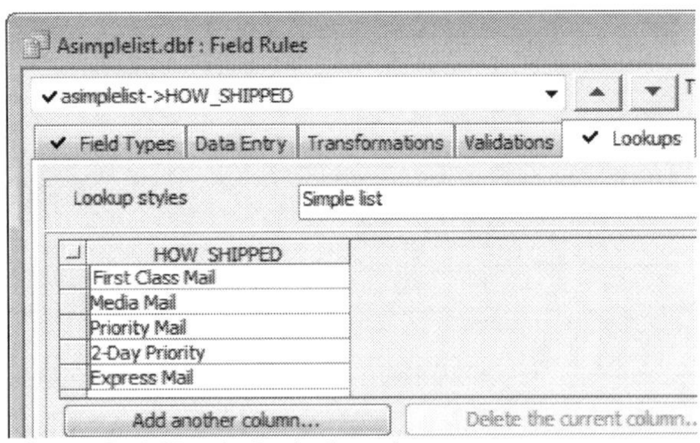

Figure 2-1 Simple list before changes

3. Click on the box to the left of the 2-Day Priority option, then drag the entry to the top of the list.

4. Move the Express Mail option up, below the 2-Day Priority option.

Add Another Column To The List

The list may be more useful if each option displayed the delivery time.

1. Click the **ADD ANOTHER COLUMN** button, then select the Delivery Time field, as shown in Figure 2-2.

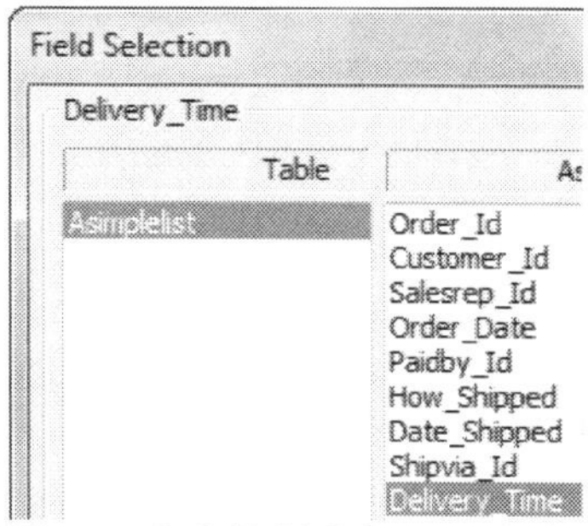

Figure 2-2 Field Selection dialog box

2. Type the values shown in Figure 2-3 in the Delivery Time column.

   Now when the How Shipped field is used on a form or browse, these are the values that will be displayed in the drop-down list.

Lookup styles: Simple list

HOW_SHIPPED	DELIVERY_TIME
2-Day Priority	2 days
Express Mail	2 days
First Class Mail	3-5 days
Media Mail	5-15 days
Priority Mail	2-3 days

Figure 2-3 Second column of values added to the Simple list

Exercise 2.2: Allow Records To Be Added To The Lookup Table

In this exercise, you will modify the Sales Rep ID field by creating a field rule that allows the user to add new sales reps to the list.

1. Duplicate the Orders table. Save it as `aTableLookup`.

   Clear the Dictionary and Field rules options shown in Figure 2-4.

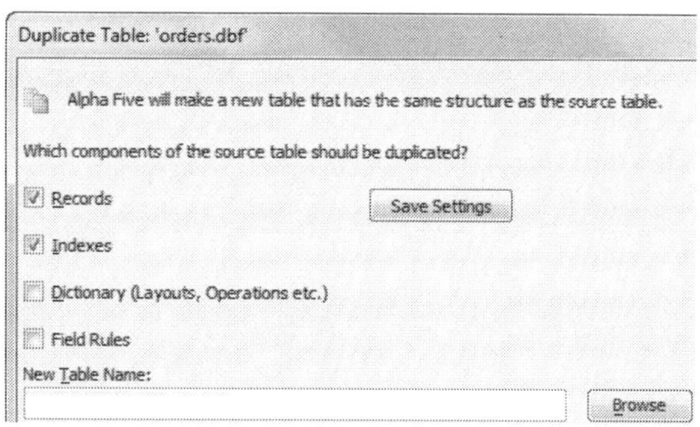

Figure 2-4 Duplicate Table dialog box

2. On the Field Rules dialog box Lookups tab, select the Salesrep ID field.

   Select the Table Lookup option, then select the options shown in Figure 2-5.

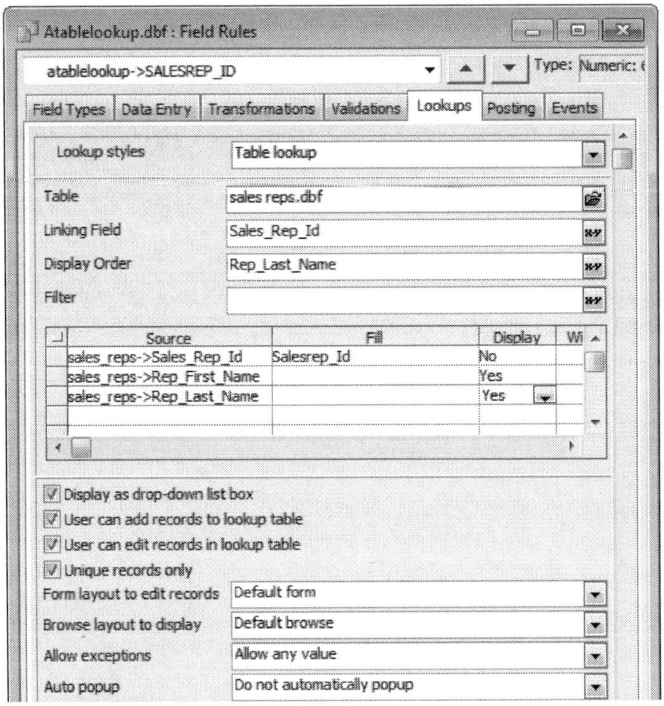

Figure 2-5 Table Lookup options

3. Display the aTableLookup table in the Default Form, then open the Sales Rep ID field drop-down list, which should look like the one shown in Figure 2-6.

   The reason that you see the Rep First Name in the field instead of the Sales Rep ID is because the ID field was not selected to be displayed in the drop-down list.

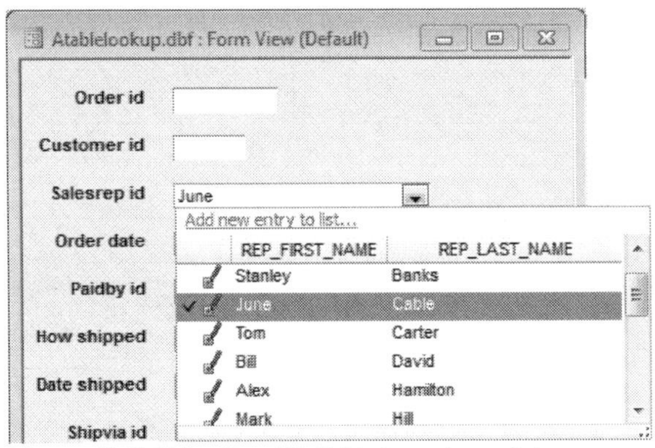

Figure 2-6 Sales Rep ID field drop-down list

4. Click the **ADD NEW ENTRY TO LIST** link and add yourself as a sales rep.

Using Previous Values

This type of lookup can save time because the lookup displays values that have already been entered in the field. This will allow the user to select one of the existing values or enter a new value.

Exercise 2.3: Create A Previous Values Lookup

In this exercise you will learn how to create a previous values lookup field rule for the Product ID field in a table that stores the products that are on each order.

1. Save the Order Detail table as `aPreviousValues`.

2. Select the Lookups tab options shown in Figure 2-7 for the Product ID field. When you view the Product ID field in the aPreviousValues table in a form or browse, you will see a list of the values already entered in the field (from previous records) in a drop-down list, as shown in Figure 2-8.

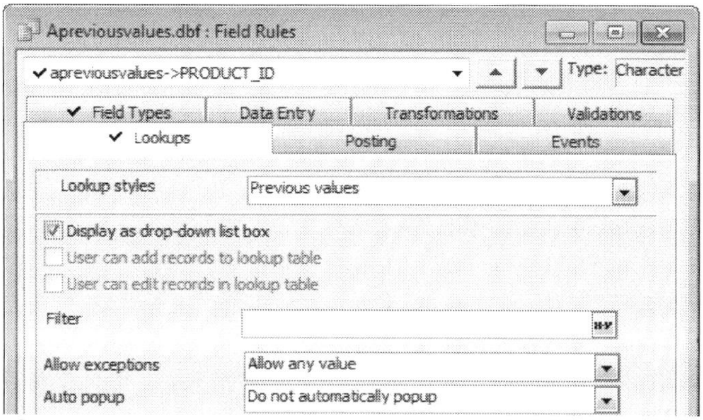

Figure 2-7 Previous values lookup options

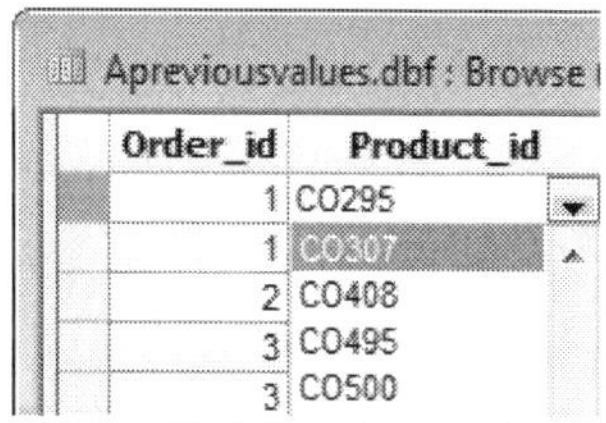

Figure 2-8 Previous values displayed in the drop-down list

Cascading List Lookup

This type of lookup is best suited when there are a lot of values to be displayed that can be categorized. This lookup type is used to create submenus. The down side to this type of lookup is that the values in the submenu are not stored in a table.

This lookup style is very easy to create and is best suited for values that do not change. Type each entry on a separate line. Type the category, then type the entries for the category. These entries must be preceded by a + (plus sign).

Exercise 2.4: Create A Cascading List Submenu

In this exercise you will learn how to create a lookup field rule that resembles a submenu.

1. Save the Products table as `aCascadingSubmenu`.

2. Type the options shown in Figure 2-9 on the Lookups tab for the Product Name field.

   The cascading menu should look like the one shown in Figure 2-10 and Figure 2-11 when viewed on a form.

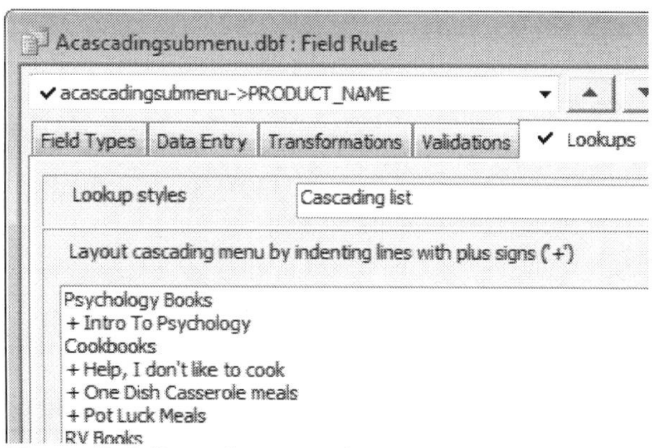

Figure 2-9 Cascading menu layout

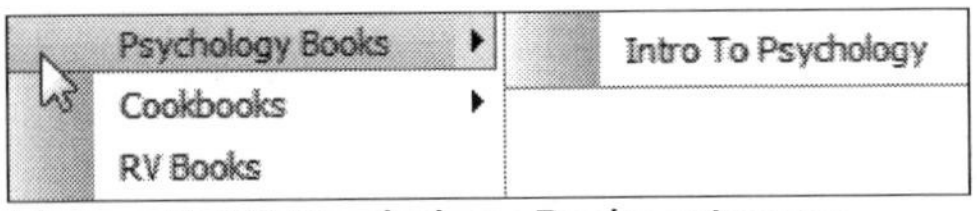

Figure 2-10 Psychology Books category

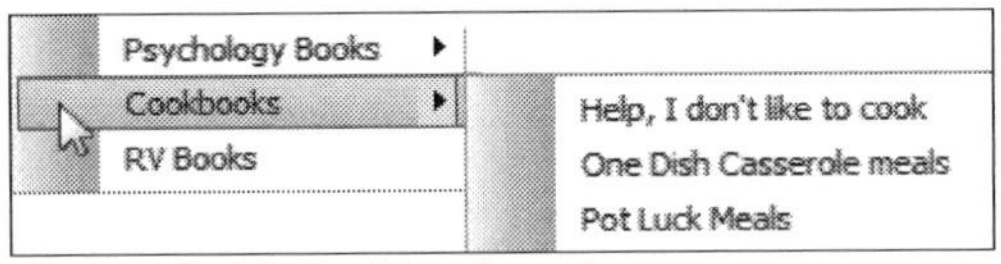

Figure 2-11 Cookbooks category

If you change the Cookbooks entries to look like the ones shown in Figure 2-12, the cascading menu will look like the one shown in Figure 2-13.

Typing ++ before an entry places the entry on a new submenu.

```
Cookbooks
+Help, I don't like to cook
+One Dish Casserole meals
++Casserole meals for the slow cooker
++Casserole meals for the frying pan
+Pot Luck Meals
```

Figure 2-12 Additional list entries

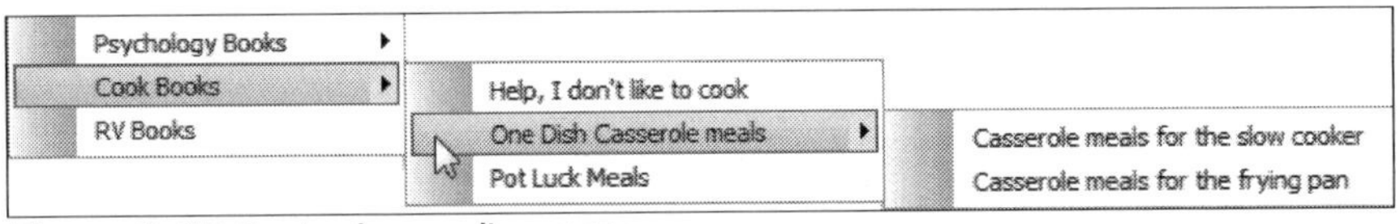

Figure 2-13 Revised cascading menu

Field Rules Posting Tab

During data entry, the options shown in Figure 2-14 are used to change (replace, add or subtract) the value in a field in one table with the value in a field in a different table. The options on this tab are used to create a condition on which the value in a field is automatically changed. This is different then using a **POST OPERATION** because the changes happen immediately, on a record by record basis, when using the options on the Posting tab, instead of being processed as a group when a Post operation is run.

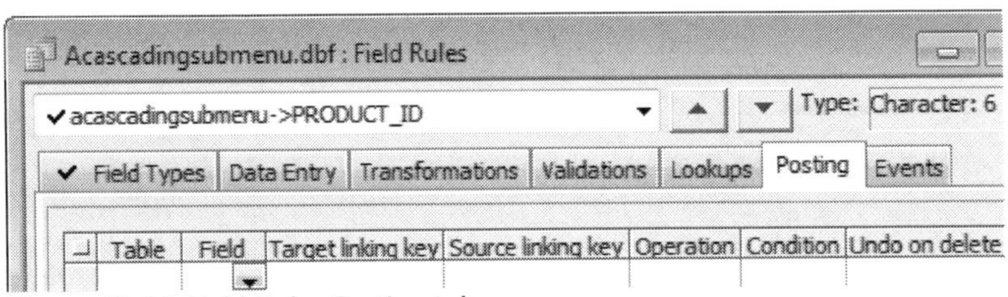

Figure 2-14 Field Rules Posting tab

Posting Tab Options

The columns in the grid on the Posting tab are used to select the following:

① The table and field that will be updated.
② The linking field (target and source) or expression for the tables.
③ The type of change (See Operations below).
④ Criteria (the condition) that the table being updated must meet.
⑤ Whether or not the data change from the posting field rule should be undone in the target table if the corresponding record in the source table is deleted.

> Posting field rules only work when data is changed on a form or browse. The posting rules do not work in web applications or from an Xbasic operation.

Operations

The three types of operations are explained below.

① **REPLACE** Overwrites the value in the target table field with the value from the source table field.
② **ADD** Adds the value in the source table field to the value in the target table field. (1)
③ **SUBTRACT** Subtracts the value in the source table field from the value in the target table field. (1)

(1) This option is only available for numeric fields.

Exercise 2.5: Create A Posting Field Rule To Update Contact Record Zip Codes

In this exercise you will learn how to create a posting field rule that will replace the zip code of records in the Contacts table, when the corresponding record in the Customer table has a zip code change. In this exercise the change will only occur if the state equals PA.

1. Save the Customers table as `aPostingRule`.

2. On the Posting tab, select the Zip Code field in the drop-down list.

3. Click the button at the end of the Table column and select the Contacts table. This is the table that will be updated. (This is the **TARGET TABLE**.)

4. Select the following options. Some of the options can be selected on the Expression Builder.
   Field column - Postal Code field
   Target Linking Key column - Contact ID field
   Source Linking Key column - Customer ID field
   Operation column - Replace

5. In the Condition column create the expression shown in Figure 2-15.

   You should have the options shown in Figure 2-16. Save the changes.

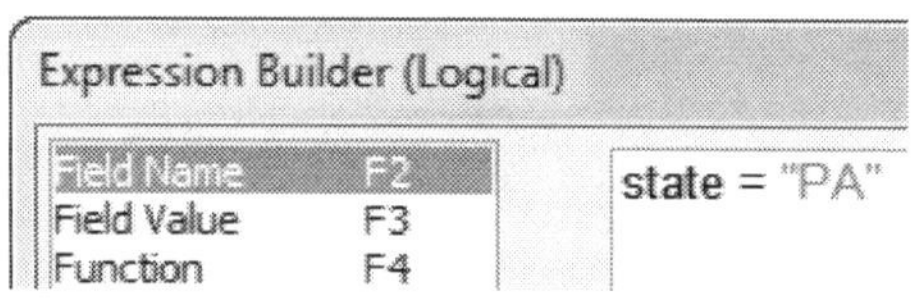

Figure 2-15 Expression to limit changes to records in PA

Table	Field	Target linking key	Source linking key	Operation	Condition	Undo on delete
contacts.dbf	contacts->Postal_Code	Contact_Id	Customer_Id	Replace	state = "PA"	

Figure 2-16 Posting field rule

Test The Posting Field Rule

1. Write down the ID numbers of the records that you are about to change. In the aPostingRule table, change the zip code for a record in PA and a record not in PA.

2. View the Contacts table in a browse. Look at the zip code for the records that you changed. The record in PA should have the new zip code that you entered. The record not in PA that you changed, should not have the new zip code that you typed in.

Field Rules Events Tab

The options shown in Figure 2-17 are used to create a field or record event. The options in the **EVENT** drop-down list are used to select when you want the event to occur. The options available depend on whether the Field Events or Record Events option is selected.

The **OPEN CODE EDITOR** button is used to create a script if you do not want to type or paste it in the box at the bottom of the dialog box. The options are explained below.

① **ACTION SCRIPTING** Using this option creates an action script, then automatically pastes the code in the box at the bottom of the Events tab. This action script is saved with the table, not as a separate object, like the action scripts are that are created from the Code tab on the Control Panel. Figure 2-18 shows the shortcut menu for the box at the bottom of the dialog box.

② **XBASIC** Opens the Code Editor to create the script.

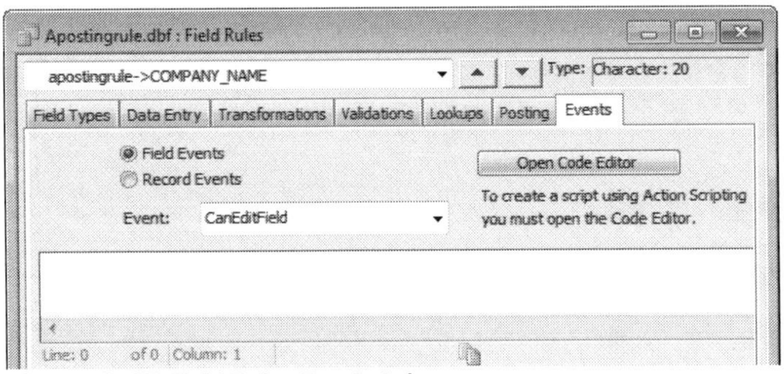

Figure 2-17 Field Rules Events tab

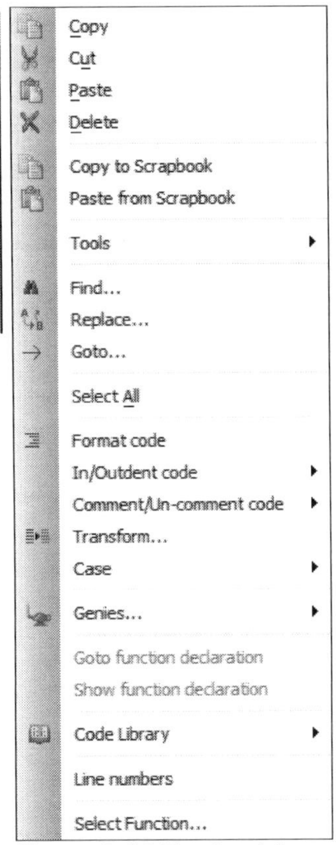

Figure 2-18 Event script shortcut menu

Calculated Field Rules

In Exercise 2.5 you learned one way to update data in a table using a posting field rule. Calculated field rules go further because you can create an expression to fill in the value in a field and using another table is not a requirement.

Exercise 2.6: Calculate The Line Item Total

In this exercise you will create a field rule to calculate the total amount (Quantity * Price) for each item ordered and store the total amount in a field. Calculated field rules are created on the Field Types tab on the Field Rules dialog box. In the real world you would not store a line item total amount in a field in a table. It is done here for illustration purposes.

1. Save the Order Detail table as `aCalculatedFieldRule`.

2. Create a numeric field in the aCalculatedFieldRule table named `Line Total`. Make the Width 8 and Decimal places 2.

3. On the Field Rules dialog box, select the Line Total field, then select the Calculated option on the Field Types tab.

   Type the formula `Qty * Price` in the **CALCULATED FIELD EXPRESSION** field shown at the bottom of Figure 2-19.

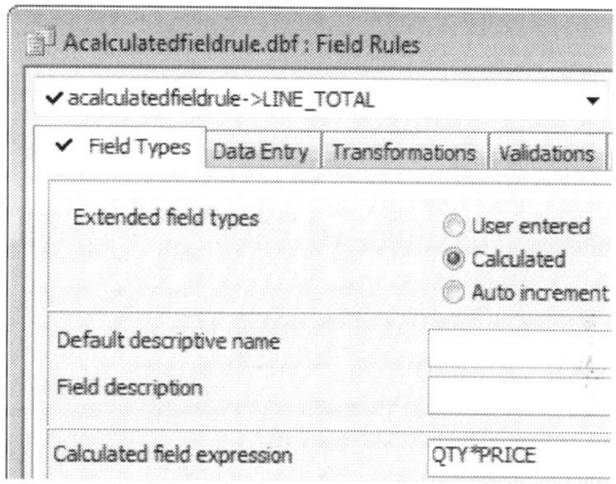

Figure 2-19 Calculated field expression

4. Display the aCalculatedFieldRule table in the Default Browse. Add a record to the table. The Line Total field should have automatically been filled in.

> **Recalculate Field Rules**
> As you saw at the end of the previous exercise, the Line Total field for the records already in the table before the calculated field was created, were not automatically updated. If you want the field rule applied to records already in the table, select one of the options below.
> ① Right-click on the table ⇒ Utilities ⇒ Recalculate Calc Fields.
> ② Open the Field Rules dialog box ⇒ Rules menu ⇒ Re-Evaluate Rules.

Mapped Tables

A mapped table is a virtual table that contains data from at least two tables. You can select fields from the tables to create a mapped table. All of the links used to create a mapped table must be one-to-one relationships. You can also create calculated fields that will be saved in the mapped table.

Like the other tables on the Tables/Sets tab, you can use a mapped table to create forms, reports and more. Mapped tables can be read-only or updatable. Only data in fields from the parent table can be changed by the user. Below are some scenarios of when you may need to create a mapped table.

① You need to use data from more than one table to create a Table Lookup field rule. This is because the Field Rules dialog box does not allow you to select a set as the data source.

② You need to export data from two or more tables to Excel or need a calculated field as part of the export. You can use a Layout Table report to export data from two or more tables.

Exercise 2.7: Create A Mapped Table

In this exercise you will learn how to create a mapped table that has fields from three tables: Orders, Customers and Sales Reps.

Select The Tables For The Mapped Table

1. On the Tables/Sets tab, New button ⇒ New Mapped Table.

2. On the Tables tab, click the **ADD TABLE BUTTON**, then select the Orders table on the dialog box shown in Figure 2-20.

   Notice that the Orders table is listed as the Top level table in the Link Properties section on the Create Mapped Table dialog box.

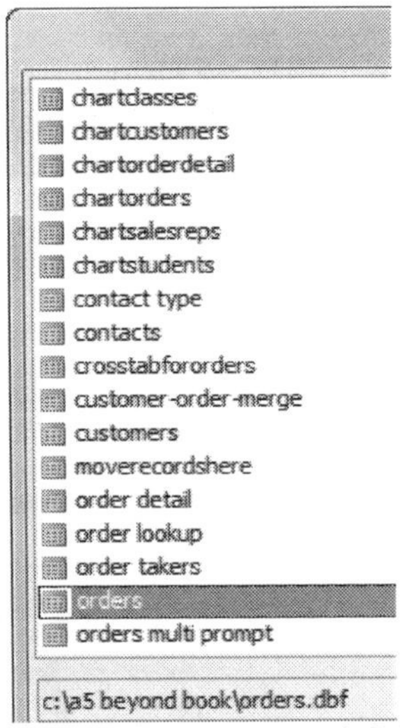

Figure 2-20 Unnamed dialog box to select a table

3. Repeat step 2 to add the Customers table.

4. Click on the Orders table, then add the Sales Reps table.

Tables Tab Options

The default **LINK PROPERTIES** shown in Figure 2-21 are correct for the Customers table. The Link Properties options are explained in Table 2-1.

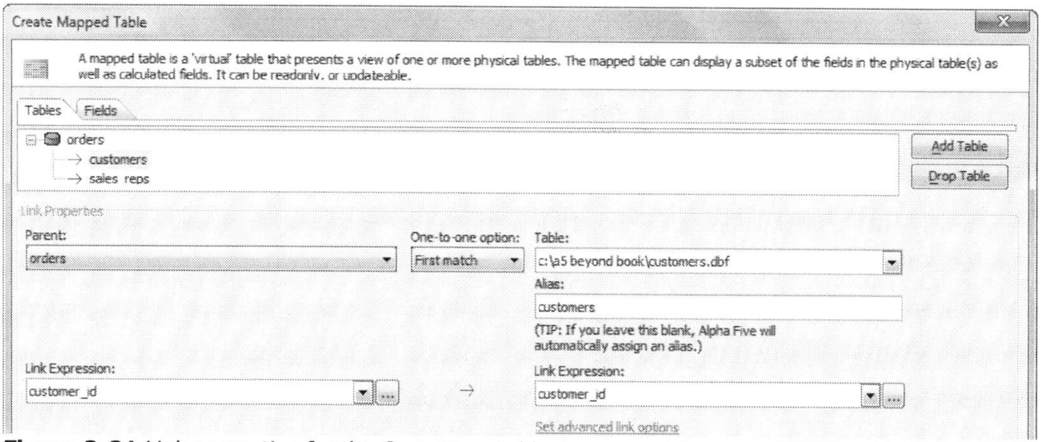

Figure 2-21 Link properties for the Customers table

Option	Description
Parent	Name of the Parent table. The fields selected from this table can be updated.
One-to-one option	[See Table 2-2]
Table	Displays the path to the child table.
Alias	Defaults to the table name. You can change this option if you need to refer to the table by a different name.
Link Expression	Is used to select the field from the table that will be used to link the parent and child tables. By default, if both tables have a field with the same name, it will be selected as the field to link on. If necessary, you can change the field or create an expression to link on by clicking the button at the end of the field.
Set advanced link options	[See Advanced Link Options Dialog Box]

Table 2-1 Link properties options explained

One To One Options

The options in this drop-down list are used to select which matching record to use to link the tables.

Option	Description
First Match	The first matching record found in the child table will be linked to, even if there are more matching records.
Closest Match	The closest matching record in the child table will be linked to, if no exact match is found.
Last Match	Only the last matching record found in the child table will be linked to.

Table 2-2 Link properties options explained

Select The Link Expression Options

When the Sales Reps table was added, it was not automatically linked to the Orders table.

1. Click on the Sales Reps table.

2. Open the Link Expression drop-down list for the Parent table and select the Salesrep ID field.

3. Open the Link Expression drop-down list for the Child table and select the Sales Rep ID field. You should have the options shown in Figure 2-22 for the Sales Reps table.

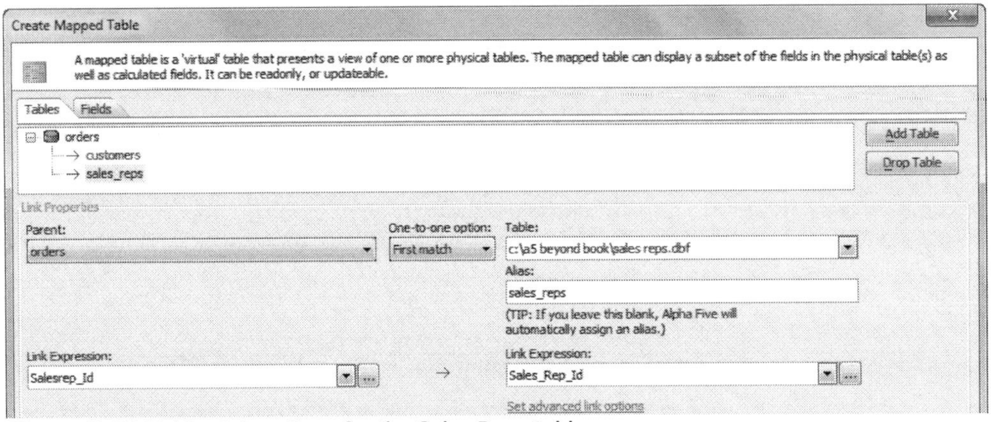

Figure 2-22 Tables tab options for the Sales Reps table

> **Linking Child Tables**
> In addition to creating relationships with the parent table, relationships can be created with the child table, as illustrated in Figure 2-23, as long as it is a one-to-one relationship. This is the same functionality as the **GRANDCHILD TABLE** in a set.

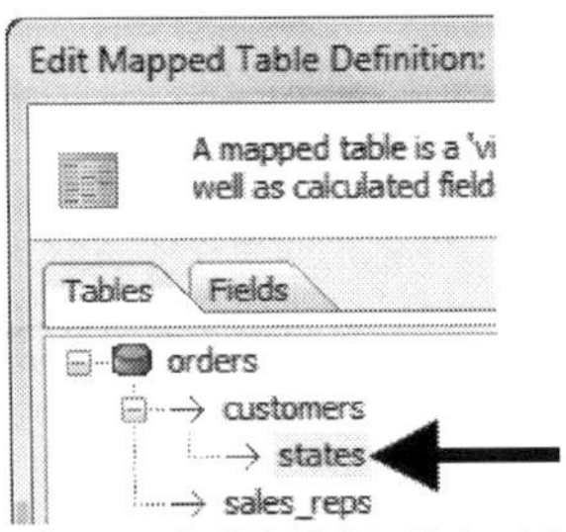

Figure 2-23 Table linked to a child

Advanced Link Options Dialog Box

The options shown in Figure 2-24 are used to select whether or not records from the parent table should be displayed if there is no matching record in the child table. The options are explained below.

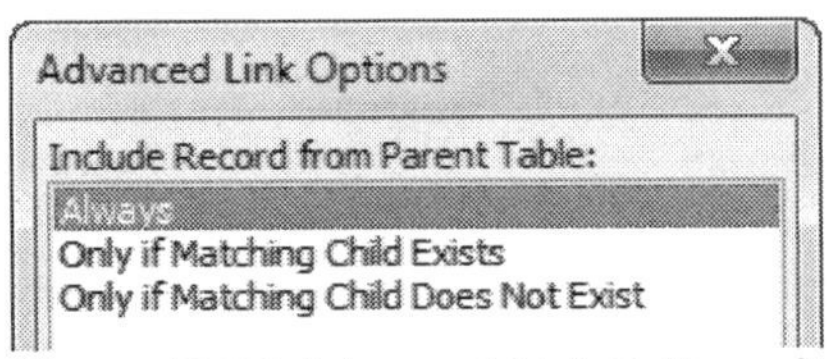

Figure 2-24 Advanced Link Options dialog box

- ☑ **ALWAYS** Is the default. This option will always include the parent record even if no matching child records are found.
- ☑ **ONLY IF MATCHING CHILD EXISTS** Only include the parent record if a matching child record is found.
- ☑ **ONLY IF MATCHING CHILD DOES NOT EXIST** Only include the parent record if there is no matching child record. This option in my opinion, is useful on a report that is being used to clean up data. Records that appear on this type of report indicate a problem with the data.

Fields Tab Options

The options on the tab shown in Figure 2-25 are used to select the fields that will be added to the mapped table. The options are explained below.

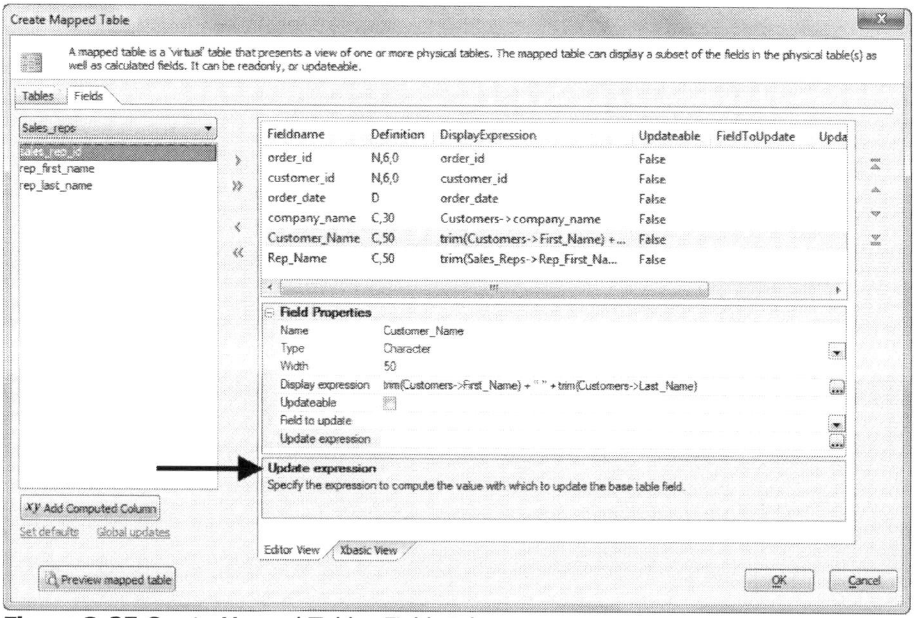

Figure 2-25 Create Mapped Tables Fields tab

① The **MOVE BUTTONS** are on the right side of the dialog box. They are used to rearrange the order of the fields that will be added to the mapped table.

② The **XY ADD COMPUTED COLUMN BUTTON** opens the Define Calculated Field dialog box shown in Figure 2-31. The options are used to create a calculated field that will be added to the mapped table.

③ The **SET DEFAULTS LINK** opens the dialog box shown in Figure 2-26. Selecting the option on this dialog box allows new fields that you add to the mapped table to automatically be set to updateable.

④ The **GLOBAL UPDATES LINK** displays the message shown in Figure 2-27. Clicking Yes will change all fields marked as updateable to Not-updateable.

⑤ The **XBASIC VIEW TAB** shown in Figure 2-28 displays the code that was automatically created based on the options selected on the **EDITOR VIEW TAB**.

⑥ Once a field has been selected to be added to the mapped table, the **PREVIEW MAPPED TABLE BUTTON** will display the data that will be added to the mapped table, as shown in Figure 2-29.

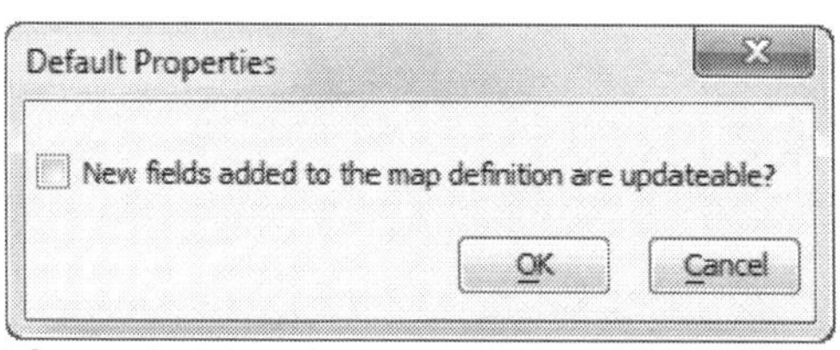

Figure 2-26 Default Properties dialog box

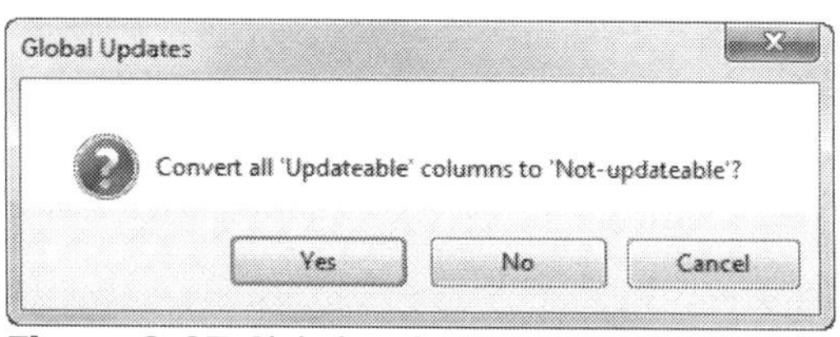

Figure 2-27 Global update message

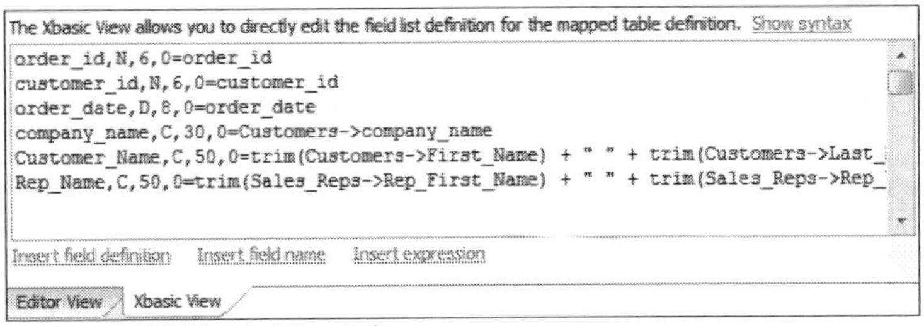

Figure 2-28 Xbasic View tab

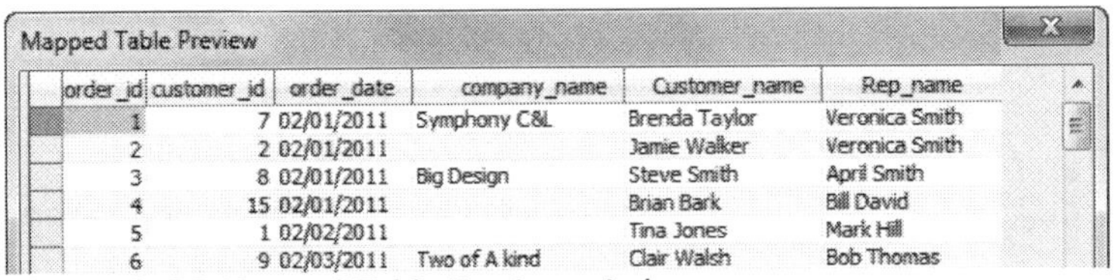

Figure 2-29 Mapped Table Preview window

Select The Fields For The Mapped Table

1. Add the following fields from the Orders table to the list on the right side of the Fields tab: Order ID, Customer ID and Order Date.

2. Open the drop-down list under the Fields tab and select the Customers table. Add the Company Name field.

Create A Computed Column Field

In this part of the exercise you will create an expression that combines the customer first and last name fields into one field that will be added to the mapped table.

1. Click the **ADD COMPUTED COLUMN BUTTON**, then type `Customer_Name` in the Field Name field.

2. Select Character as the Type, then type `50` in the Width field.

3. Click the Build button. Type the formula shown in Figure 2-30. You should have the options shown in Figure 2-31.

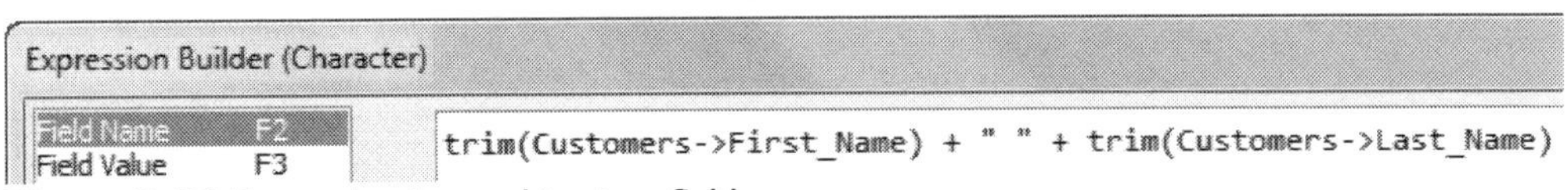

Figure 2-30 Expression to combine two fields

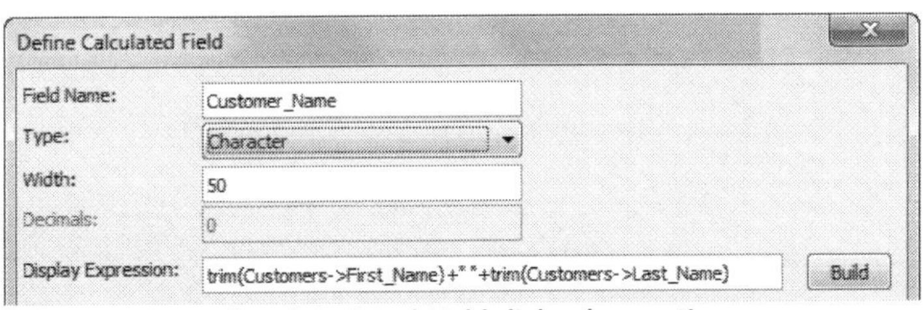

Figure 2-31 Define Calculated Field dialog box options

4. Repeat the steps above to create the Rep Name field that combines the sales rep first and last name fields, as shown in Figure 2-32.

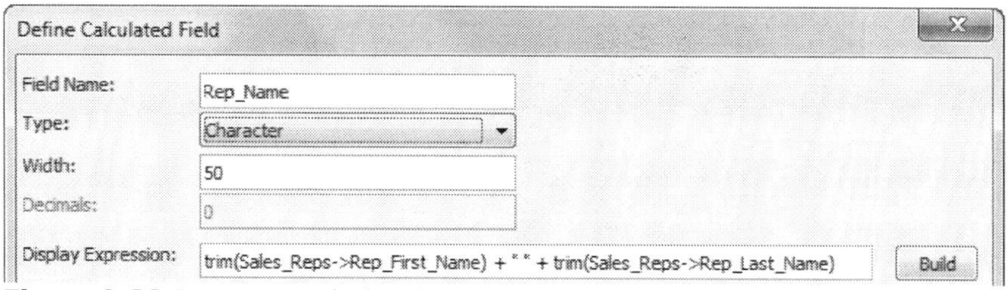

Figure 2-32 Rep name calculated field options

Field Properties

After you have selected the fields for the mapped table, you should review this section of the Create Mapped Table dialog box to see if there is anything that you need to change. If you click on one of the Update properties, you will see a description below the Properties section, as illustrated earlier in Figure 2-25.

Selecting the **UPDATEABLE** option on the Create Mapped Table dialog box opens the dialog box shown in Figure 2-33.

The options are used to select the field to update and create the expression that will be used to select the records that will be updated.

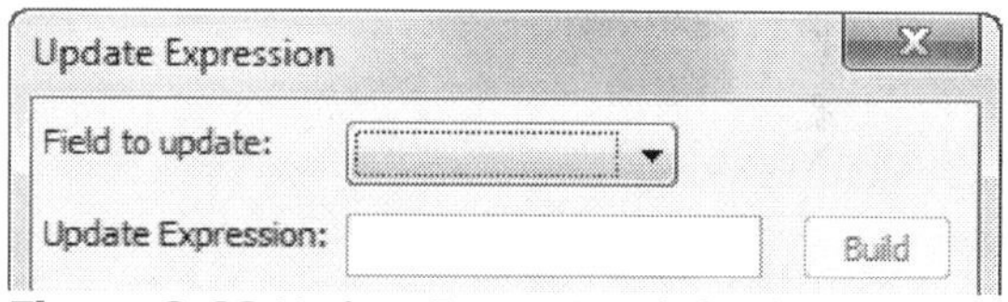

Figure 2-33 Update Expression dialog box

View And Save The Mapped Table

1. You should have the options shown earlier in Figure 2-25. Click the Preview Mapped table button. Your table should look like the one shown earlier in Figure 2-29.

2. Click OK. Type `aMappedTable` in the Table Name field on the **SPECIFY TABLE NAME DIALOG BOX**. Click No, to not view the mapped table. The mapped table will be created.

Viewing And Editing A Mapped Table Definition

At some point, you may need to view or edit the options for a mapped table. Fortunately, the Create Mapped Table dialog box works like the Report Genie, meaning that you can reopen the dialog box and change your options.

Figure 2-34 shows the shortcut menu options for a mapped table.

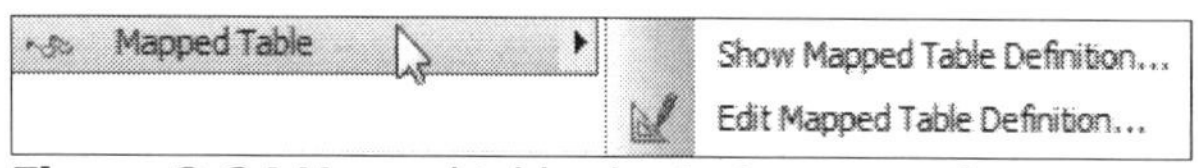

Figure 2-34 Mapped table shortcut menu options

These options are also on the Table menu when a mapped table is selected on the Tables/Sets tab. The options are explained below.

① The **SHOW MAPPED TABLE DEFINITION** option opens the dialog box shown in Figure 2-35. This dialog box is a quick view that displays the parent table, alias name and fields in the mapped table and the table relationships.

② The **EDIT MAPPED TABLE DEFINITION** option opens the dialog box shown in Figure 2-36. It has the same functionality as the Create Mapped Table dialog box shown earlier in Figures 2-22 and 2-25.

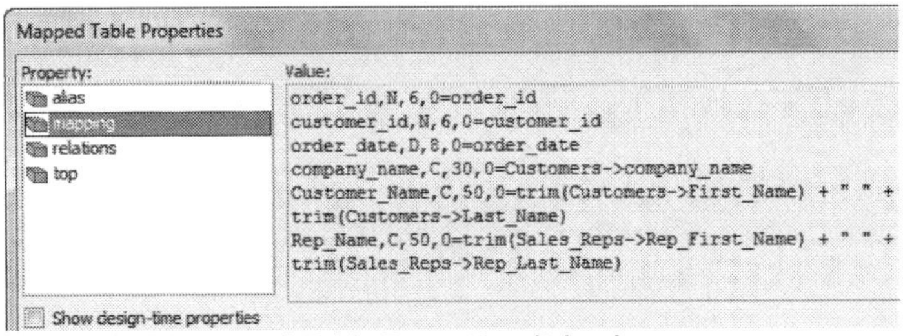

Figure 2-35 Mapped Table Properties dialog box

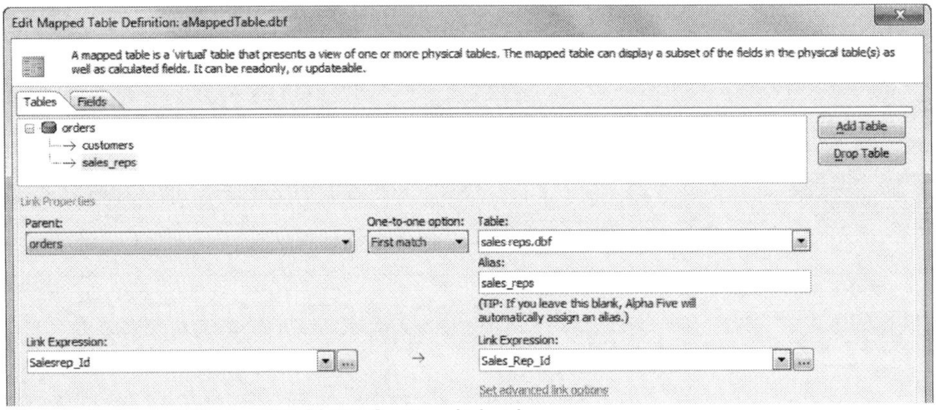

Figure 2-36 Edit Mapped Table Definition dialog box

Linking On More Than One Field To Create A Set

There may be a time when you need to create a link on two or more fields to retrieve the data that you need. More than likely, these will not be ID fields if the ID fields contain numeric values. Keep in mind that referential integrity options cannot be used with multiple links. Creating multiple links is painless <smile>, as explained below.

1. Open a new or existing set, then select the Add a child table option.

2. Select the appropriate link type, then select the table to link to.

3. Select the fields to link on, similar to what is shown in Figure 2-37.

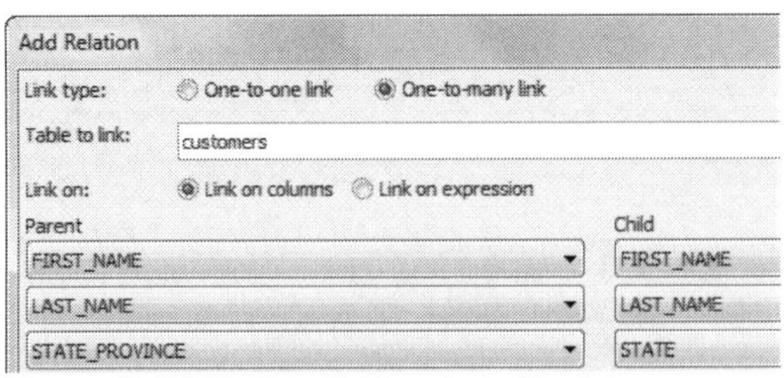

Figure 2-37 Multiple fields selected to link on

Set Level Calculated Fields

Earlier in Exercise 2.6 you create a calculated field rule. This type of calculated field will automatically be applied to every layout that the table is used in. Most of the time, you will create calculated fields in a layout. Calculated fields created at the set level appear in the Calculated Fields section of the Drag Drop List panel. This means that the expression is not automatically applied to every record.

> **Set Editor Calculated Fields Tab**
> Creating a calculated field at the set level is done on the Calculated Fields tab on the Set Editor. I don't know if I am doing some wrong or if this is how the **EXPRESSION BUILDER** button is suppose to work, but until I type the calculated field name and an equal sign, the button does not work. The **FIELDS** and **FUNCTIONS** buttons do work.

> **Using The Fields Button On The Calculated Fields Tab**
> If you can create the expression on your own, but just need the fields, click the F2 - Fields button (because it does not require the equal sign to work) instead of using the Expression Builder button.

Exercise 2.8: Create A Calculated Field In A Set

In this exercise you will create the Line Item calculated field that you created earlier in Exercise 2.6.

1. Save the Order detail-products set as `aCalculatedSetLevelField`, as shown in Figure 2-38.

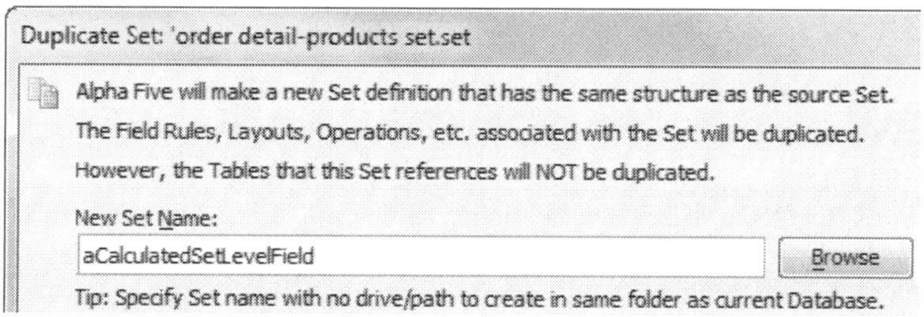

Figure 2-38 Duplicate Set dialog box

2. On the Set Editor Calculated Fields tab, type `Line_Total =`.

3. Click the Expression Builder button, then create the expression Qty * Price.

   The calculated field should look like the one shown in Figure 2-39.

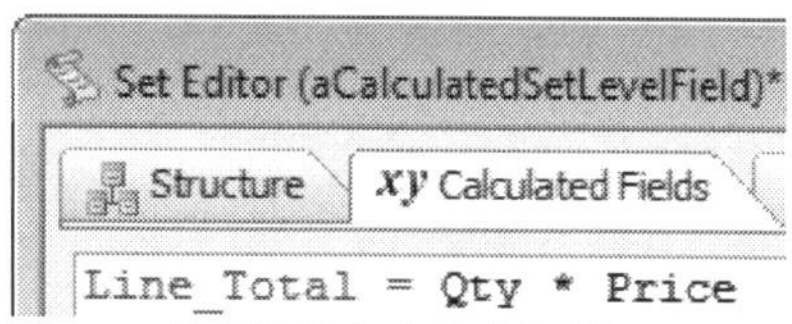

Figure 2-39 Calculated field expression

If you create a form or report based on this set, you will see the field that you just created in the Drag Drop List panel, as illustrated in Figure 2-40.

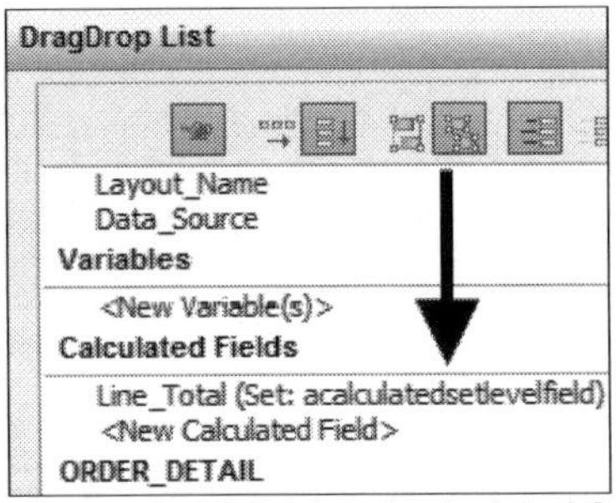

Figure 2-40 Set level calculated field in the Drag Drop List panel

Exercise 2.9: Create An Image Field

In this exercise you will add a **.JPG IMAGE FIELD** to the Contacts table, then add an image to the field for a few records.

1. Right-click on the Contacts table and select Edit Structure.
2. Create a field named `Display image`, then select the Jpeg image type.
3. View the table in the Default Browse. Scroll over to the Display image column, then click the button at the end of the field.
4. Navigate to your folder and select one of the .jpg image files. You may have to select the .jpg file type from the drop-down list near the bottom of the File name dialog box.
5. Add a different image to the second and third record in the browse.

Configure The Image Field

In this part of the exercise, you will resize the image field so that the images are displayed correctly.

1. Display the Contacts table in the Default Form in Design mode.
2. Right-click on the Display image field and select **UNGROUP**.
3. Resize the image field so that it is approximately one inch wide and 1.5 inches high.
4. On the Field Properties dialog box Setup tab, change the **DISPLAY MODE** to Best Fit.
   On the Border tab, select a Border Style and Border color, then change the Border Width to 7.
5. Save the form as `aDisplayImage`.

   When you view the image file on the form, you should be able to see the entire image, as shown in Figure 2-41.

Figure 2-41 Image displayed on the form

DATABASE MAINTENANCE

In this chapter you will learn about the following database maintenance features:

- ☑ Tables and Sets utility options
- ☑ Table menu Utilities options

CHAPTER 3

Overview

The topics covered in this chapter may not be glamorous, but they will help keep your applications running smoothly.

Table And Set Utilities

On the tables and sets shortcut menu is an option called Utilities. It displays the submenu shown in Figure 3-1 if a table is selected and Figure 3-19 shown later, if a set is selected.

Utilities Submenu For Tables

The options shown in Figure 3-1 are explained in Table 3-1.

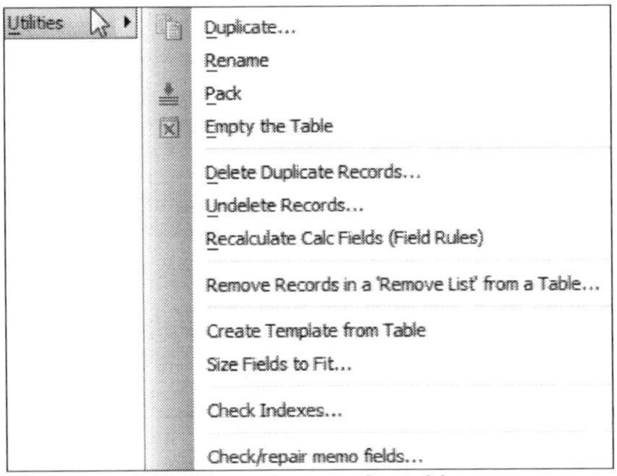

Figure 3-1 Utilities submenu for tables

Option	Description
Duplicate	[See Chapter 2, Duplicating Objects tip box]
Rename	Is used to change the name of the table.
Pack	[See Exercise 3.1: Packing Tables And Sets] (1)
Empty the Table	[See Deleting Data From A Table] (1)
Delete Duplicate Records	[See Exercise 3.2: Delete Duplicate Records]
Undelete Records	[See Undeleting Records]
Recalculate Calc Fields	[See Chapter 2, Recalculate Field Rules tip box]
Remove Records in a 'Remove List' from a Table	Using the records in one table as the list of records to delete in another table, as shown in Figure 3-2.
Create Template from Table	[See Exercise 3.3: Create A Template From A Table] (1)
Size Fields to Fit	[See Sizing Fields] (1)
Check Indexes	[See Check Indexes] (1)
Check/Repair Memo fields	Is only available if the selected table has a memo field. [See Checking Memo Fields] (1)

Table 3-1 Utilities submenu for tables options explained

(1) This option is not available for a mapped table.

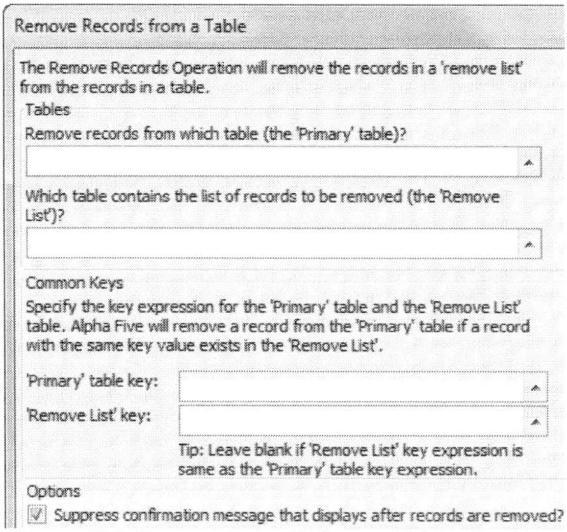

Figure 3-2 Remove Records from a Table dialog box

Exercise 3.1: Packing Tables And Sets

When tables are packed, the following tasks are completed: Records marked for deletion are removed from the table and memo fields are compressed. You should pack tables when you have made a lot of design changes to the database. **ONCE YOU PACK A TABLE, RECORDS CAN NO LONGER BE UNDELETED**. The reason to pack tables is to reduce the table size, which in turn makes the database run quicker. In this exercise you will learn how to pack tables and sets.

How To Pack A Table

If you have several tables to pack and know that some or all of them are used in the same set, use the Set option to pack them because the Set option allows more than one table to be packed at the same time.

1. Select the Pack option shown earlier in Figure 3-1 for a table in the a5beyond database. You will see the message shown in Figure 3-3. Click OK. You will then see a message that says that the table has been packed.

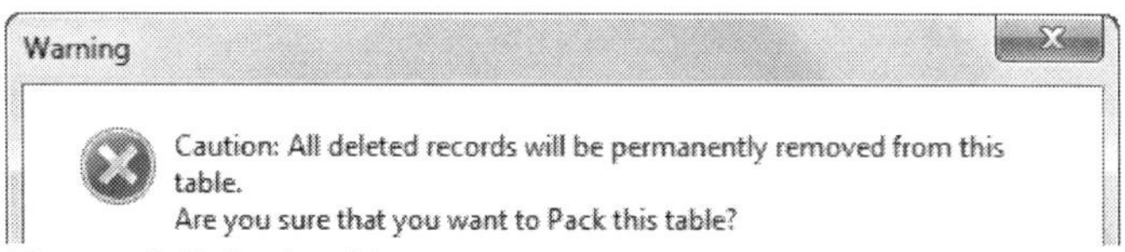

Figure 3-3 Pack table message

How To Pack A Set

1. Right-click on a set on the Tables/Sets tab ⇒ Utilities ⇒ Pack Set.

2. On the dialog box shown in Figure 3-4, select the tables that you want to pack.

   Click OK.

   On the warning screen that lists the tables that will be packed, click Yes.

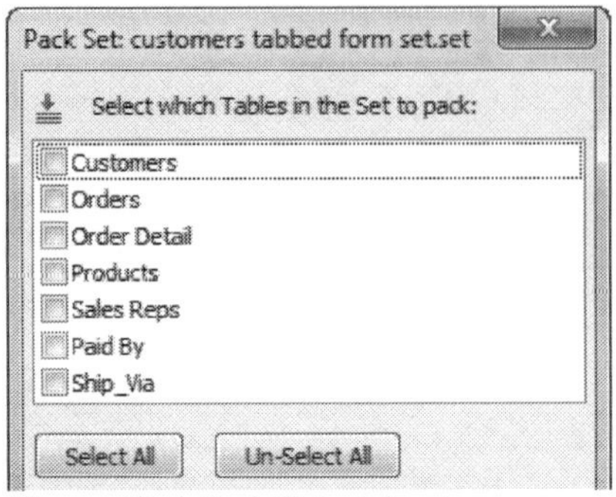

Figure 3-4 Pack Set dialog box

Deleting Data From A Table

If you have the need to delete all of the records in a table, select the **EMPTY THE TABLE** option on the Utilities submenu.

You will see the message shown in Figure 3-5. It warns you that all records in the table will be permanently deleted.

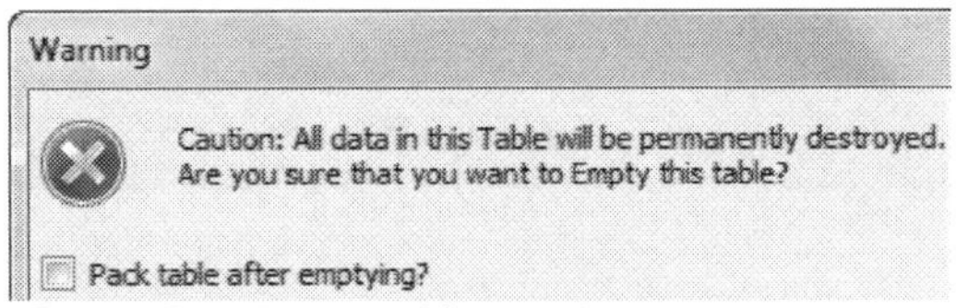

Figure 3-5 Empty table warning message

Check the **PACK TABLE AFTER EMPTYING** option if you want the table to be packed after the records are deleted. Click OK. All of the data will be deleted from the table.

> **Action Scripting Option For Deleting Data**
> If you have the need to delete data from a table on a regular basis, the **WORKSPACE UTILITIES ZAP (EMPTY) TABLE** action (on the New button ⇒ Script (Using Action Scripting) option on the Code Tab) can be set up and saved.

Find Duplicate Records Dialog Box

The options shown in Figure 3-6 are used to set up parameters to check for duplicate records. The options are explained below.

① **METHOD** Is used to select whether a list of fields or an expression will be used to determine if there are duplicate records in the table.
② The **FIELD** drop-down lists are used to select the field(s) that will be checked for duplicate values.
③ **OPTIONS BUTTON** Opens the dialog box shown in Figure 3-7. The options are used to select how much of the field will be used to check for duplicate information.
④ **IGNORE RECORDS . . .** If checked, records that do not have data in a field being used to check for duplicate values are skipped.
⑤ **FILTER THE TABLE . . .** If checked, an expression can be created on the Filter Builder to select or exclude records from being checked for duplicate data.

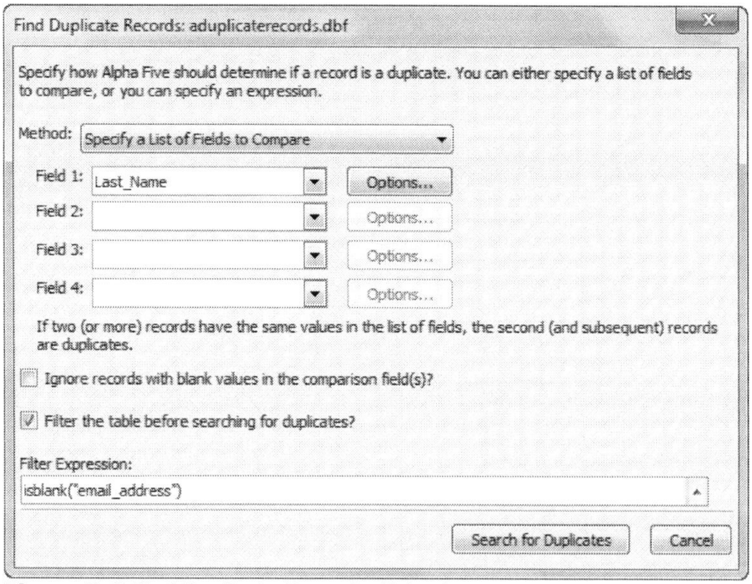

Figure 3-6 Find Duplicate Records dialog box

Exercise 3.2: Delete Duplicate Records

Over time, tables that are the basis for forms or browses that are used for data entry may contain duplicate records. From time to time you should check tables for duplicate records. This exercise will show you how to use the options that are available to find and delete duplicate records. The options selected in this exercise are for illustration purposes only.

Create The Search Criteria

1. Save the Customers table as `aDuplicateRecords`.

2. Select the **DELETE DUPLICATE RECORDS** option on the Utilities submenu. You will see the dialog box shown above in Figure 3-6.

3. Open the Field 1 drop-down list and select Last Name.

   Click the Options button.

   Select the Characters option, then change the Number of characters to 3, as shown in Figure 3-7.

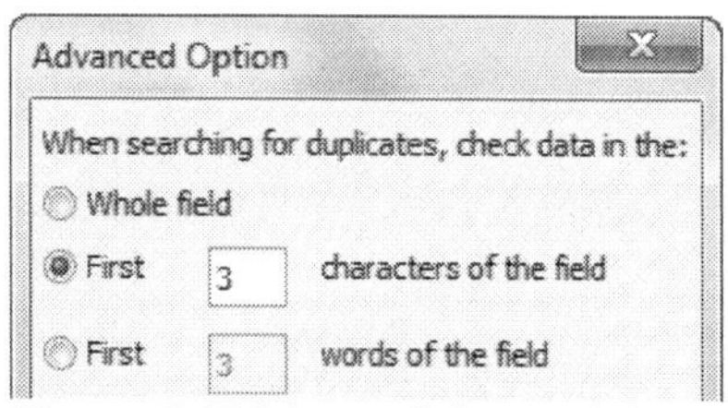

Figure 3-7 Advanced Option dialog box

4. Check the Filter the table option, then click the Filter Expression field button.

5. Create a filter to check if the Email address field is blank. You should have the expression shown earlier at the bottom of Figure 3-6.

6. Click the **SEARCH FOR DUPLICATES** button. When you see the warning message that records will be un-marked, click Yes.

Process The Potential Duplicate Records

The dialog box shown in Figure 3-8 is used to select how you want to handle the potential duplicate records.

Unless you have memorized all of the data in the table, it is safest to preview the records that have been marked as duplicate.

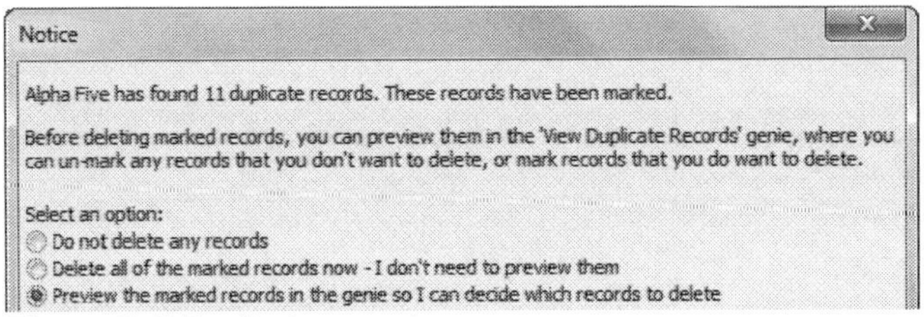

Figure 3-8 Duplicate records message

1. Click OK on the dialog box shown above in Figure 3-8. You will see the dialog box shown in Figure 3-9.

   The options shown in the figure are used to view the records that have been marked as duplicate, based on the criteria that you selected.

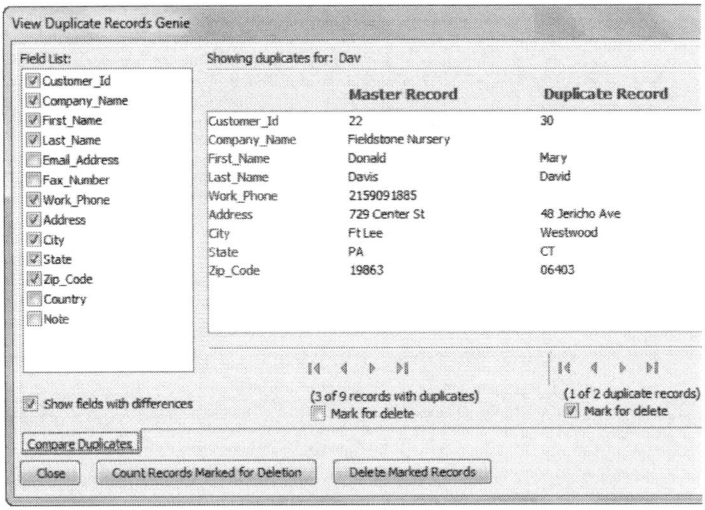

Figure 3-9 View Duplicate Records Genie

2. Select different options on the genie to get a feel for how they work. You can delete records from this table because it is only used in this exercise.

Undeleting Records

The options shown in Figure 3-10 are used to restore records that have been marked as deleted. Keep in mind that when you delete records, they are not removed from the table, unless you pack the table or compact the database.

You can restore all marked records or select specific records to restore. The **MARK RECORDS THAT ARE UNDELETED** option is used to view the records (in a browse) that are restored from the undelete process.

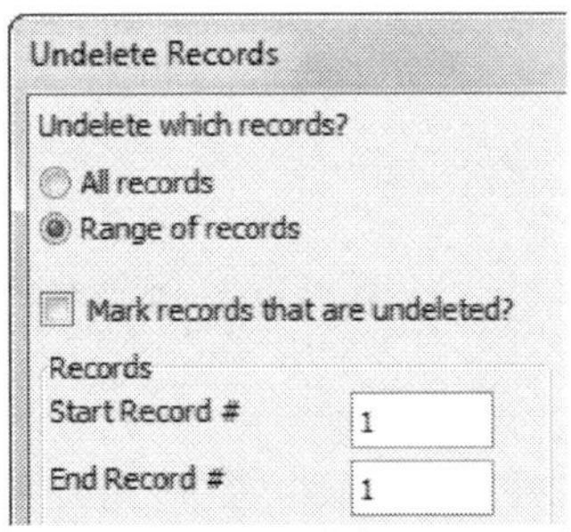

Figure 3-10 Undelete Records dialog box

If you want to restore a range of consecutive records and know the record numbers that you want to restore, enter the range in the **START RECORD NUMBER** and **END RECORD NUMBER** fields.

After you click OK, you will see the message shown in Figure 3-11, that informs you of how many records were undeleted (restored).

Figure 3-11 Undelete records message

Exercise 3.3: Create A Template From A Table

This tool is useful if you have created a table that has forms, browses, reports etc., based on a table that you would like to use in other databases. The template that you create will be available for other databases, just like the templates that come with Alpha Five.

In this exercise you will create a template that will include layouts and sample data. The reason that the template that you will create can have layouts is because the table that will be used to create the template, already has these objects, prior to creating the template.

1. Right-click on the Contacts table, then select the Create Template from Table option on the Utilities submenu.
2. On the dialog box shown in Figure 3-12, type `aMyTemplate` in the field.

   Select both Include options, then click OK.

   You will see a message saying that the template was created.

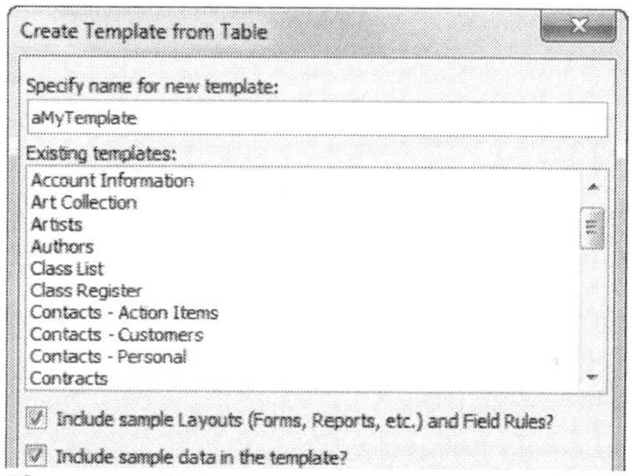

Figure 3-12 Create Template from Table dialog box

3. Control Panel ⇒ New button ⇒ Create Using Genie.

   On the dialog box shown in Figure 3-13, select the template that you created and select both Include options, then click Next.

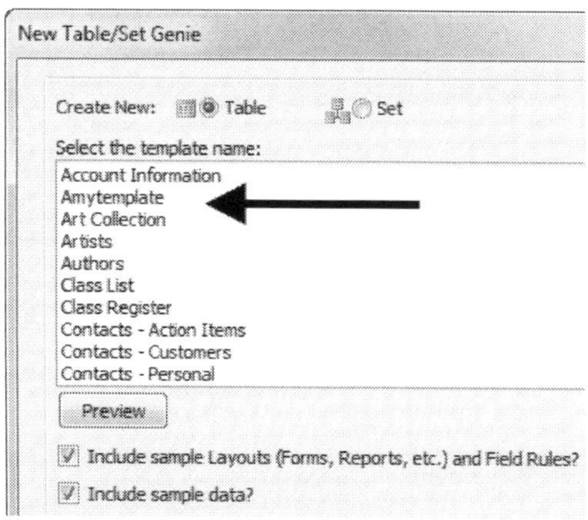

Figure 3-13 New Table/Set Genie

4. On the screen shown in Figure 3-14, type `aContacts` in the Table Name field, then click Finish.

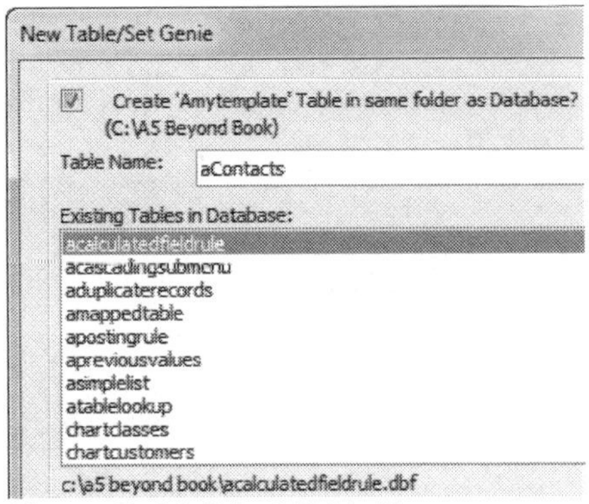

Figure 3-14 Select Table Name screen

5. Click on the aContacts table in the list on the Control Panel, then click the View button. You will see that the table has forms, browses and reports already created, as shown in Figure 3-15.

   If there are layouts that you do not need or want, click on the corresponding tab and delete the layout that has aContacts in the Tables/Sets column.

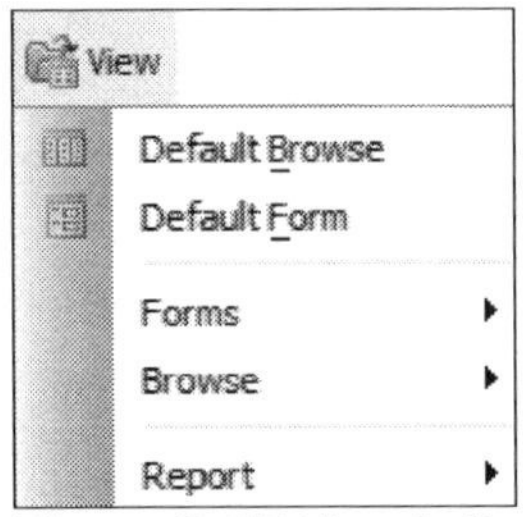

Figure 3-15 View button menu

> **Deleting Templates That You Create**
> If you decide that you no longer want or need a template that you created, the path to the templates is C:\Program Files (x86)\A5V11\Templates\Tables. An alternate path would be without the (x86). A5V11 refers to the version of Alpha Five that you are using.

Sizing Fields

The options shown in Figure 3-16 are used to change the width of fields to make them as small as possible. This is useful to make the table size smaller, which saves space.

The **PADDING OPTIONS** are used to add space to fields.

The **CREATE A BACKUP COPY** option, if checked will make a copy of the table before any changes are made. The backup copy is placed on the Tables/Sets tab with **_BACKUP** at the end of the table name.

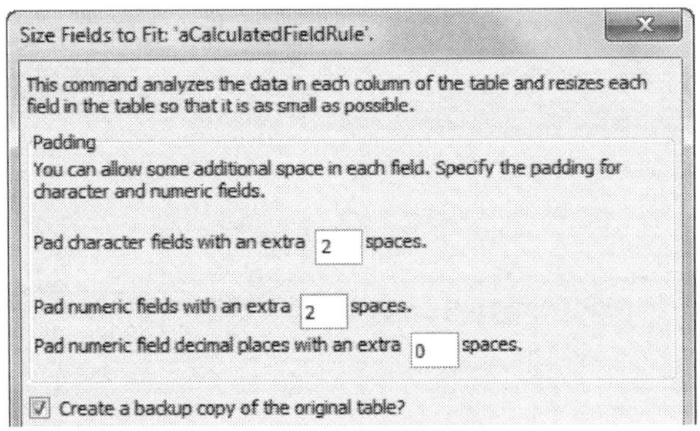

Figure 3-16 Size Fields to Fit dialog box

Check Indexes

The dialog box shown in Figure 3-17 is used to select the tables that you want to check the indexes of. This feature is helpful if the sort is not working as expected.

To check an index, no one else can have the table open. Select the table to verify, then click OK.

Click the **TEST ALL BUTTON** to check all tables.

Click the **TEST SELECTED BUTTON** to select specific tables to check.

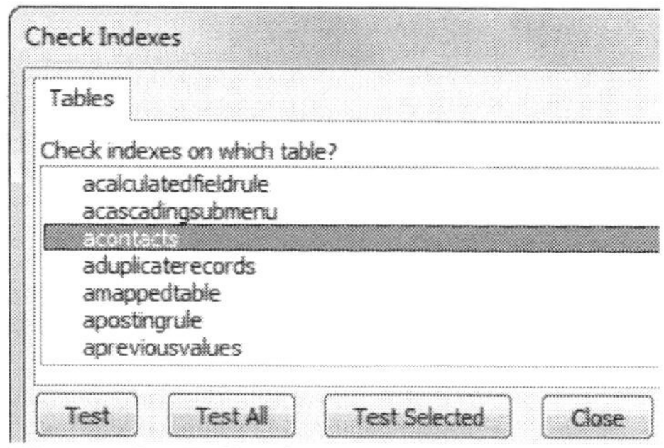

Figure 3-17 Check Indexes dialog box

Checking Memo Fields

The dialog box shown in Figure 3-18 is used to check the memo fields in the selected table for errors.

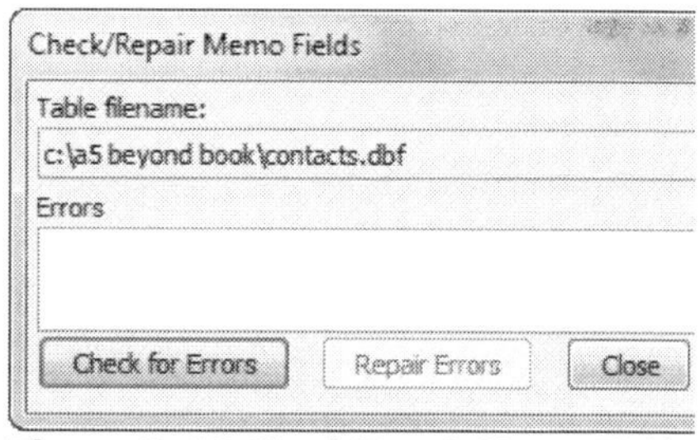

Figure 3-18 Check/Repair Memo Fields dialog box

Set Utilities

Figure 3-19 shows the Utilities submenu for sets.

A benefit to using the Set Utilities is that the same tasks can be performed on more than one table at the same time.

The options that work differently for sets then they do for tables are explained below.

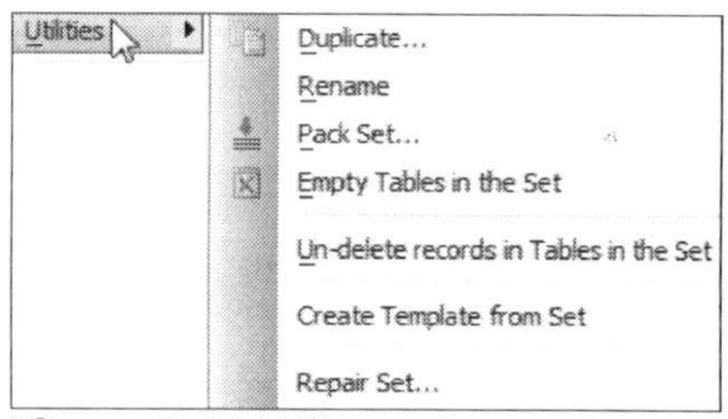

Figure 3-19 Utilities submenu for sets

Duplicate A Set

The dialog box shown in Figure 3-20 is used to duplicate a set.

Type a name for the new set, then click OK.

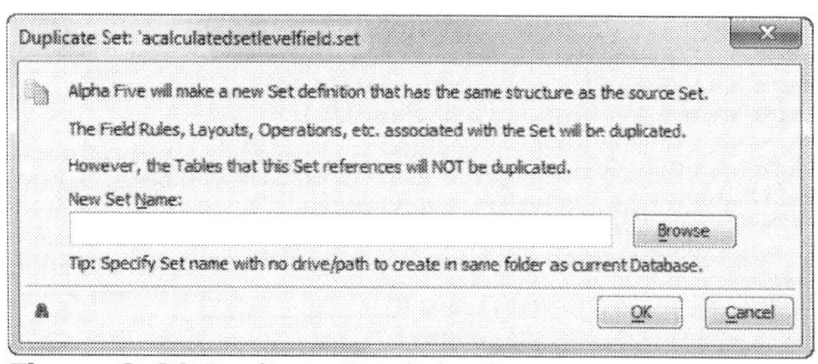

Figure 3-20 Duplicate Set dialog box

Pack Set

The dialog box shown in Figure 3-21 is used to select the tables that you want records that are marked for deletion removed from the table.

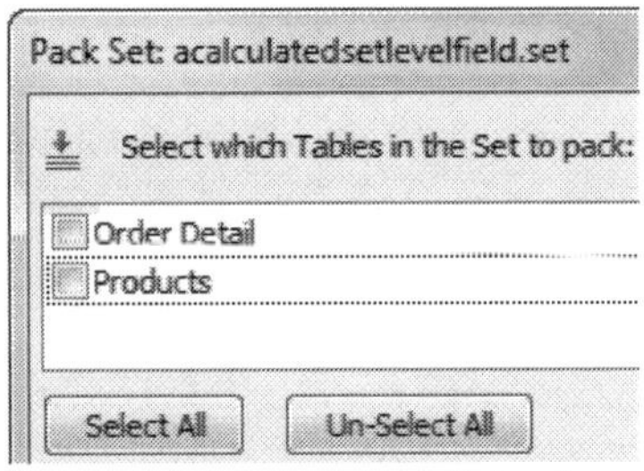

Figure 3-21 Pack Set dialog box

Empty Tables In The Set

The dialog box shown in Figure 3-22 is used to select which tables in the set that you want all of the records deleted from.

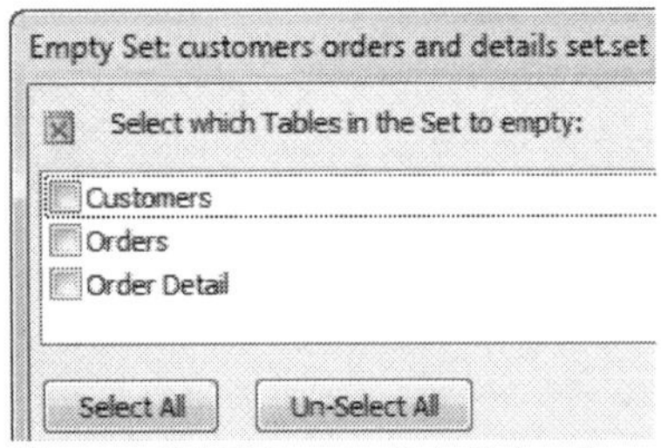

Figure 3-22 Empty Set dialog box

Un-Delete Records In Tables In The Set

The dialog box shown in Figure 3-23 is used to select the tables that you want to restore records (that have been marked as deleted) from. Unlike the Undelete option for a table, you cannot select any criteria for which records in a table will be restored.

The dialog box displayed in Figure 3-24 appears after the process has run. The number of records restored per table is displayed.

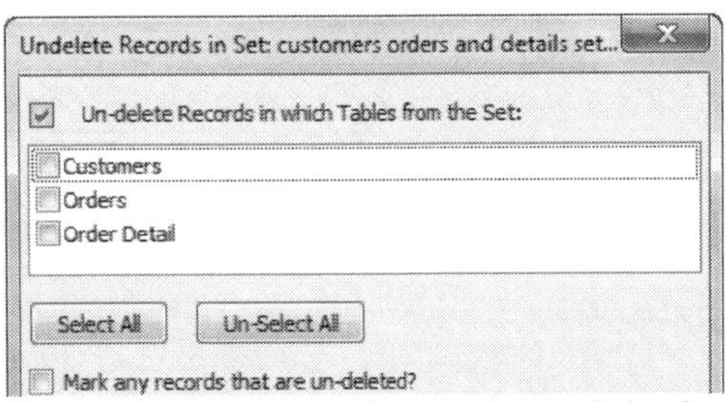

Figure 3-23 Undelete Records in Set dialog box

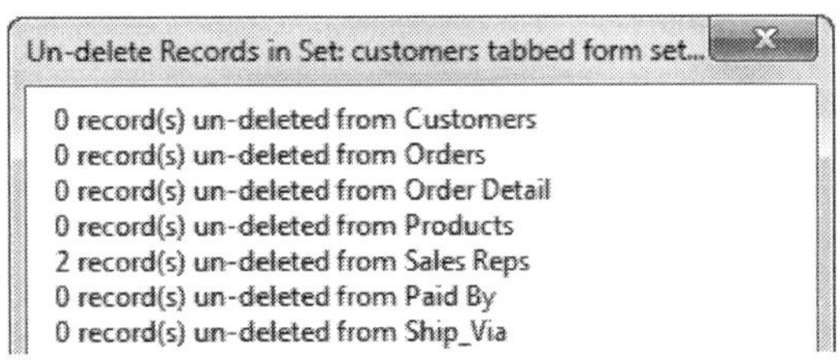

Figure 3-24 Result of records restored

Create A Template From A Set

The options shown in Figure 3-25 are used to create a template from a set. When you select the Set option on the New Table/Set Genie, you will see the set(s) that you created. Sets that you create are stored in this location: C:\Program Files (x86)\A5V11\Templates\Sets.

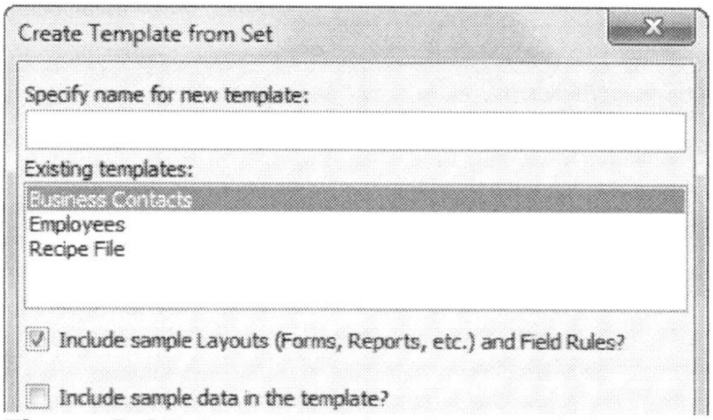

Figure 3-25 Create Template from Set dialog box

Repair Set

Select this option when the location of a table in the set has changed. The dialog box shown in Figure 3-26 is used to fix table references in a set. Each table in the set is checked. As shown in the figure, the Order detail table used in the set cannot be found.

Open the **REPLACE TABLE WITH** drop-down list and select the table, then click OK.

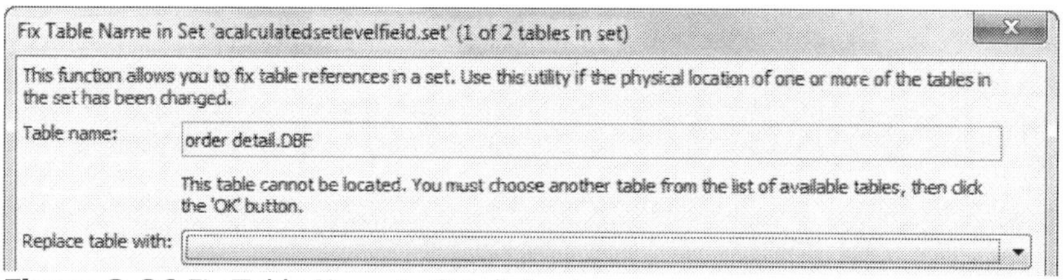

Figure 3-26 Fix Table Name in Set dialog box

The Close (X) button in the upper right corner of the Fix Table Name in Set dialog box does not work.

Aliases

This feature is used when the application needs to be transportable. Usually, this option is used when the application uses images that are stored in a folder.

View ⇒ Settings ⇒ System ⇒ Aliases, displays the options shown in Figure 3-27.

The **IMAGE FILE REFERENCE** field type is a good example because this field type stores the path to an image file. If the current path to an image file is C:\A5 Book\my_pix\ and you move the database to drive Q, the paths in the Image File Reference field would not be correct. To fix this, you would create an alias.

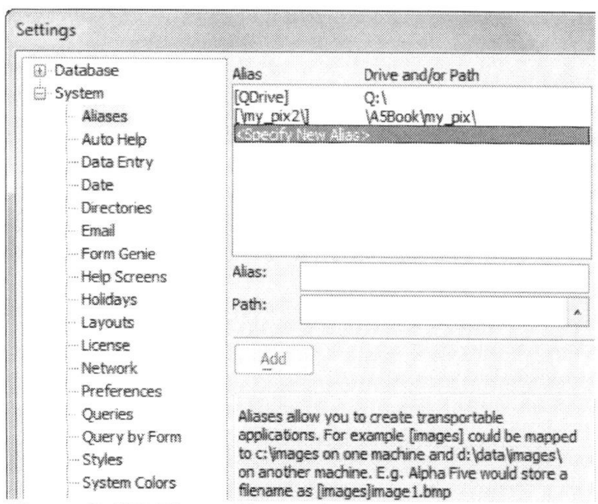

Figure 3-27 Alias setting options

The alias shown in the figure will look on the Q drive and the path Q:\my_pix2\ for the images. This means that on one computer, Alpha Five will look in C:\A5 Book\my_pix\ for the images and on a different computer, Alpha Five will look in Q:\my_pix2\ for the same images. If you are not sure of the current path for a folder, click the **PATH FIELD** button to look for it.

Deleting Temporary Files

Alpha Five creates temporary files that are not deleted when Alpha Five is closed. The temporary file names start with $$ and have the file extension **.MPX**, as shown on the right side of Figure 3-28.

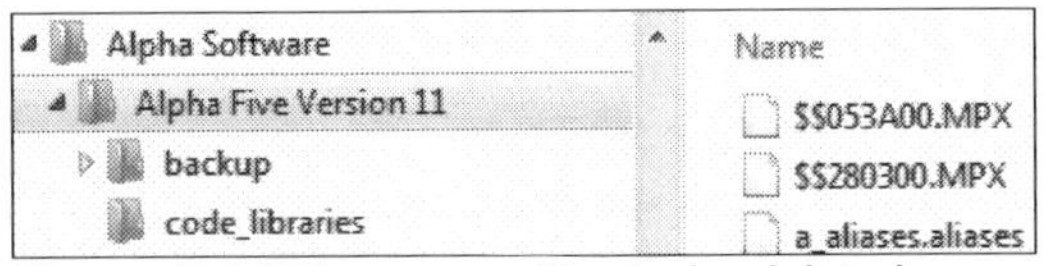

Figure 3-28 Temporary files to be deleted

You will find some of these files in this location:
C:\Users\your account name\App Data\Roaming\Alpha Software\Version.
Other temporary files may be in the folder that the database is in. If you search for .mpx in Windows Explorer, you will see a list of where these files are on your hard drive.

> **Renaming Tables**
> If you try to rename a table and get a message that says that the table is in use and you know that it is closed, delete the temporary files and try renaming the table again.

Table Menu Utilities

The table topics covered so far in this chapter are for the selected table.

The Utilities options shown in Figure 3-29 are for all tables.

To display these options, click on a blank space on the Tables/Sets tab ⇒ Table ⇒ Utilities.

The options are explained below.

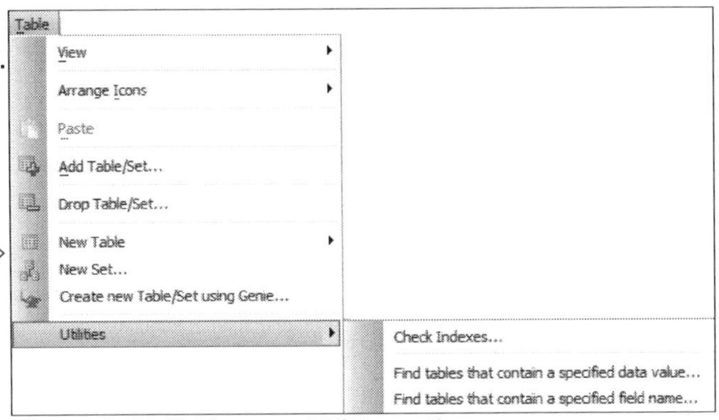

Figure 3-29 Table menu Utilities options

CHECK INDEXES [See Check Indexes, earlier in this chapter]

FIND TABLES THAT CONTAIN A SPECIFIED DATA VALUE Displays the dialog box shown in Figure 3-30. The options are used to search all tables or the tables that you select, for specific data. The field(s) that have the search criteria are displayed at the bottom of the dialog box, as shown. The search criteria can be saved to a text file.

What I could not figure out is why there is no option to select saved search criteria, so I am not sure how useful it is to save the search criteria.

FIND TABLES THAT CONTAIN A SPECIFIED FIELD NAME Displays the dialog box shown in Figure 3-31. The options are used to find tables that have a specific field. The downside is that the search field does not have a drop-down list that contains all of the fields in the database. If you select a table, then click the **SHOW ALL FIELDS** button, you will see the dialog box shown in Figure 3-32, which displays the fields in the table that you selected.

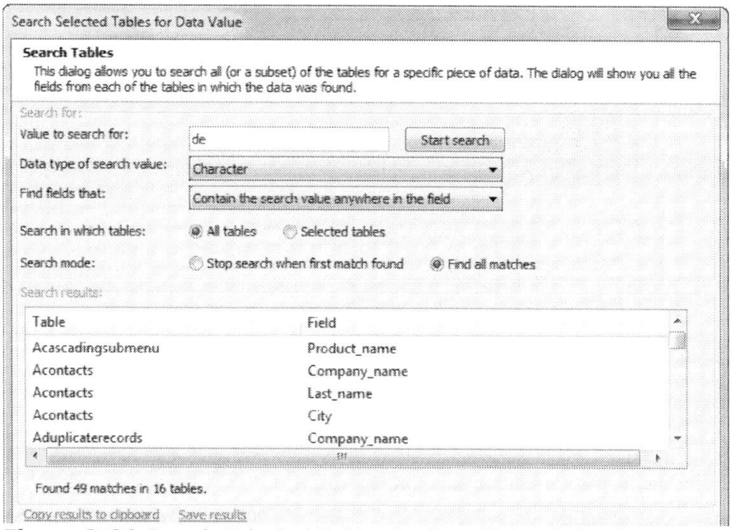

Figure 3-30 Search Selected Tables for Data Value dialog box

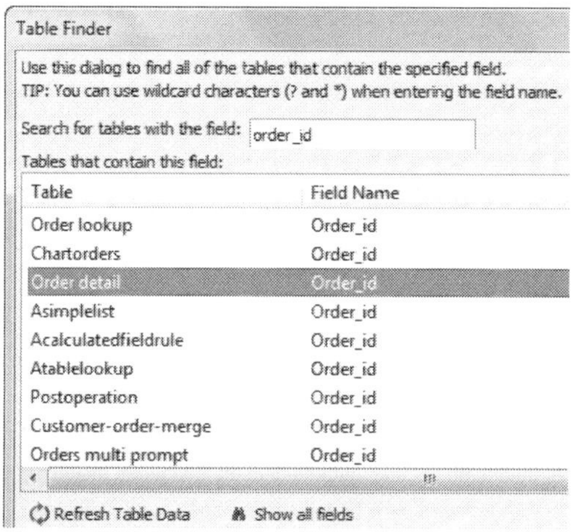

Figure 3-31 Table Finder dialog box

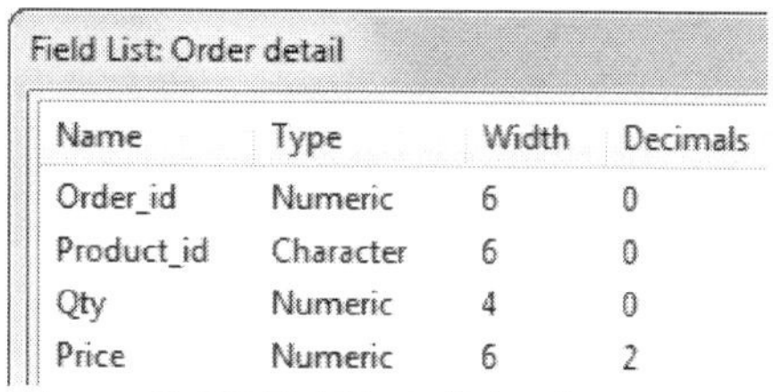

Figure 3-32 Field List dialog box

VIEW, RECORDS AND TOOLS MENU OPTIONS

In this chapter you will learn about options on the View, Records and Tools menus, including the following:

- ☑ The Trace Window
- ☑ Marking and Un-Marking records
- ☑ Creating zip files
- ☑ Backing up and restoring databases

CHAPTER 4

Overview

The topics covered in this chapter are common to forms and browses.

Exercise 4.1: Using The Trace Window

This tool is on the View menu. One use for this tool is to view warnings and errors. In this exercise you will view a form that has warnings.

1. Click on the form, Browse copied to a form, then click the View button. You should see a warning message.

2. View ⇒ Trace Window. At the bottom of the list on the Error tab, you should see the warnings shown in Figure 4-1.

   These messages let you know that there is a problem with some of the fields on the form.

   If you look at these fields on the form, you will see the word "Error".

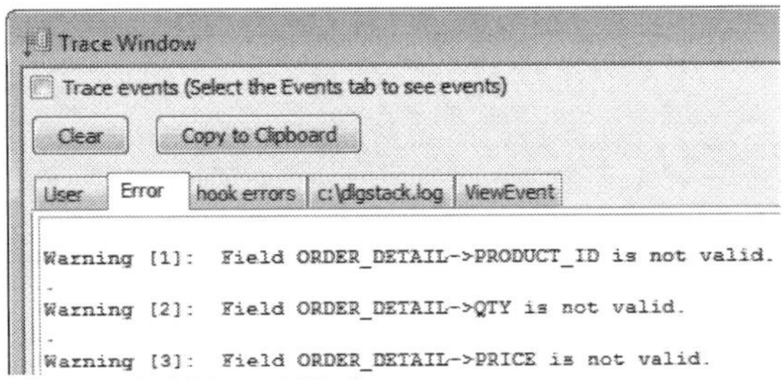

Figure 4-1 Trace Window

   If this was for real, you would have to figure out what is wrong with these fields and fix the problem so that the data for these fields would display on the form.

Records Menu

When a table or set is viewed on a form or browse, this menu is available. The following options on the Records menu are covered in this chapter: Mark, Unmark, Delete/Mark/Un-Mark selected records.

Marking And UnMarking Records

The **MARK** option is used to manually select records. Alpha Five maintains a list of records that are marked in a table. The reason to mark records is to create a group, if you will, that will be used to perform an action, like update a field in all of the marked (selected) records or copy the records to another table.

In a form, marked records display a check mark in the status bar section of the form. On a browse, marked records display a square before the first column. Keep in mind that when a record is marked, it is displayed as such, regardless of the form or browse that the record is displayed in. I find it easier to mark records using a browse.

Exercise 4.2: Marking Records Manually

In this exercise, you will learn how to mark records that will be moved to a new table later in this book. [See Chapter 13, Exercise 13.4]

1. View the Orders table in the Default Browse.

2. Click on the row for Order ID 5. Records ⇒ Mark, or press Ctrl+M.

3. Repeat step 2 to mark the records for Order ID's, 8, 10, 11, 13, 135 and 136.

4. You should see boxes to the left of these records, as illustrated in Figure 4-2. Close the browse. If you viewed the Orders table in a form and displayed any of the records that you marked, you will see the check mark illustrated in Figure 4-3.

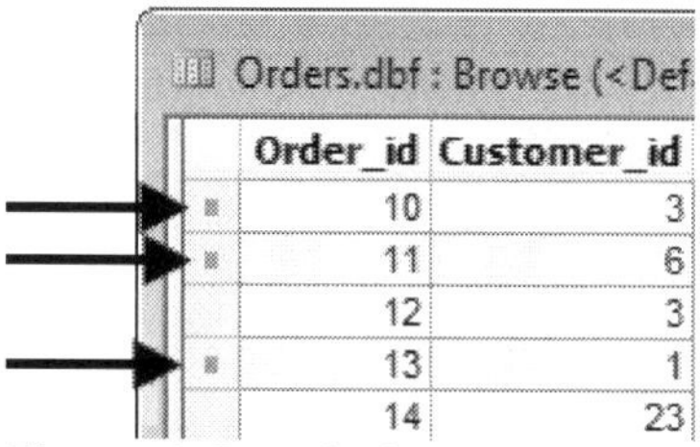

Figure 4-2 Marked records illustrated in a browse

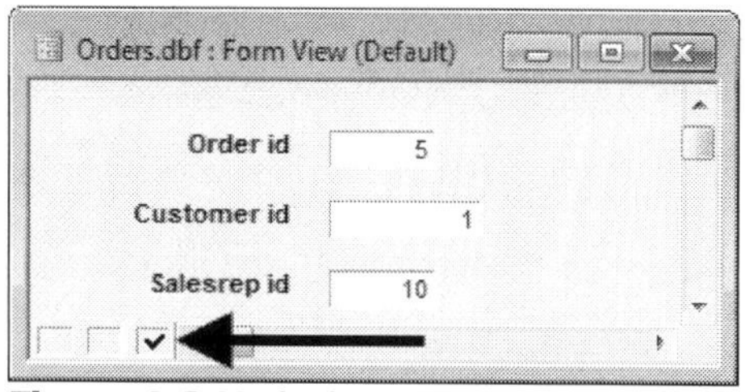

Figure 4-3 Marked record symbol illustrated in the status bar section of the form

Un-Marking Records

To remove a mark, select the record in a form or browse, then Records ⇒ Unmark or press Ctrl+U.

Delete/Mark/Un-Mark Records

Earlier you learned how to mark and unmark records manually. If you need to mark, unmark or delete all of the records in a table, select this option on the Records menu. The dialog box shown in Figure 4-4 is used to select one of these options.

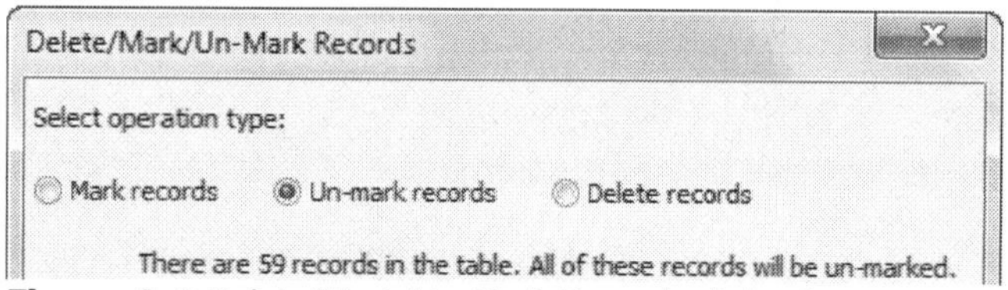

Figure 4-4 Delete/Mark/Un-Mark Records dialog box

Tools Menu

The options on this menu are used to enhance and maintain the database. The options covered in the rest of this chapter are used to zip, send, back up and restore workspaces.

What Is A Zip File?

A zip file is a file that stores other files in a compressed format. The primary reason to create a zip file is to have the ability to provide a copy of two or more files to be used or viewed from a location that is different from where the files are currently stored.

An example of this is the zip file for this book. I created the files in the zip file on my laptop. Unless I grant you access to my laptops hard drive <not gonna happen, smile>, you would not have a way to get the files. Putting all of the files for this book into a zip file, makes it easy for you to get them and download them at one time, instead of having to download the files one by one.

Using The Zip Workspace Dialog Box

The Zip Workspace tool, shown in Figure 4-5 is used to put tables, sets or the database in a zip file. The options are explained in Table 4-1.

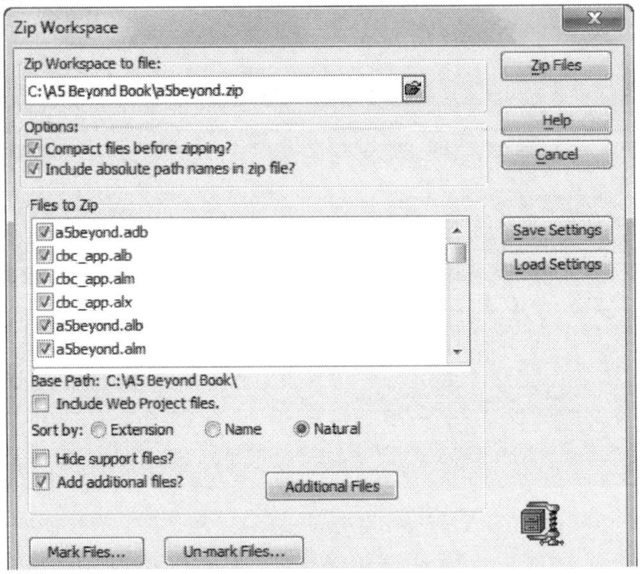

Figure 4-5 Zip Workspace dialog box

Option	Description
Zip Workspace to file	Is used to select the name and location of the zip file that will be created. The default location is the same location as the database that is open. The default zip file name is the name of the database that is open.
Compact files before zipping	Check this option to reduce the size of the files that will be added to the zip file.
Include absolute path names in zip file	Check this option if you want the files to be unzipped to the same location (folder structure) that they are currently in. If the folder structure does not exist in the location where the files will be unzipped to, the folder structure will automatically be created.
Files to Zip	By default, all of the files in the database are displayed in this list. If you do not want some files to be added to the zip file, clear the check mark for the file. If you only want certain file types added to the zip file, see Mark Files To Add To The Zip File, later in this chapter.
Include Web Project files	Check this option if there are web files used in the application and you want them included in the zip file.
Sort by	The extension, name and natural (the order that the files were created in) options are used to select the order that the files will be displayed in on the Control Panel.
Hide support file	If checked, only the database **.DBF FILES** will be displayed in the Files to Zip list.
Add additional files	Check this option if you want to add files that are not in the Files to Zip list on the dialog box.
Additional Files button	Is only enabled when the Add additional files option is checked. [See Add Files To The Zip File]

Table 4-1 Zip Workspace dialog box options explained

Option	Description
Mark Files button	[See Mark Files To Add To The Zip File]
Un-mark Files button	[See Un-Mark Files]
Zip Files button	Click this button to create the zip file.
Save Settings button	[See Save Zip File Settings]
Load Settings button	[See Load Zip File Settings]

Table 4-1 Zip Workspace dialog box options explained (Continued)

Save Zip File Settings

If you know that you will create a zip file for the database with the same options on a regular basis, click the **SAVE SETTINGS BUTTON** on the Zip Workspace dialog box after you have selected all of the options needed to create the zip file.

After clicking the button, you will see the dialog box shown in Figure 4-6. Type in a name for the zip file settings, then click OK.

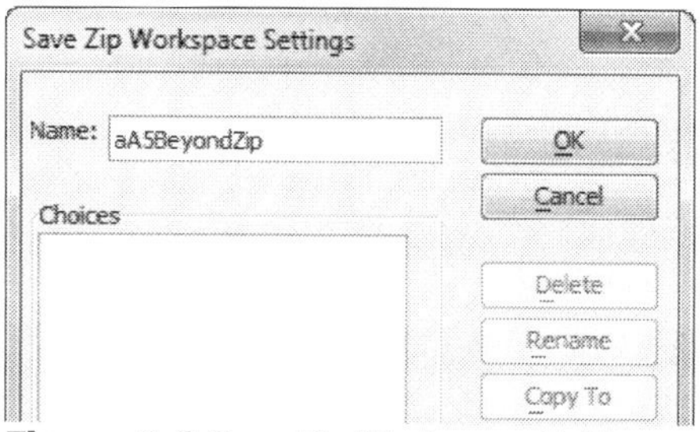

Figure 4-6 Save Zip Workspace Settings dialog box

The next time that you need to create a zip file for the database, click the Load Settings button and select the settings file. These settings can also be used on the **SEND WORKSPACE DIALOG BOX**.

Modifying Saved Settings

If the saved settings are not exactly what you need for the zip file that you are creating now, you can change them by loading the settings and changing the options as needed. You can save the changes that you make to the saved settings or you can use the changes for the current zip file that you are creating and then discard the changes.

Load Zip File Settings

Click the **LOAD SETTINGS BUTTON** on the Zip Workspace dialog box if you already have saved settings to create a zip file for the database that is currently open.

You will see the dialog box shown in Figure 4-7. Select the settings that you want to use, then click OK. If you need to change the saved settings, you can.

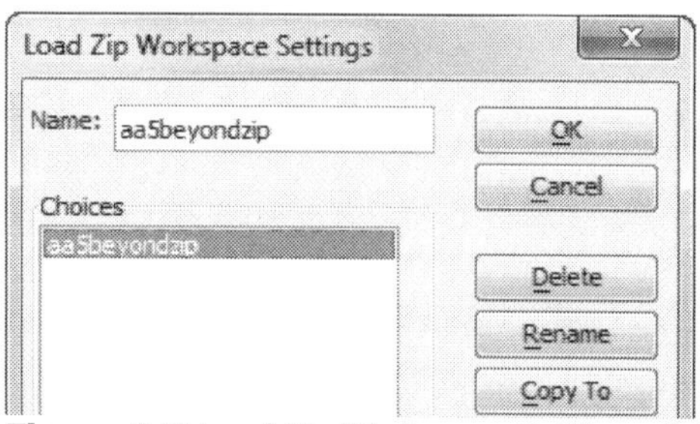

Figure 4-7 Load Zip Workspace Settings dialog box

Add Files To The Zip File

When you need to add files to the zip file that are not part of the database, select the Add additional files option on the Zip Workspace dialog box, then click the Additional Files button. The dialog box shown in Figure 4-8 is used to select the additional files that you want to add to the zip file. Click the Select Files button and select the file(s) that you want to add to the zip file.

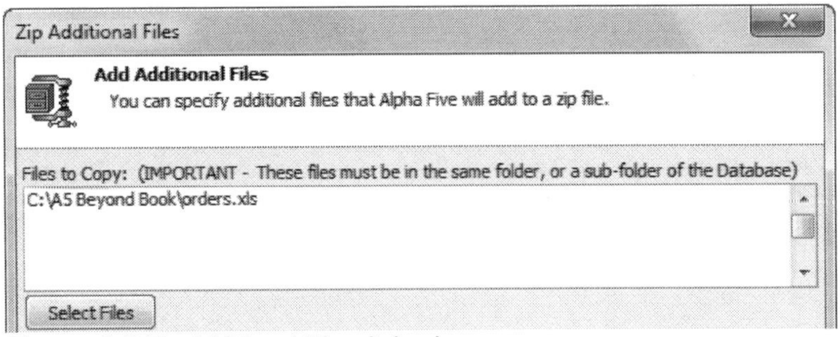

Figure 4-8 Zip Additional Files dialog box

Mark Files To Add To The Zip File

Click the Mark Files button to select a specific type of file in the database to add to the zip file.

The dialog box shown in Figure 4-9 is used to select the type of file that will be added to the zip file.

If the **DATA FILES ONLY** option is selected, you can select whether or not the index files should be included in the zip file.

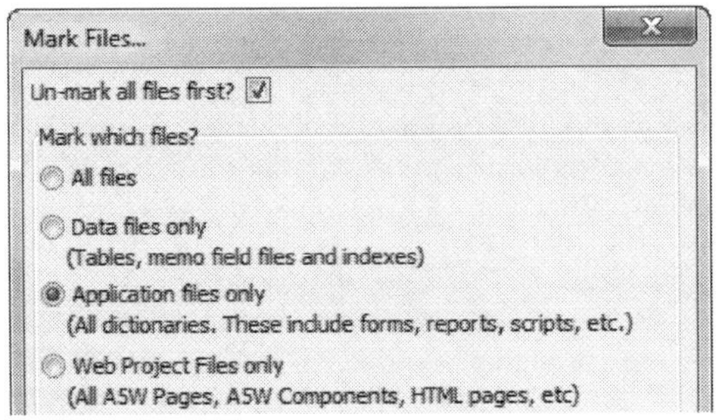

Figure 4-9 Mark Files dialog box

Clear Files From The Zip File

If you want to stop a file type from being added to the zip file, click the Un-Mark Files button.

On the dialog box shown in Figure 4-10, select the file type that you do not want added to the zip file.

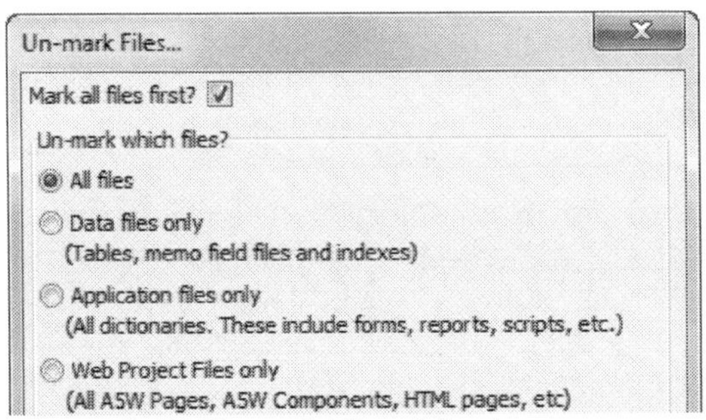

Figure 4-10 Un-mark Files dialog box

Only Sending Forms Or Reports
Keep in mind that when the zip file is opened in the new location, existing files in that location are overwritten. If you made changes to forms or created new reports for example, you should probably only include those files in the zip file. [See Mark Files To Add To The Zip File, earlier in this chapter]

Exercise 4.3: Create A Zip File

In this exercise you will learn how to create a zip file that contains a database.

1. Tools ⇒ Zip Workspace.

2. Check both options at the top of the dialog box. Check the Add additional files option, then click the Additional Files button.

3. On the Zip Additional Files dialog box, click the Select Files button, then select the orders.xls file in your folder. You should see the file, as shown earlier in Figure 4-8.

4. Click the Mark Files button. On the Mark Files dialog box, select the **APPLICATION FILES ONLY** option, as shown earlier in Figure 4-9.

5. Click the Save Settings button. Type `aA5BeyondZip` in the Name field, as shown earlier in Figure 4-6. Click the Zip Files button. If you look in your folder, you will see the zip file.

Email A Zip File

The **SEND WORKSPACE** option on the Tools menu is used to automatically create a zip file and send it via email.

The options on the dialog box shown in Figure 4-11 work the same as the Zip Workspace dialog box covered earlier in this chapter.

The one difference is explained in the next section.

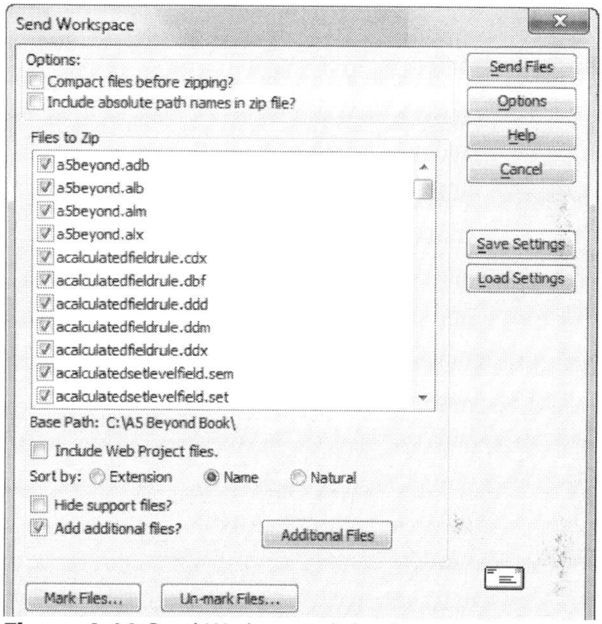

Figure 4-11 Send Workspace dialog box

Selecting The Email Software

To send the zip file via email, Alpha Five needs to know what email client (software) you want to use. The default email client is the one that you have already installed and use.

If you want to use the email client in Alpha Five, click the Options button on the Send Workspace dialog box.

On the dialog box shown in Figure 4-12, select the **ALPHA FIVE E-MAIL CLIENT** option.

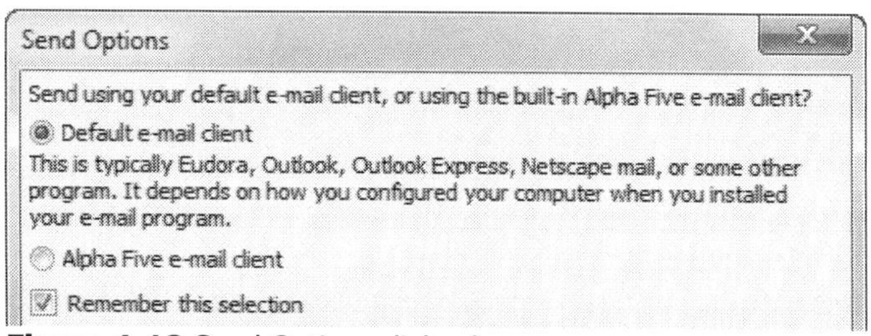

Figure 4-12 Send Options dialog box

Backing Up And Restoring Databases

Backing up databases is very important and should be done on a regular basis. If your databases are stored on corporate servers, more than likely, your database is already being backed up at least once a day. If that is the case, you can skip this section.

The options on the Tools menu shown in Figure 4-13 are used to backup or restore a database. They are explained below.

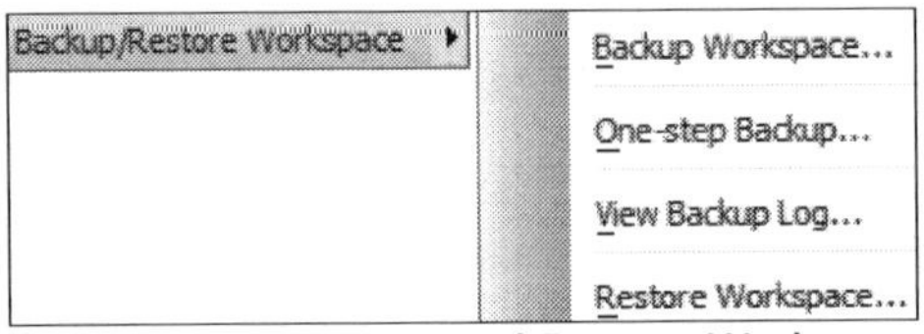

Figure 4-13 Backup and Restore Workspace options

Backup Workspace

This option opens the dialog box shown in Figure 4-14.

The options are used to configure the backup. They are explained in Table 4-2.

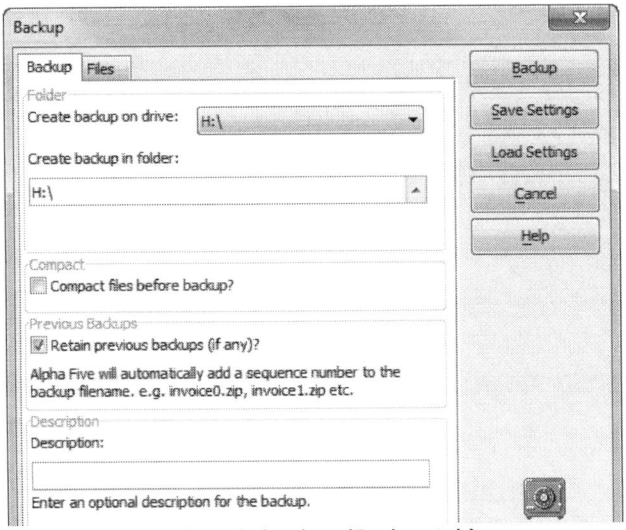

Figure 4-14 Backup dialog box (Backup tab)

Option	Description
Create backup on drive	Is used to select the drive to put the backup copy of the database on. A good rule of thumb is to put the backup copy on a different drive, then the live database.
Create backup in folder	Is used to select the folder to place the backup file in. There is no way to create the folder from this dialog box. If you need a new folder to put the backup file in, create it in Windows Explorer, then reopen the Backup dialog box.
Compact files before backup	Check this option to reduce the size of the files that will be backed up. Compacting removes the space from the files selected to be backed up, which is how the file size is reduced. Doing this also increases the performance of the database.
Retain previous backups	Check this option if you want to keep the previous backup files of this database.

Table 4-2 Backup dialog box options explained (Backup tab)

Option	Description
Description	Is one way to distinguish this backup copy from other backup files for the database. For example, if the backup file only includes certain files, you may want to list the files in this field.
Backup button	Creates the backup file. When the backup is complete, you will see the message shown in Figure 4-15. The log shown later in Figure 4-19 lists every file that was backed up and the status of each file.
Save Settings button	Saves the options selected for this backup. To save the settings, right before you click the Backup button, click the Save Settings button. Only one set of settings can be saved for a database. You cannot select a name for it.
Load Settings button	[See Load Zip File Settings, earlier in this chapter]

Table 4-2 Backup dialog box options explained (Backup tab) (Continued)

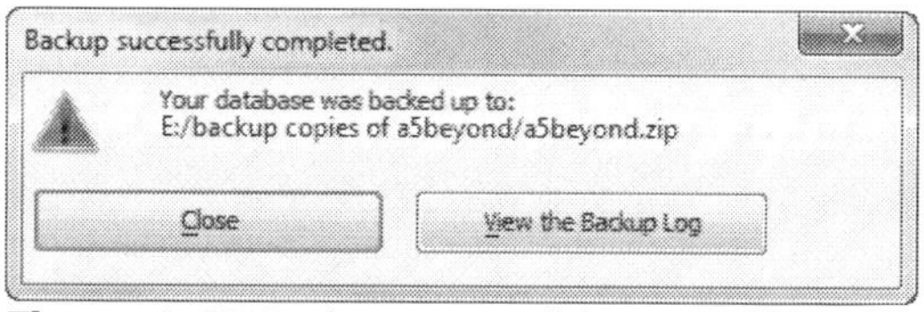

Figure 4-15 Backup successful message

Files Tab Options

The majority of options shown in Figure 4-16 work the same as they do for zip files. [See Using The Zip Workspace Dialog Box, earlier in this chapter]

The differences are explained below.

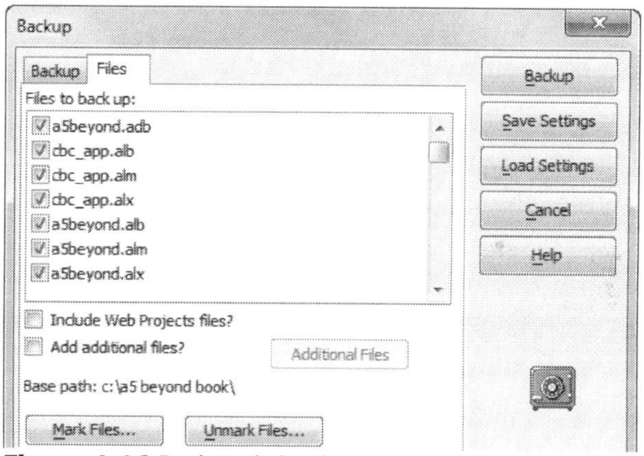

Figure 4-16 Backup dialog box (Files tab)

Mark Files And Unmark Files Buttons

Both buttons open the dialog box shown in Figure 4-17. Selecting the **FILES WITH SPECIFIED EXTENSIONS** option opens the dialog box shown in Figure 4-18. The options are used to select by extension, which files will be backed up.

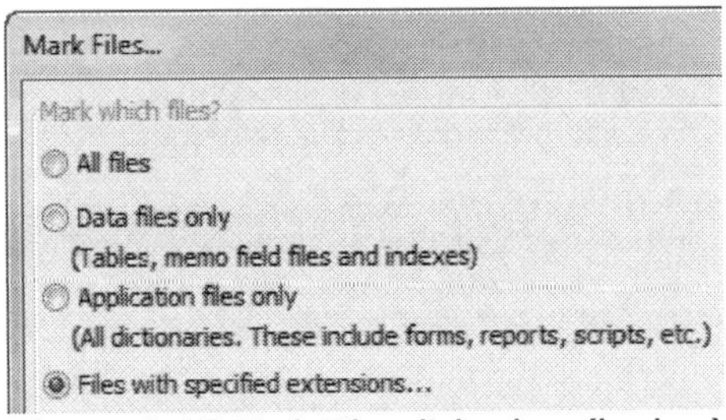

Figure 4-17 Mark Files dialog box (backup)

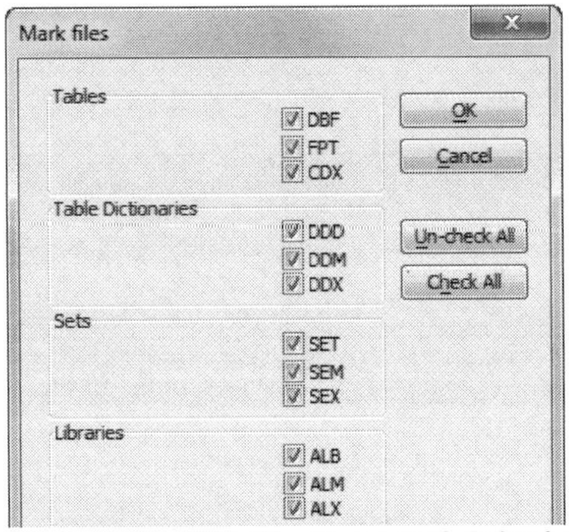

Figure 4-18 Mark Files (extension) dialog box

One Step Backup

If you saved the settings for a previous backup of the database, selecting this option on the menu shown earlier in Figure 4-13, will automatically run the backup using those settings.

View Backup Log

Selecting this option on the menu shown earlier in Figure 4-13 opens the dialog box shown in Figure 4-19.

The files that were backed up are displayed.

Figure 4-19 Backup Log

Restoring A Database/Workspace

The options shown in Figure 4-20 are used to bring back a previous copy of the database.

Once you have selected the options and files to restore, click the Restore button.

This dialog box is similar to the one when Tools ⇒ Restore Workspace is selected, when no databases are open.

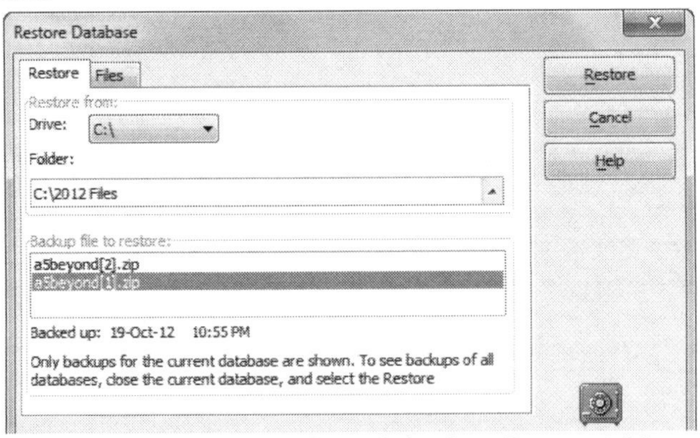

Figure 4-20 Restore Database dialog box (Restore tab)

The difference is that the dialog box opened when no databases are open also has the Destination tab shown in Figure 4-21. The options are explained below.

Restore Tab

DRIVE Is used to select the drive that has the backup copy that you want to restore.

FOLDER Is used to select the folder that has the backup file to restore.

The entries in the **BACKUP FILE TO RESTORE** list display all of the backup files that are in the folder that you selected.

Files Tab

The options on this tab work the same as they do on the Files tab on the Backup dialog box. [See Files Tab Options, earlier in this chapter]

Destination Tab

The tab shown in Figure 4-21 is only available when a database is not open.

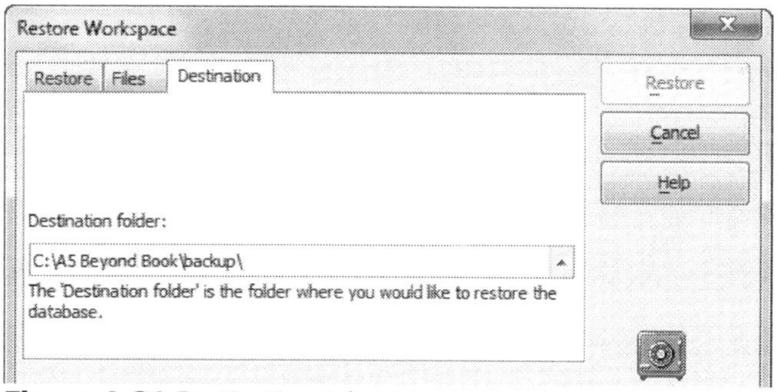

Figure 4-21 Destination tab

USING FUNCTIONS

After completing the exercises in this chapter you will be able to use some of the more common functions in Alpha Five.

CHAPTER 5

Overview

Expressions and functions are some of the most powerful features in Alpha Five. Ironically, many people that are first learning Alpha Five think that expressions and functions are some of the most dreaded features because there is math and logic involved <smile>. If you fall into this category, hopefully this chapter will help you overcome some of the fear.

As part of the report design process, you know that all fields that are needed for a report do not exist in tables. You will learn that summary fields are not stored in tables. While summary fields provide a quick way to create totals, that is about as far as they go.

For example, summary fields will not let you add two fields together, nor can you multiply a field in a table by a constant value, like calculating the sales tax for an order. When you have exhausted all other math related options, it is time to turn to expressions and functions. Expressions are most often created using the Expression Builder, but they can be created on other dialog boxes.

Table 5-1 explains the type of functions in each category. The goal of this chapter is to introduce you to some of the more common functions and demonstrate how these functions can be used to enhance reports.

> **Formulas**
> They are what Alpha Five calls **EXPRESSIONS**. They are one in the same.

What Is The Difference Between Expressions And Functions?

This is one of the questions that I am asked a lot. Expressions are calculations or some type of data manipulation that you create. Functions have already been created. If there is a function that meets your needs, use it because there is no point in reinventing the wheel, as they say. If you have created or used formulas or functions in spreadsheet software, you are already familiar with the basics of creating expressions in Alpha Five.

I like to think of functions as an extension, template or shortcut to creating formulas from scratch. What I like about functions is that when you add one to your formula, the syntax (commas and parentheses) is also added. The commas indicate that an argument is required.

Expressions

Expressions can be used on forms, browses and reports, by using the **NEW CALCULATED FIELD** option on the Drag Drop List panel for forms and reports. Browses have the **FIELDS PANEL** (which has the Calculated Field option) instead of the Drag Drop List panel. Yes, it would be nice if all three had the same panel name. You have to name each calculated field that you create. If you are going to have a title for the calculated field that will be displayed, it is a good idea to use what you want displayed as the calculated field name.

Expressions are used to create new fields. If you need to include data on a report that is not stored in tables, many times you will need to create an expression to get the data. An example of this would be the line item total on an order report. A line item total is sometimes referred to as the **EXTENDED PRICE**. Line item information is not stored in an Order Detail table, but the price and quantity ordered are stored in the table. These are the fields that you would use to create the expression to calculate the line item total. Expressions are used to create the following types of calculations, comparisons, manipulations and much more.

① Solve math problems
② Convert data from one format to another
③ Compare or evaluate data
④ Combine two or more text fields into one field
⑤ Combine text and data fields

You may be thinking or asking why all of this information is not stored in tables. There are many reasons including the ones listed below, why data that falls into these categories is not stored in tables.

① It would take a lot of hard drive or server space to store all of the data for these fields.
② Applications that share data have slightly different data needs, which means that some tables would have empty fields.
③ Some data is only needed once or the data changes constantly, so it is more efficient to calculate it when it is needed.
④ The more data that has to be written (added or changed) to a table, the slower the application will run. This "slowness" is often referred to as a performance issue.

Functions

Alpha Five comes with hundreds of functions that you can use. Functions are pre-written, built-in formulas or procedures that have been designed to complete a specific task. This does not mean that if there is bad data in a table that you won't have a problem with the function. If you do not follow the syntax rules or fill in the arguments correctly when using the function, an error will be generated.

How Functions Evaluate

When functions are evaluated, they return one of the following:

① **A VALUE** like a number or a combination of text and numeric data. For example, the **MONTH FUNCTION** displays the month name in numeric format.
② **TRUE OR FALSE** These options come from logical expressions. For example, the **ISBLANK FUNCTION** checks a field to see if it is blank.

Field Type Conversion

Each field in a table has a field type. Some expressions require fields to be a certain type. When this is the case, Alpha Five automatically converts numeric, logical and date field types to the character field type. The reason that this type of conversion is automatic is because the character field type can contain any type of data. If the expression requires fields to be numeric, logical or date type, the conversion is manual. This is most often because the field was defined as character, but has numeric data. There are functions that convert fields from one type to another. Both types of conversions are temporary.

The examples below show automatic and manual conversions. The first line is the expression. The lines after the expression explain the expression.

Example #1 Numeric To Character Type Conversion (Automatic)

"Product #" + Product_ID + " is in the " + Product_Category + " category"

The Product ID field is numeric, but is converted to character.
This character expression will display both of the following:
Product #2 is in the hat category
Product #5 is in the glove category

Example #2 Date To Character Type Conversion (Automatic)

"The order was shipped on " + Date_Shipped

The Date Shipped field is a date field, but is converted to character.
If the current value in this field is 9/19/2012, the expression will display the following:
The order was shipped on 9/19/2012.

Example #3 Character To Date Type Conversion (Manual)

Ship_Date - CTOD("9/19/2011")

This example uses a function to convert data that is in character format (in quotes) to the date type. If the Ship Date is 11/1/2011, the result of the date expression is 43 days.

Expression Builder Tips

If you are new to using the Expression Builder, the tips below will hopefully make using the Expression Builder easier.

- ☑ Functions are displayed in green.
- ☑ Text is enclosed in quotation marks.
- ☑ The + (plus sign) is used to join parts of the expression.
- ☑ Use " " (quotes) to add space between fields.
- ☑ Dates that you type in the Expression Builder must be enclosed in { } brackets, without quotes.

Expression Creation Tools

There are two primary tools (**DEFINE CALCULATED/SUMMARY FIELD DIALOG BOX** and the Expression Builder) that are used to create expressions, as explained below.

Define Calculated/Summary Field Dialog Box

The dialog box shown in Figure 5-1 is used to create a calculated or summary field. The options are explained below.

① **NAME** Type the name for the calculated or summary field that you are creating.

② **EXPRESSION** Type the expression (formula).

③ **SHOW NAMES OF EXISTING CALCULATED FIELDS** This link displays the dialog box shown in Figure 5-2. It shows the other calculated fields that the layout has.

④ **XY BUTTON** Opens the dialog box shown in Figure 5-3. Use this option if you want help creating the expression.

⑤ **ARGUMENT BUTTON** Opens the dialog box shown in Figure 5-4. It is used to help create a calculated field. The options are used to select the argument that you want to display the value of.

⑥ **PRINT WHAT? OPTIONS** The options in this section are used to create a summary field. If selected, the **COUNT OF THE RECORDS** and **OTHER SUMMARY FUNCTION** options display the expression created by the option selected in the field illustrated in Figure 5-1.

⑦ **ADVANCED OPTIONS BUTTON** Opens the dialog box shown in Figure 5-5. The options are used to change the default count options. If the expression illustrated in Figure 5-1 is correct, you will not need to make any changes on this dialog box.

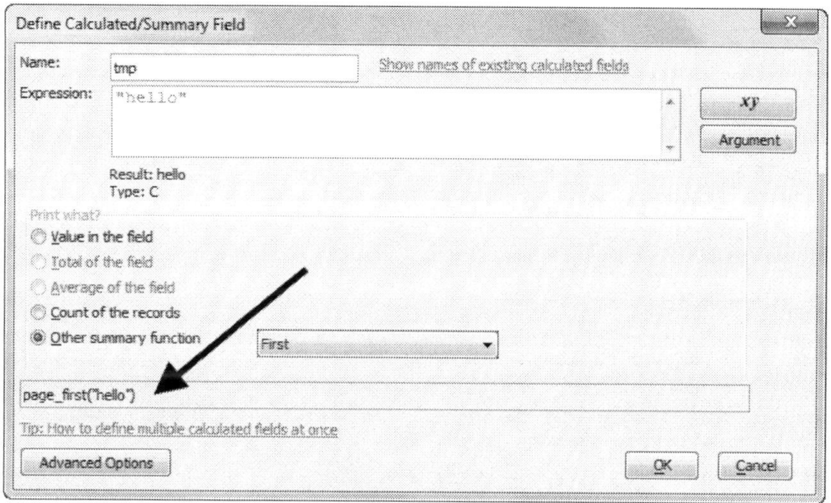

Figure 5-1 Define Calculated/Summary Field dialog box

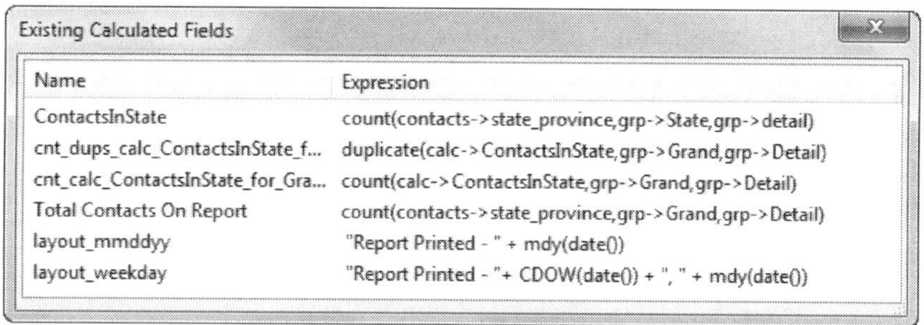

Figure 5-2 Existing Calculated Fields dialog box

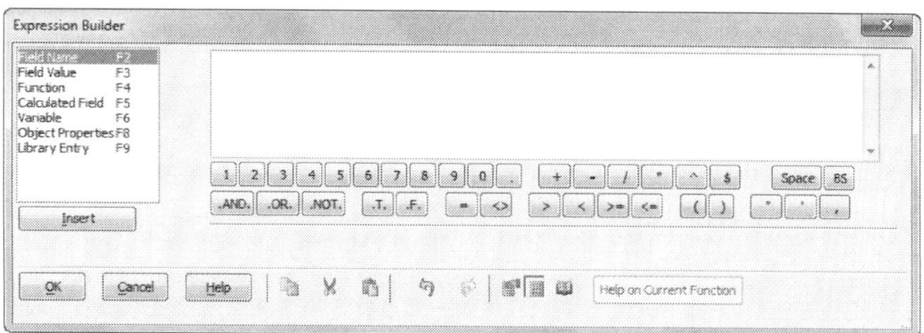

Figure 5-3 Expression Builder

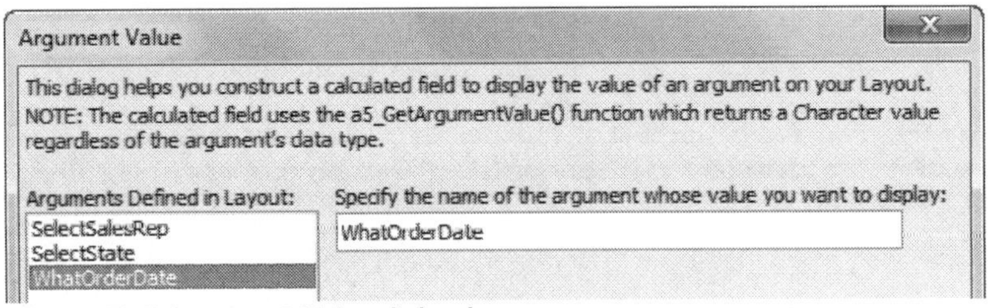

Figure 5-4 Argument Value dialog box

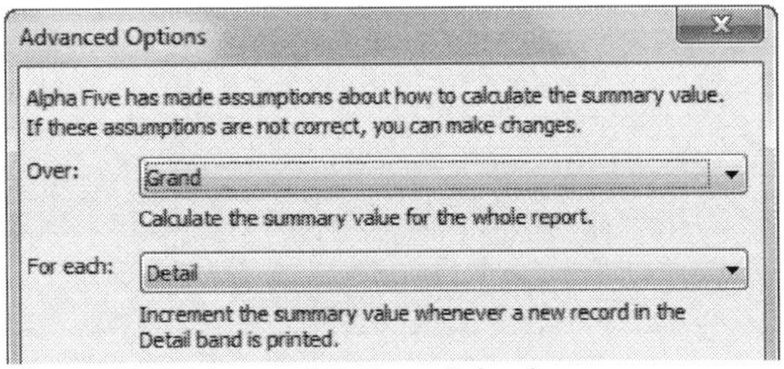

Figure 5-5 Advanced Options dialog box

Use The Update Genie To Create Expressions
As you will see throughout this chapter, the operations Update Genie can be used to create an expression that you can copy and modify as needed. This includes assigning a value to a logical field and assigning a calculated value to a field. Operations are covered in detail in Chapter 13.

Function Categories

Each of the categories discussed in Table 5-1 have several functions. The functions covered in this chapter are not all of the functions available in Alpha Five.

Category	The Functions Are Used To . . .
Table	Get the table name, field length, record information, as well as, provide linking, data entry validation, record size and disk space.
Character	Alter or manipulate the content in character data type fields.
Numeric	Create mathematical calculations.
Summary	Create summary fields, like count, total and variances.
Date and Time	Format, convert and calculate date and time fields.
Logical	Evaluate an expression.
Record Query	Extract the top, bottom and Nth records from the result of a query.
Report	Enhance the appearance of reports.

Table 5-1 Function categories explained

Table Functions

The functions in this category provide information about a table. Some of the functions are explained in Table 5-2.

Function	Description	Format
CURRENT_ FILTER_EXPN	Displays the current filter of the primary table. This function can be used on a form or report.	CURRENT_FILTER_ EXPN()
DBF	Displays the name of the current table.	DBF()
ISBLANK	Checks records to see if a field is blank. Evaluates to true for records that the field is blank. (1)	ISBLANK ("Customer_Name")
ISNOTBLANK	Checks records to see if a field is not blank. Evaluates to true for records that the field is not blank. (1)	ISNOTBLANK ("Customer_Name")
LEN	Displays the length of a field.	LEN(Customer_Name)
RECCOUNT	Counts the number of records in the current or primary table in the current layout or the table listed in the expression, which can be a different table.	RECCOUNT(Customers)
TABLE	Displays the name of the current primary table.	TABLE()

Table 5-2 Table functions explained

(1) This is a logical expression.

Exercise Tips
As you will see, many of the steps in the exercises are repetitive. The tips below explain the repetitive steps.

① Unless stated otherwise, for the exercises in this chapter, make sure that the **BRING UP FIELD GENIE BUTTON** on the Drag Drop List panel or Fields panel is selected before dragging the **<NEW CALCULATED FIELD>** option to the layout.
② Right before the step that reads "Type <calculated field name>" as the name, drag the <New Calculated Field> option to the form or report section specified.
③ The step that starts with "Type <name> as the name" means to type the <name> in the Name field on the Define Calculated/Summary Field dialog box. Type the expression in the Expression field on the dialog box.
④ Some of the calculated fields need to have an option changed. These options are on the Setup or Format tab on the Field Properties dialog box, which is referenced as the "properties dialog box" in the exercises.

Exercise 5.1: Display The Table Name

In this exercise you will create a calculated field on a form and a browse that displays the table name.

Use The DBF Function On A Form

1. Display a Default Form based on the Contacts table. Save it as aFunctionDBF.

2. Type dbf_function as the name.

   Type the expression dbf(), as shown in Figure 5-6.

   When you view the form, you will see the field shown at the top of Figure 5-7, with the table name displayed.

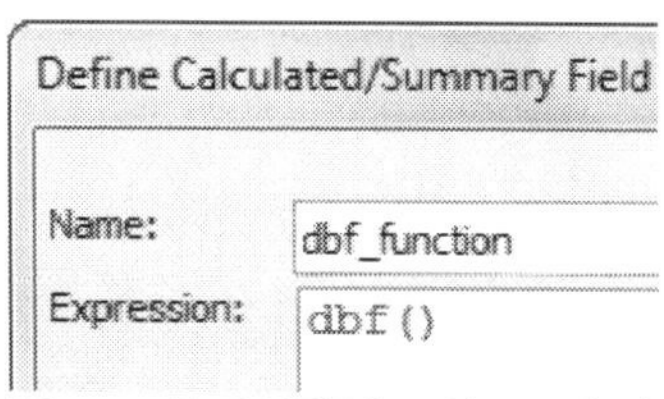

Figure 5-6 DBF function calculated field

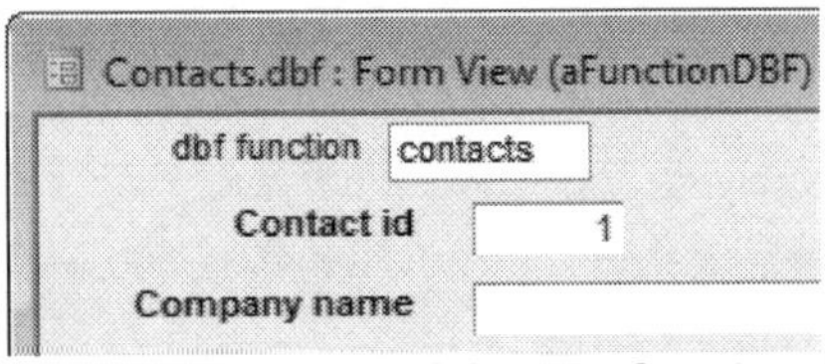

Figure 5-7 Result of the DBF function displayed on a form

Use The DBF Function On A Browse

In this part of the exercise you will create the same calculated field that you created for the form. The difference is that you will add the calculated field to a browse.

1. Save the Orders multi table set browse as `aFunctionDBF`.

2. From the Fields panel, add a calculated field to the browse and place it after the Order ID field.

3. Repeat step 2 from the forms part of this exercise to create the expression.

   When you view the browse, you should see the calculated field after the Order ID field, as shown in Figure 5-8.

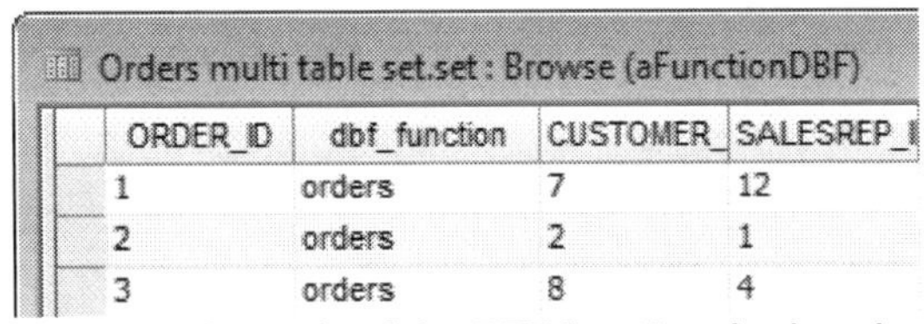

Figure 5-8 Result of the DBF function displayed on a browse

Exercise 5.2: Check To See If A Field Is Empty

In this exercise you will use the **ISBLANK** function to determine whether or not a field is blank. You will also create custom messages that will be displayed based on whether or not the field is empty.

1. Save the Find By Form form as `aFunctionISBLANK`.

2. Move all of the fields down on the form.

3. Type `isblank_function` as the name.
   Type the expression `isblank("company_name")`

   When you view the form, a "T" will be displayed in the calculated field if the Company Name field is empty, as shown in Figure 5-9. An "F" will be displayed in the field if the Company Name field has data.

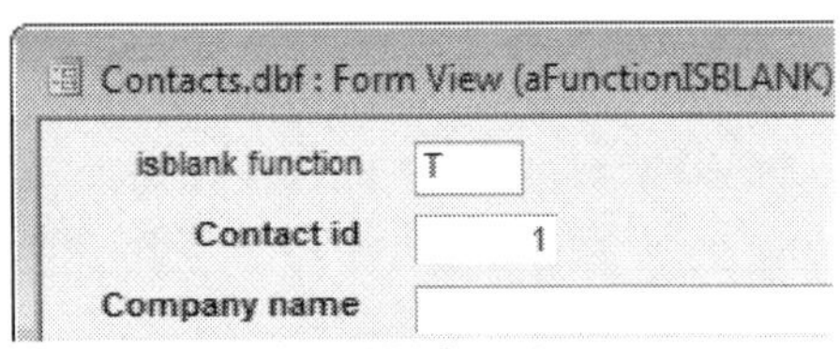

Figure 5-9 ISBLANK function

Customize The ISBLANK Function

In this part of the exercise you will learn how to display a different message in the calculated field based on whether or not a condition is met. This requires using the **IF OPERATOR**, which is covered in detail later in this chapter.

1. Save the aFunctionISBLANK form as `aFunctionISBLANKCustom`.

2. Move all of the fields down except the calculated field.

3. Add a calculated field to the form below the ISBLANK calculated field.

   Type `isblank_custom` as the name.
   Type the expression `if(isblank("Company_Name"), "No Company Name", "Has Company Name")`, as shown in Figure 5-10.

   This expression says "If the Company Name field is empty, display No Company Name in the calculated field, otherwise, display Has Company Name" in the calculated field.

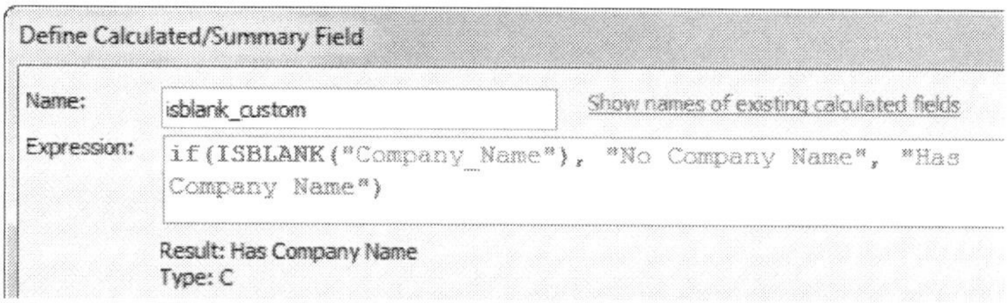

Figure 5-10 Expression to customize the ISBLANK function

4. On the properties dialog box for the ISBLANK custom field, change the Display Format Width to 20, as illustrated in Figure 5-11.

   Changing this option allows more characters to be displayed in the field. When you view a record that has data in the Company Name field, the ISBLANK custom calculated field displays the message shown in Figure 5-12.

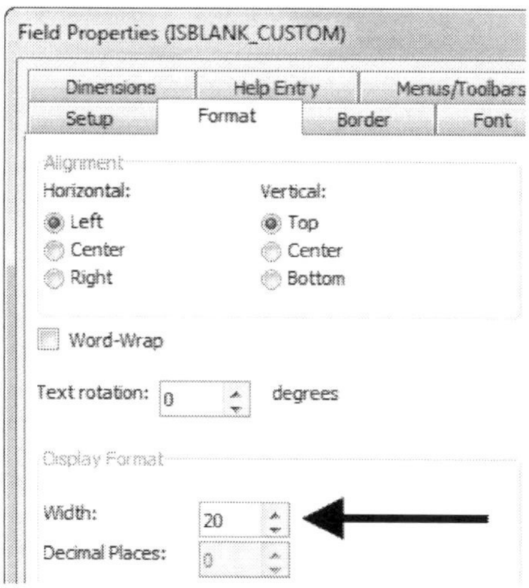

Figure 5-11 ISBLANK custom field properties

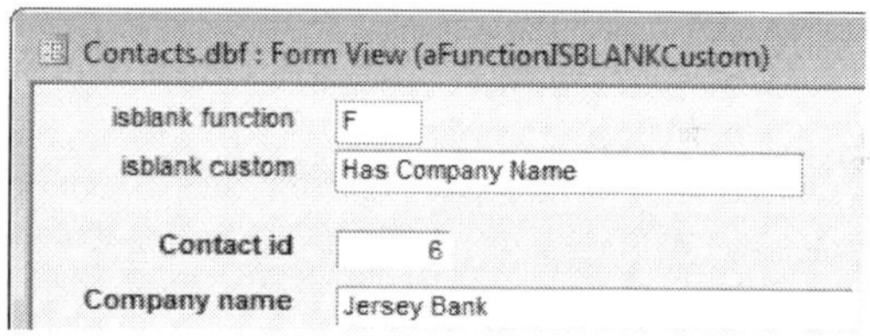

Figure 5-12 ISBLANK calculated field message

Add Color To The Calculated Field

If you wanted to go a step further and change the font color and/or background color of a calculated field, follow the steps below.

1. On the properties dialog box for the custom function field, check the **COLOR EQUATION** option, then click the button at the end of the field. The options on the first row shown in Figure 5-13 will change the font color to red and display a yellow background if the Company Name field is empty.

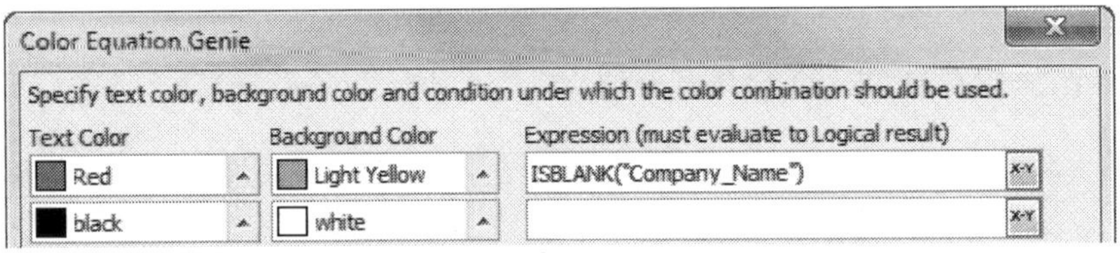

Figure 5-13 Color Equation Genie options

Exercise 5.3: Count The Number Of Records In A Table

In this exercise you will use the **RECCOUNT FUNCTION** to display the number of records in the primary table that this report is based on. In this exercise, the primary table is the customers table.

1. Save the Group totals report as `aFunctionReccount`.

2. Add a calculated field to the Report Footer section.

3. Type `reccount_function` as the name.

   Type the expression `reccount()`

   When you preview the last page of the report, you will see the number of records in the Customers table, as shown in Figure 5-14.

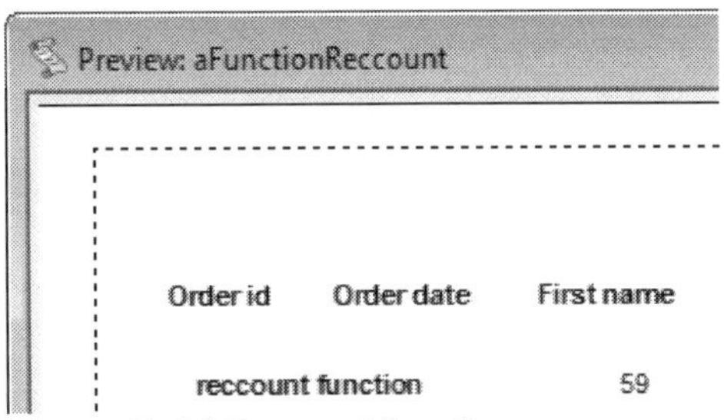

Figure 5-14 Reccount function

Count The Number Of Records In A Different Table

In the previous part of this exercise you created a count of records for the primary table of the set that the report was based on. The Reccount function can display a count of records of any table in the database, even if the table is not used in the current layout. In this part of the exercise, you will learn how to do just that.

1. Add the calculated field to the Report Footer section.
   Type `reccount_difftable` as the name.

2. Type the expression `reccount(`, then press the Page Down key on your keyboard. You will see a list of tables, as shown in Figure 5-15. Scroll down the list and select the Order lookup table.

The expression should look like the one shown in Figure 5-16. Notice that the result of the expression is displayed. When you view the last page of the report, you will see the same count for the (Order Lookup) table, as illustrated in Figure 5-17.

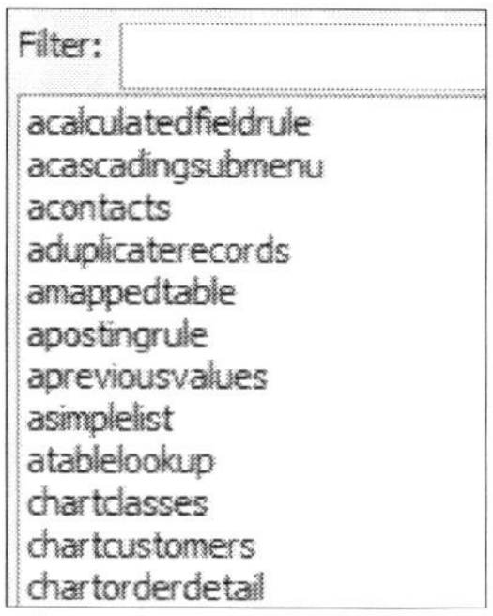

Figure 5-15 List of tables

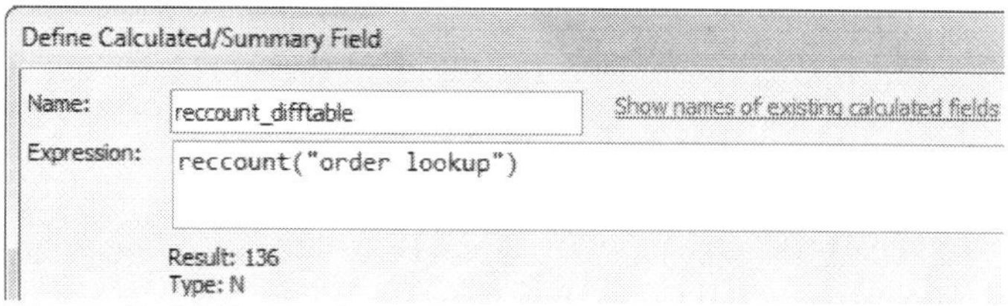

Figure 5-16 Expression to count records in a different table

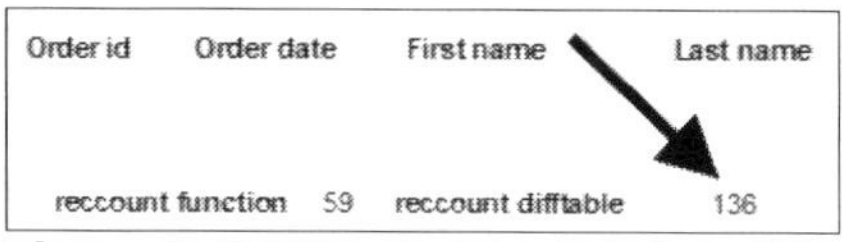

Figure 5-17 Count of records in a different table illustrated

Character Functions

The functions in this category are used to alter or manipulate the content in character fields. The functions in Table 5-3 are some of the most common character functions.

Function	Description	Format
ALLTRIM	Removes spaces from the beginning and end of the field.	ALLTRIM(Company)
F_UPPER	Converts the first character in the field to uppercase.	F_UPPER(Company)
LEFT	Extracts characters starting from the left (the beginning) of the field.	LEFT(Company,3)
LEN	[See Table 5-2]	LEN(Customer_ID)
LOWER	Converts all characters in the field to lower case.	LOWER(Company)
RIGHT	Extracts characters starting from the right (the end) of the field.	RIGHT(Company,5)
TRIM	Removes spaces from the end of the field.	TRIM(Company)
UPPER	Converts all characters in the field to upper case.	UPPER(Company)
VAL	Converts the characters in the field to a numeric value so that the value can be used in a math formula.	VAL(Customer_ID)+2

Table 5-3 Character functions explained

Using Operations To Create Character Expressions
In addition to using the Expression Builder and Define Calculated/Summary Field dialog box to create expressions, some of the Operation genies can be used to create character expressions. Some of the operations include: Search and replace, Update records and convert case of fields.

Changing The Case Of Text In A Field

The functions **LOWER**, **UPPER** and **F_UPPER** are used to format the text in a character field. These functions are useful when you need to change the case of the data stored in the field.

> **Using Case Functions**
> Unless you know for sure that data in character fields is formatted in the case that you need, it is a good idea to use one of the three functions discussed above to force the formatting.

> **Convert Case Of Fields Operation**
> This operation provides the same functionality as the Lower, Upper and F_Upper functions.

Exercise 5.4: Change The Case Of Data In A Character Field

In this exercise you will create three formulas that will change the case of the same field. Using the same field for all three formulas will make it easier to see how each function changes the content of the field.

1. Create a default form for the Products table, then save it as `aFunctionConvertText`.

2. Delete all of the fields on the form except the Product Name field, then move the Product Name field up to the top of the form.

3. Create the three calculated fields in Table 5-4.

   The report should look like the one shown in Figure 5-18.

Name	Expression
lower_function	lower(product_name)
upper_function	upper(product_name)
f_upper_function	f_upper(product_name)

Table 5-4 Calculated fields to create

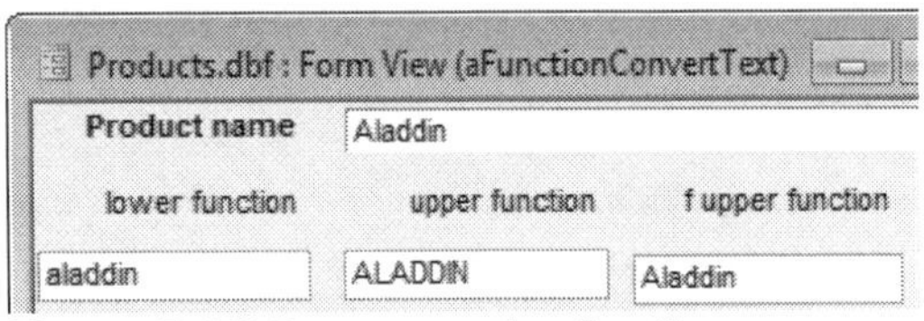

Figure 5-18 Case conversion functions

Retrieving Part Of The Data In A Field

You may have the need to only display part of the data in a field. For example, because of horizontal spacing concerns, you may only be able to display the first 20 characters of a field on the report. To ensure that only the first 20 characters are displayed, you would use the **LEFT FUNCTION**.

Exercise 5.5: Retrieve Part Of The Data In A Character Field

In this exercise you will learn how to extract part of the data in a field. You will extract the first three characters in the Last Name field.

1. Save the Find By Form form as `aFunctionLeft`.

2. Type `left_function` as the name.

   Type the expression
   `left(last_name, 3)`

   Figure 5-19 illustrates the result of the Left function applied to the Last name field.

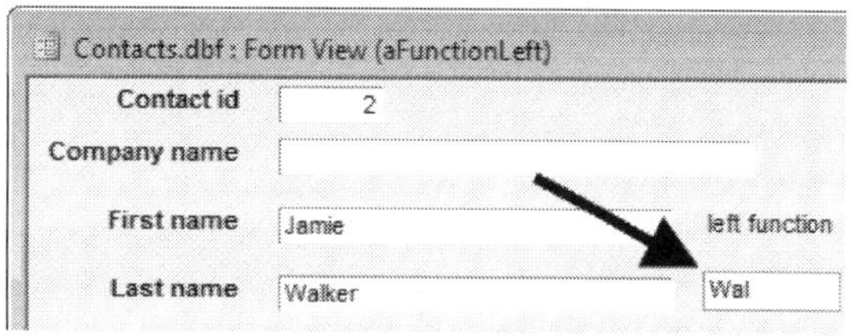

Figure 5-19 Left function

Comparison Operators

The operators in Table 5-5 are used to compare values. These operators are often used with the **IF FUNCTION** to create filters or search criteria.

The result must be a logical value, like True or False.

Operator	Finds Records That Are . . .
=	Equal to a value.
>	Greater than a value.
>=	Greater than or equal to a value.
<	Less than a value.
<=	Less than or equal to a value.
<>	Not equal to the value.

Table 5-5 Comparison operators explained

> **Comparison And Logical Operators**
> These operators are not referenced consistently throughout Alpha Five. For example, when creating an argument, you will see them referenced to as **CRITERIA**. I just wanted to let you know that regardless of what the comparison or logical operators are called, they work the same way that they are explained in this chapter. For example, the Filter Builder uses the **IS ON OR AFTER THE DATE OPERATOR**. This is the same as the **IS GREATER THAN OR EQUAL TO OPERATOR** that is used on the QBF Helper in Chapter 11, Figure 11-15.

Numeric Operators

The numeric operators in Table 5-6 are used to create mathematical calculations.

Operator	Description
+	Adds the values in the fields together.
-	Subtracts the value in one field from the value in another field.
*	Multiplies the values in the fields.
/	Divides the value in one field by the value in another field.

Table 5-6 Numeric operators explained

Expression Evaluation Order

Many of the expressions that you create will use more than one operator. The order that the expression is written in from left to right may not be the order that the expression is calculated or evaluated in. Some operators are processed first, regardless of where they are in the expression. This is known as the **ORDER OF PRECEDENCE**. The expression evaluation order is:

① The portion of the expression that is in parenthesis.
② Exponential
③ Multiplication and division (2) (3)
④ Addition and subtraction (2)

(2) If the operators in 3 and 4 above are on the same level, they are evaluated from left to right. See the examples below.

Example #1 3 + 4 / (2 + 19) = 3.19
Example #2 3 + (4 / 2) + 19 = 24

The first example calculates (2+19) first, then divides that by 4 and then adds 3.
The second example calculates (4/2) first, then adds 3 and then adds 19.

(3) Percents are evaluated at the same level as multiplication and division.

> **Expression Creation Tips**
> On your own, you may find it helpful to write the expression on paper and use data in the tables to test the expression to see if you get the results that you are expecting from the expression. As you saw in the examples above, the same data and operators can produce different results.
>
> I have noticed in the workplace and in classes that I have taught, that creating expressions is one area where many people have a lot of trouble. I think this is because they are not willing to write out the expression and test it prior to typing it. Yes, I am fully aware that doing this takes more time up front, but experience shows that the more time that you spend "preparing", the less time you will spend "debugging" in the future. Trust me, a year from now, you will not remember why you wrote an expression the way that you did <smile>. Keep the following in mind when creating expressions:
>
> ① Expressions must have an equal number of left and right parenthesis.
> ② Arguments must be the same data type.

Exercise 5.6: Create The Line Item Total Calculation

The line item total will calculate the quantity times price for each item on an order. The quantity and price fields are in the Order detail table.

1. Create a new blank free-form report using the Order detail table as the data source.

2. Add a Page Header section to the report.

   Create the report layout shown in Figure 5-20.

   Save the report as `aLineItemTotal`.

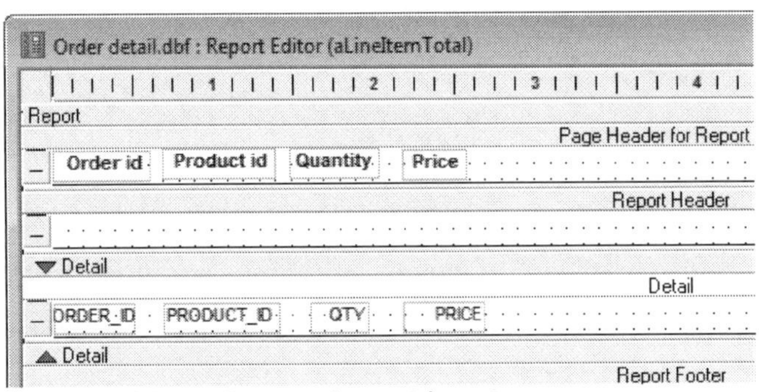

Figure 5-20 Line item total report layout

3. Add a calculated field to the Detail section.

   Type `line_total` as the name.

   Type the expression `qty * price`

   The report should look like the one shown in Figure 5-21.

   This report shows the total amount for each item on each order.

Order id	Product id	Quantity	Price	line total
1	CO295	10	79.95	799.50
1	CH007	10	14.95	149.50
2	LA044	1	29.95	29.95
3	CH100	25	12.95	323.75
3	CH101	10	12.95	129.50
3	CO200	3	129.00	387.00
3	LA048	20	29.95	599.00
3	CH220	15	12.95	194.25
4	CO888	1	129.00	129.00

Figure 5-21 Line item total calculation

Exercise 5.7: Create A Sales Tax Calculation

In this exercise you will create a 7% sales tax calculation for each item on a report.

1. Save the aLineItemTotal report as `aSalesTax`.

2. Add a calculated field to the Detail section.
   Type `sales_tax` as the name.
   Type the expression `line_total * .07`

3. On the properties dialog box for the Sales tax field, change the **DECIMAL PLACES** field to 2, as shown in Figure 5-22.

   Doing this is the same as rounding the cents to two decimal places.

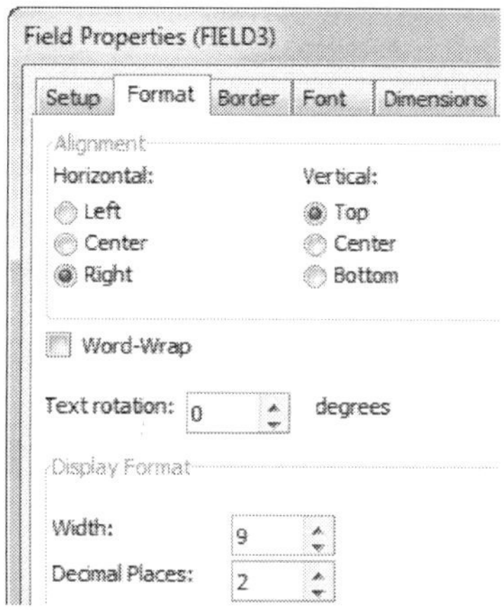

Figure 5-22 Field Properties Format tab options

4. On the properties dialog box for the Line Item field, change the **FORMAT STYLE** to $123,456.78 [blank if zero]. (4)

   The report should look like the one shown in Figure 5-23.

Order id	Product id	Quantity	Price	line total	sales tax
1	CO295	10	79.95	$799.50	55.97
1	CH007	10	14.95	$149.50	10.47
2	LA044	1	29.95	$29.95	2.10
3	CH100	25	12.95	$323.75	22.66
3	CH101	10	12.95	$129.50	9.07
3	CO200	3	129.00	$387.00	27.09
3	LA048	20	29.95	$599.00	41.93
3	CH220	15	12.95	$194.25	13.60
4	CO888	1	129.00	$129.00	9.03

Figure 5-23 Sales tax calculated field

(4) **Numeric Format Style**
Selecting a format style that has the **[BLANK IF ZERO]** option is the same as using the **ZBLANK FUNCTION**, which is used to display a blank in the field if the number is zero.

Numeric Functions

So far, this chapter has covered functions that are mostly used for fields that have text in them. Date functions are for fields that have dates in them. Numeric functions are for fields that have numeric data. These fields are often used in a math expression, which is used to answer a question. In addition to multiplication, division and subtraction, numeric functions include percents, averages, rounding, Nth largest and count.

The numeric functions in Table 5-7 use some or all of the five arguments listed below.
[See the Format column in Table 5-7 for the arguments] If no records that match the key are found, a zero is displayed in the field.

Numeric Function Arguments

① **LOOKUP TABLE** The table that will be searched.

② **INDEX TAGNAME** The field in the Lookup table that will be searched for the Key Value.

③ **KEY VALUE** The value (or field in the Lookup table that has the value) that will be searched for in the Index Tagname.

④ **LOOKUP EXPRESSION** The field in the Lookup table that the function will be applied to.

⑤ **FILTER** Criteria that the record must meet to be included in the calculation. The filter must evaluate to True or False.

Function	Description	Format
DBAVG	Searches the Lookup table for records that match the Key Value, then calculates the average of the values in the Lookup expression.	DBAVG("Lookup table", "Index Tagname", "Key Value", "Lookup Expression")
DBCOUNT	Counts the number of records in the Lookup table that have the Key Value.	DBCOUNT("Lookup table", "Index Tagname", "Key Value")
DBMAX	Finds the highest value in the records that are selected.	DBMAX("Lookup table", "Index Tagname", "Key Value", "Lookup Expression")
DBMIN	Finds the lowest value in the records that are selected.	("Lookup table", "Index Tagname", "Key Value", "Lookup Expression")
DBSUM	Searches the Lookup table for records that match the Key Value, then sums the values in the Lookup expression.	DBSUM("Lookup table", "Index Tagname", "Key Value", "Lookup Expression")
ROUND	Rounds the value up, based on the number of decimal places listed in the expression.	ROUND(Price,2)
TABLEAVG	Searches the Lookup table for records that match the filter, then calculates the average of the values in the Lookup expression. [See TABLEAVG Function Examples]	TABLEAVG("Lookup table", "Filter", "Lookup Expression")

Table 5-7 Numeric functions explained

Function	Description	Format
TABLECOUNT	Counts the number of records in the Lookup table that match the filter. [See TABLECOUNT Function Examples]	TABLECOUNT("Lookup table", "Filter", "Lookup Expression")
TABLEMAX	Finds the highest value in the table.	TABLEMAX("Lookup table", "Filter", "Lookup Expression")
TABLEMIN	Finds the lowest value in the table.	TABLEMIN("Lookup table", "Filter", "Lookup Expression")
TABLESUM	Searches the Lookup table for records that match the filter, then sums the values in the Lookup expression. [See TABLEAVG Function Examples. The expressions are the same. Replace TABLEAVG with TABLESUM in the expression]	TABLESUM("Lookup table", "Filter", "Lookup Expression")

Table 5-7 Numeric functions explained (Continued)

Using Operations To Create Numeric Expressions
The Update (Records) Genie can create the following numeric expressions that you can customize: Perform numeric calculations, Assign a constant value to a field and Assign serial (sequential) numbers to a field.

TABLEAVG Function Examples

The examples below show how to use the function depending on the data type. Each of the examples calculates the average of the values in the Price field in the Order detail table.

① **GENERAL EXPRESSION** The following expression calculates the average of the values in the Price field. TABLEAVG("Order_detail", ".T.", "Price")

② **EXPRESSION USING A LOGICAL VARIABLE FILTER** The following expression calculates the average of the Price field if the By Check field equals true. TABLEAVG("Order_detail", "By_check", "Price")

③ **EXPRESSION USING A CHARACTER FILTER** The following expression performs the calculation when the sales rep equals Johnson. TABLEAVG("Order_detail", "Rep = 'Johnson' ", "Price")

④ **EXPRESSION USING A NUMBER FILTER** The following expression performs the calculation when the price is less than $200. TABLEAVG("Order_detail", "Price < 200.00", "Price")

⑤ **EXPRESSION USING A DATE FILTER** The following expression performs the calculation when the order date is greater than 9/19/2012. TABLEAVG("Order_detail", "Order_date" > {09/19/2012}", "Price")

TABLECOUNT Function Examples

The examples below show how to use the function depending on the data type. Each of the examples count the number of records that meet the condition.

① **GENERAL EXPRESSION** The following expression counts all of the records in the Order detail table. TABLECOUNT("Order_detail", ".T.")

② **EXPRESSION USING A LOGICAL VARIABLE FILTER** The following expression counts the record when the By Check field equals true. TABLECOUNT("Order_detail", "By_check", "Price")

③ **EXPRESSION USING A CHARACTER FILTER** The following expression counts the number of records that have the rep named Johnson. TABLECOUNT("Orders", "Rep = 'Johnson' ")

④ **EXPRESSION USING A NUMBER FILTER** The following expression counts the number of records in the Order detail table that have a price less than $200. TABLECOUNT("Order_detail", "Price < 200.00", "Price")

⑤ **EXPRESSION USING A DATE FILTER** The following expression counts the number of records whose order date is greater than 9/19/2012. TABLECOUNT("Order_detail", "Order_date" > {09/19/2012}", "Price")

Exercise 5.8: Calculate The Average Value

In this exercise you will use the **DBAVG FUNCTION** to calculate the average quantity ordered of a specific product.

1. Save the aLineItemTotal report as `aFunctionDBAVG`.

2. Add a calculated field to the Page Header section above the field titles.
   Type `average_quantity` as the name.
   Type the expression `dbavg("Order_detail", "Product_ID", "LA048", "qty")`

3. On the report, change the fields title to
   `Avg quantity ordered for product LA048.`

4. On the properties dialog box for the calculated field, change the Decimal Places to zero.

   The top of the report should look like the one shown in Figure 5-24.

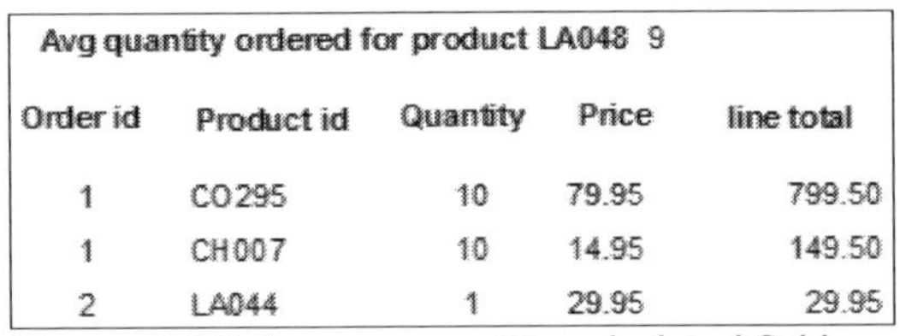

Avg quantity ordered for product LA048 9

Order id	Product id	Quantity	Price	line total
1	CO295	10	79.95	799.50
1	CH007	10	14.95	149.50
2	LA044	1	29.95	29.95

Figure 5-24 Average quantity calculated field

Exercise 5.9: Use The SUM Functions

In this exercise you will create expressions using the **DBSUM** and **TABLESUM FUNCTIONS**. The DBSUM function will be used to get a total quantity sold of the product LA048. The TABLESUM function will be used to calculate the total price of orders where the item price is $15 or less.

1. Save the aLineItemTotal report as `aFunctionSUM`.

2. Add a calculated field to the Page Header section above the field titles.
   Type `dbsum_function` as the name.
   Type the expression `dbsum("order_detail", "product_id", "LA048", "qty")`

3. Add a calculated field to the Page Header section below the field that you just created.
   Type `tablesum_function` as the name.
   Type the expression `tablesum("order_detail", "price <= 15.00", "price")`

4. On the properties dialog box for the tablesum calculated field, change the Format Style to display a dollar sign.

   The result of the expressions should look like the ones shown at the top of Figure 5-25.

dbsum function 240

tablesum function $1,214.50

Order id	Product id	Quantity	Price	line total
1	CO295	10	79.95	799.50
1	CH007	10	14.95	149.50
2	LA044	1	29.95	29.95
3	CH100	25	12.95	323.75

Figure 5-25 Sum calculations

Exercise 5.10: Use The TABLECOUNT Functions

In this exercise you will use this function to calculate how many orders a specific customer placed.

1. Create a blank, free-form report that uses the Orders table as the data source.

2. Add a Page Header section.

3. Create the report layout shown in Figure 5-26.

   Save the report as `aFunctionTABLECOUNT`.

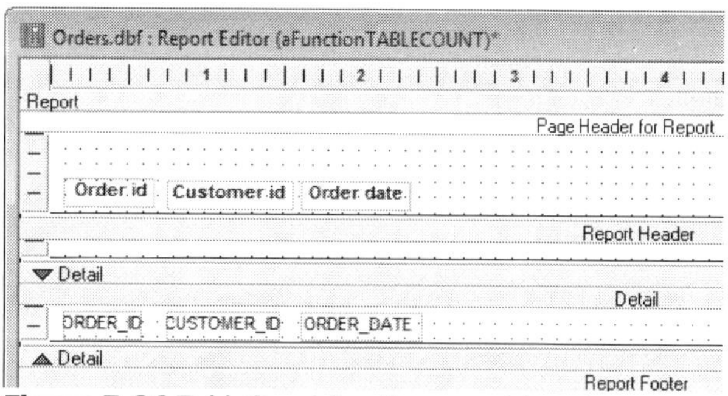

Figure 5-26 TableCount function report layout

4. Add a calculated field to the Page Header section above the field titles.
   Type `tablecount_function` as the name.
   Type the expression `tablecount("orders", "Customer_ID = 8")`

5. On the properties dialog box, change the Display Format Width option to 4.

   The report should look like the one shown in Figure 5-27.

tablecount function 6

Order id	Customer id	Order date
1	7	02/01/2011
2	2	02/01/2011
3	8	02/01/2011
4	15	02/01/2011

Figure 5-27 TABLECOUNT calculation report

Because you just created the report, you know that the TableCount function displays the number of orders for customer 8. If this report was going into production, it would need to be sorted on the Customer ID field, so that all of the orders for each customer are displayed together. The report would also need to display which customer the count is for.

Summary Functions

Summary functions are a sub category of numeric functions. These functions are used to get a count, total or average of values in a field. Some of the summary functions are explained in Table 5-8.

Function	Description	Format
AVERAGE	Calculates the average value of the selected records.	(5)
COUNT	Counts the number of records.	(5)
RUN_COUNT	Creates a running total of the selected records.	(5) (6)
TOTAL	Creates a total (sum of) the selected records.	(5)
RUN_AVERAGE	Is used in the Detail section of the report to create a running average for the records in the group.	(5)
RUN_TOTAL	Creates a total sum of the selected records.	(5) (6)

Table 5-8 Summary functions explained

(5) The format for this function is Function Name(Expression, Grp -> Group, Grp -> Sub-group).
(6) This is like a grand total.

Summary Arguments

The arguments for summary functions are different then other functions. The arguments are explained in Table 5-9.

Argument	Is Used To Select . . .
Expression	The field(s) from the current table or set that you want to summarize.
Grp -> Group	When to use the expression. (7)
Grp -> Sub_group	When to reset the value to zero that is created by the function. (7)

Table 5-9 Summary arguments explained

(7) This argument is optional. It is used to select the range of records to summarize. Examples of this argument are listed below.

- ☑ **NAME OF THE CURRENT TABLE.** Include all records in the table.
- ☑ **NAME OF A TABLE IN THE CURRENT SET.** Include all records in the set.
- ☑ **GROUP** Include all records in the group.
- ☑ **DETAIL** Include all records in the Detail section.
- ☑ **GRAND** Include all records in the table or set.

Calculated Values Dialog Box

The dialog box shown in Figure 5-28 is used to view, edit and create calculated fields. It is primarily used with reports, but can be used with other types of layouts. You can use it instead of the Define Calculated/Summary Field dialog box to create a calculated field. To open this dialog box, click the XY (Calculated Fields) button on the toolbar. The buttons at the bottom of the dialog box are explained in Table 5-10.

As illustrated in the lower left corner of the dialog box shown in Figure 5-28, you will see a letter and a value if the cursor is on a line with an expression. The letter represents the type of value (character, numeric etc.) and the value that the expression returns. In the figure, the line total expression is selected. It is numeric and returns the value 799.5.

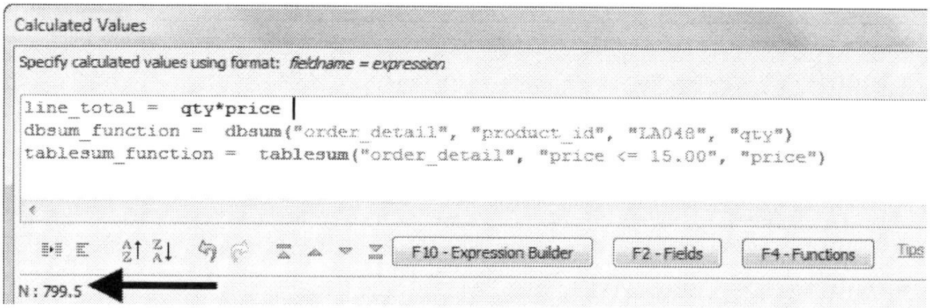

Figure 5-28 Calculated Values dialog box

Option	Description
Line up columns	Is used to space out the columns by lining up the equal signs, as shown in Figure 5-29. This may make it easier to read the expressions.
Do not line up columns	This is the default option. The expressions are displayed just like you typed them, as shown above in Figure 5-28.
Sort calculated values in ascending order	Sorts the expressions in ascending order by the calculated field name.
Sort calculated values in descending order	Sorts the expressions in descending order by the calculated field name.
Undo last edit	Removes the last change made on the dialog box.
Redo last edit	Adds the last change back.
Move to top	Moves the calculated field that has the mouse insertion point to the top of the list.
Move up one row	Moves the calculated field that has the mouse insertion point up one row.
Move down one row	Moves the calculated field that has the mouse insertion point down one row.
Move to bottom	Moves the calculated field that has the mouse insertion point to the bottom of the list.
F10 - Expression Builder button	Opens the Expression Builder.
F2 - Fields button	Opens the dialog box shown in Figure 5-30. It displays the fields for the table used in the report. You can select the field(s) that you need to create the expression. If the report is based on a set, the dialog box shown in Figure 5-31 is displayed.
F4 - Functions button	Opens the dialog box shown in Figure 5-32. This dialog box is used to search for a function.

Table 5-10 Calculated Values dialog box buttons explained

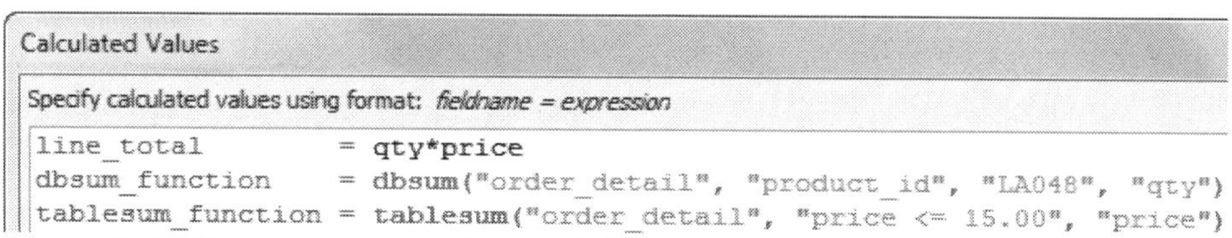

Figure 5-29 Line up columns option applied to the expressions

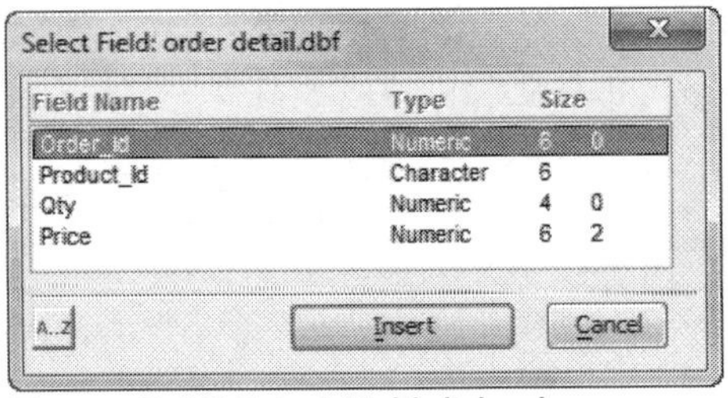

Figure 5-30 Select Field dialog box (for a table)

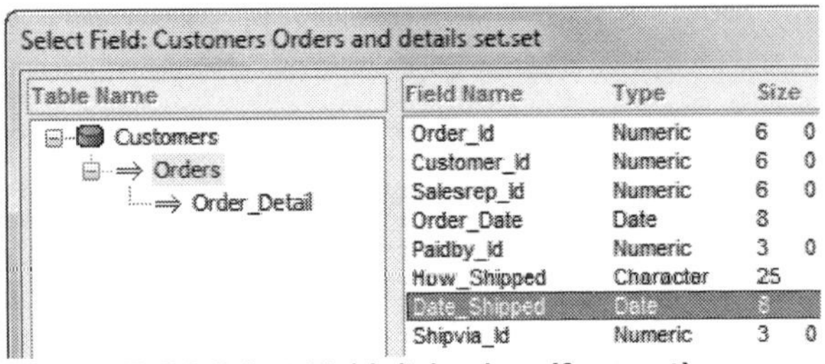

Figure 5-31 Select Field dialog box (for a set)

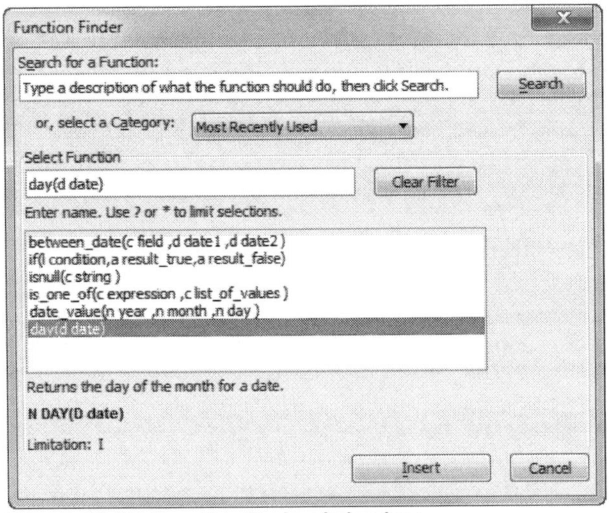

Figure 5-32 Function Finder dialog box

Exercise 5.11: Summary Functions

In this exercise you will use four summary functions. This will let you see the value that each function produces.

Create The Report

1. Create a blank free-form report based on the Orders-Order detail set. Save the report as `aFunctionSummary`.

2. Delete the Report Header section, then add the Page Header section.

3. Create a group for the Order ID field.

4. Add the fields shown in Figure 5-33 to the report.

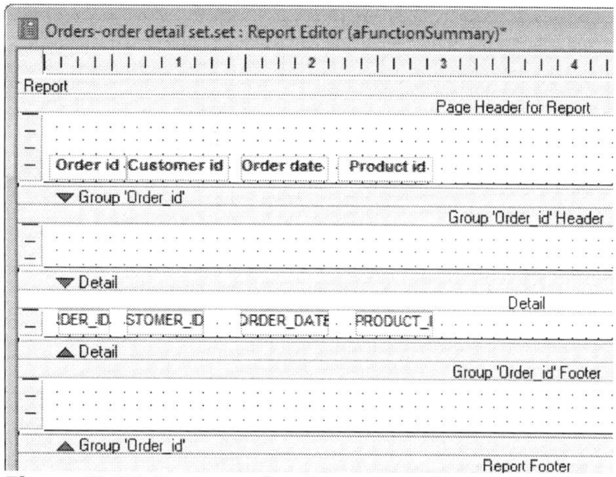

Figure 5-33 Summary functions report layout

Use The COUNT Function

This function will be used to count the number of different products per order. Yes, you could use the Field Genie and add the Product ID field to the Group Footer section to calculate the count, but I want to demonstrate how to use the COUNT function.

1. Add a calculated field to the Group Footer section.
2. Type `product_count` as the name.
   Type the expression `count(order_detail->product_id,grp -> orders)`

Use The RUN_COUNT Function

This function will be used to create a count that totals all of the products. It will be placed in the Group Footer section. This expression is similar to the COUNT expression, so I will show you a shortcut to create this expression.

1. Open the Calculated Values dialog box.
2. Select the product_count expression. Copy it, then paste it on the next line.
3. Type `running` in front of the expression name, product_count.
4. Type `run_` in front of the function.
5. At the end of the expression, change the word orders to `GRAND`. The expression should look like the one on the second line shown in Figure 5-34.

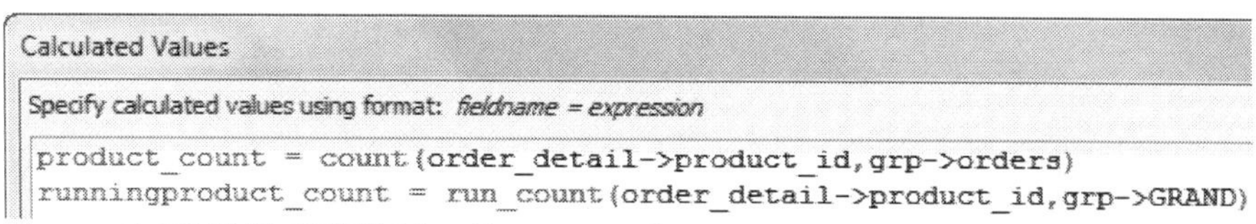

Figure 5-34 RUN_COUNT function expression

6. Add the runningproduct count calculated field to the Detail section. Put the title in the Page Header section.

Use The TOTAL Function

This function will be used to create a sub total for each order. To do this, you need to create the line item total calculated field that you created earlier in Exercise 5.6. You may be tempted to paste the expression from that report into this report. In this exercise, that would not work because that report only used one table and this report uses a set.

1. Create a calculated field named `line_item`, that uses the expression shown in Figure 5-35.

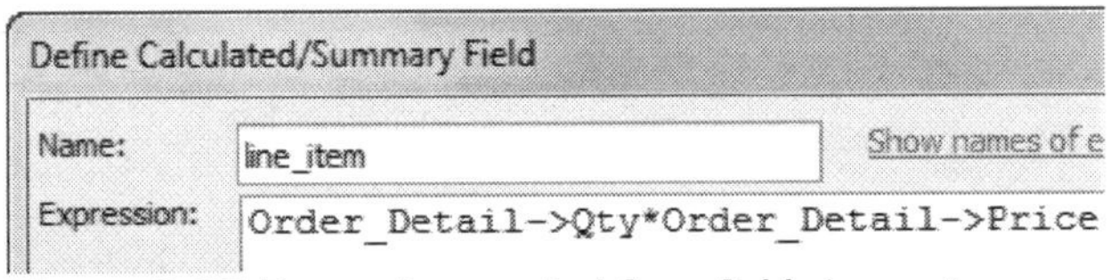

Figure 5-35 Expression created from fields in a set

2. Add the calculated field to the Detail section after the Product ID field.

3. Create a calculated field named `order_total`.
   Type the expression `Order_total = TOTAL(calc -> line_item, grp -> order_id, grp -> detail)`

> **Calc Argument**
> The calc -> argument indicates that the field is a calculated field instead of a field in a table.

4. Add the calculated field to the Group Footer section, aligned with the Line item field on the properties dialog box. Format the field to display two decimal places and use the third option in the Format Style drop-down list.

Use The RUN_TOTAL Function

This function will be used to create a running total of the line item amount.

1. Add a calculated field to the Detail section.

2. Type `runningorder_total` as the name.

   Type the expression `run_total(calc -> line_item)`

   Your report should look like the one shown in Figure 5-36.

Order id	Customer id	Order date	Product id	line item	runningproduct count	runningorder total
1	7	02/01/2011	CO295	799.50	1	799.50
1	7	02/01/2011	CH007	149.50	2	949.00
product count 2			order total	$949.00		
2	2	02/01/2011	LA044	29.95	3	978.95
product count 1			order total	$29.95		
3	8	02/01/2011	CH100	323.75	4	1302.70
3	8	02/01/2011	CH101	129.50	5	1432.20
3	8	02/01/2011	CO200	387.00	6	1819.20
3	8	02/01/2011	LA048	599.00	7	2418.20
3	8	02/01/2011	CH220	194.25	8	2612.45
product count 5			order total	$1,633.50		

Figure 5-36 Summary functions

Notice that the values in both running calculated fields increases with each record, which is what should happen.

Date Formatting Characters

Table 5-11 explains some of the more common date formatting options. Table 5-12 provides examples for the date 6/1/11.

Character	Displays The . . .
d	Day of the month in numeric format without a leading zero.
dd	Day of the month in numeric format with a leading zero if necessary.
Weekday	Name of the day spelled out.
M	Month in numeric format without a leading zero.
MM	Month in numeric format with a leading zero if necessary.
Month	Name of the month spelled out.
y or yy	Last two digits of the year.
yyyy	Year with four digits.

Table 5-11 Date formatting character options explained

This Mask . . .	Displays . . .
dd, MM, yy	01, 06, 11
Month dd yyyy	June 01 2011
Weekday Month d, yyyy	Wednesday June 1, 2011
M, d, yy	6, 1, 11

Table 5-12 Date formatting examples

Typing Dates In An Expression
There will be times when you need to type in a date in the expression instead of selecting a date field. When that is the case, enclose the date in brackets. {9/19/2012} and {Jun 9, 2012} are the acceptable formats to type dates in.

Date Operators

The operators in Table 5-13 are used to add and subtract values from a date field or from a specific date.

Operator	Description
+	Adds a (constant) value to the date. (8)
-	Subtracts one date from the other date or subtracts a (constant) value from a date field. (9)

Table 5-13 Date operators explained

(8) Sample addition expression if the Order Date is 9/19/12. Order_Date + 5.
9/24/12 would be displayed.

(9) Sample subtraction expressions if the Order Date is 9/19/12.
Expression #1 Order_Date - 5. 9/14/12 would be displayed.
Expression #2 {9/19/12} - {6/24/10}. 818 (days) would be displayed.

Date And Time Functions

A large number of reports that you will create will display date fields and use date fields as selection criteria. Often, dates are stored in this format MM/DD/YYYY, but need to be displayed as September 2011 or the year portion of the field is needed for a calculation. Many of the date functions extract a portion of the date. The functions explained in Table 5-14 are some of the more popular date and time functions.

Function	Description	Format
AGE	Calculates the age based on a date.	AGE(Birthdate)
BUS_DAYS_BETWEEN	Calculates the number of business days between the dates. Business days are Monday to Friday.	BUS_DAYS_BETWEEN (Order_Date, Ship_Date)
CDATE	Displays the date in this format YYYYMMDD.	CDATE(Order_Date)
CDOW	Displays the day of the week for the date.	CDOW(Order_Date)
CMONTH	Displays the month portion of the date.	CMONTH(Order_Date)
CTOD	Converts data in a character field to a date.	CTOD("9/19/2012")
CYEAR	Displays the year portion of the date. This function is often used when you need to display the year of the date field with text.	CYEAR(Order_Date) (10)
DATE()	Displays today's date, which comes from the system settings on the computer using the form, report or browse.	DATE()
DATE_FORMAT	Displays the date in the format that you specify.	DATE_FORMAT (Order_Date, "Month DD, YYYY")
DTOC	Converts the date or time to the character data type.	DTOC(date())
ISDATE	Checks the value in the field to see if it is a valid date.	ISDATE(character field)
MOD	Divides one number by another number and returns the remainder, instead of the result of the division.	MOD()
MONTH	Displays the month name in numeric format.	MONTH(Order_Date)
TIME	Displays the current system time.	TIME(Format String) -> "Date Time Value" (11)
TOTIME	Formats the time based on the number of seconds past midnight.	TOTIME(Number of seconds, Format Code, Decimal Places)
YEAR	Displays the year portion of a field in this format YYYY.	YEAR(Order_Date)

Table 5-14 Date and Time functions explained

(10) Sample expression - "The year born is " + CYEAR(birthdate).
(11) Sample expression - TIME("Month dd yyyy") -> "September 19 2012".

> **Using Operations To Create Date And Time Expressions**
> The Update (Records) Genie can create the following date and time expressions that can be customized. Calculate the number of days between two date values, Calculate the number of seconds between two time values and Set a date field to a specific date.

Exercise 5.12: Calculate The Age

In this exercise you will learn how to calculate a persons age based on their birth date.

1. Create a blank, free-form report based on the Sales Reps table.

2. Delete the Report Header section, then add a Page Header section.

3. Add the following fields to the Detail section: Rep First Name, Rep Last Name and Birthdate.

4. Save the report as `aFunctionAge`.

5. Add a calculated field to the Detail section.

   Type `age_function` as the name.

   Type the expression `age(birthdate)`

   The report should look like the one shown in Figure 5-37. Some of the ages that are on your report will be higher then those shown in the figure because the birth date has passed.

Rep first name	Rep last name	Birthdate	age function
Veronica	Smith	12/08/1972	39
Alex	Hamilton	02/19/1969	43
Stanley	Banks	08/30/1971	41
April	Smith	09/19/1973	39
Karen	Williams	03/04/1975	37
Tom	Carter	07/02/1964	48
Bob	Thomas	05/29/1972	40
Bill	David	01/24/1974	38
June	Cable	03/13/1968	44
Mark	Hill	06/06/1973	39

Figure 5-37 Age function report

Exercise 5.13: Calculate The Days Between Dates

In this exercise you will use the subtraction numeric operator and the Business days between function to see the difference in the calculations.

Use The Business Days Function

1. Create a blank free-form report based on the Orders table.

2. Delete the Report Header section, then add a Page Header section.

3. Add the following fields to the Detail section: Order ID, Order Date and Date Shipped.

4. Save the report as `aFunctionDates`.

5. Add a calculated field to the Detail section.
   Type `busdays_function` as the name.
   Type the expression `bus_days_between(order_date, date_shipped)`

6. Change the Display Format Width option to 3.

Create The Subtract Dates Expression

1. Add a calculated field to the Detail section.

2. Type `days_between` as the name.
Type the expression `date_shipped - order_date`
The report should look like the one shown in Figure 5-38. Notice that the function and operator return different values for the same dates.

Order id	Order date	Date shipped	busdays function	days between
1	02/01/2011	02/13/2011	9	12
2	02/01/2011	02/13/2011	9	12
3	02/01/2011	02/14/2011	10	13
4	02/01/2011	02/14/2011	10	13
5	02/02/2011	03/02/2011	21	28

Figure 5-38 Days between dates report

Exercise 5.14: Display Today's Date

In this exercise you will learn how to use the **DTOC FUNCTION** to display today's date on a form.

1. Save the Display customer name form as `aTodaysDate`.

2. Add a calculated field below the orange text field at the top of the form.
Type `display_date` as the name.
Type the expression `"Today is - " + dtoc(date())`
Delete the calculated field title.

3. On the properties dialog box, border tab, change the Border Style to None (No Border).

   The date should look like the one shown in Figure 5-39.

Figure 5-39 Today's date displayed on a form

Logical Operators

The operators in Table 5-15 are used between logical expressions. They are used to select which expression evaluates to True.

Operator	Finds Records That . . .
.AND.	Match all criteria.
IF	Meet the criteria.
.NOT.	Do not match the criteria.
.OR.	Match at least one of the criteria.

Table 5-15 Logical operators explained

Conditional Expressions

Conditional expressions are used to provide different options depending on a value. If...Then...Else statements, Select Case statements and the Case function are three of the more popular ways to create conditional expressions.

> **Conditional Formatting Tips**
> The formatting that has been covered up to this point in this book has been applied to every instance (record). Conditional formatting provides the option of whether or not to apply the formatting. Some of the formatting options on the properties dialog box have a button at the end of the field. Being able to create an expression for an option, provides more control over how the option works.

IF Operator

This operator allows different actions to be taken based on a condition. It is commonly referred to an **IF THEN ELSE STATEMENT**.

If...Then...Else Statements

This is one of the most used lines of programming code. This statement is used to set different options based on what you need to happen when the data is evaluated. The syntax below is for an If Then Else statement.

If **EXPRESSION/CONDITION** Then **TRUE STATEMENTS**
Else
FALSE STATEMENTS

Parts Of The If Then Else Statement Explained

① The **EXPRESSION/CONDITION** must evaluate to true or false.
② The **TRUE STATEMENTS** will execute if the Expression/Condition is true.
③ The **ELSE** part of the statement is optional. If the Else clause is not included and the Expression/Condition is false, nothing will happen, which may be what you want. By "nothing happens", I mean that the If statement will default to the value for the data type. For example, If Field A is greater than 95, then textfield5 = "Great Job". If the variable "textfield5" was not declared to have a specific default value, the default value for a text field data type is " " (null), which is what would be displayed if Field A is not greater than 95. The rule of thumb is to use the Else keyword to avoid problems like these.
④ The **FALSE STATEMENTS** will execute if the Expression/Condition is false.

The plain English translation of an If Then Else statement is: **IF** Choice A meets this condition, **THEN** do X, **ELSE** do Y. Walk through the examples in Table 5-16 to gain a better understanding of If Then Else statements. Fill in the column on the right based on the numbers in the Choice A column.

If Choice A is greater than 25,
then Field B = 100, else Field B = 0.

Choice A	What Does Field B=
26	
1	
25	

Table 5-16 If Then Else examples

It may help to understand If...Then...Else statements if you think of them as a true or false test question. In the example above, the test question can be worded as "Is Choice A greater than 25?" There are two possible answers:

① Yes it is (True). If it is, Field B would be set to 100.

② No it isn't (False). If it isn't, Field B would be set to 0.

How Did You Do?

Table 5-17 contains the answers for the second column in Table 5-16 above. The third column in the table explains the answer.

Choice A	Field B=	Reason
26	100	The answer is 100 because 26 is greater than 25.
1	0	The answer is 0 because 1 is less than 25.
25	0	The answer is 0 because 25 is not greater than 25.

Table 5-17 Answers for Table 5-16

To complicate If statements even more, there can be multiple true and false statements in the same If Then Else statement. Statements with multiple true and false statements are known as **NESTED IF STATEMENTS**. Nested if statements are used to create multiple conditions. The Nested If statement below translates to: If the Ship Via ID field equals 1, set the field to First Class. If the Ship Via ID field equals 2, set the field to Media Mail. If the Ship Via ID field equals 3, set the field to Priority Mail.

If (Ship Via ID = "1", How Shipped = "First Class" else
If Ship Via ID = "2", How Shipped = "Media Mail" else
If Ship Via ID = "3", How Shipped = "Priority Mail" else
How Shipped = Ship Via ID)

Exercise 5.15: Create A Conditional Expression

In this exercise you will create an expression using the If...Then...Else statement. The expression will display one value if the condition is true and display a different value if the condition is false.

1. Save the aLineItemTotal report as `aIFStatement`.

2. Add a calculated field to the Detail section.
   Type `if_expression` as the name.
   Type the expression `if (calc -> line_total >= 150, "Shipped Priority Mail", "Shipped 1st Class")`

   The report should look like the one shown in Figure 5-40.

Order id	Product id	Quantity	Price	line total	if expression
1	CO295	10	79.95	799.50	Shipped Priority Mail
1	CH007	10	14.95	149.50	Shipped 1st Class
2	LA044	1	29.95	29.95	Shipped 1st Class
3	CH100	25	12.95	323.75	Shipped Priority Mail
3	CH101	10	12.95	129.50	Shipped 1st Class

Figure 5-40 IF logical operator report

Logical Functions

The functions in Table 5-18 are used to create expressions that evaluate to True or False. This includes filter expressions. These functions are usually used as part of a conditional expression.

Function	Description	Format
*LEADING	Determines if the value in a field starts with the value specified.	*LEADING(Last_Name, "B")
BETWEEN	Determines if the value in a field is between the values specified.	BETWEEN(Order_Date, {9/19/2011}, {12/31/2011})
CASE	Determines if the value in a field matches one of the values specified. This function works the same as the .OR. operator.	CASE (Order_ID = "1234", .t., Order_ID = "345", .t., Order_ID = "6789", .t.)
CCVALID	Returns true if the credit card number is valid.	CCVALID(Card_Nbr)
CONTAINS	Determines if the value specified is in the field that is being searched.	CONTAINS(State, "CA")
ISDATE	[See Table 5-14]	ISDATE("9/19/12")
ISBLANK	[See Table 5-2]	ISBLANK("Customer_Name")
ISNULL	Determines if the field is empty.	ISNULL(Company_Name)

Table 5-18 Logical functions explained

Exercise 5.16: Use The BETWEEN Function

In this exercise you will use the BETWEEN function to display a message when the date falls within a range. If the date does not fall within the range, no message will be displayed.

1. Save the aFunctionDates report as `aFunctionBetween`.

2. Add a calculated field to the Detail section.
   Type `between_function` as the name.
   Type the expression `if(between(order_date, {3/1/11}, {3/20/11}) = .t., "Ordered during a sale", " ")`

   When you view order dates in the date range, you will see the message shown in the last column in Figure 5-41.

Order id	Order date	Date shipped	busdays function	days between	between function
53	02/05/2011	03/06/2011	20	29	
54	03/12/2011	05/25/2011	53	74	Ordered during a sale
55	03/15/2011	03/15/2011	1	0	Ordered during a sale

Figure 5-41 Between function

Case Function vs Select Case Statement

Both of these options accomplish the same result. The difference is that Select Case statements cannot be used in an expression because it uses more than one line. Both options are explained below.

Select ... Case Statement

The Select Case statement is similar to the If Then Else statement because it is used to create a conditional statement. I personally find Select Case statements easier to read and understand, especially easier then Nested If statements.

```
Select
    Case Order_Amount >= 10000 Discount_Amount = "10% discount"
    Case Order_Amount >= 5000 Discount_Amount = "15% discount"
    Case Order_Amount >= 2500 Discount_Amount = "20% discount"
    Case Else Discount_Amount = "25% discount"
```

Each **CASE CLAUSE** is like its own If statement. The value after the Case clause is the condition that you are checking for. The value has to be the same data type as the field after the Case clause.

Case clauses are evaluated in the order that they are listed, from top to bottom. If you are using a range of values on the Case clause, make sure that they are in the right order because the select value is evaluated for each Case clause.

The **CASE ELSE CLAUSE** is the equivalent of the "else" part of an If Then Else statement. Enter what you want to happen if the select value does not meet any of the case conditions.

Exercise 5.17: Use The CASE Function To Select Records

In this exercise you will use the CASE function to select specific orders to display on the report. To accomplish this, a filter expression has to be created, instead of a calculated field. The expression that you will create will only display records for the following Order ID's: 3, 9, 10 and 100.

1. Save the aIFStatement report as `aFunctionCaseFilter`.

2. Report ⇒ Select Records.

3. Type the expression in the Filter field, as shown in Figure 5-42.

   ```
   case(3=order_id, .t., 9 = order_id, .t., 10 = order_id, .t.,
   100 = order_id, .t.)
   ```

   When you preview the report, you should only see records with one of the Order IDs used in the expression.

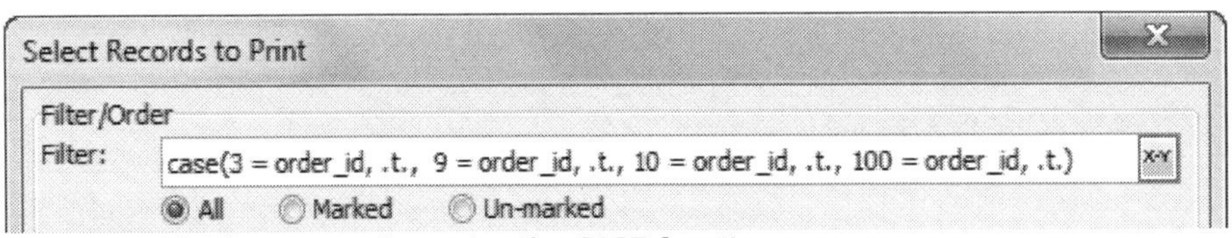

Figure 5-42 Filter expression using the CASE function

Exercise 5.18: Use The CASE Function With Range Values

Earlier you saw a sample Select Case statement. In this exercise you will use the CASE function to accomplish the same task. This is similar to the BETWEEN function that you used in Exercise 5.16 and the Nested IF statement.

1. Save the aLineItemTotal report as `aFunctionCaseRange`.

2. Delete the Report Header section.

3. Add a calculated field to the Detail section.
   Type `discount_message` as the name.

   The expression that you create must be typed on one line. It is displayed on multiple lines here to make it easier for you to read.

   Type this expression.

```
case(calc->line_total >= 1000,"10% discount",
calc->line_total >= 750, "15% discount",
calc->line_total >= 500, "20% discount",
calc->line_total >= 250, "25% discount",
calc->line_total < 250, "30% discount")
```

   The report should look like the one shown in Figure 5-43.

Order id	Product id	Quantity	Price	line total	discount message
1	CO295	10	79.95	799.50	15% discount
1	CH007	10	14.95	149.50	30% discount
2	LA044	1	29.95	29.95	30% discount
3	CH100	25	12.95	323.75	25% discount
3	CH101	10	12.95	129.50	30% discount

Figure 5-43 Case function with range values report

Record Query Functions

The majority of functions in Table 5-19 are used to create what are commonly known as **TOP N** and **BOTTOM N** reports. **N** is a number that you select. The records that these functions select from must first meet any other criteria that the report has. An example that you may be familiar with is the Top 100 songs. The equivalent of these Top and Bottom N functions.

Function	Description	Format
BOTTOM_PERCENT_RECORDS	Selects the bottom (lowest) N percent of records.	BOTTOM_PERCENT_RECORDS()
BOTTOM_RECORDS	Selects the bottom (lowest) N number of records.	BOTTOM_RECORDS()
SAMPLE_RECORDS	Selects every Nth record.	SAMPLE_RECORDS()
TOP_PERCENT_RECORDS	Selects the top (highest) N percent of records.	TOP_PERCENT_RECORDS()
TOP_RECORDS	Selects the top (highest) N number of records.	TOP_RECORDS()

Table 5-19 Record query functions explained

Report Functions

The functions in Table 5-20 are used to enhance the appearance of reports. The last two functions in this table are used to place page totals and counts on a report.

Function	Description	Format
BLANK_DUPLICATE	Hides values in a field that has the same value in two or more consecutive records.	BLANK_DUPLICATE(Expression, Grp -> Group, Grp -> Sub-group)
PAGECOUNT	Displays the total number of pages in the report.	PAGECOUNT()
PAGENO	Displays the current page number of the report.	PAGENO(Grp -> Group_Name) (12)

Table 5-20 Report functions explained

(12) The **GRP ARGUMENT** in optional. Use it on a report when you want the page number to be reset when the value in the field being grouped on changes. Put the page number calculated field in the Group Footer section. [See Exercise 5.20]

Exercise 5.19: Hide Duplicate Values

In this exercise you will learn how to use the **BLANK_DUPLICATE FUNCTION** to hide data that is repeated. Doing this can help make the report easier to read.

1. Create a blank free-form report based on the Contacts table.

2. Delete the Report Header section, then add the Page Header section.

3. Add a calculated field to the Detail section.
   Type `blank_field` as the name.
   Type the expression `blank_duplicate(state_province)`
   Change the title to `State`.

4. Add the First name, Last name and City fields to the Detail section.

5. Sort the records on the State Province field.

6. Save the report as `aFunctionBlankDuplicate`.
   The report should look like the one shown in Figure 5-44. Notice that the state field is only displayed for the first record in the state.

The No Code Way To Hide Duplicate Values
If you do not want to write code to hide duplicate or **REPEATED VALUES**, follow the steps below.

1. On the Drag Drop List panel, enable the **BRING UP GENIE** option.
2. Drag the field or calculated field that you want to hide duplicate values on, to the report.
3. You will see the dialog box shown in Figure 5-45. Check the **DON'T PRINT REPEATED VALUES** option, then click OK.

State	First name	Last name	City
CT	Clair	Walsh	Menden
	Tina	Walker	Stamford
	Tom	Smith	Wilton
	Fred	Amos	Westwood
	Louis	Riker	Tappan
	June	Brannigan	Lodi
	Mary	David	Westwood
	Jane	Downey	Westwood
	Keith	Dickerson	Tappan
	Marvin	Easterling	Tappan
FL	Tina	Jones	Ft Lee
	Stuart	Thomas	Orlando
	Todd	Green	Tampa

Figure 5-44 Blank Duplicate function

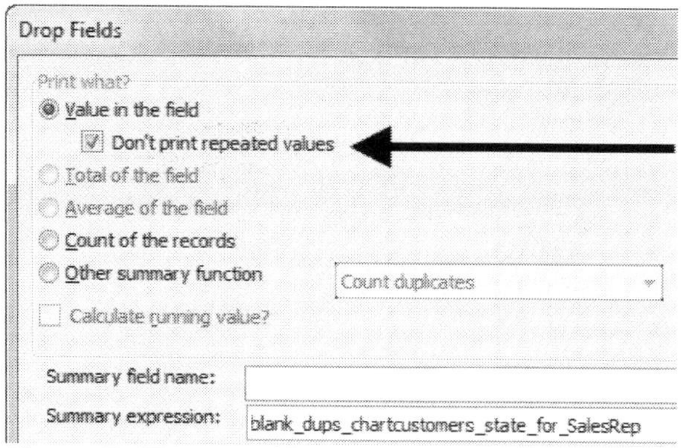

Figure 5-45 Drop Fields dialog box

Exercise 5.20: Add Page Numbers To A Report

In this exercise you will learn how to use two page number functions to display page numbers in different layouts.

Create A Basic Page Number

1. Save the aFunctionReccount report as `aFunctionPageNumbers`.
2. Delete the Customer ID Group Header section.
3. Add a Page Footer section, then add a calculated field to the section.
4. Type `basic_pagenbr` as the name.
   Type the expression `"Page " + pageno()`
   Move the title to the far left of the section, then move the calculated field below the title.
   Save the changes.

Create The X Of Y Page Number

1. Add a calculated field to the Page Footer section.
   Type `total_pagecount` as the name.
   Type the expression `"Page " + pageno() + " of " + pagecount()`
   Move the field next to the basic page number field.

Create A Page Count Per Group

The page number that you will create in this part of the exercise will be displayed in a Group Footer section. This page number will automatically be reset for each group on the report. In addition to the page number, the calculated field will also display the state (which is the field being grouped on).

1. Add a calculated field to the State Group Footer section.
   Type `group_pagecount` as the name.
   Type the expression `"Page " + pageno(grp -> state) + " for " + state`
   Change the Display Format Width to 20.

2. Add the Page Break control to the bottom of the State Group Footer section. When you view the bottom of the last page of the report for CT, you should see the three page number styles illustrated in Figure 5-46.

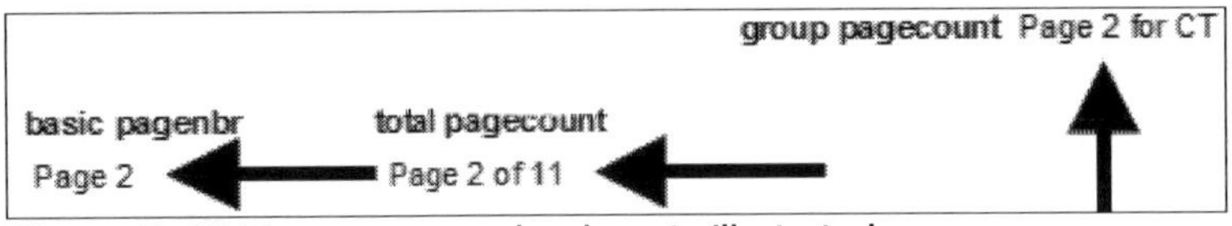

Figure 5-46 Three page number layouts illustrated

Exercise 5.21: Use The ISNULL Function

In this exercise you will learn how to use the ISNULL function with the IF function. The expression that you will create will display a message if the Company Name field is empty, otherwise, it will display the Company Name.

1. Save the aFunctionBlankDuplicate report as `aFunctionISNULL`.

2. Move the City field and title over to the right.

3. Add a calculated field to the Detail section after the Last name field.
   Type `isnull_function` as the name.
   Type the expression `if(isnull(company_name) = .t., "** No Company Name **", company_name)`

4. Move the title to the Page Header section, then change it to `Company`.

   As shown in Figure 5-47, there is only one contact in CT that has a company name.

State	First name	Last name	Company	City
CT	Clair	Walsh	Two of A kind	Menden
	Tina	Walker	** No Company Name **	Stamford
	Tom	Smith	** No Company Name **	Wilton
	Fred	Amos	** No Company Name **	Westwood
	Louis	Riker	** No Company Name **	Tappan
	June	Brannigan	** No Company Name **	Lodi
	Mary	David	** No Company Name **	Westwood
	Jane	Downey	** No Company Name **	Westwood
	Keith	Dickerson	** No Company Name **	Tappan
	Marvin	Easterling	** No Company Name **	Tappan

Figure 5-47 ISNULL function

COMMON TOOLBOX PANEL CONTROLS

In this chapter you will learn about the controls on the Toolbox panel.

CHAPTER 6

Overview

The Toolbox panel shown in Figure 6-1 is available for all layouts except Browses and Layout Table reports. Browses have the Browse Controls panel instead of the Toolbox panel. These **CONTROLS** are primarily used to create new objects. (The figure does not display all of the controls.)

Table 6-2 lists the controls and which layout types support it. The controls that are common to all layout types are covered in this chapter. Some of these controls can be accessed from the **OBJECT MENU** in the Layout Editor.

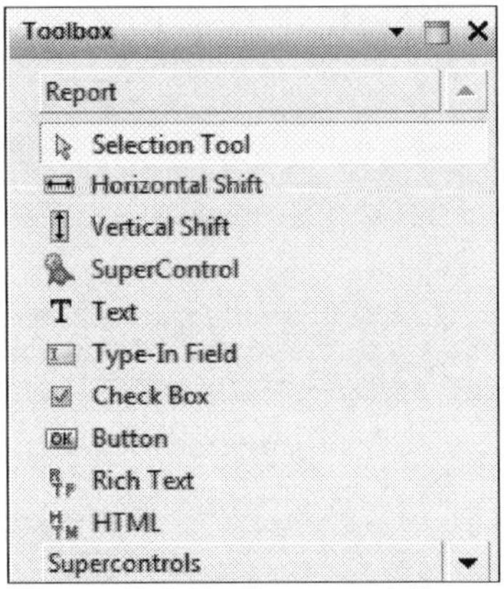

Figure 6-1 Toolbox panel (for reports)

Toolbox Panel Section Shortcut Menu

The shortcut menu shown in Figure 6-2 is displayed when you right-click on one of the sections (Report or Supercontrols for example), as shown above in Figure 6-1. The options are explained below in Table 6-1.

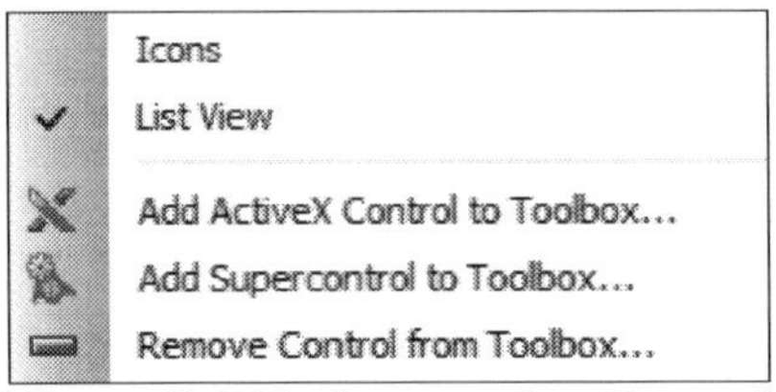

Figure 6-2 Toolbox panel section and control shortcut menu

Toolbox Panel Control Shortcut Menu

This shortcut menu is displayed when you right-click on a control in the Toolbox panel. It has the options shown above in Figure 6-2, except the last option. The options are explained in Table 6-1.

Option	Description
Icons	Only displays icons for the controls in the Toolbox, as shown in Figure 6-3.
List View	Displays the Toolbox with text and icons, as shown earlier in Figure 6-1.
Add ActiveX Control to Toolbox	Opens the dialog box shown in Figure 6-4. This dialog box is used to add ActiveX controls to the Toolbox. If you use the same ActiveX controls on a regular basis, add them to the Toolbox.
Add Supercontrol to Toolbox	Opens the dialog box shown in Figure 6-5.
Remove Control from Toolbox	(Only available on the Toolbox panel section shortcut menu.) This option does not seem to work.

Table 6-1 Toolbox shortcut menu options explained

Figure 6-3 Toolbox in icon view

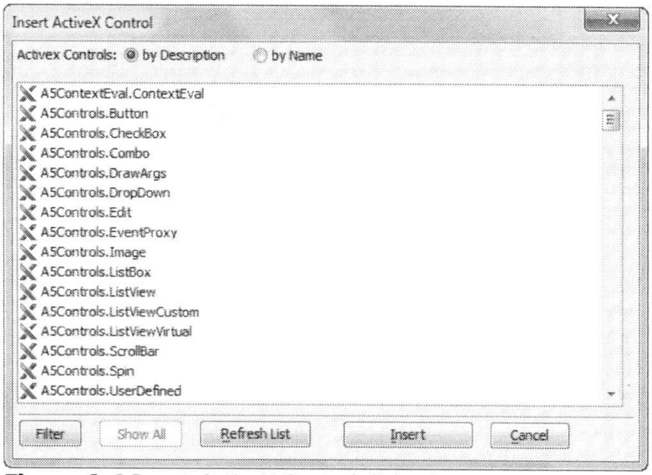

Figure 6-4 Insert ActiveX Control dialog box

Add Supercontrol Dialog Box

The dialog box shown in Figure 6-5 is used to add Super Controls to the Toolbox.

These are the same controls that are already in the Super Controls section of the Toolbox.

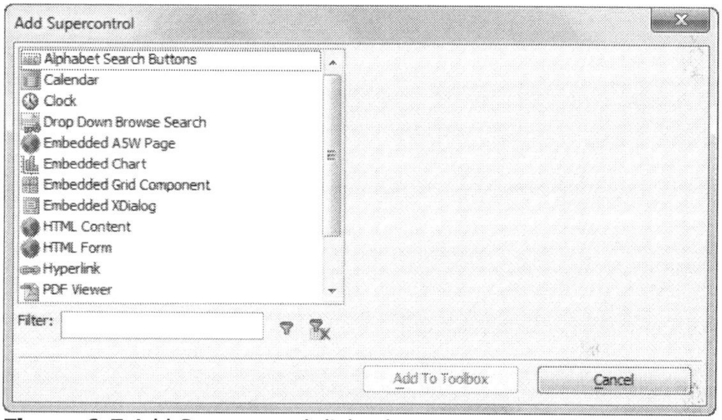

Figure 6-5 Add Supercontrol dialog box

Toolbox Panel Controls

To activate a control, click on it in the Toolbox panel, then draw a box on the layout. In addition to being located on the Toolbox panel, many of these controls can also be accessed from Object ⇒ New, in the Layout Editor. Some of the controls have slightly different names on the New Object dialog box.

Control	Forms	Reports	Letters	Labels
Selection Tool	X	X	X	X
Horizontal Shift	X	X	X	X
Vertical Shift	X	X	X	X
Text	X	X	X	X
Type-In Field	X	X	X	X
Radio Button (1) (2)	X			

Table 6-2 Toolbox panel controls

Tool/Control	Forms	Reports	Letters	Labels
Check Box (2)	X	X	X	X
Combo Box (1) (2)	X			
List Box (1) (2)	X			
Record-List Edit Combo Box (1) (2)	X			
Record-List List Box (1) (2)	X			
Tree Control (1) (2)	X			
Drop-down Tree Control (1) (2)	X			
Two-state Button (1) (2)	X			
Multi-state Button (1) (2)	X			
Button	X	X	X	X
Rich Text	X	X	X	X
HTML	X	X	X	X
Browse (1)	X			
Sub-Form (1)	X			
Bitmap	X	X	X	X
OLE Object	X	X	X	X
Frame	X	X	X	X
Line	X	X	X	X
Page Break	X	X	X	X
Conditional Object	X	X	X	X
Tabbed Object (1)	X			
Hot Spot Object	X	X	X	X
User Control	X	X	X	X
ActiveX Control	X	X	X	X
Embedded Chart	X	X	X	X
Sub-Report		X		
Linked Report		X		

Table 6-2 Toolbox panel controls (Continued)

(1) This control is covered in Chapter 7.
(2) The control can be used in place of the Type-In Field control.

Control Shortcut Menu

When added to a layout, controls have the shortcut menu shown in Figure 6-6. Some controls have one or two different options on the shortcut menu then those shown in the figure. For example, controls attached to a field that has field rules have an option to edit the field rules, as illustrated in Figure 6-7. Super Controls have the **SUPER CONTROL DESIGNER** option that opens the corresponding genie-like dialog box for that type of control.

Selection Tool Control

Is used to select an object on the layout to resize, move, modify or delete the object. This control is the same as clicking on the object. This control also removes the focus from any other control. (3)

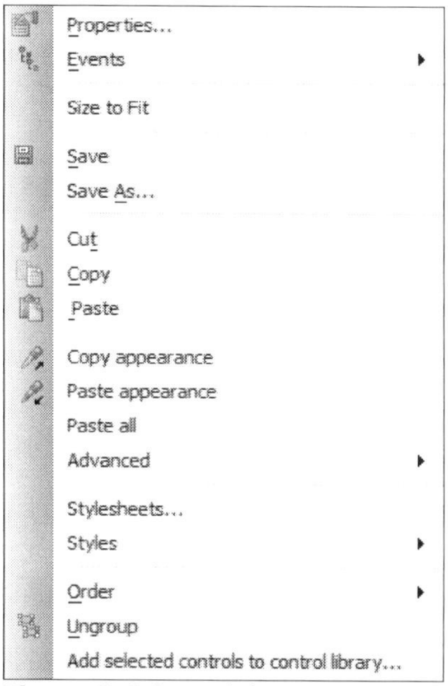

Figure 6-6 Control shortcut menu

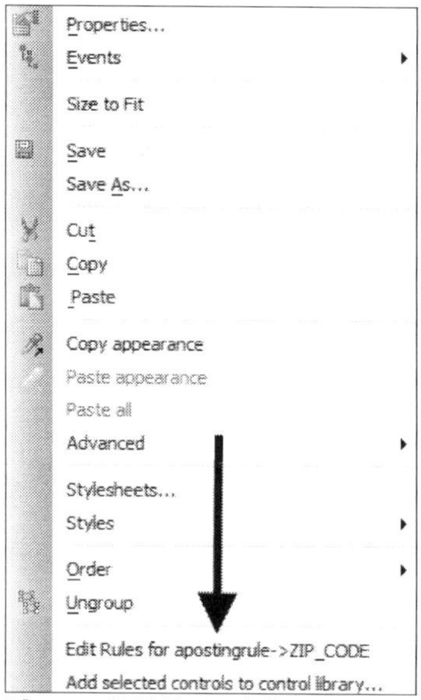

Figure 6-7 Control shortcut menu for a field with a field rule illustrated

Horizontal Shift Control

Selects all objects to the right of where you click on the layout. When you hold the mouse pointer over the layout, it will change to horizontal double arrows, as shown in Figure 6-8. When you click on the layout, objects will be selected. When you drag the mouse pointer left or right, the selected objects will move. (3)

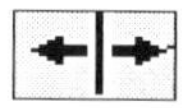

Figure 6-8 Horizontal Shift mouse pointer

Vertical Shift Control

Selects all objects below where you click on the layout. When you hold the mouse pointer over the layout, it will change to vertical double arrows, as shown in Figure 6-9. When you click on the layout, objects will be selected. When you drag the mouse pointer up or down, the selected objects will move. (3)

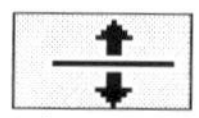

Figure 6-9 Vertical Shift mouse pointer

(3) More than likely, you will not have a lot of use for this tool.

Text Control

This control adds a text object to a form or report. This is a free form control which is used to enter the content that you need to display that is not in a table, variable or calculated field.

Type-In Field Control

This (field type) control is used to display and edit text, date, time, numeric and logical fields. By default, when a field from a table or a calculated field is added to a layout, it has the Type-In Field control type. Fields that use this control type can be switched for a control in Table 6-2 that has the footnote (2). Figure 6-20 shown later, displays all of the control types.

Check Box Control

This control toggles between selected (on) and not selected (off). It is most often used in logical fields, like Yes/No values.

Exercise 6.1: Use The Check Box Control

In this exercise you will add a logical field to a table, then add the Check Box control to the logical field on a form.

Add A Field To The Orders Table

1. Create the following field in the Orders table.
   Field Name - `By Check`
   Type - Logical

Change The Control Type Of A Field

1. Create a blank form using the Orders table.

2. Add the following fields without using the Field Genie on the Drag Drop List panel: Order ID, Customer ID, Order Date and By Check.

3. Save the form as `aCheckBoxControl`.

4. On the properties dialog box Setup tab for the By Check field, open the Control Type drop-down list and select Check Box.

Choices Tab

The options shown in Figure 6-10 are used to customize the checkbox. The options are explained below.

CHECKBOX TEXT Is used to enter the text if any, that you want to appear to the right of the check box. This field could be used to display instructions for the check box, as illustrated in Figure 6-11.

Typing **<AUTO>** in this field is used to select what text will be displayed to the right of the check box, based on whether or not the check box is checked.

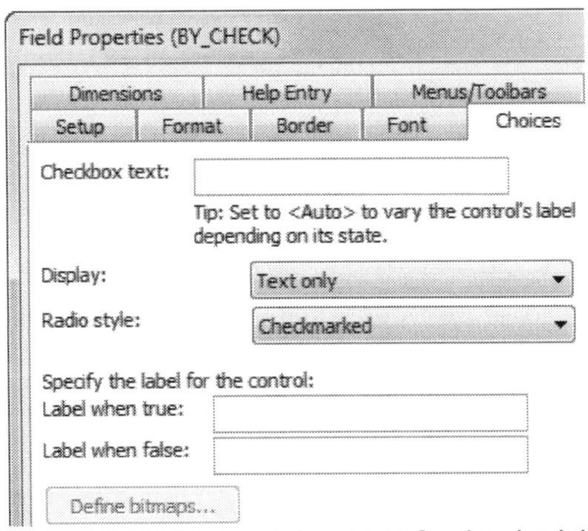

Figure 6-10 Choices tab options for the check box control

DISPLAY Is used to select whether or not an image, text or combination is displayed. Selecting any option in the drop-down list that has the word "button" in it enables the Define Bitmaps button.

RADIO STYLE Is used to select how the check mark will be displayed. Figure 6-11 illustrates the **INDENTED DIAMONDS RADIO STYLE.**

LABEL WHEN TRUE Is used to type in what text should be displayed when the check box is checked. (4)

LABEL WHEN FALSE Is used to type in what text should be displayed when the check box is not checked. (4)

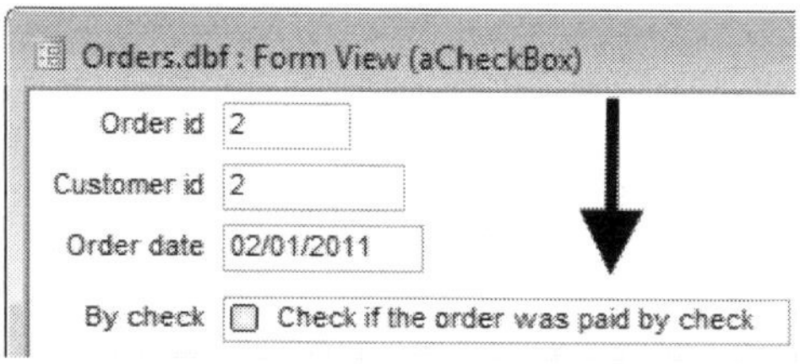

Figure 6-11 Text added to check box

Figure 6-12 Indented diamonds style illustrated

(4) This option is enabled when **<AUTO>** is entered in the Checkbox text field.

The options shown in Figure 6-13 will display the text shown in Figure 6-14 when the check box is checked and Figure 6-15 when the check box is not checked. It is not a requirement to enter text in both of the label fields.

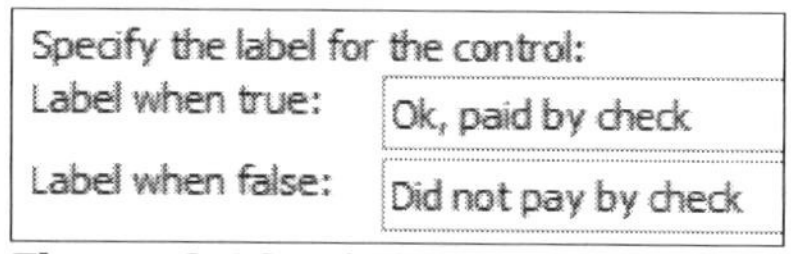

Figure 6-13 Label text

Figure 6-14 Label text when the check box is checked

Figure 6-15 Label text when the check box is not checked

DEFINE BITMAPS BUTTON Displays the dialog box shown in Figure 6-16. It is used to select the default pressed (check box is checked) and indeterminate (check box is not checked) options.

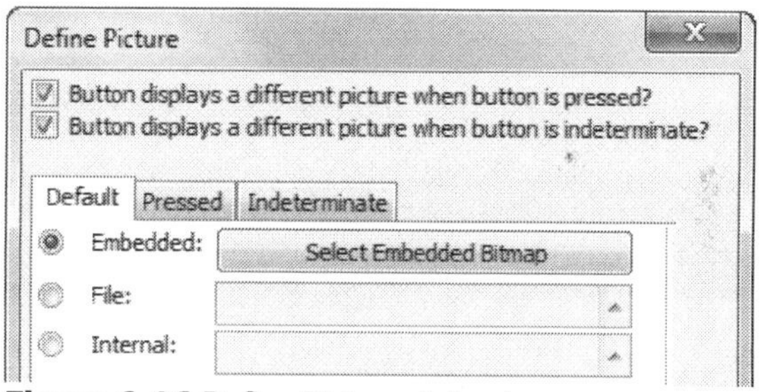

Figure 6-16 Define Picture dialog box

Add The Check Box Control To The Form

In the previous part of the exercise, you changed the control type of a field that was already on the form. In this part of the exercise you will add the Check Box control from the Toolbox to the form.

Field Select Dialog Box

The options shown in Figure 6-17 are used to select the field that will be used as a check box. The **SYSTEM TABLE** contains some of the fields that are in the System section of the Drag Drop List panel.

The **ADD VARIABLE BUTTON** opens the dialog box shown in Figure 6-18, which is used to create a variable that will be used with the check box, if needed.

Figure 6-17 Field Select dialog box

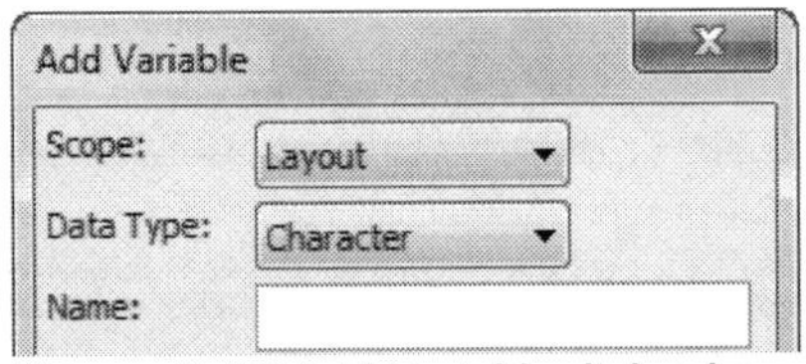

Figure 6-18 Add Variable dialog box

1. Click on the Check Box control in the Toolbox, then draw a square below the fields on the form. You should see the dialog box shown above in Figure 6-17.

2. Select the By Check field, then open the Field Properties dialog box.

   On the Setup tab, you will see the Control Type field, as shown in Figure 6-19.

   Control fields can be customized like fields in a table. As shown earlier in Figure 6-10, the **CHOICES TAB** contains options specifically for the check box.

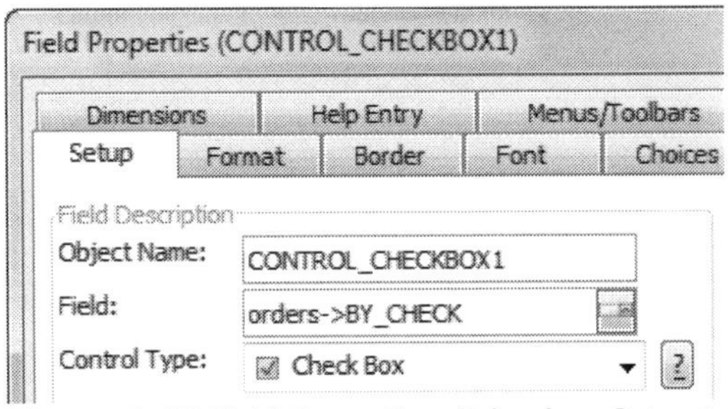

Figure 6-19 Field Properties dialog box Setup tab

Control Types

Figure 6-20 displays all of the control types that are available. The Control Type field is useful when you want to select or change how a field already on a form is displayed.

For example, a form already has the Company field on it. If you want to change the field to a drop-down list, you do not have to delete the field from the form, then add the drop-down list control and attach it to the Company field. Instead, select the Company field on the form, open the properties dialog box and select the control type from the list shown in Figure 6-20.

Clicking on the question mark button to the right of the Control Type field shown above in Figure 6-19, displays the dialog box shown in Figure 6-21. This dialog box is used to test the different control types.

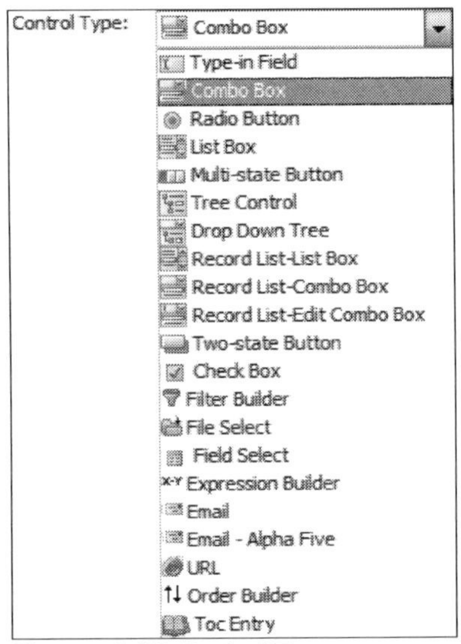

Figure 6-20 Control Types

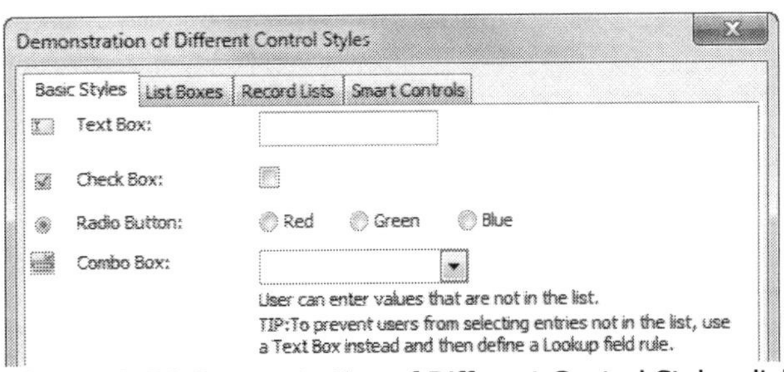

Figure 6-21 Demonstration of Different Control Styles dialog box

Button Control

This control is used to create a button like the ones on toolbars. They can have an image, text or both. Buttons can execute an **ACTION SCRIPT**. You can also use the **XBASIC EDITOR** to create a script for the button. There are also pre-defined actions that you can add to the button.

Like the other controls, the Button control is added to the form. Buttons are helpful in an application where the default menus and toolbars have been removed, but you need to provide some of the functionality or you have custom features that you want to add to a form.

Exercise 6.2: Use The Button Control

In this exercise you will learn how to set up a button to use a pre-defined action.

Use The Zoom To Record Pre-Defined Action

In this part of the exercise you will configure the Button control to use the **ZOOM TO RECORD** action. This action requires an embedded browse that will be used to select the record that will be displayed on the form when the button is clicked. The forms that are available were created from the same table or set that the form with the embedded browse was created from.

1. Save the Customers tabbed form as `aZoomButtonControl`.

2. Display the Orders tab. Click the Button control in the Toolbox, then draw a box to the left of the first browse on the form.

Define Button Dialog Box

The options shown in Figure 6-22 are used to create a custom button using a script.
The options shown in Figure 6-23 are used to select a pre-defined action for the button.

The categories in this list are the menus that are displayed by default when the form is viewed. The actions that you can select are the options on these menus. The options in the **APPEARANCE** section change, depending on the action that is selected. For example, compare the appearance options shown in Figure 6-23 to the options shown in Figure 6-26.

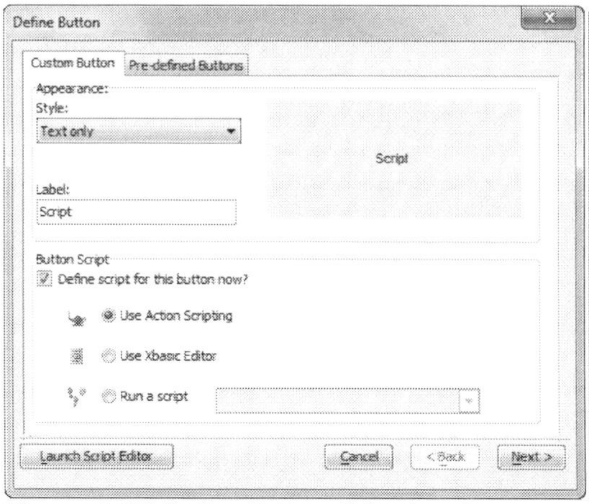

Figure 6-22 Define Button dialog box (custom options)

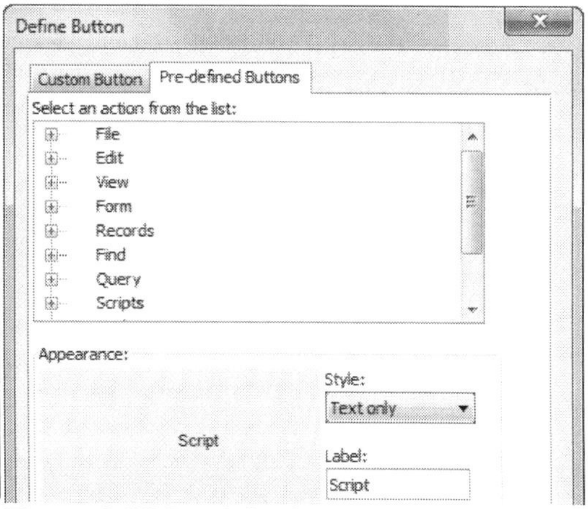

Figure 6-23 Pre-defined Buttons actions

3. On the Pre-defined Buttons tab, open the Form category, then select the Zoom To Record action.

   The **STYLE** and **DEFINE PICTURE** options are used to select what will appear on the button. The options are the same as the ones discussed earlier in the Choices Tab section.

4. Open the Style drop-down list and select Picture only, if it is not already selected.

5. Click the Define Picture button.

   The **INTERNAL** option should be selected. Click the button at the end of the field.

   On the dialog box shown in Figure 6-24, select an image from the System, Addin or Windows Images options, then click the Insert button.

   Click OK.

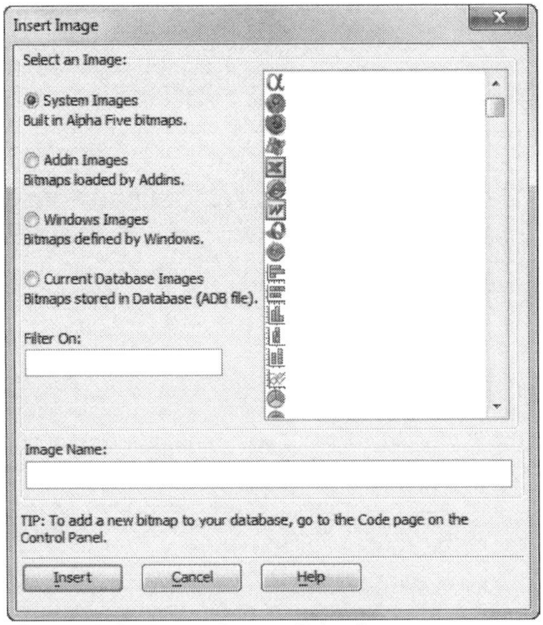

Figure 6-24 Insert Image dialog box

> Once you close the **DEFINE BUTTON DIALOG BOX** you cannot reopen it to edit the control. If you need to make changes to the control, open the properties dialog box.

6. On the Pre-defined Buttons tab, click OK, then save the changes.

Using The Button Control

7. View the Orders tab on the form, then click on a row in the top browse.

If you click on a row in a browse (in this exercise the button works with both browses on the Orders tab), then click the Zoom button, the dialog box shown in Figure 6-25 is displayed.

8. Click the button. You will see the dialog box shown in Figure 6-25.

   Select one of the forms, then click OK.

   You will see all of the data in the table for the row that you selected on the embedded browse.

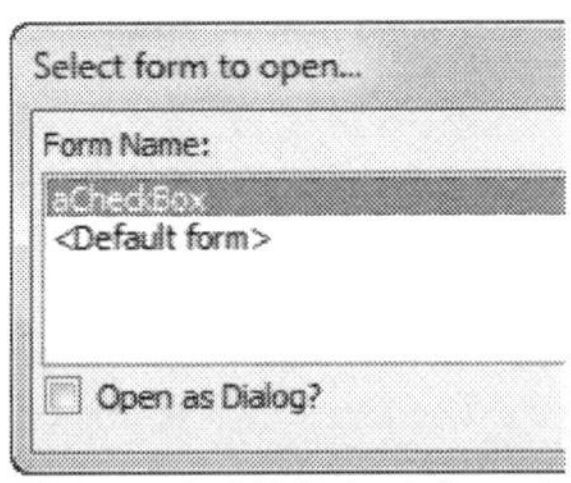

Figure 6-25 Select form to open dialog box

Exercise 6.3: Use The Export To Excel Pre-Defined Action

In this exercise you will configure the Button control to use the Export to Excel action.

1. Save the Find By Form form as `aExcelExportButton`.
2. Add the Button control to the right of the Contact ID field.
3. On the Pre-Defined Buttons tab, open the Tools category, then select the Export to Excel action.
4. Open the Style drop-down list and select **PICTURE OVER TEXT**.
5. Change the Label field to `Export data to Excel`, as shown in Figure 6-26.

   Click OK.

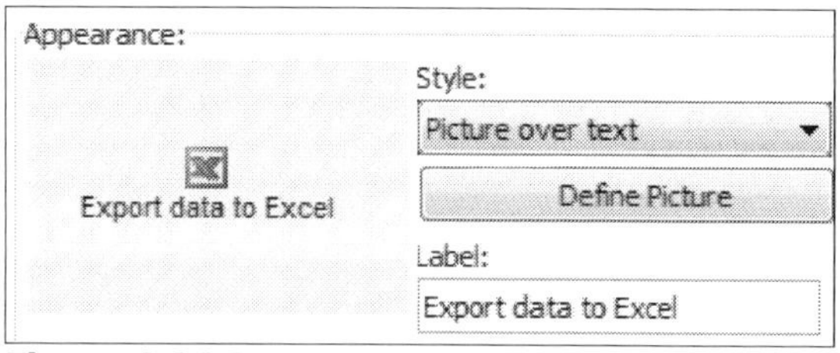

Figure 6-26 Export to Excel action options

6. Make the button large enough to see all of the words.

When you click the button shown in Figure 6-27, the data in the table is exported, Excel opens and displays the data in a spreadsheet that has the name of the table. By default, the export file is saved in the folder listed in the **PRIVATE PATH** field on the Settings dialog box. [See Chapter 1, Figure 1-3]

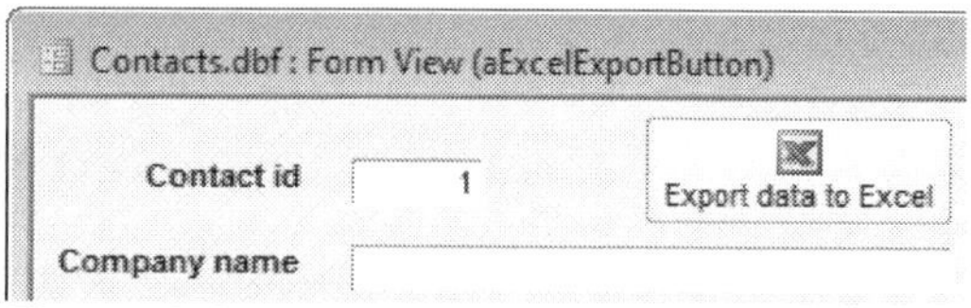

Figure 6-27 Export data to Excel button

Rich Text Control

This control is used to create a text field that you need to provide more formatting to, then the Text control discussed earlier in this chapter provides.

Figure 6-28 shows the toolbar that is displayed when the Rich Text control is used. It provides options to format the text that will be added to the field.

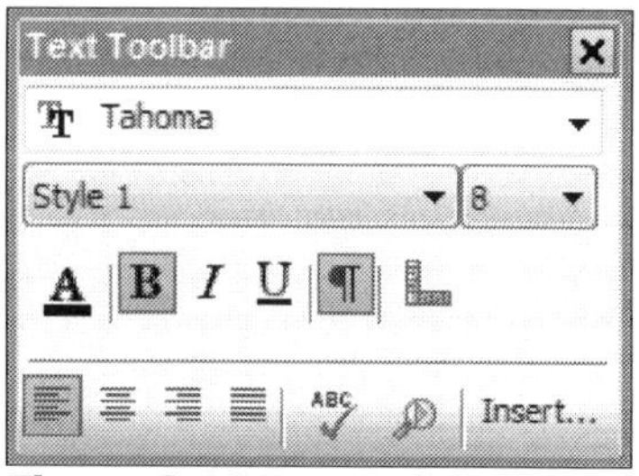

Figure 6-28 Text toolbar

Rich Text Control Shortcut Menu

In addition to the Text toolbar discussed in the previous section, the shortcut menu shown in Figure 6-29 is available for this control.

The **PROPERTIES** option opens the **RICH TEXT PROPERTIES** dialog box.

The options on the **INSERT** submenu shown in the figure are the same options when you click the Insert button on the Text toolbar which displays the **RTF INSERT COMMAND** toolbar.

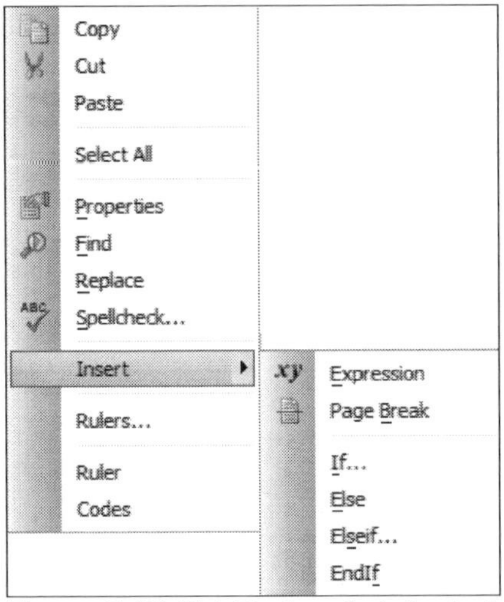

Figure 6-29 Rich Text control shortcut menu

Rich Text Control vs Text Control

These controls seem similar because text can be added to both. There are some differences, as explained below.

① The content in a Text control cannot be changed by the user. If enabled, the content in a Rich Text control can be changed by the user.
② All of the content in a Text control is formatted the same way. The content in a Rich Text control can be modified on a character by character basis, if needed.
③ Fields can be added to a Rich Text control.

Exercise 6.4: Adding Text And A Field To A Rich Text Control

In Chapter 5 you created expressions that combined text and a calculated field. All of the expression had to be formatted the same way. In this exercise, you will add text and a field to a Rich Text control and format them independently.

1. View the Chart Customers table in the Default Form. Delete the fields starting with the Email Address field to the end of the form. Save the form as `aRichTextControl`.

2. Add the Rich Text control to the form below the Last Name field.

3. Type `Last years order total is $`, then press the space bar.

4. Drag the Last Years Sales field from the Drag Drop List panel to the Rich Text control and place it after the dollar sign.

5. Double-click in the Rich Text control after the field that you just added. Press the space bar. Type `amount has different formatting`. Make the control long enough to view all of the content on one line.

6. Select the text at the beginning of the control. Change the font to Century Schoolbook, size 10 and bold.

7. Select the dollar sign and the Last Years Sales field.

   Change the font size to 10, bold and red.

   When you view the form, the Rich Text control should look like the one shown in Figure 6-30.

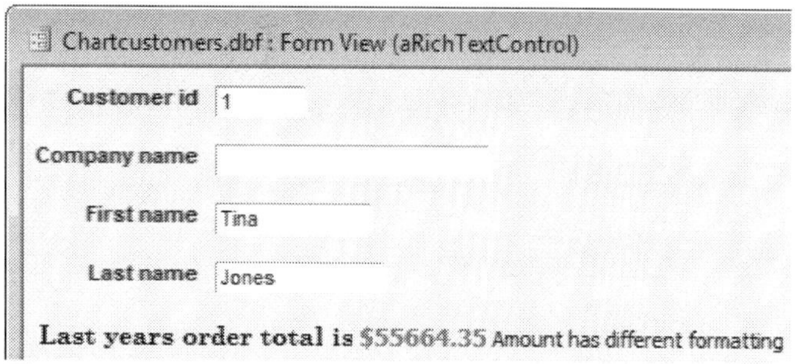

Figure 6-30 Rich Text control with text and a field

HTML Control

This control is automatically added to HTML Memo fields. At the end of a HTML Memo field on a form, you will see an icon. Click on the icon to open the editor.

This editor shown in Figure 6-31 is used to create content in a Memo field in HTML format. The editor displays the name of the HTML Memo field in the top left corner of the dialog box. The options illustrated are explained in Table 6-3.

Figure 6-31 HTML Editor (for a Memo field)

Button	Description
1	**INSERT IMAGE** Opens the dialog box shown in Figure 6-32. The options are used to select and size the image.
2	**INSERT TABLE** Opens the dialog box shown in Figure 6-33. The options are used to create a table that will be added to the HTML Memo field.
3	**INSERT HYPERLINK** Opens the dialog box shown in Figure 6-34. The options are used to create a link to a web page or to a file.
4	**INSERT CURRENT DATE** Adds the current date to the HTML Memo field.
5	**INSERT CURRENT TIME** Adds the current time to the HTML Memo field.

Table 6-3 HTML Memo field editor options explained

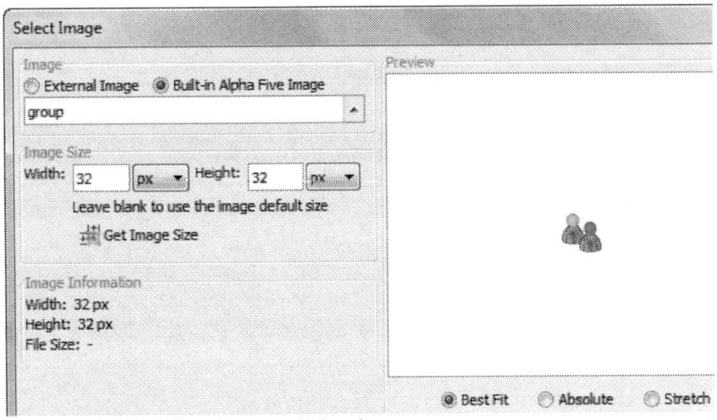

Figure 6-32 Select Image dialog box

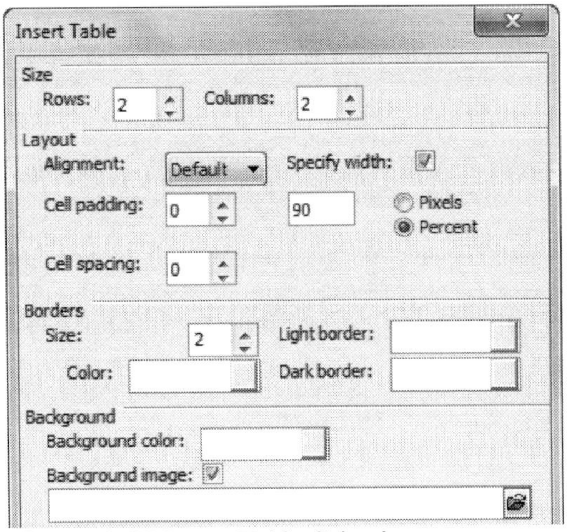

Figure 6-33 Insert Table dialog box

Figure 6-34 Hyperlink dialog box

Bitmap Control

This control is used to add an image to the form. After you add the control to the form, open the properties dialog box.

The options shown in Figure 6-35 are used to select the image and how it will be displayed. The options are explained in Table 6-4.

The file format of the image can be **.BMP**, **.JPG** or **.PNG**.

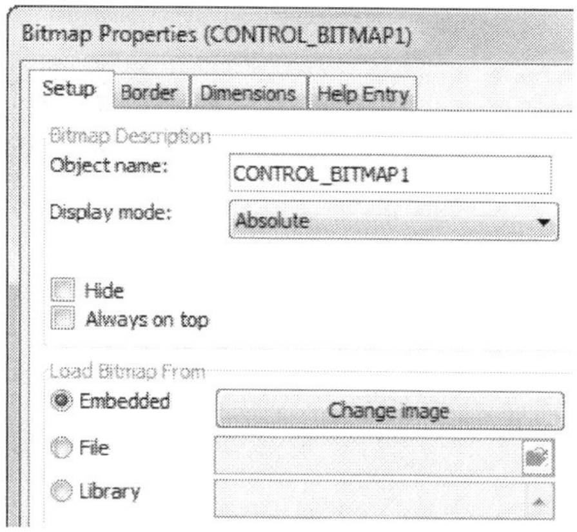

Figure 6-35 Bitmap Properties Setup tab

Option	Description
Display mode	Is used to select how the bitmap is displayed. There are four options in the drop-down list: **ABSOLUTE** displays one image pixel for each printer pixel. This option usually is not used for reports. **STRETCH** resizes the image horizontally and vertically to fill the control. This option can distort the image file. **TILE** repeats the image to fill the control. **BEST FIT** resizes the image without distorting it to fill the control.
Embedded	Is used to select an image file, which will be embedded in the layout.
File	Is used to select an image file.
Library	Is used to select an icon image file from the images that come with Alpha Five, as shown earlier in Figure 6-24.

Table 6-4 Backdrop tab options explained

OLE Object Control

This control is used to add functionality from an external source. This control has very few customization options. When the person using the form double-clicks on the OLE control, the dialog box shown in Figure 6-36 is displayed.

The user would select the type of object that they want to view.

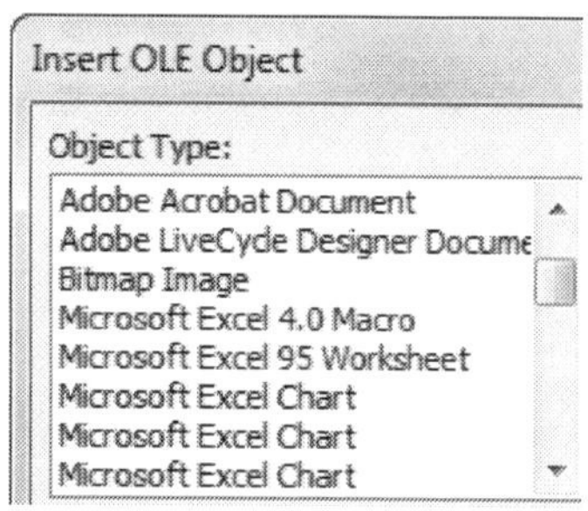

Figure 6-36 Insert OLE Object dialog box

None of the Microsoft Excel Chart options worked for me.

Frame Control

This control is used to add a frame around objects on the form. This control is often used when you want to give the appearance that some objects are grouped. It is also used to display alternating colors for the background of the Detail section of the report.

Adding A Frame

To add a frame, follow the steps below.

1. After you click on the control in the Toolbox, draw a box around the objects that you want inside of the frame.
2. On the dialog box shown in Figure 6-37, enter the text that you want to appear in the upper left corner of the frame. An example of Frame Text are the words "Frame Style" shown on the dialog box. Doing this is optional.

   If the **FRAME HEADING** field is left blank, the frame will not display any text, which may be what you want.

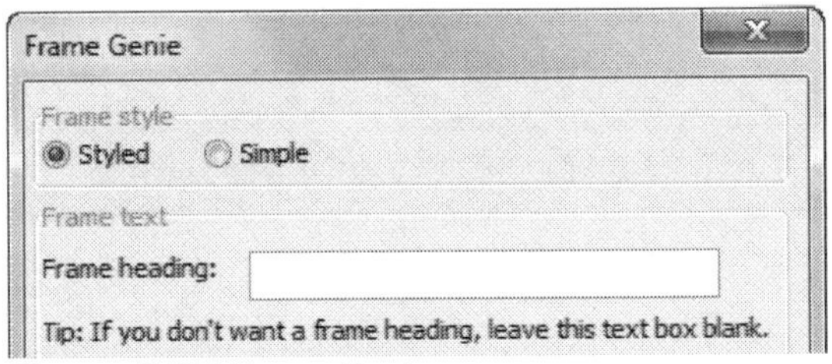

Figure 6-37 Frame Genie

Frame Properties Dialog Box

The properties shown in Figure 6-38 are used to customize the frame. The **ADVANCED FRAME TITLE BUTTON** opens the dialog box shown in Figure 6-39.

Figure 6-38 Frame Properties dialog box

Advanced Text Properties Dialog Box

The options on this dialog box are used to add text, images or buttons to the frame title.

The form shown in Figure 6-40 is the output of the options in the Selected Controls list shown in Figure 6-39.

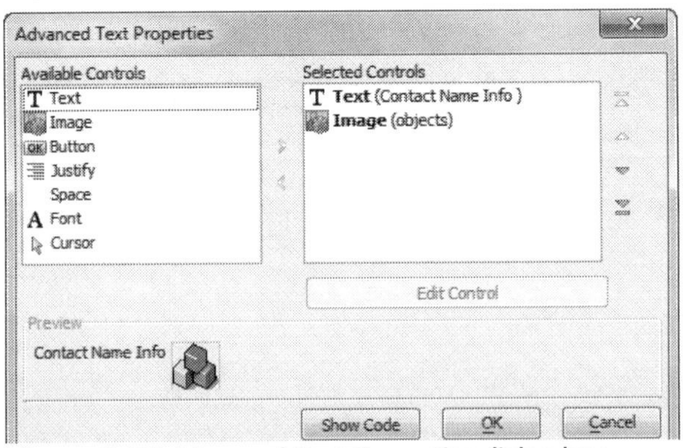

Figure 6-39 Advanced Text Properties dialog box

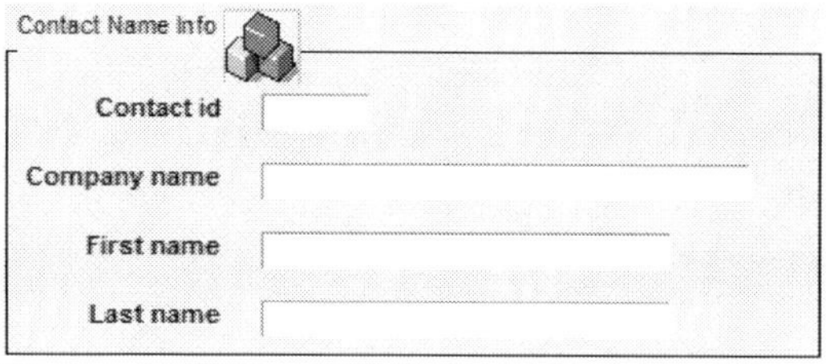

Figure 6-40 Result of frame options selected

Exercise 6.5: Use The Frame Control

1. Display a Default Form based on the Contacts table. Move the fields down about ¼ inch. Save the form as `aFrameControl`.

2. Add the Frame control around the fields shown above in Figure 6-40.

3. Click OK on the Frame Genie dialog box.

4. On the Frame Properties dialog box Setup tab, click the Advanced Frame Title button.

   Add the Text control to the Selected Controls list, then enter text for the frame on the dialog box shown in Figure 6-41.

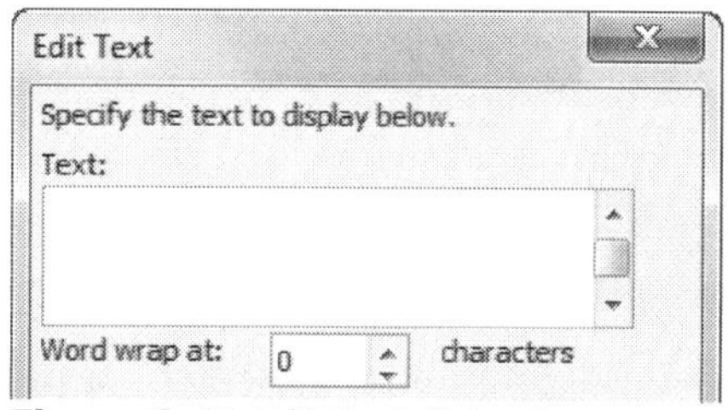

Figure 6-41 Edit Text dialog box

5. Add the Image control to the Selected Controls list. On the dialog box shown in Figure 6-42, click the Image Name field button and select an image.

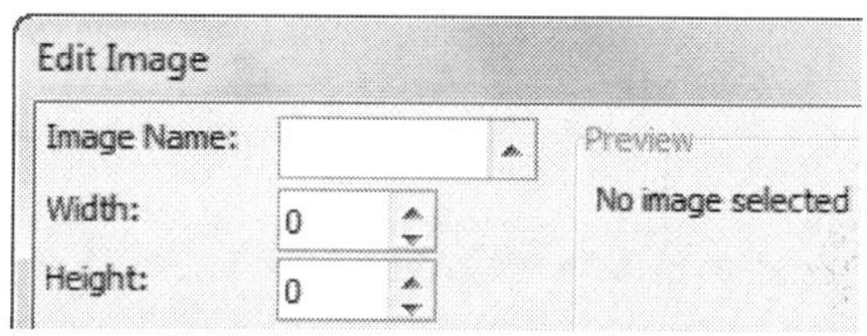

Figure 6-42 Edit Image dialog box

6. Save the changes. Your form should look similar to the one shown earlier in Figure 6-40.

Line Control

This control is used to add a line to the form. Once the line is drawn on the form, the dialog box shown in Figure 6-43 opens. The options are used to select the thickness of the line.

If you need to change the style or color of the line, use the properties dialog box.

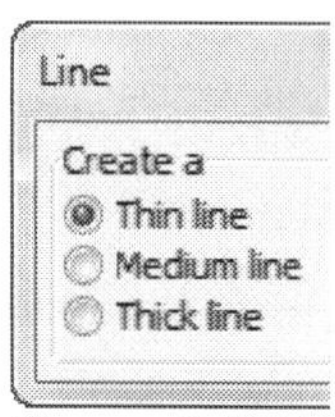

Figure 6-43 Line dialog box

Page Break Control

This control is used to select where a form or report should break if printed. The properties shown in Figure 6-44 are used to customize the page break.

You will probably use this control on reports more than on a form. In Chapter 5, Exercise 5.20, you used this control on a report.

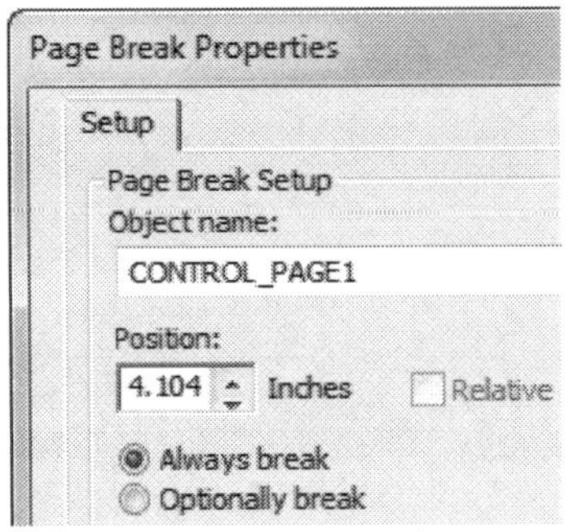

Figure 6-44 Page Break Properties dialog box

Conditional Object Control

This control is used to display other controls, based on the variables value.

The properties shown in Figure 6-45 are used to set up the conditions for the controls that will be displayed in this control.

Figure 6-45 Conditional Object Properties dialog box

Hot Spot Object Control

This control is used to create an invisible area (like on a button) that when clicked on, runs a script. It can also be used to set the values for variables. Most of the time, this control is placed on an image. When the mouse pointer is placed over a hot spot, it changes to a hand.

Exercise 6.6: Use The Hot Spot Object Control

In this exercise you will place a hot spot control over the image that you added to the Frame control in the previous exercise. You will also learn how to use the **SCRIPT GENIE** to have the Hot Spot control run the Mail Merge action.

Place The Hot Spot Object Control Over An Image

1. Save the aFrameControl form as `aHotspotControl`.

2. Click on the Hot Spot control in the Toolbox, then draw a box around the image on the form.

3. On the dialog box shown in Figure 6-46, accept the default option **USE SCRIPT GENIE**, then click Next.

   The Use Script Genie option uses **ACTION SCRIPTING**, which you will learn more about in Chapter 9.

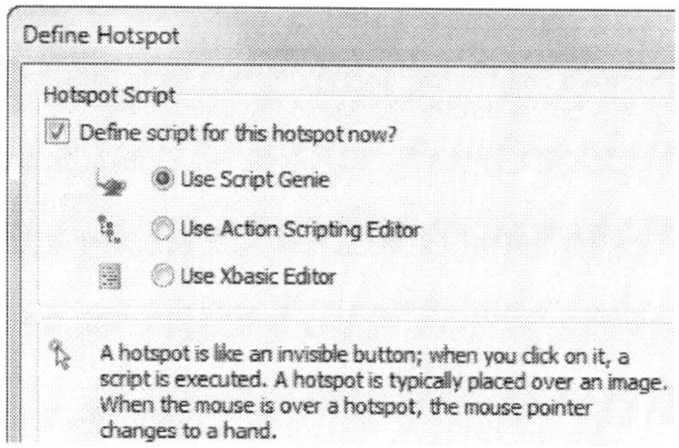

Figure 6-46 Define Hotspot genie

4. Click the **ADD NEW ACTION BUTTON**.

5. On the dialog box shown in Figure 6-47, scroll down the Action list and select the **MAIL-MERGE WITH MICROSOFT WORD** action. Clicking the **SEARCH** button to the right of the Action list opens the dialog box shown in Figure 6-48. Click OK.

The Filter Actions dialog box is used to enter a word to narrow the list of actions that are displayed. All categories will be searched. Selecting an option in the Category list on the Select Action dialog box, also filters the actions.

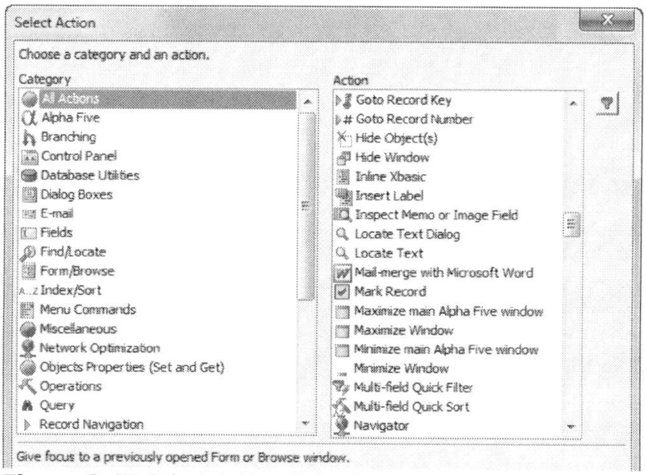

Figure 6-47 Select Action dialog box

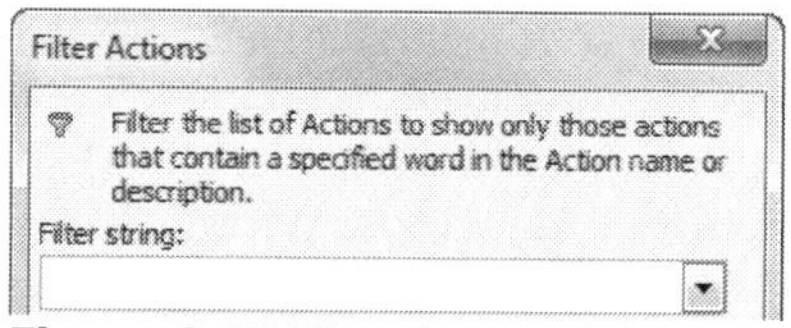

Figure 6-48 Filter Actions dialog box

Mail-Merge With Microsoft Word Script Genie

The genie shown in Figure 6-49 is used to select the options for the Mail Merge action.

To provide the most flexibility for the user, it is best to select the **DISPLAY THE "MICROSOFT WORD MERGE" DIALOG BOX** option in the first drop-down list.

The **PRE-DEFINE THE MERGE** option is used to select the merge options instead of letting the user select the options.

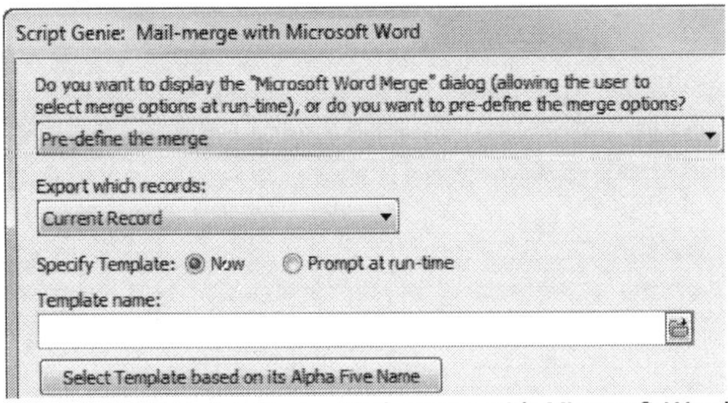

Figure 6-49 Script Genie: Mail-merge with Microsoft Word

The other options on the genie are explained below.

① **EXPORT WHICH RECORDS** The options in this drop-down list are used to select the records for the merge.

② **SPECIFY TEMPLATE** Selecting **NOW**, is used to select the template. Selecting **PROMPT AT RUN-TIME** lets the user select the template.

③ **TEMPLATE NAME** Is used to select the template for the mail merge. Clicking the button at the end of this field to select a template outside of the database.

④ **SELECT TEMPLATE BASED ON ITS ALPHA FIVE NAME** Clicking this button opens the dialog box shown in Figure 6-50. Select the table or set that has the template that you want to use.

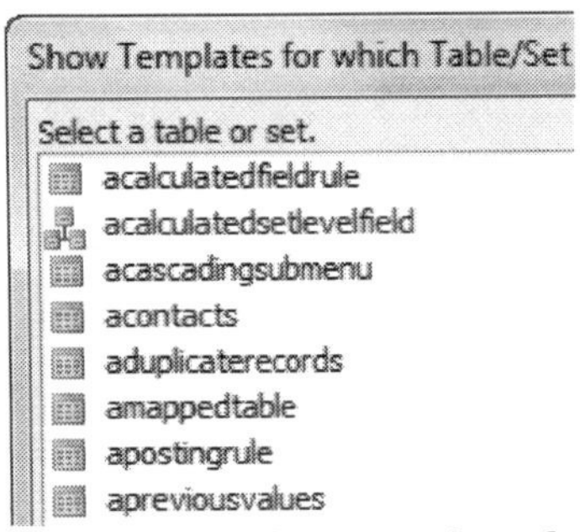

Figure 6-50 Show Templates for which Table/Set dialog box

Script Genie Dialog Box
The options on this dialog box change based on the action selected on the Select Action dialog box, shown earlier in Figure 6-47.

1. Select the Display the "Microsoft Word Merge" dialog box option from the first drop-down list, then click Finish.

2. You should see the dialog box shown in Figure 6-51.

   The **EDIT ACTION** option reopens the dialog box shown earlier in Figure 6-49.

   Click Finish.

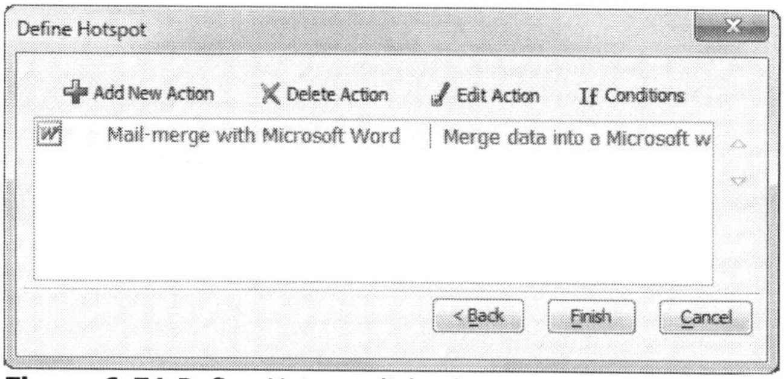

Figure 6-51 Define Hotspot dialog box

3. You will see a frame around the image on the form.

   When you view the form and click on the image, you will see the dialog box shown in Figure 6-52. This dialog box is used to select the options for the mail merge.

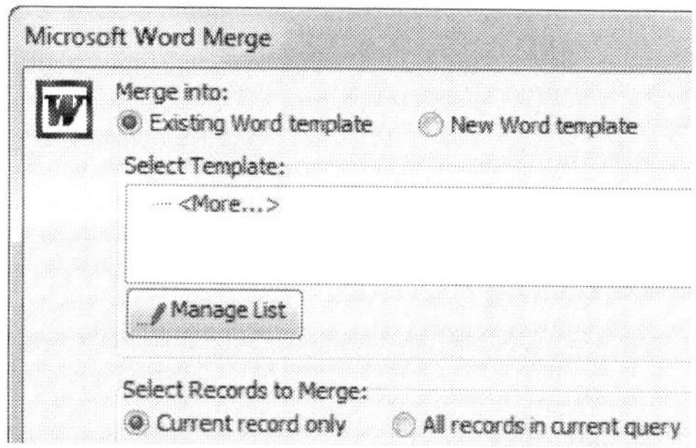

Figure 6-52 Microsoft Word Merge dialog box

User Control

This control is used to add functionality to an application. The Setup tab properties for the control are shown in Figure 6-53.

The control is not visible on the form. You can add an action to an event for the control. If you need an action to happen automatically when a form is closed, you can use this control and attach the action to the **ON EXIT EVENT**.

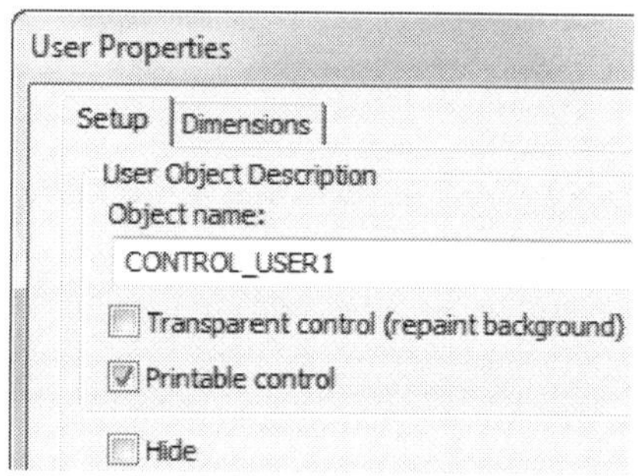

Figure 6-53 User Properties dialog box

Active X Control

These controls are small programs (also known as **ADD-ONS**). Usually they are used to enhance a web browser. Like the OLE control, Active X controls are used to display a file created in another software package in the application. When this control is added to the form, you will see the dialog box shown earlier in Figure 6-5. These are the Active X controls that are on your computer that can be added. Because Active X controls are not part of the distribution of an application created in Alpha Five, they may need to be installed and registered on a users computer. The developer license key must be embedded in the form.

Embedded Chart Control

This control is used to create and add a chart to a form or report.

FORM TOOLBOX PANEL CONTROLS

After completing the exercises in this chapter you will be able to use many of the form specific controls.

CHAPTER 7

Overview

In the previous chapter you learned about the controls that are common to almost all layout types. In this chapter you will learn about the controls that are specific to forms. The purpose of the controls covered in this chapter is to make data entry on forms easier and to help reduce errors. You have probably used many of the control types covered in this chapter, either at work or online.

When you add a field to a form, it is displayed as a text box. Without field rules, almost anything can be typed into a Text control. Many of the other control types can be pre-populated, which allows the user to select an option from a list or from a group of values. There are a lot of controls to select from. You should keep the following in mind when selecting a control type.

① Some control types only work with certain field data types.

② Some control types like the List Box and Radio Button are better suited for shorter lists, while the Combo Box is great for longer lists.

③ If you need to use the same list of values for more than one form or on a form and a browse for example, it may be best to define the list as a field rule, like you learned how to do in Chapter 2.

Radio Button Control

This control is used when only one value should be selected from a group of values.

Exercise 7.1: Use The Radio Button Control

In this exercise you will use this control to let the user select how the order is being paid for, by selecting one of the radio button options.

1. Save the aCheckBoxControl form as `aRadioButtonControl`.

2. Delete the Check Box controls. Add the Radio Button control to the form to the right of the Order ID field.

3. On the Field Select dialog box, select the How Shipped field, then make the control larger so that all of the options are visible, as shown in Figure 7-1.

   If you click on the radio button options, you will see that only one option can be selected.

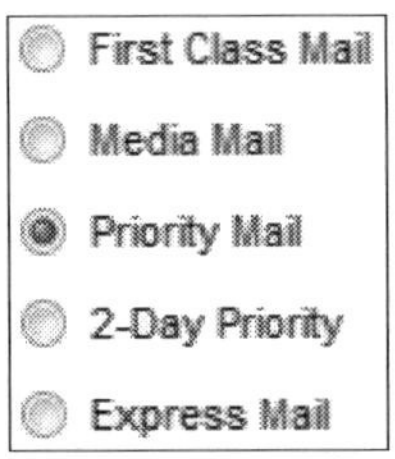

Figure 7-1 Radio Button control

Change The Radio Button Control Text

If the field that you select on the Field Select dialog box does not display the text that you want displayed next to each radio button, you can change the text by following the steps below. This example will show you how to modify some of the text displayed above in Figure 7-1.

1. On the properties dialog box Choices tab for the Radio Button control, open the **CHOICES FOR CONTROL ARE** drop-down list and select User Defined.

2. Change the Radio style to **INDENTED DIAMONDS**.

The content in the box shown in Figure 7-2 are the current options from the table. The first option in the row is what is displayed on the form. This is what would be changed. The option after the | (**VERTICAL BAR**) is the actual value.

```
First Class Mail|First Class
Media Mail|Media Mail
Priority Mail|Priority Mail
2-Day Priority|2-Day Priority
Express Mail|Express Mail
```

Figure 7-2 Current radio button options

3. Change the text before the vertical bar for one or two options.

   When you view the form you should see the changes, as shown in Figure 7-3.

   Compare this figure to Figure 7-1, shown earlier.

Figure 7-3 Radio buttons

Combo Box Control

This control is used to create a drop-down list that contains the values that can be selected for the field. The drop-down list can be populated from the values in a field in a table or set. They can also be typed in to create the list. The other option is to use Xbasic.

Exercise 7.2: Create The List For The Combo Box Manually

In this exercise you will learn how to manually create the list of values for the combo box.

1. Create a default form for the Order Lookup table, then save the form as `aComboBoxManualControl`.

2. Delete the How Shipped field and title, then add the Combo Box control to the form where the How Shipped field was.

3. On the Field Select dialog box, select the How Shipped field.

4. Open the properties dialog box for the Combo Box control. On the Choices tab, open the drop-down list and select **USER DEFINED**.

5. Type `Flat Rate` at the beginning of the Priority Mail option. Type `Overnight` at the beginning of the Express Mail option.

6. Click the **SORT ASCENDING** button that is to the left of the list.

   Your list should look like the one shown in Figure 7-4.

```
2-Day Priority|2-Day Priority
First Class Mail|First Class
Flat Rate Priority Mail|Prior
Media Mail|Media Mail
Overnight Express Mail|Expres
```

Figure 7-4 Manual list for the combo box

> The reason that the values were automatically filled in the list is because the field has lookup field rules.

7. Add a Text control to the left of the combo box on the form and type `How Shipped`.

   Make the text bold.

   When you view the form and open the drop-down list, you should see the options shown in Figure 7-5.

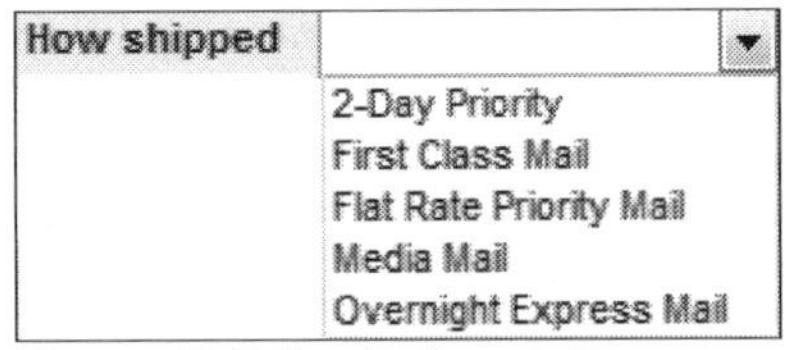

Figure 7-5 Combo box options

Exercise 7.3: Use A Field In A Table To Create The Combo Box List

In the previous exercise the entries for the combo box list were created manually. In this exercise you will use a field in a table to supply the values for the list. This means that the list can grow automatically when unique values are added to the field in the table that has the values for the Combo Box list.

> If the field that you want to apply one of the **CONTROL TYPES** to is already on the form, you do not have to add the control from the Toolbox to the form. You can change the control type on the Field Properties dialog box, as long as the field is not grouped to its title.
>
> As you read earlier, fields that have lookup field rules will automatically fill in values from the lookup. This exercise will include removing the lookup field rules for the field that will use a combo box. This will let you learn how to create a combo box from scratch.

> **Ungroup Control**
> The **DON'T GROUP CONTROLS** option on the Drag Drop List panel will not ungroup fields and titles that were not added to the form from the Drag Drop List panel. To ungroup them, right-click on the grouped field and select **UNGROUP**, to remove the group.

The one thing to keep in mind when using a combo box is that the values in the drop-down list are the values that will be added to the table that the drop-down list field is in.

This means that the drop-down list field must be a matching data type for the values displayed in the drop-down list.

If the data type does not match, you will see the error message shown in Figure 7-5 or a similar message.

Figure 7-6 Data type invalid message

1. Save the Order Lookup table as `aComboBox`. Clear the Dictionary and Field Rules options on the Duplicate Table dialog box.

2. Change the Paid By ID field type to Character, with a width of 25.

3. Create a default form based on the aComboBox table, then ungroup the Paid By ID field. Make the field longer.

4. Save the form as `aComboBoxList`.

5. Open the properties dialog box for the Paid By ID field. Open the Control Type drop-down list and select Combo Box.

6. On the Choices tab, open the drop-down list and select **COMPUTED AUTOMATICALLY**.
   Open the Source drop-down list and select **VALUES FROM A TABLE/SET**.
   Open the From Table drop-down list and select the Paid By table.
   Open the Field/Expression values to display drop-down list and select the Paid By field.

7. Change the Display order to sort by the Paid By field.

   You should have the options shown in Figure 7-7.

   Clicking the **PREVIEW BUTTON** displays the combo box drop-down list and the values that will be displayed in it.

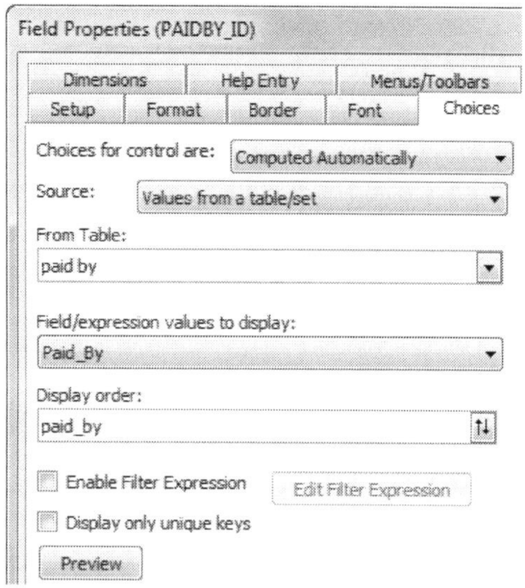

Figure 7-7 Combo Box Choices tab options

8. View a new record on the form, then open the Paid by drop-down list. You should see the values shown in Figure 7-8.

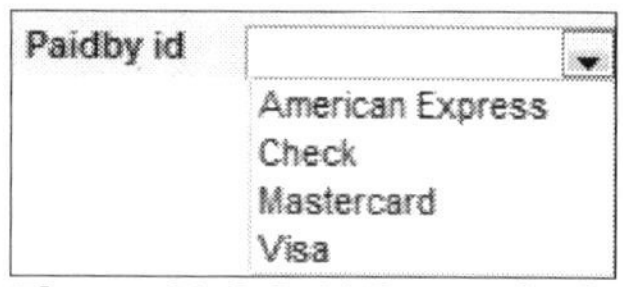

Figure 7-8 Paid By combo box drop-down list

The reason that you see a number in the Paid By field is because the field was numeric before this exercise, so it has the equivalent of the options shown in Figure 7-8. From this point forward, the field will contain one of the values shown above in Figure 7-8.

List Box Control

This control is similar to the Combo Box control and can be used interchangeably with the Combo Box control. The difference is in the appearance. Instead of a drop-down list, the List Box control has up and down arrows that are used to move through the values, as shown in Figure 7-9.

I use the List Box control instead of the Combo Box control when space on the form is limited. The List Box control has the same options on the Choices tab that the Combo Box control has.

Figure 7-9 List Box control

Record-List Edit Combo Box Control

This control is similar to the Combo Box control. One difference is that this Record-List control can display more than one column of data in the drop-down list. The other differences are explained below.

① This control provides a dynamic view of the fields and records in a table or set.

② Users can add or edit values in the list.

Exercise 7.4: Use The Record-List Edit Combo Box Control

In this exercise you will learn how to use this control to display several fields in the drop-down list.

1. Save the aComboBoxList form as `aRecordListEditControl.`

2. Delete the Salesrep ID field, not the title. Change the title to `Sales Rep`, then add the Record-List Edit Combo Box control to the form in place of the field.

3. Select the Salesrep ID field.

Record-List Choices Tab Options

The options shown in Figure 7-10 are used to select the source of the values for the list and how they should be filtered and displayed. The options are explained in Table 7-1.

The **RECORD-LIST LIST BOX CONTROL** has the same options.

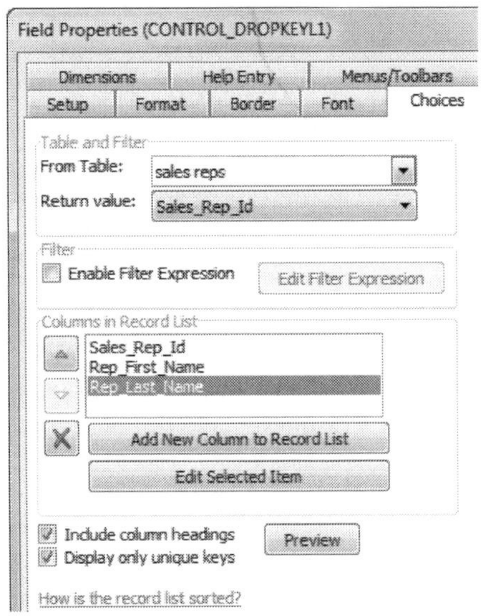

Figure 7-10 Record List Choices tab options

Option	Description
From Table	Is used to select the table that has the values to display in the list. The **<CURRENT TABLE>** option will select values from the table that the form is based on.
Return value	Is used to select the field (from the table selected in the From Table field) that has the value that will be saved in the field that the Record-List control is attached to. An expression can also be created to select the value to be saved. An example of when to use an expression would be if the values in two fields combined is what should be saved with the record.
Enable Filter Expression button	Opens the dialog box shown in Figure 7-11. The options are used to create criteria to select which records appear in the list.

Table 7-1 Record List Choices tab options explained

Option	Description
Add New Column To Record List button	Opens the dialog box shown in Figure 7-12. The options are used to select a field from the table in the From Table field to display in the list. (1)
Edit Selected Item button	Opens the **EDIT EXISTING RECORD LIST FIELD DIALOG BOX**, which is used to modify the selected field. This dialog box is identical to the Add New Record List Field dialog box, shown in Figure 7-12.
Include column headings	If checked, the heading(s) that you set up in the Add New Record List dialog box will be displayed as the first row in the drop-down list.
Display only unique keys	If you do not want to display all of the records that have the same ID field, select this option.
Preview button	Clicking this button displays how the drop-down list will look when viewed.
How is the record list sorted?	Clicking on this link displays the dialog box shown in Figure 7-13. It explains how the values in the record list are sorted.

Table 7-1 Record List Choices tab options explained (Continued)

(1)

Select A Field And Hide It In The Drop-Down List
You may have the need to add a field to the list but not display it. When that is the case, change the **WIDTH** of the field on the dialog box show in Figure 7-12 to zero.

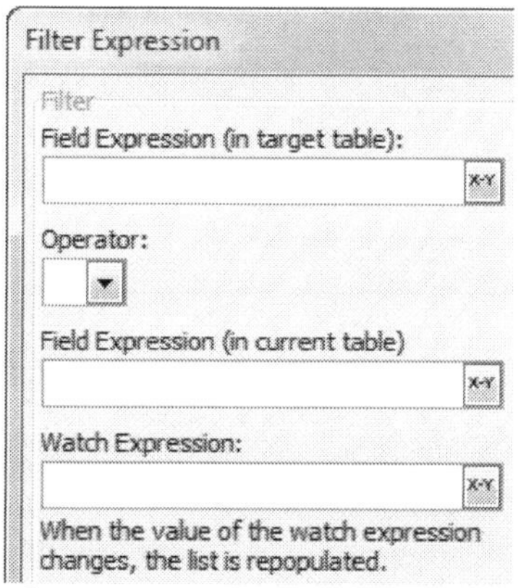

Figure 7-11 Filter Expression dialog box

Figure 7-12 Add New Record List Field dialog box

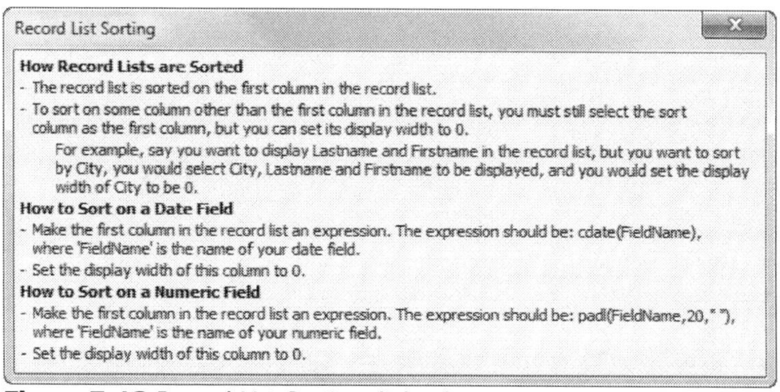

Figure 7-13 Record List Sorting dialog box

Select The Choices Tab Options

1. On the Choices tab, open the From Table drop-down list and select the Sales Reps table. Open the Return value drop-down list and select the Sales Rep ID field.

2. Click the Add New Column to Record List button.

3. Open the Field drop-down list and select the Sales Rep ID field. Type `Rep ID` in the Header field, then change the Width to 6, as shown earlier in Figure 7-12.

4. Repeat the step above to add the Rep First Name field. Use `First Name` as the heading. Do not change the width.
   Add the Rep Last Name field. Use `Last Name` as the heading.

5. Select the Include column headings and Display only unique keys options. You should have the options shown earlier in Figure 7-10.

   When you open the Sales Rep drop-down list on the form, you should see the list shown in Figure 7-14.

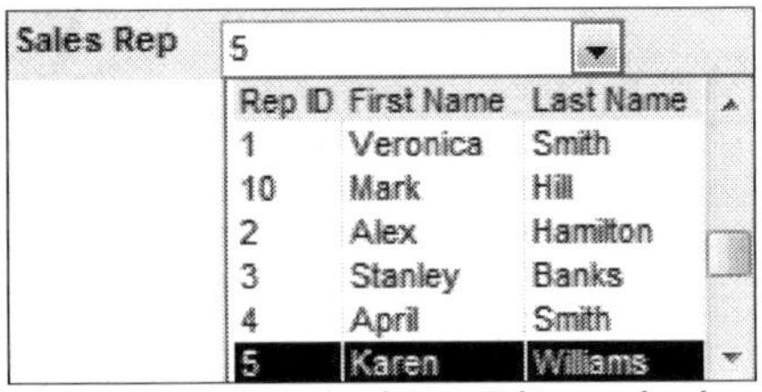

Figure 7-14 Record-List Edit combo box

It is not a requirement to display the value (Sales Rep ID) that will be added to the table (or set) that the form is based on.

Record-List List Box Control

This control displays multiple columns of data in the Record-List Edit Combo box. It has the same options on the Field Properties dialog box Choices tab that the Record-List Edit Combo Box control has. The difference is that there is no drop-down list. Some of the rows are always displayed on the form, as shown in Figure 7-15.

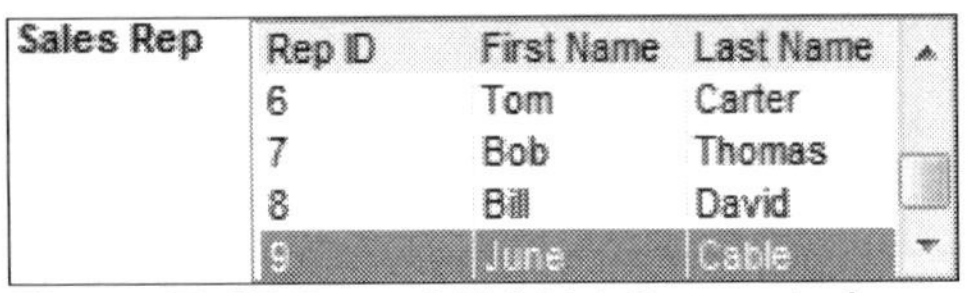

Figure 7-15 Record-List List Box control

Tree Control

This control displays options in a folder structure, like the one used in Windows Explorer. Use this control when the options to select from can be categorized. It has the same options on the Choices tab that the Combo Box control has. [See Figure 7-7, earlier in this chapter]

This control may be best suited for values that do not change often, if you use the **USER DEFINED CONTROL** option on the Choices tab. If you want to use this control for values that change, my advice is to type the list in a word processing document, then paste the entries in on the Choices tab.

Exercise 7.5: Use The Tree Control With The City Field

In this exercise you will change the City field to use the Tree control. This is how users will select the city for the contact. Doing this will prevent typos for a field that is often used to sort on.

1. Save the aHotspotControl form as `aTreeControl`.

2. Ungroup the City field if it is grouped.

3. On the properties dialog box for the City field, change the Control Type to Tree Control.

4. On the Choices tab, select User Defined in the drop-down list.

5. Type the entries shown in Figure 7-16, in the Text box.

   What The Entry Means
   Example - CT.Tappan|Tappan
   CT is the category
   .Tappan is an option in the CT category
   |Tappan is the value that you want saved in the field. This is optional. If you do not enter anything after the vertical bar, CT.Tappan will be saved in the field.

```
NV.Las Vegas|Las Vegas
FL.Ft Laud|Ft Laud
PA.Ramsey|Ramsey
NY.Norwood|Norwood
PA.Ft Lee|Ft Lee
CT.Tappan|Tappan
NV.Bogota|Bogota
NJ.Wilson|Wilson
CT.Westwood|Westwood
```

Figure 7-16 Entries for the Tree control

6. Click the Sort Ascending button to sort how the entries will be displayed in the control.

7. Make the Tree control longer. It should look like the one shown in Figure 7-17.

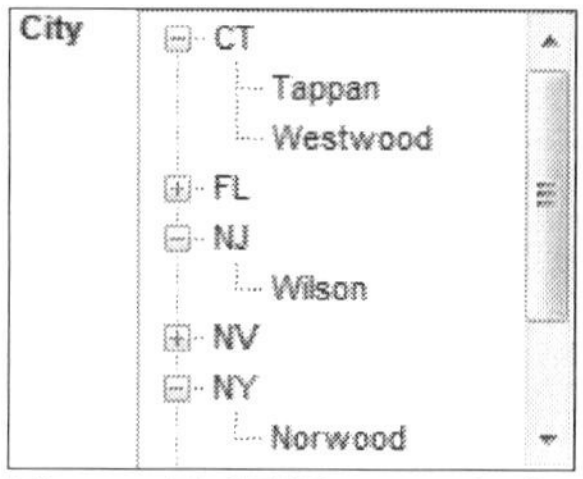

Figure 7-17 Tree control options

Drop-Down Tree Control

This control works like the Tree control covered in the previous exercise. The difference is that the options are displayed in a drop-down list, as shown in Figure 7-18. Use this tree control option when there are space limitations on the form.

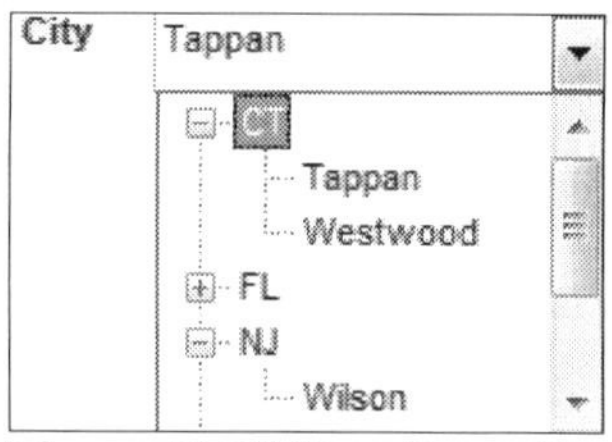

Figure 7-18 Drop Down Tree control

Two-State Button Control

This control works like the Check Box control and has the same options. [See Chapter 6, Check Box Control]

Exercise 7.6: Use The Two-State Button Control

In this exercise you will use this control to display whether or not the order was paid by check. You will create an expression to change the background color of the control. To test this control, data needs to be added to a field.

1. Open the Orders table in the Default Browse. Make the browse large enough to see all of the columns. For orders 1, 3 and 4, type `F` in the By Check field.

2. Save the aCheckBoxControl form as `a2StateButtonControl`.

3. Delete the two By Check fields on the form. Add the Two-State Button control to the form, then select the By Check field.

4. On the properties dialog box Setup tab, check the **COLOR EQUATION** option, then click the button at the end of the field.

5. On the first row, change the Background Color to Gold, then create an expression that checks the By Check field to see if it is equal to .T. (for true). If necessary, you can click the button at the end of the Expression field to create the expression on the Expression Builder.

6. Change the Background color at the bottom of the dialog box to Bright Green.

   You should have the options shown in Figure 7-19.

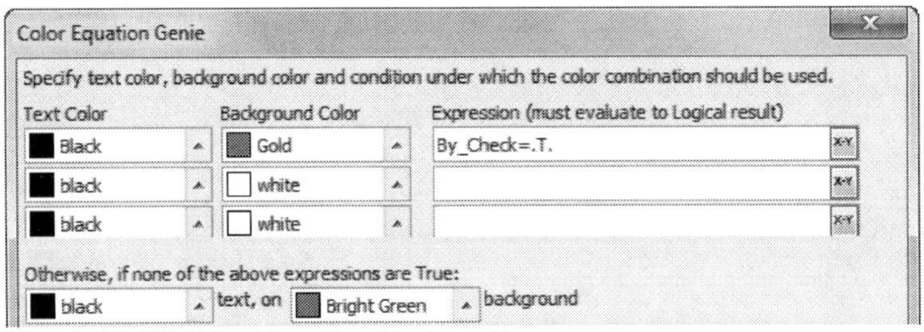

Figure 7-19 Color Equation Genie options

7. On the Choices tab in the Checkbox text field type `<auto>`.

8. In the Label when true field, type `Paid by check`. In the Label when false field, type `Not paid by check`. When you view the form, the background color of the Two-State button should be gold and have the phrase "Paid by check" for Order IDs 2 and 3.

Multi-State Button Control

This control is similar to the List Box control because they both have the following options.

① The **STORED VALUE** can be different from the value that is displayed.
② The **SELECTED VALUE** is always displayed.
③ There are at least two pre-defined values.

Multi-State Button Control vs List Box Control

While these controls have the similarities explained above, they do have some differences. The Multi-State Button control has the features explained below that the List Box control does not have.

① They can be displayed horizontally or vertically.
② They can display an image instead of text, including displaying a different image when the button is clicked.
③ A button is displayed for each pre-defined option, as shown in Figure 7-20.

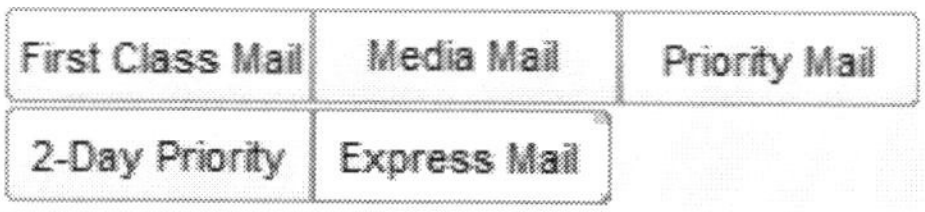

Figure 7-20 Multi-State buttons for the How Shipped field

Browse Control

The **BROWSE CONTROL** is not the same control as the **DROP DOWN BROWSE SUPER CONTROL.**

This control is used to create a browse window on the form. It produces the same results as using the Form Genies Custom option with a set. The differences are explained below.

① Using a set is not a requirement.

② An existing browse created from the same table or set can be used with the Browse control. If the Browse control is added to this form, the options shown in Figure 7-21 are available.

The **SAVED BROWSE LAYOUT** drop-down list displays existing browse objects that are based on the Contacts table. They can be used for the Browse control.

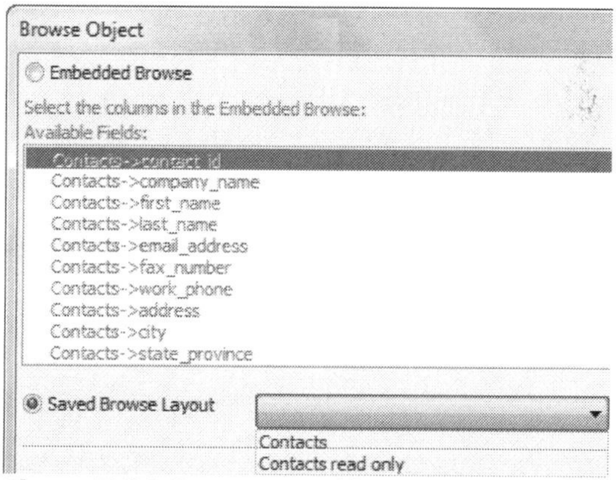

Figure 7-21 Browse control layout options

Exercise 7.7: Use The Browse Control

In this exercise you will use this control to create the embedded browse that will be added to the form.

1. Save the Customers Orders form as `aBrowseControl`.

2. Delete the embedded browse.

3. Add the Browse control to the bottom of the form.

   The options shown in Figure 7-22 are used to select fields from the main table or an existing browse layout that will be used to create the embedded browse.

   Select the One-to-Many Link option.

   Open the Saved Browse Layout drop-down list, then select the Order Header info layout, as shown in the figure.

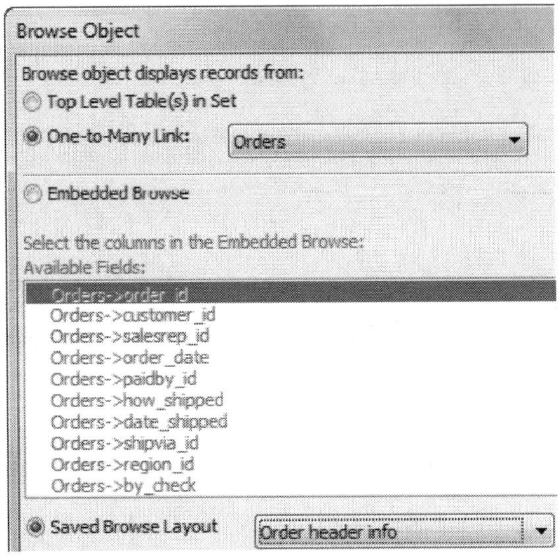

Figure 7-22 Browse control existing layout options

4. Open the Form Properties dialog box, then remove all of the restrictions on the Form tab. The embedded browse should look like the one shown in Figure 7-23.

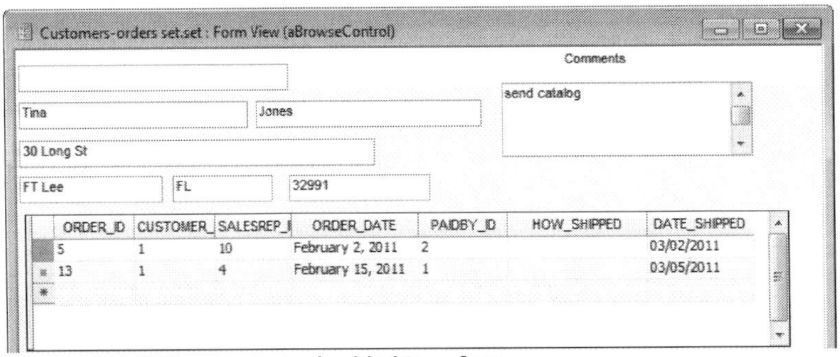

Figure 7-23 Browse control added to a form

Sub-Form Control

This control is similar to the Browse control covered in the previous exercise. The difference is that a form will be used to create the sub form instead of a browse.

Sub-Form Control Options Based On A Table

When a Sub-Form control is added to a form based on a table, the dialog box shown in Figure 7-24 is displayed.

You can create the sub form as a default form or select an existing form that is based on the same table to be used as the sub-form.

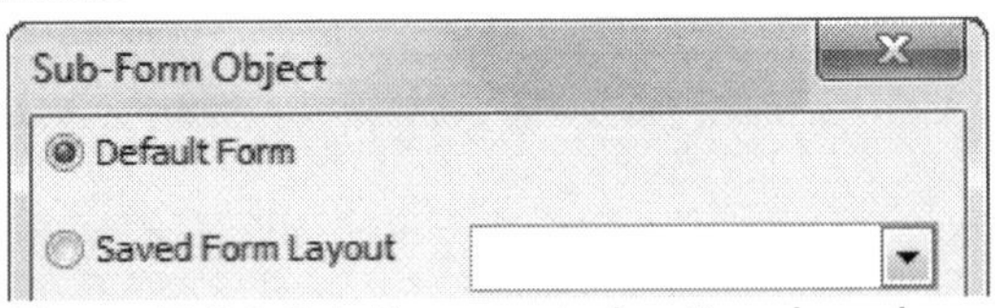

Figure 7-24 Sub-Form control options based on a table

Sub-Form Control Options Based On A Set

When a Sub-Form control is added to a form based on a set, the dialog box shown in Figure 7-25 is displayed.

The **DEFAULT FORM** option creates a form with all of the fields in the table selected at the top of the dialog box.

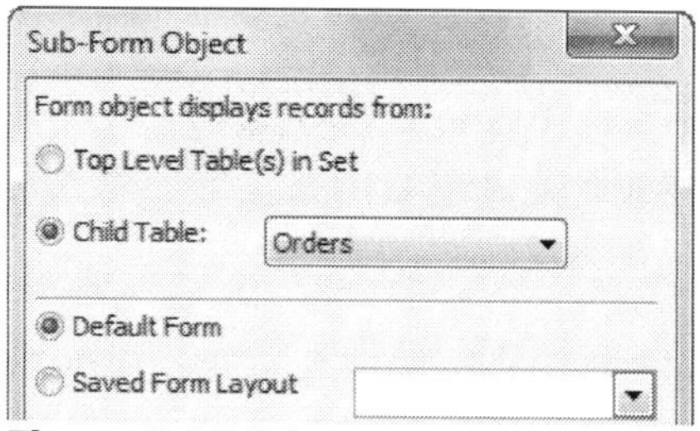

Figure 7-25 Sub-Form control options based on a set

Exercise 7.8: Use The Sub-Form Control

In this exercise you will use a default form as a sub form on the main form.

1. Save the aBrowseControl form as `aSubformControl`.

2. Delete the embedded browse.

3. Add the Sub-Form control to the bottom of the form. Make the box about 2½ inches long and 3½ inches wide.

4. Select the Child Table option. The Orders table should be in the drop-down list. Select the Default Form option. You should have the options shown earlier in Figure 7-25. Click OK.

5. The options shown in Figure 7-26 are used to customize the sub form. The form should look like the one shown in Figure 7-27.

Figure 7-26 Sub-Form Properties dialog box

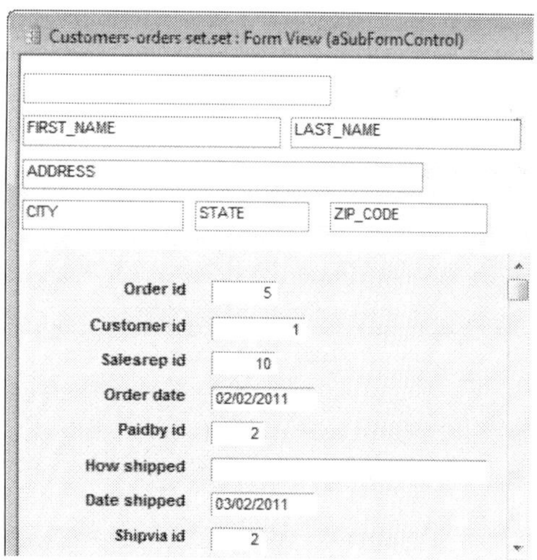

Figure 7-27 Form with a sub form

Tabbed Object Control

This control creates the same layout that can be created when the Custom Form and Tabbed layout style options are selected on the Form Genie. The difference is that the Tabbed Object control can be added to an existing form. Figures 7-28 and 7-29 show the options that can be used to customize the Tabbed Object control.

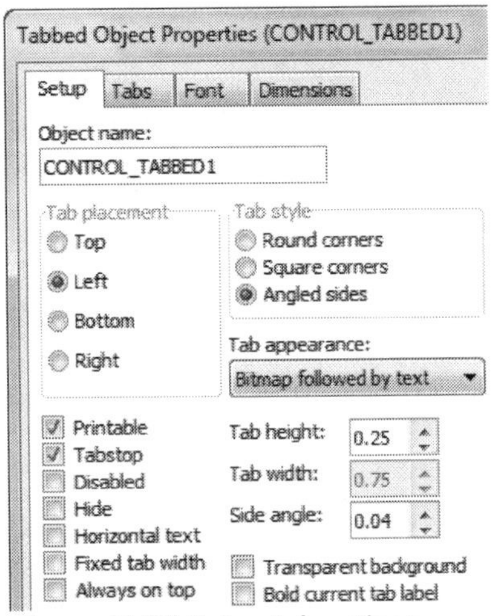

Figure 7-28 Setup tab options

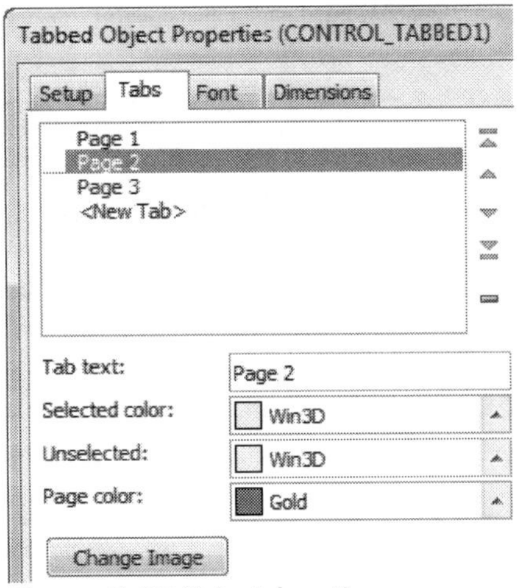

Figure 7-29 Tabs tab options

SUPER CONTROLS

In this chapter you will learn about the super controls on the Toolbox.

CHAPTER 8

Overview

In the previous two chapters you learned about the common controls in the Toolbox. In this chapter, you will learn about the controls in the Supercontrols section of the Toolbox. These controls provide more functionality then the other controls in the Toolbox. Like the controls covered in the previous two chapters, an existing field on a form can be changed to a super control. The Super Controls are listed in Table 8-1.

Super Control	Forms	Reports	Letters	Labels
Hyperlink	X	X	X	X
Calendar	X	X	X	X
Clock	X	X	X	X
Embedded XDialog	X			
Embedded Grid Component	X	X	X	X
HTML Content	X			
HTML Form	X			
PDF Viewer	X			
Record Navigator	X			
Report Preview	X			
Web Content	X			
Alphabet Buttons Search	X			
Drop Down Browse	X			

Table 8-1 Super Controls

Hyperlink Super Control

This control is used to create a clickable link like the type that are on web pages. What you will see is that being able to use Xbasic to create the hyperlink will add a lot of flexibility. Yes, I know what you may be saying, "I don't know how to write Xbasic code". Believe it or not, that may be okay.

As you know, Xbasic code is automatically created for many objects like operators, forms and buttons that you created. If the object already exists that has the Xbasic code that you need, you can copy the code from the object or you can create the object, then copy the code to the hyperlink.

Hyperlinks can be used interchangeably with buttons. That means that if you can't write code in Xbasic, use the Button control, which has a genie, to create the task that you want the hyperlink to perform, then paste the code into the Hyperlink control. The Hyperlink control does not have a genie.

Exercise 8.1: Create Hyperlinks

In this exercise you will create two hyperlinks: One to open an external file and another to let the user open a different database.

Create The Button To Generate The Code To Open A Spreadsheet

In this part of the exercise you will add a button to a form temporarily so that you can use the Button Genie to create the code to open an external file.

1. Save the Sales Reps form as `aHyperlinkControl`, then make the form larger.

2. Add the Button control to the bottom of the form. If it is not already selected, select the Use Action Scripting option on the Define Button dialog box, then click Next.

3. Click the **ADD NEW ACTION BUTTON**. Scroll down the Action list and select **OPEN A NON-ALPHA FIVE FILE**, then click OK.

4. Click the File Name field button, then navigate to your folder and select the Orders.xls file.

   You should have the options shown in Figure 8-1.

   Click Finish.

Figure 8-1 Script Genie: Open a Non-Alpha Five file screen

Copy The Action Script Code To The Hyperlink

1. On the Define Button screen, right-click on the script and select View Xbasic, as illustrated in Figure 8-2.

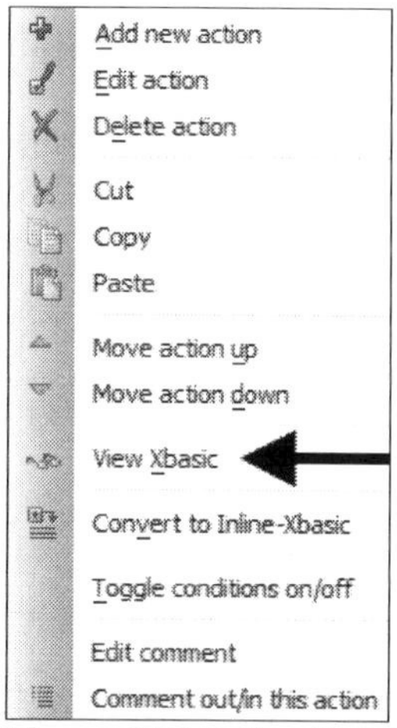

Figure 8-2 Action Script shortcut menu

2. Click the **COPY CODE TO THE CLIPBOARD BUTTON** at the bottom of the dialog box shown in Figure 8-3, then close the Define Button dialog box.

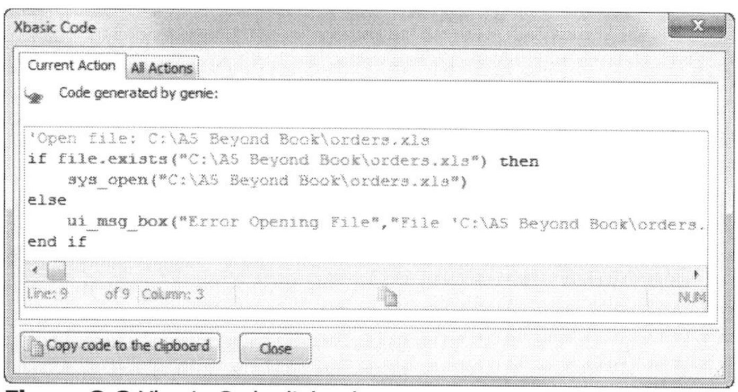

Figure 8-3 Xbasic Code dialog box

3. Add the Hyperlink super control to the form across from the Sales Rep Nbr field.

4. In the Text field, type `Click here to open the Orders spreadsheet.`

5. In the **EVENT BOX**, press Enter at the end of the first line, then press Ctrl+V.

   You should have the options shown in Figure 8-4.

   Click OK.

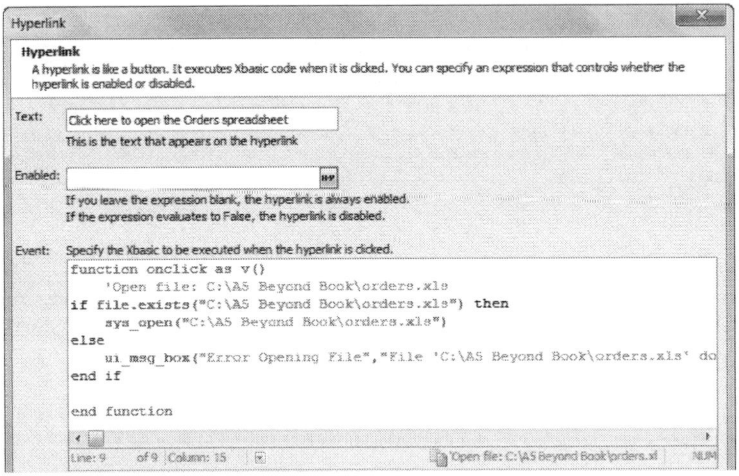

Figure 8-4 Hyperlink dialog box

6. Make sure that all of the text in the hyperlink control is displayed.

   Your form should look like the one shown in Figure 8-5.

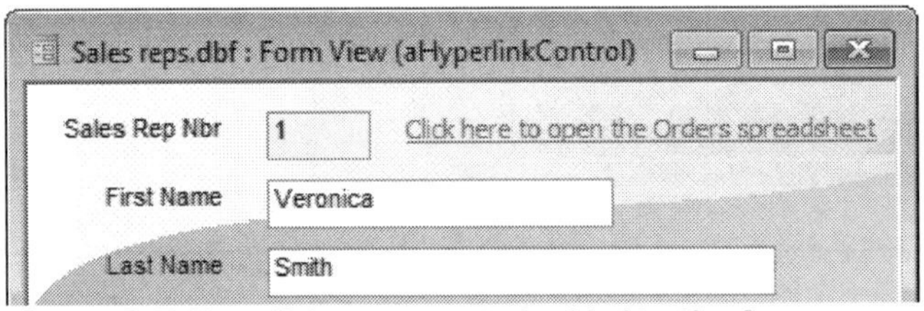

Figure 8-5 Hyperlink super control added to the form

If you have Excel installed and click on the hyperlink, the Orders spreadsheet will open.

In Design mode, the Hyperlink button shown at the end of the field in Figure 8-6 opens the dialog box shown earlier in Figure 8-4.

Figure 8-6 Hyperlink super control

Create The Button To Generate The Code To Open Another Database

In the previous part of this exercise, the script that you created selected the file that would be opened when the link was clicked on. In this part of the exercise you will create a button to generate the code to allow the user to select which database that they want to open. Yes, as the developer, this means that you are giving up a little control. <smile>

1. Add a Button control to the aHyperlinkControl form.

2. Click Next on the Custom Button tab, then click the Add New Action button. On the Select Action screen, scroll down the Action list and select **OPEN ANOTHER WORKSPACE**.

3. At the top of the Script Genie window, select the **PROMPT FOR NAME OF DATABASE TO OPEN AT RUNTIME** option shown in Figure 8-7, then click Finish.

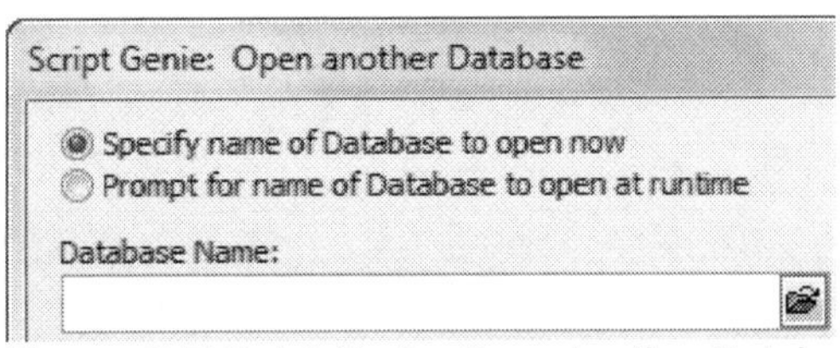

Figure 8-7 Script Genie: Open Another Database screen

4. View the Xbasic code. Click the Copy code to the clipboard button. Click Cancel to close the Define Button dialog box.

5. Add the Hyperlink super control to the form to the right of the Rep First Name field.

6. In the Text field type `Open another database`.

   Paste the Action Script below the first line in the Event box.

   You should have the options shown in Figure 8-8.

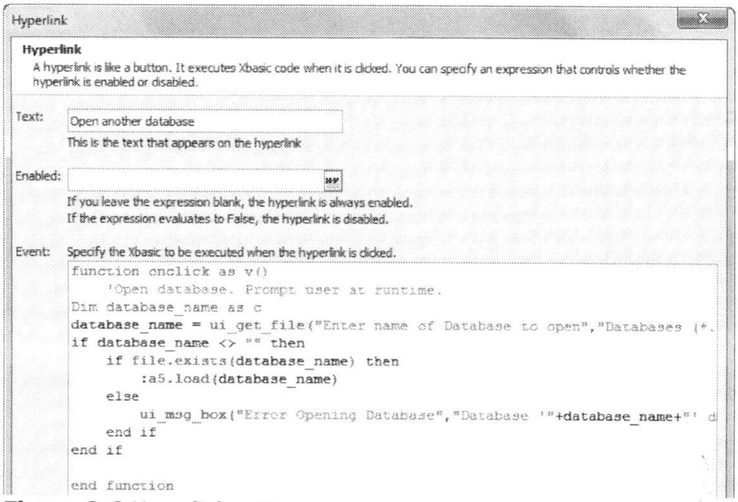

Figure 8-8 Hyperlink options

> **Suggestions For Modifying The Xbasic Code In Figure 8-8**
> If you know how to modify the code, you could change the Enter name of Database portion of the **DATABASE_NAME VARIABLE** to display something more suited to your application. You could also change the **UI_MSG_BOX VARIABLE** to display a different error message.

7. When you click on the link, the dialog box shown in Figure 8-9 opens so that the user can select the database that they want to open.

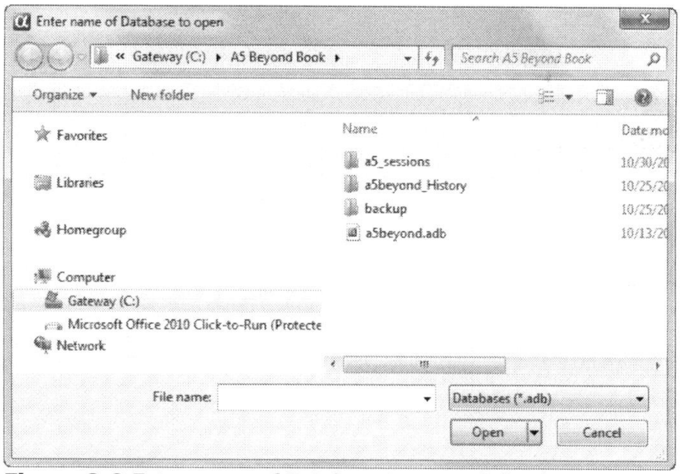

Figure 8-9 Enter name of Database to open dialog box

Calendar Super Control

As you know, the Calendar **SMART CONTROL** is automatically added to date fields on a form or browse. The Calendar super control is used to bind a calendar to a date field or a variable. Like the Calendar smart control, the Calendar super control will let the user select the date instead of typing it in. The date displayed on the calendar is updated automatically when a different record is displayed. If the date is changed on the calendar, the date field or variable is automatically updated. The benefit that the calendar super control has is that it can be customized.

Exercise 8.2: Add The Calendar Super Control To A Date Field

In this exercise you will learn how to customize the calendar super control.

1. Save the aComboBoxManualControl form as `aCalendarControl`.

2. Add the Calendar super control to the form.

3. On the Date Picker Builder, when you open the **BIND TO** drop-down list, you will see all of the date fields in the underlying table or set. This option is used to select the field that you want to add the Calendar control to. Open this drop-down list and select the Date Shipped field.

> **Description Of Options On The Date Picker Builder**
> Other then the Bind To option, when you click on an option, you will see a description at the bottom of the dialog box.

4. Check the **START WEEK ON MONDAY** and **USE RANGE** options.

> **Selecting The Month Or Year Date Options**
> The month and year options on the Start Date dialog box shown in Figure 8-10 and the End Date dialog box are drop-down lists. They are very useful when you need to select a month or year that is not close to the current date. This is faster then clicking the arrow buttons to change the month and year. The **TODAY BUTTON** selects and displays the current month, day and year.

Figure 8-10 Start Date dialog box

5. Click the Start Date field button, then select the date September 19, 2012.

6. Click the End Date field button, then select the date December 31, 2019. You should have the options shown in Figure 8-11. Click OK. Adding a start and end date range to the control will only allow dates in the range to be entered.

7. Move the control to the bottom of the form, then make it larger. The control should look like the one shown in Figure 8-12. This control will be used to select a date for the Date Shipped field in addition to the smart control. The control should be placed as close to the field that it is for, as possible.

When viewing records, the date in the Date Shipped field on the form will be displayed on the calendar.

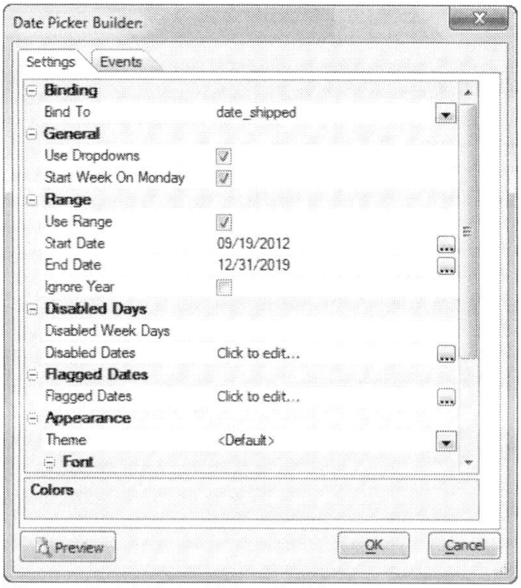

Figure 8-11 Date Picker Builder

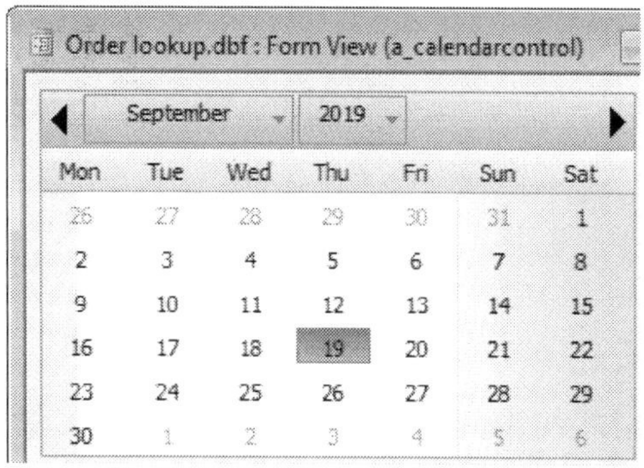

Figure 8-12 Calendar control added to the form

Calendar Super Control Customization Options

Below are some of the options on the Date Picker Builder, shown above in Figure 8-11, that can be used to customize the calendar control.

DISABLED DAYS OPTIONS The options in this section are used to prevent specific days of the week or specific dates from being used.

The **DISABLED DATES OPTION** button opens the dialog box shown in Figure 8-13.

This dialog box is used to select specific dates that will not be available on the control.

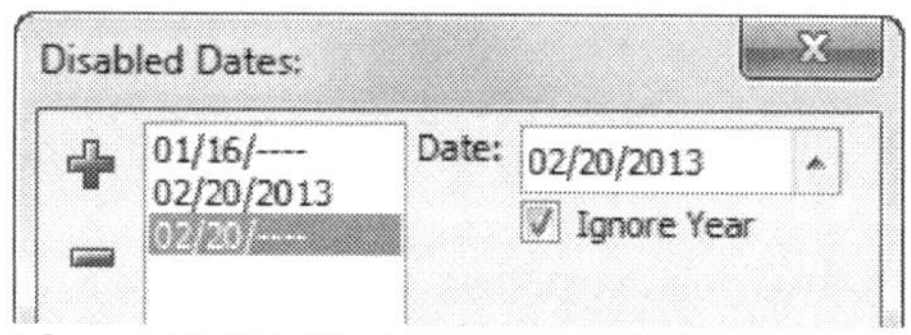

Figure 8-13 Disabled Dates dialog box

FLAGGED DATES OPTIONS The options shown in Figure 8-14 are used to select dates that you want highlighted on the Calendar super control. Figure 8-15 illustrates a flagged date on the control.

Figure 8-14 Flagged Dates dialog box

COLOR OPTIONS Figure 8-16 shows all of the parts of the calendar that you can change the color of.

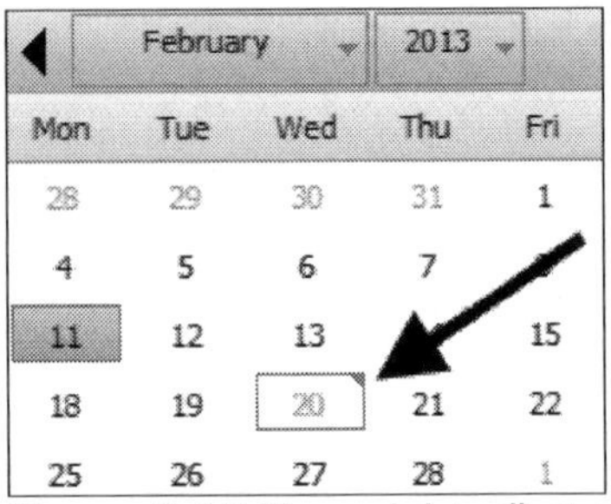

Figure 8-15 Flagged date illustrated

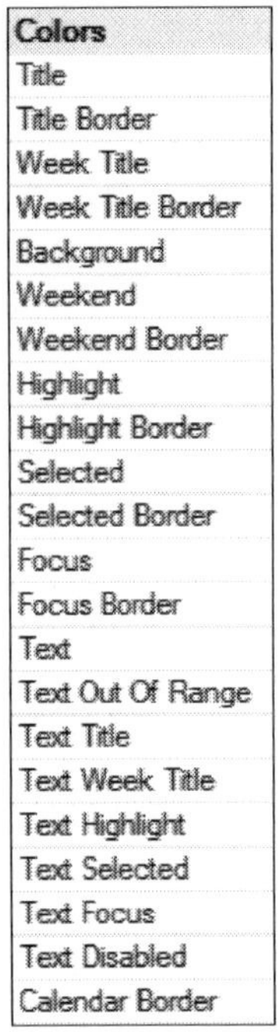

Figure 8-16 Calendar color options

Clock Super Control

This control is used to add a clock to a variable, time or short time field. The time displayed on the clock is updated automatically when a different record is displayed. If the time is changed on the clock, the time field or variable is automatically updated.

The hands on the clock can be moved to change the time in the field on the form.

Like the date field, the time field has a smart control, as shown in Figure 8-17.

The Short time control does not display the calendar shown in Figure 8-17.

If the form that you are adding the control to does not have a time field or variable, you will see a message that lets you know that.

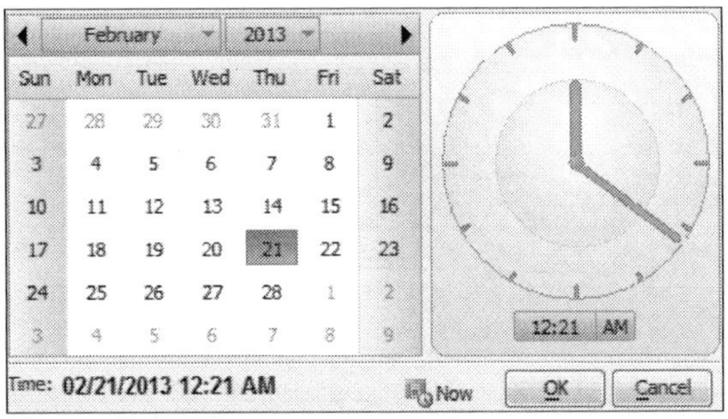

Figure 8-17 Time smart control

The dialog box shown in Figure 8-18 is used to customize the clock. It is similar to the Date Picker Builder shown earlier in Figure 8-11.

If checked, the **SHOW NUMERIC INPUT** option causes the time to be displayed below the clock, as shown in Figure 8-19.

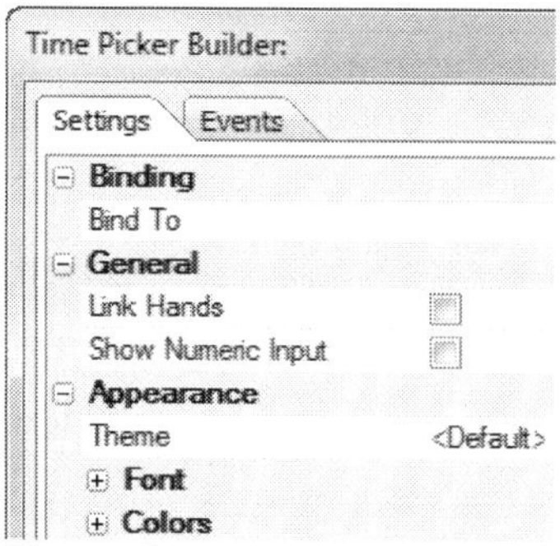

Figure 8-18 Time Picker Builder

Figure 8-19 Show Numeric Input option applied to the clock control

Embedded XDialog Super Control

This control adds an XDialog (a dialog box) to the form. This dialog box is often used to display information, a warning or prompt the user for information. Figure 8-20 shows the dialog box used to customize this control. Using this super control requires writing Xbasic code.

The definition that you create can be saved as a **GLOBAL SCRIPT** or it can be saved in the form. Like the calendar and clock super controls, the Xdialog control can be bound to fields on the form.

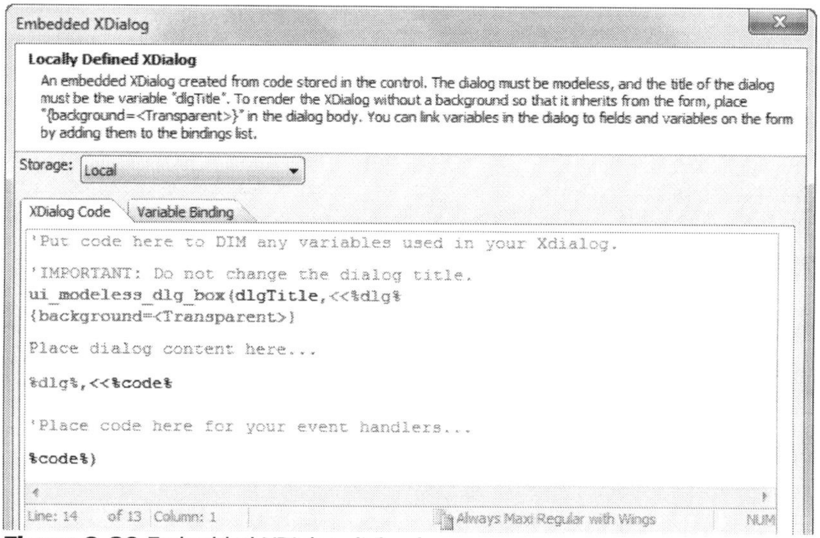

Figure 8-20 Embedded XDialog dialog box

Embedded Grid Component Super Control

This super control is used to place a grid component on a form. Grid components are created in the Web Projects module of Alpha Five. They are used to create web components. This is necessary because forms created in the Desktop module of Alpha Five cannot be used on the web because they cannot be viewed with a web browser.

Grid components can be embedded in a desktop form. I find the word "grid" confusing and misleading because the content displayed in a grid component does not have to look like an embedded browse. It can look like a form.

When embedded on a desktop form, a grid component will display the "form" if you will, that is displayed on a web page.

The good thing is that you do not need to know how to create a web component to be able to embed a grid component on a form.

Figure 8-21 shows the dialog box that is used to add a grid component (that contains a web component) to a form.

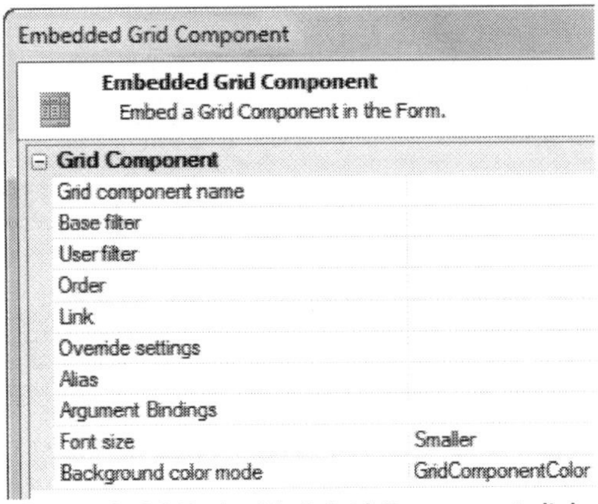

Figure 8-21 Embedded Grid Component dialog box

HTML Content Super Control

This control is used to add a field to the form or report that displays static HTML content (content that doesn't change). An expression is created to display the content in HTML format. Having some HTML programming language knowledge is necessary to use this super control. Some expressions that this control supports are explained below.

① Display one line of text with a normal font and underlined and display another line in bold.
② Display a field like a notes field that has HTML content.
③ Display a file that has HTML content.

Exercise 8.3: Add HTML Content To A Form

In this exercise you will learn how to use this control to display the first line of content in bold and the second line of content underlined.

1. Save the Contact Type form as `aHTMLContentControl`.
2. Add the HTML Content super control below the date field.
3. On the Expression Builder type `"<B>This line is bold</B> <P> <U>This line is underlined</U>"`.

   When previewed, the control will display the content shown in Figure 8-22.

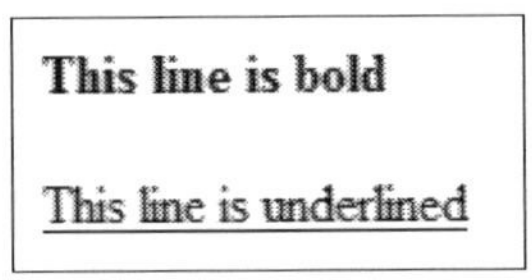

Figure 8-22 HTML content on a form

HTML Form Super Control

This control is used to add an HTML form (that looks like a web page) to a form. Like the HTML Content super control, the HTML Form super control requires HTML programming knowledge.

The objects on the HTML form can be bound to fields in the table(s) that the form is based on. When this control is added to the form, the editor shown in Figure 8-23 is displayed. The tabs are explained in Table 8-2.

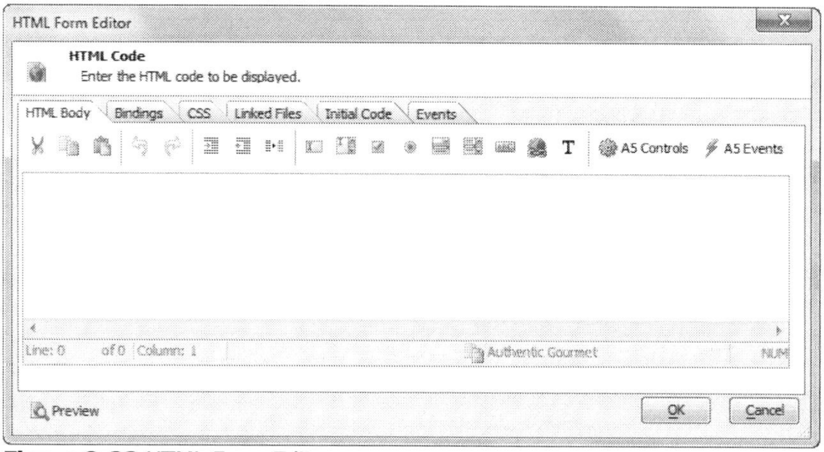

Figure 8-23 HTML Form Editor

Option	Description
HTML Body	Is used to create the layout of the HTML form, as shown above in Figure 8-23.
Bindings	The options shown in Figure 8-24 are used to bind fields on the HTML form to fields in the table that the (desktop) form is based on.
CSS	The tab shown in Figure 8-25 is used to create any CSS that is needed for the HTML form.
Linked Files	The tab shown in Figure 8-26 is used to select, remove or edit the files that have CSS or Java Script that the HTML form will use.
Initial Code	The tab shown in Figure 8-27 is used to create code that is run before the HTML form is displayed.
Events	The tab shown in Figure 8-28 is used to create Xbasic code for events that the HTML form will use.

Table 8-2 HTML Form Editor tabs explained

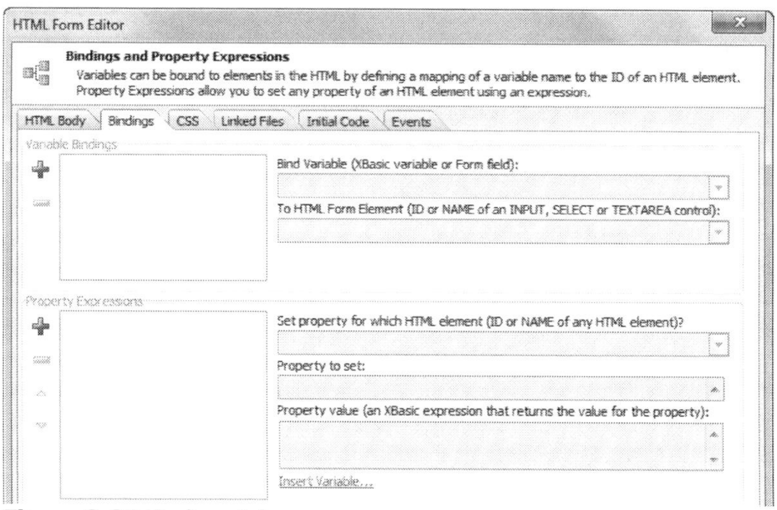

Figure 8-24 Bindings tab

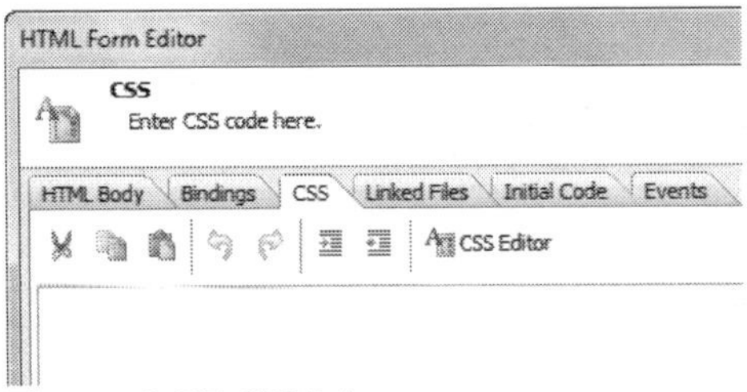

Figure 8-25 CSS tab

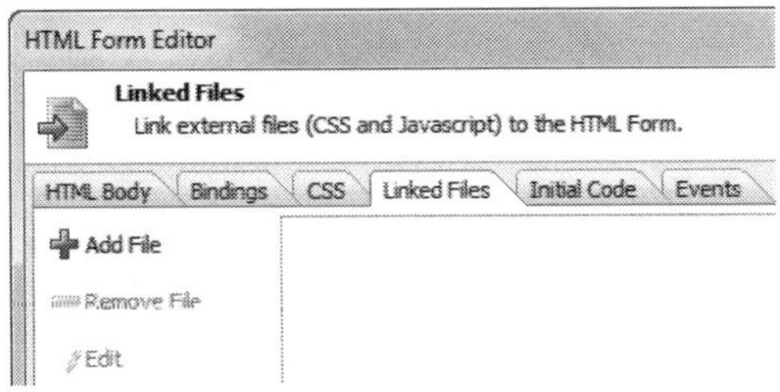

Figure 8-26 Linked Files tab

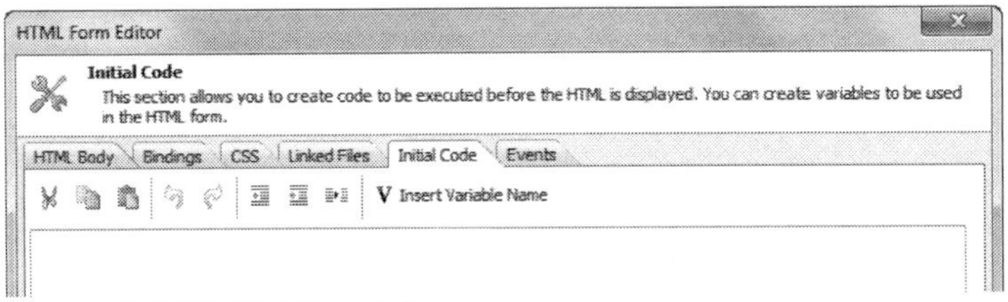

Figure 8-27 Initial Code tab

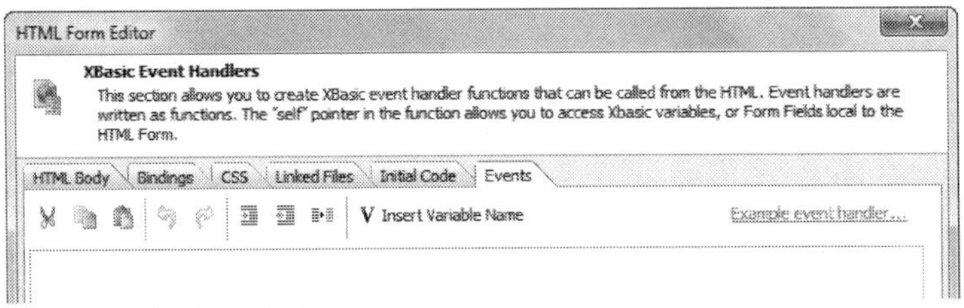

Figure 8-28 Events tab

A5 Controls

On the HTML Form Editors HTML Body tab is a button labeled A5 Controls. When clicked, the dialog box shown in Figure 8-29 is displayed. These controls are specifically for HTML pages. Some of the controls have a dialog box similar to the one shown in Figure 8-30 that will help you configure the control.

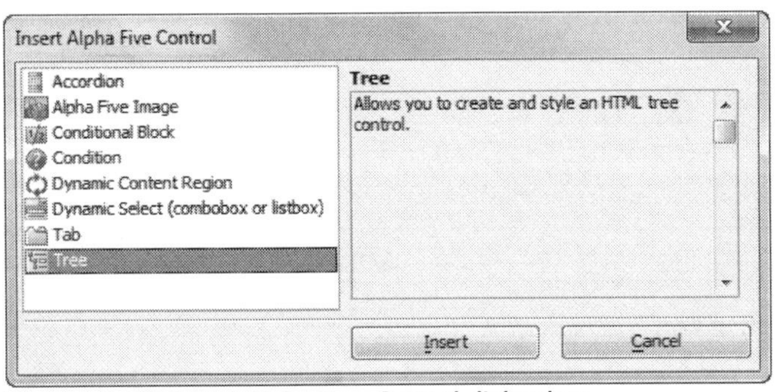

Figure 8-29 Insert Alpha Five Control dialog box

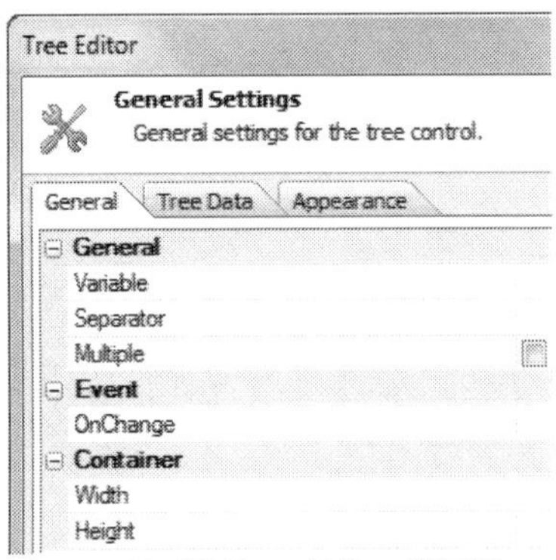

Figure 8-30 Tree Editor (HTML Form)

PDF Viewer Super Control

This control is used to display a PDF file on a form. The person using a form that has this control needs to have the free Adobe Reader or full version of Adobe Acrobat installed.

Exercise 8.4: Add PDF Functionality To A Form

In this exercise you will modify a tab on a form to display a PDF file.

1. Save the Change Title Bar caption form as `aPDFViewerControl`.
2. Add another tab to the form and name it `PDF Viewer`.
3. On the new tab add the PDF Viewer super control. Make the control almost as large as the bottom portion of the tab, then click the **SELECT PDF FILE** link.
4. On the PDF File dialog box select the file, PDF file.pdf.

   You should have the options shown in Figure 8-31.

   Click OK.

   The **PREVIEW BUTTON** displays the PDF file at the bottom of the dialog box, as shown in the figure.

   When you view the PDF Viewer tab on the form, you should see the PDF file, as shown in Figure 8-32.

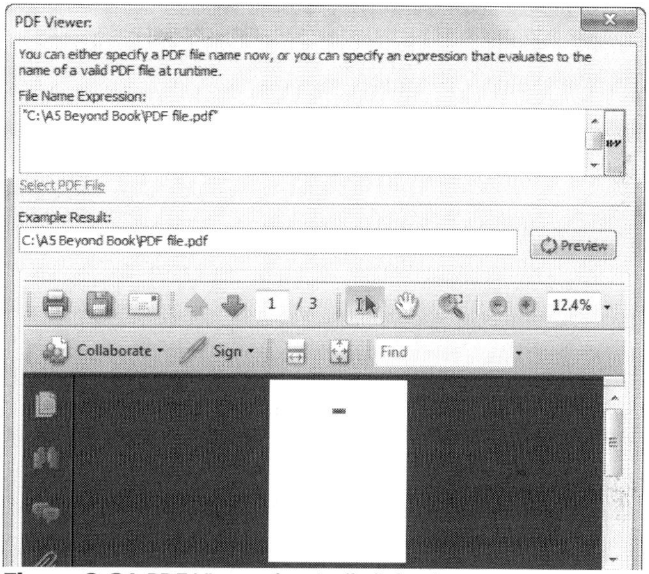

Figure 8-31 PDF Viewer (control) dialog box

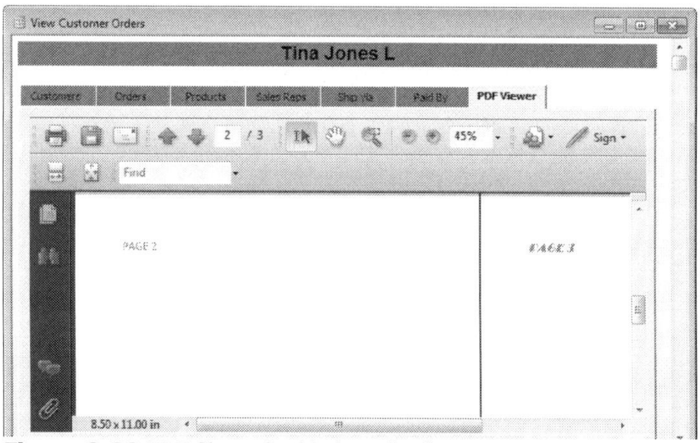

Figure 8-32 PDF file embedded on the form

Record Navigator Super Control

This control adds a scrollbar or trackbar to the form that is used to display different records. This control is helpful if you are not displaying the default menus and toolbar that are available when the form is viewed.

Exercise 8.5: Add Record Navigation To A Form

In this exercise you will add the Record Navigation super control to a form and customize it.

1. Save the aTreeControl form as `aRecordNavigatorControl`.

2. Add the Record Navigator super control to the form across from the fields in the frame, by drawing a vertical square on the form.

Record Navigator Dialog Box

The options shown in Figure 8-33 are used to configure the Record Navigator control.

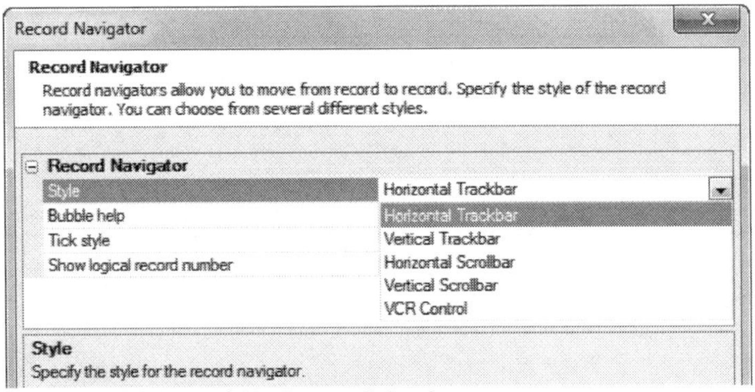

Figure 8-33 Record Navigator dialog box

Record Navigator Options

The options discussed below are used to select and customize the navigator.

① **STYLE** The options in this drop-down list shown above in Figure 8-33, are used to select the appearance of the navigator. The two **TRACKBAR OPTIONS** display a navigator that has a button that slides to display a record. The two **SCROLLBAR OPTIONS** display a slider like the one displayed vertically on the right side of windows in Alpha Five and other software. There are no customization options for the scrollbar styles on this dialog box. Trackbars and scrollbars can be placed vertically or horizontally on the form. **VCR CONTROL OPTION** [See VCR Control Style Record Navigator]

② **BUBBLE HELP** If checked and the data is sorted by something other than the record number, the key value of the record that is displayed appears next to the trackbar button, while you are dragging it. (1)

③ **TICK STYLE** The options in this drop-down list are used to select where the tick marks on the trackbar will be displayed. (1)

④ **SHOW LOGICAL RECORD NUMBER** If checked, the record count and logical record number values will be displayed in the Bubble help. The logical record number is the invisible counter used when a record is added to a table. This is different then the ID field in a table. (1)

(1) This option is only available for trackbars.

VCR Control Style Record Navigator

The options shown in Figure 8-34 are used to select the buttons that will be available on the VCR Navigator, as shown in Figure 8-35.

This navigator can only be displayed horizontally.

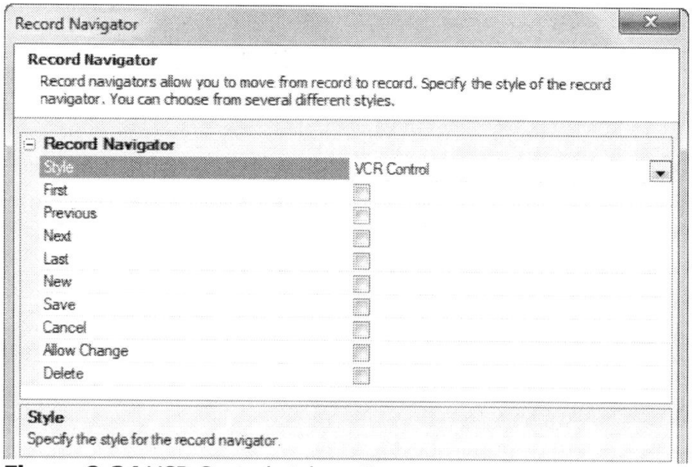

Figure 8-34 VCR Control style options

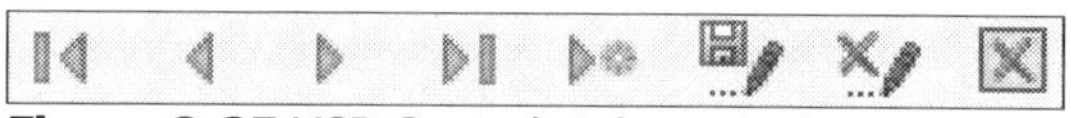

Figure 8-35 VCR Control style navigator

Configure The Record Navigator

In this part of the exercise you will select the options for the trackbar.

1. On the Record Navigator dialog box, open the Style drop-down list and select **VERTICAL TRACKBAR**, if it is not already selected.

2. Open the Tick Style drop-down list and select Right.

3. Open the Record Navigator Properties dialog box, then select the following options, as shown in Figure 8-36. The Record Navigator should look like the one shown in Figure 8-37.

   Style - Long Dashes
   Color - Red
   Width - 5

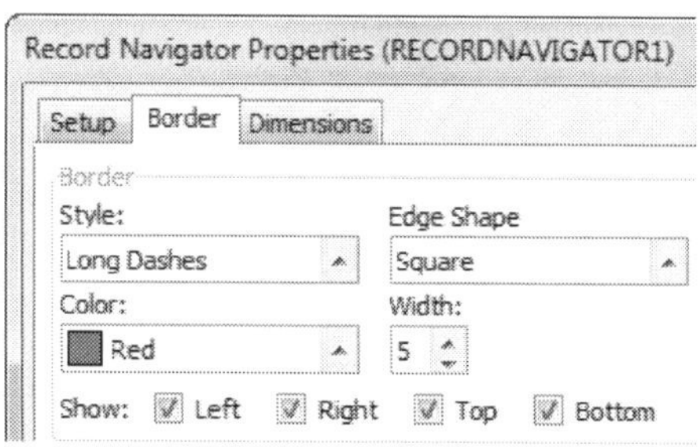

Figure 8-36 Record Navigator Properties dialog box

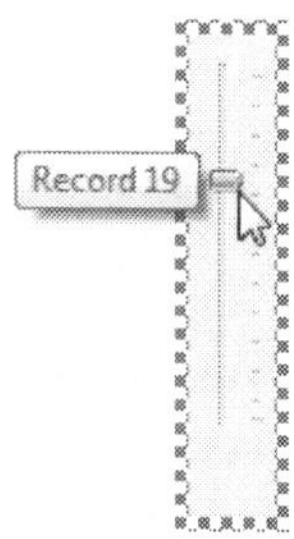

Figure 8-37 Record navigator

The data in the form is sorted by last name.

Notice the difference in what is displayed in the Bubble help in Figure 8-38, compared to what is displayed in Figure 8-37.

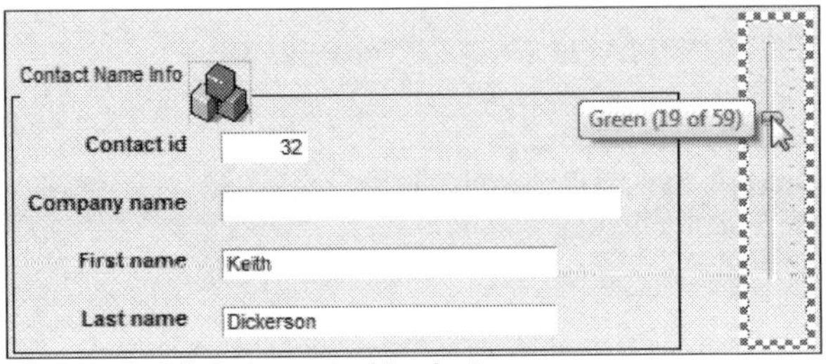

Figure 8-38 Data sorted by last name

Report Preview Super Control

This control is used to add a window to a form that will display a report, letter or label. The report displayed can be filtered by the record displayed on the form or not. If filtered, as different records are displayed on the form, the data displayed on the report will change. The report does not have to be linked to a field on a form, meaning that a report can be displayed that doesn't have any data in common with the data on the form.

Exercise 8.6: Display A Report In A Window On A Form

In this exercise you will add a report that is linked to a field on the form.

1. Save the Customer Order Details form as `aReportPreviewControl`.

2. Drag the right border of the form layout to the 13.5 inch mark (or wider if you have a 17 inch screen).

3. Add the Report Preview super control to the form. Make the control as wide as you made the form in step 2 above. Make the control at least five inches long. If you can't make the control this size now, you can resize it after you close the Report Preview dialog box.

Report Preview Dialog Box

The options on this dialog box are used to select and customize the report that will be displayed on the form.

Select The Report To Be Displayed On The Form

In this part of the exercise you will select the report that will be displayed in the control. You will also create the filter, select the link field for the form and report and select the sort order. The options shown in Figure 8-39 are used to accomplish these tasks. The options are explained below.

① **REPORTS** The options in the upper left corner are the reports, letters and labels in the database that you can select from to display on the form.
② The **TYPE**, **NAME** and **LOCATION** options in the upper right corner display information about the report that was selected to be displayed on the form.
③ The **REFRESH PREVIEW BUTTON** near the bottom of the dialog box will display the report based on the options selected on this dialog box.

1. Select the Grouped by order date report.

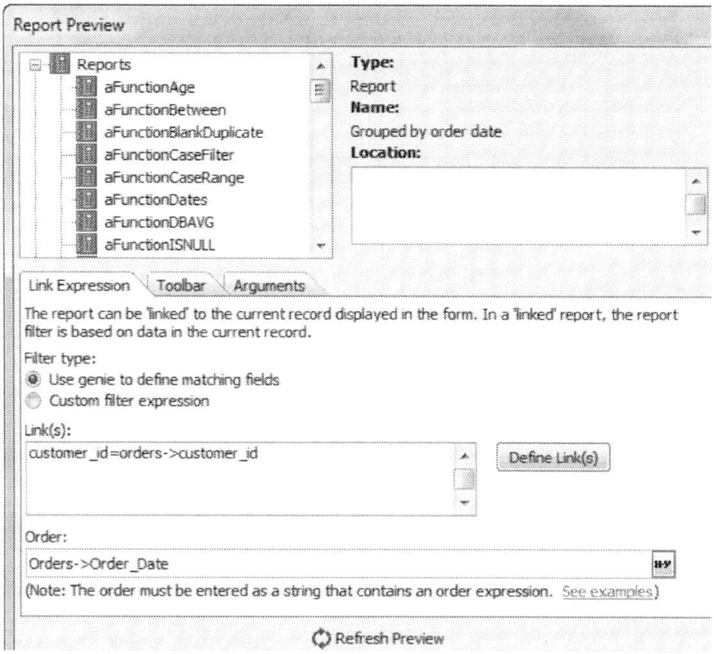

Figure 8-39 Report Preview dialog box and Link Expression options

Link Expression Tab

The options on this tab are used to select the filter type, links between the form and report and the sort order for the records displayed on the report.

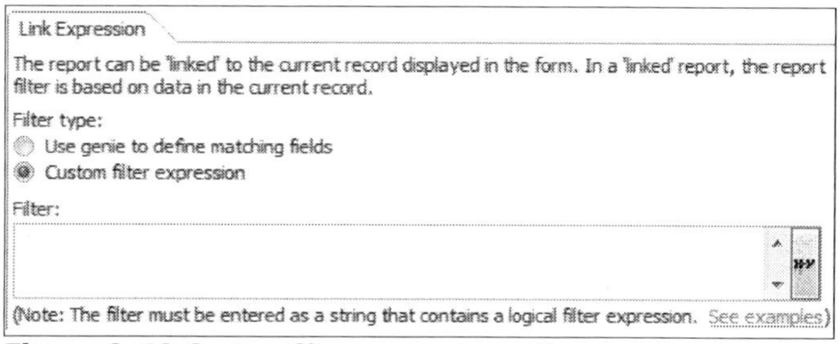

Figure 8-40 Custom filter expression option

Selecting the **CUSTOM FILTER EXPRESSION** option displays the Filter field shown in Figure 8-40. This option is used to create a logical filter expression.

The **DEFINE LINK(S)** button opens the Link(s) dialog box shown later in Figure 8-41. The options are used to select the field(s) that are needed to link the report to the form.

1. Select the **USE GENIE TO DEFINE MATCHING FIELDS** option if it is not already selected, then click the **DEFINE LINK(S) BUTTON.**

2. Open the Report Field drop-down list and select the Customer ID field. Open the Form Field drop-down list and select the Customer ID field in the Orders table. In this exercise, you could select the Customer ID field in the Customers table in the Form Field drop-down list. You should have the options shown in Figure 8-41.

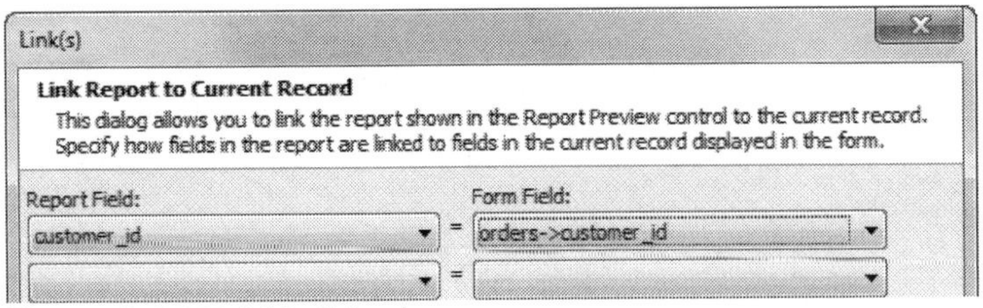

Figure 8-41 Link(s) dialog box

3. Click the Order field button, then click the Insert button.

   Select the Order Date field on the dialog box shown in Figure 8-42.

   You should have the options shown in earlier Figure 8-39.

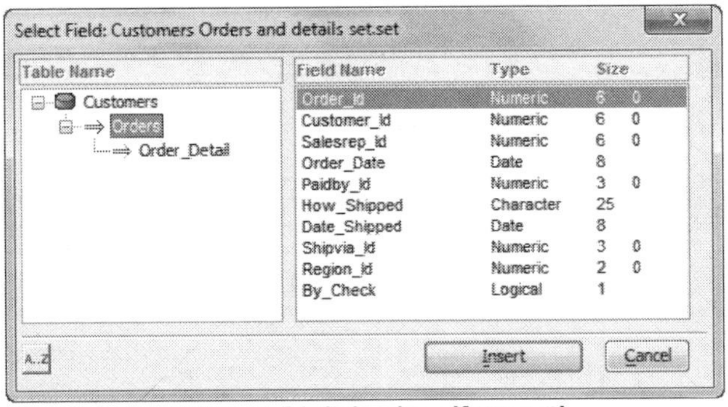

Figure 8-42 Select Field dialog box (for a set)

Toolbar Tab

The options shown in Figure 8-43 are used to add buttons to the window that will display the report. Doing this is optional.

The green plus sign button displays the shortcut menu shown in Figure 8-44.

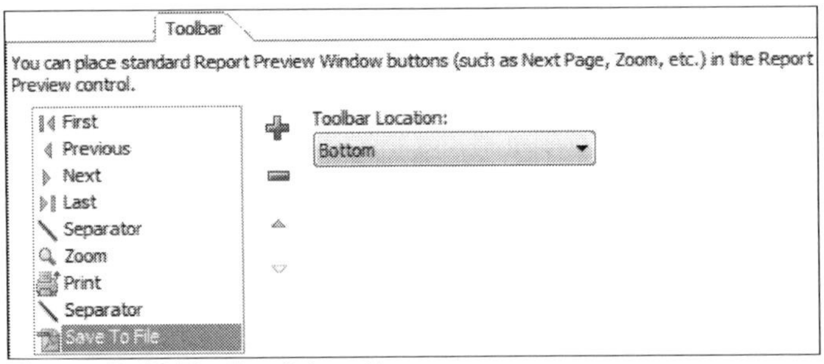

Figure 8-43 Toolbar tab options

The **TOOLBAR LOCATION** option is used to select where the toolbar will be placed in relation to the report.

1. Select the following options from the shortcut menu shown in Figure 8-44. First, Previous, Next, Last, Separator, Zoom, Print, Separator, Save To File.

> It would be nice if there was an option to add all of the buttons to the toolbar at one time.

2. Open the Toolbar Location drop-down list and select Bottom. You should have the options shown earlier in Figure 8-43. Click OK.

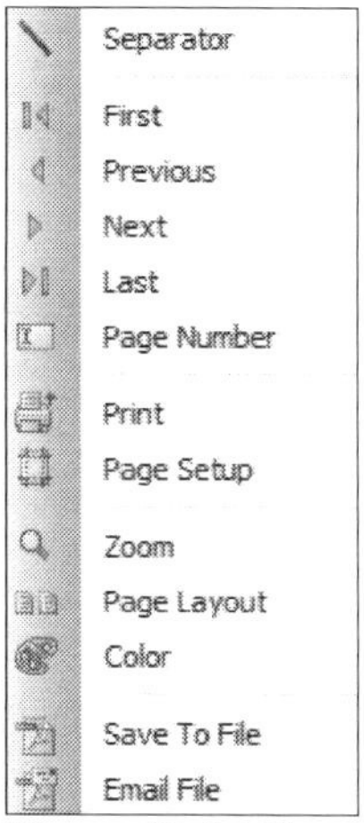

Figure 8-44 Shortcut menu of buttons that can be added to the Report Preview control toolbar

Arguments Tab

The options shown in Figure 8-45 are used to create arguments that will be used to filter the data displayed on the report.

The **CUSTOM FILTER EXPRESSION** option on the Link Expression tab must be selected to create an argument.

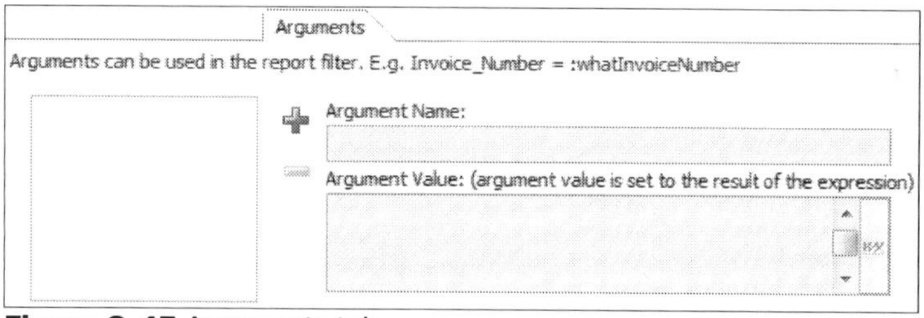

Figure 8-45 Arguments tab

Finish Customizing The Report

1. On the Report Preview Properties dialog box, click on the Border tab. Change the Border Style and Color to a combination that you like.

2. Change the Width to 5. Your form should look similar to the one shown in Figure 8-46.

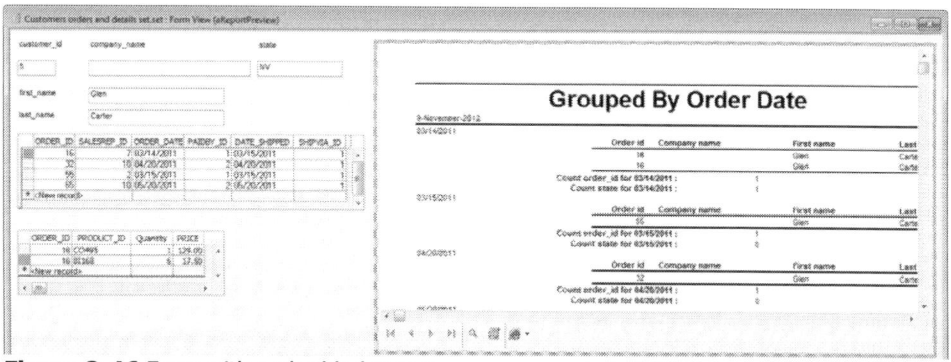

Figure 8-46 Form with embedded report

When you view different records on the form, the corresponding Order IDs will be displayed on the report. If you want to view the part of the report that displays a specific order, click on the Order ID on the form. For example, view the record for Customer ID 8 on the form. This customer has placed several orders. More than likely, you cannot see the data for Order ID 61 on the report. You could scroll down the report to look for it or you could click on the row for Order ID on the form. Doing this displays the corresponding page in the report.

Web Content Super Control

The dialog box shown in Figure 8-47 is used to display a web page in a window on the form. The web page that is displayed can be **STATIC** (the same web page for every record displayed on the form) or **DYNAMIC** (the web page changes for each record displayed on the form, based on the data in the table). The options are explained below.

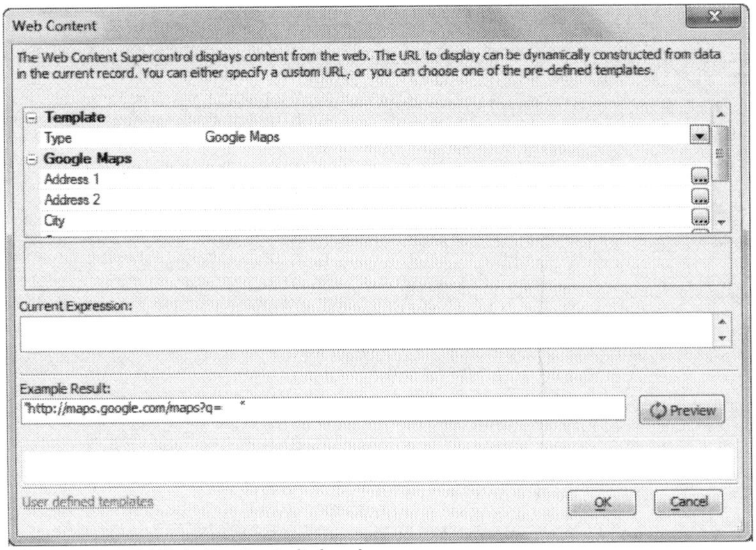

Figure 8-47 Web Content dialog box

Predefined Templates

Alpha Five comes with the following web content templates: Google Image Search, Google Maps, Google Search, MSN Maps and Yahoo Maps. Each of these templates displays fields that can be mapped to, which means that the web content displayed is specific for the record that is displayed.

Generic Template

The **USER DEFINED URL EXPRESSION** template type is used when you want to display content from a web site other then the ones that have predefined templates. This option can be used to create a static or dynamic link by creating an expression.

Custom Web Content Templates

You can create your own template by clicking on the **USER DEFINED TEMPLATES** link in the lower left corner of the Web Content dialog box, then selecting New Template. The dialog box shown in Figure 8-48 is used to create the template.

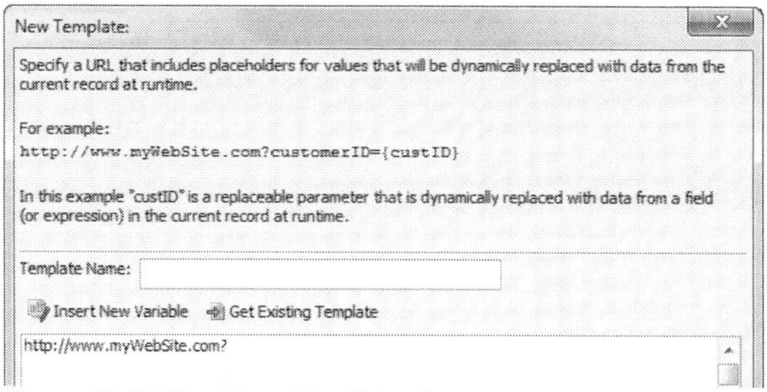

Figure 8-48 New Template dialog box

Exercise 8.7: Display Web Sites On A Form

In this exercise you will learn how to use the Web Content super control to display a web page based on the data in a field. You need to be connected to the Internet to be able to view the content in this control.

1. Open the Contacts table and create a character field named `Web site`, with a width of 50.
2. View the Contacts table in the Default Form. Delete the fields starting with the Email address field through the Note field. Move the web site field up, then save the form as `aWebContentControl`.
3. Type in a web site that you visit for the first two records in the table.
4. Make the form at least seven inches wide and six inches long.

Add The Web Content Super Control To The Form

1. Add the Web Content control to the bottom of the form. Make it as wide and long as the form.
2. Open the Type drop-down list and select **USER DEFINED URL EXPRESSION**.
3. Click the URL Expression field button. Select the Website field.
4. When you view the first two records in the table, you should see the web sites in the control.

Alphabet Buttons Search Super Control

This is probably one of the most popular controls and is often referred to as **A TO Z BUTTONS**. It can display the letters of the alphabet and numbers 0 to 9 as buttons or links. When you click on a button, the data is searched and records that match the letter or number of the button that was clicked on are displayed.

Alphabet Buttons Search Dialog Box

The dialog box shown in Figure 8-49 is used to customize the alphabet buttons.

The options that you will use most are explained in Table 8-3.

The other options on this dialog box are used to customize the buttons appearance on the control.

There are options to change the alignment, color, border and shape of buttons when they are hovered over with the mouse pointer, disabled or clicked on.

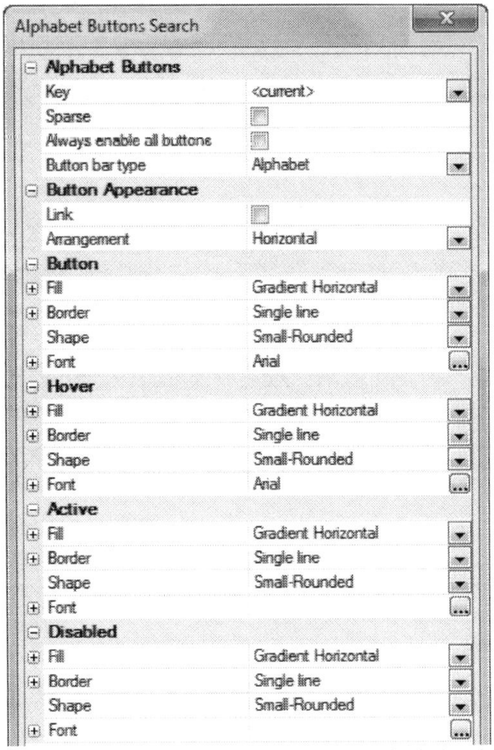

Figure 8-49 Alphabet Buttons Search dialog box

Option	Description
Key	The options in this drop-down list contain the fields in the primary table that the form is based on. Select the field that the buttons will search. The **<CURRENT>** option will use the field that is currently being used as the sort field.
Sparse	If checked, only buttons that have records that match the letter will be displayed.
Always enable all buttons	If checked, buttons that do not have matching records are disabled. I personally like this option enabled because I don't want to click on a button that does not have any matching records.
Button bar type	[See Button Bar Types]
Link	If checked, the buttons will be displayed as hyperlinks.

Table 8-3 Alphabet Buttons Search dialog box options explained

Button Bar Types

The four options discussed below are the type of alphabet style buttons that can be displayed.

① **ALPHABET** This is the default and probably the most used. The buttons display the letters of the alphabet. [See Figure 8-55]

② **NUMERIC** Displays the numbers 0 to 9 on the buttons, as shown in Figure 8-50.

③ **ALPHA-NUMERIC** Displays the alphabet characters and numbers on buttons, as shown in Figure 8-51. This option is helpful when the first character in the field being searched could be numeric. For example, some company names start with a number.

④ **RANGED BUTTONS** Is used to create buttons that use a range of values as the search criteria. When this option is selected, the Ranged Buttons field illustrated in Figure 8-52 is displayed. Clicking the button at the end of the Ranged Buttons field, opens the dialog box shown in Figure 8-53.

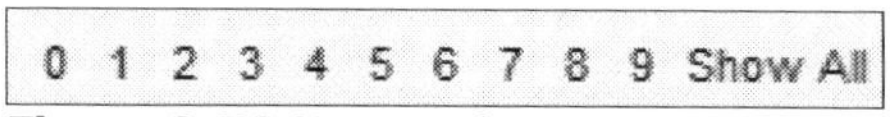

Figure 8-50 Numeric button type

Figure 8-51 Alpha-Numeric button type

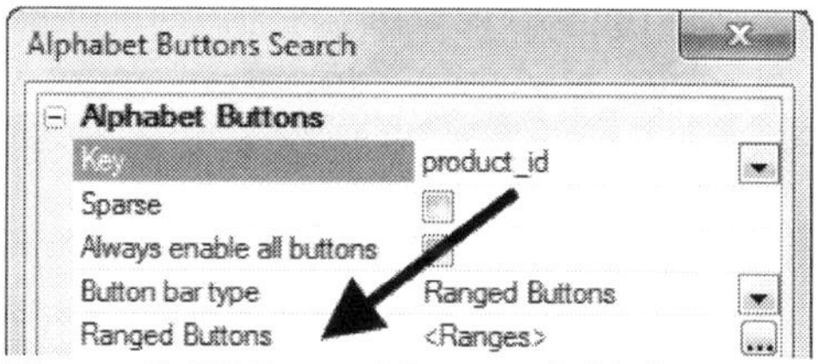

Figure 8-52 Ranged Buttons field illustrated

Edit Range Buttons

The dialog box shown in Figure 8-53 is used to type in the custom range values or click the **PREDEFINED RANGES** link to select a range for the alphabet buttons, as shown in Figure 8-54.

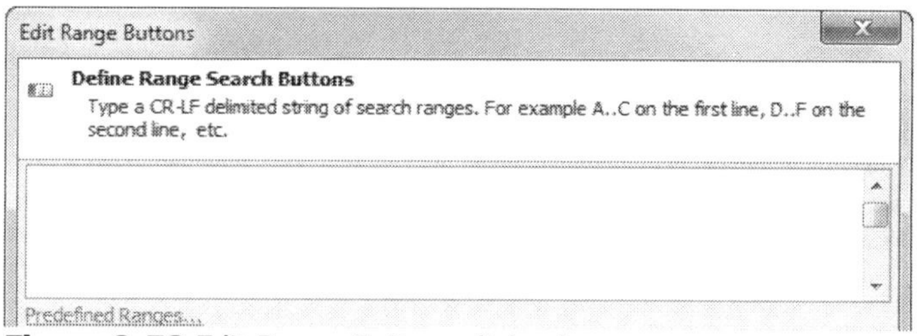

Figure 8-53 Edit Range Buttons dialog box

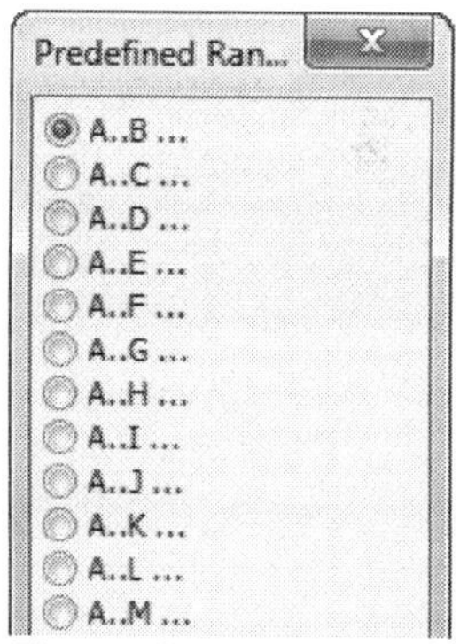

Figure 8-54 Predefined Range dialog box

Exercise 8.8: Add Alphabet Search Buttons To A Form

In this exercise you will learn how to use the options on the Alphabet Buttons Search dialog box to add the alphabet search buttons to a form.

1. Create a default form for the Customers table, then save it as `aAlphabetButtonsControl`.

2. Move all of the fields on the form down, then add the Alphabet Buttons Search super control to the top of the form.

3. Select the following options: Key - Last name, then clear the check mark for the Always enable all buttons option.

4. Make the changes in Table 8-4 to display the buttons in different colors. The last three columns in the table refer to the section of the Alphabet Buttons Search dialog box that the option is in. The buttons should look like the ones shown in Figure 8-55. Notice that some letters are not enabled. When the mouse pointer hovers over a letter, the background and border color changes.

Option	Button	Hoover	Active
Fill	Gradient Horizontal	Gradient Radial Bottom Left	Gradient Horizontal Capsule
Fill Color		Yellow	Sky Blue
Fill Accent Color		Turquoise	Dark Blue
Font Size	10, Bold		30, Bold, Underline
Font Color	Red		Blue

Table 8-4 Button appearance options

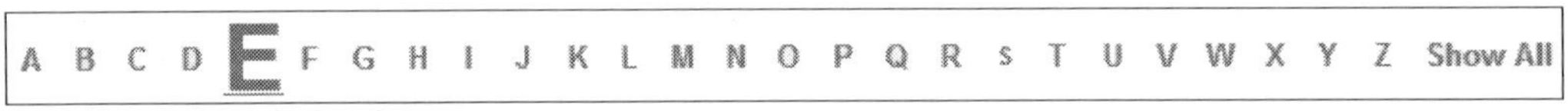

Figure 8-55 Alphabet buttons

> **Saving The Changes**
> When you make changes to the Alphabet Buttons control, you should save the changes before viewing the form.

> **Border And Shape Options**
> It may be something I did wrong when selecting these options because the options did not appear on the buttons, even though I saved the changes.

5. Click on a few of the enabled buttons to display records where the last name starts with a letter that you clicked on.

Drop Down Browse Super Control

This control displays a drop-down list that has the values from at least one field in the table that the form is based on. This control will remind you of the Simple list and Table lookup field rule drop-down lists. The difference is that the option selected in the Drop Down Browse control displays the corresponding record on the form.

What I like about this control is that more than one can be used on the same form. The value in one control can be used to filter the values displayed in another control. You may know this as the **CASCADING EFFECT**.

Drop Down Browse Dialog Box

The options shown in Figure 8-56 are used to configure the drop-down list. The options are explained below.

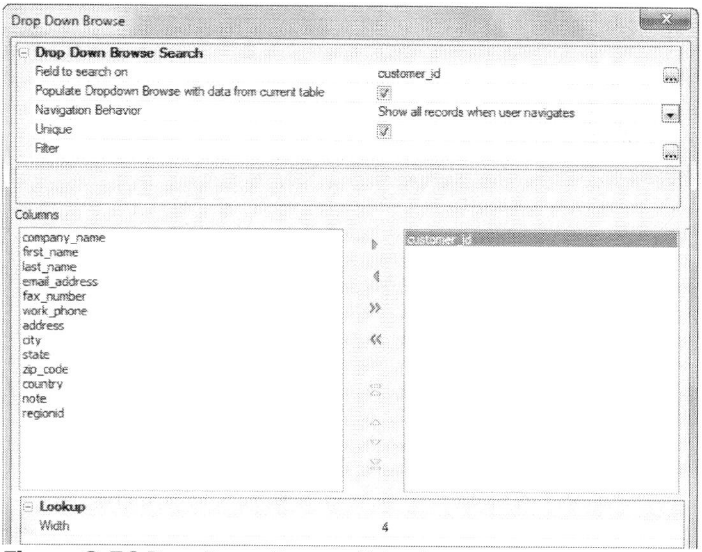

Figure 8-56 Drop Down Browse dialog box

① **FIELD TO SEARCH ON** Is used to select the field in the top level table (that the form is based on) to search on. **TOP LEVEL TABLE** is the terminology used when the form is created from a set. All fields in the set can appear on the form.

② **POPULATE DROP DOWN BROWSE WITH DATA FROM THE CURRENT TABLE** If checked, the values displayed in the drop-down list will come from the table (or set) that the form is based on. Clearing the check mark allows any field in the database to be used. The Table and Link options (explained below) are enabled when the check mark is cleared. The options illustrated in Figure 8-57 are used to select the table. The **TABLE** option is used to select the table that has the values that you want to display in the drop-down list. The **LINK** option is used to select the field in the table that the form is based on. This may sound like you have more options for selecting fields, but I was not able to find a good use for this option.

③ **NAVIGATION BEHAVIOR** The options in this drop-down list are used to select what the drop-down browse list should do. The options are explained in Table 8-5.

④ **UNIQUE** If checked, only unique values will be displayed in the drop-down list.

⑤ **FILTER** Clicking the button at the end of this field displays the dialog box shown later in Figure 8-58. It is used to create a filter for the values that will be displayed in the drop-down list. These values will be based on the value in another drop-down browse list that has already been set up on the form.

⑥ The **COLUMNS** list in the middle of the dialog box displays the available fields.

⑦ The **WIDTH** field displays the length of the field selected in the (unnamed) list to the right of the Column list. If necessary, you can change the width of a field.

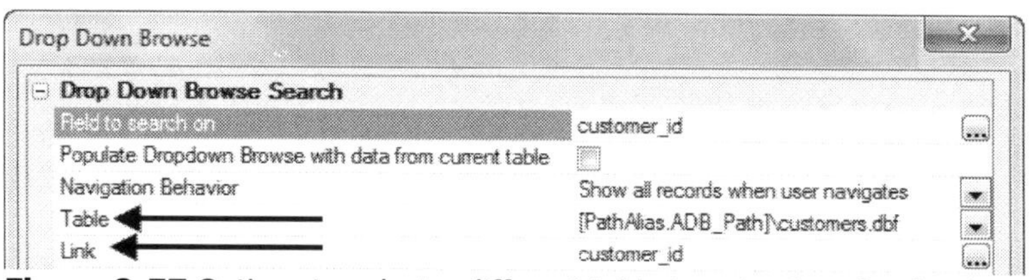

Figure 8-57 Options to select a different table to get values for the drop-down list illustrated

Navigation Behavior Options

Option	Description
Show all records when user navigates	This is the default option. After an option is selected in the drop-down list on the form, if there is a filter applied, the filter is removed. The records are not reordered.
Query when user navigates	After an option is selected in the drop-down list on the form, a query is run instead of the Find By Key search method. This option is automatically used by Active Link tables.
Restrict navigation to records in the current filter	The drop-down list on the form will only display records in the current filter.

Table 8-5 Navigation Behavior options explained

Exercise 8.9: Add The Drop Down Browse Super Control To A Form

In this exercise you will learn how to use this control to let the user select orders by customer name and date to select the record to view. The records will be restricted to orders on or after a specific date.

1. Create a default form for the Customers-Orders-Set. Save the form as `aDropDownBrowseControl`.

2. Move the fields down on the form, then add the Drop Down Browse super control to the top of the form.

3. Click the Field to search on button, then select the Order Date field.

4. Click the Filter field button. On the Build Drop Down Browse Filter dialog box, click the **EDIT AS EXPRESSION** link. Create an expression to check if the Order Date is greater than or equal to 3/2/2011.

> **Build Drop Down Browse Filter Dialog Box**
> On the dialog box shown in Figure 8-58, I was not able to create the expression needed for this exercise with the options at the bottom of the dialog box because the Operator drop-down list does not have an option for greater than. Nor do the options on this dialog box support a comparison using a literal. The options are explained below.

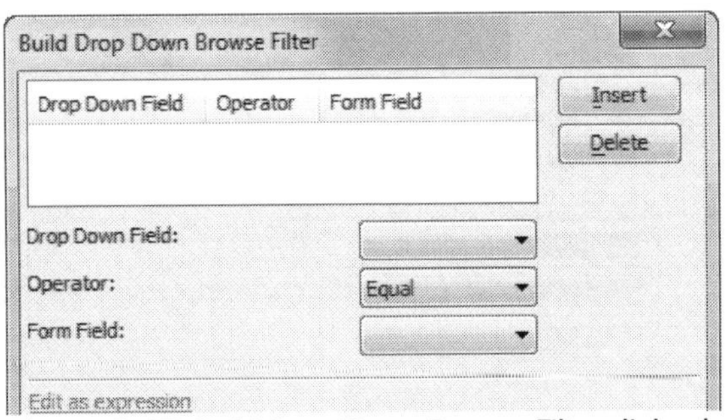

Figure 8-58 Build Drop Down Browse Filter dialog box

① **DROP DOWN FIELD** Select a field that you want to create a filter for.

② **OPERATOR** Select the Equal, Not equal or Contains operator based on the filter that you need to create. If none of these operators meet your needs, click the Edit as expression link to create the filter.

③ **FORM FIELD** Select a field that the form is based on.

④ The **EDIT AS EXPRESSION** link opens the Expression Builder, where you can create the expression for the filter, if needed.

5. Add the First and Last Name fields to the list on the right before the Order Date field.

6. Add the Product Name field to the list after the Order Date field.

   You should have the options shown in Figure 8-59.

   Your Drop Down Browse should have the options shown in Figure 8-60.

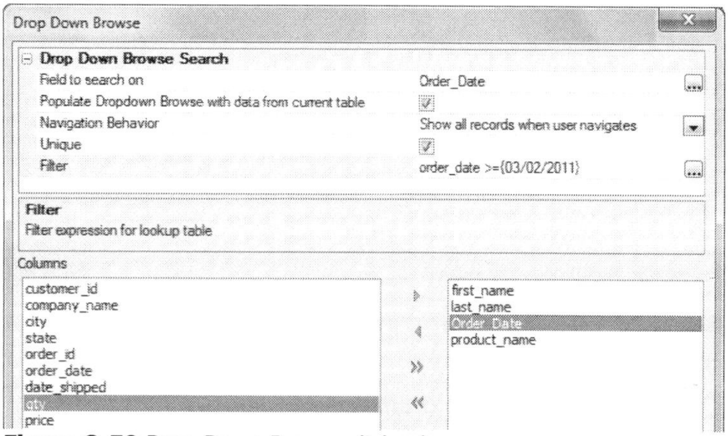

Figure 8-59 Drop Down Browse dialog box

Notice that the Order Date for all records displayed is greater than or equal to 3/2/2011.

When you select a row in the drop-down list, the corresponding data will be displayed on the form.

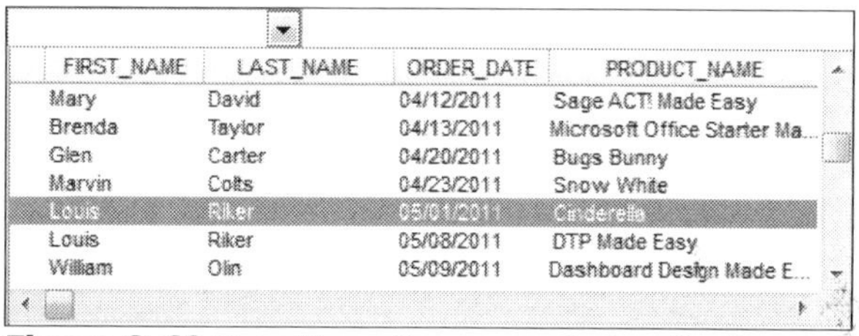

Figure 8-60 Drop Down Browse control on the form

Using Two Drop Down Browse Controls On A Form

In the previous section you learned how to add and configure a single Drop Down Browse control. Using one control may work for a lot of forms, but you may find that you need more than one control to let the user select the record(s) that they want to view.

You can use two controls on a form independent of each other or you can have the values in one control determine what values are displayed in the second control. An example of this is state and city. The first drop-down list contains all of the states in the table. When a state is selected in the first drop-down list, the second drop-down list will only display cities in the state that was selected in the first drop-down list.

Exercise 8.10: Use One Drop Down Browse Control To Filter Another One

In this exercise you will add two Drop Down Browse controls to the form and configure one control to filter the other one, as discussed in the previous section.

1. Save the Customer Order Details form as `a2DropDownBrowseControls`.

2. Add the City field to the form below the State field, then move all of the fields down on the form.

3. Add the Drop Down Browse super control to the form.

4. Select the State field as the Field to search on.

Create The Filter For The Second Drop Down Browse Control

In this part of the exercise you will add another drop down control to the form and create a filter for the second control.

1. Add another Drop Down Browse control to the form, next to the one for the State field.

2. Select the City field as the Field to search on.

3. Click the Filter field button.

4. Open the Drop Down Field drop-down list and select the State field.

   Open the Form Field drop-down list and select the State field.

   You should have the filter options shown in Figure 8-61.

   You should have the control options shown in Figure 8-62.

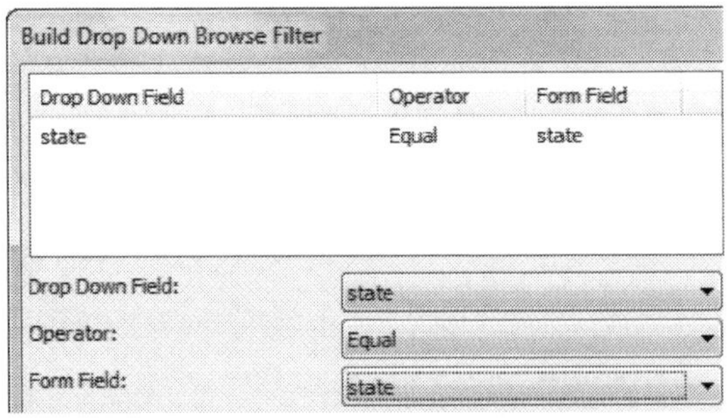

Figure 8-61 City drop-down list filter options

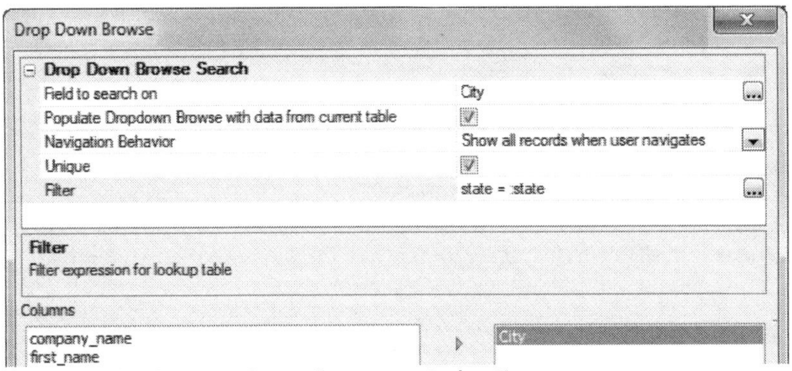

Figure 8-62 City Drop Down Browse control options

5. Open the State drop-down list on the form and select a state. When you open the second drop-down list (for the City field) you will only see cities for the state that you selected. It would be helpful to add labels for the drop-down lists so that the user knows what each drop-down is for.

ENHANCING FORMS

In this chapter you will learn about the following features that can be used to enhance forms.

- ☑ HTML Bubble Help
- ☑ Action Scripting
- ☑ Alphabet Buttons Search Super Control
- ☑ Drop Down Browse Super Control
- ☑ Images

CHAPTER 9

Overview

The controls that were covered in the previous three chapters are helpful for making data entry easier. The topics covered in this chapter are used to give forms more functionality and some expand on topics covered in the previous three chapters.

Edit Bubble Help

The dialog box shown in Figure 9-1 is used to create the content for the bubble help in HTML format.

This dialog box is similar to the HTML Editor for memo fields.

[See Chapter 6, Figure 6-31]

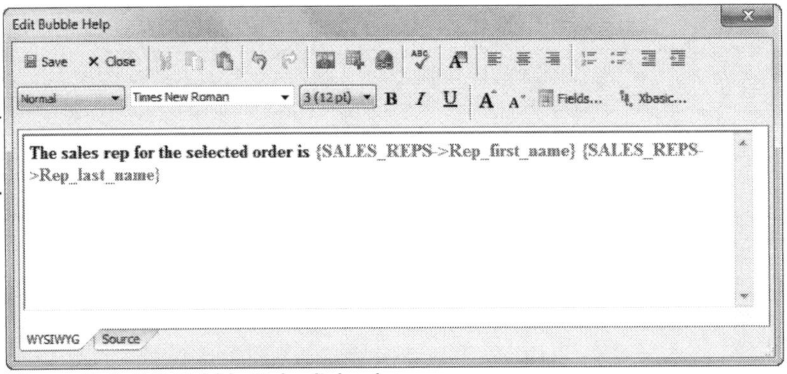

Figure 9-1 Edit Bubble Help dialog box

Exercise 9.1: Add HTML Bubble Help To A Field

In this exercise you will learn how to create bubble help in HTML format. The help message that you will create will display data from a different field then the one the help message is applied to.

1. Save the Display Customer Name form as `aHTMLBubbleHelp`.

2. Open the properties dialog box for the Company name field. On the Help Entry tab, click the Edit button.

3. Select the **USE HTML** option, then click in the blank line below the **<BODY>** tag.

4. Click the **EDIT IN HTML EDITOR** button.

   Type `The sales rep for the selected order is.`

   Press the space bar, then click the **FIELDS** button.

   On the dialog box shown in Figure 9-2, drag the Rep first name field to the editor, then press the space bar.

   Drag the Rep last name field to the editor.

Figure 9-2 Drag Fields Into Editor dialog box

5. Select all of the text and make it bold.

6. Select both fields and change the color to blue. The content should look like it does in Figure 9-1. Click the Save button. Your HTML code should look like the code shown in Figure 9-3. Click OK twice to close both dialog boxes.

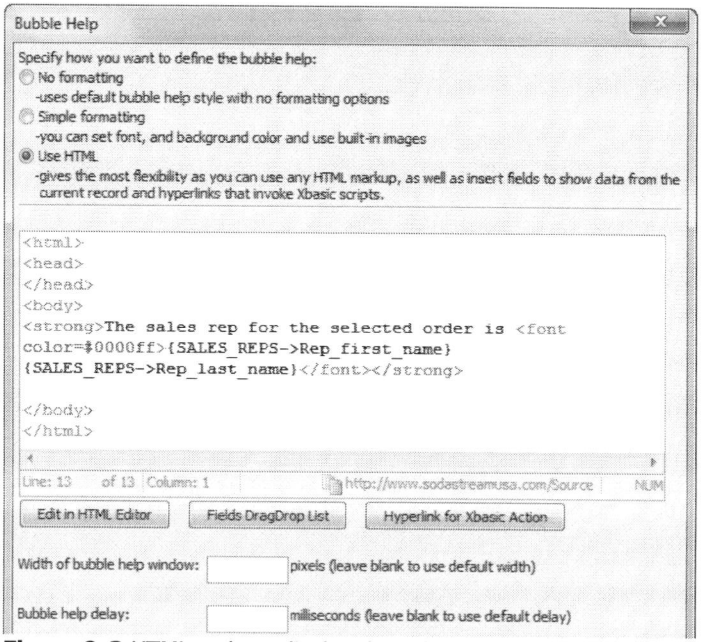

Figure 9-3 HTML code to display the sales rep name

> **Delay The Bubble Help Display**
> The last option shown above in Figure 9-3 is used to select how long it will take the bubble help message to display after the mouse pointer hovers over the field. I thought that I was seeing things when I saw that this option uses milliseconds. Really? I could not figure out what the default display value is, but if you want to use this option, the following may be helpful. 1 second = 1000 ms, 5 seconds = 5000 ms, 10 seconds = 10000 ms

View The Help Message

When you hold the mouse pointer over the Company name field, you will see the bubble help message shown in Figure 9-4.

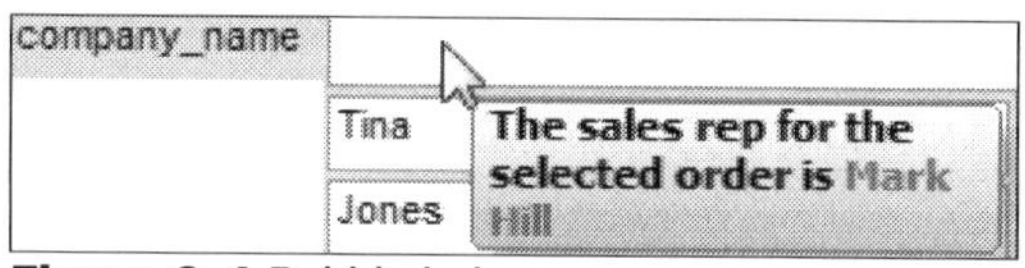

Figure 9-4 Bubble help message

If you click on the Orders tab, you will see that the first order has the Sales rep shown above in Figure 9-4. Click on Order ID 13, then click on the Customers tab. Hold the mouse pointer over the Company name field. You will see that the correct sales rep is displayed in the bubble help message.

Fly-Over Effect

This effect is displayed when the mouse pointer is hovered over a button. The default options for this effect are a white background with black text, which is why you did not notice it in Chapter 6, Exercise 6.2, when you added a button to a form. The options shown in Figure 9-5 are the properties that can be applied to the Fly-Over effect.

What The Buttons Do

OK Saves the selections and closes the dialog box.

APPLY Saves and applies the changes.

RESET Undoes the changes saved the last time the Apply button was clicked.

CANCEL Closes the dialog box without saving any changes that were not previously applied or saved.

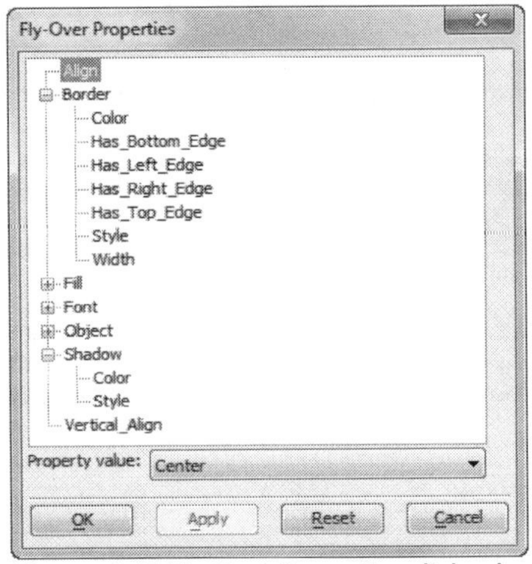

Figure 9-5 Fly-Over Properties dialog box

Exercise 9.2: Apply Fly-Over Effects To A Button

In this exercise you will apply some of the options shown above in Figure 9-5 to a button.

1. Save the aExcelExportButton form as `aFlyoverButton`.

2. On the properties dialog box for the button, click the **SET FLY-OVER APPEARANCE** button.

   Make the changes in Table 9-1, then click OK twice.

Option	Change To
Border Color	Orange
Border Style	Large Rounded Dots
Border Width	10
Fill Backcolor	Light Orange
Shadow Color	Blue
Shadow Style	Medium Soft

Table 9-1 Fly-over options to change

3. View the form. When you hover the mouse pointer over the button, it should look like the one shown in Figure 9-6.

Figure 9-6 Button with fly-over effects

Copying Button Effects
While you can use the options on the **COPY FORMAT TOOLBAR** to copy effects to other buttons, you may get unexpected results, especially if the button that will receive the copied fly-over effect properties already has properties selected. A better solution, in my opinion, is to use the **COPY SELECTED PROPERTIES DIALOG BOX** (Right-click on the button ⇒ Advanced ⇒ Copy selected properties) because as its name indicates, you can select which properties to copy.

Introduction To Action Scripting

Yes, I know what you are thinking, "Why is this topic in a chapter named Enhancing Forms, especially when I have already used this feature earlier in this book?". One reason is because action scripting works well with buttons. Another reason is because it is easier to use action scripting then it is to write Xbasic code. A third reason is because this feature is used to automate and customize an application.

Using Action Scripting will remind you of using a genie because it has screens that are used to select options. It is the front end, if you will, to Xbasic. This means that you do not have to write code. Behind the scenes, the Xbasic code is automatically created for you. In Chapter 6, Exercise 6.2 and 6.3, you learned how to use **PRE-DEFINED ACTION SCRIPTS**.

Action scripts can have more than one action. What I like about action scripts is that you can go back and edit them, similar to how you can go back and edit a report layout that was created using the Quick Report Genie.

Exercise 9.3: Configure The Button Control To Run A Report

In Chapter 6 you learned how to use the Button control. In this exercise you will enhance a button by using action scripting. The button that you set up will be used to run a report from a form.

1. Save the Customer order details form as `aActionScriptButton`.
2. Add a Button control to the form below the State field.
3. On the Define Button dialog box in the Label field, type `View Filter By Month Report`. Select the Use Action Scripting option, then click Next.
4. Click the **ADD NEW ACTION** button. Scroll down the Category list and select the Reports category. In the Action list select the **PREVIEW A LAYOUT** option, then click OK.
5. Scroll down the **LAYOUT NAME LIST** on the dialog box shown in Figure 9-7 and select the Filter by month report.

   The **ONLY SHOW LAYOUTS FOR CURRENT TABLE/SET** option is used to filter the layouts to only display the ones that were created from the table or set that the layout that you are currently using was created from.

   If checked, the **DISPLAY PRINT/PREVIEW PROMPT AT RUNTIME?** option causes the dialog box shown later in Figure 9-14 to open before the report selected on this tab opens, when the button is clicked.

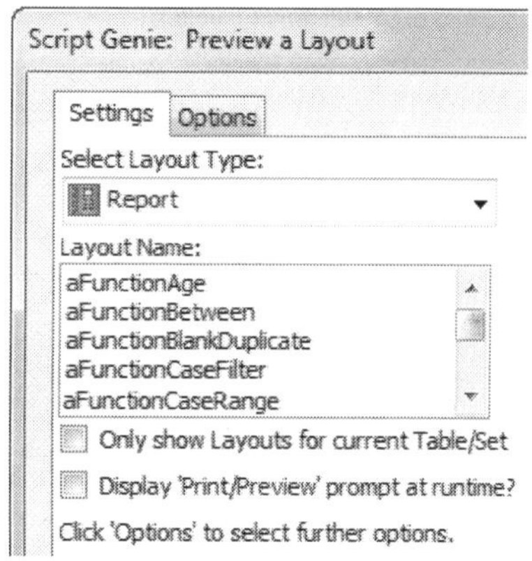

Figure 9-7 Script Genie: Preview a Layout dialog box (Settings tab)

6. Select the Display Print/Preview . . . option, then click Next.

Options Tab

The options shown in Figure 9-8 are used to add more customization to the button. The options selected on this tab will also be included in the Action Script.

The options in the **PRINT METHOD** drop-down list are used to select the output format for the layout that you selected on the Settings tab.

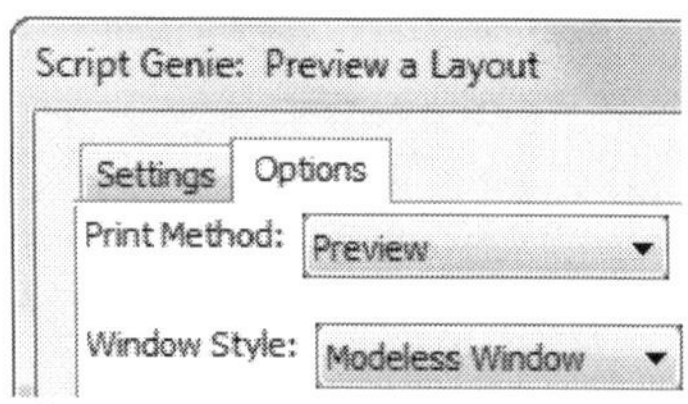

Figure 9-8 Options tab on the Preview a Layout Script Genie dialog box

Selecting The Records To Print

The options at the top of the screen shown in Figure 9-9 are used to select the records that you want to be displayed on the layout. The options at the bottom of the screen change depending on the option selected at the top of the dialog box. For example, compare the options at the bottom of Figure 9-9 to the options at the bottom of Figure 9-10.

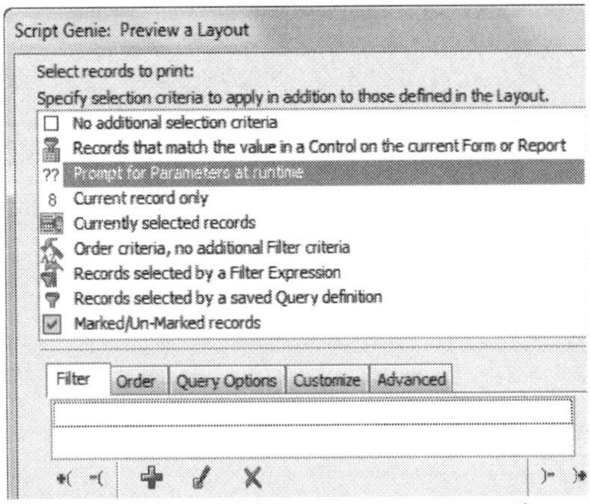

Figure 9-9 Prompt for parameters at run time options

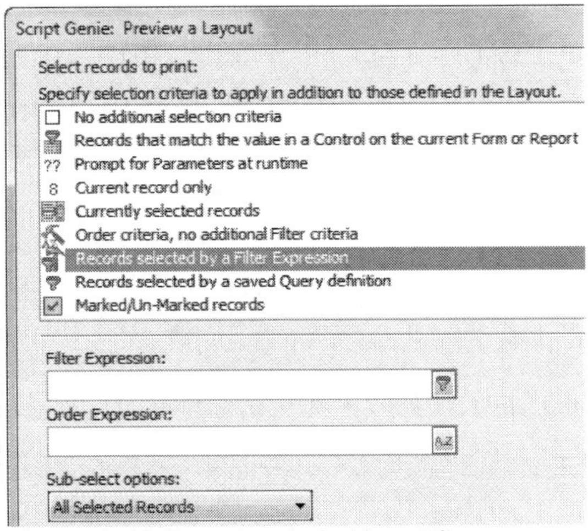

Figure 9-10 Records selected by a Filter Expression options

7. Select the **NO ADDITIONAL SELECTION CRITERIA** option on the screen shown above in Figure 9-10, if it is not already selected, then click Finish.

   You should see the Preview a layout script on the dialog box shown in Figure 9-11.

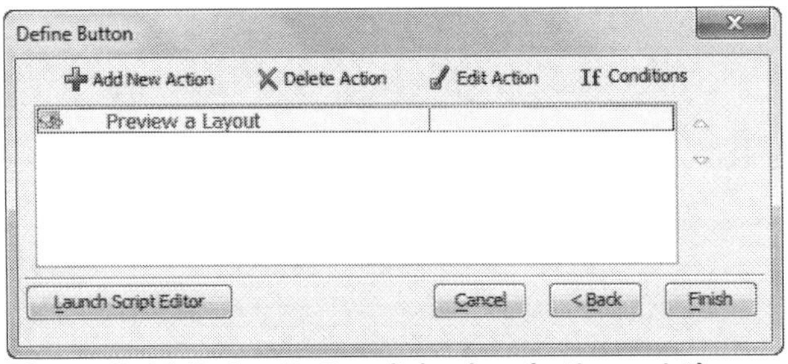

Figure 9-11 Define Button dialog box (action script)

If the script needed more actions, you would click the Add New Action button to select and configure another action.

The (Script) Code Editor

Clicking the **LAUNCH SCRIPT EDITOR BUTTON** shown above in Figure 9-11 opens the dialog box shown in Figure 9-12. Don't click this button now because you can't get back to the Define Button dialog box.

8. Click the Finish button on the Define Button dialog box, then resize the button if necessary so that all of the words are visible.

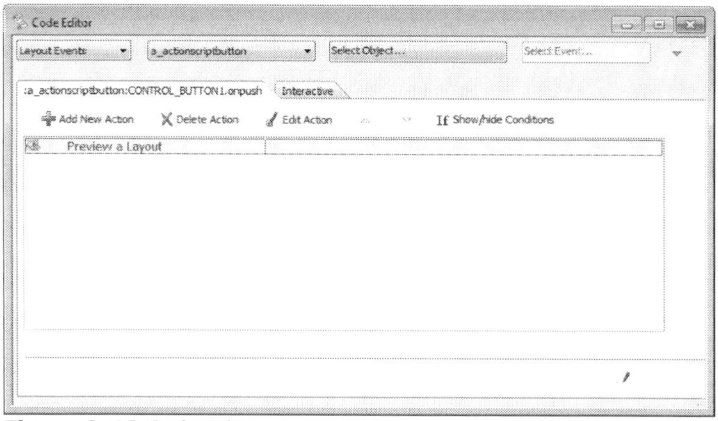

Figure 9-12 Code Editor

Test The Button

1. View the form. You should see the button shown in Figure 9-13.

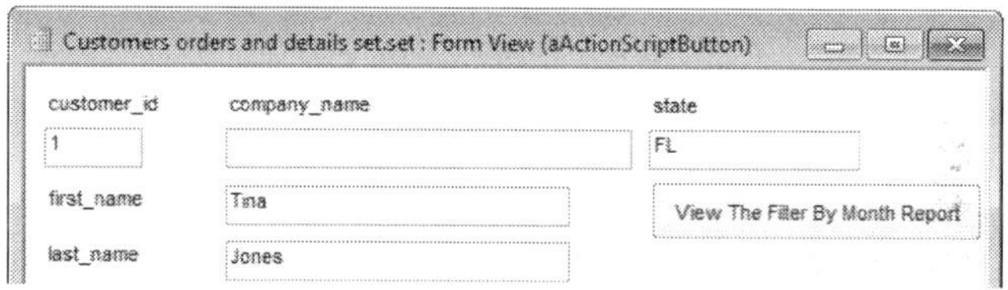

Figure 9-13 Form with a button

2. Click the button. The dialog box shown in Figure 9-14 appears because the Display Print/Preview prompt at run time option was selected when the script was created.

   Accept the Preview option, then click OK. You should see the Filter by month report.

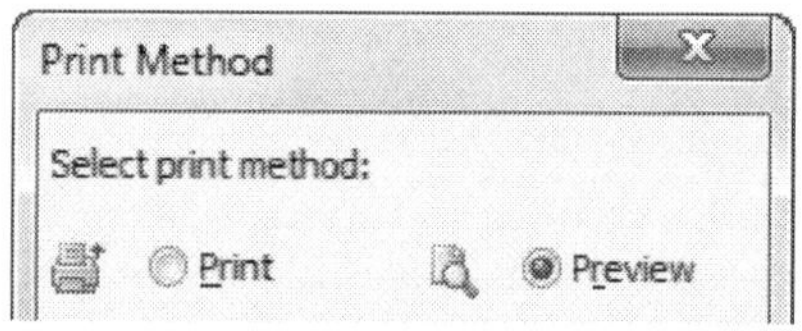

Figure 9-14 Print Method dialog box

View The Xbasic Code

In case you are curious and want to see the code that was generated from the Action Script that you created, follow the steps below.

1. In Design mode click on the button on the form, then press the **F11 KEY**.

2. On the dialog box shown in Figure 9-15, right-click on the action, then select **VIEW XBASIC**.

   The shortcut menu shown in the figure is also available on the Define Button dialog box.

   The dialog box shown in Figure 9-16 displays the code created by the options that you selected using the Action Script Genie.

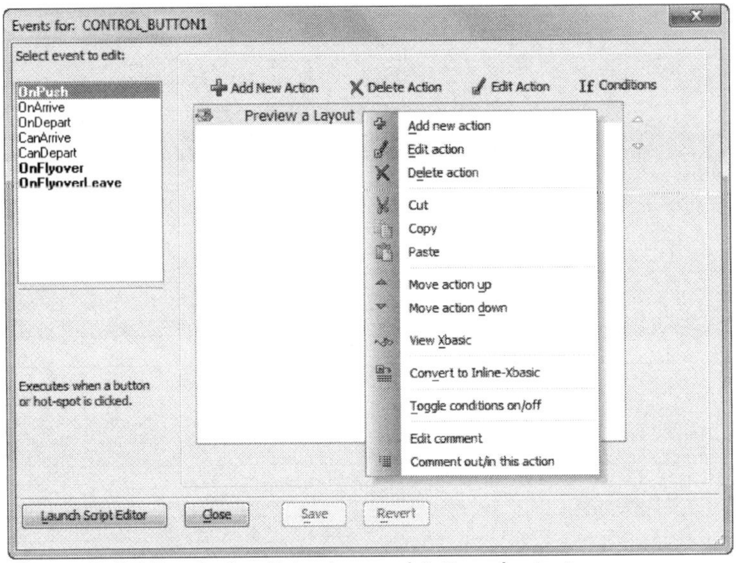

Figure 9-15 Events for dialog box and Action shortcut menu

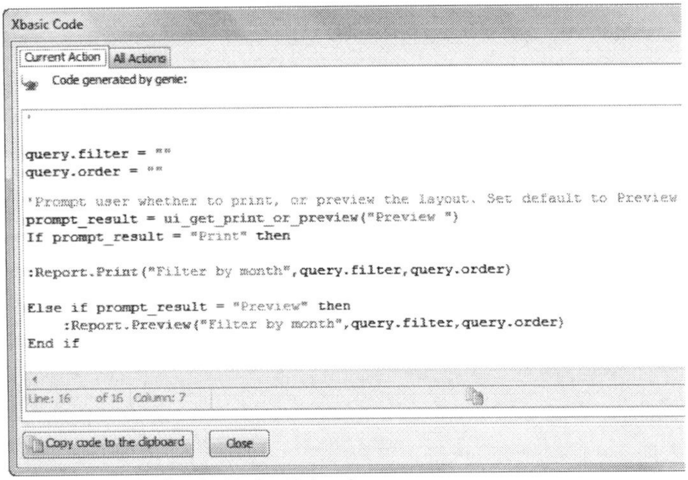

Figure 9-16 Xbasic Code dialog box

Adding A Comment To An Action

It is a good idea to add a comment to actions that you create because when you need to edit it, you will have something to read that reminds you why the action script was created the way that it was. To add a comment, follow the steps below.

1. On the shortcut menu shown earlier in Figure 9-15, select **EDIT COMMENT**.
2. On the dialog box shown in Figure 9-17, type in a comment for the action. The comment will be displayed to the right of the action on the Events for dialog box. It will also be displayed on the Define Button dialog box and the Code Editor.
3. Click the Save button, then click Close.

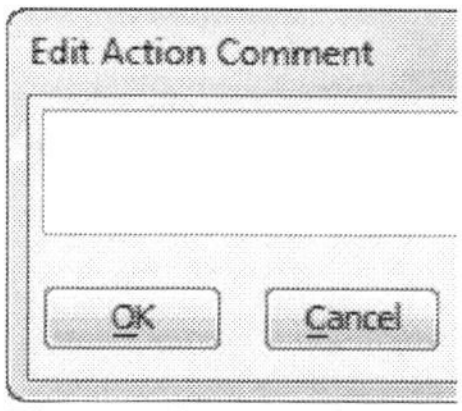

Figure 9-17 Edit Action Comment dialog box

Exercise 9.4: Use The Rich Text Control To Display Data

In this exercise you will learn how to display data for the selected product on an embedded browse.

1. Save the Display customer name form as `aRichTextControl`, then make the light yellow portion of the form a little longer.

2. On the Orders tab, add the Rich Text control to the bottom of the form. Make it long enough to display two lines of text.

3. Type `Quantity in stock:`, then press the space bar. Drag the Qty_in_stock field in the Products table and place it next to the text. Accept the Value option, then click OK.

4. On the next line in the Rich Text control, type `Quantity on order:`, then press the space bar. Drag the Qty_on_order field in the Products table and place it next to the text. Accept the Value option, then click OK.

5. Select all of the Text and change the color to red, then make the font bold.

6. Click on the border of the control. On the properties dialog box change the Border Style to No border. Change the Fill Color to Pale yellow.

7. View the form. Display the customer Stuart Thomas.

   On the Orders tab, click on different products in the second browse.

   You will see the values in red at the bottom of the form change, as shown in Figure 9-18.

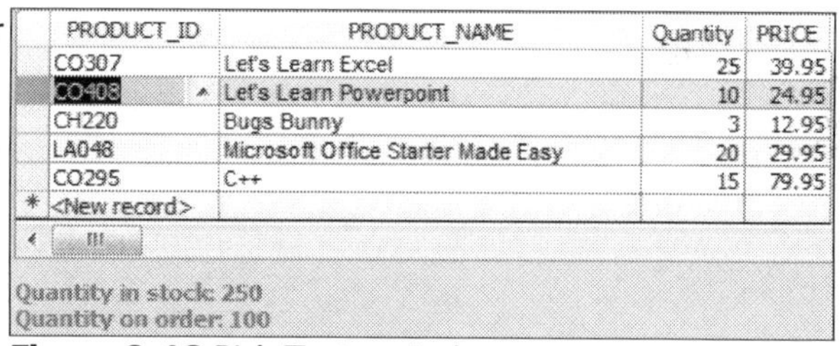

Figure 9-18 Rich Text control

Enhancing The Alphabet Buttons Search Super Control

In Chapter 8, you learned how to set up a basic search using this super control. As you read, there is more than one way to display these buttons. This control is very helpful on forms that will be used to do a lot of searching. One thing to keep in mind when using this control on a form that is created from a set is that the search is only performed on records in the Parent table. Keep in mind that a control can be added to a form more than once.

Exercise 9.5: Enhance The Alphabet Button Search Super Control

In Exercise 8.7 you added this control to a form that is based on a table. In this exercise you will use a form that is based on a set. Most of the time, forms that are primarily used to search or query, display the data in a browse layout format. To go a step further, the browse portion of the form will allow the user to click a button to display detail information. This control will be added to the form a few times to accomplish the following:

- ☑ Change the sort order.
- ☑ Search by company.
- ☑ Search by state by selecting a range.
- ☑ Search by state by selecting the state from a drop-down list.

Add More Data To Tables

To get a better feel for how this control is useful, having more data in the Customers, Orders and Order Detail tables would be helpful. If you want to add more data to these tables, follow the steps below.

1. On the Operations tab, you will see append record operations for the three tables discussed above.

2. Select an append operation, then click the **DESIGN** button.

3. Change the **TRANSACTION TABLE** file to the corresponding table in the more data folder.

4. Append all fields in the Transaction table file, as shown in Figures 9-19 to 9-21.

   There are 180 customer records, 326 order records and 752 order detail records to append.

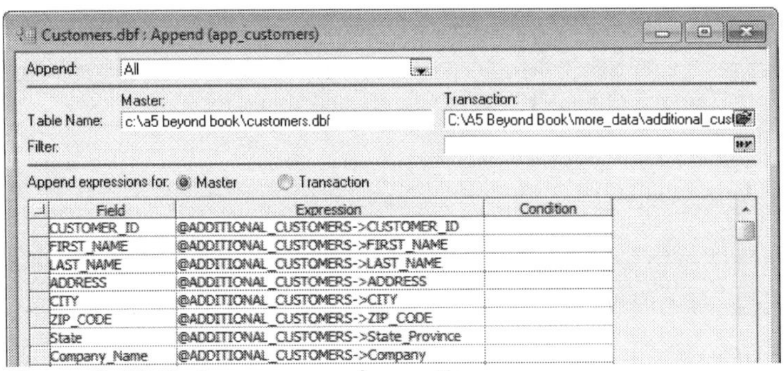

Figure 9-19 Customers append operation

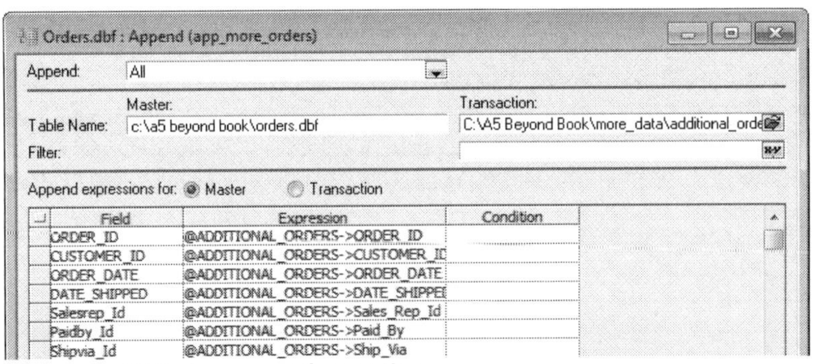

Figure 9-20 Orders append operation

Figure 9-21 Order detail append operation

Create The Form

In this part of the exercise you will create a form that has an embedded browse. The browse will be used to view all of the records, as well as the records retrieved from the search. To create this form, you will add a **BROWSE CONTROL** to the form.

1. Create a blank form based on the Customers orders and details set.

2. Add the Browse control to the form. Start it 2 inches down on the form.

3. Add the following fields from the Customers table: Company name, First name, Last name, City and State.

4. On the Browse tab of the properties dialog box for the browse, clear the check mark for all of the options in the **RESTRICTIONS** list.

5. Open the **COLUMN TITLE CLICK BEHAVIOR** drop-down list and select Click sorts by column.

6. Resize the columns in the browse, then resize the browse so that it looks like the one shown in Figure 9-22.

   Save the form as `aAlphabetBtnsEnhanced`.

Figure 9-22 Embedded browse resized

Active Button Options

For each Alphabet Button control added to the form, select the options shown in Figure 9-23 on the Alphabet Buttons Search dialog box. Selecting these options will let you know which button on the control is currently selected.

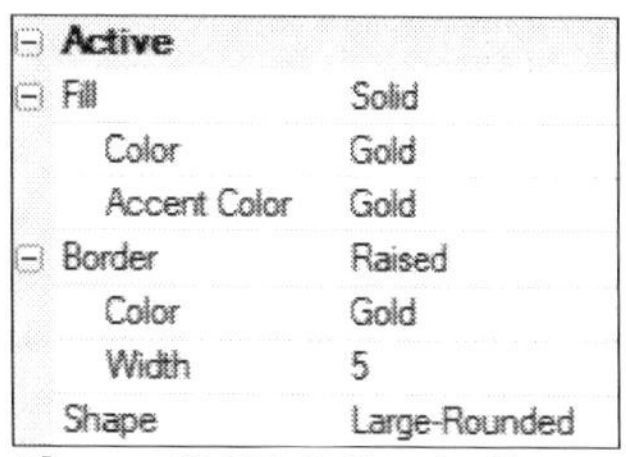

Figure 9-23 Active button options

Display Records Based On The Column Being Sorted On

In this part of the exercise you will configure the alphabet buttons to display customer records based on the column in the browse that is currently used to sort the records. When an alphabet button is clicked on, only records that start with that letter will be displayed. For example, if the records are being sorted by company name and the B button is clicked, only records with a company name that starts with a B will be displayed.

1. Add the Alphabet Buttons Search super control to the top of the form. Start it as the one inch mark and about ¼ inch down. Make the box at least five inches wide.

2. On the Alphabet Buttons Search dialog box, check the **SPARSE** option.

3. Add a text object above the control with the text, `Search on selected column in the browse.`

4. View the form. Click on the State column, then click the M button. If you scroll down the list of records displayed in the browse, you will see that all of the records are in a state the starts with the letter M.

5. Click on the Company name column, then click the E button. You should see the three records whose company name starts with the letter E.

If you view the form without a column being selected on the browse, you will see the message, shown at the bottom of Figure 9-24, instead of the alphabet buttons.

Figure 9-24 Message when no column is selected

Display Records By Company

In this part of the exercise, you will configure the alphabet buttons to display records in the browse by company name.

1. Add a text object with the text `Find By Company`, below the Alphabet Button control.

2. Add the Alphabet Buttons super control below the text field.

3. Open the Key drop-down list and select the Company Name field, then check the Sparse option.

   Select the Alpha-Numeric Button bar type, as shown in Figure 9-25.

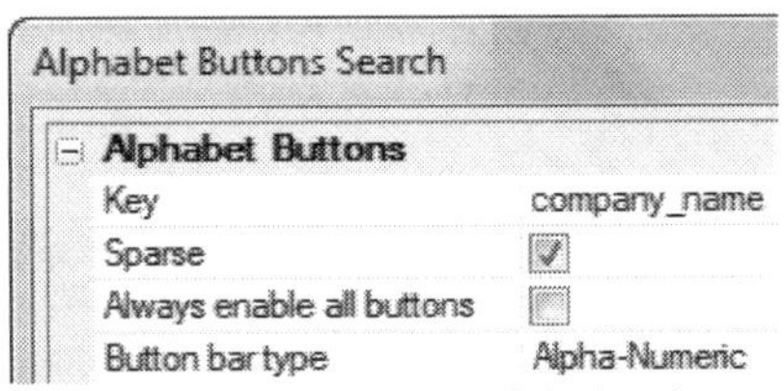

Figure 9-25 Company alphabet button options

4. View the form. Notice that a company name starts with a number. The reason that you see the number with the alphabet buttons, as shown in Figure 9-26 is because the alpha-numeric button bar type option was selected.

When you use the first set of alphabet buttons, no records with a company name that started with a number could be displayed by selecting a button. When you click on a button in the second set of buttons, companies that start with a number or letter are displayed on the embedded browse.

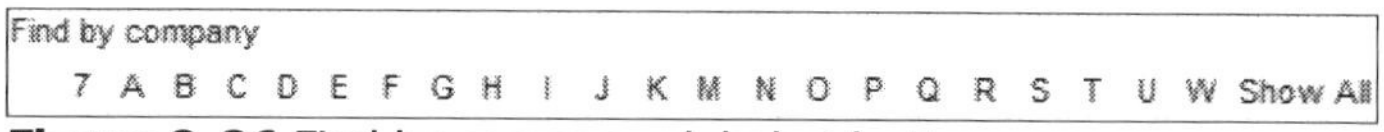

Figure 9-26 Find by company alphabet buttons

Create Buttons That Use A Range

In this part of the exercise you will learn how to use the Ranged Buttons bar type option to search by state. This button bar type would look better if it was displayed vertically.

1. Add a Text object to the left of the button bars and type `Find by state`.
2. Add the Alphabet Buttons Search super control below the text object.
3. Open the Key drop-down list and select the State field.
4. Select the Ranged Buttons Button bar type. Click the Ranged Buttons option button. On the **EDIT RANGE BUTTONS** dialog box, click the Predefined Ranges link.
5. Select the A...D... option, then click OK.

   You should see the ranges shown in Figure 9-27.

   Click OK.

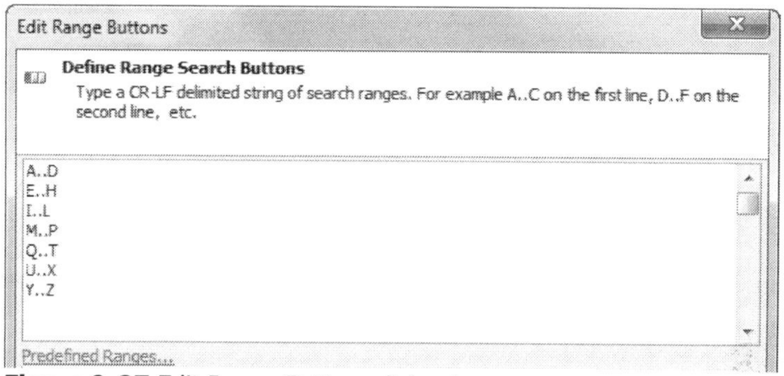

Figure 9-27 Edit Range Buttons dialog box

6. Open the Arrangement option drop-down list and select Vertical.
7. The control should look like the one shown in the upper left corner of Figure 9-28.

   The button at the bottom of the list is the Show All option.

   When you select an option, all records that have a state that starts with one of the letters in the range will be displayed in the browse.

Figure 9-28 Range buttons

Exercise 9.6: View Detail Information

In the previous exercise you learned how to search for records by using the Alphabet Button Search super control. The embedded browse displayed customer information. Once the customer is found, it would be helpful to the user if they could view the customers orders. An easy way to provide this functionality is to add a button to the form that opens another form that displays the detail data for the customer selected in the browse. In order to do this, both forms need a common field to link on.

1. Save the aAlphabetBtnsEnhanced form as `aLinkFormsButton`.

2. Add the Customer ID field in the Customer tables to the end of the embedded browse. Make the field as small as you can, then resize the browse so that the column is not visible.

3. Add the Button control to the form above the browse. On the Define Button dialog box, type `View Customers Orders` in the Label field, then click Next.

4. Click the Add New Action button. Select the Form/Browse category, then select the **OPEN FORM OR BROWSE LAYOUT** action.

5. On the Script Genie: Open Form or Browse Layout dialog box, select the aReportPreviewControl form, then click Next.

6. Select the **RECORDS THAT MATCH THE VALUE IN A CONTROL ON THE CURRENT FORM OR REPORT** option. At the bottom of the screen, open the first drop-down list and select the Customer ID field at the top of the list. Open the next drop-down list and select the Customer ID field shown in Figure 9-29. This is the link between the forms. Click OK. You should have the options shown in Figure 9-30.

7. On the Order tab, click the **A..Z BUTTON**. Open the Sort by drop-down list and select the Orders -> Order ID field. You should have the options shown in Figure 9-31.

8. Click Finish. Click Finish again to close the Define Button dialog box. Save the changes. The form should look like the one shown in Figure 9-32.

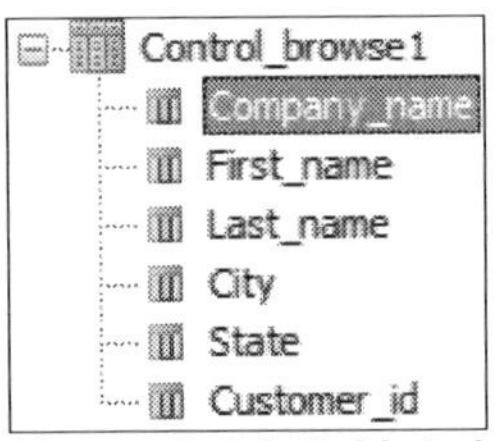

Figure 9-29 Fields in browse to select from

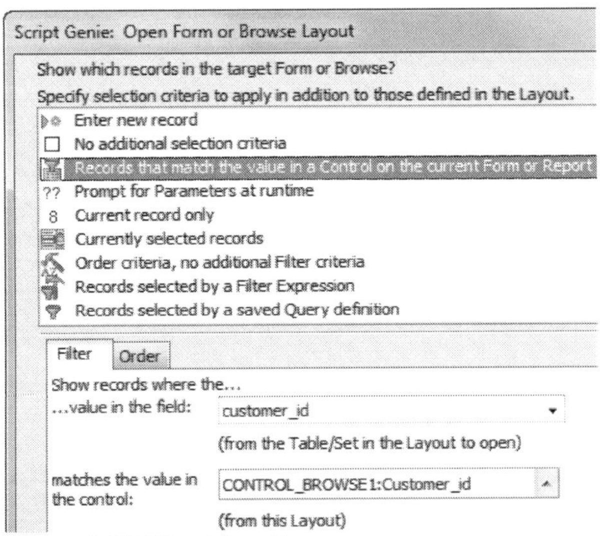

Figure 9-30 Filter tab options

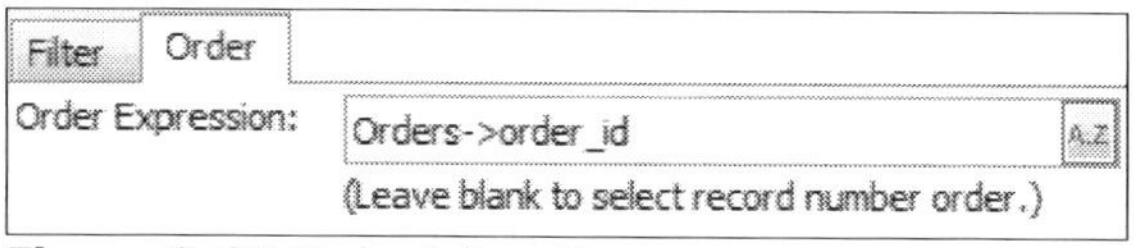

Figure 9-31 Order tab options

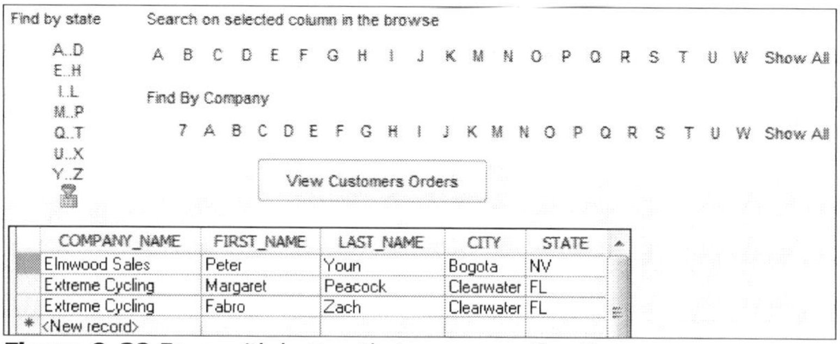

Figure 9-32 Form with button that opens another form

9. Click on any record in the browse, then click the View Customers Orders button. You should see the form with an embedded report that you created in Exercise 8.6. [See Chapter 8, Figure 8-46]

Exercise 9.7: Use The Drop Down Browse Super Control To Filter Records

In Chapter 8 you learned how to use this control to select which records were displayed on a form. This super control can also be used to select which records are displayed in a browse. In this exercise you will use this control to select the customers by state.

1. Save the aAlphabetBtnsEnhanced form as `aSelectByDropDown`.

2. Delete the <current> and company name alphabet button controls and their titles.

3. Add the Drop Down Browse super control to the form to the right of the Find by state controls.

4. Select the State field as the field to search on.

5. Change the text "Find by State" to `Use either option to find records by state`. Center the text over both controls.

6. The drop-down list should look like the one shown in Figure 9-33.

   It would be nice if there was an option to select how many items appear in the drop-down list.

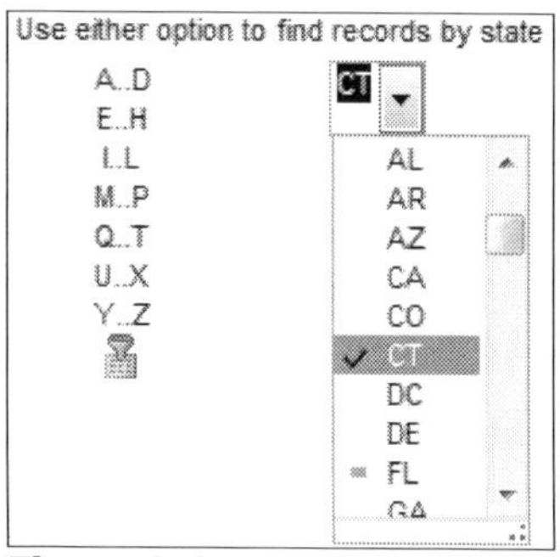

Figure 9-33 State Drop Down Browse super control

Exercise 9.8: Display A Report On A Form

In Chapter 8 Exercise 8.6, you learned how to display a report on a form. The report in that exercise displayed data based on the customer information. The aReportPreviewControl form also displays all of the orders for each customer. In this exercise you will create a form that displays customers and their order header information. The report will display order information based on the order that is selected on the embedded browse on the form.

Create The Form

1. Create a blank form based on the Customers-orders set.

2. Open the aReportPreviewControl form. Copy the customer fields and the first browse to the new form.

3. Save the form as `aReportPreview2`.

Add A Report To The Form

1. Add the Report Preview super control to the right side of the form.

2. Select the following options.
   Select the aFunctionDBAVG report.
   Click the Define Link(s) button, then select the Order ID field in the Report Field and Form Field columns.

3. On the Toolbar tab, add the following options: First, Previous, Page Number, Next and Last, as shown in Figure 9-34.

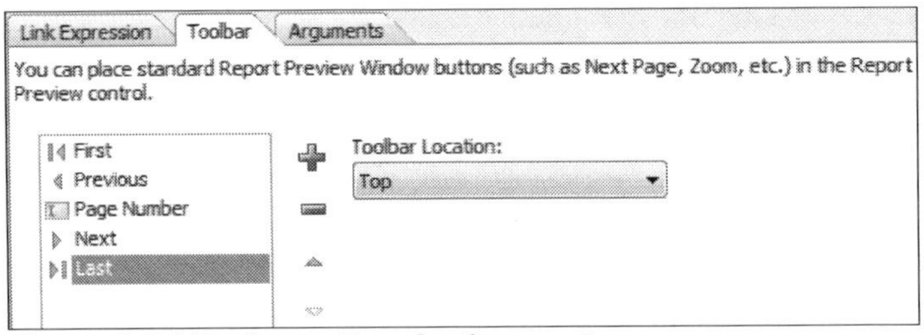

Figure 9-34 Toolbar options for the report

4. Click OK to close the Report Preview dialog box, then save the form.

5. View the form and display the record for Stuart Thomas. In the browse, click on the row for Order ID 10. You should see the report shown in Figure 9-35. If you click on Order ID 12, you will see the part of the report shown in Figure 9-36. If you view the aFunctionDBAVG report, you will see that it displays all orders.

Avg quantity ordered for product LA048 9

Order id	Product id	Quantity	Price	line total
10	CO307	25	39.95	998.75
10	CO408	10	24.95	249.50
10	CH220	3	12.95	38.85
10	LA048	20	29.95	599.00
10	CO295	15	79.95	1199.25

Figure 9-35 Report filtered for Order ID 10

Avg quantity ordered for product LA048 9

Order id	Product id	Quantity	Price	line total
12	LA044	10	29.95	299.50

Figure 9-36 Report filtered for Order ID 12

The Control Library

This tool is used to save objects and controls (usually ones that you have customized) created in one form or report that you want to be able to use on another form or report. Using this feature will remind you of copying and pasting objects from one form or report to another, like you did in Exercise 9.8. A group of objects can also be saved to the Control Library. The Control Library option is on the Object shortcut menu. Once created, the Control Library is added to the Toolbox.

Exercise 9.9: Add Objects To The Control Library

In this exercise you will learn how to use the Control Library.

1. Open the aAlphabetBtnsEnhanced form.

2. Select the three alphabet controls and their titles. Right-click on one of the selected objects and select **ADD SELECTED CONTROLS TO CONTROL LIBRARY**.

Add To Layout Control Library Dialog Box

The options shown in Figure 9-37 are used to configure the objects that are added to the Control Library.

Depending on the object(s) selected to be added, all of the options shown in the figure may not be available.

The options are explained in Table 9-2.

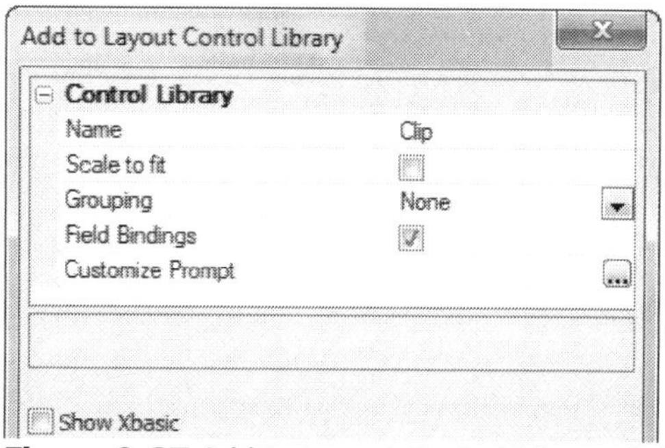

Figure 9-37 Add to Layout Control Library dialog box

Option	Description
Name	Clip is the default name for the object(s) being added to the library. You should change the name to better reflect the object(s) being added.
Scale to fit	If checked, the control(s) selected to be added to the library will automatically be resized to fit the size of the square that is drawn on the form or report. If not checked, the control(s) will stay the size that they are.
Grouping	Is used to select whether the selected objects will be saved in the library as a group. Select **NONE** if you do not want to save the objects as a group. **PRESERVE EXISTING** saves the objects as they are now. **GROUP ALL** forces the objects to be grouped when saved in the library.
Field Bindings	This option is only available if the object selected to be added to the library is a field. This option is used to automate mapping fields when added to a different form.
Customize Prompt	Is only available if the Field Bindings option is checked. It is used to customize the prompts that will be used to map the fields.
Show Xbasic	If checked, the generated code for the objects being added to the library will automatically be displayed when you click OK to close this dialog box, shown later in Figure 9-39.

Table 9-2 Add to Layout Control Library dialog box options explained

Select The Control Library Options

3. In the Name field type `alphabet buttons`, then click OK.

Add More Objects To The Control Library

In this part of the exercise you will add fields from another form to the Control Library.

1. Open the a2StateButtonControl form.

2. Select the three fields and their titles, then open the Add to Layout Control Library dialog box.

3. Select the following options.
   Name field - `Order Header fields`
   Check the Show Xbasic option
   Click the Customize Prompt field button

Customize The Control Library Prompts

The dialog box shown in Figure 9-38 is used to modify what is displayed on the dialog box shown later in Figure 9-42. The goal is to make it easier to map fields (or bind controls) on the new form to the fields in the Library Control.

This is helpful if the field names are not the same or if you are going to display the Label field on the report. This is one thing that I like to change because I do not like to see underscores in titles on a form or report.

The first column contains the fields (from the second column) that you have decided since selecting them on the form, that you do not want to add to the library.

The second column contains the field(s) that will be added to the library.

The **CONTROL LIBRARY ENTRY** column displays the name of the field, the label and help message that will be displayed during the mapping process.

The **PREVIEW** link displays the Select Fields dialog box, shown later in Figure 9-42.

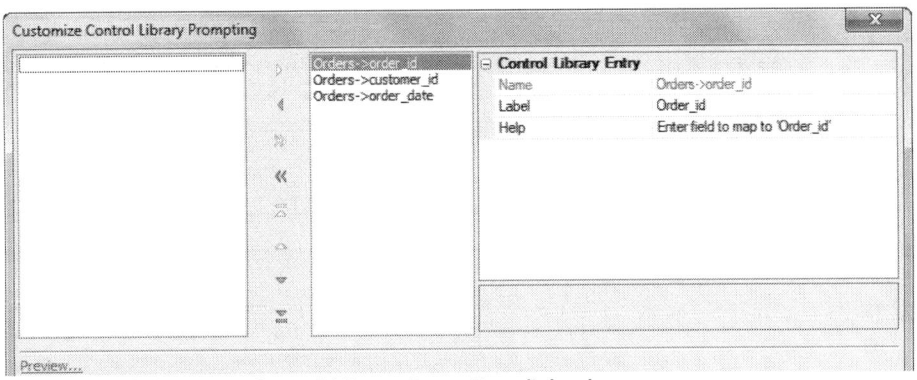

Figure 9-38 Customer Control Library Prompting dialog box

1. Change the Order ID Label to `Order ID`.

2. Change the Help message to `Select the field to map the Order ID field to`, then click OK.

3. Click OK to close the Add to Layout Control Library dialog box.

   You should see the dialog box shown in Figure 9-39.

   This is code that was automatically generated for the objects that will be added to the Control Library.

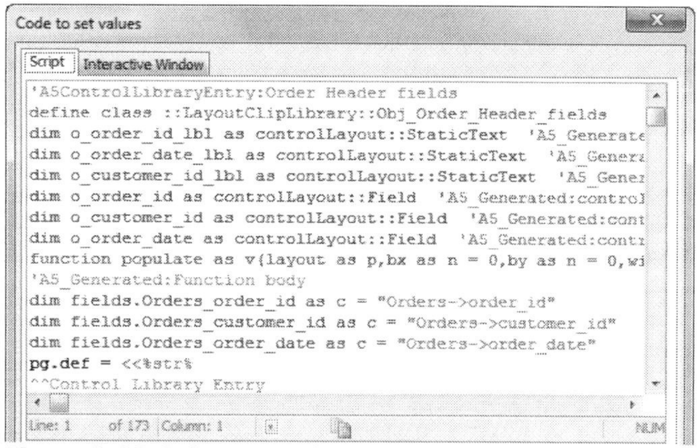

Figure 9-39 Code to set values dialog box

4. Add the Paid by check button on the a2StateButtonControl form to the Control Library. Use the following options.
   Name - PaidByCheck button
   Scale to fit - Clear the check mark

5. Add the Export button on the aExcelExportButton form to the Control Library. This button is not linked to a specific table, which means that it can be used on any form. Use the following options.
   Name - `ExportButton`
   Scale to fit - Clear the check mark

6. If you look at the bottom of the Toolbox, you will see the Control Library and the objects that you added, as shown in Figure 9-40.

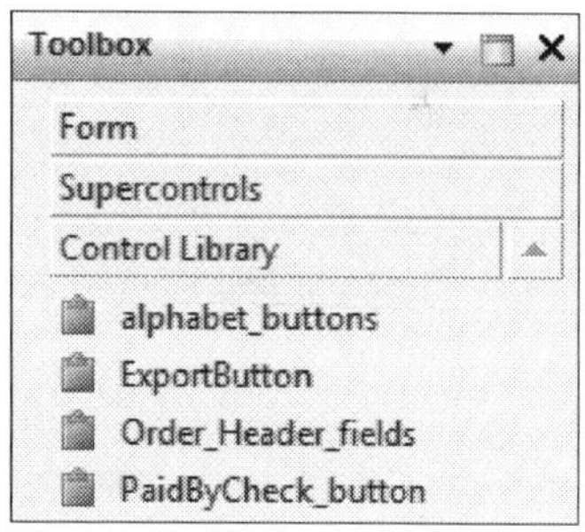

Figure 9-40 Control Library

Control Library Shortcut Menu

The shortcut menu shown in Figure 9-41 is available when you right-click on a control in the library on the Toolbox. The options are explained below.

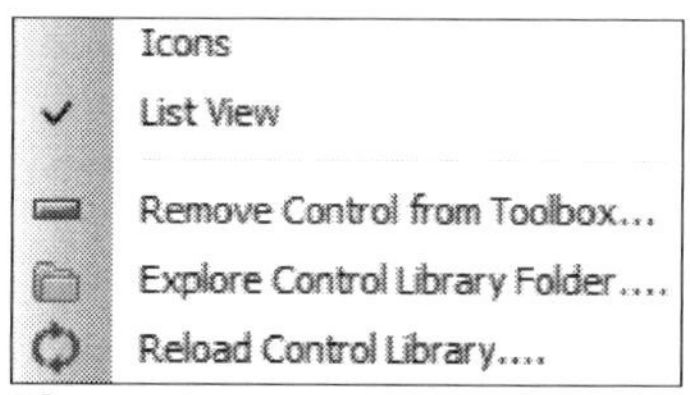

Figure 9-41 Control Library shortcut menu

① **ICONS** Displays the items in the library with icons and no text.

② **LIST VIEW** Displays the items in the library with icons and text. This is the default.

③ **REMOVE CONTROL FROM TOOLBOX** Deletes the control from the library.

④ **EXPLORE CONTROL LIBRARY FOLDER** Opens the Toolbox folder (in Windows Explorer), which displays a class file for each item in the library.

⑤ **RELOAD CONTROL LIBRARY** Refreshes the entries in the Control Library.

Add Controls From The Library To A Form

In this part of the exercise you will add controls from the library to a new form that will be based on a different table then the table that the controls are based on.

1. Create a new blank form based on the Order lookup table. Save the form as `aControlLibrary`.

2. Display the Control Library in the Toolbox.

3. Add the Order Header fields control to the form. The dialog box shown in Figure 9-42 displays the fields in the control that will be added to the form.

   Earlier in this exercise you modified the help message for a field that would be used when a control is added to a form. The bottom of the figure shows the help message that you customized.

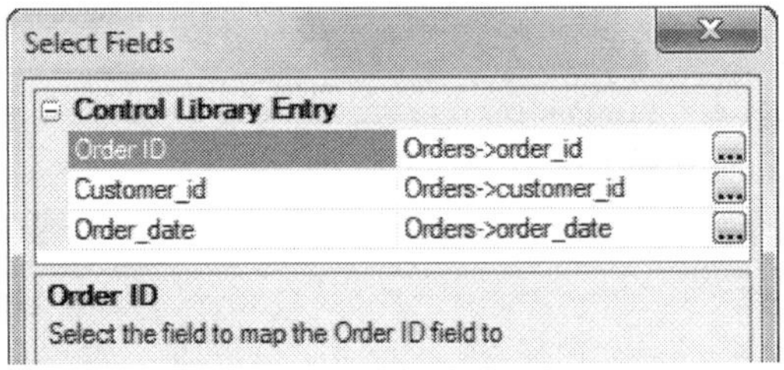

Figure 9-42 Select Fields dialog box

> **Select Fields Dialog Box**
> If you add a control that has fields from the library that does not automatically open the Select Fields dialog box, it means that the forms data source does not have the fields that the control needs to run.

Clicking the button at the end of the field (on the Select Fields dialog box) displays the table or set and fields that the form is based on, as shown in Figure 9-43.

The Orders table shown in the second column (on the Select Fields dialog box, shown above in Figure 9-42) is not the table that the form is based on, so you need to select the field from the list of fields shown in Figure 9-43.

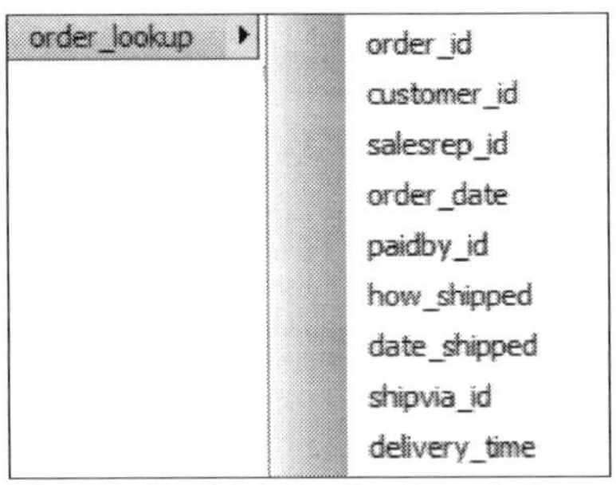

Figure 9-43 Table the form is based on

4. Select the three fields from the current table (Order Lookup) to map the fields in the control to fields in the table that the form is based on. You should have the options shown in Figure 9-44. Click OK. You should see the fields on the form.

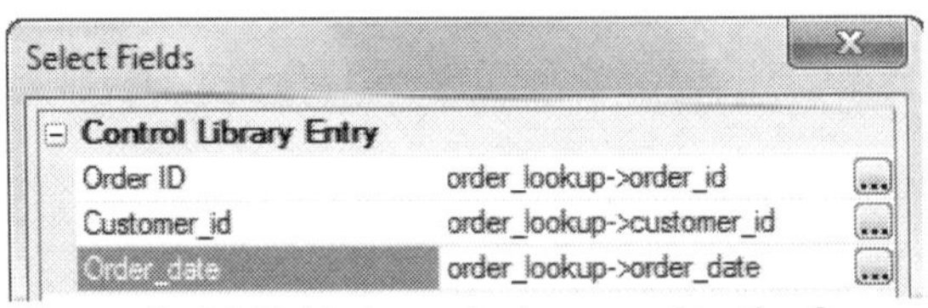

Figure 9-44 Fields in control mapped to the form

5. Add the Export button control in the library to the form, to the right of the fields, then save the changes.

   The form should look like the one shown in Figure 9-45.

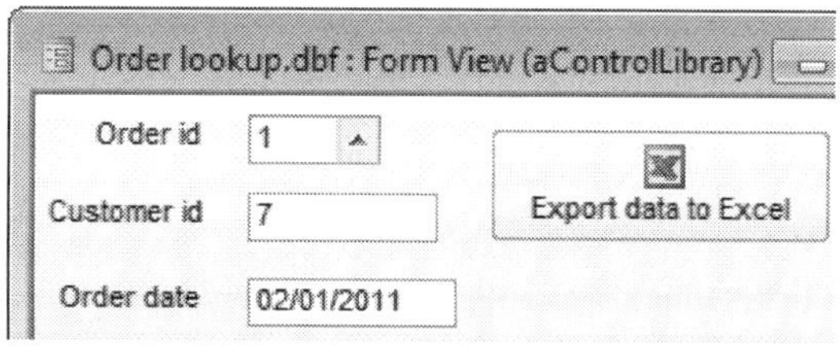

Figure 9-45 New form with Control Library objects

Adding Images To Layouts And Buttons

Images, like photos and logos can be added to a form, report, letter or label. Images can be used to enhance forms and provide a visual cue on buttons. Adding a company logo to a form or report is a common task. Adding an image to a button may help the user know what task the button will perform.

Reference vs Embedded Images

There are two ways to add a custom image, as explained below.

① **REFERENCE** This option links to the image file. Select this option when the image needs to be changed from time to time. For example, the current logo image file has a blue background. For a promotion next month, you want the logo to have a different color background. You will create the new image and save it with the same file name as the current logo. (Rename the current logo file first <smile>.) That would update the image every place in the application that it is used.

② **EMBEDDED** This option adds the image file to the application. If changes are made to the image file outside of the Alpha Five application, the changes will not be reflected in the application. Select this option when you do not need to change the image file.

Options For Adding Images

There are several ways to add images to a layout or button, as explained below.

① **BITMAP CONTROL** This option only allows the image file to be used on the selected layout or button.

② **GLOBAL BITMAP** This option stores the bitmap file in the databases library file, which means that the image file is available wherever you need it in the application. Once the global bitmap has been set up, you can access it from the **BITMAP PROPERTIES DIALOG BOX**, library option.

Exercise 9.10: Set Up A Global Bitmap

In this exercise you will learn how to set up a global bitmap. If the image will be used on a button, it may need to be resized before it is set up as a global bitmap.

1. Control Panel ⇒ Code tab ⇒ New button ⇒ Bitmap.

Create Global Bitmap Dialog Box

The dialog box shown in Figure 9-46 is used to set up a global bitmap. The options are explained below.

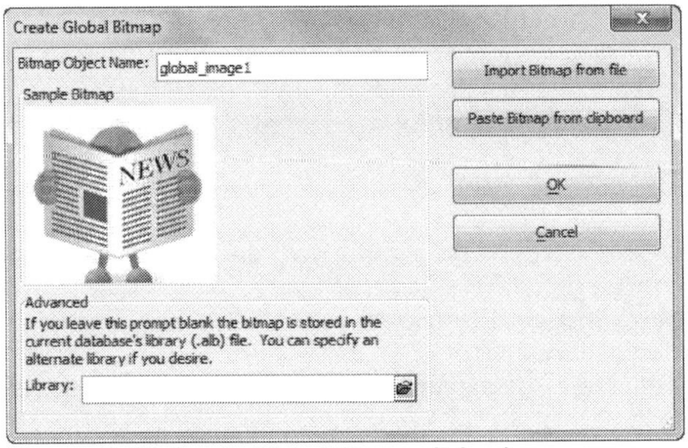

Figure 9-46 Create Global Bitmap dialog box

① **BITMAP OBJECT NAME** Type in a name for the image.

② **IMPORT BITMAP FROM FILE BUTTON** Is used to select an existing image file, that is in **JPEG**, **JPG**, **BMP** or **PNG** format.

③ **PASTE BITMAP FROM CLIPBOARD BUTTON** Is most often used for images that you have copied from another file or web page.

④ **LIBRARY** Is used to select a database other then the one that you have open now, as the location to save the global bitmap file.

2. In the Bitmap Object Name field type `global_image1`.

3. Click the Import Bitmap from file button, then select the image7.jpg file in your folder.

4. You should see the image shown earlier in Figure 9-46.

   Click OK. You should see the file shown in Figure 9-47 on the Code tab. Now the image file can be used any place in the application.

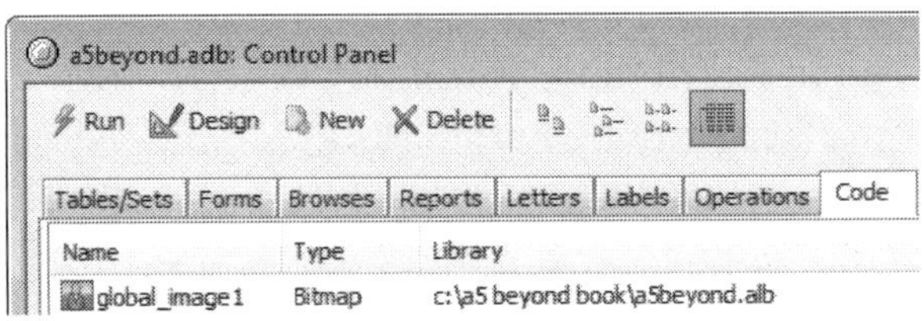

Figure 9-47 Global bitmap image

Exercise 9.11: Add A Global Bitmap File To A Form And Button

In the previous exercise you learned how to set up a global image file. In this exercise you will learn how to add the image file to a form and a button.

Add The Image To A Form

1. Save the a2StateButtonControl form as `aGlobalImage`.

2. Move all of the objects on the form over to the right so that they start at the 1.5 inch mark on the ruler.

3. Add the Bitmap control to the form to the left of the field titles, then select the following options. On the properties dialog box Setup tab, change the Display mode to Best Fit. Select the **LIBRARY** option in the Load Bitmap From section, then click the button at the end of the field.

4. On the Insert Image dialog box, select the **CURRENT DATABASE IMAGES** option.

   You should see the global image file that you set up in the previous exercise, as shown in Figure 9-48.

   Click on the file, then click the Insert button. You should see the image at the bottom of the Setup tab on the properties dialog box.

   Click OK.

   When you view the form, you should see the image to the left of the fields.

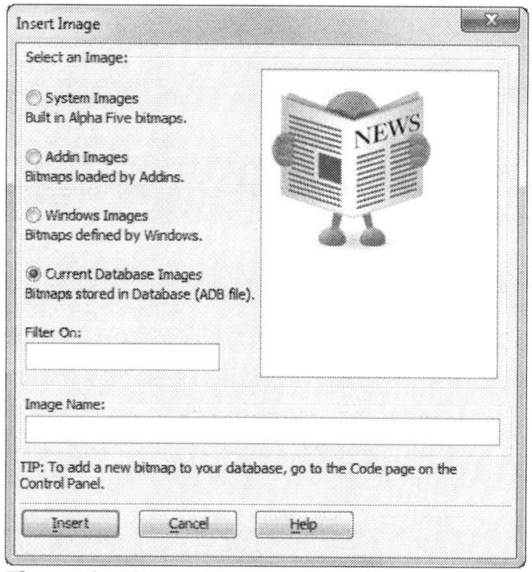

Figure 9-48 Insert Image dialog box

Add The Image To A Button

1. On the Choices tab of the properties dialog box for the button (on the aGlobalImage form), change the **DISPLAY OPTION** to Text followed by bitmap.

2. Click the **DEFINE BITMAPS BUTTON**. On the Define Picture dialog box, select the Internal option, then click the button at the end of the field.

3. On the Insert Image dialog box, select the Current Database Images option, then select the image.

   You should have the options shown in Figure 9-49.

   Click OK.

   If checked, the **BUTTON DISPLAYS A DIFFERENT PICTURE WHEN BUTTON IS PRESSED** option displays the **PRESSED TAB**, which has the same options as the Default tab. You should select the image that you want displayed when the button is clicked.

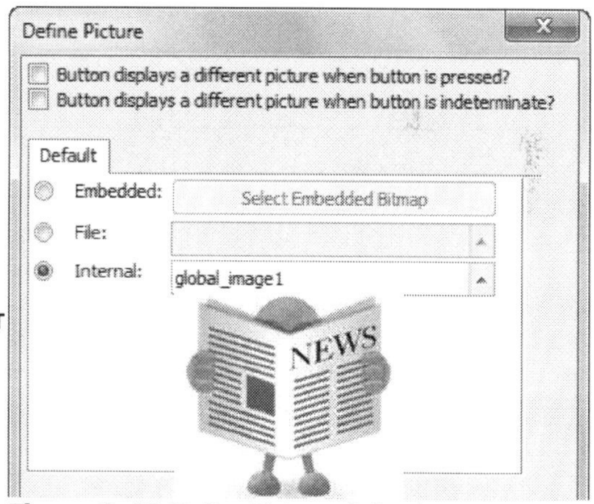

Figure 9-49 Define Picture dialog box

   If checked, the **BUTTON DISPLAYS A DIFFERENT PICTURE WHEN BUTTON IS INDETERMINATE** option (not known, meaning when the button is not being clicked and is not in its default state) displays the **INDETERMINATE TAB**. Use the options on this tab to select the image that you want displayed when the state of the button is unknown.

4. On the Format tab, change the horizontal alignment to left.

5. Resize the button as needed, so that the text and image are visible.

   When you view the form, it should look like the one shown in Figure 9-50.

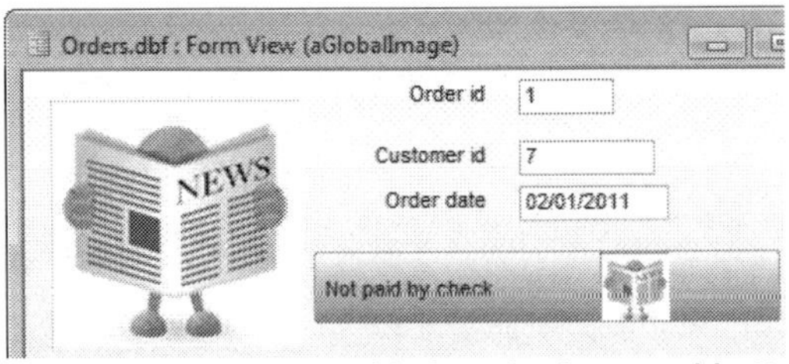

Figure 9-50 Image added to the form and button

ENHANCING A BROWSE

In this chapter you will learn about the following features that can be used to enhance a browse.

- ☑ Zoom to Record
- ☑ Browse Controls

CHAPTER 10

Overview

The topics covered in this chapter are used to give a browse more functionality.

Viewing A Browse Based On A Set

When you view a browse that is based on a set, the Browse menu has two additional options, as shown in Figure 10-1, that a browse based on a table does not have. The options are explained below.

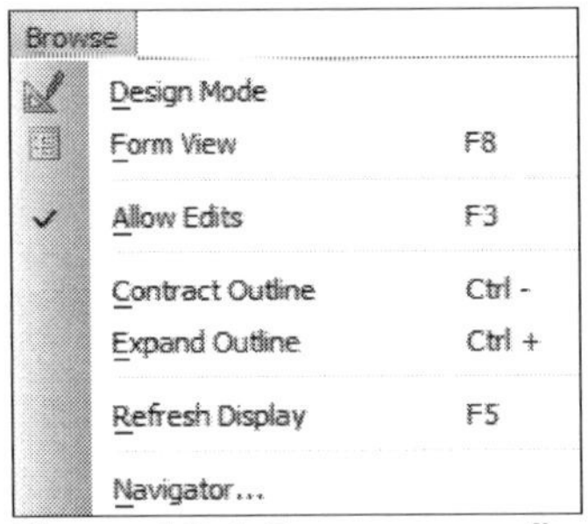

Figure 10-1 Browse menu (based on a set)

CONTRACT OUTLINE Hides rows that have a duplicate value in the parent tables primary key field. Most of the time, this will be the first column in the browse, as it is often the primary key field.

EXPAND OUTLINE Displays all the rows that were hidden by the Contract Outline option.

Zoom To Record Action

Often, a browse does not display all of the fields that are needed. The Zoom To Record action script is only available for an embedded browse and is usually added to an event.

The options shown on the menu in Figure 10-2 (except for the last option) are the events that the action script can be added to.

This script allows the user to open a form.
What makes this action script useful is that when run, the form opens and displays the corresponding record. The form can be basic (like the Default Form) or as customized as needed. The form can be based on a table or set.

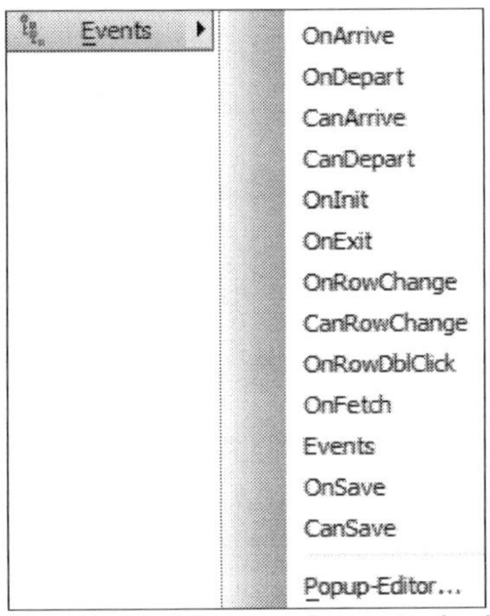

Figure 10-2 Events for an embedded browse

Exercise 10.1: Use The Zoom To Record Action

In Chapter 6, Exercise 6.2 you learned how to add the Zoom To Record Pre-defined action to a button on the form. The difference between the pre-defined action and the script is that the script has a few more features.

In this exercise you will create a form that has an embedded browse that displays some fields in the Customers table. You will also create a form that will display all of the fields in the Customers table.

1. Create a default form based on the Customers table. Save the form as `aZoomForm`.
   This is the form that will open when the script is run.

2. Create a blank form based on the Customers table. Save the form as `aZoomToRecord`.

3. Add the Browse control to the aZoomToRecord form.

   Add the following fields to the browse. Customer ID, Company name, First name and Last name, as shown in Figure 10-3.

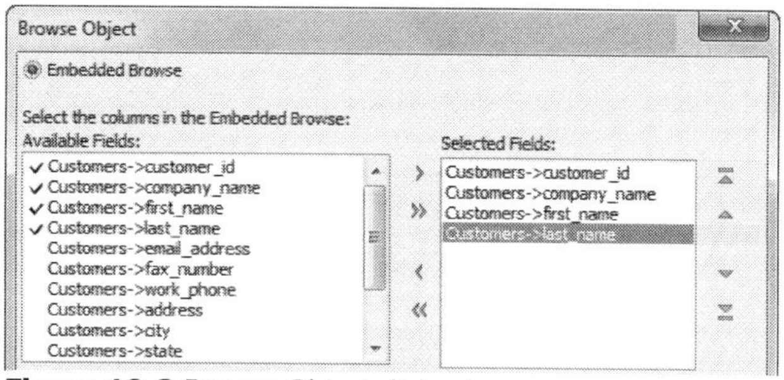

Figure 10-3 Browse Object dialog box

4. Resize the browse so that all of the columns are visible, then save the changes.

Add The Zoom To Record Script To An Event

1. Right-click on the Browse ⇒ Events ⇒ **ONROWDBLCLICK**. This event is activated when a row in the browse is double-clicked on.

   On the dialog box shown in Figure 10-4, accept the default option shown, then click OK.

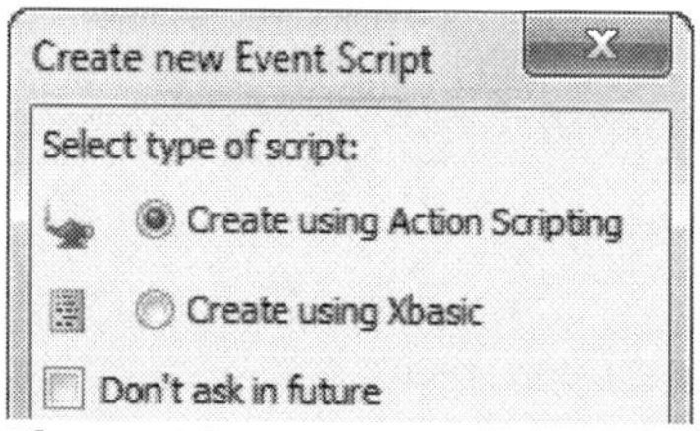

Figure 10-4 Create New Event Script dialog box

2. On the Code Editor, click the Add New Action button. Select the Form/Browse category, then select the **ZOOM TO RECORD** action. Click OK.

3. On the screen shown in Figure 10-5, select the **SPECIFY TARGET FORM NOW** option. Scroll down the **FORM NAME** list at the bottom of the dialog box and select the form aZoomForm. Click Next. The **FILTER FORMS** button opens the dialog box shown in Figure 10-6. This dialog box is used to select the table or set that you want to see the forms for. The available forms will be displayed in the Form Name list.

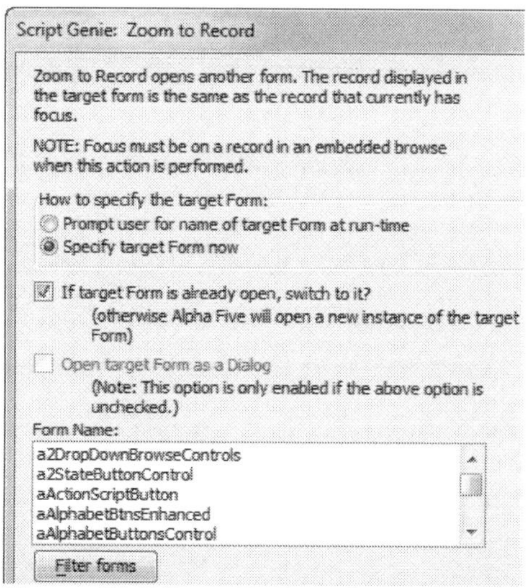

Figure 10-5 Zoom To Record script form options

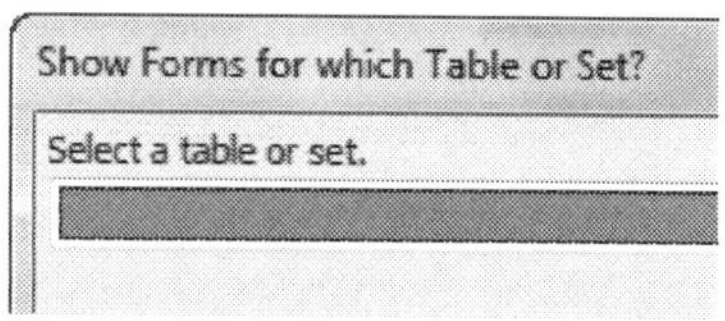

Figure 10-6 Show Forms for which Table or Set? dialog box

4. On the screen shown in Figure 10-7, the options are used to name the pointer variable and select where the variable can be used. The default options shown are appropriate.

   Click Next.

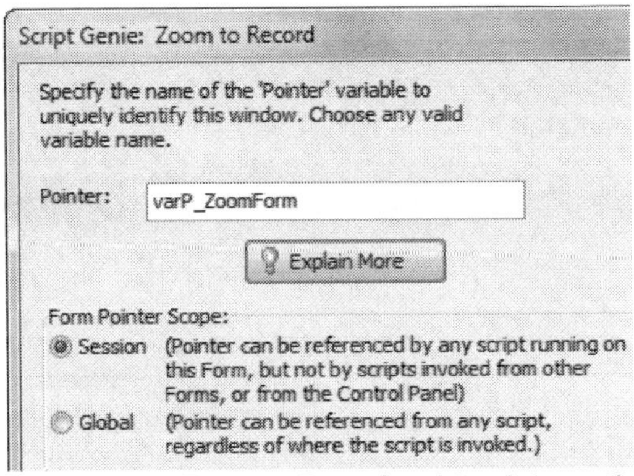

Figure 10-7 Zoom to Record script pointer options

5. Change the comment to `Opens the form aZoomForm`, as shown in Figure 10-8, then click Finish.

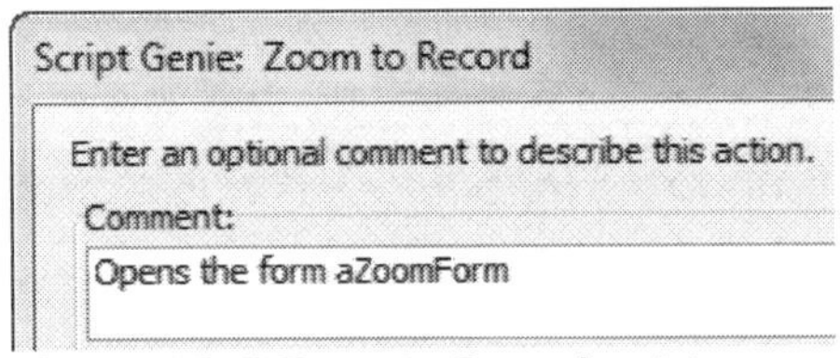

Figure 10-8 Zoom to Record script comments

6. Click the Save button on the toolbar, then close the Code Editor. Save the changes to the form.

7. When you view the form, double-click on a row in the browse. The form aZoomForm will open and display the record for the row that you double-clicked on.

Add A Button That Closes The Form

In this part of the exercise you will add a button to the aZoomForm form that will let the user close the form.

1. Open the aZoomForm form.

2. Add a Button control to the right of the Customer ID field. In the Label field type `Close Form`, then click Next.

3. Click the Add New Action button. In the Action list, select the **CLOSE FORM/BROWSE** action. Click OK.

4. Accept the options shown in Figure 10-9, then click Finish.

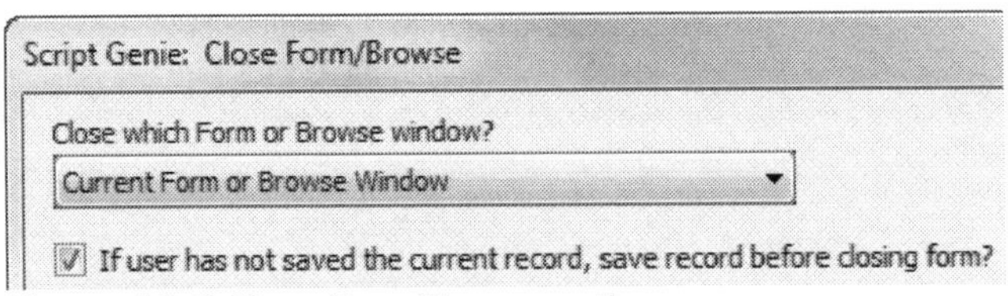

Figure 10-9 Close Form/Browse options

5. On the Define Button dialog box, click Finish, then save the changes to the form. Now when the aZoomForm form is opened, there is an easy way to close it. If you leave this form open and double-click on another record in the browse on the aZoomToRecord form, the corresponding record will be displayed on the aZoomForm form.

Browse Column Options

The columns in a browse can be customized individually.

Browse Column Shortcut Menu

Right-clicking on a column in a browse displays the shortcut menu shown in Figure 10-10.

The **EDIT DISPLAY FORMAT** option opens the Browse Cell Display Format Builder covered later in this chapter.

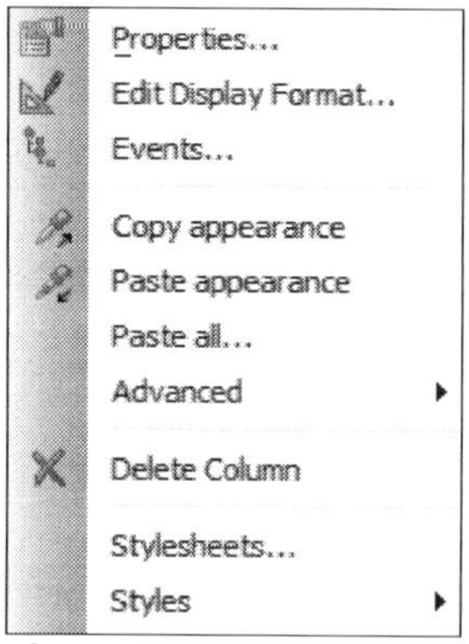

Figure 10-10 Browse column shortcut menu

Column Properties

The dialog box shown in Figure 10-11 is used to customize the column.

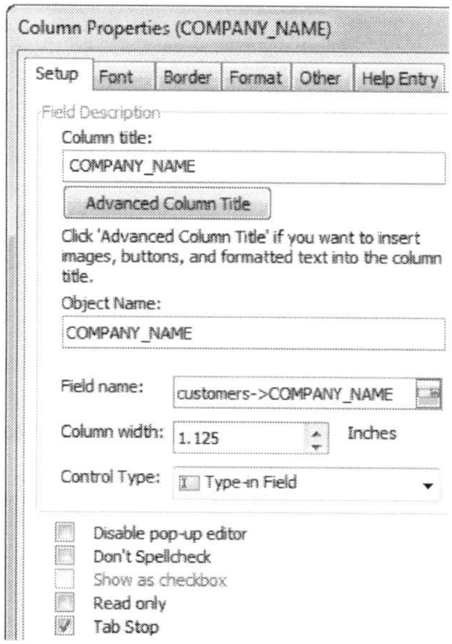

Figure 10-11 Column Properties dialog box

Browse Controls Panel

The panel shown in Figure 10-12 are the controls that can be placed in **STAND ALONE** and **EMBEDDED BROWSES**.

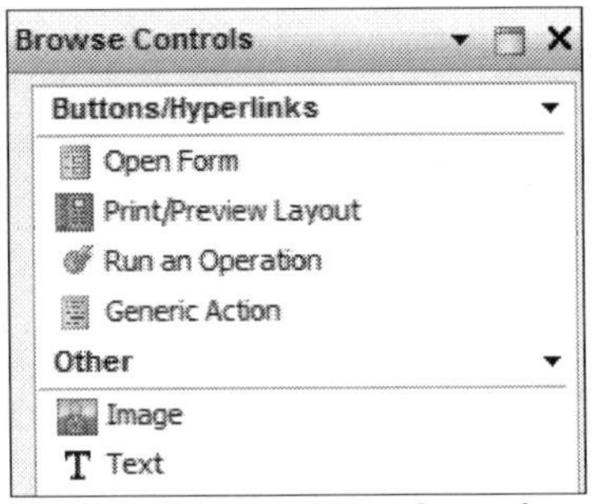

Figure 10-12 Browse Controls panel

This panel is the equivalent of the Toolbox panel that forms and reports have.

If you have a browse file open in Design mode, you should see the Browse Controls panel in the lower right corner of the workspace. This panel does not have a button on the toolbar. If you do not see the panel, select one of the following options:

① Task List ⇒ Browse Controls.
② Click on the down arrow button on the Toolbox and select Browse Controls, as shown in Figure 10-13.

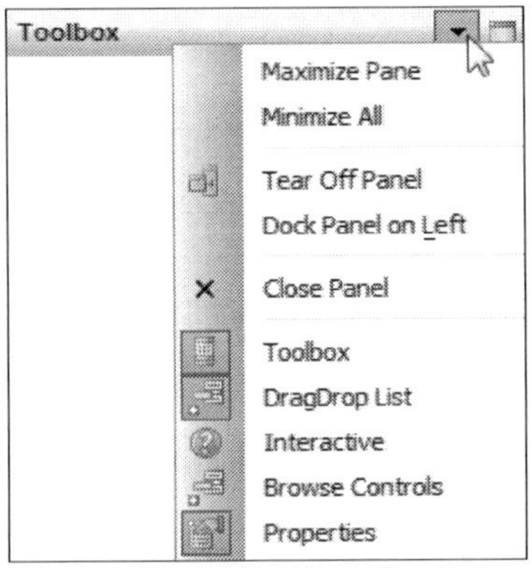

Figure 10-13 Toolbox shortcut menu

Browse Controls

Browse controls are buttons, hyperlinks and images that can be added to a cell in the browse. Like controls in the Toolbox, Browse controls also have a genie that is used to configure the control. Once the options for the control are selected, a new column is added to the browse. When a Browse control is clicked, an action will happen. The controls are explained below.

① **OPEN FORM** Opens a form and displays records from another table or set that are related to the record in the browse. (1)
② **PRINT/PREVIEW LAYOUT** Allows a report or other layout to be printed or previewed. Reports can be filtered based on the data in the row in the browse that the control is in. (1)
③ **RUN AN OPERATION** Runs an operation. [This feature is covered in Chapter 13, Using Operations] (1)
④ **GENERIC ACTION** Runs XBasic code or a script. This option requires writing code or at least copying code from another source. (1)
⑤ **IMAGE** Adds an icon to the cell. The icon represents a value. The image can be static (doesn't change) or dynamic (the image changes based on the value in another cell). (2)
⑥ **TEXT** Adds static or dynamic text to the cell. Static text will replace the contents of the cells. (2)

(1) This control adds a button or hyperlink to a cell.
(2) The dynamic value is based on a value in the current record.

Unbound System Field

Unlike other columns on a browse, a column created by using a browse control is bound to the **SYSTEM UNBOUND FIELD**, as illustrated in Figure 10-14.

An unbound field is one that is not bound to a field in a table or calculated field. When initially displayed on a browse, the column does not have a width. You will have to make the column wider.

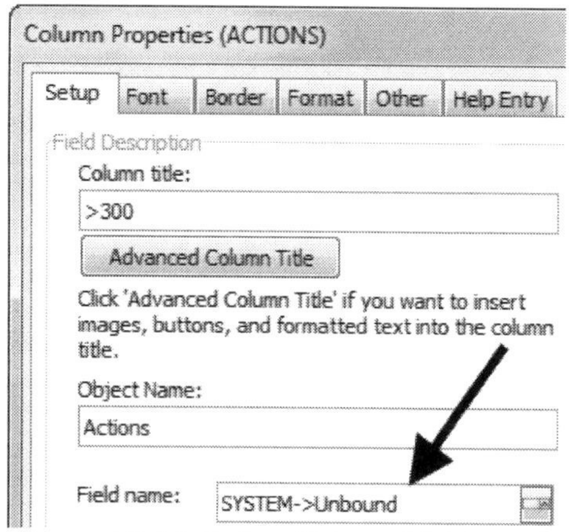

Figure 10-14 System Unbound field illustrated

Exercise 10.2: Use The Open Form Control

In this exercise you will create a browse that will be added to a Browse control.

1. Browses tab ⇒ New button ⇒ Select the Customers table, then click Next.
2. Add the following fields to the Fields in Browse list: First Name, Last Name, State and Note, then click Finish.
3. Make the first three columns smaller, then save the browse as `aCustomerBrowseControl`.

Add The Control To The Browse

In this part of the exercise you will add the Open Form Browse control to the aCustomerBrowseControl browse, which will be used o display the customers orders.

1. Drag the Open Form control from the Browse Control panel and place it after the State column.

Open Form Dialog Box

The options shown in Figure 10-15 are used to configure the Open Form control.

The options are explained below.

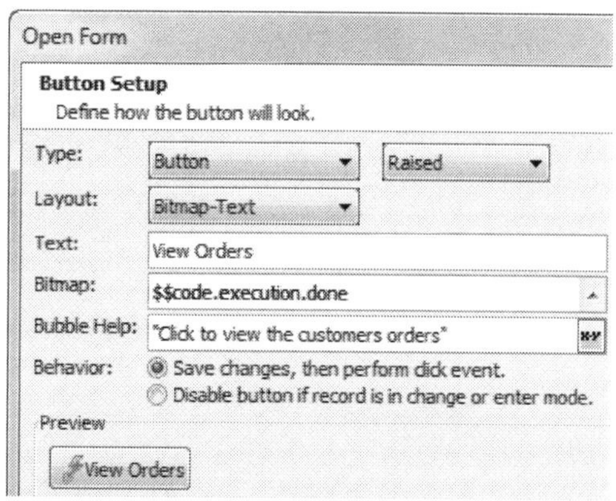

Figure 10-15 Button Setup screen

① **TYPE** Is used to select whether the control will be a button or hyperlink. The field to the right of it is only available for the button type and is used to select the appearance of the button.
② **LAYOUT** Is used to select what will appear on the button or hyperlink.
③ **TEXT** Is used to type in the characters that will appear on the button or hyperlink.
④ **BITMAP** Click the button to open the Insert Image dialog box, which is used to select an image.
⑤ **BUBBLE HELP** Is used to create a help text message for the button or hyperlink.
⑥ **BEHAVIOR** Is used to select if the button saves the changes or is disabled.
⑦ **PREVIEW SECTION** Shows what the button or hyperlink will look like.

Set Up The Button

1. In the Text field, type `View Orders`.

2. Click the Bitmap field button. Scroll through the list of images and select one that you like, then click the Insert button.

3. In the Bubble Help field, type `"Click to view the customers orders"`.
   You should have the options shown earlier in Figure 10-15. Click Next.

Select The Form And Its Options

The screen shown in Figure 10-16 is used to select the form that you want the control to open.

1. Select the Customers Orders form, then click Next.

Figure 10-17 shows the options that will determine what happens to the form when it is opened. The options are explained below.

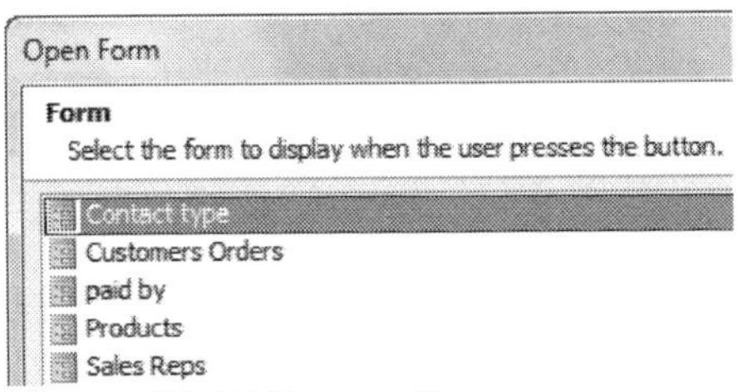

Figure 10-16 Form options

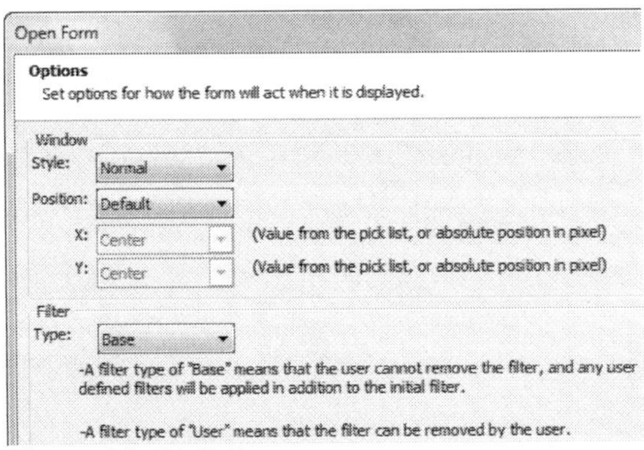

Figure 10-17 Options screen

① **STYLE** Is used to select the border of the form. **NORMAL** displays the form as it currently looks. **DIALOG** changes the border of the form to resemble a dialog box. I could not get this option to work.
② **POSITION** Is used to select where the form will be displayed on the screen. Selecting **OVERRIDE** enables the X and Y options, which are used to select a specific position on the screen.
③ **FILTER TYPE** Is used to select whether or not the user can remove the filter.

2. None of the options shown above in Figure 10-17 need to be changed. Click Next.

Create The Filter

The options shown in Figure 10-18 are used to create a filter and sort order for the records that will be displayed on the form.

Clicking the **DEFINE LINK(S)** button opens the Links Genie, which is used to create the filter.

The link is what will cause the form to only display matching records for the row in the browse that the button was clicked for.

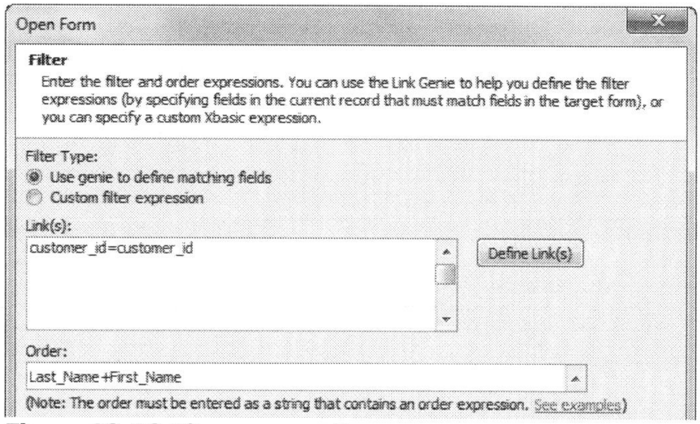

Figure 10-18 Filter screen options

1. Click the Define Link(s) button.

2. Open the first drop-down list in both columns and select the Customer ID field, as shown in Figure 10-19, then click OK.

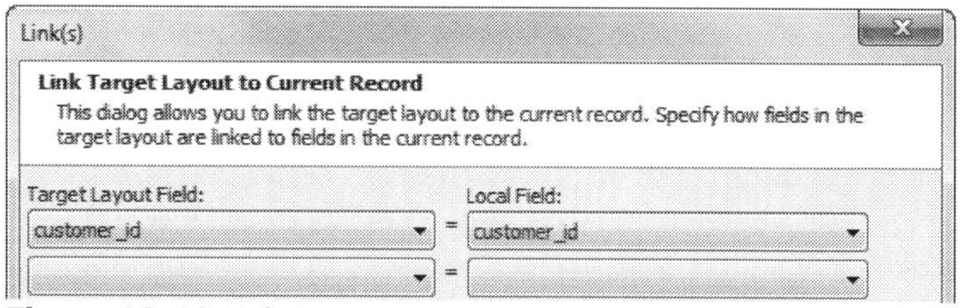

Figure 10-19 Link Target Layout to Current Record screen

Select The Sort Order

The sort order for the form is last name and first name.

1. Click the Order field button on the Filter screen.

2. Click the Insert button on the Expression Builder. Select the Last Name field from the Customers table, then click the Insert button.

3. Type a plus sign.

4. Click the Insert button again. Select the First Name field, then click the Insert button.

5. Type a quote at the beginning and end of the expression.

   You should have the expression shown in Figure 10-20.

   Click OK.

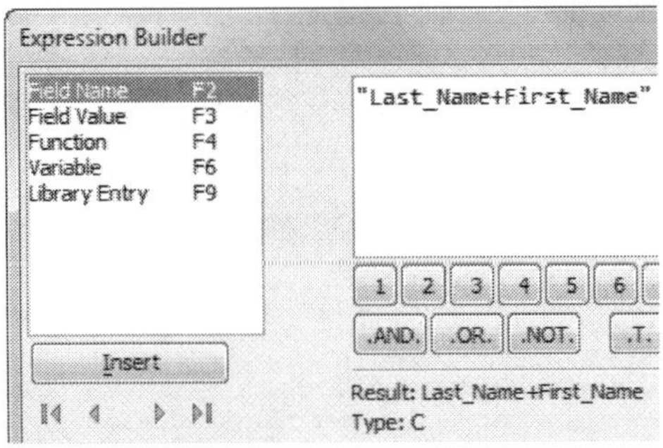

Figure 10-20 Sort order expression

6. You should have the options shown earlier in Figure 10-18 on the Filter screen. Click Finish, then save the changes.

Change The Column Name

1. Click on the Open Form column, then open the Column Properties dialog box.
2. Change the Column title field to `More Detail . . .`, then click OK. Save the changes.

View And Test The Control

When you view the browse, it should look like the one shown in Figure 10-21. Notice the Bubble help over the button.

Click the View Orders button. You will see the Customers Orders form. Notice that the form displays the orders for the customer that you selected on the browse.

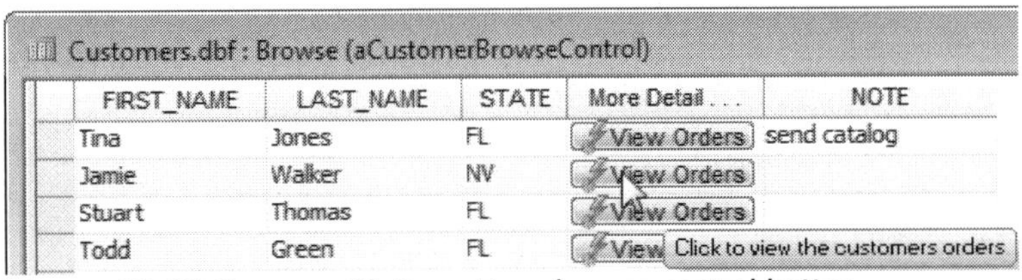

Figure 10-21 Browse with Open Form browse control button

Exercise 10.3: Use The Print/Preview Layout Browse Control

In this exercise you will use the control to preview a report from a browse.

1. Open the Order header info browse, then drag the Print/Preview Layout browse control to the browse after the Order ID field.
2. Open the second Type drop-down list and select Modern. In the Text field type `View Line Items`, then click Next.
3. On the Layout screen, select the aLineItemTotal report, then click Next.
4. Click the Define Link(s) button, then select the Order ID field for the Target Layout and Local Field options. Click OK, then click Finish.

5. Save the browse as `aPreviewBrowseControl`.

   View the browse. When you preview the report, you will see the detail records for the order that you selected on the browse, as shown in Figure 10-22.

Order id	Product id	Quantity	Price	line total
3	CH100	25	12.95	323.75
3	CH101	10	12.95	129.50
3	CO200	3	129.00	387.00
3	LA048	20	29.95	599.00
3	CH220	15	12.95	194.25

Figure 10-22 Report added to the browse

Exercise 10.4: Use The Image Browse Control To Display Images Dynamically

In this exercise you will use the Image control to graphically display whether a value in a cell on the browse is greater than or less than a specific value.

> **Selecting Images**
> If you know the file name of the image that you want to use, you can type it in the Image Name field on the Insert Image dialog box. In this exercise you can also type the image file name on the Images dialog box.

1. View the Products table in the Default Browse. Save the browse as `aImageBrowseControl`.

2. Delete the On Back Order column.

3. Add the Image control after the Product ID field.

   On the dialog box shown in Figure 10-23, select the **DYNAMICALLY SELECTED IMAGE** option, then click Next.

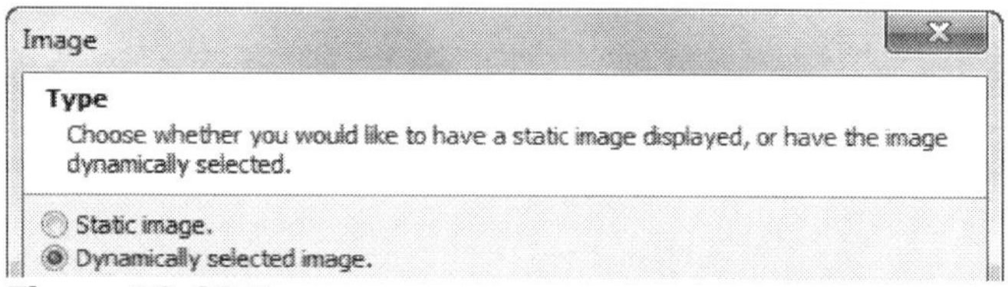

Figure 10-23 Type screen

4. Click the Image field button, then scroll down the list of images and select the red plus sign. The image name is $$code.debug.line.breakpoint.conditional. Click the Insert button.

5. Click the Expression field button.

   Create an expression to check if the Qty In Stock field is >=300, as shown in Figure 10-24, then click OK.

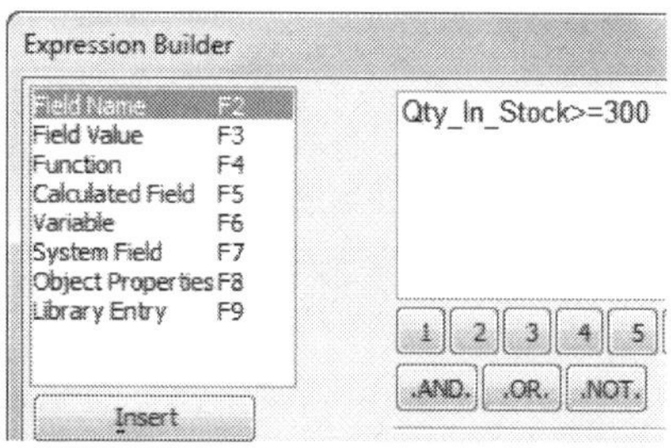

Figure 10-24 Expression to check Qty In Stock field value

6. Open the second Image drop-down list and select the $$web.download.image file. (It's near the bottom of the list).

7. Create the expression shown in Figure 10-25, then click Finish.

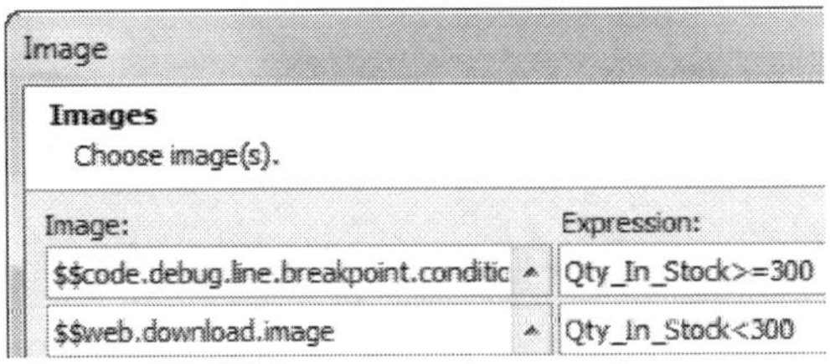

Figure 10-25 Images and expressions

8. Make the column wider, then open the Column Properties dialog box for the Image column. Change the Column title field to >300.

9. On the Format tab, select the Center alignment option.

   Save the changes.

   The browse should look like the one shown in Figure 10-26. The symbols indicate whether the Qty in stock is greater or less than 300.

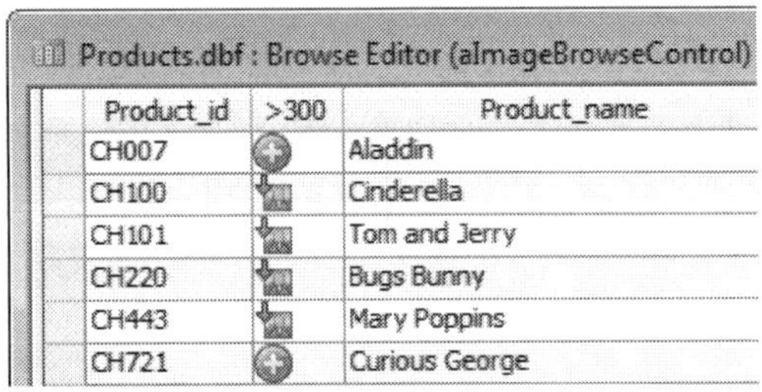

Figure 10-26 Browse with dynamic images

Multiple Browse Controls In The Same Cell

You may have the need to place more than one Browse control in the same cell. When that is the case, follow the steps below.

① On the Browse Controls panel, select all of the controls that you want to add to the cell.
② Drag the selected controls to the browse. You will see the dialog box shown in Figure 10-27.
③ When you have edited each control, the icon next to the control will turn green and the **INSERT CONTROLS** button will be enabled.

The **EDIT** button opens the genie for the selected control.

The **MOVE UP** and **MOVE DOWN** buttons are used to change the order of the controls.

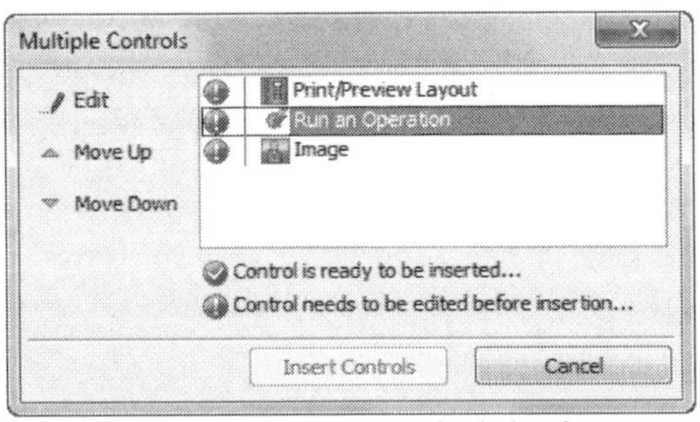

Figure 10-27 Multiple Controls dialog box

Using The Browse Cell Display Format Builder

In the previous exercise you learned how to dynamically display images by creating a condition for the browse control. The same functionality can be created on the Browse Cell Display Format Builder. With a browse open (in Design view), there are several ways to open this dialog box, as explained below.

① Right-click on a column ⇒ Edit Display Format
② Right-click on a cell ⇒ Edit Display Format
③ Right-click on a column ⇒ Properties ⇒ Other tab ⇒ Edit Display Format button
④ Right-click on a cell ⇒ Properties ⇒ Other tab ⇒ Edit Display Format button
⑤ Column ⇒ Properties ⇒ Other tab ⇒ Edit Display Format button

The dialog box shown in Figure 10-28 is used to format columns in a browse.

Click the Add button to add another browse control or condition to the column.

The options on this dialog box are explained below.

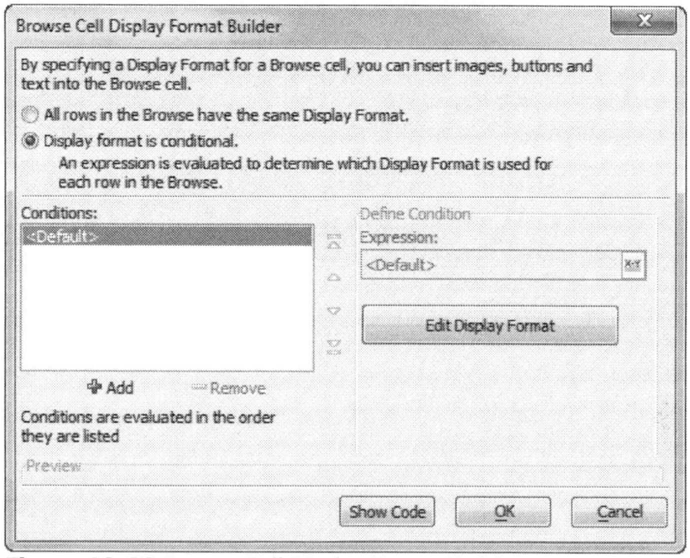

Figure 10-28 Browse Cell Display Format Builder

The **ALL ROWS IN THE BROWSE HAVE THE SAME DISPLAY FORMAT** option is used to apply the formatting created on this dialog box to every cell in the column.

The **DISPLAY FORMAT IS CONDITIONAL** option displays the options shown above in Figure 10-28. The options shown are used to create, edit and remove conditional formatting. They are also used to conditionally add the following to a column in a browse, based on values in the table or set. This is similar to adding a browse control to the browse.

① Formulate text.
② Add buttons or images.

Selecting either option above, then clicking the Edit Display Format button, opens the dialog box shown in Figure 10-29. The options on the Advanced Text Properties dialog box are used to add a control in the list on the left side of the dialog box to the column.

Each control has its own genie, as shown in Figures 10-30 to 10-36. Notice that there are controls here that are not available from the Browse Controls panel. To add a control to the column, add it to the Selected Controls list, click on it, then click the Edit Control button.

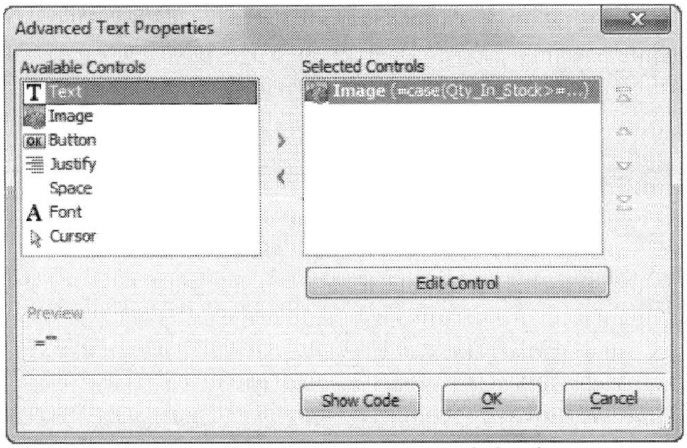

Figure 10-29 Advanced Text Properties dialog box

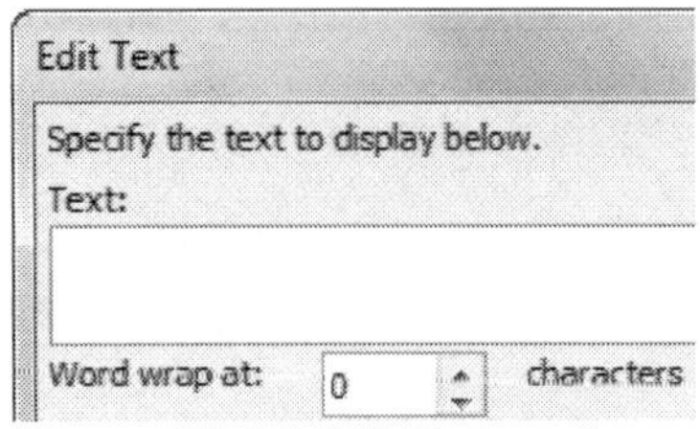

Figure 10-30 Edit Text genie

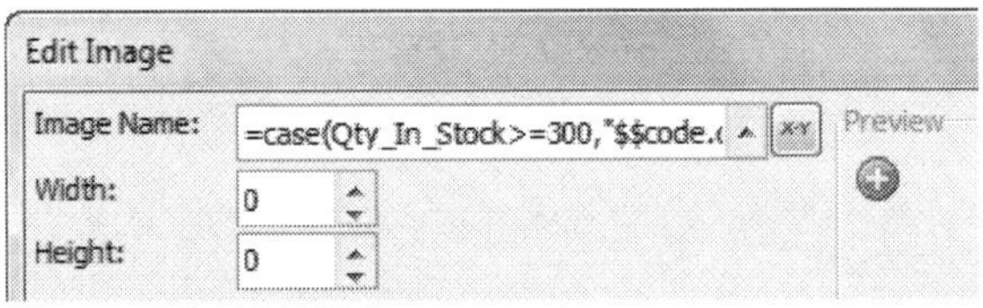

Figure 10-31 Edit Image genie

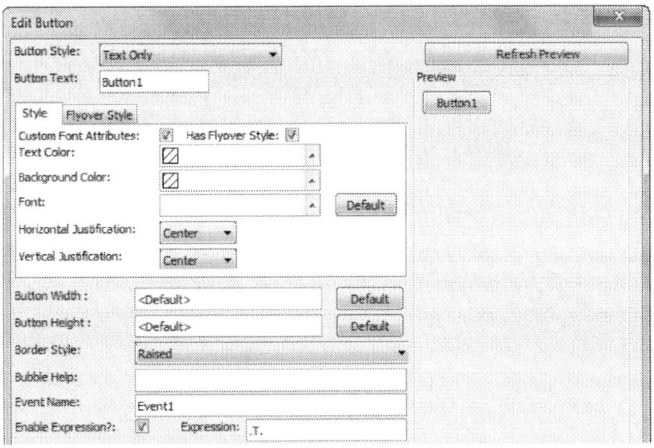

Figure 10-32 Edit Button genie

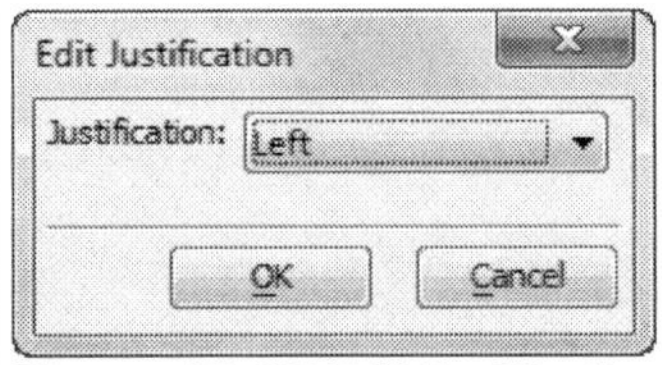

Figure 10-33 Edit Justification genie

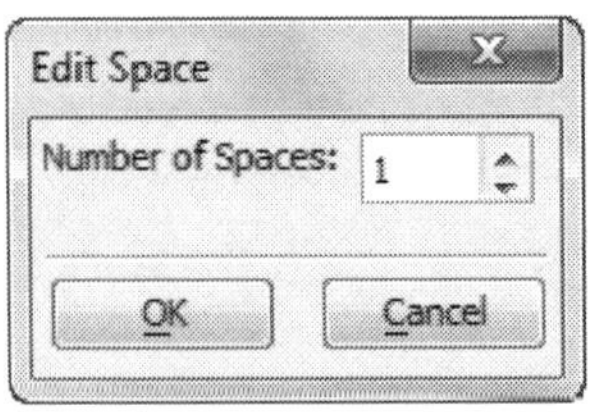

Figure 10-34 Edit Space genie

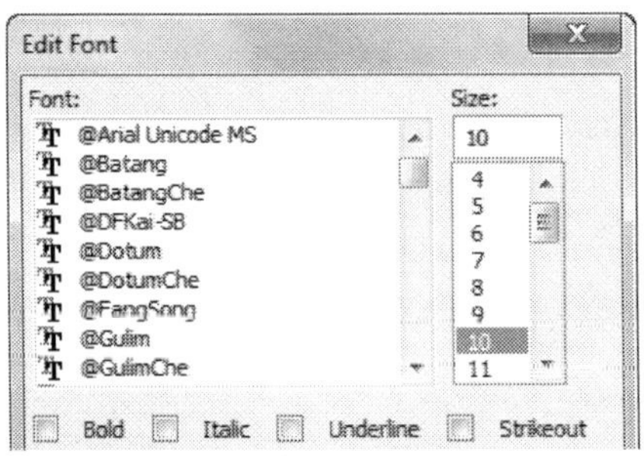

Figure 10-35 Edit Font genie

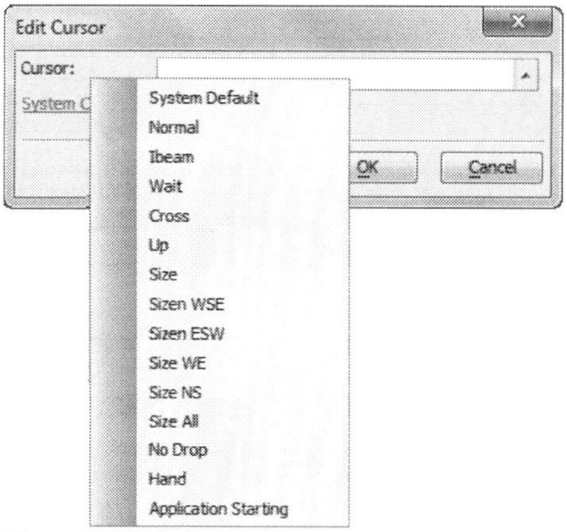

Figure 10-36 Edit Cursor genie

Change The <Default> Genie Expression

If you want to follow along, open the aImageBrowseControl browse, then open the Browse Cell Display Format Builder for the conditional column (greater than 300).

As shown earlier in Figure 10-28, the selected column in the browse already has at least one control. This is denoted by the <Default> option in the Conditions list. To edit the condition(s), follow the steps below.

1. Click the Edit Display Format button on the Browse Cell Display Format Builder. You will see the Advanced Text Properties dialog box shown earlier in Figure 10-29.

2. The control in the Selected Controls list (on the Advanced Text Properties dialog box) contains the code from the browse control(s). To view the code, click the **SHOW CODE** button. You will see the dialog box shown in Figure 10-37. You can view the code, but not change it here.

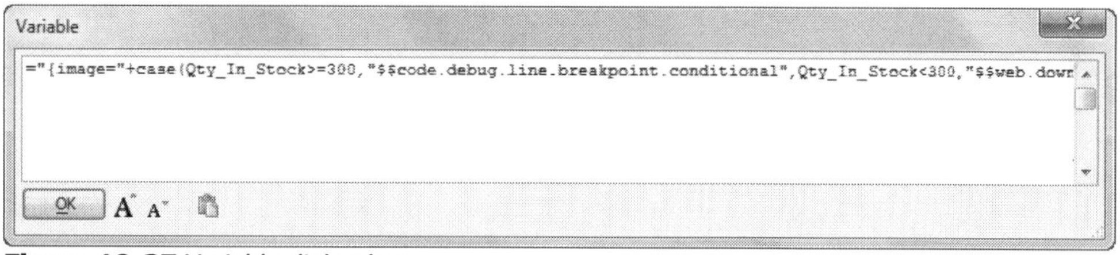

Figure 10-37 Variable dialog box

3. Click the Edit Control button on the Advanced Text Properties dialog box. You will see the dialog box shown earlier in Figure 10-31. Clicking the X-Y button displays the code for the control that you can modify, as shown in Figure 10-38.

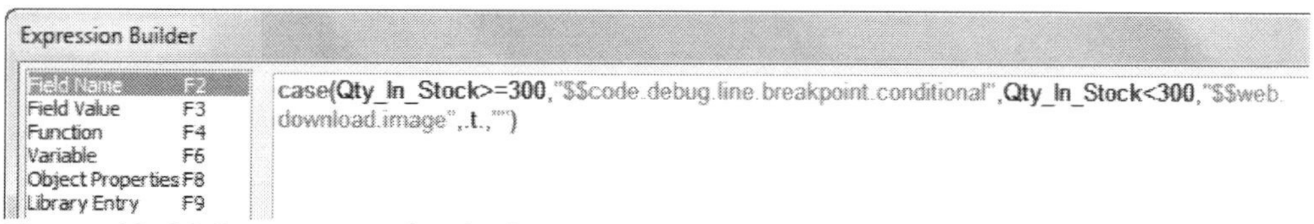

Figure 10-38 Browse control code that can be modified

Changing An Image
If you need to change or add an image, you need to know the file name before opening the Expression Builder because there is no option to select an image from a list or dialog box.

SORTING, FILTERING AND QUERYING DATA

As the title of this chapter indicates, you will learn sorting and filtering data techniques. You will also learn several ways to query data.

CHAPTER 11

Overview

Some of the topics covered in this chapter may seem like they are better suited for people that will use the application rather then people that develop applications. My rationale for including the topics in this chapter is to give you a different view of why expressions are created. The topics covered revolve around searching for records on a form or browse.

Often, you will need to create filters for reports that will search tables to retrieve the records to display on reports. You will also need to know how to use expressions to display data on charts. Hopefully, you will see the connection between understanding how to sort and filter records from a user perspective and creating expressions from a developers perspective so that the data is in the order that you need to create reports and charts. Being able to create queries will help you understand logic, which will be very helpful in creating reports and charts.

Sorting Data

There are several ways to sort data on a form or browse. One of the easiest ways to sort in a browse is by clicking on a column heading. This section covers more advanced ways to manually sort data. Keep in mind that when creating an expression, "ordering records" is the same as sorting records.

Indexes

In addition to being able to manually sort data, Alpha Five automatically creates indexes. An example of when an index is automatically created is when you click on a column heading in a browse and sort on it. These indexes are another type of sorting. The default index is named Record Number.

Creating Indexes

When you create a table, there is an option to designate a field as an index field. Indexes can also be created after the table has been created.

Using The Index Builder

The Index Builder is used to view and modify the indexes already in the table, as well as, create new indexes. If you need to display data in a browse or form in a specific order, you can short the data in the form or browse or you can create an index and display the data in order by the index. A benefit of using an index in a set is that the retrieval process is faster.

Right-click on a table in the Control Panel and select **DEFINE INDEXES**. You will see the dialog box shown in Figure 11-1.

The **_A5_RECOR INDEX** is the default index that is automatically created.

The **BUILD** button rebuilds all of the indexes in the table.

The **FULL TEXT SEARCH** button displays the dialog box shown in Figure 11-2.

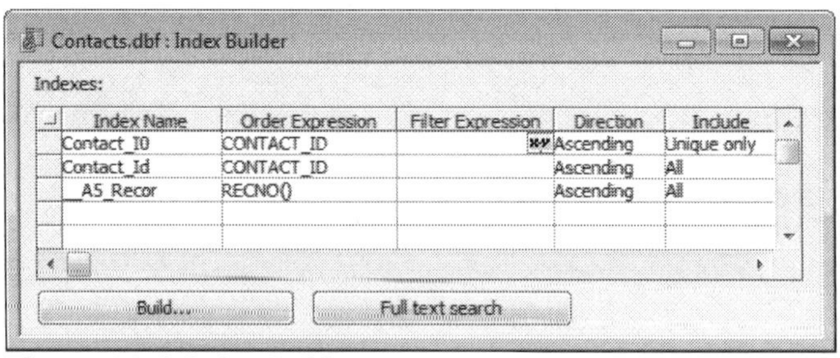

Figure 11-1 Index Builder

This dialog box is used to select fields that have words that you want to use as an index.

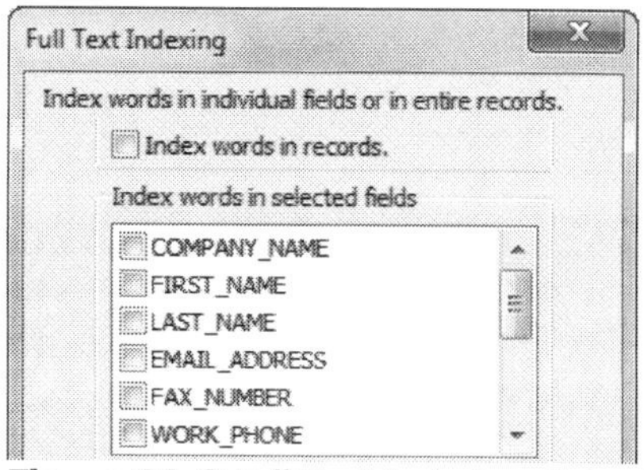

Figure 11-2 Full Text Indexing dialog box

Viewing Indexes

In addition to using the Index Builder to view indexes, the dialog box shown in Figure 11-3 can also be used to view and apply an index.

View a form or browse ⇒ Query ⇒ Select Index/Query, opens this dialog box.

Indexes like Customer_0 and Order_ID have the key icon and Temporary Queries have the Q icon and the words "Temporary Query".

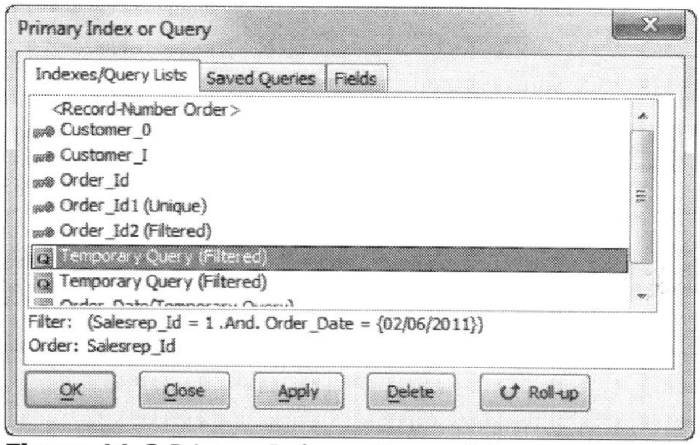

Figure 11-3 Primary Index or Query dialog box

Notice that the Filter and Order Expressions for the form or browse that has focus are displayed at the bottom of the dialog box for the selected index or query.

> **Find By Key**
> The Find By Key tool has an option to select an index.

Sorting On More Than One Field

You will have the need to sort data on more than one field when creating reports. The good thing is that you can sort on fields from different tables in a one-to-many set. The downside to sorting is that the sort criteria cannot be saved.

Exercise 11.1: Sort On Multiple Fields

In this exercise you will sort the records in a browse. The sort will use fields from two tables.

1. View the Orders Multi Table set browse.

2. Query ⇒ Multi-Field Sort.

The options shown in Figure 11-4 will sort the data by these fields: Sales Rep ID, Order Date, State, Last Name and First Name.

This criteria would be good for a report that needed to display orders by sales rep in order date order.

The maximum number of fields that can be sorted on is six.

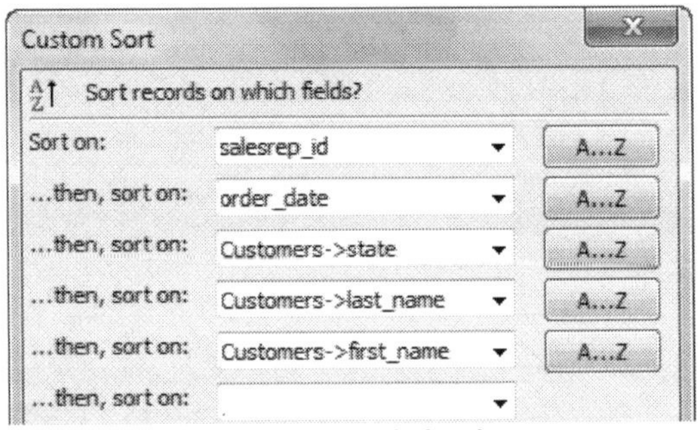

Figure 11-4 Custom Sort dialog box

The fields at the top of the drop-down list that do not have a table name are fields in the primary table in the set.

If you select a field to sort on, then change your mind, open the drop-down list and select the blank option at the top of the drop-down list.

3. Select the options shown above in Figure 11-4, then click OK. The records should be in order by the fields that you sorted on.

Sorting In Descending Order

In the previous exercise, the sort that you created was in ascending (low to high) order, which is the default sorting option. There will be times when you will need to sort in descending (high to low) order. For example, if you create a Top N report, the top level field that you sort on, must be in descending order.

The **DESCENDING SORT** button on the toolbar and Query ⇒ Descending Sort, are used to sort on one column.

The Custom Sort dialog box has A...Z buttons which default to ascending.

If you click on this button, it will change to Z...A, as shown in Figure 11-5. This will sort the corresponding field in descending order.

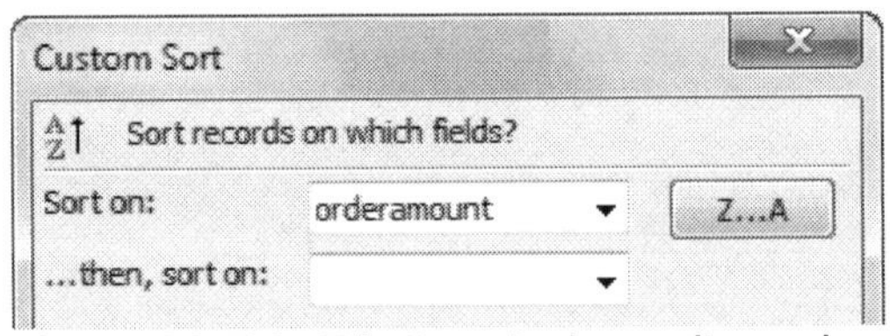

Figure 11-5 A...Z buttons in descending order

Order Builder

The Order Builder also has the A...Z buttons. You will see this dialog box in a variety of places including forms, browses, reports and genies. Open the Form or Browse Properties dialog box. Select the Filter/Order tab shown in Figure 11-6, then click the Order Expression button to display the Order Builder shown in Figure 11-7. This dialog box works the same as the Custom Sort dialog box. The difference is that the Order Builder only allows a maximum of three fields to be sorted on.

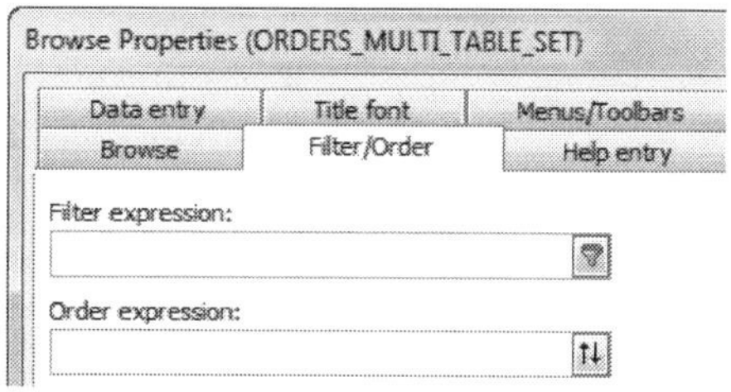

Figure 11-6 Filter/Order tab

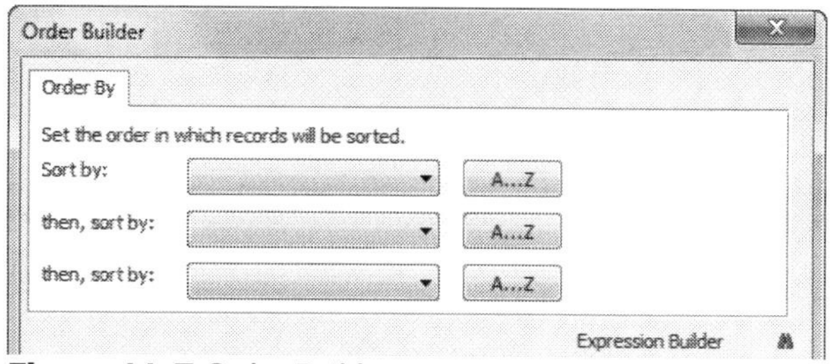

Figure 11-7 Order Builder

Using The Descending Sort Option As A Field Rule

Technically, the Field Rules dialog box does not have a "Descending" sort option like the Order Builder has, but you can use the function explained below to sort in descending order on the Field Rules dialog box.

Invert Function

This function works the same as the descending option does. This function is not just for the Field Rules dialog box. It can be used any place that you can create an expression. If you know that a lookup field needs to always be sorted in descending order, follow the steps below.

1. Open the Field Rules dialog box for the table that has the lookup field that you want to always be sorted in descending order.
2. On the Lookup tab, select the field that you want to sort in descending order.
3. In the **DISPLAY ORDER** field, type `invert(fieldname)`, as illustrated in Figure 11-8.

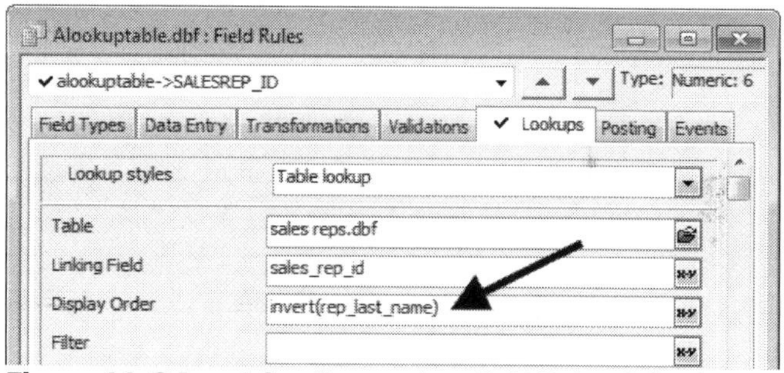

Figure 11-8 Invert function used on Field Rules dialog box

Actually, when you click on an A...Z button to switch to descending, the code behind the Z...A button uses the Invert function. For example, instead of typing the function in the Display Order field, click the button at the end of the field, then click the Create Order using Genie button (on the Expression Builder). The Order Builder will be displayed.

Filtering Data

Filtering data (also known as **QUERYING DATA**) is used to find records that meet criteria that you select. Alpha Five does provide the option to exclude records that meet the criteria that you select. I personally do not use the exclude option because it can be confusing, especially if you are looking at the criteria in a hurry <smile>.

Three filter options that you may find helpful are explained below. While these options can be used on a form, I find it easier to use filter options on a browse, where I can see more than one record at a time.

① **QUICK FILTER** This tool is easy to use. Click on the value that you want to use as the filter value, then click on the Quick Filter button on the toolbar.

② **MULTI-FIELD QUICK FILTER** This tool works similar to the Multi-Field Sort option covered earlier in this chapter. It is used to select values for more than one field to filter on. The fields that you select must have the values that you want to filter on. For example, if you wanted to see all orders that were paid by check and shipped via First Class mail, you could use this tool to create the filter.

If you wanted to see all orders paid by check after a certain date, you could not use this tool because it does not have an option to select a range, like greater than. This option can only filter on one field. The two things that I found interesting about this tool is that if you cannot find a record that has the criteria (data value) that you want to use, you have to use the **FIND BY KEY** tool to select the field and criteria before you use the Multi-Field Quick Filter.

③ **MULTI-SELECT** This tool is used to select more than one value in a field to filter on. For example, if you want to see orders that do not have anything in common, select the record number and add them to the dialog box shown in Figure 11-9.

Figure 11-9 Multi-Select Records dialog box

Exercise 11.2: Use The Quick Filter

In this exercise you will use the Quick Filter to find customers in a specific state.

1. View the Customers table in the Default Browse.

2. Click in a cell in the State column that has FL.

3. Click the Quick Filter button on the toolbar. You should now only see records that have FL in the State column.

   If you look in the lower right corner of the workspace, you will see the number of records that meet the filter criteria that you selected, as shown in Figure 11-10.

Figure 11-10 Count of records that match the filter criteria

4. If you click in a cell in the City column that has Ft Laud and then click the Quick Filter button, you will only see customers in Ft Laud, FL. To view all of the records in the browse, click the **SHOW ALL** button on the toolbar.

Exercise 11.3: Use The Multi-Field Quick Filter

In this exercise you will use the Multi-Field Quick Filter to find orders for a sales rep on a specific day.

1. Display the Orders table in the Default Browse.

2. Click the Find By Key button on the toolbar, then click the Search by button and select the Sales Rep ID field on the Fields tab.

3. On the Find By Key dialog box type 1, then click the Find button. Close the dialog box.

4. In the Order date column, click on the first 2/6/2011 date for Sales Rep ID 1.

5. Query ⇒ Multi-Field Quick Filter.

   Check the Sales Rep ID and Order Date fields, as shown in Figure 11-11.

   The dialog box selects the values in the row selected on the browse. At the bottom of the dialog box you will see the values in the fields that you checked.

   The options in the drop-down list at the bottom of the dialog box are used to select the filter criteria.

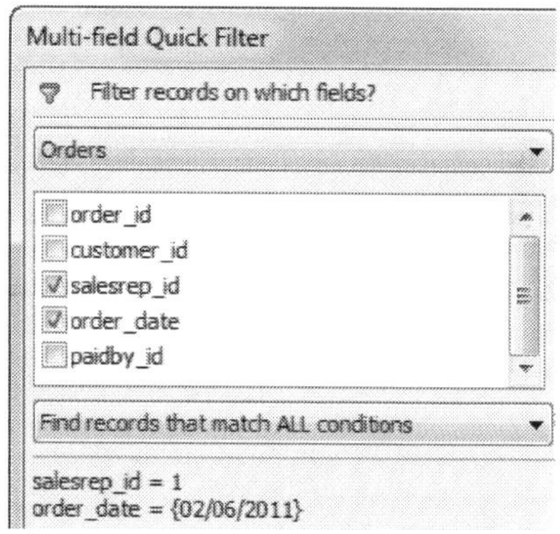

Figure 11-11 Multi-Field Quick Filter

6. Click OK. You should see two records. Both will be for Sales Rep 1, with an order date of 2/6/2011. It may be me, but wouldn't it be less steps to sort by sales rep, then by order date? <smile>

Querying Data

Queries take sorting and filters one step further because you can save the criteria and use it again and again. Alpha Five provides several ways to create a query including the following:

① Query By Form
② Options on the Select Filter dialog box
③ QBF Helper

Using The Query By Form Tool

The option displays a default form that shows all of the fields in the table or set. Type the value that you want to search for in a field on the form. This query option also has a toolbar and can use the QBF Helper. The Query By Form option is only available when viewing a form. The default form or form that you create can be used to query by form. To access this option, display the form in form view, then click the Query By Form button on the Form View toolbar. You can also sort on more than one field.

> **Query By Form And Sets**
> As useful as the Query By Form is, it does not allow you to use fields from a table that is designated as the "many" table in a one-to-many relationship.

Query By Form Toolbar

The options on the toolbar shown in Figure 11-12 are available when the form is open. The buttons specific to the Query By Form tool are explained in Table 11-1.

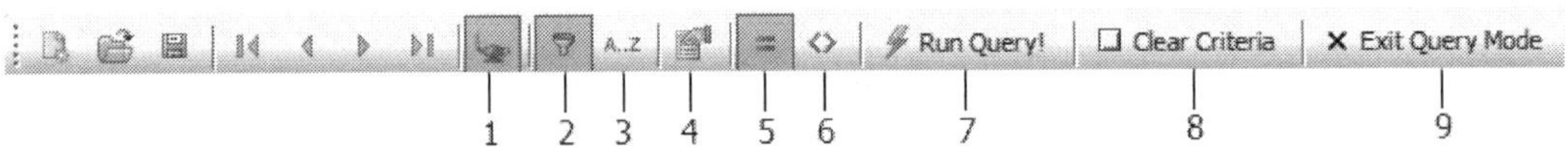

Figure 11-12 Query by form toolbar

Option	Description
1	**QBF** Displays and hides the QBF Helper shown later in Figure 11-15. Click this button when you need to create filter or order criteria.
2	**FILTER CRITERIA** Is used to create a filter expression. You can type the expression in the field or use the QBF Helper. (1)
3	**ORDER CRITERIA** Displays buttons on the form as shown in Figure 11-13. Click on the buttons in the order that you want to sort on. (1)
4	**SHOW EXPRESSIONS** Displays the dialog box shown in Figure 11-14. It displays the filter and order criteria that has been set up so far.
5	**INCLUDE RECORDS THAT SATISFY CRITERIA** If clicked, the query that you create will be used, as is. This is the default.
6	**EXCLUDE RECORDS THAT SATISFY CRITERIA** If clicked, the query criteria that you created will be reversed. That means that if your query should select dates in a range, records with dates outside of the range will be selected and displayed when the query is run.
7	**RUN QUERY** Runs the query that you created.
8	**CLEAR CRITERIA** Removes the query criteria that you selected.
9	**EXIT QUERY MODE** Returns back to form view.

Table 11-1 Query by form toolbar buttons explained

(1) The Filter criteria and Order criteria buttons cannot be selected at the same time.

The arrows next to the buttons on the form shown in Figure 11-13, indicate ascending (Up arrow) and descending (Down arrow) order.

One field can be sorted in descending order and another field in ascending order.

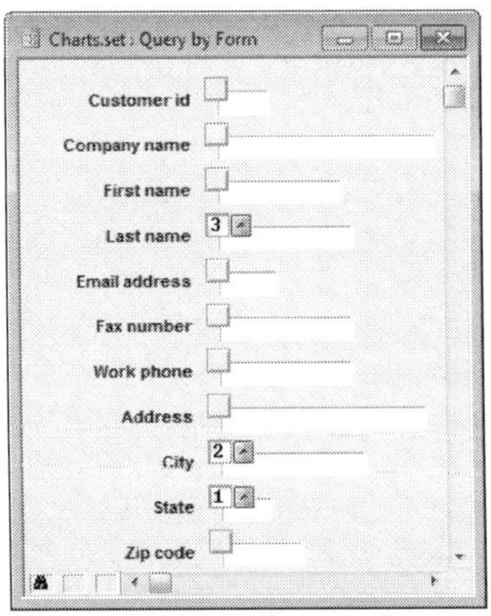

Figure 11-13 Order criteria option

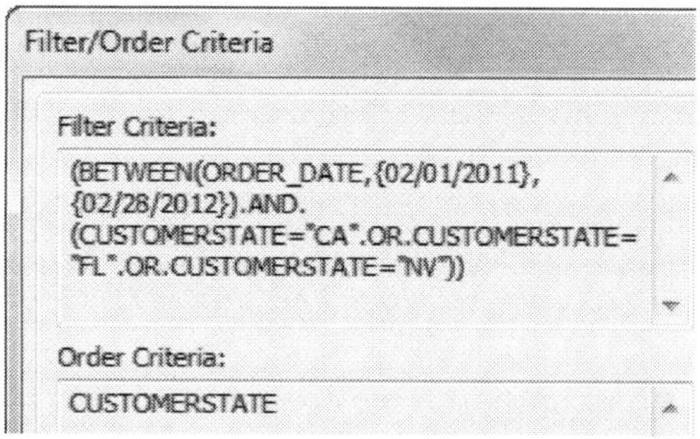

Figure 11-14 Filter/Order Criteria dialog box

The QBF Helper

The genie shown in Figure 11-15 displays operators that you can use to create queries. The options are used to create filter and order expressions when using the Query By Form tool.

Notice that the field name is at the top of the dialog box.

The buttons that appear on this dialog box will vary slightly depending on the field type that is selected. For example, if the field is numeric, the **CONTAINS CHARACTERS** and **SOUNDS LIKE OPERATORS** shown in Figure 11-15 are not available.

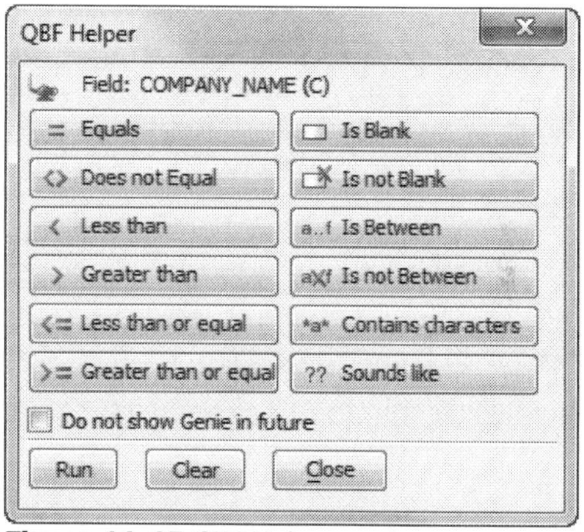

Figure 11-15 QBF Helper genie

Each button on the QBF Helper displays the operator that it will create. Most buttons have their own dialog box, as shown in Figures 11-16 to 11-18 that is specific to the operator.

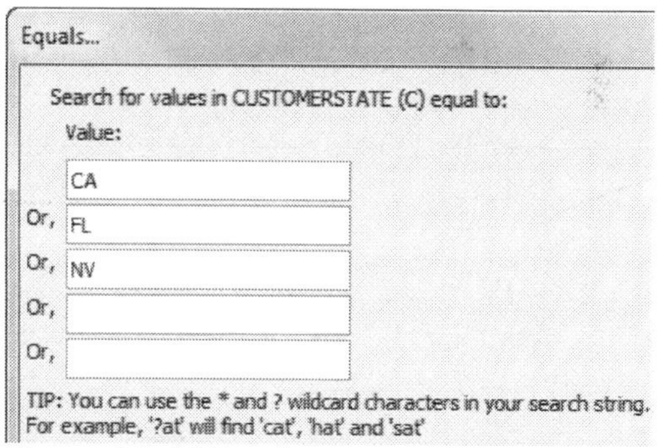

Figure 11-16 Equals operator dialog box

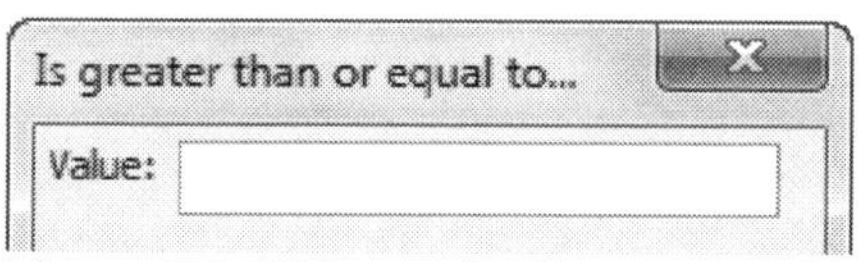

Figure 11-17 Is greater than or equal to operator dialog box

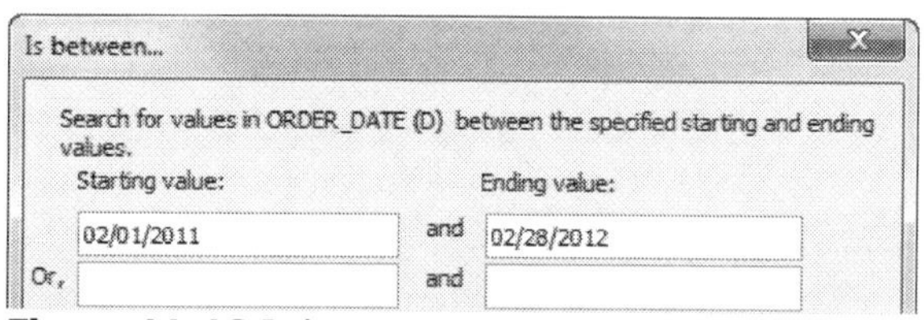

Figure 11-18 Is between operator dialog box

Exercise 11.4: Use The Query By Form Tool

In this exercise you will query a form to find records in a certain date range and in one of three states. The query will sort the data by state. You will also learn how to save the query.

1. Save the Chart Orders table in the Default Form layout. Save it as `aQueryByForm`.
2. View the form ⇒ Query ⇒ Query By Form. Leave the QBF Helper dialog box open.
3. Click the Order Criteria button, then click the button for the Customer State field.
4. Click the Filter Criteria button, then click in the Order Date field. On the QBF Helper, create criteria to select records with an order date between 2/1/2011 and 2/28/2012, as shown earlier in Figure 11-18.
5. Click in the Customer State field. Create criteria to select records in CA, FL or NV, as shown earlier in Figure 11-16. You should have the criteria shown earlier in Figure 11-14.
6. Click the Save button on the toolbar, then type `QueryChartOrders` as the name.
7. Run the query. In the bottom right corner of the workspace, you should see that 71 records were retrieved.

View And Open Saved Queries

Depending on when you try to view a saved query, you will find it in different locations, as explained below.

① If you saved and ran the query, it will only be on the Indexes/Queries List tab on the Primary Index or Query dialog box, as shown in Figure 11-19. In Form View, click the Select Index/Query button on the toolbar.

② Once you close and reopen the database, the query is available in the following locations:
1. On the Saved Queries tab on the Primary Index or Query dialog box. Select the query, then click the Apply button.
2. On the Control Panels Operations tab. What's cool about the query being on this tab is that it can be used to filter a report or it can be added to a browse or button on a form, as long as it is created from the same data source that the query is based on.
3. In Form View ⇒ Query ⇒ Run Saved Query, as shown in Figure 11-20. If you select the Run Saved Query option without closing Alpha Five, you will get an error message. Why the database has to be closed and reopened is beyond me.

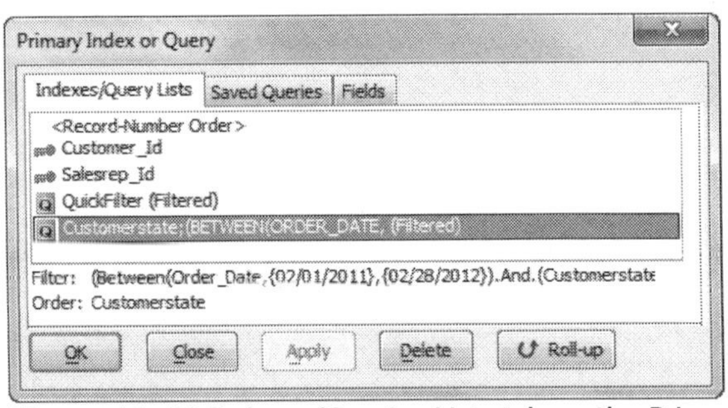

Figure 11-19 Indexes/Queries Lists tab on the Primary Index or Query dialog box

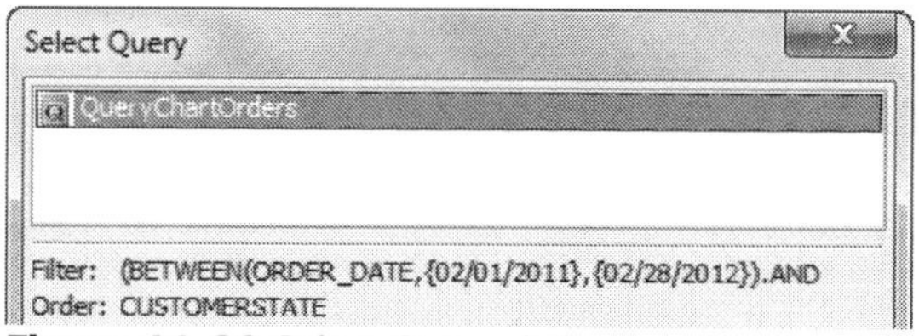

Figure 11-20 Select Query dialog box

How To Edit A Saved Query

When you have the need to edit a saved query, follow the steps below.

1. On the Operations tab, click on the query that you want to edit, then click the Design button.

   On the tab shown in Figure 11-21 you can type in the changes or click the button at the end of the expression that you want to modify and make the changes on the Expression Builder.

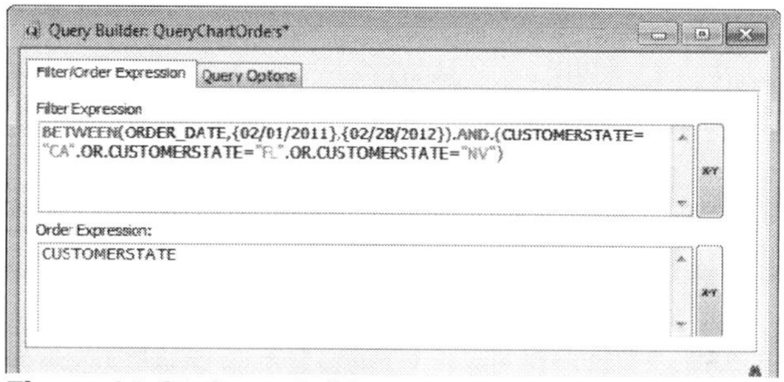

Figure 11-21 Query Builder

2. When you are finished, click the Save button on the toolbar.

Select Filter Dialog Box

The options shown at the top of Figure 11-22 are pre-defined filter expressions. The expressions are explained in Table 11-2. Many of these expressions are also on the **SELECT RECORDS DIALOG BOX** that reports have access to and on the Action Script Genie, which you may already be familiar with.

> These queries are also known as **SPECIAL QUERIES**.

In Form View, Query ⇒ Special Queries, opens this dialog box.

The bottom half of the dialog box explains the query or filter that is selected and provides the options (criteria) for you to select and configure.

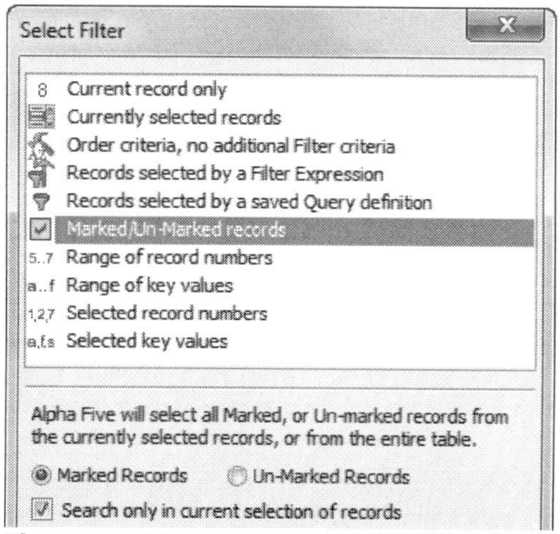

Figure 11-22 Select Filter dialog box

Option	Creates A Query That . . .
Current record only	Only returns the current record. I don't see the value of this option.
Currently selected records	Is based on all of the records in the current query list or current index. (2)
Order criteria, no additional Filter criteria	Is based on the order expression that you create. Filter criteria will not be applied.
Records selected by a Filter Expression	Uses a filter or order expression. (2)
Records selected by a saved Query definition	Uses an existing query. (2)
Marked/Un-Marked records	Uses marked or un-marked records from the entire table or the records that are currently selected.
Range of record numbers	Retrieves all records that have a record number in the range that you select.
Range of key values	Retrieves records that have the key value(s) in the range that you select. This option has the same functionality as the **IS BETWEEN OPERATOR**.
Selected record numbers	Retrieves the records that have the record numbers that you select. In addition to being able to select non consecutive record numbers, this option can also be used to select a range of record numbers.
Selected key values	Retrieves all of the records that have one of the values that you select. This option has the same functionality as the **IS ONE OF OPERATOR**.

Table 11-2 Select Filter dialog box options explained

(2) This option can also be used to create a Top N, Bottom N or N percent query.

Cross-Level Queries

This type of query is used to search tables, including child tables that are in a one-to-many relationship in a set. To create this type of query, you have to use the Query By Expression tool shown in Figure 11-23 or Query Genie shown in Figure 11-24. This means that criteria can be created for a field in a child table. The query excludes records in the parent table that do not have a record in the child table that meets the criteria.

For example, in a set that has the orders and order detail tables, you could create the query Qty >=10, where the Qty field is in the order detail (child) table. The result of this query will display orders that have at least one item where the Qty is >= 10.

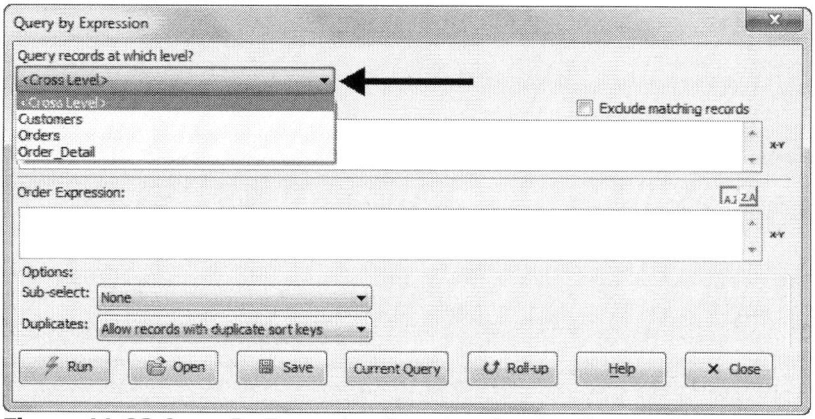

Figure 11-23 Query By Expression Cross Level option illustrated

Clicking the **<CROSS LEVEL>** button on the Query Genie, displays the **SELECT LEVEL DIALOG BOX** shown in the figure.

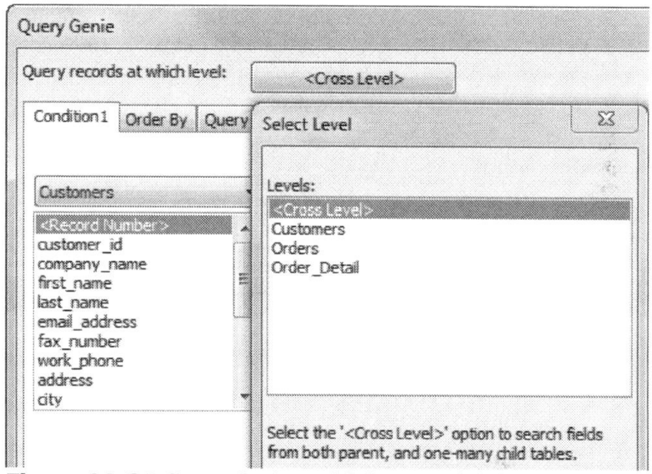

Figure 11-24 Query Genie and Select Level dialog boxes

Query By Expression

This tool can be used when viewing forms and browses.

It is used to filter and sort records by typing in the expression, as shown in Figure 11-25.

Query ⇒ Query By Expression, opens this dialog box.

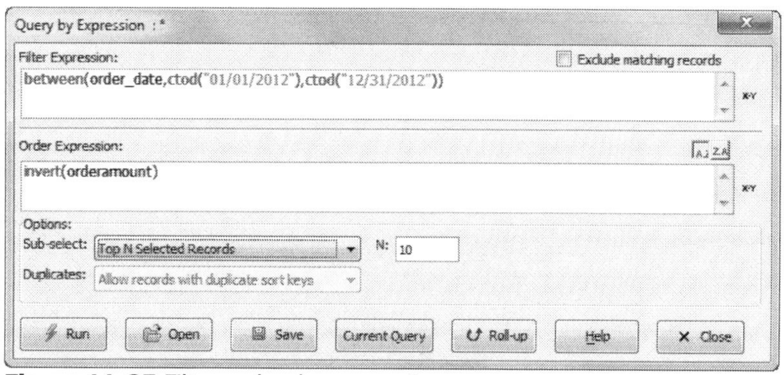

Figure 11-25 Filter and order expressions

What I like about this dialog box is that you can leave it open while you are working. There is a Query By Expression button on the toolbar when a browse is open.

The options in the **SUB-SELECT DROP-DOWN LIST** are the Top N options that you will learn about later in this book.

The options in the **DUPLICATES DROP-DOWN LIST** are used to select what you want to do with records that have duplicate sort key values.

"Technically", this dialog box does not have a genie, but you can access the **FILTER BUILDER** and **ORDER BUILDER** genies with a few mouse clicks.

Like the Query By Form tool, you can save queries created on the Query by Expression dialog box, as well as, open an existing query.

Exercise 11.5: Use The Query By Expression Dialog Box

In this exercise you will create and save a query that finds the top 10 orders in 2012.

1. Save the Chart Orders table with the Default Browse layout as `aQueryByExpression`.
2. View the browse, then click the Query By Expression button on the toolbar.
3. Click the Filter Expression field button, then click the Create Filter Using Genie button.
4. Create a filter expression to only select orders placed in 2012.
5. Create an order expression to sort the records in descending order by order amount.
6. Open the Sub-select drop-down list and select the **TOP N SELECTED RECORDS** option. You should have the options shown earlier in Figure 11-25.
7. Click the Save button. Type `QueryTop10In2012` as the query name.
8. Click the Run button. You should see the 10 orders in descending order based on the Order Amount field, as shown in Figure 11-26.

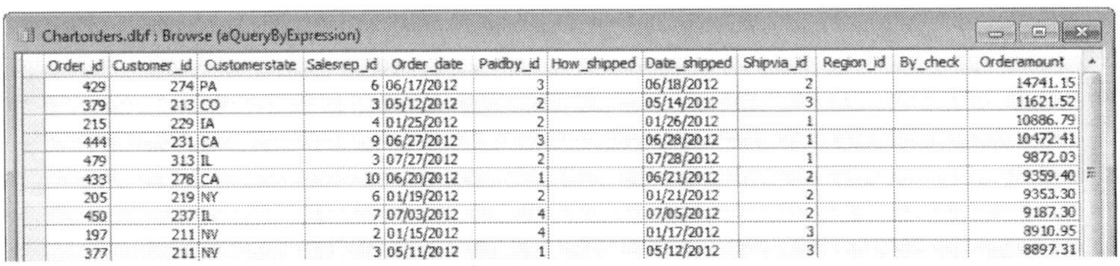
Chartorders.dbf : Browse (aQueryByExpression)

Order_id	Customer_id	Customerstate	Salesrep_id	Order_date	Paidby_id	How_shipped	Date_shipped	Shipvia_id	Region_id	By_check	Orderamount
429	274	PA	6	06/17/2012	3		06/18/2012	2			14741.15
379	213	CO	3	05/12/2012	2		05/14/2012	3			11621.52
215	229	IA	4	01/25/2012	2		01/26/2012	1			10886.79
444	231	CA	9	06/27/2012	3		06/28/2012	1			10472.41
479	313	IL	3	07/27/2012	2		07/28/2012	1			9872.03
433	278	CA	10	06/20/2012	1		06/21/2012	2			9359.40
205	219	NY	6	01/19/2012	2		01/21/2012	2			9353.30
450	237	IL	7	07/03/2012	4		07/05/2012	2			9187.30
197	211	NV	2	01/15/2012	4		01/17/2012	3			8910.95
377	211	NV	3	05/11/2012	1		05/12/2012	3			8897.31

Figure 11-26 Result of Top 10 In 2012 query

Query Genie

This genie, shown in Figure 11-27 will remind you of the Filter Builder. The biggest difference is the toolbar in the lower right corner. The buttons are used to save and open queries. That may make this tool a little easier to use then the Filter Builder.

Exercise 11.6: Use The Query Genie

In this exercise you will create a Cross-Level query that is based on a set that has a one-to-many relationship.

1. Save the Chart Customer Orders set in the Default Browse as `aCrossLevelQuery`.

2. View the browse. Click the Query Genie button on the toolbar. On the Condition 1 tab, create a filter to select order dates in 2011.

3. Click the **ADD CONDITION BUTTON.**

   On the Condition 2 tab, create a condition using the Product ID field in the Chart Order Detail table for these Product ID's: CH007, CH100, CH101, CH220 and CH443, as shown in Figure 11-27.

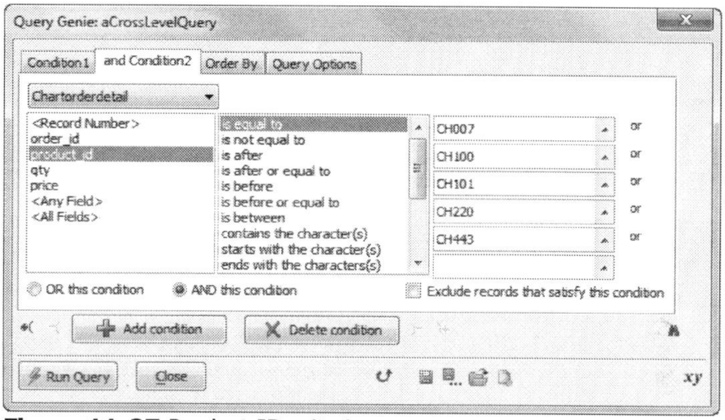

Figure 11-27 Product ID criteria

4. On the Order By tab, sort on the Chart Orders Customer ID field, then sort on the Chart Orders Order ID field.

5. Save the query as `aCrossLevelQuery`. Run the query.

You will see that 70 records meet all of the criteria. Not all of the records displayed have one of the Product ID's that you selected. If you look at all of the rows for a particular Order ID, you will see that at least one of the products has one of the Product IDs in the query. This is what should happen because if you were going to print these orders, you would want to print all of the items for the order.

Editing A Query

To open the query that you just created, follow the steps below.

1. Open the Query Genie.

2. Click the **LOAD A SAVED QUERY** button on the toolbar in the lower right corner of the dialog box.

3. Select the query that you want to edit.

   If you are not sure which query is the one that you want to edit, the filter and order criteria is displayed at the bottom of the dialog box, as shown in Figure 11-28.

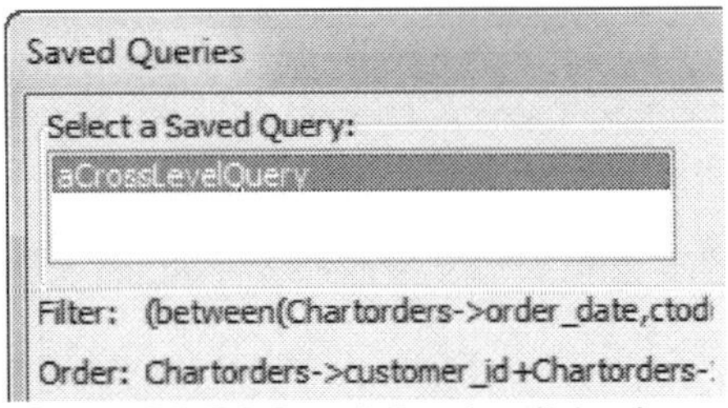

Figure 11-28 Saved Queries dialog box

If you edit the query, you will see the options shown in Figure 11-29 when you click the Run Query button.

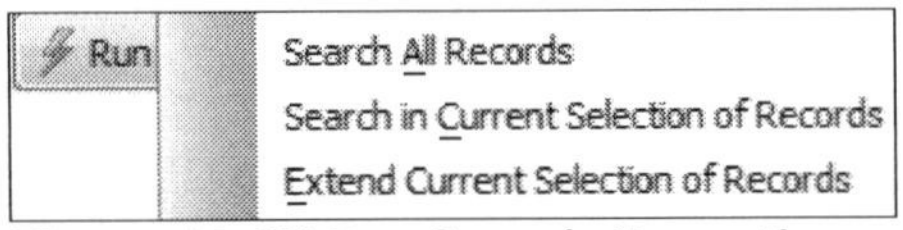

Figure 11-29 Run Query button options

The options are used to select the record set for the query, as explained below.

① **SELECT ALL RECORDS** Means to run the query against all of the records in the table or set.

② **SEARCH IN CURRENT SELECTION OF RECORDS** If a query was already run, selecting this option means that the query will run only using the records retrieved from the previous query. This option will reduce the number of records displayed. (3)

③ **EXTEND CURRENT SELECTION OF RECORDS** Selecting this option means that the current record set could grow, based on the result of running the query. (3)

(3) If no prior query was run, this option will work the same as using the Select All Records option.

IMPORTING DATA

In this chapter you will learn about the options available to import data into an Alpha Five database.

CHAPTER 12

Overview

One task that is done often, especially when a database is first created, is bringing data from external data sources into Alpha Five tables. The Import operation will be of great assistance in bringing data into Alpha Five. If the data that you need for one table in Alpha Five exists in multiple spreadsheets, you can import the data from multiple spreadsheets at the same time into one table.

Create New Operation Dialog Box

The dialog box shown in Figure 12-1 is displayed when the New button on the Operations tab is clicked.

Select the operation that you want to create, then click on the table or set from the list on the right that you want to apply it to.

This chapter covers importing options.

The other operations are explained in Chapter 13, Table 13-2.

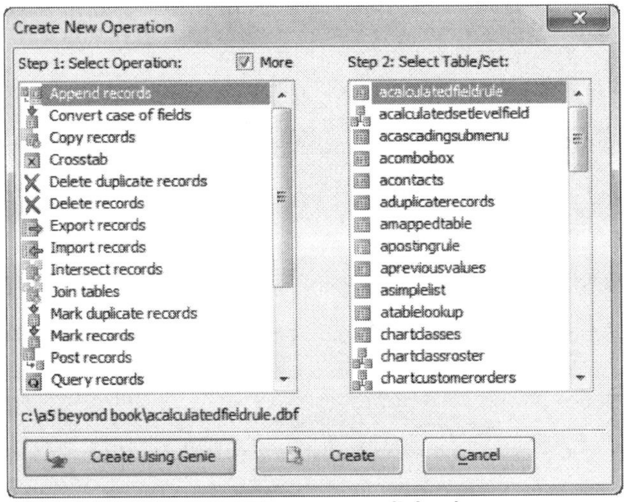

Figure 12-1 Create New Operation dialog box

Import Records Operation

This may be the most used operation because it allows data to be brought into an Alpha Five application.

The Create Using Genie and Create buttons on the Create New Operation dialog box both display the dialog box shown in Figure 12-2.

The options are explained below.

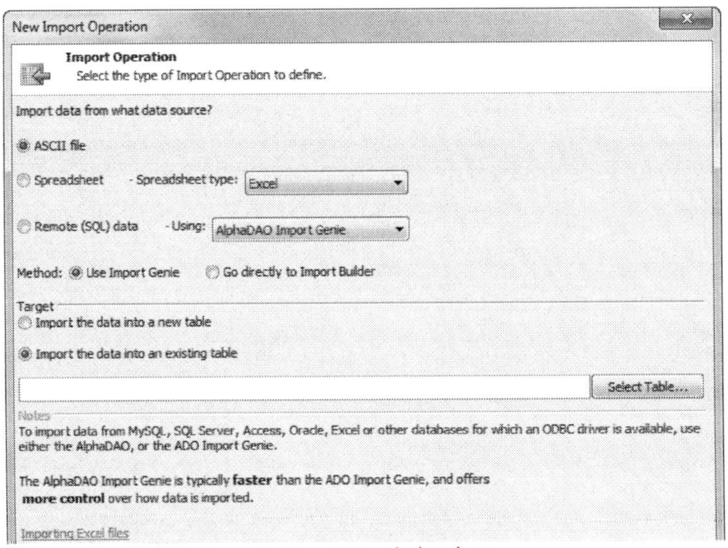

Figure 12-2 New Import Operation dialog box

① The **ASCII FILE** option is most often used for importing comma delimited text files. **.CSV FILES** are an example.

② The **SPREADSHEET** option only imports the first sheet in a workbook. It can import Excel 2000 and earlier and Lotus spreadsheets. If you need to use this import option and the sheet that you want to import is not the first sheet in the workbook, move the sheet so that it is the first sheet. After the import is complete, you can move the sheet back in the workbook if necessary.

③ The **REMOTE (SQL) DATA** option is used to import data from databases that have an **ODBC DRIVER** like SQL and Access databases. Excel 2000 and higher workbooks, including ones with multiple sheets can be imported into the same or different tables at the same time.

④ **METHOD** Select the **USE IMPORT GENIE** option if you want help creating the import operation. Select the **GO DIRECTLY TO IMPORT BUILDER** option shown above in Figure 12-2 if you do not need any help. (1)

⑤ **TARGET** Select this option if the data that will be imported should be added to a new or existing table. If the data will be added to an existing table, click the Select Table button to select the table. (1)

(1) This option is not available for the Remote (SQL) data option.

Operation Exercise Tips

① Unless stated otherwise, prior to starting an operation exercise, open the Create New Operation dialog box shown earlier in Figure 12-1.

② Click the Create Using Genie button after selecting the options on the Create New Operation dialog box.

Exercise 12.1: Use The Spreadsheet Import Option To Create A New Table

In this exercise you will use the Spreadsheet Import option to import data into a new table. The spreadsheet that you will use has three sheets, but this import option will only import data on the first sheet in the workbook.

1. Select the **IMPORT RECORDS** option. Select the Spreadsheet option, then click Next.

2. Click the button at the end of the field (right before the Field Names label) illustrated below in Figure 12-3, at the top of the Import Operation screen, then select the Import3Sheets Excel file. This is the file that has the data to import.

3. Open the **FIELD NAMES** drop-down list and select the Use Field names option. Selecting this option will use these field names when the table is created. You should have the options shown in Figure 12-3. Click Next.

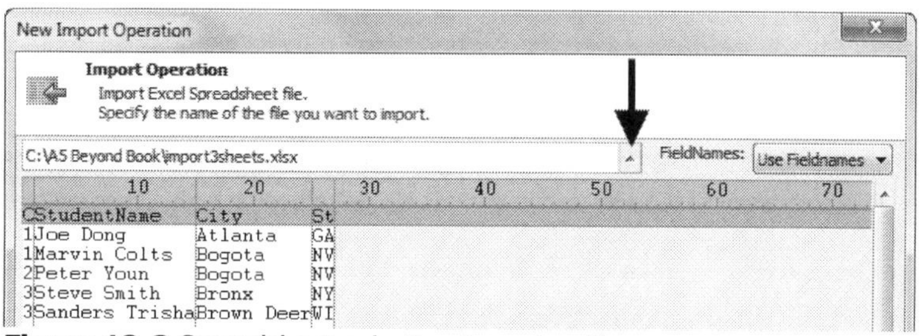

Figure 12-3 Spreadsheet selection import options

Change The Field Settings

When importing data you have the opportunity to select the field settings, which are the same options (on the Table Structure dialog box) used when you create a new table in Alpha Five. It is a good idea to check the options before importing the data. To view the settings for a field, click on the column heading for the field.

1. View the Field settings for the first column, the Class Nbr field, by clicking on the column heading. This is the small column to the left of the Student name column.

   Change the Width to `4`, as illustrated in Figure 12-4.

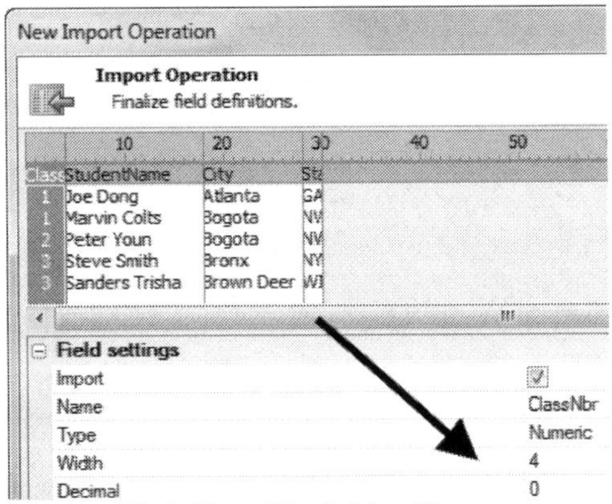

Figure 12-4 Class Nbr field settings

2. Change the Width of the Student Name and City fields to `30`, then click Next.

3. The default Run option, selected in Figure 12-5, is the one you want.

   Click Finish.

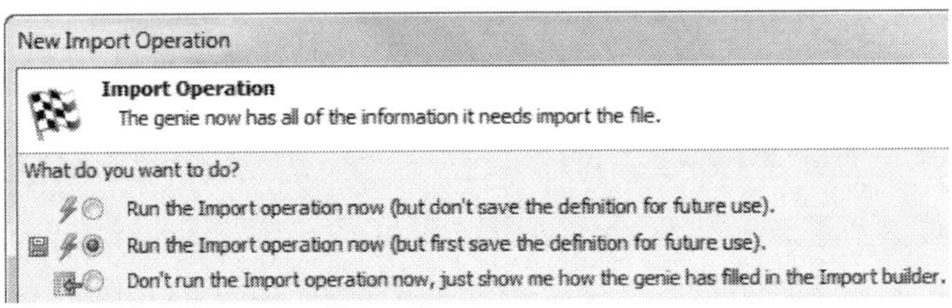

Figure 12-5 Run operation options

> **Don't Run Option**
> If you select the Don't run option, there is no way to get back to the Import Genie.

4. Type `aImportExcelSheet` as the operation file name, then click OK.

   The dialog box shown in Figure 12-6 displays how many records were imported and the name of the table that the records were imported into.

   Clicking the **VIEW RESULT** button displays the new table with the records.

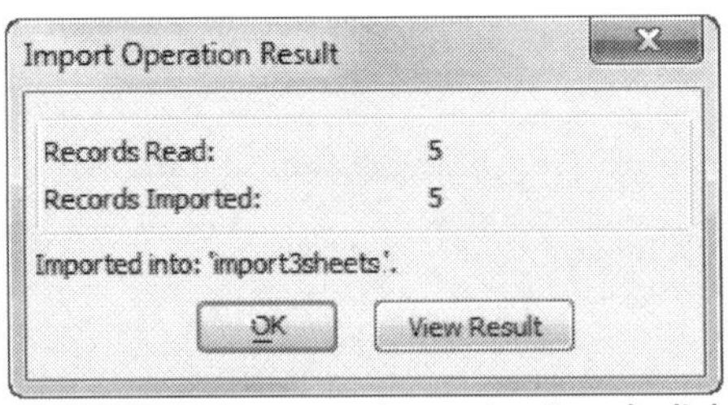

Figure 12-6 Import Operation Result dialog box

5. Rename the import3sheets table to `aImport3Sheets`.

> **No Option To Select A Name For The Table**
> Did you notice that there is no option to select a name for the new table to import the data into? On the first Import Operation Genie screen (shown earlier in Figure 12-2) there is an option to select that you want to import the data to a new table, but no place to type in a name for the new table. The default table name is the name of the spreadsheet. Really? If you use the **IMPORT BUILDER** you can type in a table name. If this was the "real world", you would rename the table right after importing the data if you needed a specific table name. Selecting the last option shown earlier in Figure 12-5 displays the Import Builder, shown in Figure 12-7. To save the operation from the Import Builder, click the Save button on the toolbar.

Import Builder

The Import Builder is another way to import data into Alpha Five. The buttons are explained below.

The **DUPLICATE RECORD SETTINGS** button opens the dialog box shown in Figure 12-8.

The **IMPORT PROPERTIES** button opens the dialog box shown in Figure 12-9.

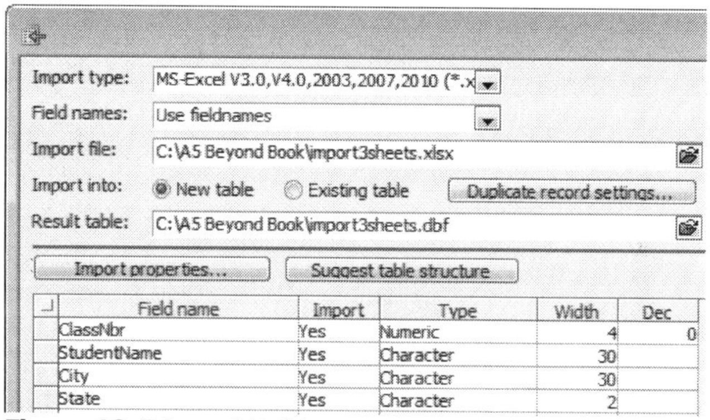

Figure 12-7 Import Builder

The **SUGGEST TABLE STRUCTURE** button changes the options in the grid shown above in Figure 12-7 to what Alpha Five thinks they should be. The problem that I have with this option is that it does not let you select which of its suggestions to use or not use. There is also no way to undo the suggestions without starting over. My advice is to use this option with caution.

The options on this dialog box are used to select how you want to determine if a record is a duplicate.

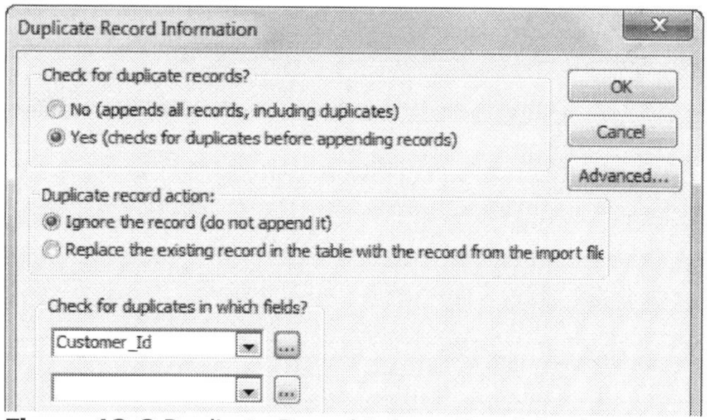

Figure 12-8 Duplicate Record Information dialog box

This dialog box is used to select whether or not the table, if it already exists should be overwritten.

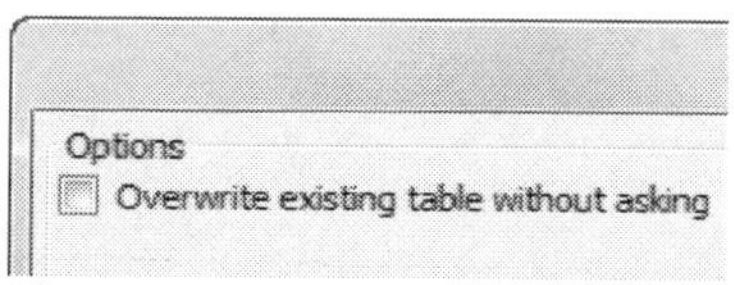

Figure 12-9 Import Properties dialog box

Exercise 12.2: Use The Spreadsheet Import Option To Add Records To A Table

This import option will remind you of the append operation because the records will be added to an existing table. This means that the fields that you want to import have to have the same field names as the ones in the table.

1. Duplicate the Order Lookup table. Save it as `aImportOperation`.

2. Select the Import Records operation, then click the Create Using Genie button. Select the Spreadsheet import option.

3. Select the Import the data into an existing table option, then click the Select Table button and select the aImportOperation table. Click Next.

4. Select the Orders spreadsheet, then select the Use Field names option. Click Next.

Select The Fields To Import

If there are fields that you do not want to import, you can skip them during the import process.

5. Clear the check mark for the **IMPORT** Field Settings option illustrated in Figure 12-10 for the Paid By ID and How Shipped fields, then click Next.

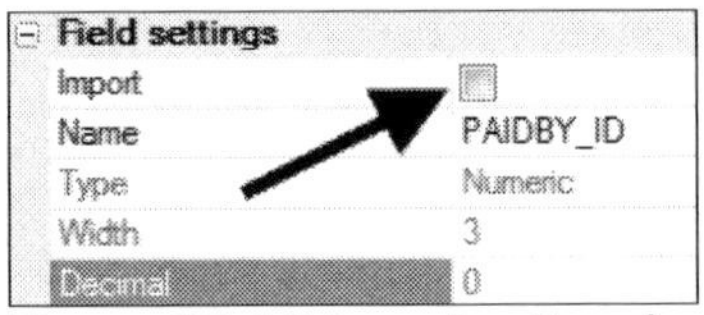

Figure 12-10 Import option check mark cleared

Checking For Duplicate Records

Any time that you add records to an existing table, there is a possibility that there will be duplicate records.

The options shown in Figure 12-11 are used to check for duplicate records.

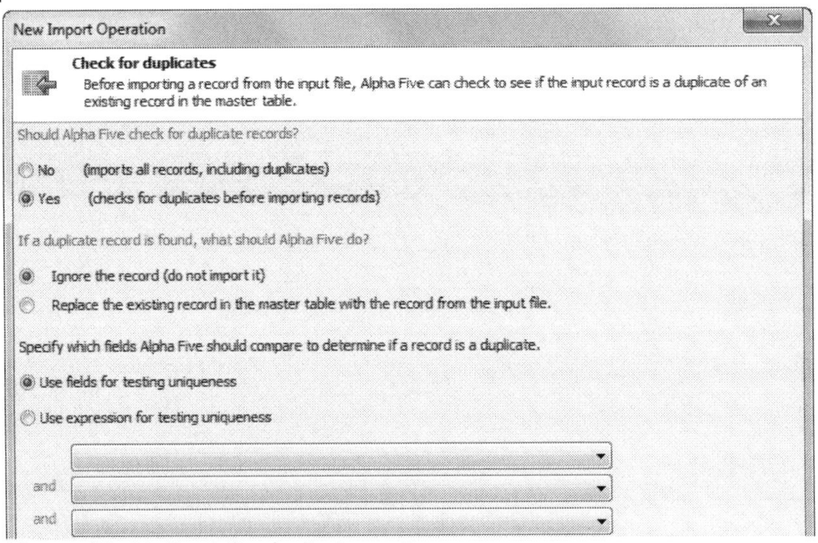

Figure 12-11 Check for duplicates options

6. Select the options shown above in Figure 12-11, then click Next.

7. Select the Don't run option, then click Finish. On the Import Builder, you should see that two fields will not be imported because the Import column has No in it.

8. Click the Save button. Type `aImportExcelToTable` as the operation name.

9. Click the Run Import Operation button on the toolbar. Click OK when you see the message saying 20 records will be imported.

Remote (SQL) Data Options

The two remote data connection options are explained below. Both options can import data from all versions of Excel and data from any sheet in the workbook can be imported.

① **ALPHA DAO IMPORT GENIE** (DAO stands for Data Access Objects) This is the default remote data option. It provides the most control over the data that will be imported. Select this option if the database has an **ODBC DRIVER** or if you want to import more than one sheet of a workbook into the same or different tables at the same time.

② **ADO IMPORT GENIE** (ADO stands for Microsoft's ActiveX Data Objects) In addition to supporting databases like SQL that have an ODBC driver, databases that have an ADO provider are also supported.

Alpha DAO Import Genie

The dialog box shown in Figure 12-12 has three sections, as illustrated. The sections are explained below.

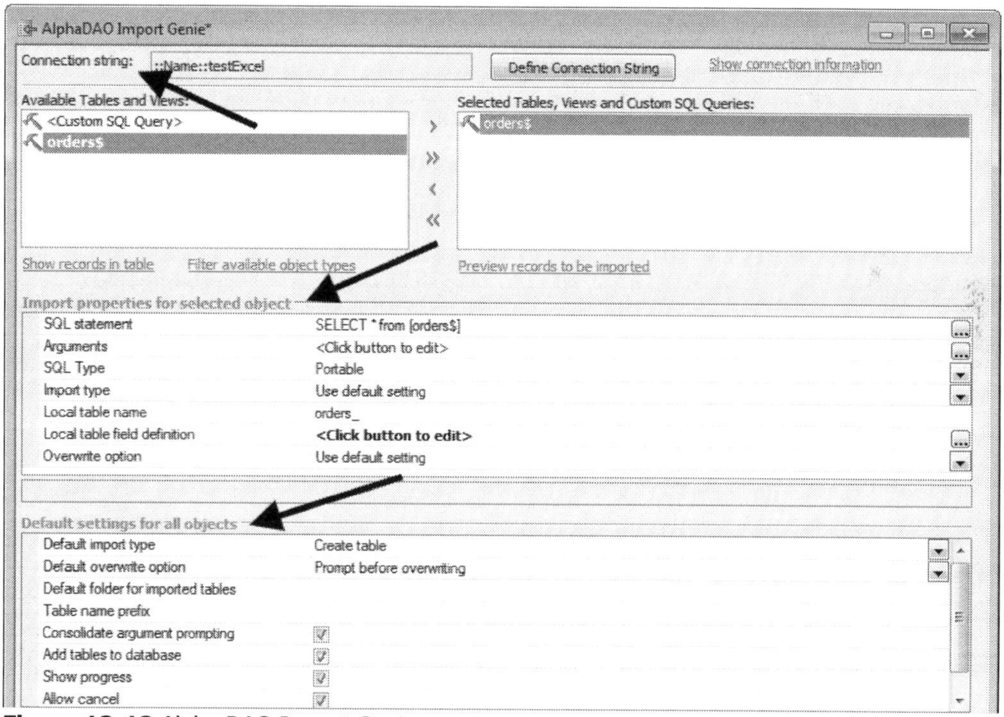

Figure 12-12 Alpha DAO Import Genie

① **CONNECTION TO A DATA SOURCE** The first thing that you will see when you open this dialog box is a message that informs you that there is no connection, as illustrated in Figure 12-13. A connection needs to be created to select the source of the import file.

② **IMPORT PROPERTIES FOR SELECTED OBJECT** For example, a specific table or sheet.

③ **DEFAULT SETTINGS FOR ALL OBJECTS** For all files being imported.

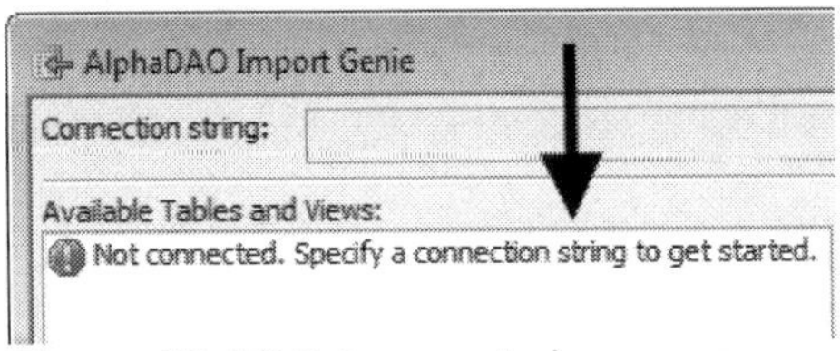

Figure 12-13 Not connected message

Section 1: Connection String

The options in this section are used to select, create and edit connections, as well as view and filter the data that will be imported. The options are explained below.

CONNECTION STRING This field displays the name of the connection string that will be used for the import. Once a connection string is selected, the name appears in this field.

The **SHOW CONNECTION INFORMATION** link is available after a connection string has been selected. Clicking on this link displays the dialog box shown in Figure 12-14.

The **AVAILABLE TABLES AND VIEWS** list is just that. It is a list of the tables and views in the data source that you can select to import data from. **VIEWS** are stored in a database and are like tables, but they do not have the physical characteristics of a table. For example, records cannot be added to or deleted from a view. Fields cannot be added to a view or the length of a field cannot be changed in a view.

The **SELECTED TABLES, VIEWS AND CUSTOM SQL QUERIES** list displays the names of the objects that you selected to import data from.

The **SHOW RECORDS IN TABLE** link displays the data in the table or view selected in the Available Tables and Views list, as shown in Figure 12-15.

The **FILTER AVAILABLE OBJECT TYPES** link displays the options shown in Figure 12-16 that are additional data sources that can be used to import data from.

The **PREVIEW RECORDS TO BE IMPORTED** link displays the records from the data source selected in the Selected Tables list that will be imported.

This dialog box provides information about the connection that you may need to know.

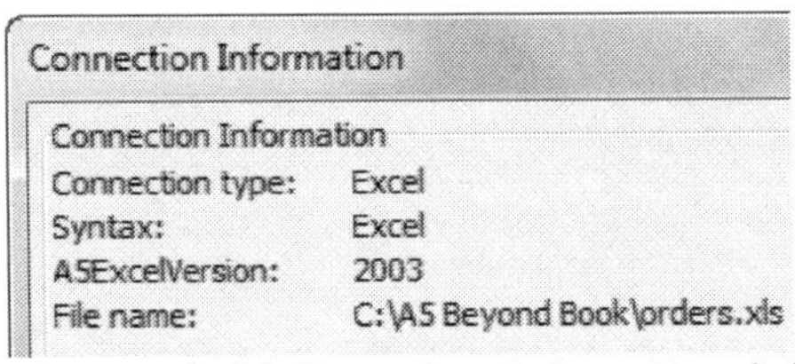

Figure 12-14 Connection Information dialog box

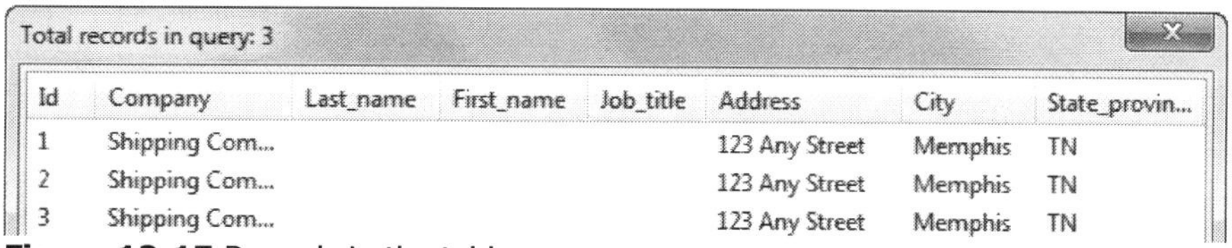

Figure 12-15 Records in the table

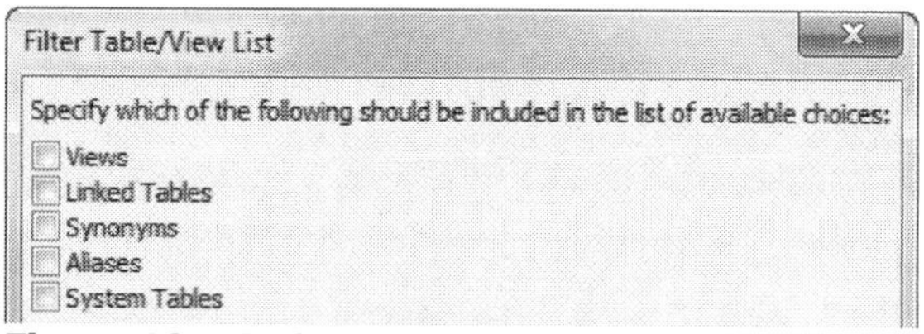

Figure 12-16 Filter Table/View List dialog box

Creating A Connection String

This is less painful then it sounds <smile>. A connection string is the way to let a process know where the data is that should be used. Alpha Five has no way of knowing where any data is unless you let it know.

Clicking the **DEFINE CONNECTION STRING** button opens the dialog box shown in Figure 12-17.

The options are used to select an existing connection string, edit an existing connection string, create a new connection string, select an Access database or select an Excel file. Why do I get the feeling that you feel much better about this connection stuff already <smile>.

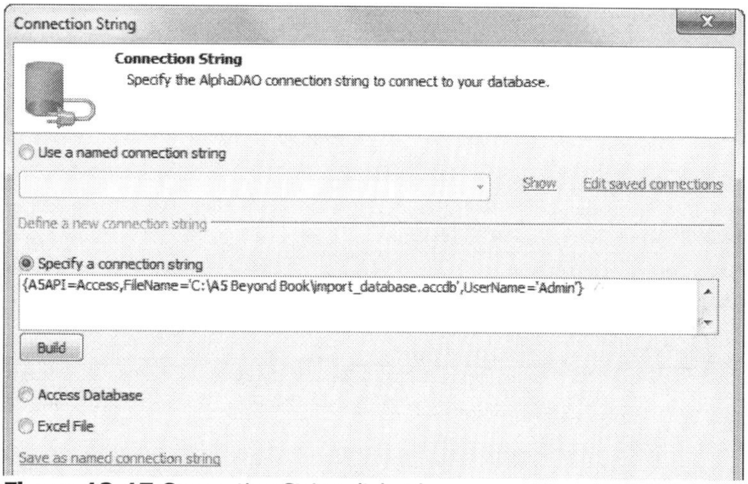

Figure 12-17 Connection String dialog box

Access Database Connection Tip
For Access databases, you only have to use the connection string option if the database is password protected. If the Access database that you are going to import from does not have a User ID and password, select the **ACCESS DATABASE** option, then select the database. If you want to create a new Alpha Five database based on an Access database and want to bring in all of the records in the tables, see the Access Import tip at the end of this chapter.

Connection Options

The options for selecting or creating a connection string are explained below.

Use A Named Connection String Option

Select this option when a connection string already exists for the data source. Open the drop-down list and select the connection string for the data source that you need.

Build Button

If you cannot create a connection string on your own (many people can't), click the **BUILD** button.

The dialog box shown in Figure 12-18 is like a genie because it helps you select the options for the data source that you need to connect to.

The **CONNECTION TYPE** drop-down list has options for the most popular data sources. The other options on the dialog box change, based on the connection type that is selected.

The text in the **CONNECTION STRING** field is what Alpha Five uses to connect to the data source.

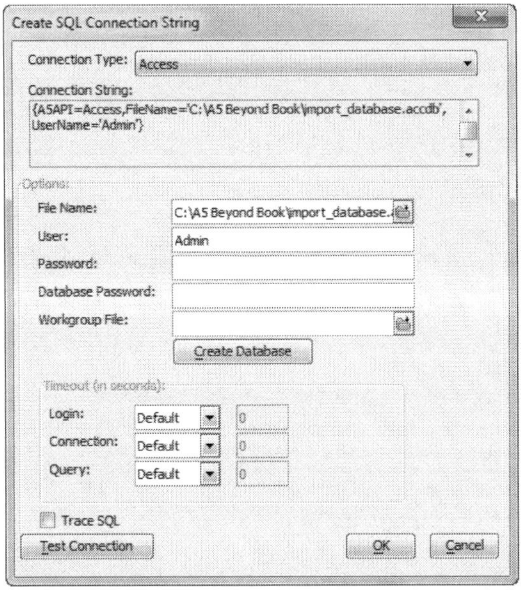

Figure 12-18 Create SQL Connection String dialog box

Edit Saved Connections Link

Clicking on this link on the Connection String dialog box, displays the dialog box shown in Figure 12-19.

A new connection can be created and an existing connection can be modified.

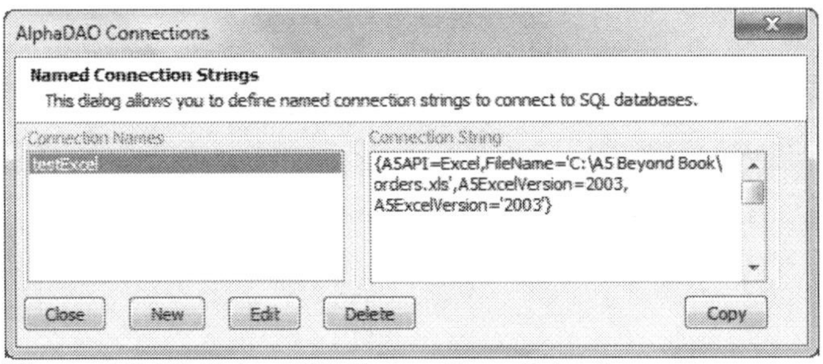

Figure 12-19 Alpha DAO Connections dialog box

Section 2: Import Properties For Selected Object

The options in this section are used to select the import properties for the object selected in the Selected Tables, Views and Custom SQL Queries list. If you are only importing one table or sheet, this is the section to use. The options are explained below.

① **SQL STATEMENT** Is the equivalent of a filter and order expression combined. Use this option when you do not want to import all of the records. There are several dialog boxes that help you create the SQL statement. Clicking the button at the end of the field displays the dialog box shown in Figure 12-20.

② **ARGUMENTS** Opens the Define/Edit Arguments dialog box.

③ **SQL TYPE** The options are Portable, Native and Stored Procedure. Because SQL syntax varies between vendors, the Portable option works with the Portability functions, which SQL and Xbasic both understand. Unless you are using a stored procedure (code already written to select records), use the Portable option.

④ **IMPORT TYPE** Is used to select where the imported data will go. Selecting any of these options (Append to existing table, Create ASCII file, Create XML file) displays different properties then those shown below this option on the Alpha DAO Import Genie (See Figure 12-12). For example, selecting the Create XML file option, only displays the File name option.

⑤ **LOCAL TABLE NAME** The default value is the name of the table or sheet that will be imported. You can change the name.

⑥ **LOCAL TABLE FIELD DEFINITION** Is used to override the field type and size of the imported fields that Alpha Five will select. It is probably a good idea to at least check to see what Alpha Five selects. Figure 12-24, shown later, displays the options.

⑦ **OVERWRITE OPTION** The options in this drop-down list are used to select how you want to be notified during the import process for records that will be overwritten.

SQL Statement Options

The dialog box shown in Figure 12-20 is used to create an SQL statement to select the records.

Select the field(s) from the table that you want to import. If checked, the ***(ALL COLUMNS)** option will add all of the columns to the import.

Clicking the **WHERE** button displays the dialog box shown in Figure 12-21.

Clicking the **ORDER BY** button displays the dialog box shown in Figure 12-22.

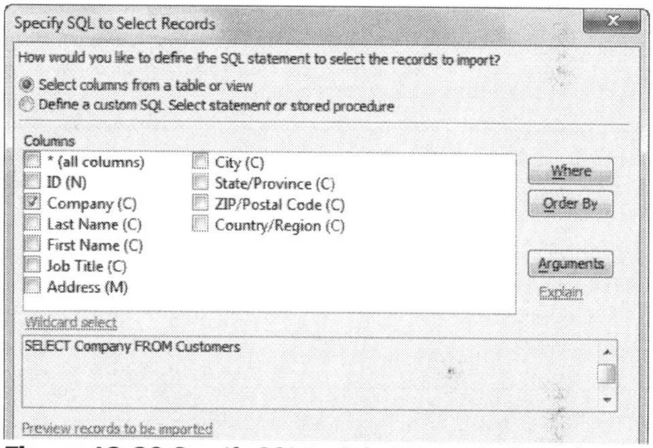

Figure 12-20 Specify SQL to Select Records dialog box

Clicking the **ARGUMENTS** button displays the Define/Edit Arguments dialog box, which was covered earlier in this book. This is pretty cool because you can let the user select the criteria for which records to import at run-time.

The **WILDCARD SELECT** link displays the dialog box shown in Figure 12-23.

The options on this dialog box are used to create conditions that the data must meet to be imported.

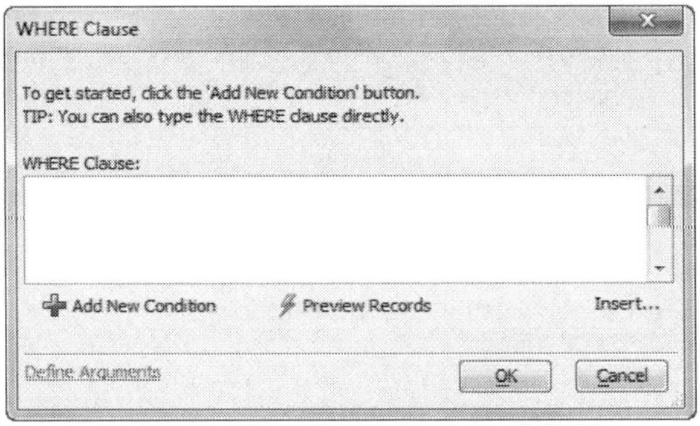

Figure 12-21 WHERE Clause dialog box

The options on this dialog box are used to select how the imported records will be sorted before they are added to the table in Alpha Five.

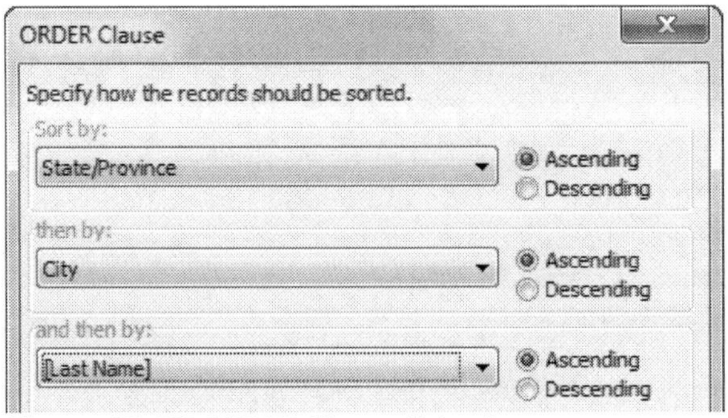

Figure 12-22 ORDER Clause dialog box

The options on this dialog box allow you to use wildcard characters as part of the criteria to select the records to import.

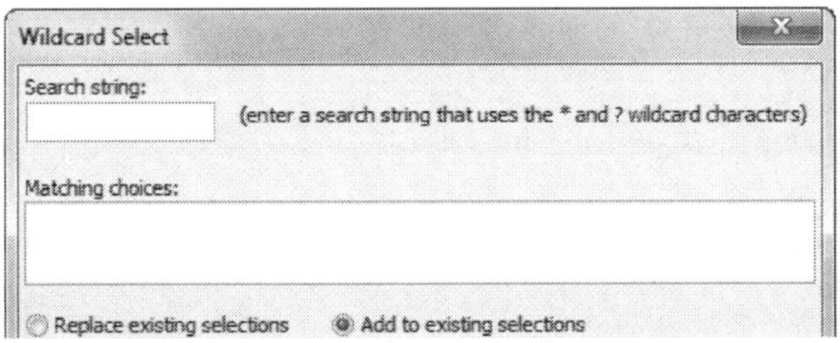

Figure 12-23 Wildcard Select dialog box

Local Table Field Definition

The first two options shown in Figure 12-24 are applied to all fields that are imported that have that field type.

Selecting the Override field definition option, then clicking the Field Definitions button allows you to view and change the definition of each field, as shown in Figure 12-25.

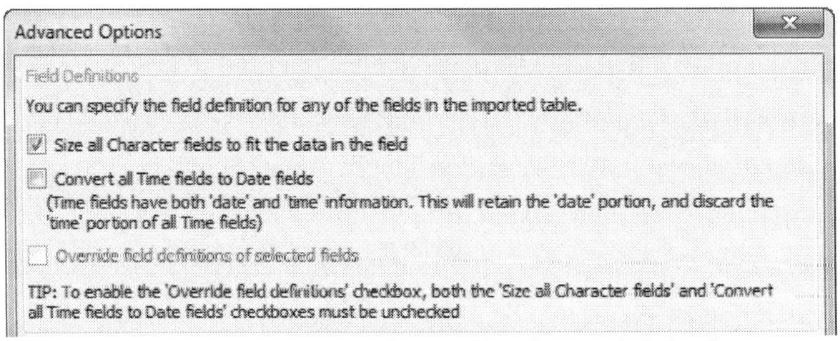

Figure 12-24 Advanced Options (for Field Definitions) dialog box

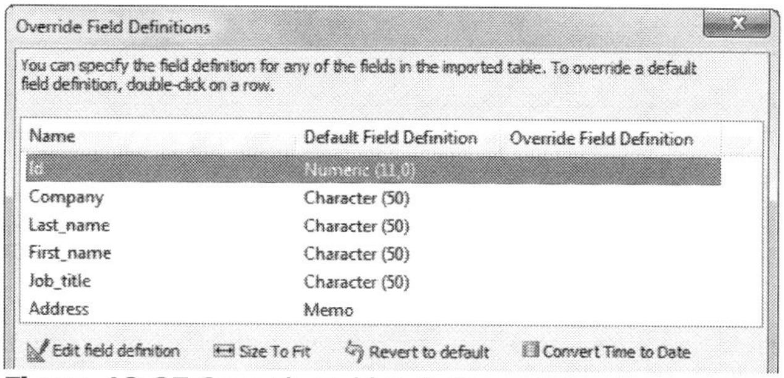

Figure 12-25 Override Field Definitions dialog box

Section 3: Default Settings For All Objects

The options in this section will be applied to all of the objects in the Selected Tables, Views and Custom SQL Queries list. The options are explained below.

① **DEFAULT IMPORT TYPE** [See the Import Type option in Section 2 above]

② **DEFAULT OVERWRITE OPTION** [See the Overwrite option in Section 2 above]

③ **DEFAULT FOLDER FOR IMPORTED TABLES** If you want the new table that will store the imported data stored in a different location then the current database, type in the path to the folder where you want to store the table in this field.

④ **TABLE NAME PREFIX** If you want the tables that will store the imported data to have characters in front of the table name (like IM_Customers), type the prefix (for example, type IM_) in this field.

⑤ **CONSOLIDATE ARGUMENT PROMPTING** If more than one table that you are importing data into has prompts (arguments), checking this option causes all of the prompts to be displayed on one dialog box, instead of a separate dialog box for each table.

⑥ **ADD TABLES TO DATABASE** If checked, the new tables will automatically be added to the current database.

⑦ **SHOW PROGRESS** If checked, a progress bar will be displayed when the data is being imported. This is more helpful if you are importing tens of thousands of records.

⑧ **ALLOW CANCEL** If checked, the import can be cancelled while it is running.

ADO Import Genie

This genie imports data from sources that have an ADO provider. This genie has less options than the Alpha DAO Import Genie, as shown in Figure 12-26. The options are explained below.

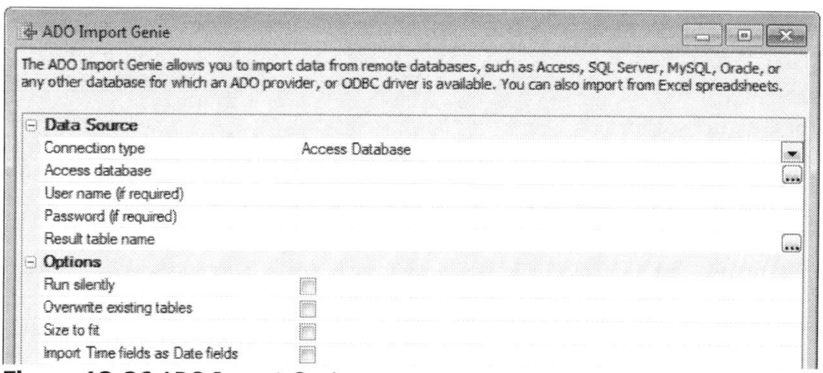

Figure 12-26 ADO Import Genie

Data Source Options

① **CONNECTION TYPE** Is used to select the type of database that you want to connect to or to create a connection string.

② **ACCESS DATABASE** The name of this option changes to match the connection type that is selected. This option is used to select the connection string, database or Excel spreadsheet that data will be imported from.

③ **USER NAME** and **PASSWORD** These options are only used if the database or spreadsheet is password protected.

④ **RESULT TABLE NAME** Is used to select the name of the new table that the data will be imported into. If the table name already exists, any data in the table will be overwritten.

Options Section Options

① **RUN SILENTLY** If checked, errors and prompts will not be displayed when the import is running.

② **OVERWRITE EXISTING TABLES** If checked, existing tables will be overwritten automatically.

③ **SIZE TO FIT** If checked, after the import, the field size will automatically be resized to be as small as possible.

④ **IMPORT TIME FIELDS AS DATE FIELDS** If checked, Date/Time fields will be imported as Date fields.

Exercise 12.3: Import Three Excel Worksheets

In this exercise you will learn how to import three Excel worksheets at the same time. One sheet of data will be added to an existing table and two sheets of data will be used to create two new tables.

Create The Connection To An Excel Workbook

1. On the Import Operation screen, select the Remote (SQL) data - Alpha DAO Import Genie option, then click OK.

2. Click the Define Connection String button.

3. On the Connection String screen, select the Excel File option, then open the **VERSION** drop-down list and select Excel 2010.

4. Click the Excel File field folder icon button, then select the Import3Sheets spreadsheet.

5. Click the **TEST EXCEL CONNECTION** link. You should see the Success message.

6. Click the **SAVE AS NAMED CONNECTION STRING** link, then type `3Sheets` as the Connection name field, as shown in Figure 12-27.

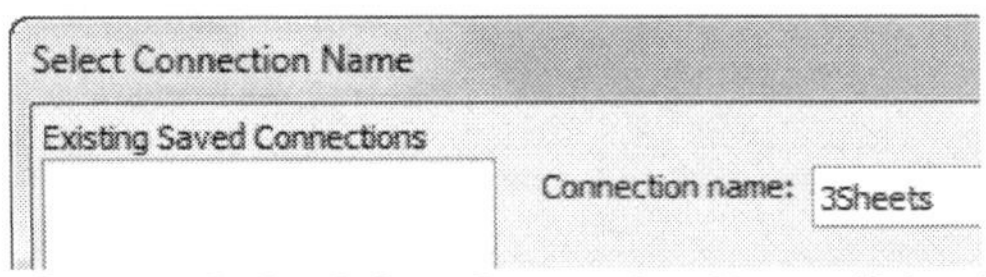

Figure 12-27 Select Connection Name dialog box

7. You should see the connection name in the Use a named connection string field. If you want to view the contents of the connection string, click on the **SHOW** link. You will see the dialog box shown in Figure 12-28. Click Close, then click OK.

Figure 12-28 Connection string dialog box

On the Import Genie, in the Available Tables and Views list, you should see the Orders, Purchase Orders and Students lists.

If the sheets are not renamed in Excel before starting the import, they will look like the ones shown in Figure 12-29. Looking at these sheet names, you have no idea what data they contain.

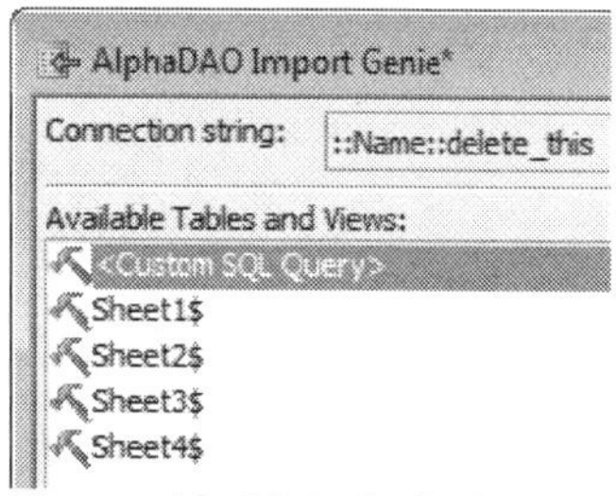

Figure 12-29 Default sheet names

Select The Import Options For The Orders Sheet

In this part of the exercise you will create an SQL statement that selects specific sales reps records to import.

1. Add the three sheets to the list on the right, then click on the Orders sheet.

2. Click the SQL statement field button. Check all of the fields except the Paid By ID and How Shipped fields. This part of the SQL statement says which fields to select for the import, as shown at the bottom of the dialog box.

3. Click the Where button, then click the Add New Condition button. On the Add New Condition dialog box, open the Select a column drop-down list and select the Sales Rep ID field.

4. Open the Select an operator drop-down list and select the **IS EQUAL TO** operator.

5. Click the **CLICK HERE TO SPECIFY MULTIPLE VALUES** link. Type `4`, `5`, `7` and `8`, as shown in Figure 12-30. The **SELECT** button displays the values in the field, as shown in Figure 12-31. You can select the fields on this dialog box instead of typing them in.

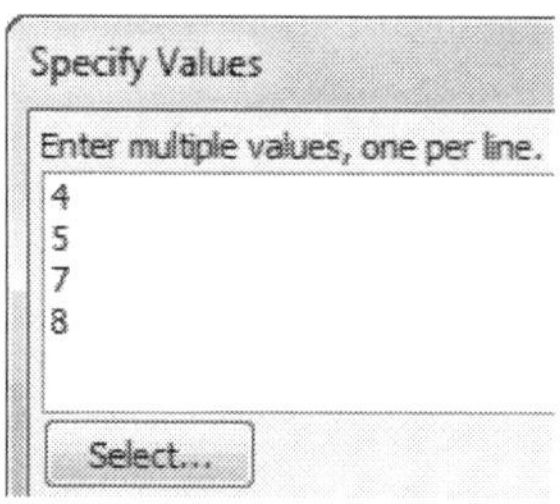

Figure 12-30 Specify Values dialog box

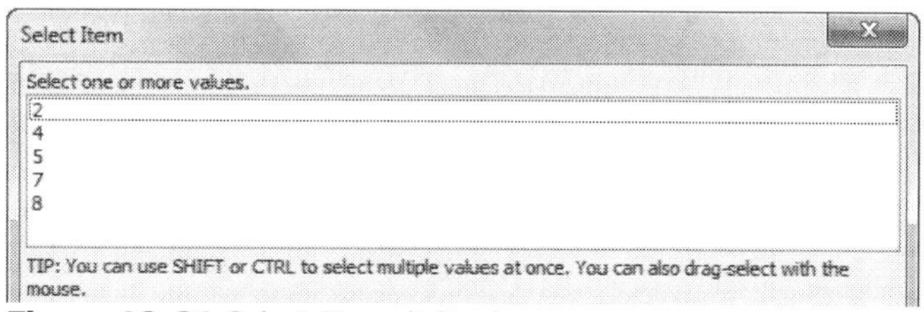

Figure 12-31 Select Item dialog box

6. You should have the options shown in Figure 12-32. Click OK. The WHERE clause should look like the one shown in Figure 12-33. Click OK. The SQL statement should look like the one shown in Figure 12-34.

As shown at the bottom of Figure 12-34, the options on the WHERE Clause dialog box were added to the end of the SQL statement. The statement says which fields to select and what requirements the records must meet in order to be imported. And to think, you did not want to learn how to create SQL statements <smile>. If you want to view the records that will be imported, click the Preview records to be imported link. You will see the dialog box shown earlier in Figure 12-15.

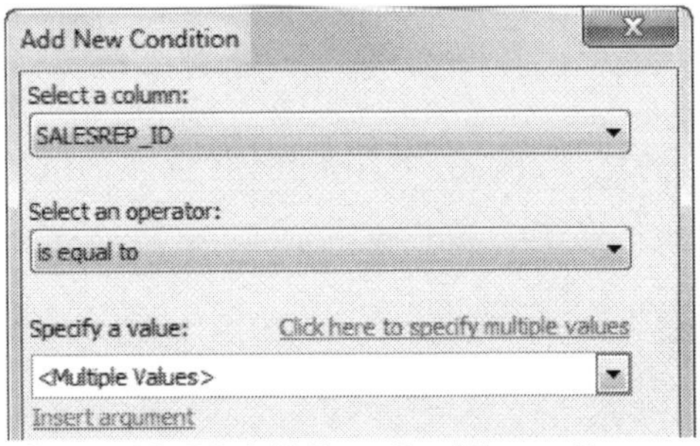

Figure 12-32 Add New Condition options

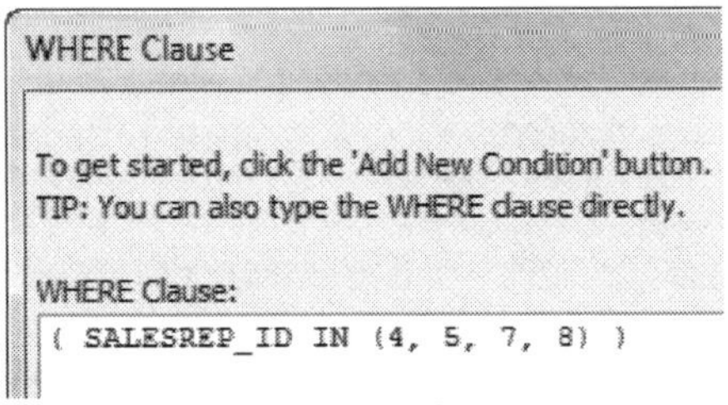

Figure 12-33 WHERE Clause

```
SELECT ORDER_ID, CUSTOMER_ID, SALESREP_ID, ORDER_DATE, DATE_SHIPPED, SHIPVIA_ID
FROM [orders$] WHERE SALESREP_ID IN (4, 5, 7, 8)
```

Figure 12-34 SQL statement

7. On the Import Genie, open the Import type field drop-down list and select **APPEND TO EXISTING TABLE**.

8. Open the Master table name field drop-down list and select the aImportOperation table.

Map The Fields

This process matches the fields in the Transaction table (the table that has the records to import) to fields in the Master table (the table that records will be added to). In this exercise all of the fields in the Transaction table (the Orders tab on the spreadsheet) will be imported. The Map Fields dialog box makes this process easy and will attempt to match the fields for you, if you want.

1. Click the Field Map field button, then click the **SUGGEST MATCHES** link.

As shown in Figure 12-35, the majority of fields were mapped.

The Paid By ID and How Shipped fields do not have a match because they were not selected to be imported. If you open the drop-down list for these fields, you will not see them, which is correct.

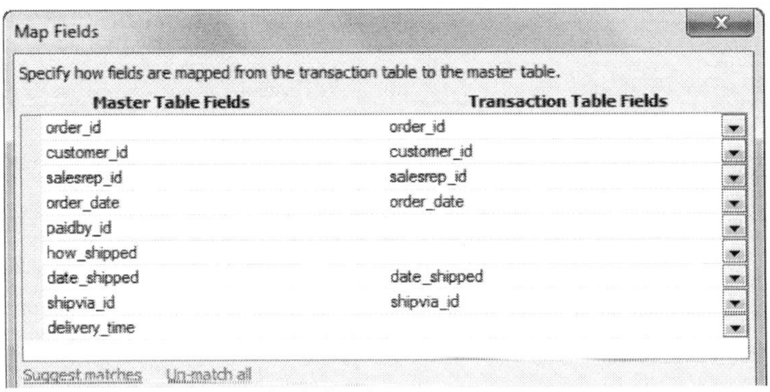

Figure 12-35 Map Fields dialog box

The Delivery time field is not in the Transaction table. If it was there with a different name, you would select it.

2. Click OK. Click the Save button on the toolbar. Type `aImport3ExcelSheets` as the name of the import operation.

Select The Import Options For The Purchase Orders Sheet

This sheet will be used to create a new table.

1. Click on the Purchase Orders sheet in the list in the upper right corner of the dialog box.
2. Change the Import type to Create table.
3. Change the Local table name field to `aPurchaseOrders`.
4. Click the Local table field definition field button. Select the Override option, then click the Field Definitions button.
5. Select the Purchase Order ID field, then click the **EDIT FIELD DEFINITION** button.
6. Change the Data type to Numeric, then change the Width to `8`, as shown in Figure 12-36.

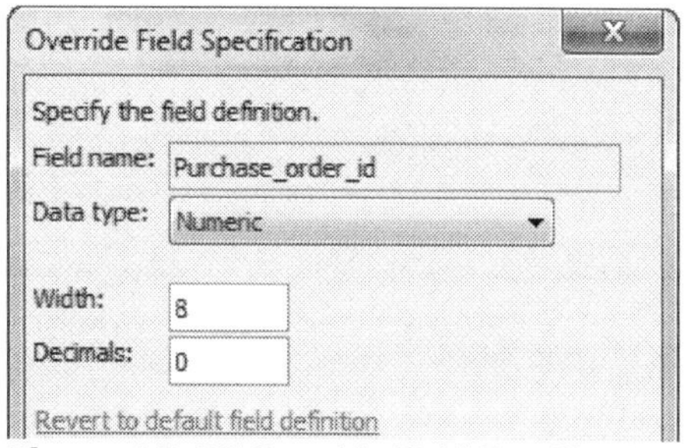

Figure 12-36 Override Field Specification dialog box

7. Change the Creation date and Submitted date fields to the Date data type by selecting the field, then clicking the **CONVERT TIME TO DATE** button. You should have the options shown in Figure 12-37.

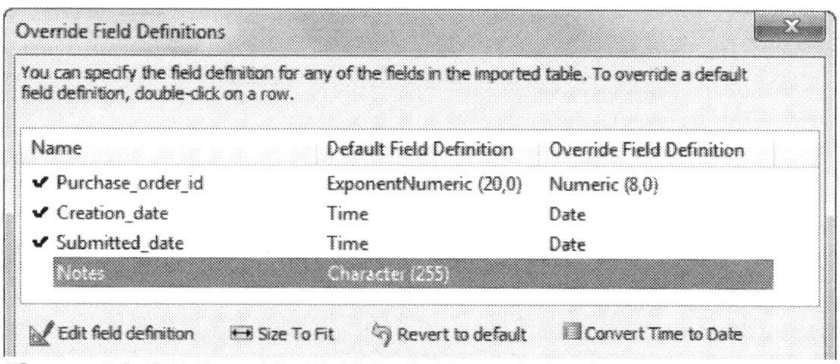

Figure 12-37 Override Field Definitions dialog box

Select The Import Options For The Students Sheet

1. Select the Students sheet, then change the properties in Table 12-1.

Property	Change To
Import type	Create table
Local table name	aNewStudents
Local table field definition	Remove the check mark for the Size all characters option on the Advanced Options dialog box.

Table 12-1 Import properties for the Students sheet

> **SQL Tip**
> The SQL Select statement shown in Figure 12-38 will select all of the records and import all of the fields on the sheet.

Figure 12-38 SQL statement

Run The Import

1. Save the changes, then click the Run button on the toolbar.

   When finished, you will see the dialog box shown in Figure 12-39. It displays the status of the import.

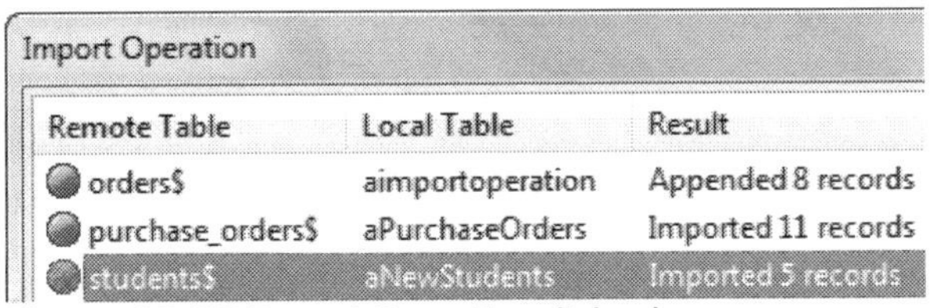

Figure 12-39 Import Operation dialog box

   Green icons indicate that the import operation was successful. If there was a problem, the icon would be red. Notice that the Result column indicates the number of records and how they were added to the database.

2. Close the Import Genie. If you look on the Tables/Sets tab, you will see the two new tables created from the import. The aImportOperation table has more records now.

Exercise 12.4: Create A Connection For An Import From Scratch

In the previous exercise you set up a connection to an Excel workbook. This exercise will show you how to create a connection to a database from scratch.

1. On the Operations tab, click the New button ⇒ Import Records ⇒ Create Using Genie button.
2. Select the Remote (SQL) data option, the Alpha DAO Import Genie option, then click OK.
3. Click the Define Connection String button. On the Connection string screen select the **SPECIFY A CONNECTION STRING** option, then click the Build button.
4. On the Create SQL Connection String dialog box, select the Access connection type option, if it is not already selected.

5. Click the File Name field button. Change the File type (drop-down list in lower right corner of the **SELECT ACCESS DATABASE** dialog box) to Access 2007 database (*.accd*), then select the Import_Database database.

6. You should have the options shown in Figure 12-40.

   Click the **TEST CONNECTION** button. You should see a message with the word "Succeeded".

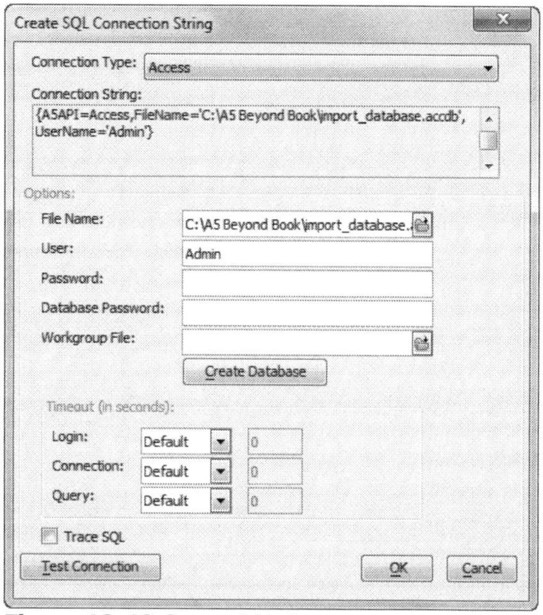

Figure 12-40 Create SQL Connection String dialog box

7. On the Connection String dialog box, click the **SAVE AS NAMED CONNECTION STRING** link. Type `Access_Connection`, as the Connection name. You should have the options shown in Figure 12-41. Click OK.

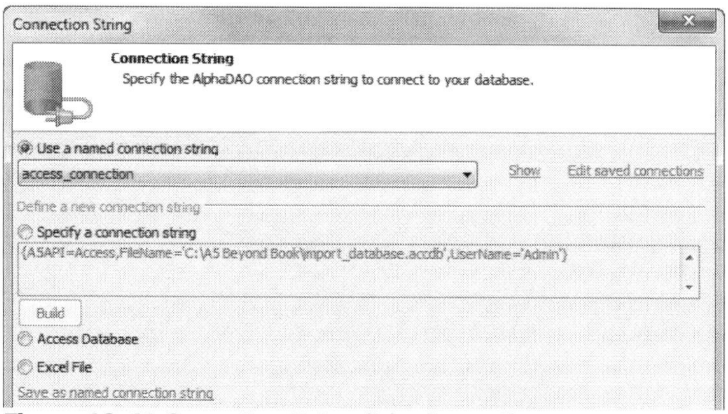

Figure 12-41 Connection String dialog box options

8. Change the Local table name to aCustomersImport.

9. Add the Customers table to the list on the right, then save the import connection as `aImportAccessDB`. Close the genie. If you wanted to practice, you could select the import property options, then import the table. Doing this is optional, as the data is not needed for the rest of this book.

Importing Layout Definitions

Alpha Five provides a feature to import layouts (forms, reports, etc). This is helpful if there is a layout in another Alpha Five database that you want to use in the current database. Layouts are stored in a file with the extension **.A5PKG**.

Exercise 12.5: Import A Report Layout

In this exercise you will import a report layout file.

1. From any layout tab, Layout ⇒ Import Layout.

2. Select the Orders by State report package in your folder, then click the Open button. If you click on the Reports tab, you should see the Orders by state report.

Access Database Import Tip
If you are creating a new Alpha Five database and want to import all records in the table(s), follow the steps below.
1. On the Select Workspace dialog box, click on the **CREATE A WORKSPACE FROM IMPORTED DATA** option.
2. Click the folder button at the end of the Microsoft Access Database field, then select the Access database that you want to import data from. You should see the database that you selected in the field, as shown in Figure 12-42.
3. Click OK. Navigate to the folder where you want to save the new Alpha Five database. In the File name field, type the name for the new database, then click Save.
4. On the dialog box shown in Figure 12-43, select the tables, views, etc., that you want to import, then click OK. The objects that you selected will be imported. You will see the Import Operation dialog box, shown earlier in Figure 12-39.

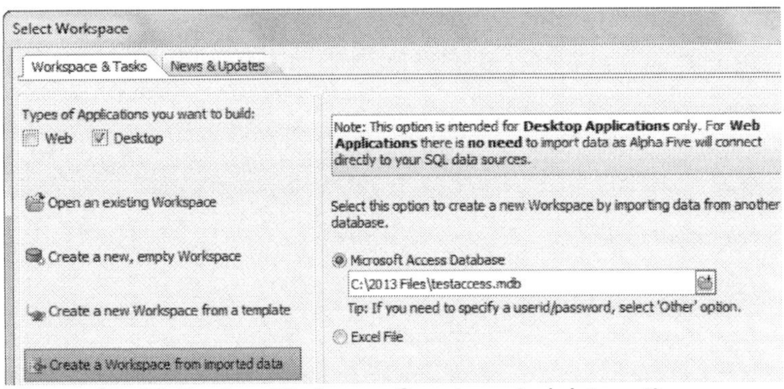

Figure 12-42 Create a Workspace from imported data options

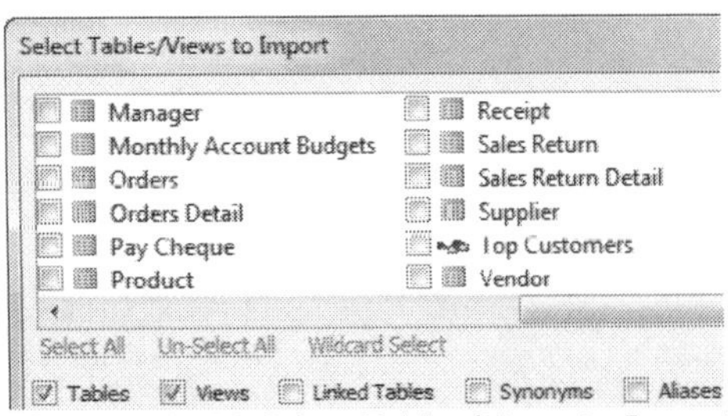

Figure 12-43 Select Tables/Views to Import dialog box

USING OPERATIONS

In this chapter you will learn how to create the following operations:

- ☑ Ad-Hoc
- ☑ Convert case of fields
- ☑ Search and Replace
- ☑ Join Tables
- ☑ Mark Duplicate Records
- ☑ Crosstab
- ☑ Post Records

CHAPTER 13

Overview

In Chapter 11, you learned how to create queries and save them. When the queries were saved, they were saved as operations. If you have the need to manipulate data and do not really want to write code to do it, this chapter will be very useful. Alpha Five comes with several operation genies, if you will, that you can customize to meet your needs. Some of the operation genies use functions to complete the task. You can copy the expression created by the genie and modify it to meet your needs. You may find this easier then creating expressions from scratch, in some cases.

What Are Operations And How Will They Help Me?

Operations are pre-built scripts that are used to manipulate data in records and specific fields. The operations can be used to add data to fields, add or delete rows of data, import data (covered in Chapter 12), create new tables, export data and much more. This means that you have the ability to add or change hundreds or thousands of records at the click of a button. Using operations will keep you from having to write Xbasic code to accomplish the same task. Each operation has its own genie to help you select the options. Even better, you can link operations together by adding them to a button on a form.

AD-HOC Operations

There may be times when you only need to use an operation once and do not have the need to save it.

When that is the case, an ad-hoc operation may be the solution, even though they cannot be saved.

The Ad-Hoc operations are on the Records menu, as illustrated in Figure 13-1, when viewing a form or browse. They are explained in Table 13-1.

What you will like about Ad-Hoc operations is that they usually have less steps then creating an operation that can be saved. They have a subset of the features that the operations created from the Operations tab have.

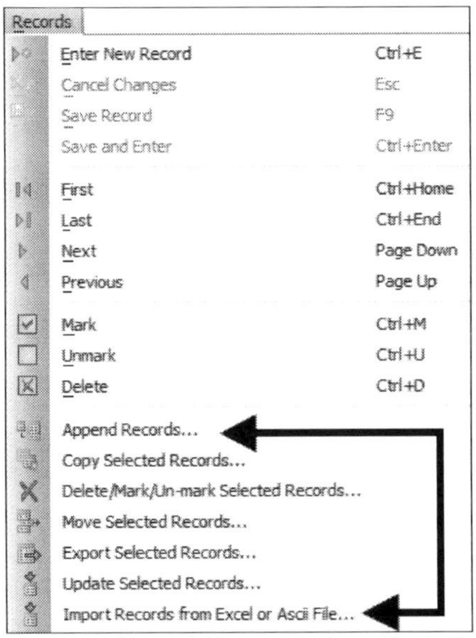

Figure 13-1 Ad-Hoc operations illustrated

Operation	Description
Append Records	Adds records in one table to another table. The field names in both tables have to be the same. If they aren't, you have to use the Append operation on the Operations tab. You can select to append all records, unique records only or unique records and replace existing records.
Copy Selected Records	Copies the selected records in the form or browse to a new or existing table. The form or browse can be based on a table or set.

Table 13-1 Ad-Hoc operations explained

Operation	Description
Delete/Mark/Un-mark Selected Records	Deletes, marks or un-marks the selected records by selecting an option on the dialog box shown in Figure 13-2. Unless you want to delete, mark or un-mark all of the records, create a filter to select the records, then select this option. Marking records creates a pseudo group, if you will. I say that because records in a group have something in common. Marked records do not have to have anything in common. On the Operations tab there are individual operations for Delete, Mark and Un-mark.
Move Selected Records	Moves the selected records to an existing table and then deletes them from the current table. There is no corresponding option on the Operations tab. The closest option on the Operations tab is the **SUBTRACT RECORDS OPERATION**. The **TARGET TABLE** is the one that the records will be moved to and must have the same fields as the **SOURCE TABLE** that they are being moved from.
Export Selected Records	Copies the selected records to another file format by selecting options on the dialog box shown in Figure 13-3.
Update Selected Records	Updates the value in up to five fields at the same time. You can select the records on the browse that you want to update, then open this operation to update the selected records.
Import Records from Excel or ASCII File	Add records to the current table from an Excel or comma delimited file by selecting options on the dialog box shown in Figure 13-15.

Table 13-1 Ad-Hoc operations explained (Continued)

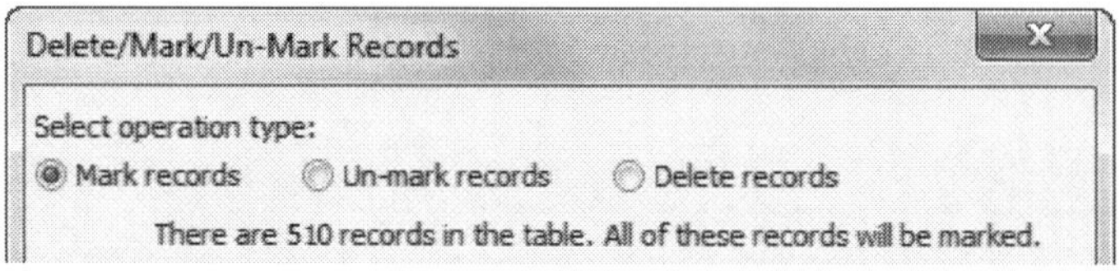

Figure 13-2 Delete/Mark/Un-Mark Records dialog box (Ad-Hoc operation)

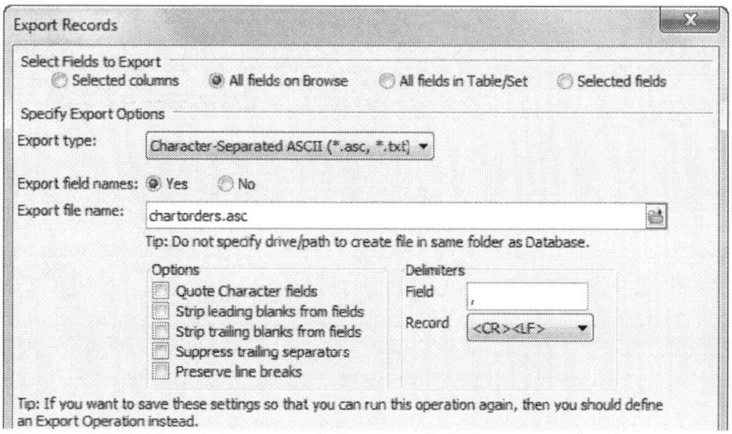

Figure 13-3 Export Records dialog box (Ad-Hoc operation)

Operation Exercise Notes

① Some of the exercises will have you duplicate a table. When you duplicate the table, only duplicate the records. Do not duplicate the indexes, dictionary or field rules.

② When instructed to view a table, view it in the Default Browse.

Exercise 13.1: Use The Append Records Ad-Hoc Operation

In this exercise you will learn how to append records based on a filter.

1. Duplicate the Order Detail table. Save it as `aAdHocAppend`.
2. View the aAdHocAppend table. Records ⇒ Append Records.
3. Click the Select button, then select the aPreviousValues table.
4. Check the **FILTER RECORDS BEFORE APPENDING?** option, then create an expression to select records if the Qty is greater than or equal to 10.
5. You should have the options shown in Figure 13-4.

   Click OK.

   You should see a message that says 347 records will be appended.

   Click Yes.

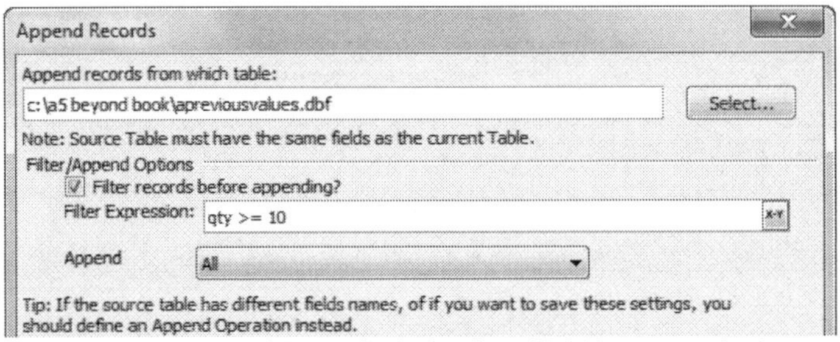

Figure 13-4 Append Records dialog box (Ad-Hoc operation)

The **UNIQUE RECORDS ONLY** and **UNIQUE RECORDS AND REPLACE EXISTING RECORDS** append options display the Common Key field shown in Figure 13-5. This option is used to sort the records that will be appended by using the Order Builder or creating an order expression on the dialog box shown in Figure 13-6.

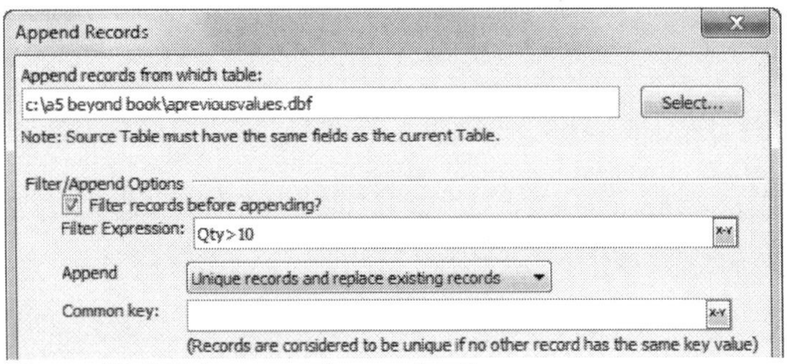

Figure 13-5 Unique record append options

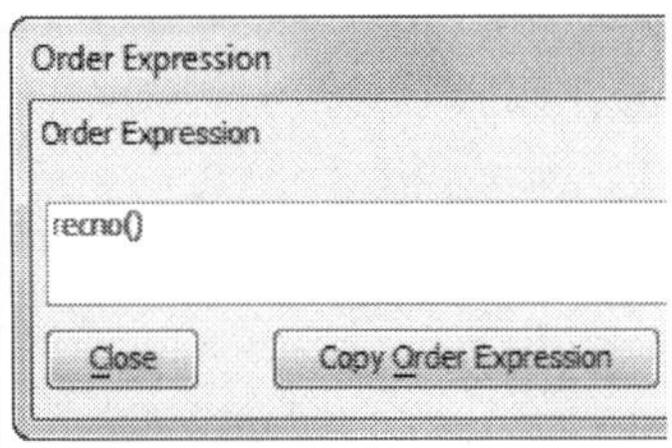

Figure 13-6 Order Expression dialog box

Exercise 13.2: Use The Copy Selected Records Ad-Hoc Operation

In this exercise you will use this operation to copy some fields in a set to a new table. Using a set as the data source means that you can select fields from any of the tables in the set.

1. View the Chart Customer Orders set in the Default Browse, then Records ⇒ Copy Selected Records.

2. In the Table name field type `aAdHocCopyNewTable`.

Select Fields To Copy Options

The options in this section are used to select what fields will be copied to the new table. The options are explained below.

① **SELECTED COLUMNS** Will only copy the columns that are highlighted (selected) before this dialog box was opened.

② **ALL FIELDS ON BROWSE** Is the default option. All of the fields and records displayed on the browse will be copied. This means that you can create a filter on the browse to select the records that will be copied to the table, then open this dialog box.

③ **ALL FIELDS IN TABLE/SET** Copies all fields in the underlying table or set.

④ **SELECTED FIELDS** Is used to select the fields that will be copied. If you are copying the records to a new table, you can also select the order of the fields that will be added to the new table.

3. Select the Select Fields option, then click the Select Fields button.

   Add the fields in the order shown in the Selected Fields column in Figure 13-7.

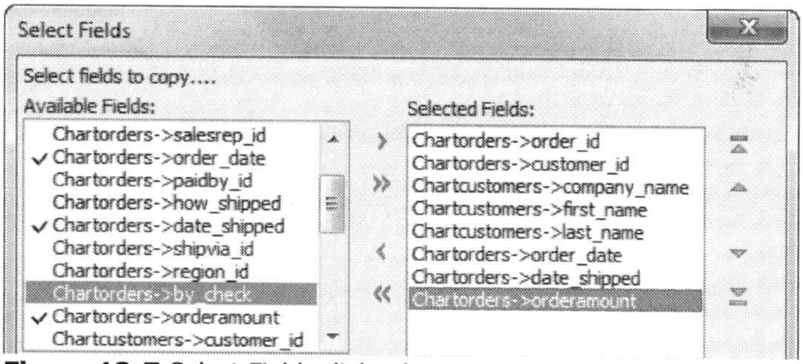

Figure 13-7 Select Fields dialog box

4. Clear the **COPY DICTIONARY** option shown in Figure 13-8, then click OK.

   Click OK when prompted to copy records.

   Click Yes to view the aAdHocCopyNewTable table.

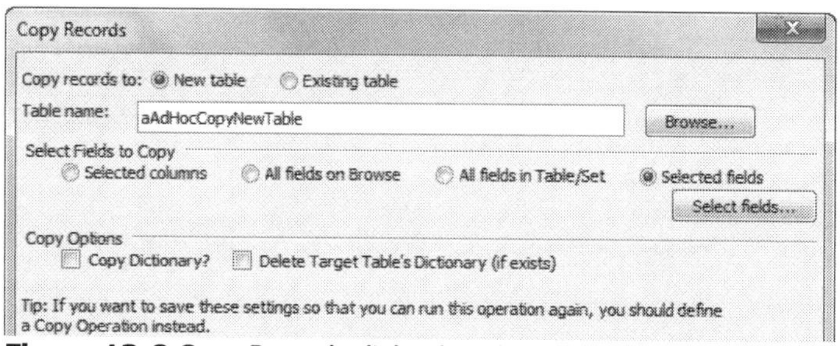

Figure 13-8 Copy Records dialog box (Ad-Hoc operation)

Copying Records To An Existing Table

Selecting the **EXISTING TABLE** option displays the options shown in Figure 13-9. If you select a table that does not have the same structure, you will see the dialog box shown in Figure 13-10.

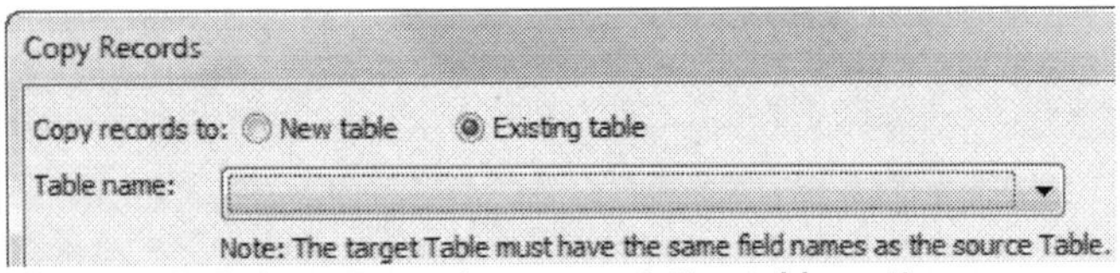

Figure 13-9 Copy Records to an existing table options

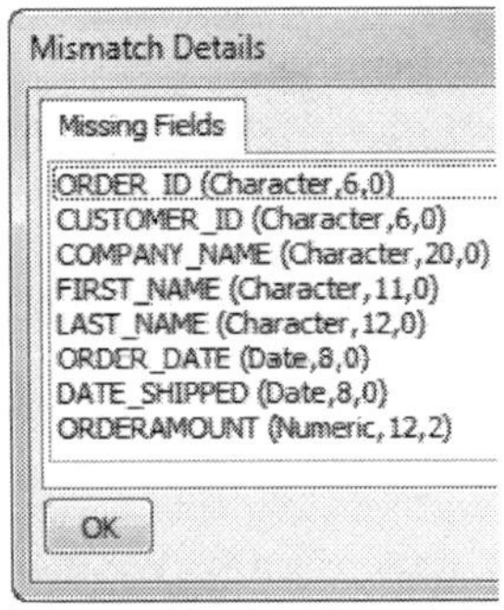

Figure 13-10 Mismatch Details dialog box

Exercise 13.3: Use The Move Selected Records Ad-Hoc Operation

In this exercise you will create a filter that selects the records that will be moved to another table.

1. Open the table structure of the aAdHocCopyNewTable table. Change the Type of the Order ID and Customer ID fields to numeric.

2. Display the aAdHocCopyNewTable in the Default Browse.

3. Create and run a query that selects records where the Company name field is blank. These are the records that will be moved to another table.

Move The Selected Records To A New Table

1. Records ⇒ Move Selected Records.

2. Open the Target Table drop-down list and select the Move Records Here table, as shown in Figure 13-11.

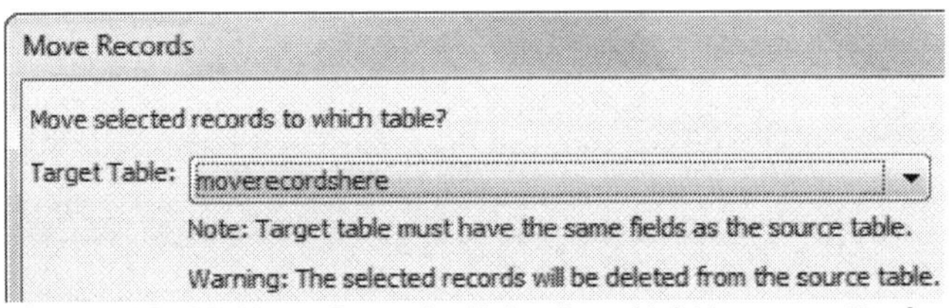

Figure 13-11 Move Records dialog box (Ad-Hoc operation)

3. Click OK twice, then click Yes to view the records that were moved. Notice that the Company name field is blank (in the Move Records Here table), which is correct.

4. Re-open the aAdHocCopyNewTable table in the Default Browse. All of the records in the table have a value in the Company name field, which is correct.

Exercise 13.4: Move Records To Another Table

The source and target tables in this exercise do not have the same fields, so one table will have to be modified before records can be moved.

1. Save the Orders table as `aMoveSource`. Save the Order lookup table as `aMoveTarget`.

2. Delete the By Check field from the aMoveSource table.

3. View the aMoveSource table in the Default Browse. Records ⇒ Move Selected Records.

4. Select the aMoveTarget table on the Move Records dialog box, then click OK.

   The message shown in Figure 13-12 displays how many records will be moved. Click Yes.

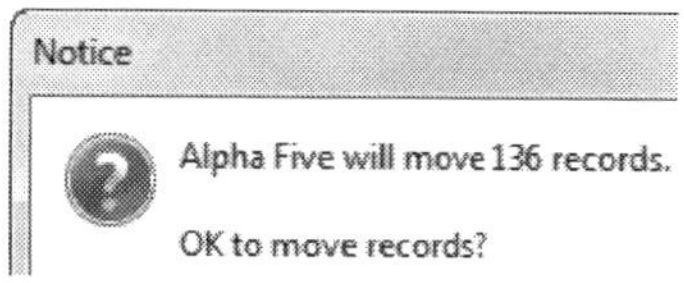

Figure 13-12 Move Records message

5. Click Yes to view the target table.

Exercise 13.5: Updating Fields

When a field is updated, any data already in the field is overwritten. In this exercise you will update the Country field to "USA".

1. View the aContacts table in the Default Browse, then Records ⇒ Update Selected Records.

2. Open the Field name drop-down list and select the Country field.

3. In the Update Expression field type `"USA"`, as shown in Figure 13-13, then click OK.

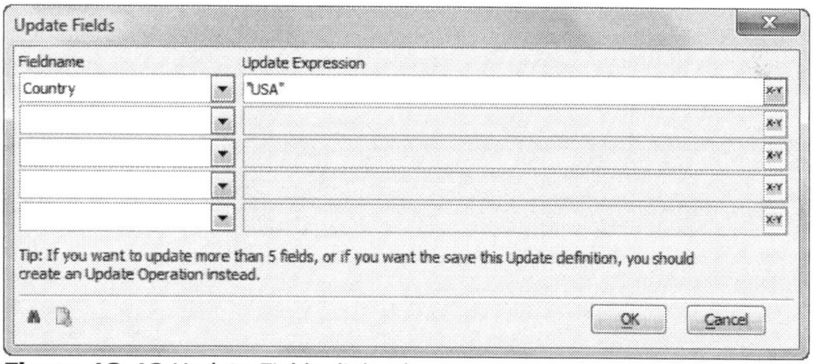

Figure 13-13 Update Fields dialog box

4. When prompted that 59 records will be updated, click Yes. If you check the Country field in the aContacts table, you will see that all records have USA in the field.

Exercise 13.6: Use The Update Selected Records Ad-Hoc Operation For Selected Records

In the previous exercise you used the Update Selected Records operation to update a field for all of the records in a table. In this exercise you will select (highlight) a few records in the browse, then change the value of a field for the selected records, not all of the records in the table.

1. View the Move Records Here table in the Default Browse, then select the first 10 records.

2. Records ⇒ Update Selected Records.

3. Open the Field name drop-down list and select the Company name field.

4. In the Update Expression field type `"*Get company name*"`, as shown in Figure 13-14.

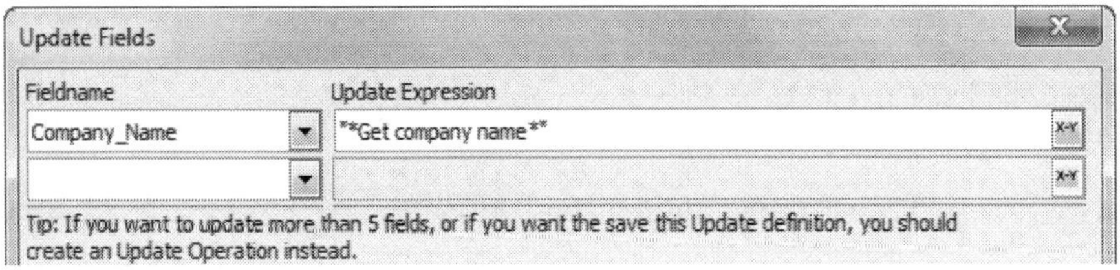

Figure 13-14 Update Fields dialog box (Ad-Hoc Operation)

5. Click OK. Click Yes to update the 10 records. You should see that the records that you selected now have something in the company name field.

Exercise 13.7: Import Records

In the previous chapter you learned how to customize the import process. The import process covered in this exercise is geared towards one time only importing of data from an Excel spreadsheet or ASCII file because there are not a lot of options to select and the import options cannot be saved.

A lot of people keep data in an spreadsheet that needs to be added to a database application. Instead of retyping the data in the database, spreadsheet data can be added to a table in the database. The key to using the Ad-Hoc Import option on the Records menu is that the file that has the data to import has to have the same field names. Only fields with matching names will be imported.

The fields in the file to import do not have to be in the same order as they are in the table in the database. As you will see, the data being imported does not have the Region ID field. When fields do not have the same name, create an Import operation or rename the columns in the spreadsheet and save the spreadsheet with a new name.

1. Save the Orders table as `aImportedData`, then preview the table in the Default Browse.

2. Records ⇒ Import Records from Excel or ASCII file.

3. Click the Select button, then select the orders.xls spreadsheet in your folder.

4. You should have the options shown in Figure 13-15.

   Click OK.

   Figure 13-16 displays the records that will be imported.

   Click the OK - Import Records button.

   The records will be imported.

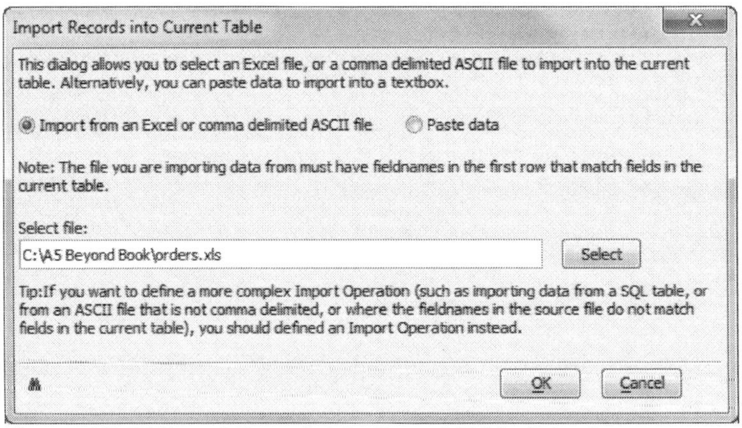

Figure 13-15 Import Records into Current Table dialog box

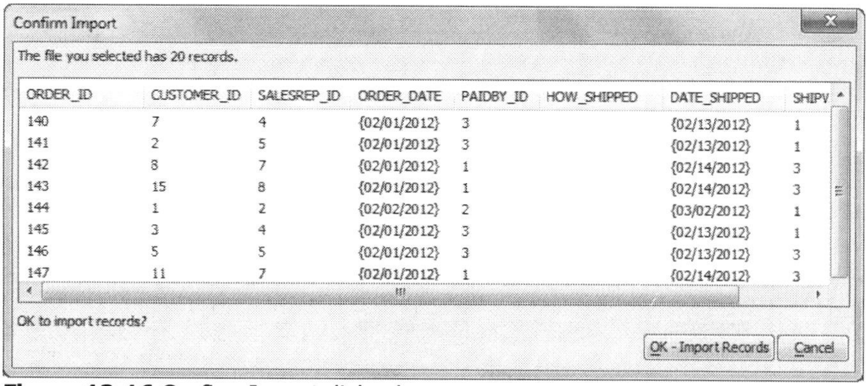

Figure 13-16 Confirm Import dialog box

Operations

So far, the operations that you created in this chapter could not be saved. The operations explained in Table 13-2 can be saved. These operations are accessed from the New button on the Operations tab on the Control Panel.

Operation	Is Used To . . .
Append Records	[See Table 13-1, Append Records]
Convert case of fields	Change text to lower case, upper case or mixed case. This operation has the same functionality as the **LOWER**, **UPPER** and **F_UPPER FUNCTIONS** that you learned about in Chapter 5. (1)
Copy Records	[See Table 13-1, Copy Selected Records]
Crosstab	Create a table that has summarized data. Usually the data summarized would be in the Detail section of the report.
Delete Duplicate Records	Find and delete records that have the same value in fields that you select.
Delete Records	Delete the selected records.
Export Records	Save data to a different file format or to a remote SQL database.
Import Records	Import data that is not in Alpha Five format into an Alpha Five table. [See Chapter 12, Importing Data]
Intersect Records	Create a new table from data that is in two other tables. This operation only adds records that are in both tables in the new table. This means that you can select from the records that are in both tables to create the new table.
Join Tables	Combine two tables that have at least one field in common to create a new table.
Mark Duplicate Records	Find duplicate records based on criteria that you select and mark the records as duplicate.
Mark Records	[See Table 13-1, Delete/Mark/Un-Mark/Selected Records]
Post Records	Update the values in a field in one table with values in a field from a different table.
Query Records	Create filter and sort criteria to select records.
Search and Replace	Look for a value in a field and replace it with a different value. (1)

Table 13-2 Operations explained

Operation	Is Used To . . .
Subtract Records	Create a new table from either of the following: ① From records in the master table (current data) that are not in the transaction table (new data). This option lets you know which records in the master table are not in the transaction table. ② From records in the transaction table (new data) that are not in the master table (current data). This option lets you know which records from the transaction table were added to the master table.
Summarize Records	Create a new table by summarizing data based on groups that you select. The new table will contain one row of data for each unique value for the field(s) being grouped on.
Unmark Duplicate Records	Find duplicate records that are marked and remove the marked tag from the records.
Unmark Records	Remove the marked tag from records that are selected.
Update Records	[See Table 13-1, Update Selected Records]

Table 13-2 Operations explained (Continued)

(1) This operation does not have a builder. [See How To Create An Operation, below]

How To Create An Operation

There are two ways to create an operation, as explained below.

① **USE THE GENIE** I suspect that this is the most popular way to create an operation, because the options that you need to select are presented to you.

② **USE THE BUILDER** In addition to each operation having its own genie, most operations have their own builder.

The builders display the options on one screen for you to select. Figures 13-17 to 13-19 show some of the builders.

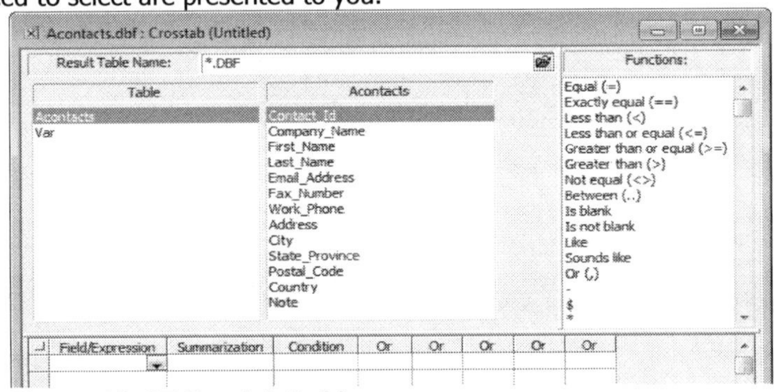

Figure 13-17 Crosstab Builder

Figure 18-18 Join Builder

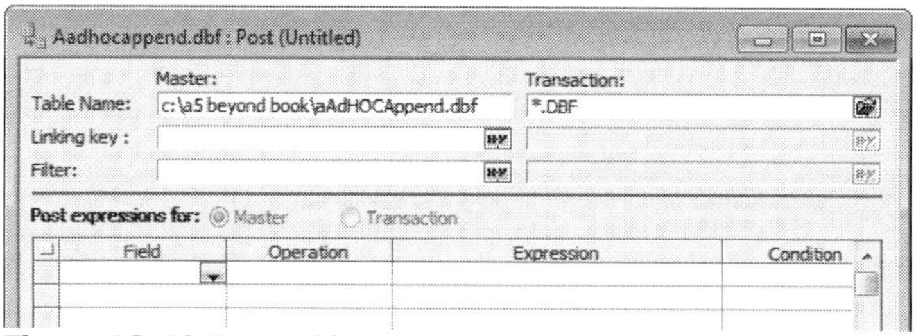

Figure 13-19 Post Builder

Operation Menu And Toolbar

The majority of options on the Operation menu and toolbar are the same as the ones on the Form View toolbar. Figure 13-20 shows the menu when no operation is selected.

Clicking on a saved operation replaces the Operation menu shown in Figure 13-20 with one for the type of operation that is selected. Figure 13-21 shows the menu when a Query operation is selected on the Operations tab.

When an operation is open in Design mode, a menu and toolbar similar to the ones shown in Figure 13-22 is displayed.

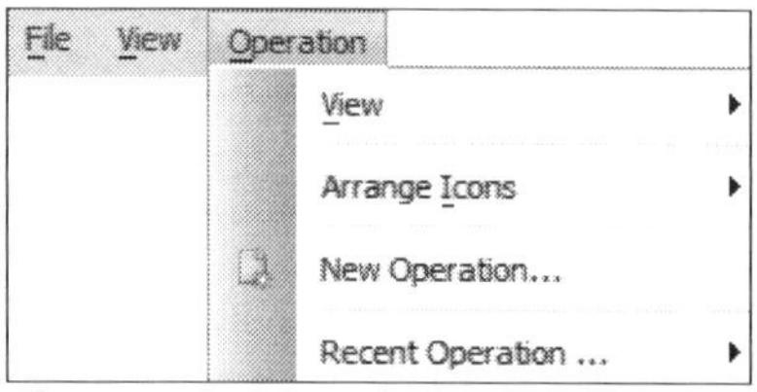

Figure 13-20 Default Operation menu

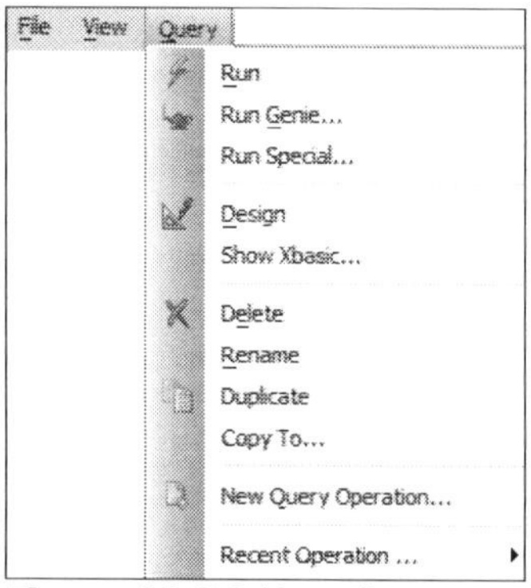

Figure 13-21 Menu for a specific operation type

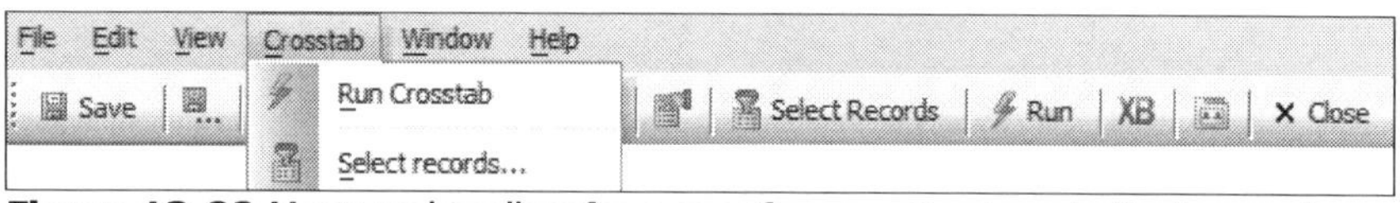

Figure 13-22 Menu and toolbar for a specific operation type in Design mode

The Back Button Becomes Disabled In The Convert Case Of Fields Operation
The downside to using this operation is that even though you can change the case of more than one field at a time, once you select the options for one field, the Back button is disabled. This prevents you from going back to view or change the options that you selected for a previous field.

Exercise 13.8: Use The Convert Case Of Fields Operation

In this exercise you will change the case of three character fields.

1. On the Operations tab, click the New button. Select the **CONVERT CASE OF FIELDS** operation, then select the aImport3Sheets table.

2. Select the Student name field shown in Figure 13-23, then click Next.

   On this screen, more than one field can be selected. Select all of the fields that you want to apply the case conversion to.

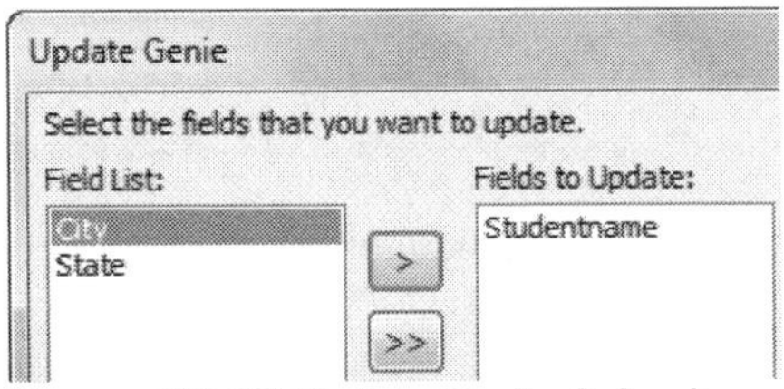

Figure 13-23 Update Genie dialog box

3. On the screen shown in Figure 13-24, select the **UPPER CASE ALL CHARACTERS** option, then click Next.

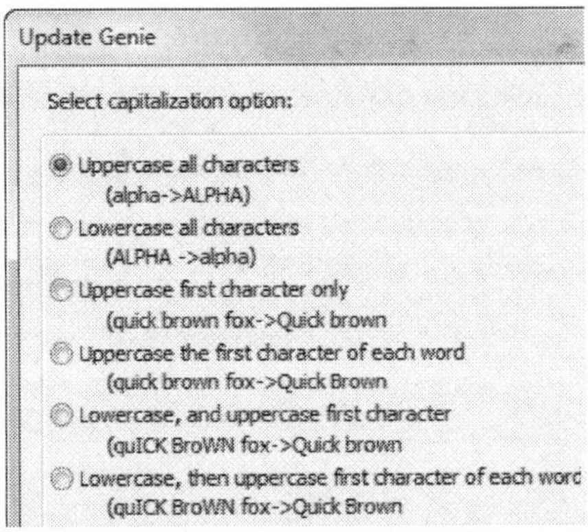

Figure 13-24 Capitalization update options

4. On the screen shown in Figure 13-25, select Yes to update (change the case of) more fields, then click Next. Notice on the screen shown in Figure 13-26 that the Back button is disabled. This is what I am referring to in the warning message right before the beginning of this exercise. In this exercise all of the changes are capitalization of text, so the option selected in Figure 13-26 is correct. Click Next.

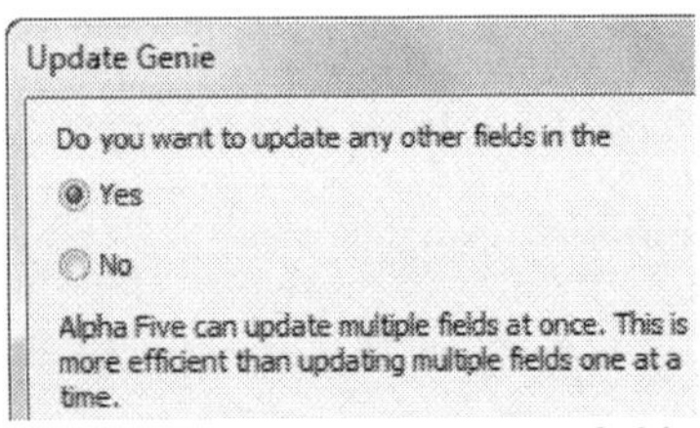

Figure 13-25 Update more fields screen

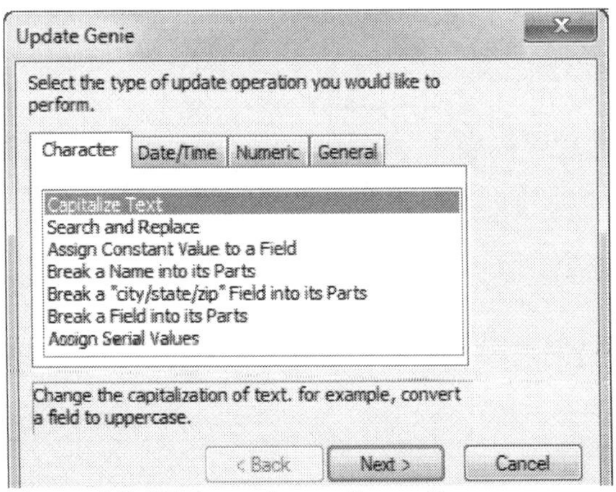

Figure 13-26 Type of operation options

5. Select the City field, then click Next. Select the **UPPERCASE FIRST CHARACTER ONLY** option, then click Next.

6. Select Yes to update another field, then click Next twice.

7. Select the State field, then click Next. Select the **LOWERCASE ALL CHARACTERS** option, then click Next.

8. Select No, to not apply any more updates, then click Next.

Select The Records To Apply The Conversions To

In this exercise you will apply the Convert Case option to all records. If you want to select which records to apply the conversion to, you can create a filter or select one of the built-in queries shown in Figure 13-27.

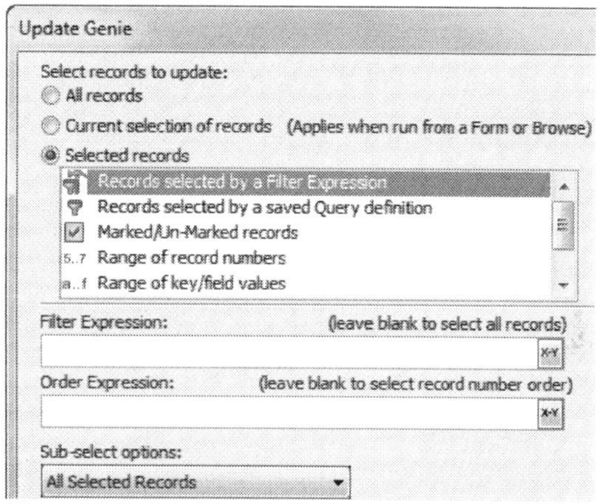

Figure 13-27 Select records to update options

1. Select the All Records option, then click Next. Click Finish to save the operation.

2. Type `aConvertCase` as the operation name. You will see a message that says five records will be updated. Click OK.

3. View the records.

   The Student name should be all capital letters.

   The City should only have the first letter of the first word capitalized and the State should be all lower case, as shown in Figure 13-28.

Classnbr	Studentname	City	State
1	JOE DONG	Atlanta	ga
1	MARVIN COLTS	Bogota	nv
2	PETER YOUN	Bogota	nv
3	STEVE SMITH	Bronx	ny
3	SANDERS TRISHA	Brown deer	wi

Figure 13-28 Result of Convert Case operation

> The **SEARCH AND REPLACE OPERATION** works strange to me. When prompted to select a field to update, I was expecting to see all of the fields in the table or set. Only a few fields were displayed. Naturally, the one I needed was not displayed <smile>, but I did find a work around.

Exercise 13.9: Use The Search And Replace Operation

In this exercise you will search for a specific date and replace it with another date based on the value in another field. By first appearance, this operation appears to only work for character replacement. It can be used for numeric and date search and replace functionality also.

One problem is that you have to enter data where you don't need it if the search you are doing is not a character search and replace.

If you view the aImportOperation table in the Default Browse and sort the data in ascending order on the Date Shipped field, you will see 21 records with a Date Shipped value of 4/11/2011. Out of these 21 records, the only ones that will have the date changed are those where the Paid By ID field equals 2, which means that five records will be changed.

1. Select the Search and replace operation, then select the aImportOperation table.

2. In the Find what field, type `04/11/2011`. In the Replace with field type `04/18/2012`, as shown in Figure 13-29. Click Next.

   For a date search and replace, you can really type in anything you want on this screen. You really do not need to enter anything on this screen, but you can't go to the next screen without entering something.

   Another thing that I do not understand is why this operation is separate from the **UPDATE RECORDS OPERATION** on the Create New Operation dialog box, when they both use the **UPDATE GENIE**.

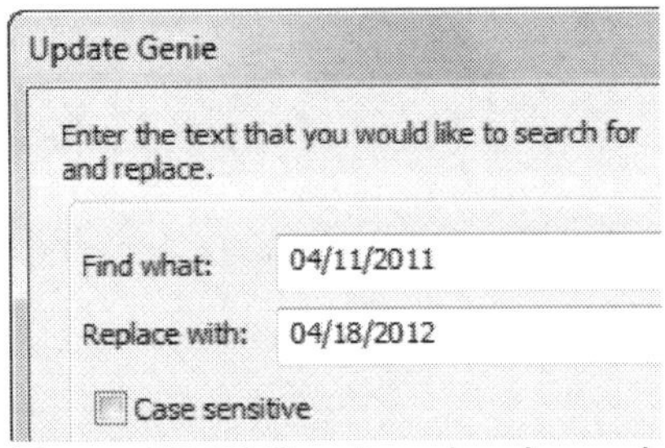

Figure 13-29 Search and replace values

   The difference is that the Update Records operation does not display the screen shown in Figure 13-29.

   This is where the operation gets more weird to me. Most of the fields in the table are not displayed, as shown in Figure 13-30.

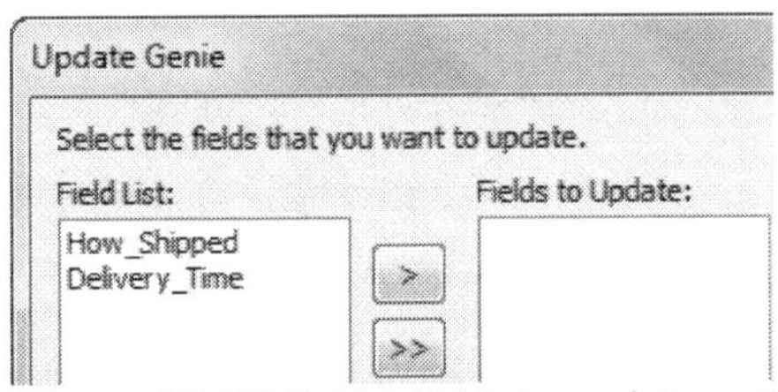

Figure 13-30 Select fields to update options

3. Add the How Shipped field to the **FIELDS TO UPDATE** list, then click Next. You will see that you can change the field to update. Click Yes on the update any other fields screen, then click Next.

4. On the Date/Time tab, select the **ASSIGN CONSTANT VALUE TO A FIELD** option shown in Figure 13-31, then click Next.

5. Open the drop-down list and select the Date Shipped field. Select the **ENTERED VALUE** option, then type `04/18/2012` in the field, as shown in Figure 13-32. Click Next.

6. Click Next on the Update any other fields screen.

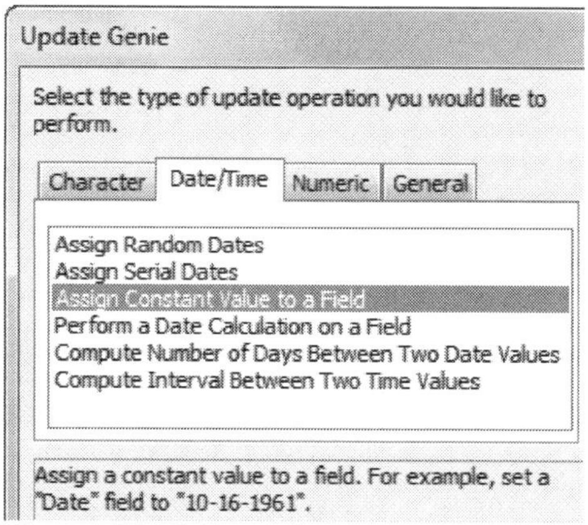

Figure 13-31 Type of update operation options

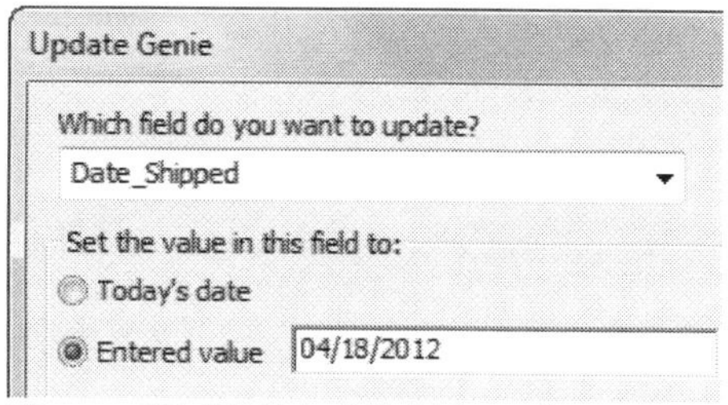

Figure 13-32 Select field to update options

Create The Filter Criteria

1. Select the **SELECTED RECORDS** option. Create a filter expression to select records if the Date Shipped field equals 4/11/2011 and the Paid By ID field = 2.

> **Filter Builder Date Field Operators**
> As you will see, some of the date operators are different from the date operators that you are use to seeing. Why? I have no idea. The **IS ON THE DATE(S) OPERATOR** shown in Figure 13-33 is the same as the **IS EQUAL TO OPERATOR.**

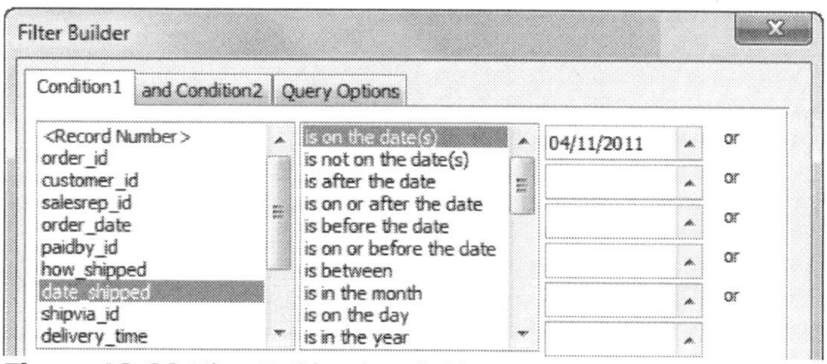

Figure 13-33 Filter Builder date field operators

2. Your expression should look like the one shown in Figure 13-34. Click Next on the Select Records to update screen.

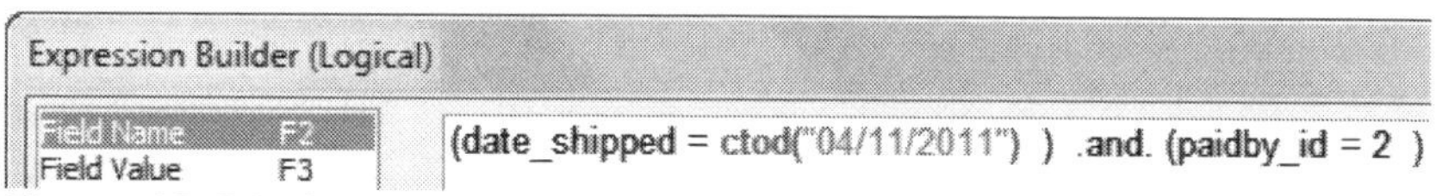

Figure 13-34 Filter expression for the search and replace operation

Normally you would select the second option to save, then run the operation. Because the operations logic does not allow you to select the type of search and replace (See Figure 13-31 earlier) that you want to perform earlier in the process, there are currently two fields that will be updated, which is not what you want.

3. Select the Don't run the update now option, then click Finish.

4. On the Update Builder shown in Figure 13-35, click on the first row (the How Shipped field), then press the Delete key.

Figure 13-35 Update Builder

5. Save the operation as `aSearchAndReplaceDate`.

6. Click the Run button on the toolbar. You will see a message that says five records will be updated. Click OK. I don't know about you, but I don't have any plans to use this operation for dates <smile>. I just wanted to show you that it could be done.

Exercise 13.10: Use The Join Tables Operation

In this exercise you will create a new table by using fields from two tables. Usually, these tables have a common field, but that is not a requirement. The first screen on this genie explains the role of the Master and Transaction tables, as well as, how records will be added to the new table.

1. Select the Join tables operation, then select the Chart Order Detail table. The first table selected for this operation will be the one used as the Master table, as shown in Figure 13-36.

2. Click Next.

   Click the Transaction table field button, then select the Products table, as shown in Figure 13-36.

   Click Next.

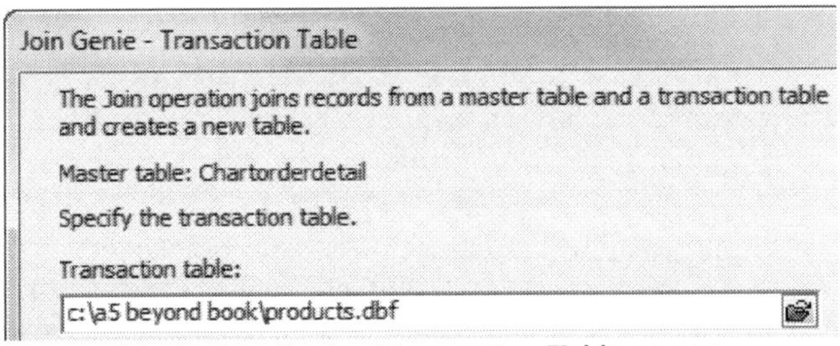

Figure 13-36 Join Genie - Transaction Table screen

3. In the Result field, type `aJoinDetailAndProducts`, as shown in Figure 13-37. The Advanced Options button is used to select what should happen if the table in the **RESULT** field already exists.

   The default is to warn you before overwriting the existing table, as shown in Figure 13-38.

   Click Next.

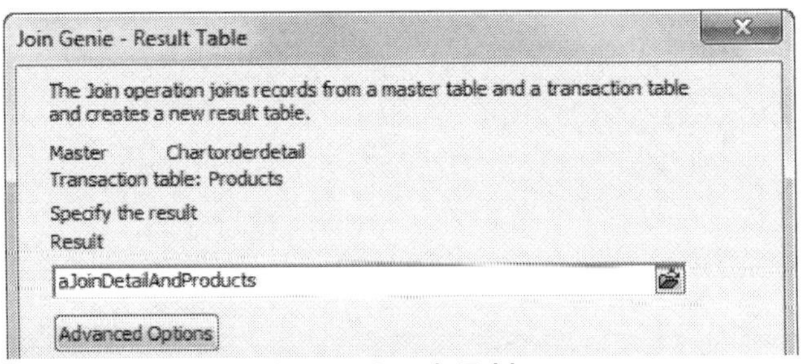

Figure 13-37 Join Genie - Result Table screen

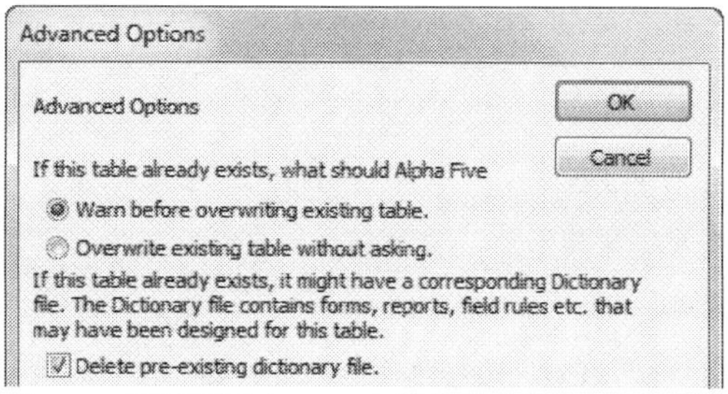

Figure 13-38 Advanced Options dialog box (Join operation)

4. Open the Master table drop-down list and select the Product ID field. Select the same field for the Transaction table, as shown in Figure 13-39. Click Next.

   The button before the word "matches" opens the dialog box shown in Figure 13-40.

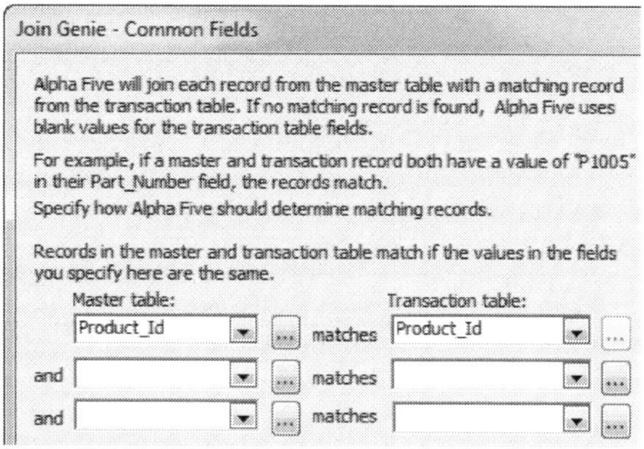

Figure 13-39 Join Genie - Common Fields screen

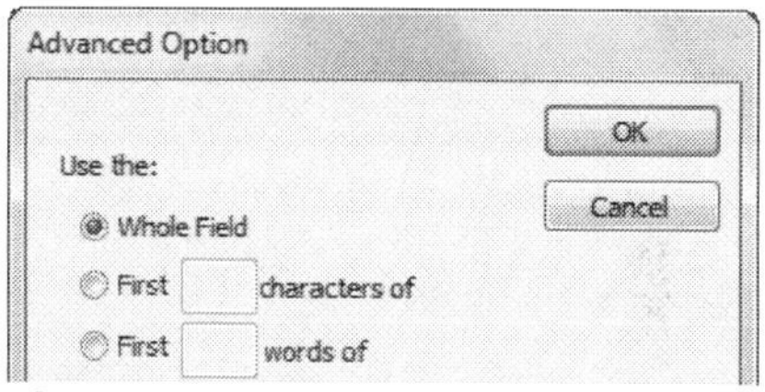

Figure 13-40 Advanced Option dialog box (for the Master table)

The button after the Transaction table field shown above in Figure 13-39 opens the dialog box shown in Figure 13-41 if a value has not been selected for the Transaction table.

If a value has been selected for the Transaction table, the dialog box shown above in Figure 13-40 is displayed.

The options on these Advanced Option dialog boxes are used to select what part of the field should be used to match the value in the other table.

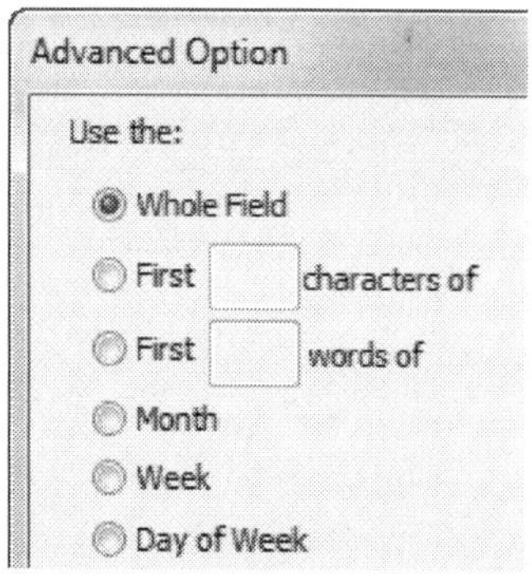

Figure 13-41 Advanced Option dialog box (for the Transaction table)

5. Add the Order ID and Product ID fields from the Master table to the Result table. Add the Product name field from the Transaction table to the Result table.

6. Add the Qty and Price fields from the Master table.

   Add the On Back Order field from the Transaction table.

   You should have the options shown in Figure 13-42.

   Click Next.

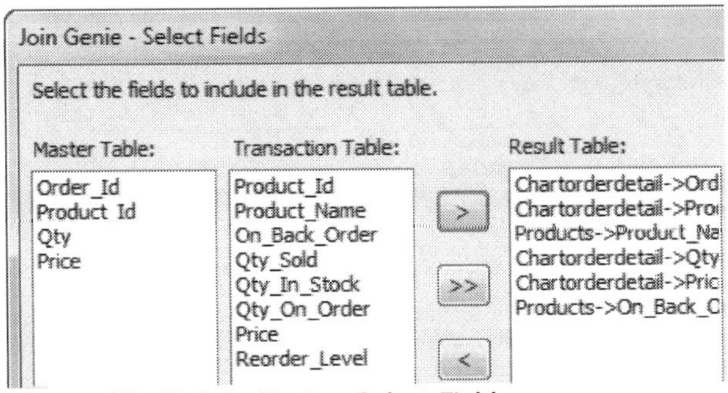

Figure 13-42 Join Genie - Select Fields screen

The screen shown in Figure 13-43 is used to select the records in the Master table to add to the new table.

The **SELECTED RECORDS** option works the same as it does for the Search and Replace operation covered in the previous exercise.

The Select Records (Transaction Table) screen has the same options shown in this figure.

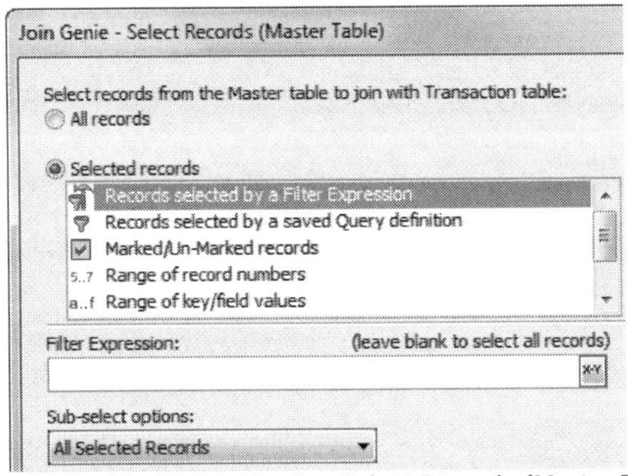

Figure 13-43 Join Genie - Select Records (Master Table) screen

7. Select the All Records option, then click Next.

8. Click Next on the Select Records (Transaction Table) screen. Click Finish.
   Type `aJoinOperation` as the operation name. Click OK when prompted to proceed.
   If you view the new table, you will see that all of the records have the Product name and On back order fields.

Checking For Duplicate Records

Being able to keep data accurate is very important. One way to do this is to check for duplicate records and then decide if the records are really duplicate. If they are, they should be deleted or at the very least, marked as duplicate.

In Exercise 3.2 you learned how to use the Delete Duplicate Records table utility as one way to find duplicate records. The Duplicate Records operation is used to save the duplicate record checking criteria. Saving the criteria means that you do not have to guess a month from now how you checked for duplicate records.

Understanding The View Duplicate Records Genie

This genie is very helpful because you can see the records that are potentially duplicate. Figure 13-44 shows the genie. The options are explained below.

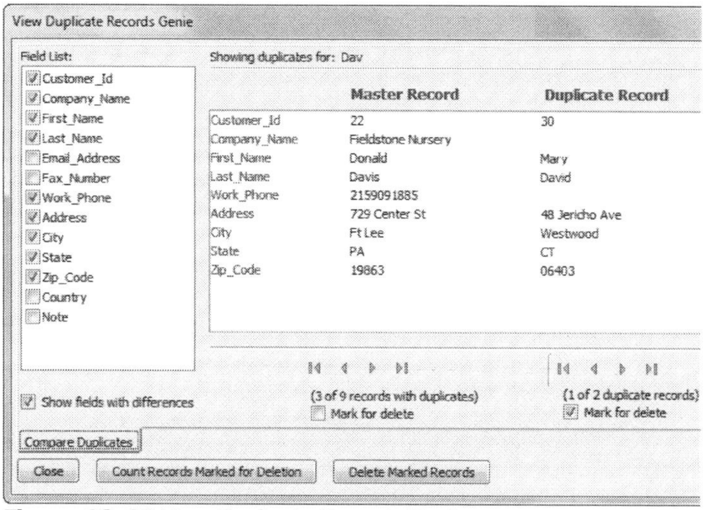

Figure 13-44 View Duplicate Records Genie

① **FIELD LIST** Displays the fields in the table that is being checked for duplicate records. Check the fields that you want the values of displayed. The order that you select them in is the order that they will appear in, on the right side of the dialog box.

② **SHOWING DUPLICATES FOR** (above the master record heading) Displays the criteria used to check for duplicate records for the records currently displayed. If you create a filter expression that selects multiple criteria, like the expression shown at the bottom of Figure 13-45, the criteria displayed will change. For the expression shown in Figure 13-45, you will see the criteria shown at the top of Figures 13-46 and 13-47, depending on the master record that you are viewing. The information shown in this field can change, record by record, based on the criteria (filter expression) that you created.

③ **SHOW FIELDS WITH DIFFERENCES** If checked, Alpha Five will automatically check for duplicate values and will place a check mark in the Field List, next to the fields that it finds duplicate values in. These fields will be displayed in the window to the right. Clear this option if you want to select the fields that will be checked for duplicate values.

④ **X OF Y RECORDS WITH DUPLICATES** This option is below the navigation buttons. It displays the total number of records that are currently marked for deletion for the corresponding master record. Each master record can have more than one duplicate record, as shown above at the bottom of Figure 13-44. When that is the case, make sure to view all of the records in the Duplicate Record column for the master record.

⑤ **MARK FOR DELETE** Check this option (under the currently displayed master or duplicate record) to indicate that you want to delete the record. Clear the check mark if you do not want the record displayed to be deleted.

⑥ **COUNT RECORDS MARKED FOR DELETION BUTTON** Click this button if you want to display a message that shows a count of the number of records (both master and duplicate) that are marked to be deleted.

⑦ **DELETE MARKED RECORDS BUTTON** Click this button to delete the marked records.

[See Chapter 3, Find Duplicate Records Dialog Box for an explanation of the options]

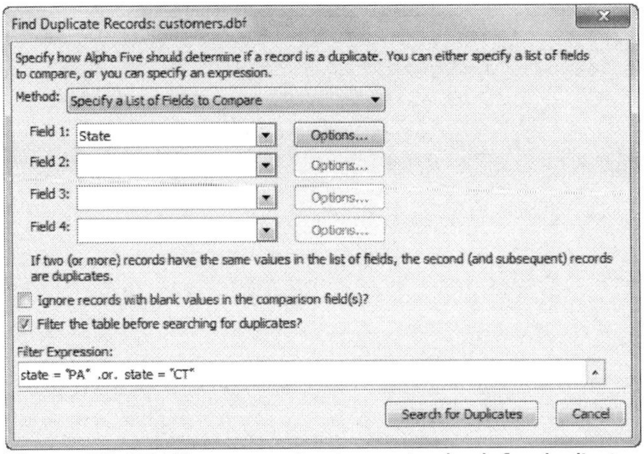

Figure 13-45 Filter expression to use to check for duplicate records

As shown above in Figure 13-45, the filter expression has two options.

One option is shown in Figure 13-46 and the other is shown in Figure 13-47.

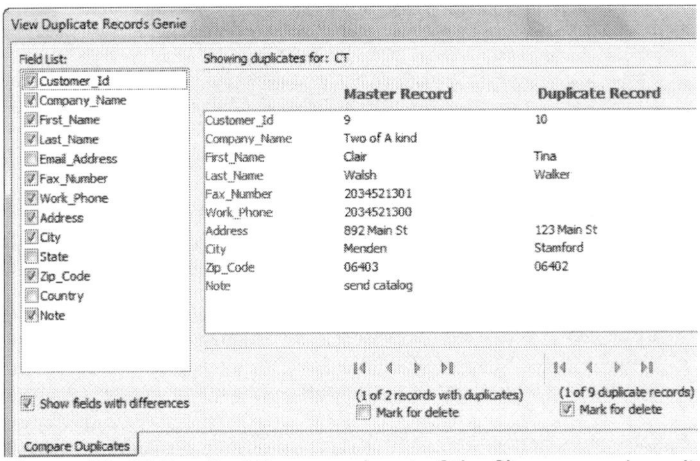

Figure 13-46 Result of the second part of the filter expression criteria

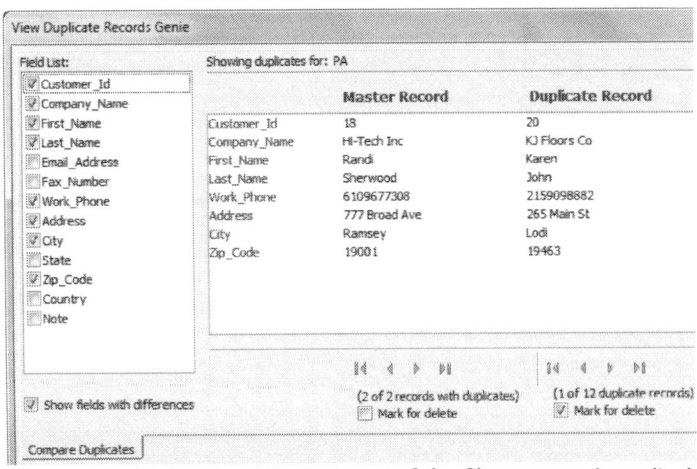

Figure 13-47 Result of the first part of the filter expression criteria

Exercise 13.11: Find, Mark And Delete Duplicate Records

In this exercise you will check a table that has potential duplicate order header information.

1. Select the Mark duplicate records operation, then select the aImportOperation table. Click Next on the first screen on the genie.

2. Open the first drop-down list and select the Order ID field, then select the Customer ID and Order Date fields, as shown in Figure 13-48.

   The buttons open the Advanced Options dialog box shown earlier in Figure 13-41.

   Click Next.

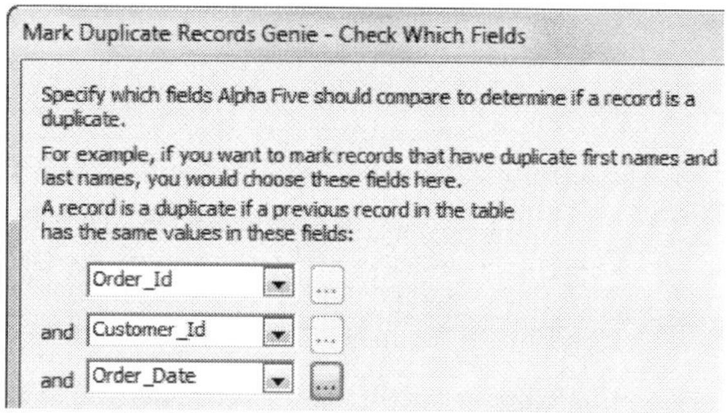

Figure 13-48 Mark Duplicate Records Genie - Check Which Fields screen

> **No Obvious Way To Clear An Option**
> If you select more than one field to check for duplicate values (on the screen shown above in Figure 13-48) and then decide that you do not want to include the field, the only way to remove it is to highlight the content in the field, then press the Delete key.

3. Click Finish. Type `aMarkDuplicateOrder` as the operation name. Click OK to proceed.

4. You will see the dialog box shown in Figure 13-49, which displays how many records were marked as duplicate.

   Click the **VIEW RECORDS IN THE 'VIEW DUPLICATES GENIE'** button.

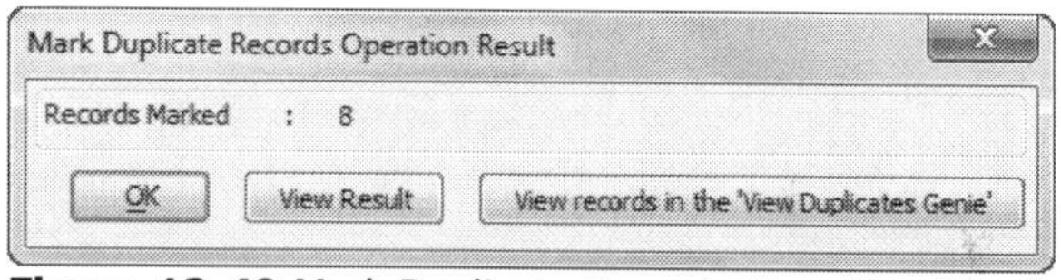

Figure 13-49 Mark Duplicate Records Operation Result dialog box

Using The View Duplicate Records Genie

1. Select the following fields in the Field List: Order ID, Customer ID, Sales Rep ID, Order Date, and Date Shipped.

2. Clear the check mark for the Show fields with differences field, then view the records that have been marked as duplicate.

   As you can see in Figure 13-50, the values in the fields are identical.

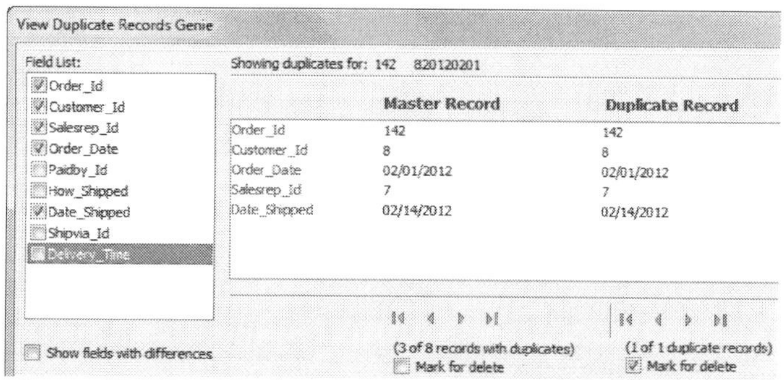

Figure 13-50 Field selected to be checked for duplicates

3. Click the Delete Marked Records button, then click Yes twice.

4. If you run the Mark Duplicate Order operation again, no duplicate records will be found based on the criteria selected in that operation. If you change the criteria, it is possible that records will be marked as duplicate.

Crosstab Operation

In Exercise 13.10 you used the Join operation to create a new table. The Crosstab operation also creates a new table. The difference is that summary values are placed in the new table. Crosstab tables can be created from a table or a set, but only the primary table in a set can be used to select the column and row headings for the new table.

Usually, crosstab grids as I call them, are placed in a report, so that is the context that I will explain crosstabs in. The Crosstab operation requires one to think in dimensions. Like spreadsheets, crosstab grids have rows and columns. Each cell in a spreadsheet contains one piece of raw data. In a crosstab grid, each cell contains one piece of summary data (count, sum, average etc.) that is the equivalent of the sub totals that are usually in the Group Footer section of the report.

The difference between a crosstab table and a spreadsheet is that the data in a crosstab table is summarized, where data in a spreadsheet displays detail rows of data and some summary information. The data in a crosstab table is often used for high level or comparison analysis.

This compact way of displaying data in a crosstab report is possible because the data is grouped on two axes. The data is summarized horizontally and vertically. Examples of crosstab reports are:

① Sales by sales rep, by year.
② Sales by region.
③ Summarizing how many orders by year and by zip code, each sales rep has.
④ Sales of a specific product by sales rep, by month.
⑤ Summarizing how many customers by region purchased certain products by month or by year.

Behind the scenes, the crosstab operation takes the detail records that you are use to seeing and summarizes the detail data and places the result in a field in the table. Hopefully the following scenario will make the concept of crosstab tables easier to understand. Figure 13-51 shows a basic list report, which has detail records. Figure 13-52 shows the same data grouped by sales rep and year.

Sales By Rep By Year

Last Name	First Name	Order Date	Order Amount	Customer Name
Davolio	Nancy	02/19/2010	$789.51	Belgium Bike Co.
Davolio	Nancy	02/19/2010	$58.00	Spokes for Folks
Davolio	Nancy	02/26/2010	$68.90	Mountain Madmen Bicycles
Davolio	Nancy	02/27/2010	$1,529.70	Cycle City Rome
Davolio	Nancy	02/27/2010	$1,079.70	Mountain Madmen Bicycles
Davolio	Nancy	02/27/2010	$2,698.53	Pedals Inc.
		. . .		
Last Name	**First Name**	**Order Date**	**Order Amount**	**Customer Name**
Suyama	Michael	02/06/2012	$5,879.70	Biking's It Industries
Suyama	Michael	02/08/2012	$863.74	Alley Cat Cycles
Suyama	Michael	02/09/2012	$5,219.55	Spokes
Suyama	Michael	02/10/2012	$659.70	Psycho-Cycle

Figure 13-51 Basic list sales report sorted by sales rep by year

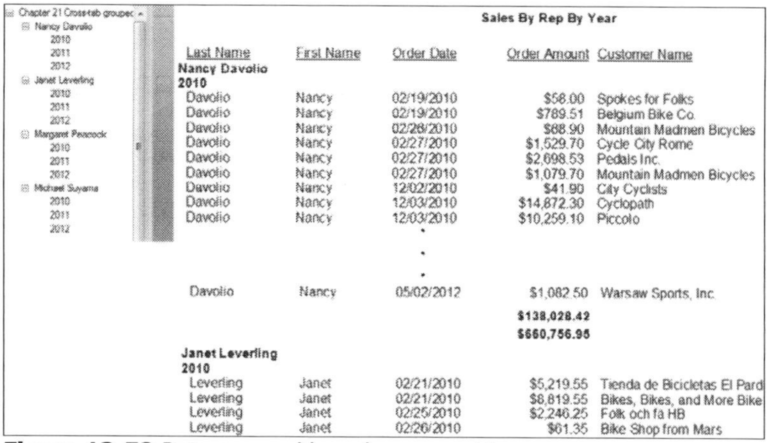

Figure 13-52 Data grouped by sales rep and by year

How To Create This Crosstab

Yes, I hear you grumbling and saying, "Great, I now see the advantages of creating a crosstab report, but how do I get the data shown above in Figures 13-51 and 13-52 into crosstab format?" Okay, here goes:

① Usually, the field down the left side of a crosstab (that creates the rows) is the data element that there are more occurrences of. In this example, there are more sales reps than years. However, you can put the sales reps across the top of the crosstab (which would create the columns) and still get the same results.

② The field that goes across the top (that creates the columns) represents the data element that there are less occurrences of.

③ The cells in the middle of the crosstab are the sum (in this example, a count) of orders that the sales rep had for the year. This is the equivalent of grouping data.

④ I have saved the best for last; the placement of the fields on the Crosstab Genie. The fields for the row and column were answered above. That leaves the field for the cells in the middle of the crosstab grid. Recall the original report criteria: Sales by sales rep, by year. You have already determined that the sales rep field (the Rep name field in the table), is what will be used for the rows. You have also determined that the Order Date will be used for the columns. The only field left is the sales (the order amount). This is what goes on the Summary field screen. In this example, the cells represent a total of the order amount.

Exercise 13.12: Create A Crosstab Table

In this exercise you will create a crosstab table that totals the order amount by sales rep and by state.

1. Select the Crosstab operation, then select the CrossTabForOrders table. Click Next on the first Crosstab Genie screen.

2. Open the Group Rows By drop-down list and select the Rep name field, as shown in Figure 13-53, then click Next.

   This means that there will be one row for each sales rep in the crosstab table.

   There is an <expression> option in the drop-down list that is used to create an expression to create the Rows value.

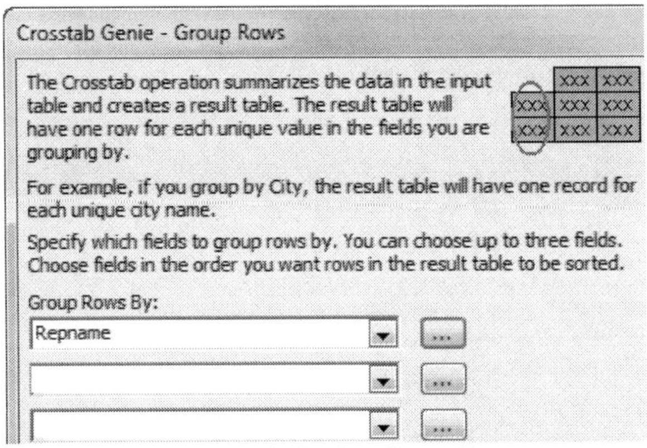

Figure 13-53 Crosstab Genie - Group Rows screen

   If the crosstab was based on a set, there would be a Table drop-down list that contains all of the tables in the set (above the Group Rows By field), as shown in Figure 13-54.

   The same is true for the Group Columns screen and Summary Field screens.

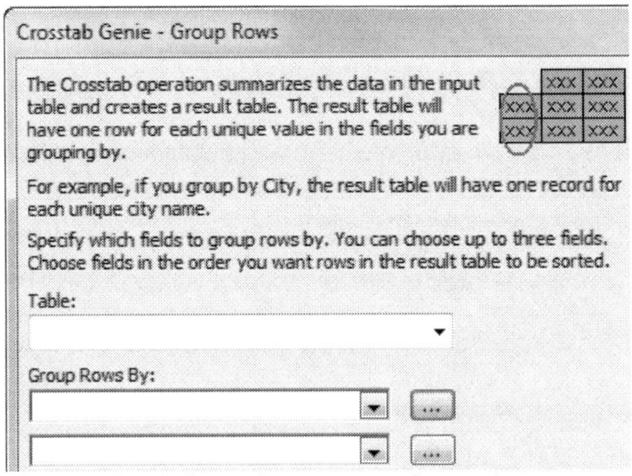

Figure 13-54 Group Rows screen for a set

3. Open the Group Columns By drop-down list and select the State field, as shown in Figure 13-55, then click Next.

   This means that there will be one column for each state in the crosstab table.

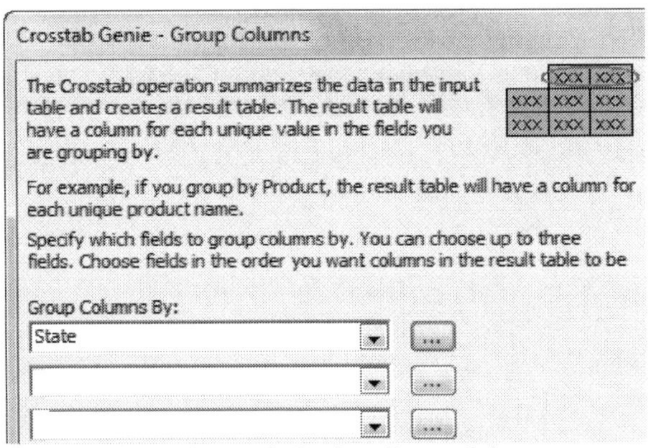

Figure 13-55 Crosstab Genie - Group Columns screen

4. Open the Field drop-down list and select the Order Amount field.

   Open the Summary calculation drop-down list and select Total, as shown in Figure 13-56.

   This will add the order amount values by state for each sales rep and put the total in the corresponding state field (column).

   Click Next.

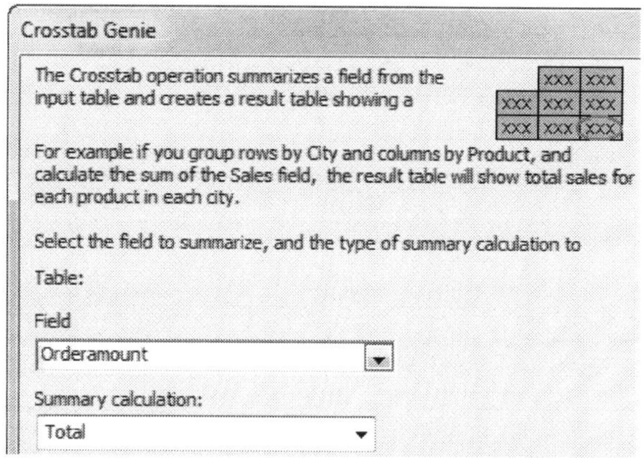

Figure 13-56 Crosstab Genie - Summary field screen

5. The table that this crosstab is based on has orders for more than one year.

   Create a filter expression that selects records with an order date in 2011, as shown in Figure 13-57, then click Next.

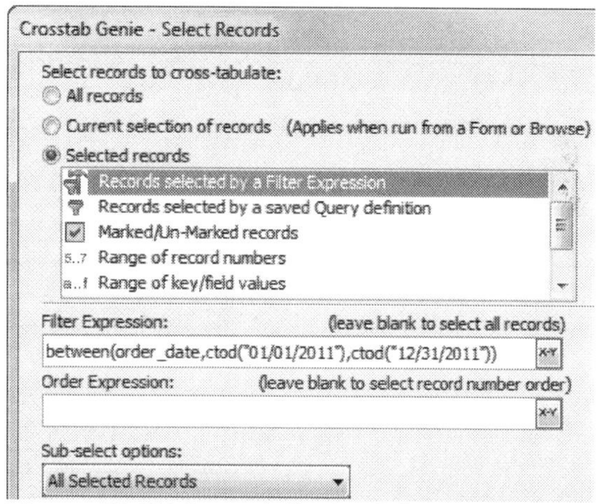

Figure 13-57 Crosstab Genie - Select Records screen

> If this crosstab table will be used for a report, a better solution for selecting the records to put in the table is to create an argument that lets the user select the date range, instead of creating the hard coded filter expression shown above in Figure 13-57.

6. Type `aCrosstabBySalesRep` in the Result table field, as shown in Figure 13-58. This is the name of the crosstab table that will be created.

   Click Next.

   The Advanced Options button opens the dialog box shown in Figure 13-59.

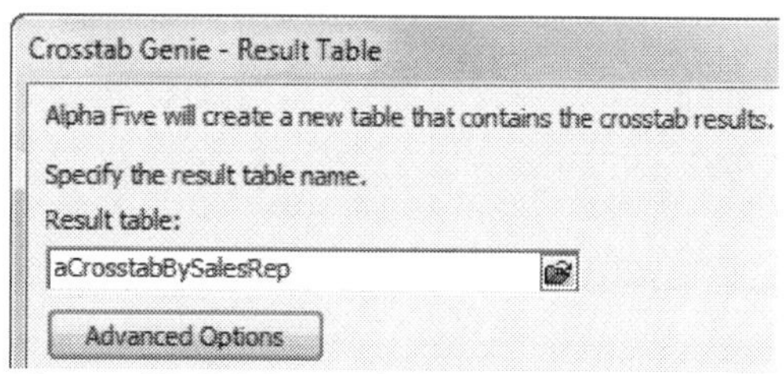

Figure 13-58 Crosstab Genie - Result Table screen

The options on this dialog box are used to select whether or not the crosstab table and dictionary should be overwritten automatically.

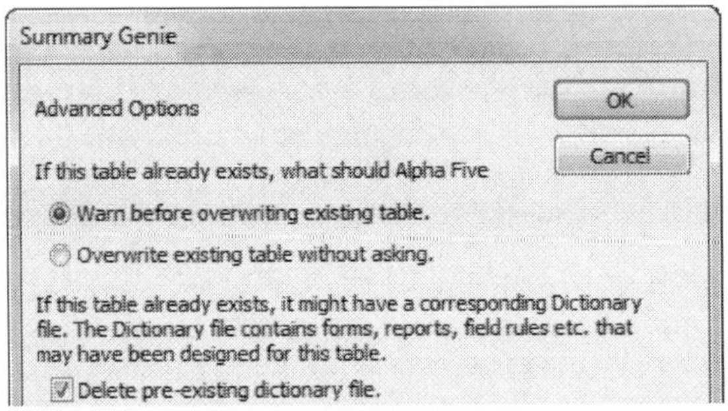

Figure 13-59 Summary Genie screen

7. Click Finish. Type `aCrosstabBySalesRep` as the operation name. Click OK to proceed.

View The Crosstab Table And Operation

1. Open the aCrosstabBySalesRep table. It should look like the one shown in Figure 13-60.

   It shows the total dollar amount of sales per rep, per state.

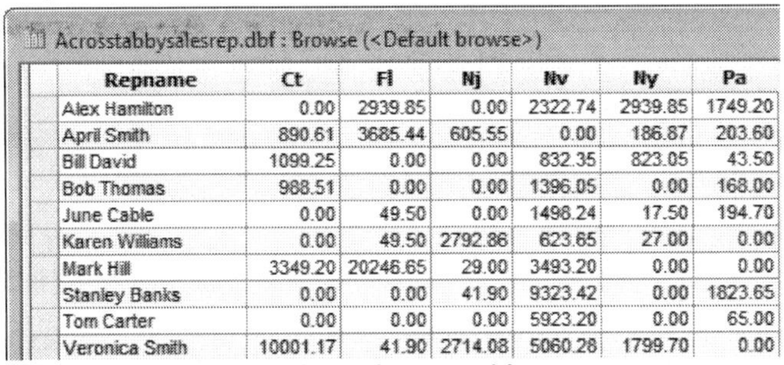

Acrosstabbysalesrep.dbf : Browse (<Default browse>)

Repname	Ct	Fl	Nj	Nv	Ny	Pa
Alex Hamilton	0.00	2939.85	0.00	2322.74	2939.85	1749.20
April Smith	890.61	3685.44	605.55	0.00	186.87	203.60
Bill David	1099.25	0.00	0.00	832.35	823.05	43.50
Bob Thomas	988.51	0.00	0.00	1396.05	0.00	168.00
June Cable	0.00	49.50	0.00	1498.24	17.50	194.70
Karen Williams	0.00	49.50	2792.86	623.65	27.00	0.00
Mark Hill	3349.20	20246.65	29.00	3493.20	0.00	0.00
Stanley Banks	0.00	0.00	41.90	9323.42	0.00	1823.65
Tom Carter	0.00	0.00	0.00	5923.20	0.00	65.00
Veronica Smith	10001.17	41.90	2714.08	5060.28	1799.70	0.00

Figure 13-60 aCrosstabBySalesRep table

2. Open the aCrosstabBySalesRep operation in Design mode.

   It should look like the one shown in Figure 13-61.

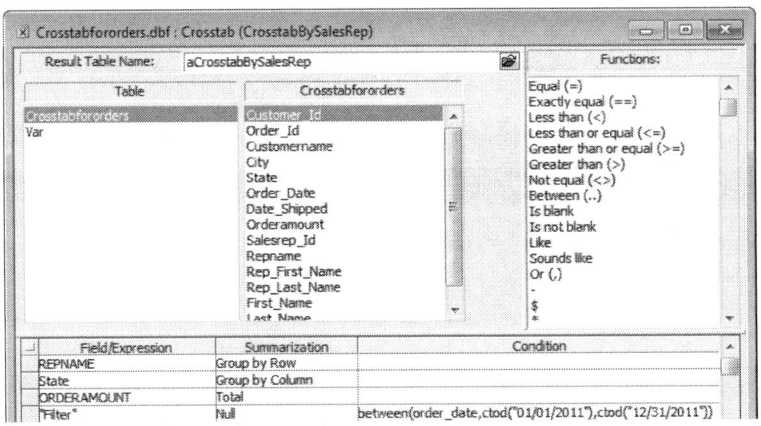

Figure 13-61 Crosstab operation

Exercise 13.13: Create A Report Based On Crosstab Data

1. Use the Quick Report Genie to create a report based on the aCrosstabBySalesRep table.

2. Add all of the fields to the report.

3. For all of the State fields, complete the following:
   - ☑ Select a format expression with a dollar sign. (**TIP:** Select the expression, right-click and select Copy, then paste it in the field for the other State fields instead of opening the Display Format dialog box over and over.)
   - ☑ Check the **TOTAL** Summary option.

4. On the Report Settings tab, clear the check mark for the **USE LAYOUT TABLES** option.

5. On the Style tab, select the **SECTION BORDERS** and **COLOR ALTERNATING ROWS** options.

6. Click the Open in Report Editor button. Select the Free form report option, then click the Save Report and Open in Report Editor button.

7. Select the State headings in the Report Header section, then change the Layout Align option to Center.

8. In the Report Footer section, add a text object to the beginning of the section, with the text `Sales rep totals by state`.

9. Save the report as `aCrosstabForSalesRep`. It should look like the one shown in Figure 13-62.

REPNAME	CT	FL	NJ	NV	NY	PA
Alex Hamilton	$0.00	$2,939.85	$0.00	$2,322.74	$2,939.85	$1,749.20
April Smith	$890.61	$3,685.44	$605.55	$0.00	$186.87	$203.60
Bill David	$1,099.25	$0.00	$0.00	$832.35	$823.05	$43.50
Bob Thomas	$988.51	$0.00	$0.00	$1,396.05	$0.00	$168.00
June Cable	$0.00	$49.50	$0.00	$1,498.24	$17.50	$194.70
Karen Williams	$0.00	$49.50	$2,792.86	$623.65	$27.00	$0.00
Mark Hill	$3,349.20	$20,246.65	$29.00	$3,493.20	$0.00	$0.00
Stanley Banks	$0.00	$0.00	$41.90	$9,323.42	$0.00	$1,823.65
Tom Carter	$0.00	$0.00	$0.00	$5,923.20	$0.00	$65.00
Veronica Smith	$10,001.17	$41.90	$2,714.08	$5,060.28	$1,799.70	$0.00
Sales rep totals by state	$16,328.74	$27,012.84	$6,183.39	$30,473.13	$5,793.97	$4,247.65

Figure 13-62 Crosstab report

Exercise 13.14: Use The Post Operation

In this exercise you will update the value in one field in a table with the value from a field in a different table. The State field in the Post Operation table has missing data and the Last Years Sales field is empty. The Chart Customers table has the data that will be used to update the data in the Post Operation table.

1. Select the Post Records operation, then select the Post Operation table. Click Next on the first Post Genie screen.

2. Select the Chart Customers table as the Transaction table, as shown in Figure 13-63.

   Click Next.

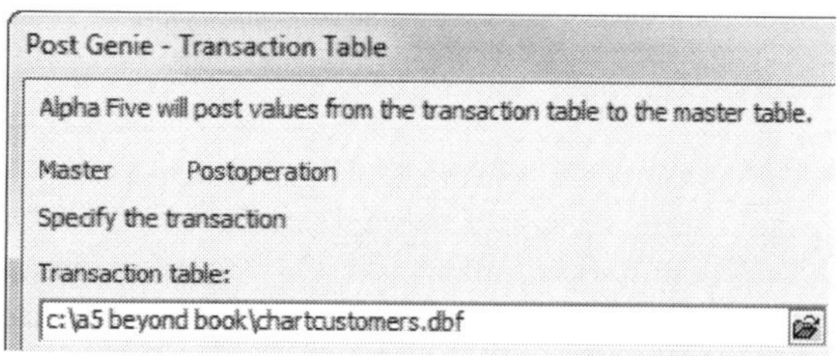

Figure 13-63 Post Genie - Transaction Table screen

3. Select the Customer ID field for the Master and Transaction tables, as shown in Figure 13-64, then click Next.

   The buttons open the Advanced Option dialog box shown earlier in Figure 13-41.

   The Advanced Options button opens the dialog box shown in Figure 13-65.

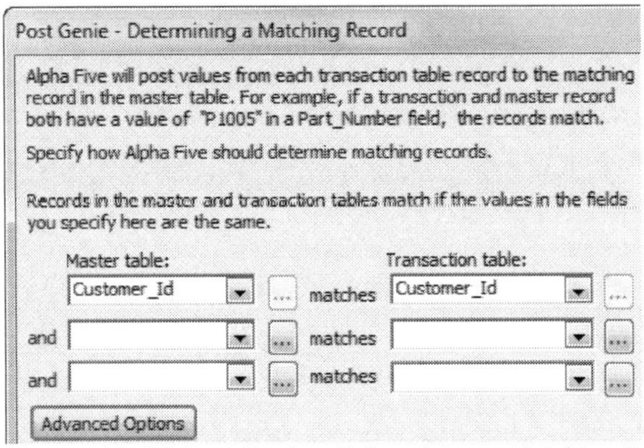

Figure 13-64 Post Genie - Determining a Matching Record screen

The options on this dialog box are used to select which records in the Master table will be updated.

For example, you could create an expression that only updates records if a certain field is empty.

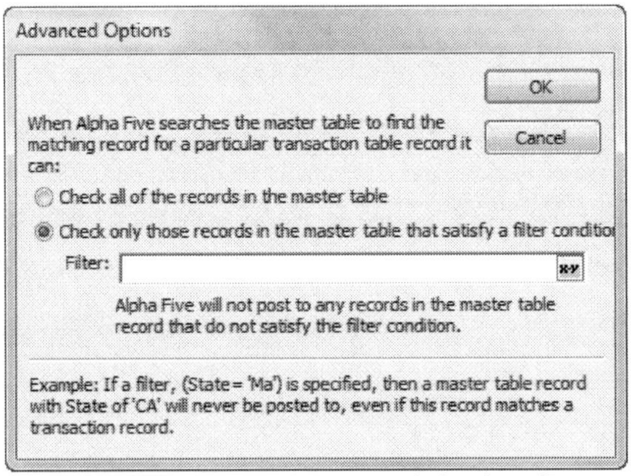

Figure 13-65 Advanced Options dialog box (Post operation)

4. Open the Update the value in drop-down list and select the Customer state field. Open the By drop-down list and select **REPLACING IT WITH**. Open the Value in drop-down list and select the State field.

5. Select the **ONLY IF THIS CONDITION IS TRUE** option, then click the button at the end of the field.

   Create an expression to select the records where the Customer State field is blank, as shown in Figure 13-66.

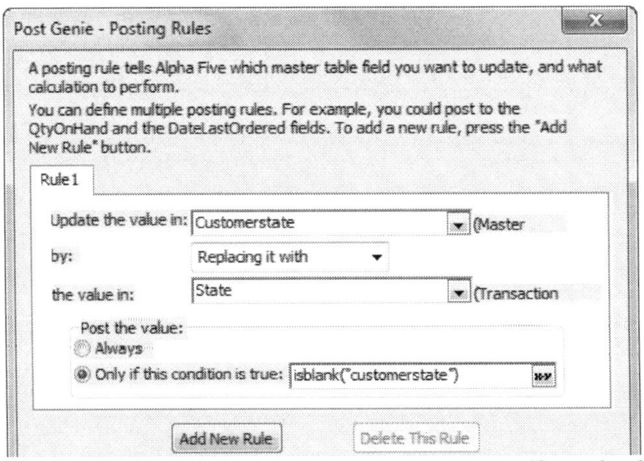

Figure 13-66 Post Genie - Posting Rules screen (for Rule 1)

6. Click the Add New Rule button.

   Create the rule shown in Figure 13-67, then click Next.

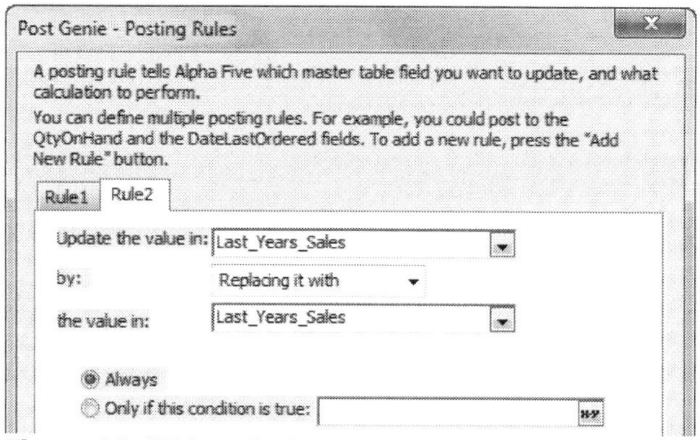

Figure 13-67 Post Genie - Posting Rules screen (for Rule 2)

7. On the Select Records screen for the Transaction table, click Next. Select No to update the fields in the Transaction table, then click Next.

8. Click Finish. Type `aPostToTable` as the operation name. Click OK to proceed.

9. You should see the dialog box shown in Figure 13-68.

   Click the View Result button.

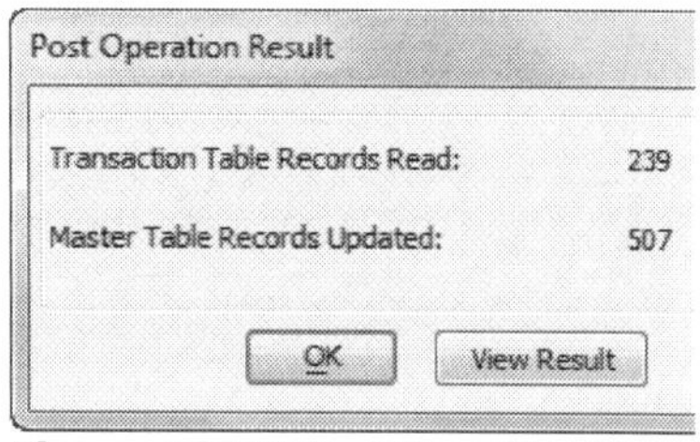

Figure 13-68 Post Operation Result dialog box

If you sort the Post Operation table on the Customer ID field, you will see that the Customer state field for Customer ID 33 is blank. That is because the Chart Customers table does not have a record for customer 33.

EXPORTING DATA

In this chapter you will learn how to export data to Excel, PDF, RTF, HTML and Text formats.

CHAPTER 14

Overview

Just like you can import data into Alpha Five tables from a variety of file formats, you can export data in Alpha Five tables to a variety of file formats. Alpha Five provides several export options.

Exporting Data To Excel

This is probably the most used export option. In Chapter 6, you learned how to use the **EXPORT TO EXCEL ACTION**. There are several ways to export data to Excel including the following: 1) Through a browse, 2) Export Records Operation, 3) Layout Table Reports and 4) Mapped Tables.

Use A Browse To Export Data To Excel

This is the easiest way to export data to Excel, but it is also the most limiting because there are no options to select, meaning for example, you cannot select the file format version of Excel that the export file will have. Formatting that is applied to the browse is not exported and you cannot select a name for the Excel file before the data is exported.

The default file name is the table name that the browse is based on. If the browse is based on a set, the name of the primary table is used as the file name. The default folder location for the exported file is the Private Path folder. [See Chapter 1, Figure 1-3] Once the export file is created, you can rename it. If you only want to export a subset of the data displayed in the browse, create a query. Only data displayed on the browse is exported.

Exercise 14.1: Export To Excel Using A Browse

In this exercise you will export data in a browse that is based on a set.

1. View the Orders Multi Table Set in the Default Browse.

2. Create a query to only display orders in 2012. Run the query. In the lower right corner of the workspace, you should see that 326 records are displayed.

3. Click the **EXPORT TO EXCEL** button on the toolbar or Tools ⇒ Export to Excel, to export the data displayed in the browse. Excel will open and display the 326 records. Notice that the Excel file name is orders0.xls. The number (zero, in this case) is automatically added when the file name already exists in the same folder. Close the browse.

Export Records Operation

In the previous chapter you learned how to use a variety of operations. I suspect that by the end of that chapter you were wondering why the Export Records operation was left out. Well, the wait is over. This operation has the following options for exporting data to Excel:

① The ability to select the Excel file format (**.XLS** or **.XLSX**).
② Select a name for the Excel export file.
③ Select fields from any table in the set.
④ Create a filter or order expression.

This operation can export data to other formats including: **.CSV**, **TXT**, **RTF**, Lotus and Symphony.

Export Operation Options

The options shown in Figure 14-1 are used to select the file format for the exported file.

The **EXPORTING EXCEL FILES** link explains the differences between the File and Remote database options.

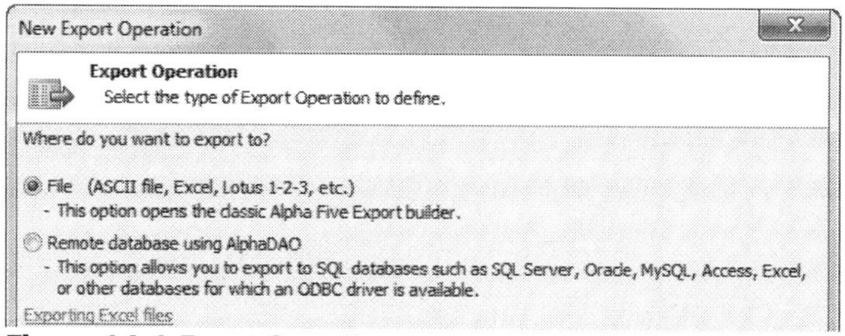

Figure 14-1 Export Operation screen

The differences explained below will probably be the ones that you use to make a decision on which export option to select.

① The **FILE OPTION** has a limit of 16,384 rows that can be exported. The Remote database option does not have a limit.

② The **REMOTE DATABASE OPTION** can create an Excel file that has a tab for each table in a set. The File option does not have this feature.

Exercise 14.2: Export To Excel Using The Export Records File Option

In this exercise you will create an operation that uses a set. You will select fields from several tables, similar to using the **COPY RECORDS OPERATION**, to create a new table.

1. Select the Export Records operation, then select the View Orders set.

2. Select the File option shown on the screen shown above in Figure 14-1, then click OK. Click Next.

3. Open the Export file drop-down list and select the MS-Excel 2007 option, shown in Figure 14-2, then click Next.

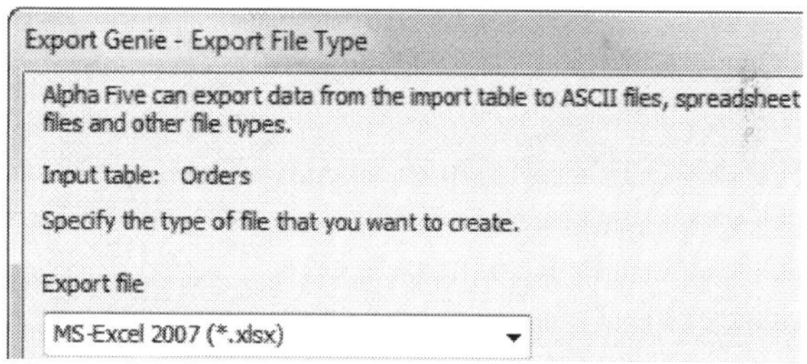

Figure 14-2 Export Genie - Export File Type screen

4. Type `ExportOrders` as the file name, as shown in Figure 14-3, then click Next.

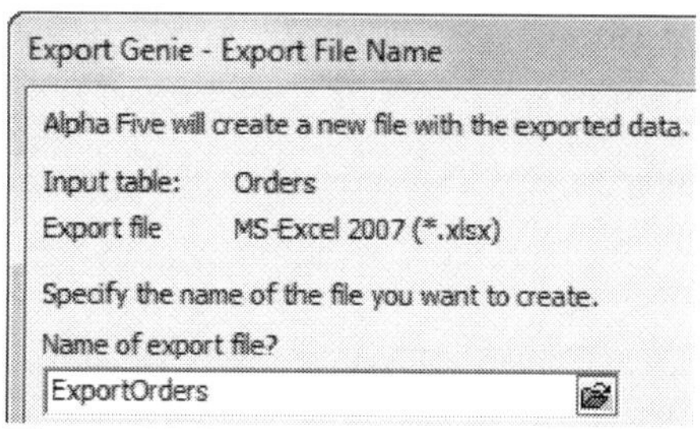

Figure 14-3 Export Genie - Export File Name screen

5. Check the option, **INCLUDE FIELD NAMES IN EXPORTED FILE.**

   Select the fields listed in Table 14-1, as shown in Figure 14-4.

Table	Fields To Select
Customers	Customer ID, First Name, Last Name, State
Orders	Order ID, Order Date
Order Detail	Product ID
Products	Product Name
Orders	Sales Rep ID
Sales Reps	Rep First Name, Rep Last Name
Orders	Date Shipped

Table 14-1 Fields to export

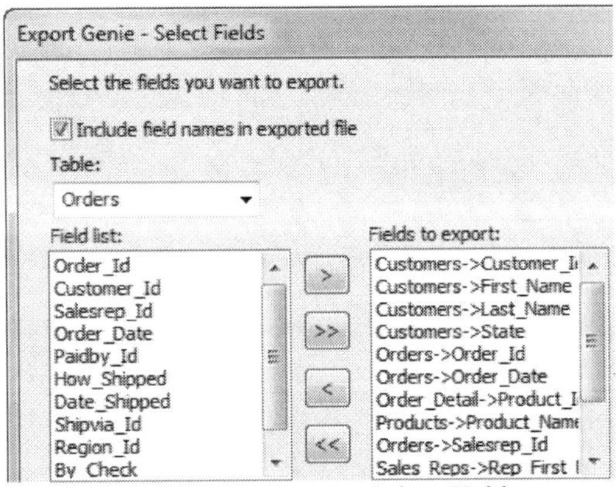

Figure 14-4 Export Genie - Select Fields screen

Because the set being used to create the export file has at least one one-to-many relationship, most notably the Order - Order Detail link, the data in many columns in the Excel export file will be the same, just as if the data was originally created in Excel. This is what happens when you take the relational data and place it in what is known as a **FLAT FILE**.

6. Create a filter expression to select orders where the Product ID field in the Order Detail table starts with the character c, as shown in Figure 14-5.

   The options on the screen shown in Figure 14-5 work the same as they do for other operations.

   The reason that you have to select the Product ID field in the Order Detail table is because you only want to retrieve records of items that were actually ordered.

   Click Next.

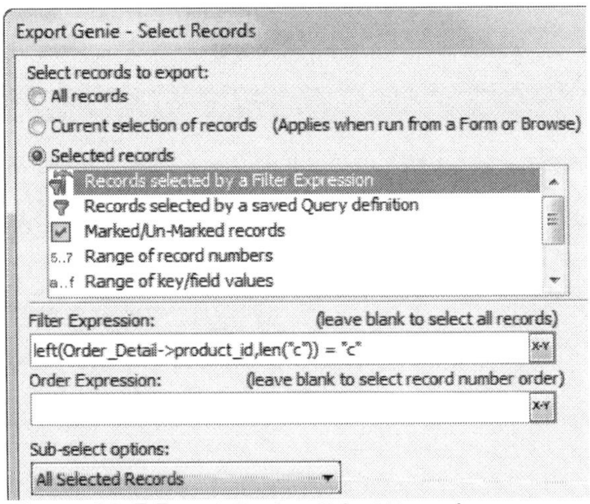

Figure 14-5 Export Genie - Select Records screen

7. Click Finish. Type `Excel File Export` as the operation name. Click OK when prompted that the records will be exported. If you view the Export Orders spreadsheet, you will see that the numeric fields are not formatted.

Exercise 14.3: Export To Excel Using The Export Records Remote Database Option

In the previous exercise you used the Export Records operation to export data to Excel. If you looked at the exported file, you probably frowned at the amount of formatting that someone will have to do. In this exercise you will use the remote option to create more than one table in the Excel Export file.

Create The Connection String

1. Select the Export Records operation. This operation does not require you to select a table or set. Click the Create Using Genie button.

2. Select the **REMOTE DATABASE USING ALPHA DAO** option, then click OK.

3. Click the **DEFINE CONNECTION STRING** button shown in Figure 14-6. Select the Excel File option. Click the Create New Excel File button. Navigate to your folder.
   Type `ExcelExportMultiSheets.xls` in the File name field.

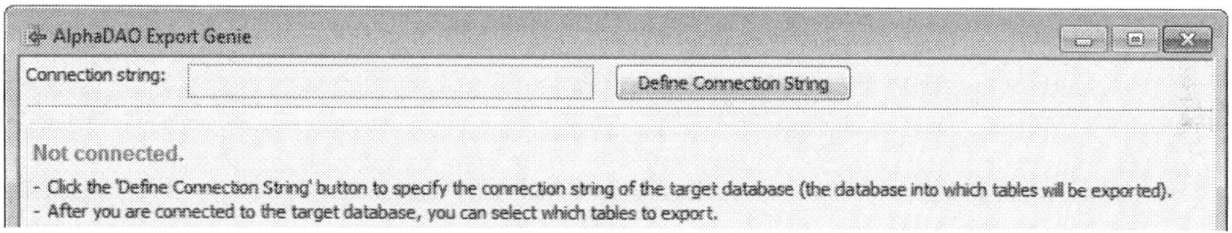

Figure 14-6 Alpha DAO Export Genie connection screen

4. You should have the options shown in Figure 14-7. Click the Test Excel Connection link, then click the **SAVE AS NAMED CONNECTION STRING** link.

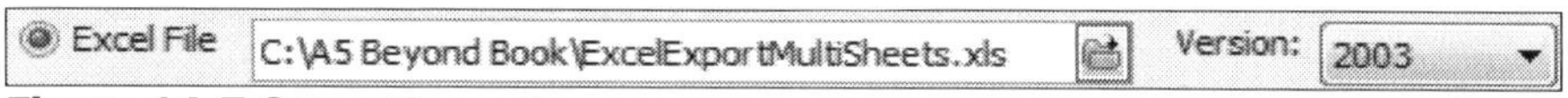

Figure 14-7 Connection options

If you want to export tables to an existing spreadsheet, click the yellow folder icon shown above in Figure 14-7 and select the spreadsheet.

5. Type `ExcelMultiSheetExport` as the connection name. Click OK on the Connection String dialog box. You will see the dialog box shown in Figure 14-8. The Alpha DAO Export Genie will remind you of the Alpha DAO Import Genie that you learned above in Chapter 12 because they look similar, as shown in Figure 14-8. The options that are different from the Alpha DAO Import Genie are explained below.

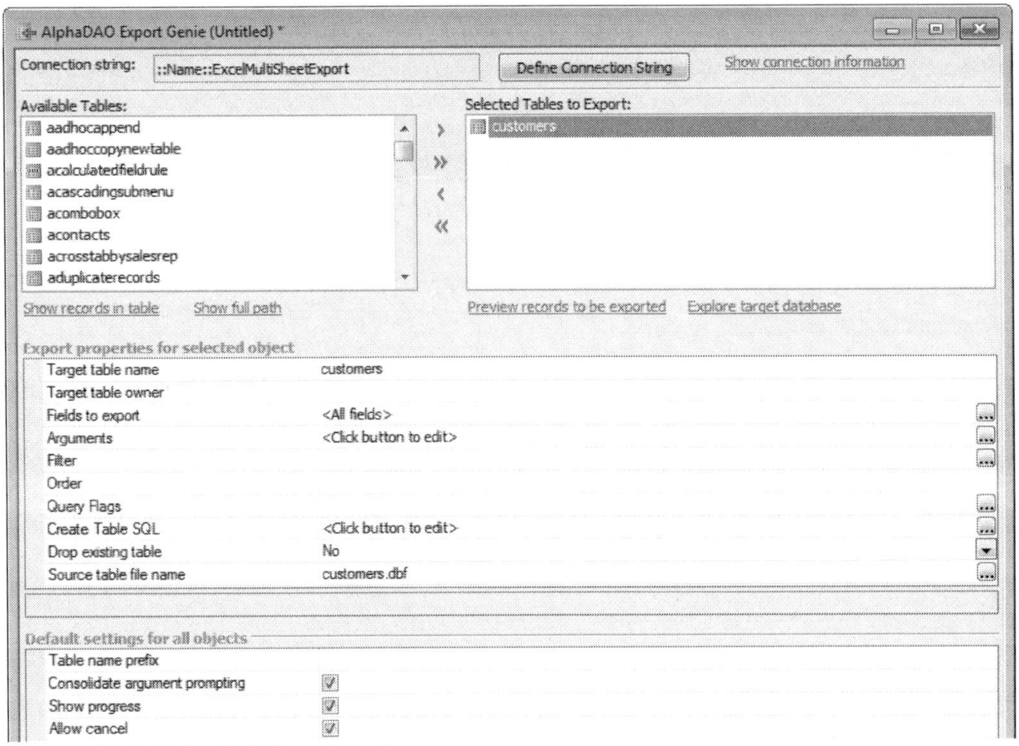

Figure 14-8 Alpha DAO Export Genie

Section 1: Connection String Options

The options in this section are used to select, create and edit connections, as well as view and filter the data that will be exported. The options are explained below.

① The **SHOW FULL PATH** link displays the path to the table in the Available Tables list that is selected, as shown in Figure 14-9.

② The **PREVIEW RECORDS TO BE EXPORTED** link displays the Records inquiry dialog box. It displays the records in the table selected in the Selected Tables to Export list. It is similar to the Total Records in Query dialog box.

③ The **EXPLORE TARGET DATABASE** link displays the dialog box shown in Figure 14-10.

Figure 14-9 Table File Name dialog box

Using The Explorer

This dialog box shown in Figure 14-10 has two sections, as explained below.

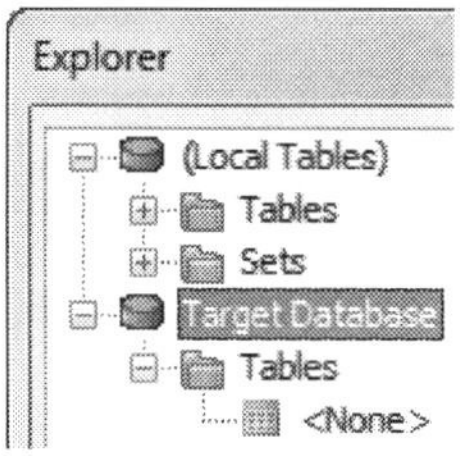

Figure 14-10 Explorer dialog box

(Local Tables) Section

This section displays the tables and sets in the database. Right-clicking on the (Local Tables) node displays the shortcut menu shown in Figure 14-11.

The **ADD DATABASE TO EXPLORER** option is used to select an existing connection or create a new connection for a database that you want to add to the Export Genie. This will let you export from multiple data sources at the same time.

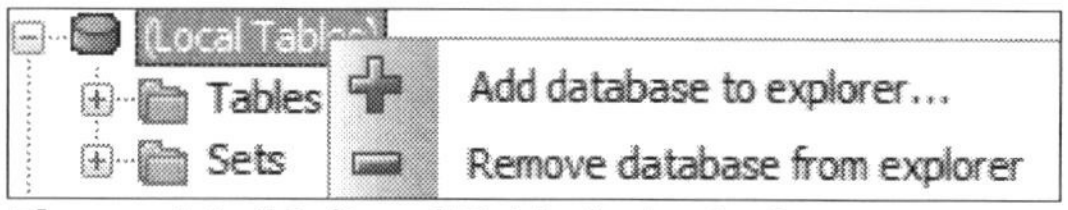

Figure 14-11 (Local Tables) shortcut menu

The **REMOVE DATABASE FROM EXPLORER** option does just that. It removes the database associated with the local table.

Right-clicking on a table name displays the shortcut menu shown in Figure 14-12. By default, the options are used to view the table in the Default Browse or Default Form. As shown, if the table has forms, browses, reports etc., that were created based on the table, you can access those as well.

Figure 14-13 shows the fields in a table with the field type and length.

Right-clicking on a set displays the shortcut menu shown in Figure 14-14. The View option displays the options shown in Figure 14-12. The **SHOW SET STRUCTURE** option displays the **SET INFORMATION** dialog box.

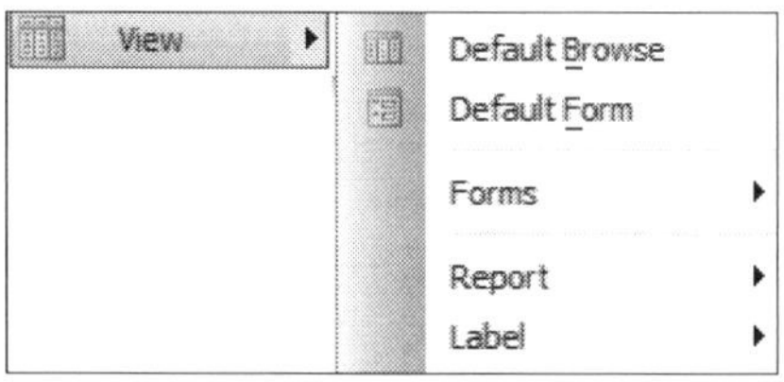

Figure 14-12 Table folder shortcut menu

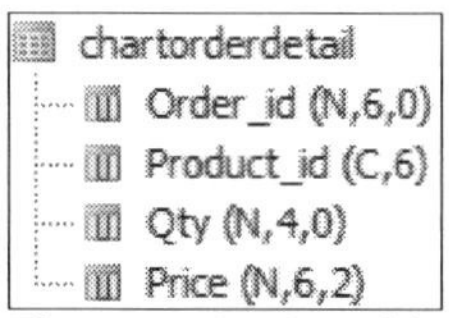

Figure 14-13 Fields in a table

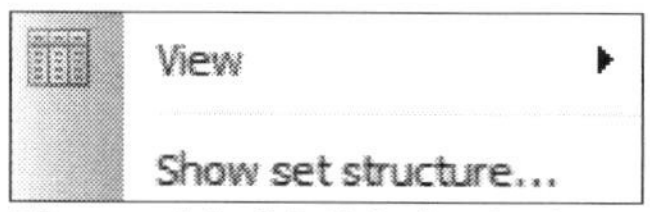

Figure 14-14 Set shortcut menu

Target Database Section

This section displays the tables that will be exported. It will be empty until you save the changes on the Alpha DAO Export Genie dialog box.

Right-clicking on the Target Database node displays the shortcut menu shown in Figure 14-15.

The options that you may not be familiar with are explained below.

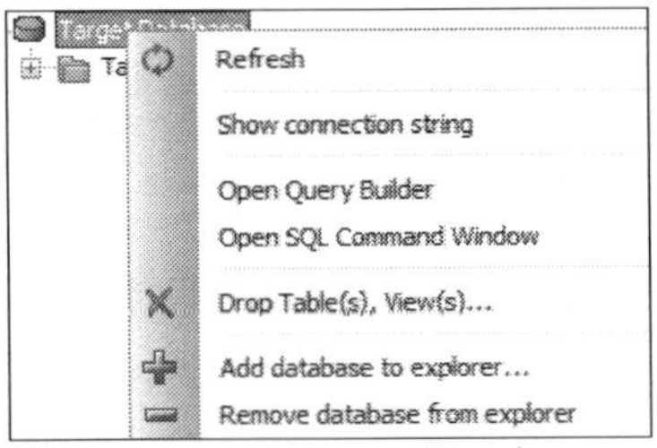

Figure 14-15 Target Database node shortcut menu

① **SHOW CONNECTION STRING** Displays the Connection String for Target database dialog box (the file that will be created when the data is exported) shown in Figure 14-16.

② **OPEN QUERY BUILDER** Displays the genie shown in Figure 14-19. It is used to create an SQL SELECT statement that uses **PORTABLE SQL**. The purpose of each tab is explained below the figure.

③ **OPEN SQL COMMAND WINDOW** Displays the dialog box shown in Figure 14-17. It is used to test SQL statements.

④ **DROP TABLE(S), VIEW(S)** Displays the dialog box shown in Figure 14-18. Right-clicking on the Tables node also displays this dialog box. It is used to remove tables, views, linked tables, synonyms and aliases from the database.

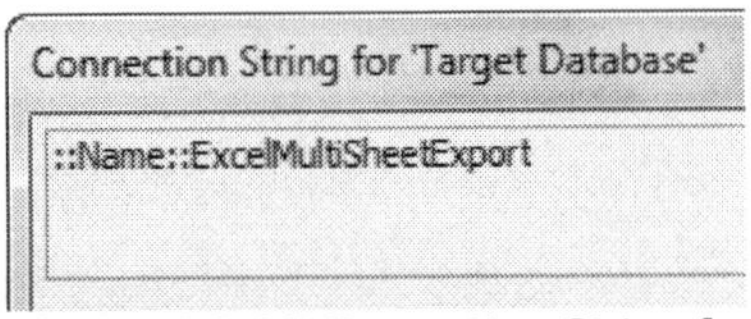

Figure 14-16 Connection String for Target Database dialog box

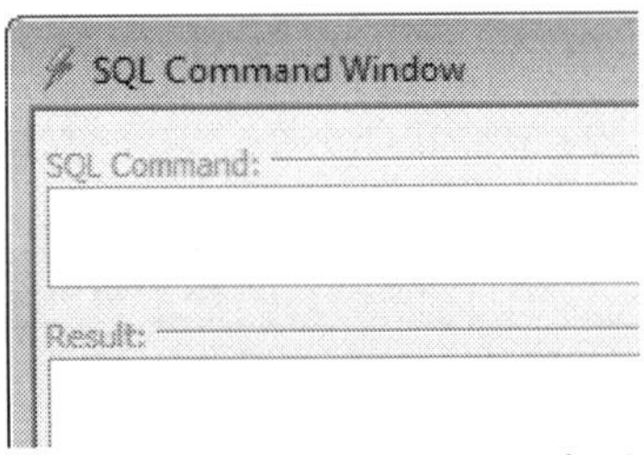

Figure 14-17 SQL Command Window

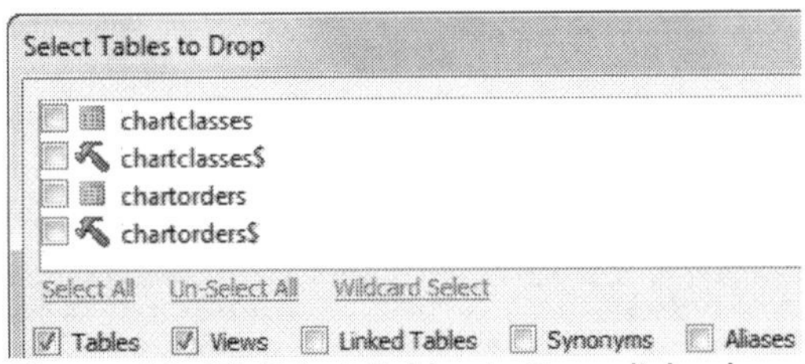

Figure 14-18 Select Tables to Drop dialog box

SQL Query Genie

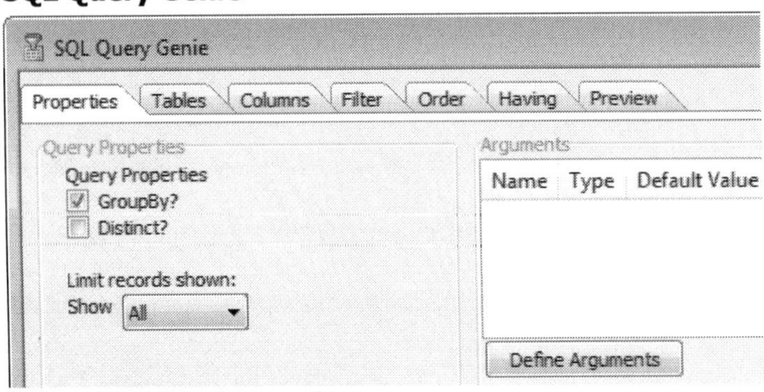

Figure 14-19 SQL Query Genie

① **PROPERTIES TAB** Is used to define arguments, set record ranges, create **GROUP BY** and **DISTINCT** clauses.
② **TABLES TAB** Is used to select the tables and define the **JOIN RELATIONSHIPS** between the tables.
③ **COLUMNS TAB** Is used to select the fields from the tables.
④ **FILTER TAB** Is used to create **WHERE CLAUSES** to filter the records that will be retrieved.
⑤ **ORDER TAB** Is used to select the sort order of the records that will be retrieved.
⑥ **HAVING TAB** Is only available when there is a Group By clause. It is used to create a filter that will select records when there is a Group By clause.
⑦ **PREVIEW TAB** Is used to view the SQL SELECT statement and records that will be retrieved.

Explorer Tables Shortcut Menu

Right-clicking on a table displays the shortcut menu shown in Figure 14-20.

This shortcut menu is only available after you have run the export.

The options are explained in Table 14-2.

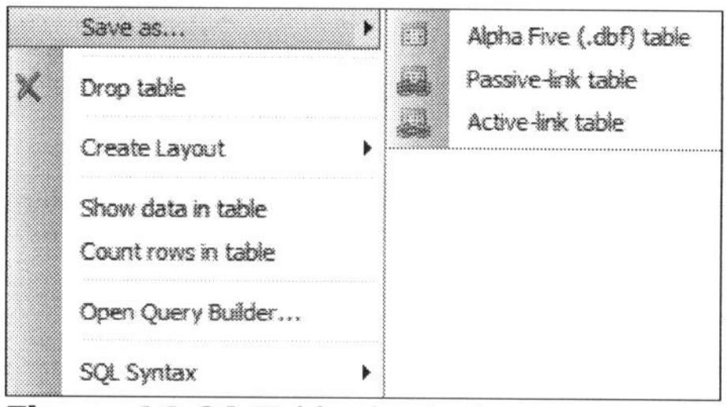

Figure 14-20 Table shortcut menu

Option	Description
Save As	Displays the options shown on the right of Figure 14-20 above. The options are formats that the exported table can be saved as.
Drop Table	Deletes the table from the export.
Create Layout	Creates a report, label or letter based on the data.
Show data in table	Displays some of the data that was exported, as shown in Figure 14-21.
Count rows in table	Displays the dialog box shown in Figure 14-22. The message displays how many records were exported.
Open Query Builder	Is used to view or modify the SQL statement that was used to create the exported table. [See SQL Query Genie, earlier in this chapter]
SQL Syntax	Displays the submenu shown in Figure 14-23. The options are used to create a CREATE TABLE statement on the dialog box shown in Figure 14-24, create an Insert, Update or Delete statement for the selected table.

Table 14-2 Explorer Tables shortcut menu options explained

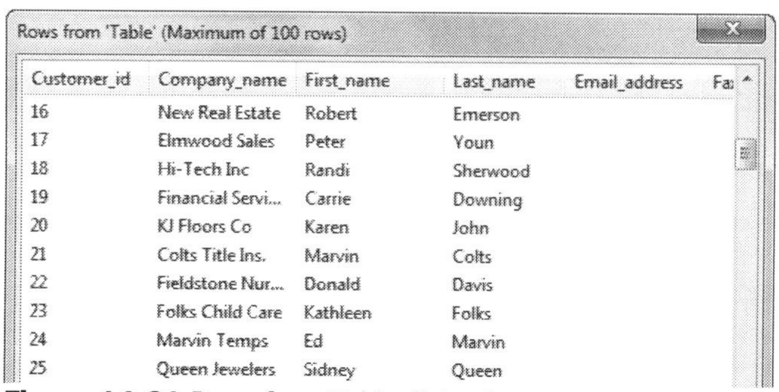

Figure 14-21 Rows from Table dialog box

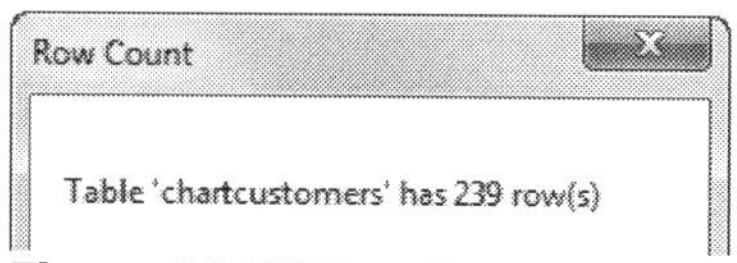

Figure 14-22 Row Count dialog box

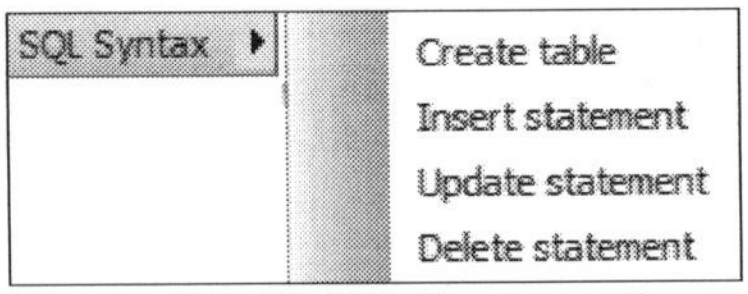

Figure 14-23 SQL Syntax options

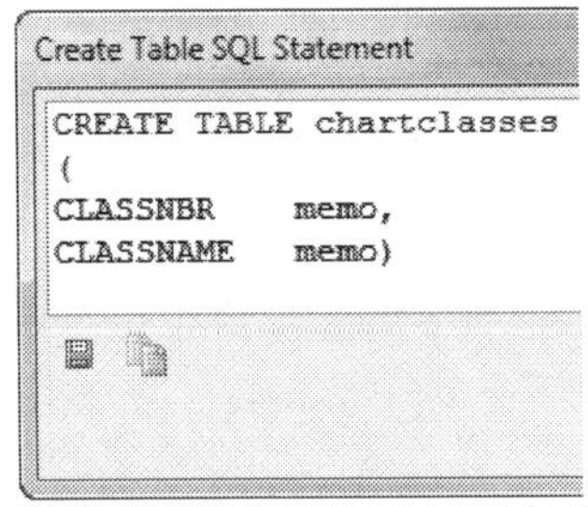

Figure 14-24 Create Table SQL Statement dialog box

Section 2: Export Properties For Selected Object

The options in this section are used to customize the export of the table selected in the Selected Tables to Export list. The options in this section work in conjunction with the default settings for all objects. Each table being exported can have different options in this section. The options are explained in Table 14-3.

Option	Is Used To . . .
Target table name	Change the name of the table that will be exported, if necessary. The default is the name of the table in Alpha Five.
Target table owner	Enter the owners name of the table if the exported table needs an owner for security purposes.
Fields to export	Select the fields that you want to export. The default is all fields. Clicking the button at the end of the field opens the dialog box shown in Figure 14-25. Select the fields that you want to export. They do not have to be exported in the same order that they are in the table.
Arguments	Create prompts for the user to select the export criteria for the table at run time. The button at the end of the field opens the **DEFINE/EDIT ARGUMENTS** dialog box.
Filter	Create a filter that selects the records in the table that will be exported. The **FILTER BUILDER** is available to help you create the filter if needed.
Order	Create an expression to sort the records that will be exported. The default sort order is by record number.
Query Flags	Control the order of which records are exported and if only unique records based on the order criteria are exported. This option works in conjunction with the order expression. Clicking the button at the end of the field displays the dialog box shown in Figure 14-26.
Create Table SQL	Create the table definition using the **CREATE TABLE** statement. By default, Alpha Five will create the table definition SQL statement. If you want to create the statement, click the button at the end of the field to use the dialog box shown in Figure 14-27.
Drop existing table	Use the options shown in Figure 14-28 to select what should happen to a table in the exported (target) database that has the same name.
Source table file name	View the name of the table that will be exported. This property cannot be changed.

Table 14-3 Export Properties for Selected Object section options explained

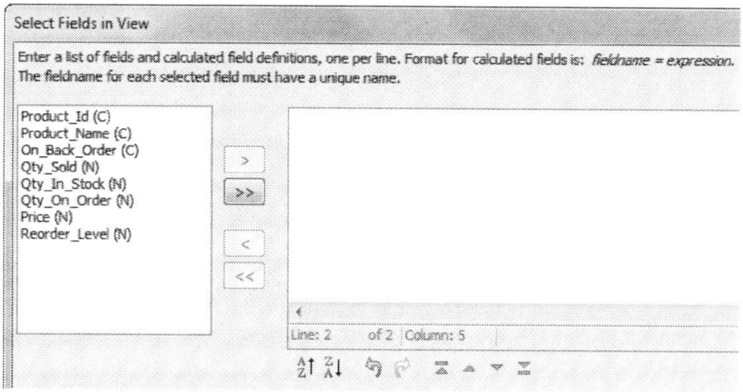

Figure 14-25 Select Fields in View dialog box

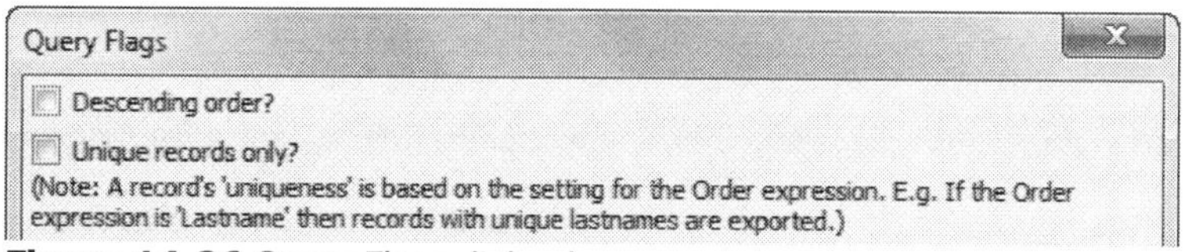

Figure 14-26 Query Flags dialog box

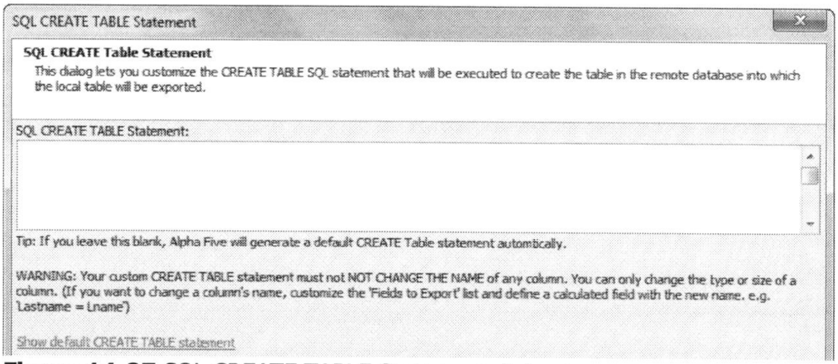

Figure 14-27 SQL CREATE TABLE Statement dialog box

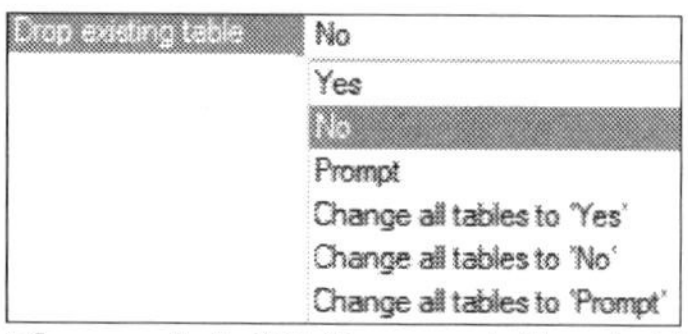

Figure 14-28 Drop existing table options

Section 3: Default Settings For All Objects

The settings in this section are automatically applied to every table that will be exported. They are the same as the ones for the Alpha DAO Import Genie. [See Chapter 12, Section 3: Default Settings For All Objects]

Select The Tables To Export

1. Select five tables of your choice to export.

2. Change the Target table name of the second table that you selected.

3. Select the first three fields in the fourth table as the fields to export.

4. Create a filter for one of the tables.

5. Use the Query Flags option on the first table that you selected to only export unique records.

6. Change the Drop existing table option for the first table that you selected, to **PROMPT** and Yes for the second table that you selected.

7. Click the Save button on the toolbar, then type `aExcelExportMultiSheet` as the operation name.

8. Click the Run button.

   When the export is finished, you should see the dialog box shown in Figure 14-29. It displays the status of each table that was exported.

   If you see that an export failed, click on the table to view the error message, as shown at the bottom of Figure 14-29.

   If you run the operation a second time, tables that you changed the Drop existing table option to Prompt, will be displayed on the dialog box shown in Figure 14-30.

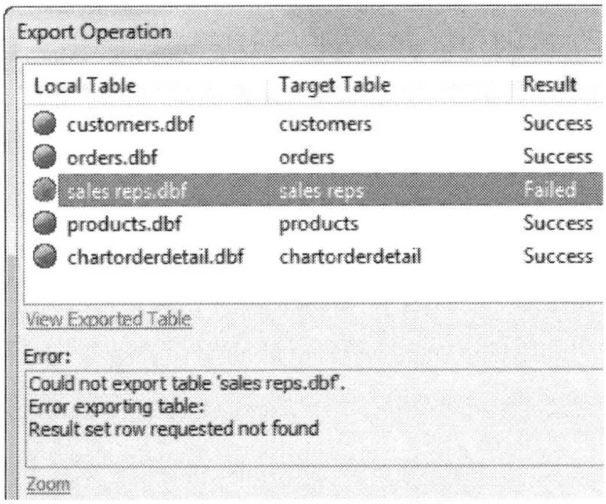

Figure 14-29 Export Operation dialog box

When you open the Excel Export Multi Sheet spreadsheet, you should see a tab for each table that you exported.

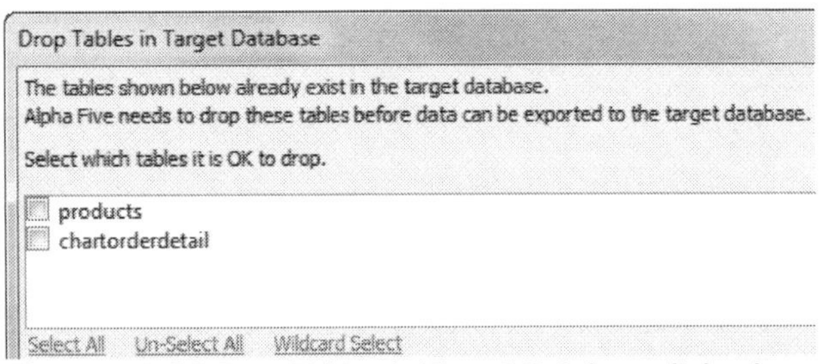

Figure 14-30 Drop Tables in Target Database dialog box

Using Mapped Tables

As you learned in Chapter 2, a mapped table contains fields from two or more tables. From that perspective, it may remind you of the **JOIN OPERATION**. Once created, mapped tables are placed on the Tables/Sets tab on the Control panel and can be used to create forms and reports, just list any other table. One reason mapped tables are used to export data is because they can export calculated fields to Excel.

Exercise 14.4: Export A Mapped Table

In this exercise you will use fields in the Order Detail and Products tables to create a mapped table. You will also create a calculated field, then export the mapped table.

1. On the Tables/Sets tab. New ⇒ New Mapped Tables.
2. Add the Order Detail and Products tables.
3. On the Fields tab, add the following fields from the Order Detail table. Order ID and Product ID.
4. Add the Product Name field from the Products table, then add the Qty and Price fields from the Order Detail table.

Create The Calculated Field

1. Click the Add Computed Column button.
2. In the Field Name field type `LineTotal`. Select the Numeric type.
3. Type `8` in the Width field and `2` in the Decimals field.
4. Click the **BUILD** button.

   Create an expression that multiplies the Qty and Price fields.

   You should have the options shown in Figure 14-31.

   Click OK.

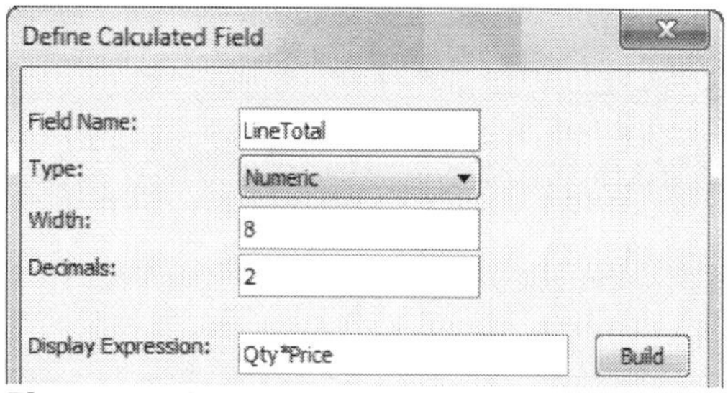

Figure 14-31 Define Calculated Field dialog box

5. Click OK. Type `aMappedOrders` as the table name on the Specify Table Name dialog box.

Export The Mapped Table To Excel

1. On the Operations tab, select the Export Records operation.
2. Select the Remote database option, then create a connection to a new Excel file named `ExportMappedTable.xls`, as shown in Figure 14-32.

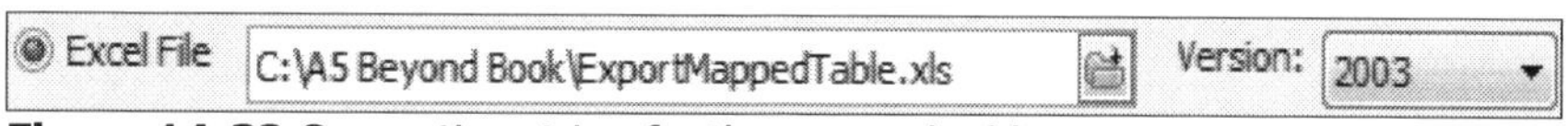

Figure 14-32 Connection string for the mapped table

3. Save the named connection string as `MappedTableExport`.
4. On the Alpha DAO Export Genie dialog box, select the aMappedOrders table as the one to export.
5. Change the Target table name to `OrderDetailExport`.

6. Save the export operation as `aMappedExport`. Run the export.

Exercise 14.5: Save A Layout Table Report To Excel

Layout table reports are well suited for exporting to Excel because the data is already in rows and columns. In this exercise you will export a contacts layout table report to Excel.

1. Preview the Contacts by State layout report.

2. Click the Save As button on the toolbar or File ⇒ Save As, then select the Excel option.

You can save the Excel file with the same name as the layout table report or you can type in the name that you want.

If checked, the **OPEN FILE WITH ASSOCIATED APPLICATION** option will cause Excel (in this exercise) to open and automatically open the spreadsheet.

3. If you want to change the Excel file name, change it now. You should have the options shown in Figure 14-33.

   The **CLICK TO SET EXCEL OPTIONS** link opens the dialog box shown in Figure 14-34. If your report has any of these features and you want them exported to the Excel file, check the item(s) that you need.

   Click OK.

   The spreadsheet will be created and opened in Excel.

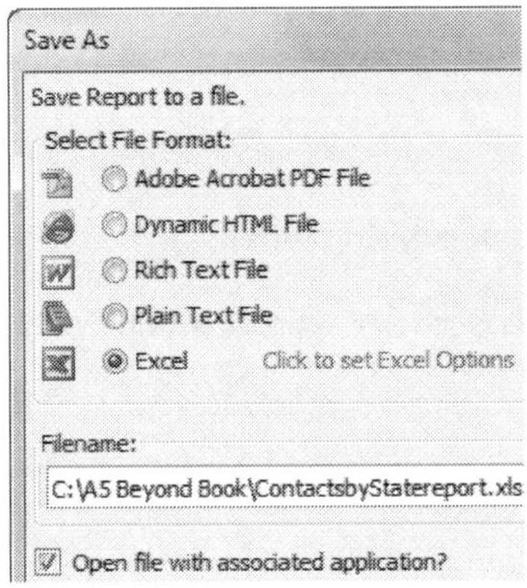

Figure 14-33 Excel Save As options

If you scroll to the bottom of the spreadsheet you will see Page 0 of 0. That is because Excel does not recognize Alpha Five system fields. On your own, you could delete this field from the layout table report before saving it as an Excel file.

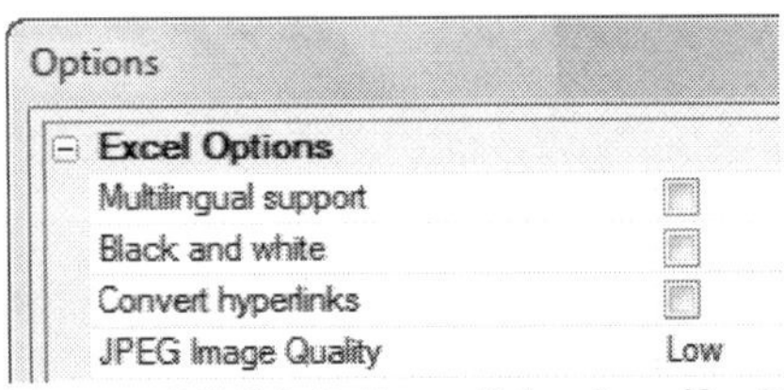

Figure 14-34 Options dialog box (for Excel)

> **Default Save As Option**
> By default, the file format option selected on the Save As dialog box (shown earlier in Figure 14-33) is the option that was used, the last time that you used this feature.

> **Saving Layout Table Reports With Linked Reports**
> This report combination can be saved to an Excel spreadsheet, just like Layout Table Reports can.

Saving In PDF Format

This file type is very popular because it saves the document exactly as it is displayed. This file type can be opened and printed from virtually every computer, regardless of the operating system that the computer has. Alpha Five has a built-in PDF driver, which means that you do not need additional software to create basic PDF files in Alpha Five. In Chapter 8, you learned how to use the PDF Viewer super control to display a PDF file on a form.

PDF Options

The options shown in Figure 14-35 are used to configure the PDF file.

These options are available when you view a PDF file. The options are explained in Table 14-4.

Select the **SAVE AS DEFAULT** option at the bottom of the dialog box if the options selected on the dialog box are the ones that you will use the majority of time to create this file type.

Each of the file formats on the Save As dialog box shown earlier in Figure 14-33, except the Plain Text File format has the Save as default option.

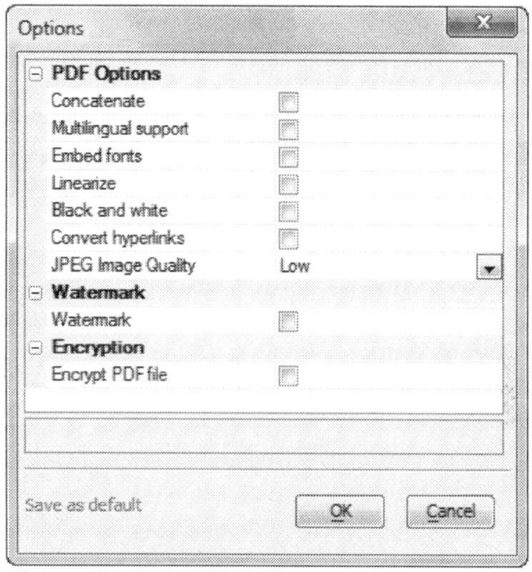

Figure 14-35 PDF Options

Option	Description
Concatenate	If checked and there is already a PDF file with the same name, the PDF file that you are creating now will be added to the existing PDF file with the same name. This is similar to the **COMBINE FILES** PDF Tool. [See PDF Tools]
Multilingual support	If checked, international character sets will be added to the PDF file.
Embed fonts	If the file that you are saving as a PDF file has fonts that do not come with Windows, you should check this option. The reason is because you cannot guarantee that every one that opens the PDF file has all of the fonts that you used. If someone opens the PDF file and does not have a font that you used, that portion of the PDF file will be displayed in a default font at best. Keep in mind that embedded fonts in a PDF file cannot be edited.
Linearize	Check this option if the report will be displayed on a web page. This option allows some of the pages to be displayed in the web browser before the entire PDF file has loaded.
Black and white	Check this option if you want all of the color in the document to be saved in black and white in the PDF file.
Convert hyperlinks	Checking this option allows the links that start with **HTTP**, in the file being exported to be clicked on in the PDF file.

Table 14-4 PDF export options explained

Option	Description
JPEG Image Quality	Is used to select the quality of any JPEG image file that will be saved in the PDF file. The higher the quality selected, the better the image file will look in the PDF file.
Watermark	[See PDF Watermark Options] (1)
Encrypt PDF file	[See PDF Encryption Options] (1)

Table 14-4 PDF export options explained (Continued)

(1) Checking this option displays more options to customize the PDF file.

PDF Watermark Options

The options shown in Figure 14-36 are used to create a watermark that will appear on every page in the PDF file. The options are explained in Table 14-5.

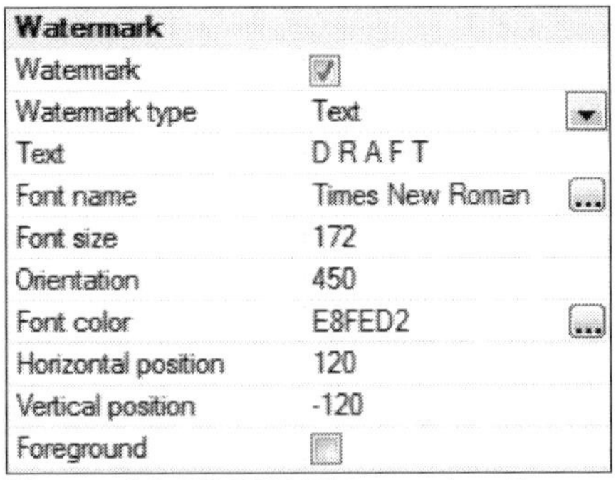

Figure 14-36 PDF Watermark options

Option	Description
Watermark	If checked, a watermark will be added to every page in the PDF file. This option enables the other watermark options.
Watermark type	Is used to select if the watermark is text or a PDF File.
Text	Text watermarks can use the default DRAFT option or you can type in the text that you want to use as the watermark. (2)
Font name	Select the font that you want the text watermark to be displayed in. (2)
Font size	Type in the font size in inches for the text watermark. (2)
Orientation	Type in how much you want the watermark rotated. The 450 default value will rotate the watermark 45 degrees. (2)
Font color	Is used to select the color for the text watermark. (2)
Horizontal position	This is the starting point measured from the left side of the page where the watermark should start. This must be a positive number. The default 120 value means that the watermark will start about one inch from the left margin. (2)
Vertical position	This is the starting point measured from the top of the page where the watermark will start. This must be a negative number. The default -120 value means that the watermark will start about two inches from the top of the page. (2)
Watermark file name	Is used to select one of the options shown in Figure 14-37. This option is only available if the watermark type is PDF.
Foreground	If checked, the watermark will appear on top of the content in the PDF file. The default is to have the watermark appear behind the content.

Table 14-5 PDF Watermark options explained

(2) This option is only available if the watermark type is text.

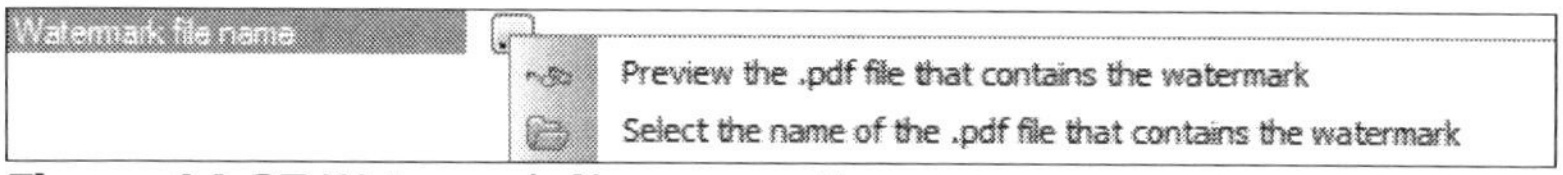

Figure 14-37 Watermark file name options

PDF Encryption Options

The options shown in Figure 14-38 are used to add security to the PDF file. They are explained in Table 14-6.

Figure 14-38 PDF Encryption options

Option	Description
Encrypt PDF file	Is used to add passwords to the to the PDF file and set permissions for the PDF file. If checked, an owner password is required. This option enables the other encryption options.
Owner password	Is used to enter the password that must be used if the permissions of the PDF file need to be changed. (3)
User password	Is used to enter the password that must be used to open the PDF file. Even if the PDF files does not have a user password, the restrictions are still enforced. (3)
Can print	If checked, the PDF file can be printed.
Can modify document	If checked, the content of the PDF file can be modified.
Can copy	If checked, the content of the PDF file can be copied. (4)
Can add notes	If checked, people that can open the PDF file can use the Comment/Add Sticky Note feature in the PDF file.
Use 128 bit key	If checked, version 5 or higher of the Adobe Reader is required to view the PDF file.

Table 14-6 PDF Encryption options explained

(3) Using a password is optional. The password is case sensitive.

(4)

PDF Can Copy Option
I don't know if this option works properly. I encrypted the PDF file, set an owner password and removed the check mark for this option and was still able to copy the content of the PDF file to a text file.

Exercise 14.6: Save A Report In PDF Format

In this exercise you will save a report that has a chart in PDF format.

Check The Printer Options
By default, the PDF tool uses the settings of your default printer. Check the printer options before creating the PDF file. Make any changes to the printer options that are needed.

1. Preview the aPieChart report. File ⇒ Save As. You will see the same Save As dialog box shown earlier in Figure 14-33.

2. Display the PDF options, then clear the Embed fonts option on the dialog box shown earlier in Figure 14-35.

Add A Text Watermark To The PDF File

1. In the Text field type `CONFIDENTIAL`.

2. Change the font to Century gothic (if you don't have this font, select another one), then change the Font size to 80.

3. Change the Orientation to 350.

4. Change the Vertical position to `-60`, then click OK.

5. Click OK on the Save As dialog box to create the PDF. If you see the dialog box shown in Figure 14-39, you can click OK and create the PDF file to see if all of the content is in it.

When I get this dialog box, I select the **TRIM** option because more times then not, the report layout is too wide and the right side of the report does not have any content. If you look at the Right printer and Report margin options shown on the dialog box, you will see what I am talking about. If not, change the settings for the printer being used to base the PDF file on or resize the report.

You see the warning message based on your settings for the overflow data option. If you selected Prompt at run time, you will see this dialog box.

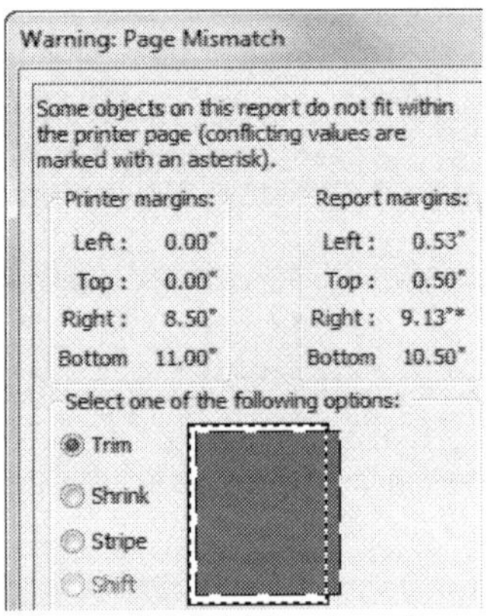

Figure 14-39 Warning: Page Mismatch message

On the first page of the PDF file you cannot see all of the watermark, as shown in Figure 14-40 because the chart is over it.

If you view the second page of the PDF file, shown in Figure 14-41, you can see the entire watermark.

I changed the font color of the text watermark so that it would be visible in the figures. Yours should not be as dark.

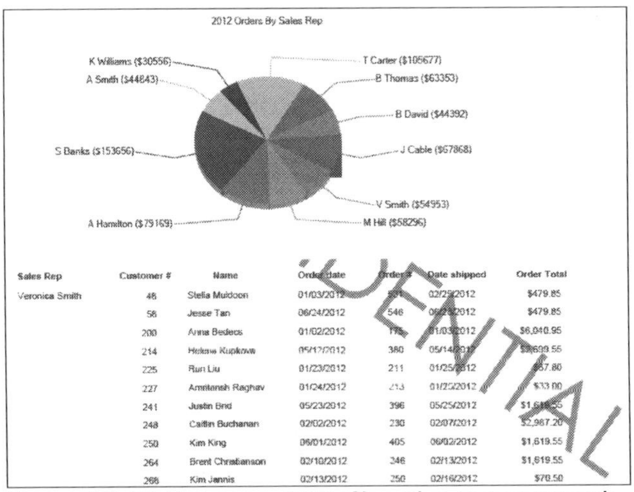

Figure 14-40 First page of PDF file with a text watermark

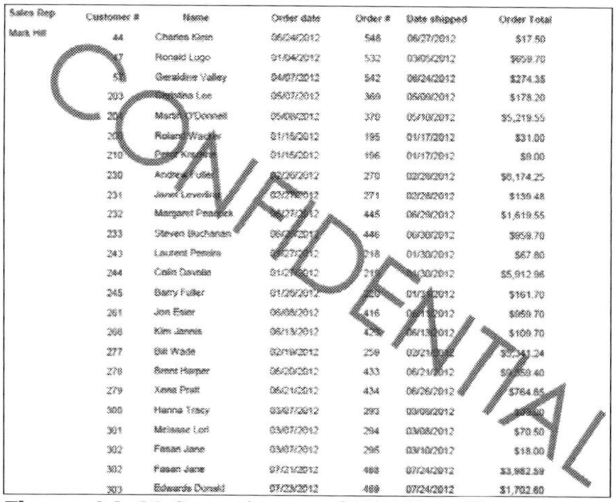

Figure 14-41 Second page of PDF file with a text watermark

Exercise 14.7: Create A PDF File With Bookmarks

If you save reports that have a Table of Contents, bookmarks or an index, in PDF format, all of those features are automatically enabled in the PDF file.

1. Preview the aIndexCustom report, then File ⇒ Save As.

2. Select the PDF File option, then display the PDF options.

3. Clear the watermark option. Click OK to create the PDF file. It should look like the one shown in Figure 14-42.

   On the left are the bookmarks for the report.

   If you click on a page number or line in the Table of Contents on the right, the corresponding page of the report will be displayed.

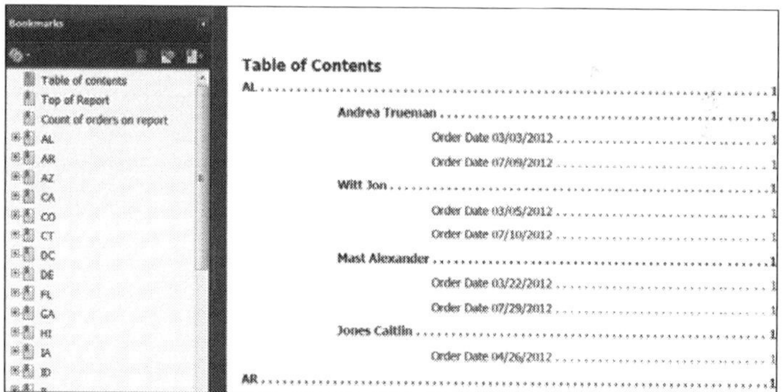

Figure 14-42 PDF file with bookmarks

4. Select a state. Select a customer in the state that you selected, then select an order number. The orders will be displayed on the right.

Interestingly enough, when you click on the Index bookmark (on the left), the beginning of the Index is displayed on the right. For me, that doesn't happen when view the report in Alpha Five.

I do wish that the highlight feature that is automatically available for reports with bookmarks came over during the conversion to PDF format.

Saving Reports As A Dynamic HTML File

The options shown in Figure 14-43 are used to configure a report to be saved as an HTML file, which will be viewed using a web browser.

The options specifically for the HTML file type are explained below. The other options were explained earlier in Table 14-4.

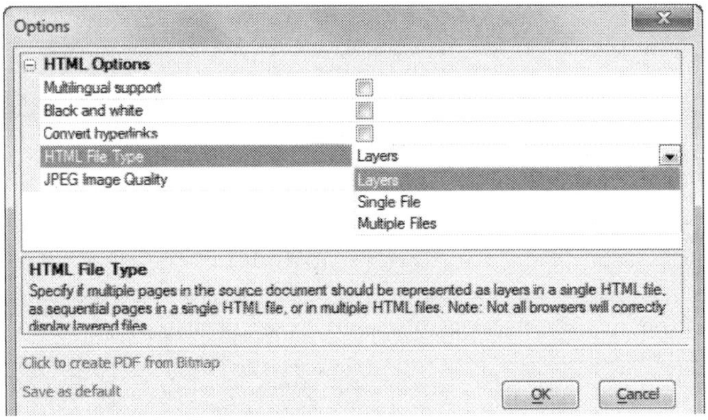

Figure 14-43 HTML options

The **CLICK TO CREATE PDF FROM BITMAP** link displays the Create PDF File From Bitmap dialog box. [See Create From Bitmap] This option is also available for Rich Text File and Excel options on the Save As dialog box.

HTML File Type Options

The options shown above in Figure 14-43 are used to select how the report should be converted to an HTML file. If the report is only one page, these options may not matter.

① Select the **LAYERS OPTION** to create one HTML page. This page has all of the report pages. A navigational system is added to the HTML file to let the user go from page to page.
② Select the **SINGLE FILE OPTION** to create multiple pages in one HTML file. The user has to scroll down to view all of the report pages.
③ Select the **MULTIPLE FILES OPTION** to make more than one HTML file from the report pages.

Exercise 14.8: Save A Report As A Dynamic HTML File

In this exercise you will create three HTML files, one for each type. You will use the same report to create each file type so that you can see the differences. Keep in mind that not all browsers display layered files.

Use The Layers HTML File Type

1. Preview the aOrdersGroupedByMonth report, then File ⇒ Save As.

2. Select the Dynamic HTML File option, then click the Click to set HTML Options link.

3. Open the HTML File Type drop-down list and select **LAYERS**.

4. Change the File name to `adynamiclayers.htm`, as illustrated in Figure 14-44.
   The HTML version of the report should look like the one shown in Figure 14-45.
   Notice the navigation buttons in the upper left corner. This is how to view the pages in the report. The blank space below the report title is where the chart is in the report. As you can see, the chart did not appear on the report in .HTML format.

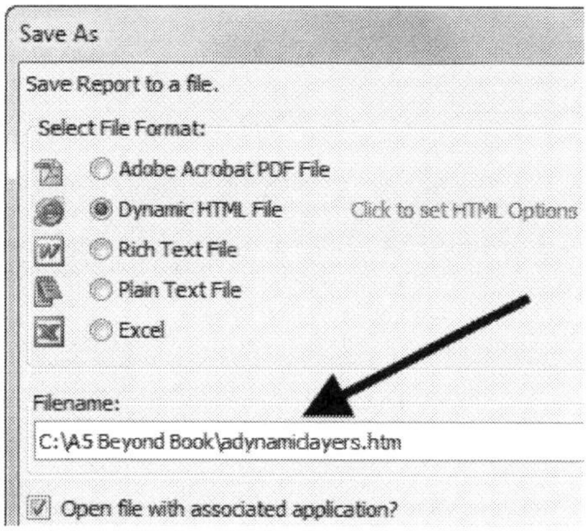

Figure 14-44 HTML file name illustrated

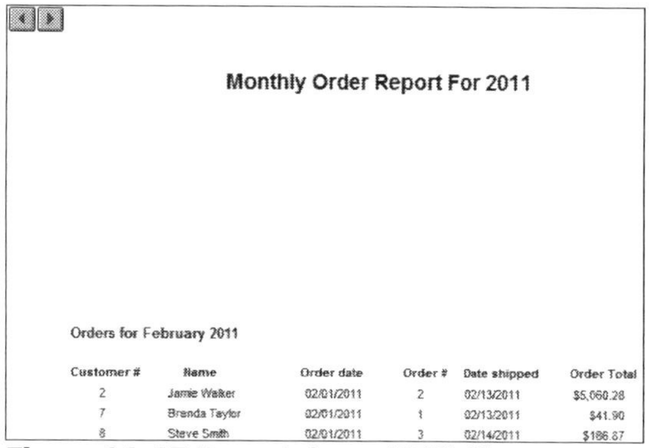

Figure 14-45 Dynamic layers HTML file type report

Use The Single Page HTML File Type

1. Preview the aOrdersGroupedByMonth report, then File ⇒ Save As.
2. Select the Dynamic HTML File option, then click the Click to set HTML Options link.
3. Open the HTML File Type drop-down list and select **SINGLE FILE**.
4. Change the File name to `adynamicsinglefile.htm`. The report looks like the layers report, minus the navigation buttons. To view the report pages, you have to scroll down the web page.

Use The Multiple File HTML File Type

1. Preview the aOrdersGroupedByMonth report, then File ⇒ Save As.
2. Select the Dynamic HTML File option, then click the Click to set HTML Options link.
3. Open the HTML File Type drop-down list and select **MULTIPLE FILES**.
4. Change the File name to `adynamicmultiplefiles.htm`.

> **Multiple File HTML File Type**
> This option is suppose to create multiple HTML pages if the report has multiple pages. During testing, only one HTML page was created, even though the report had several pages.

Saving A Report As A Rich Text File

The options shown in Figure 14-46 are used to create Rich Text files (also known as **RTF FILES**) from reports. Usually, RTF files are edited in Microsoft Word, but they can be edited in other software packages. The option specific to Rich Text files is explained below. The other options were explained earlier in Table 14-4.

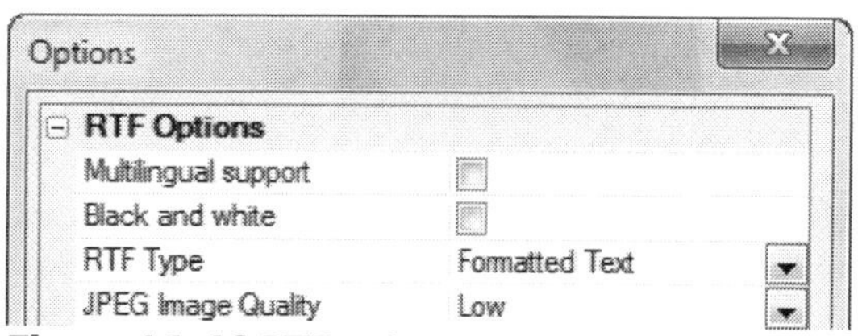

Figure 14-46 RTF options

The **RTF TYPE** option is used to select how much formatting in the report will be brought over to the exported file. Once converted, the RTF file is opened in word processing software. Select one of the following options based on the editing needs of the file.

① The **ADVANCED RTF** option supports text and graphics. Frames are used to position objects.

② The **FULL RTF** option makes the file easier to edit because it does not use frames. It does support text and graphics.

③ The **FORMATTED TEXT** option only supports text.

④ The **SIMPLE TEXT** option only supports unformatted text.

> When I tested each of these rich text options, I did not see a difference in the exported RTF files when I tested them in Word 2010.

Saving A Report As A Plain Text File

Selecting this option saves the report in a text file (**.TXT**), like files that are created in Notepad, which does not have any formatting.

PDF Tools

This option is on the Tools menu when no object on the Control Panel is open.

The options shown in Figure 14-47 are used to create PDF files and export PDF files to other formats. The options are explained below.

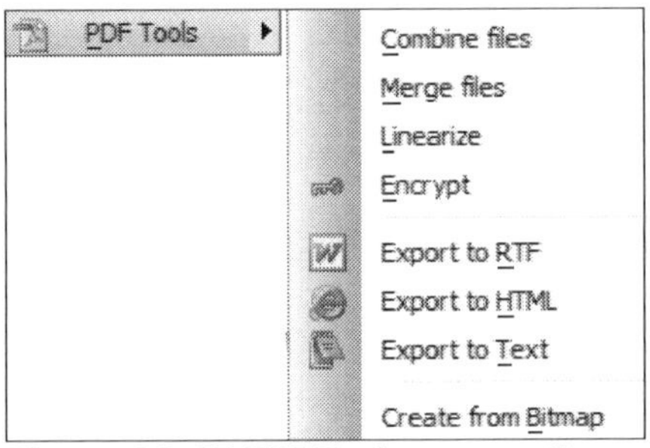

Figure 14-47 PDF Tools menu options

Exercise 14.9: Use The Combine Files Tool

The dialog box shown in Figure 14-48 is used to combine two or more PDF files into a new PDF file. In this exercise you will combine two PDF files that you created. The files will be combined in the order that they are listed in. This is similar to the **CONCATENATE PDF OPTION**, discussed earlier in this chapter.

1. Tools ⇒ PDF Tools ⇒ Combine files.

2. Click the Add File button, then select the aIndexCustom PDF file.
   Click the Add File button, then select the aPieChart PDF file.

> **Selecting Multiple PDF Files**
> It would be great if you could select more than one PDF file at a time on the Selected PDF File dialog box, instead of having to reopen the dialog box multiple times.

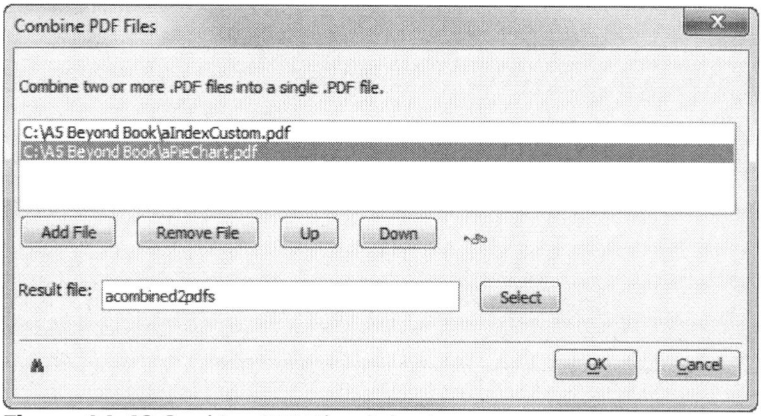

Figure 14-48 Combine PDF Files dialog box

Selecting The Result File

What may not be obvious is that by selecting an existing PDF file in the Result file field means that the files selected on the Combine PDF Files dialog box will overwrite the existing PDF file with the same name. If this field is left blank, the combined PDF file will be saved as the first file listed on the dialog box, overwriting the original.

1. In the **RESULT FILE** field, type `aCombined2PDFs`, as shown above in Figure 14-48, then click OK.

2. When prompted to view the file, click Yes. My PDF file is 65 pages. Page 55 starts the Pie Chart PDF.

Exercise 14.10: Use The Merge Files Tool

The options show in Figure 14-49 are used to add a logo or watermark in one PDF file to another PDF file.

What wasn't made clear, at least to me, is that the PDF file that has the logo or watermark should not have any other content.

In this exercise you will select the options to only apply the watermark to the first page of a PDF file.

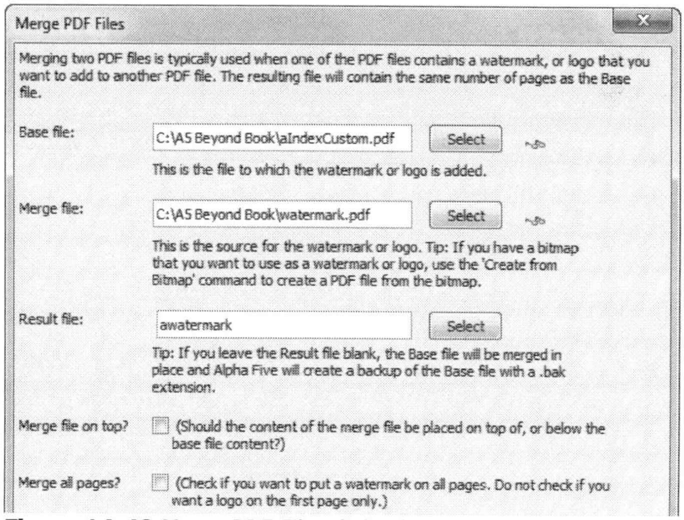

Figure 14-49 Merge PDF Files dialog box

1. Tools ⇒ PDF Tools ⇒ Merge Files.

2. Click the Base File Select button and select the aIndexCustom PDF file.

3. Click the Merge File Select button and select the Watermark PDF file.

4. In the Result file field type `awatermark`. Like the Combine Files tool, leaving this field blank overwrites the file. In this case the base file will be overwritten, but that may be what you want.

5. Clear the check mark for the **MERGE ALL PAGES** option. You should have the options shown above in Figure 14-49.

6. Click OK. Open the Adobe free reader or the full version of Adobe Acrobat to view the aWatermark PDF file. You should see that the watermark is only on the first page of the PDF file.

> According to the help file, there should be a prompt to view the PDF file. That did not happen for me.

Linearize Tool

The options shown in Figure 14-50 are used to create a PDF file that will let the user view pages of the PDF file on the web before the entire PDF file loads.

This is the same as selecting **LINEARIZE** on the dialog box shown earlier in Figure 14-35.

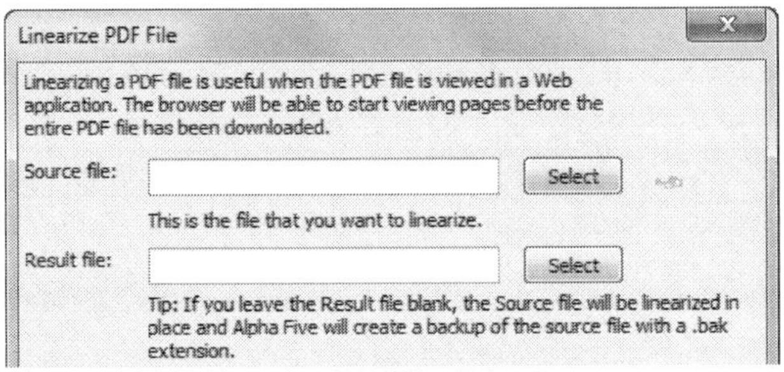

Figure 14-50 Linearize PDF File dialog box

Encrypt Tool

The options shown in Figure 14-51 are used to encrypt an existing PDF file. [See Encrypt PDF File, earlier in this chapter]

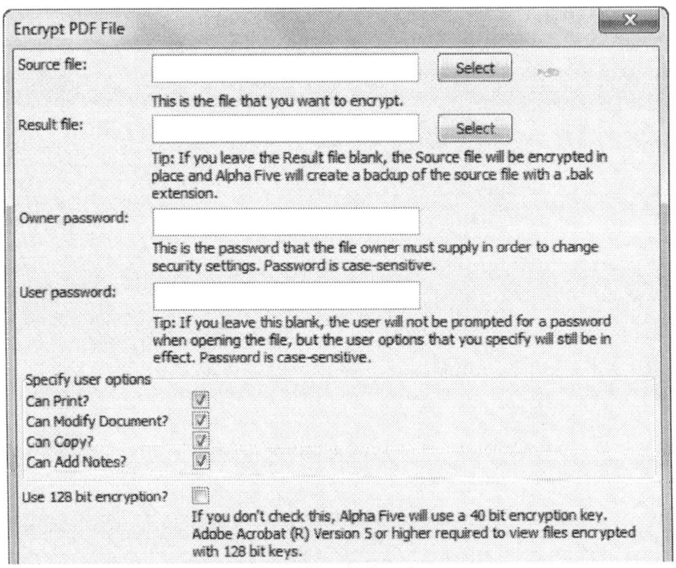

Figure 14-51 Encrypt PDF File dialog box

Exercise 14.11: Export To RTF

The options shown in Figure 14-52 are used to export a PDF file to an RTF document.

This is helpful if you need to edit the contents of a PDF file and do not have the file that the PDF was created from.

I don't know how much this would be used to modify the PDF version of Alpha Five reports.

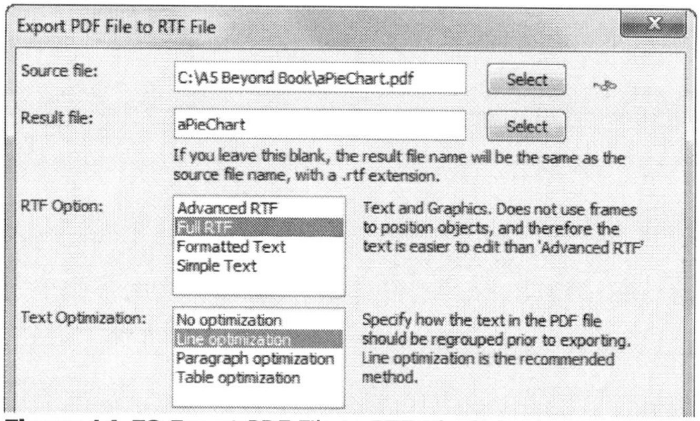

Figure 14-52 Export PDF File to RTF File dialog box

The **SHOW PDF FILE** button to the right of the first Select button will display the source PDF file that you selected.

RTF OPTION [See Saving A Report As A Rich Text File, earlier in this chapter]

> **PDF Files To Export**
> This tool is not limited to PDF files created in Alpha Five. As long as the PDF file is not encrypted, you can export it to RTF format using this option. I tested this by selecting a PDF file that I created outside of Alpha Five.

1. Tools ⇒ PDF Tools ⇒ Export To RTF.
2. Select the aPieChart PDF file as the source file.
3. In the Result file field type `aPieChartrpt`.
4. Select the RTF option, Full RTF, as shown above in Figure 14-52, then click OK. The **.RTF FILE** will be created. To view it, open Microsoft Word. When you first see the report it will be in columns. When you preview the report, it will look like the report that you originally created.

Export To HTML

The options shown in Figure 14-53 are used to export a PDF file to HTML format.

They work the same way as the Dynamic HTML file options that were covered earlier in this chapter.

The Multiple HTML Export option did not work here either for me (meaning it did not create more than one HTML file).

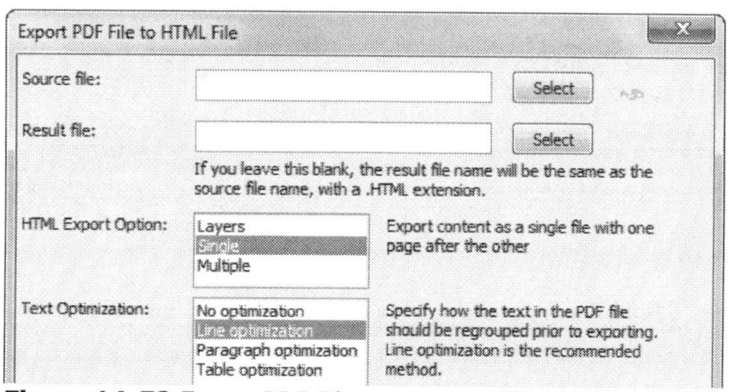

Figure 14-53 Export PDF File to HTML File dialog box

Export To Text

The options shown in Figure 14-54 are used to export a PDF file to plain text format (.TXT), like Notepad.

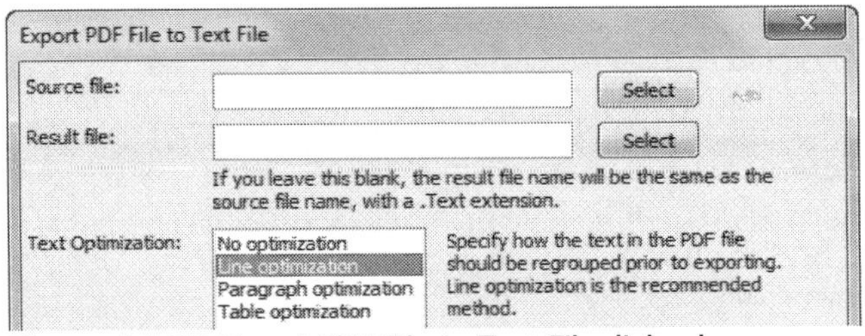

Figure 14-54 Export PDF File to Text File dialog box

Create From Bitmap

The options shown in Figure 14-55 are used to create a PDF file that would be used as a watermark or logo.

The two image file types that can be used as the watermark are **.BMP** and **.JPG**.

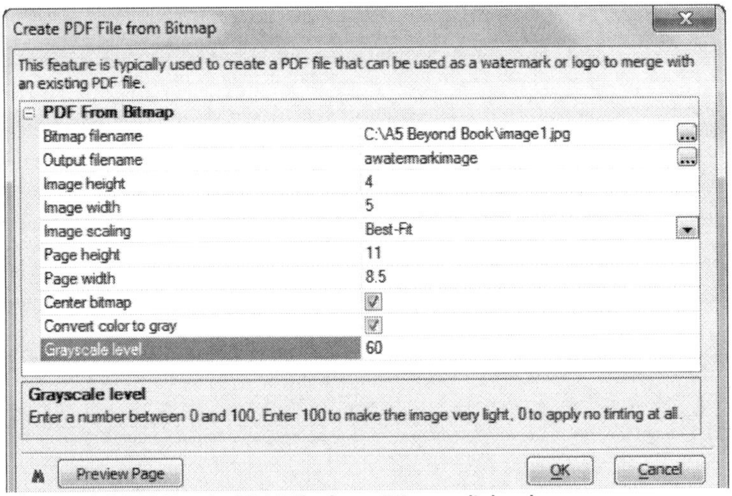

Figure 14-55 Create PDF File from Bitmap dialog box

Exercise 14.12: Create A PDF File To Use As A Watermark File

In this exercise you will create a PDF file to use as a watermark, then add it to another PDF file.

1. Tools ⇒ PDF Tools ⇒ Create from Bitmap.
2. Click the **BITMAP FILE NAME** field button, then select the image1.jpg file.
3. In the Output file name field type `awatermarkimage`.
4. Change the **GRAYSCALE LEVEL** to 60. You should have the options shown above in Figure 14-55. Click OK. If you want to preview the watermark file, click Yes.
5. Repeat Exercise 14.10 Use The Merge Files tool, with the changes below to use the watermark image PDF file that you just created.

   Step 2 - Use the awatermarkimage PDF file.
   Step 4 - Use `awatermark2`, as the file name.
   The first page of the watermark2 PDF file should have the image in the background.
   When you view the awatermark2.pdf file, you will see the image.

Exercise 14.13: Use The Print Layout Genie To Export Data

This genie can be used to export data displayed on a form or browse to any of the following file types: PDF, HTML, Rich Text or Excel. The data can be filtered and sorted before it is exported. The down side to this option is that your selections cannot be saved. You can copy the Xbasic code that is created by the options that you select, to a document to use later.

1. View the Orders Multi Table Set in the Default Browse.

2. Click the arrow on the Print button to display the menu shown in Figure 14-56, then select the **PRINT/SEND SELECTED RECORDS** option.

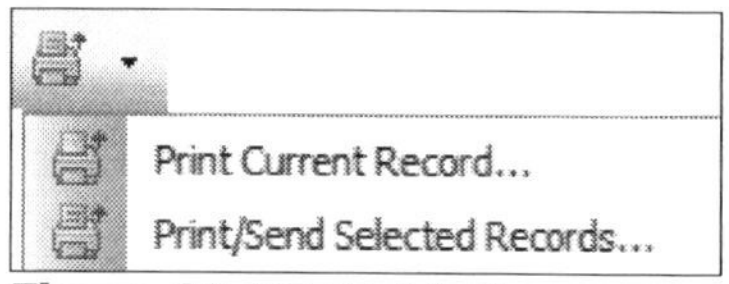

Figure 14-56 Print button menu

3. Open the Layout type drop-down list and select Browse. Because the browse that you want to use (in this exercise) is displayed, you can use the <Current Browse> option. The other layouts shown in the list are based on the same table or set.

4. Select the **SAVE TO FILE** option.

   You should have the options shown in Figure 14-57.

   Click Next.

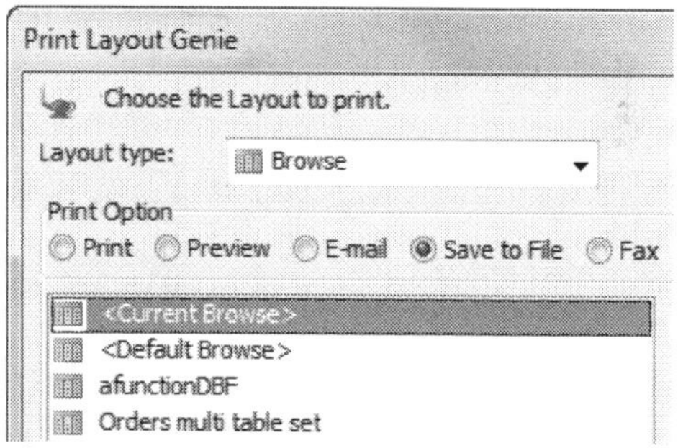

Figure 14-57 Print Layout Genie

5. Select the Records Selected by a Filter Expression option, then create an expression to select orders for Sales Rep ID's 1, 2, 3, 4 or 5, as shown in Figure 14-58.

   Click Next.

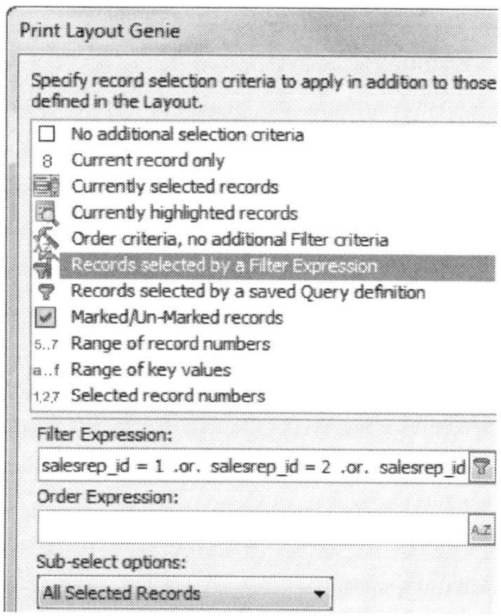

Figure 14-58 Selection criteria

6. Click the Options link, then clear the check mark for the Watermark option.

The Save As drop-down list on the Print Layout Genie contains the file formats that the data in the browse can be saved in.

7. Change the File name to `aPrintLayoutGenie`, as shown in Figure 14-59.

   Click Finish.

   You will see the records from the browse in the PDF file. What you will notice is that all of the columns do not fit on one page because there are too many of them.

   The **OPTIONS** link opens the corresponding Export dialog box based on the file type selected (in this exercise the dialog box shown earlier in Figure 14-35 would open).

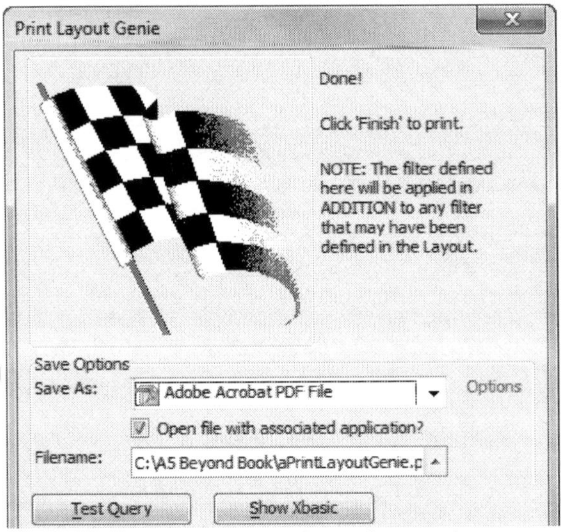

Figure 14-59 Print Layout Genie Save options

   The **TEST QUERY** button shows how many records will be displayed, based on the filter expression that you create.

Exercise 14.14: Export A Layout

In Chapter 12 you learned how to import a report layout. In this exercise you will learn how to export a report layout, which can be used in another Alpha Five database.

1. Right-click on the aSplineAreaChart report, then select **EXPORT LAYOUT**.

2. In the File name file type `aSplineAreaChartReport`, then click the Save button. If you look in the folder for this book, you will see the aSplineAreaChartReport.a5pkg file. You would open this file in the database that you needed to use the report in.

USING XDIALOG

In this chapter you will learn how to use the Xdialog Genie to create a dialog box.

CHAPTER 15

Code Tab Shortcut Menu

Figure 15-1 shows the shortcut menu when no object is selected on the Code tab.

The options for scripts, functions, menus and toolbars are explained in Table 15-1.

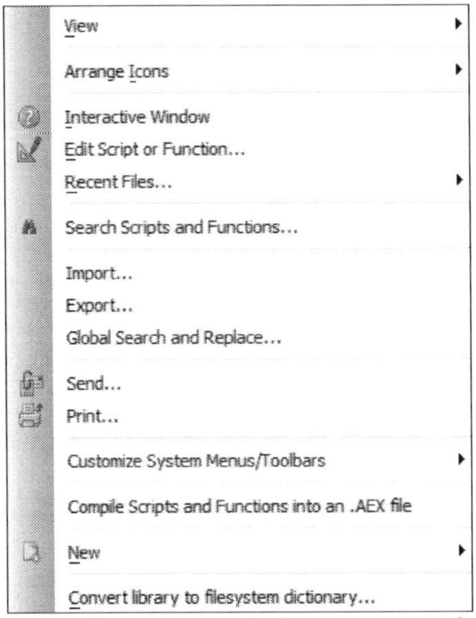

Figure 15-1 Code tab shortcut menu when no object is selected

Option	Description
Edit Script or Function	Opens the dialog box shown in Figure 15-2. By default, all of the functions, scripts, classes and enumerations on the Code tab are displayed. To find the item that you are looking for to edit, you can type part of the name in the Search field at the top of the dialog box or click one of the four **INCLUDE/EXCLUDE BUTTONS** at the bottom of the dialog box to limit the items displayed in the list.
Recent Files	Displays a list of files that were recently opened on the Code tab.
Search Scripts and Functions	Opens the dialog box shown in Figure 15-3. The options are used to search scripts, functions, classes and enumerations for a word or field.
Import	Opens the dialog box shown in Figure 15-4. The dialog box is used to import a script, function, class, enumeration, menu or toolbar.
Export	Opens the dialog box shown in Figure 15-5. The options are used to **EXPORT**, **SEND** or **PRINT** a script, function, class, enumeration, menu or toolbar.
Global Search and Replace	Opens the dialog box shown in Figure 15-6. The options are used to export all global scripts and functions in the database to a text editor to make changes, then import them back into the database.
Send	[See Export, earlier in this table]
Print	[See Export, earlier in this table]
Customize System Menus/Toolbars	Displays the submenu shown in Figure 15-7. The options are used to customize the menus and toolbars the come with Alpha Five, as shown in Figure 15-8.
Compile Scripts and Functions into an **.AEX** file	Opens the dialog box shown in Figure 15-9. The options are used to compile and encrypt scripts and functions.

Table 15-1 Code tab shortcut menu options when no object is selected explained

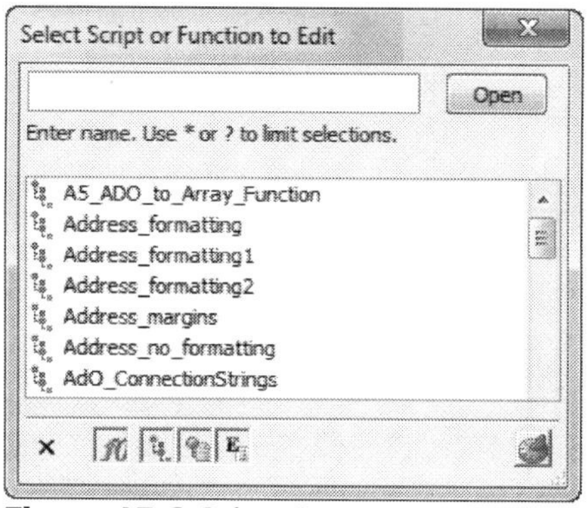

Figure 15-2 Select Script or Function to Edit dialog box

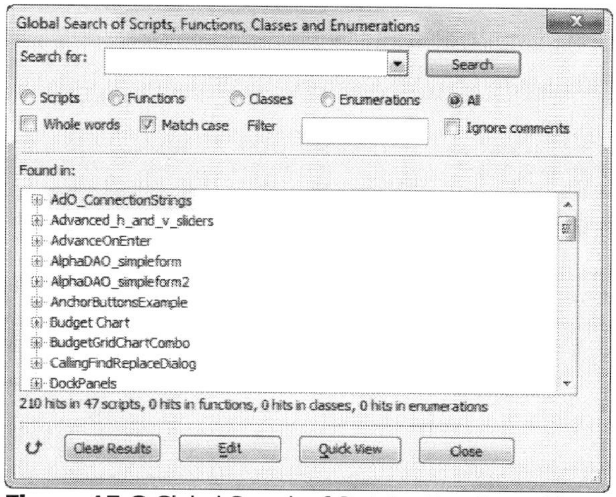

Figure 15-3 Global Search of Scripts, Functions, Classes and Enumerations dialog box

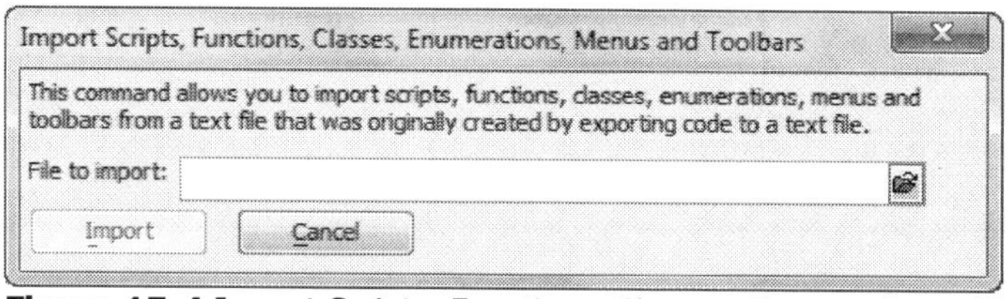

Figure 15-4 Import Scripts, Functions, Classes, Enumerations, Menus and Toolbars dialog box

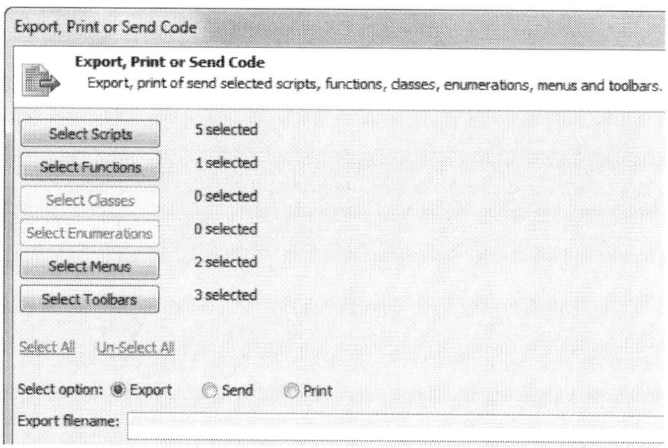

Figure 15-5 Export, Print or Send Code dialog box

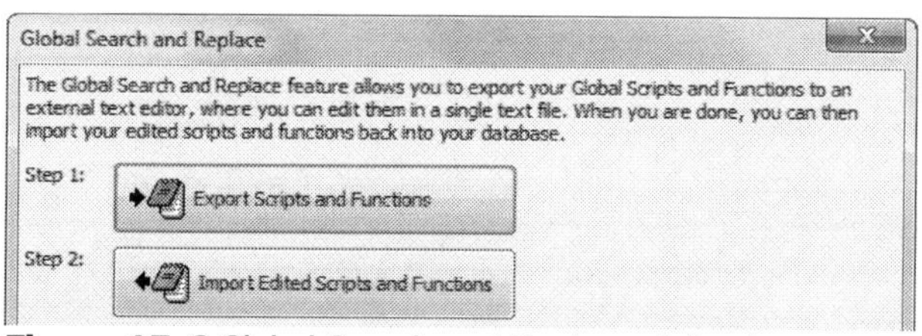

Figure 15-6 Global Search and Replace dialog box

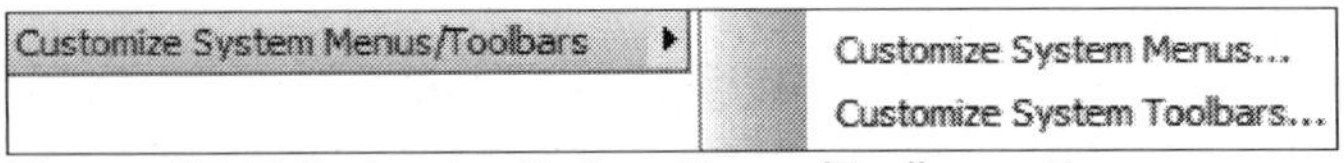

Figure 15-7 Customize System Menus/Toolbar options

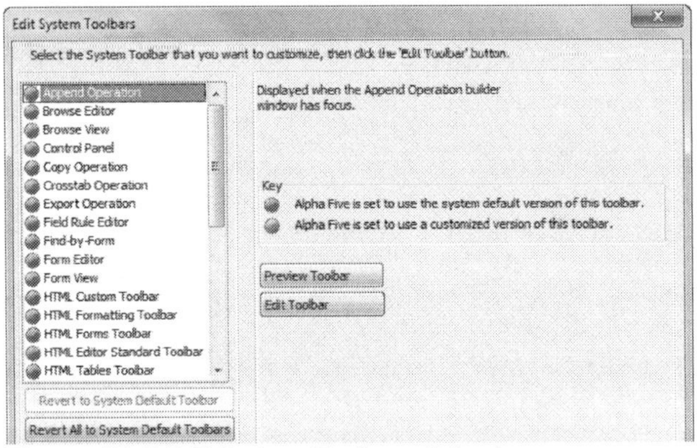

Figure 15-8 Edit System Toolbars dialog box

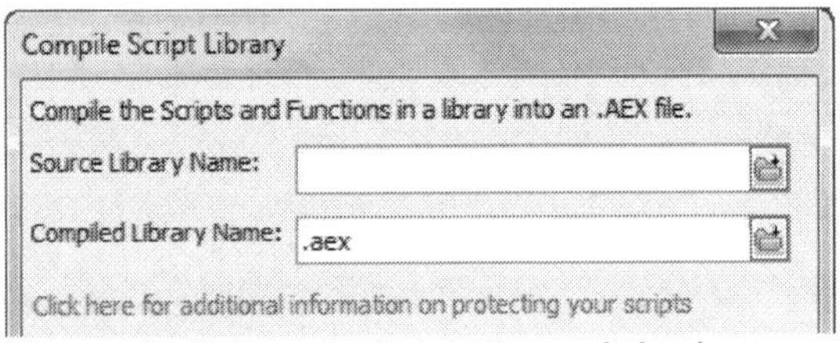

Figure 15-9 Compile Script Library dialog box

What Is Xdialog?

It is a tool that is used to create dialog boxes. The dialog boxes are used to display prompts, usually more than one on the dialog box, just like arguments. Additionally, data can also be displayed on the dialog box. The data changes based on the values selected in the prompts on the dialog box. Variables are often used to store the data gathered from the prompts. Variables can also get data from Xbasic or Action Scripts. These dialog boxes can be used instead of a form or browse.

The Xdialog tool can be used to create basic dialog boxes that only have one variable, one action and no Xbasic code or a dialog box can be created that has several variables and actions, as well as a lot of Xbasic code. It is up to you. Believe it or not, this chapter only has one exercise, but it will be enough to get you started creating your own dialog boxes and understanding the possibilities of using Xdialog.

What Are Variables?

I suspect that there are a lot of people that have created hundreds if not thousands of reports without using variables in expressions. Expressions only keep the result of their calculation until the next record is processed. This means that they cannot be used to accumulate data, like what is needed to print a total. Because expressions do not have the ability to store anything from the past or from record to record, variables are used for this purpose. Variables can be incremented, reset and store constant values. A variable is a temporary field that you create that is stored in the computers memory. Temporary in that it is only available when the report is open. Variables are not stored in tables.

I suspect that you may be asking how do I determine when I need to use a variable in a expression? The short answer is that you need a variable when you want to store data from an expression to use later in that expression, use in another expression in the same report or use in a subreport linked to the main report.

What variables have in common with fields in a table is that they both have data types (date, numeric, character, etc.). After variables are created, they can be added to a layout, by selecting it on the Drag Drop List panel, just like you add calculated field. The one exception that comes to mind is the memo field. There is no variable for this field type.

The data that variables hold changes and is not saved. For example, a variable can be created to hold the state to filter the report on. Each time the report is run, a different state is selected. The state is stored in the variable. After the report is run and closed, the data in the variable is discarded, just like it is in an argument.

Variable Names

There is no rule for naming variables. It is a good idea to use a name that represents the data that the variable will store. If the data that it will store comes from a field in a table, I use the field name. To be able to tell a variable from a field in the table, I start variable names with the letter "v". Doing that is optional.

Xdialog Genie

What you will hopefully like about this genie is that you can create the dialog box shown later in Figure 15-37 without writing code, unless you include creating short expressions, writing code. If you want to write code, you can. Like other genies, the Xdialog genie lets you click to select a lot of the options.

One thing that I like about this genie is that you can reopen it. The one thing that I do not like about this genie is that there is no option to save the changes, while the genie is open. The script can be saved when the Code Editor is open or when the Code tab on the Control Panel has focus.

Because the prompts and data are displayed on the dialog box, the form part if you will, is created using the genie. This makes the dialog box self-contained, opposed to a dialog box for the prompts (arguments) being maintained in one file and the layout(s) used to display the data maintained in other files.

The result of using this genie will be an action script that is stored on the Control Panels Code tab. The Xdialog genie actually has two genies, as explained below.

① **SCRIPT GENIE** Is used to create a variable, the variable style, the window size and the prompts for the dialog box.
② **LIST VIEW GENIE** Is used to select the data and how the data is displayed.

Exercise 15.1: Use Xdialog To Create A Dialog Box

In this exercise you will learn the basics of creating a dialog box that will let the user select a sales rep, display their sales and the detail data for each sale. You will create an action script to run a report that displays the selected sales reps orders by month and then add a button to the dialog box to run the report.

Create The Xdialog Action Script

1. Control Panel ⇒ Code tab ⇒ New button ⇒ **SCRIPT (USING ACTION SCRIPTING)**, as shown in Figure 15-10.

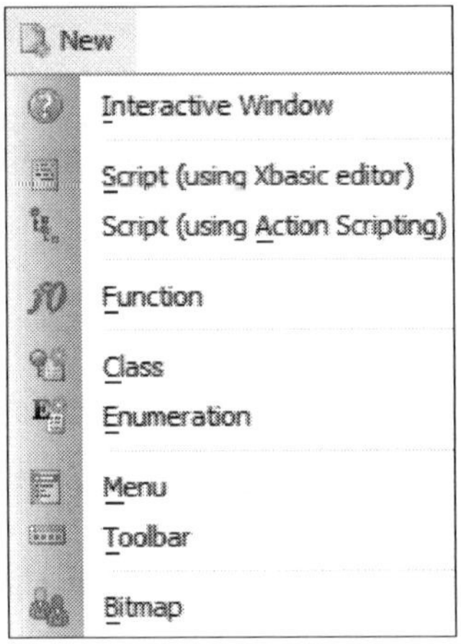

Figure 15-10 New button menu Code tab

2. On the Code Editor, click the Add New Action button. Select the **XDIALOG WINDOWS** category, then select the **DISPLAY AN XDIALOG BOX** action. Click OK.

Script Genie: Display An Xdialog Box

The screen shown in Figure 15-11 is used to create a variable and select the control that will be used to display the data for the variable. The options are explained below.

If the dialog box that you are creating needs more than one variable, you can select the options for all of the variables that you need here, then complete the other screens, or you can walk through all of the screens for one of the variables, then come back to this screen and set up the other variables. The other screens only have to be filled out once because they are for the dialog box, not a specific variable.

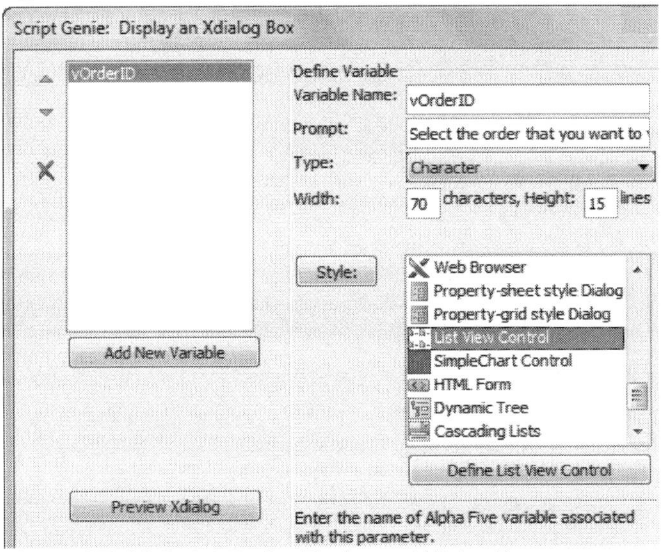

Figure 15-11 Script Genie: Display an Xdialog Box screen

① **ADD NEW VARIABLE BUTTON** Is used to create a variable for the dialog box. The Up and Down triangle buttons to the left of the variable list are used to change the display order of the prompts on the dialog box. I find this helpful because some variables need information from another variable. For example, if Variable A needs information from Variable B, I create Variable B first, then create Variable A because I have the information from Variable B. Otherwise, I would have to remember to go back to Variable A after setting up Variable B to fill in what is needed from Variable B. The red x button will delete the variable that is selected.

② **VARIABLE NAME** Is used to select the name for the variable. After the variable name is created, the other options on the screen are enabled.

③ **PROMPT** Is used to enter the text (instructions) that briefly explains to the user how to use the control.

④ **TYPE** Is used to select one of the following to define what type of data the variable will store: Character, Numeric, Date, Logical, Time or Short Time.

⑤ **WIDTH** Is used to select how many characters wide the control should be. You may have the need to change this option after the fields are selected to be displayed, if some of the information gets cut off.

⑥ **HEIGHT LINES** Is not available until a control is selected from the Control list below. Select how many rows (how many lines high) of data the control should display.

⑦ **STYLE BUTTON** Displays the Demonstration Different Control Styles dialog box, similar to the one shown in Chapter 6, Figure 6-21. The options on this dialog box display what different types of controls look like, which may help you decide which one is best suited for the variable that you are creating.

⑧ **CONTROL LIST** Is to the right of the Style button. It is used to select the control that you want to use. The controls available depend on the type of data that the variable will store.

⑨ **PREVIEW XDIALOG BUTTON** Displays the dialog box that you are creating, based on the options that you have selected so far, as shown in Figure 15-12. Each screen on the genie has a Preview button, which also displays the dialog box that you are creating.

⑩ **DEFINE LIST VIEW CONTROL BUTTON** Displays the dialog box shown in Figure 15-13.

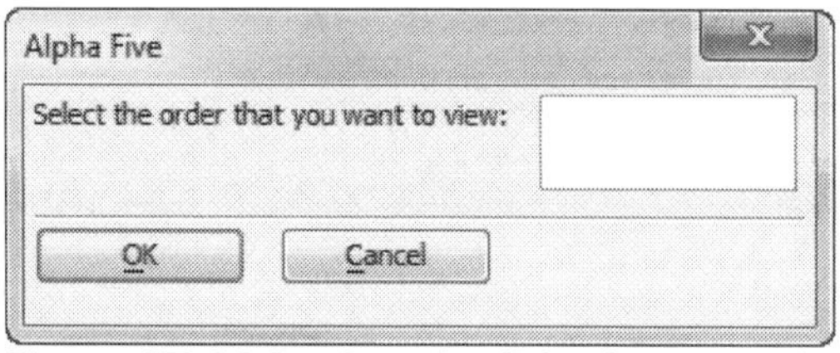

Figure 15-12 Preview of a dialog box created in Xdialog

Options In The Control List
The options in the list are not in alphabetical order.

Create The Order Variable And List Using The Script Genie

In this part of the exercise you will create the variable for the Orders table and select the fields that will be displayed in what looks like a browse on a form.

1. Select the following options.
   Variable Name - `vOrderID`
   Prompt - `Select the order that you want to view`
   Type - Character
   Width - `70`

2. Scroll to the bottom of the Control list and select the **LIST VIEW CONTROL**.

3. Change the Height option to `15`. You should have the options shown earlier in Figure 15-11.

4. Click the Preview Xdialog button. You should see the dialog box shown above in Figure 15-12.

List View Genie

Clicking the Define List View control button on the Script Genie screen shown earlier in Figure 15-11, opens this dialog box.

The options shown in Figure 15-13 are used to configure the control. The options are explained below.

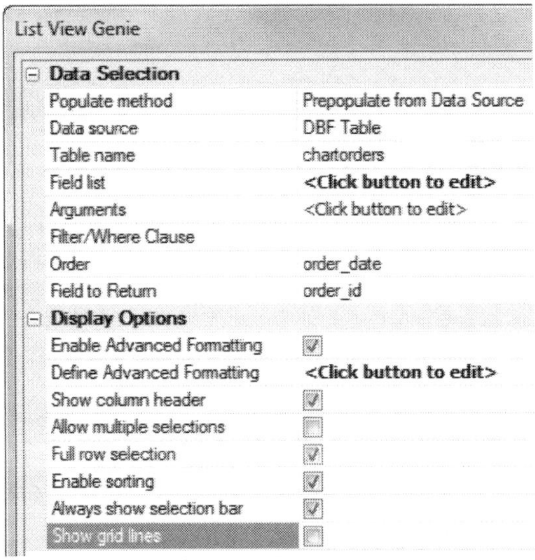

Figure 15-13 List View Genie

Data Selection Options

① **POPULATE METHOD** Is used to select how the control will get the data for the list. The options are: **PRE POPULATE FROM STATIC LIST** Select this option for data that you will type in. This option is best suited for a small amount of data that will not change. Selecting this option displays the Static Choices option shown in Figure 15-14. Clicking the Static Choices field button displays the dialog box shown in Figure 15-15. It is used to manually create the list. **PRE POPULATE FROM DATA SOURCE** Select this option if the data source is a database. **DYNAMICALLY BOUND** Select this option if the data will come from a live DBF table.

② **DATA SOURCE** Is only available if the Pre populate from Data Source option is selected. It is used to select the type of database. The options are: DBF Table, Access Database, ADO Data Source and Alpha DAO Data Source. (1)

③ **TABLE NAME** Is used to select the table that has the data to display on the control. (1)

④ **FIELD LIST** Is used to select the field(s) from the table to display on the control. (1) (2)

⑤ **ARGUMENTS** Is used to create a prompt that will be used to create a Filter Expression, Where Clause or query. This option is only available if the Populate Method is set to Pre populate from Data source or Dynamically Bound.

⑥ **FILTER/WHERE CLAUSE** Is used to create an expression to filter the data that will be displayed. (2)

⑦ **ORDER** Displays the Order Builder to select the default sort order for the data displayed in the control. (1) (2)

⑧ **FIELD TO RETURN** Is used to select a field from the table that has the value that will be returned. (1) (2)

(1) See Figure 15-13.
(2) This option is enabled after a table is selected.

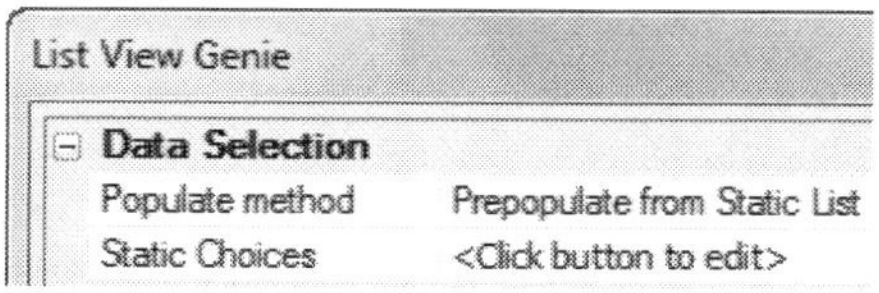

Figure 15-14 Static Choices option

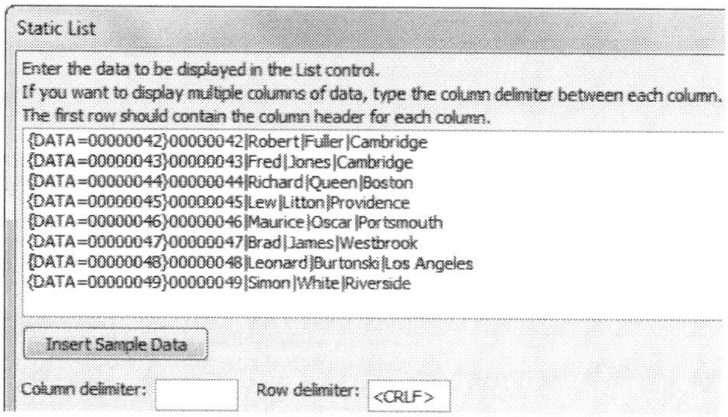

Figure 15-15 Static List dialog box

Display Options

① **ENABLE ADVANCED FORMATTING** Is used to enable the **DEFINE ADVANCED FORMATTING** option shown earlier in Figure 15-13. Clicking the Define Advanced Formatting button displays the dialog box shown in Figure 15-16. It is used to select the background and font color for the control.

② **SHOW COLUMN HEADER** If checked, the field names will be displayed on the control.

③ **ALLOW MULTIPLE SELECTORS** If checked, the user can select more than one row of data.

④ **CHECKBOX LIST** (This option is not enabled if the Enable Advanced Formatting option is enabled, which is why it is not shown in Figure 15-13 shown earlier) If checked, a check box appears to the left of the first column, as shown in Figure 15-17.

⑤ **FULL ROW SELECTION** If checked, the entire row will display a different background color when selected, opposed to just the first column displaying a different background color, as shown in the first row in Figure 15-18.

⑥ **ENABLE SORTING** If checked, clicking on a column heading will sort the data in the control in ascending order by the data in that column. Click on the same column heading again to sort in descending order.

⑦ **ALWAYS SHOW SELECTION BAR** If checked, a row in the control will always be selected (highlighted) even if the control does not have focus.

⑧ **SHOW GRID LINES** Adds horizontal lines to the control, like you see in a spreadsheet, as shown in Figure 15-18.

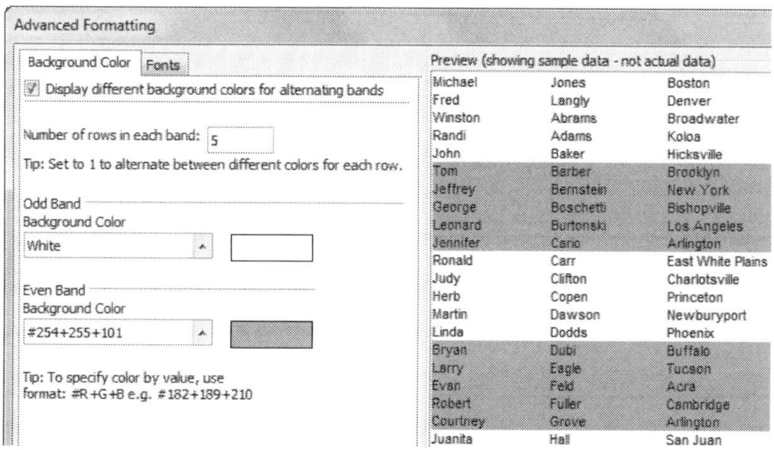

Figure 15-16 Advanced Formatting dialog box

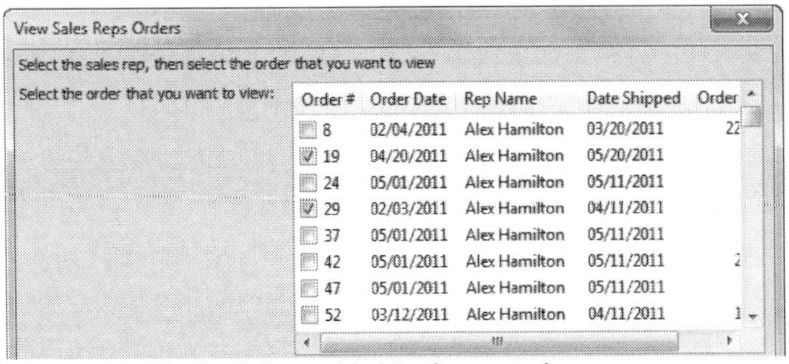

Figure 15-17 Check box added to the control

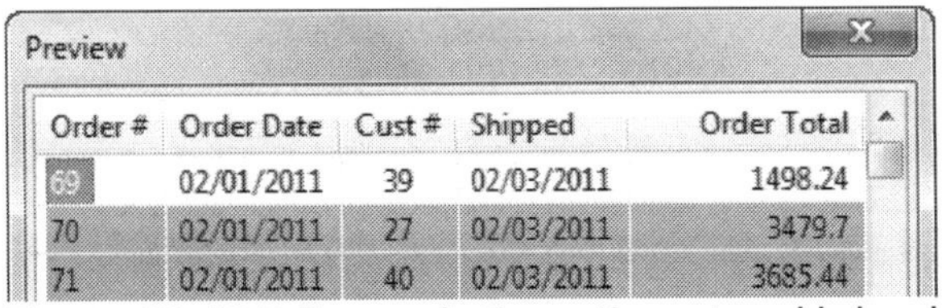

Figure 15-18 Full row selection option not enabled and grid lines added to the control

Select The Data And Display Options For The Order ID List View Control

1. Click the Define List View Control button, then select the following Data Selection options.
   Populate method - Pre populate from Data Source
   Data Source - DBF Table
   Table name - ChartOrders
   Order - Rep Full Name
   Field to Return - Order ID

2. Click the Field list button, then select the following fields: Order ID, Order Date, Rep Full Name, Data Shipped and Order Amount, as shown in Figure 15-19.

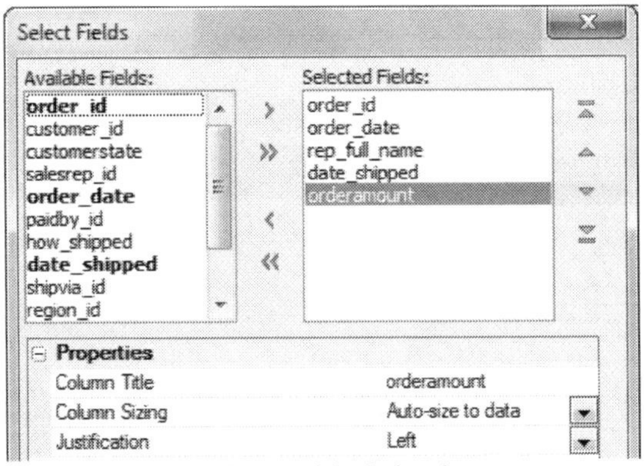

Figure 15-19 Select Fields dialog box

Field Properties

As shown above in Figure 15-19, each field has the same three properties, which are explained below.

① **COLUMN TITLE** Type in the text that will appear at the top of the column (the column heading) instead of the field name.

② **COLUMN SIZING** Is used to select how the width of the column is selected. The options are:
DO NOT AUTO-SIZE Select this option to use the default column width.
AUTO-SIZE TO DATA Sizes the column based on the longest entry in the column.
AUTO-SIZE TO COLUMN HEADER Makes the column width the size of the column title.
SPECIFY WIDTH Displays the Column Width field shown in Figure 15-20. Type the width that you want in inches.

③ **JUSTIFICATION** Is used to select how the data and column title are aligned. The options are Left, Center and Right.

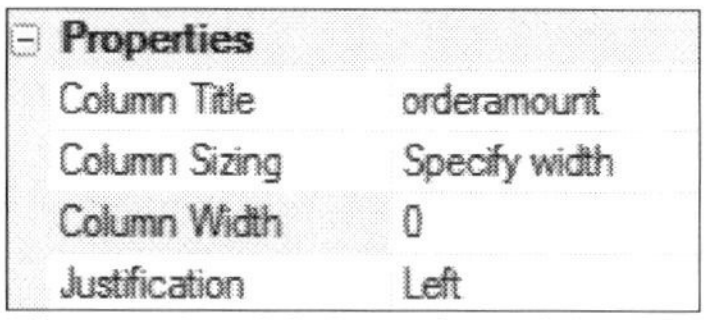

Figure 15-20 Specify width options

Select The Field Properties

1. Select the properties in Table 15-2 for the fields.

Field	Column Title	Column Sizing	Justification
Order ID	Order #	Auto-size to column header	Center
Order Date	Order Date	Auto-size to column header	Left
Rep Full Name	Rep Name	Auto-size to data	Left
Date Shipped	Shipped	Auto-size to column header	Left
Order Amount	Order Total	Auto-size to column header	Right

Table 15-2 Field properties to select

The reason that I use the Auto-size to column header option most of the time is because I want to see the entire column name displayed in the control.

Notice that the column title is displayed in parenthesis next to the field, as shown in Figure 15-21.

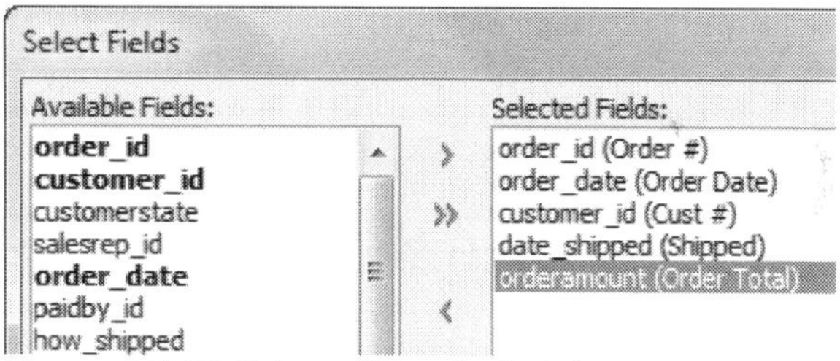

Figure 15-21 Column titles displayed

Compare the Selected Fields column to the one shown earlier in Figure 15-19.

Select The Display Options For The Order ID Variable

1. Check the Enable Advanced Formatting option, then click the Define Advanced Formatting button.

2. Click the **DISPLAY DIFFERENT BACKGROUND COLORS FOR ALTERNATING BANDS** option, then make the changes below. When done, you should have the options shown earlier in Figure 15-16. Click OK.

   Numbered rows in each band - 5
   Even band background color - Light Yellow

3. Click OK to close the List View Genie.

4. Click the Preview Xdialog button. You should see the dialog box shown in Figure 15-22.

   Click on the column title to see how the sorting works.

   Click OK, then click Next on the Script Genie screen.

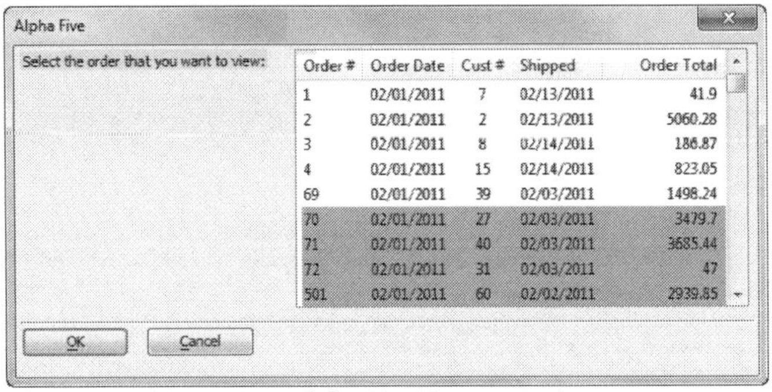

Figure 15-22 Preview of the List View control

Title, Header, Footer, Button And Background Options

The options shown in Figure 15-23 are used to customize the dialog box that is being created.

The options are explained below.

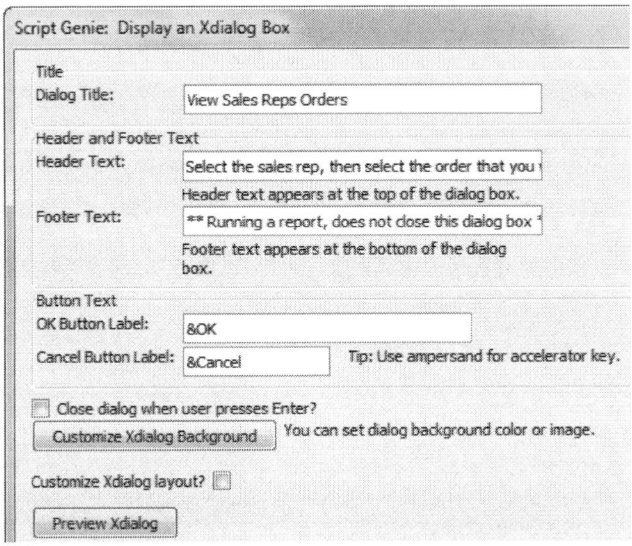

Figure 15-23 Xdialog box customization options

① **DIALOG TITLE** Enter the text that you want to appear in the Title bar of the dialog box that you are creating. In Figure 15-22 shown earlier, that would be the words "Alpha Five".

② **HEADER TEXT** Enter the text that you want to appear below the Dialog Title. For example, you can enter instructions on how to use the options on the dialog box.

③ **FOOTER TEXT** Enter the text that you want to appear right above the OK button on the dialog box that you are creating, as shown earlier at the bottom of Figure 15-22.

④ **OK BUTTON LABEL** (3)

⑤ **CANCEL BUTTON LABEL** (3)

⑥ **CLOSE DIALOG BOX WHEN USER PRESSES ENTER** If checked, any time that the user presses Enter, the dialog box will close.

⑦ **CUSTOMIZE XDIALOG BACKGROUND BUTTON** [See Customize The Dialog Box Background]

⑧ **CUSTOMIZE XDIALOG LAYOUT** If checked, the **EDIT TEMPLATE** button is displayed. When clicked, the dialog box shown in Figure 15-24 is displayed. It is used to change the layout of the dialog box that you are creating.

(3) The text on the button can be changed. The button can also be modified to perform the action of your choice, like display a report.

If your dialog box has errors, the **MISSING CONTROLS** and **UNDEFINED CONTROLS** buttons may help you resolve the problem.

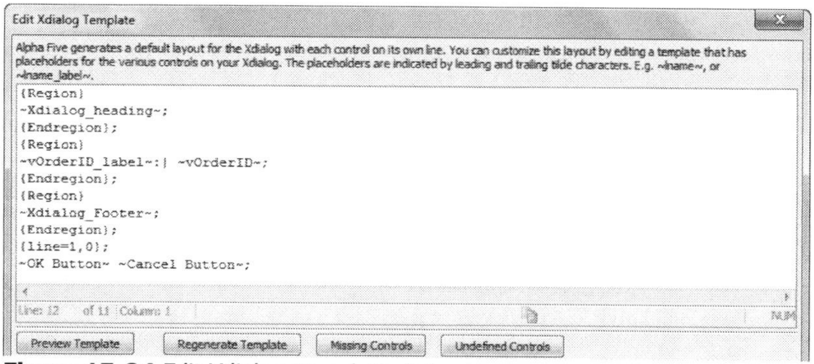

Figure 15-24 Edit Xdialog Template dialog box

Customize The Dialog Box

1. Change the following options. When done, you should have the options shown earlier in Figure 15-23.

   Dialog Title - `View Sales Reps Orders`
   Header Text - `Select the sales rep, then select the order that you want to view`
   Footer Text - `** Running a report does not close this dialog box **`
   Close dialog box when user presses Enter - Clear the check mark

Customize The Dialog Box Background

The options shown in Figure 15-25 are used to change the background of the dialog box. You can change the color or select an image to display as the background.

Check the **HAS CUSTOM BACKGROUND** option to enable the other options.

The **PREVIEW** button displays the result of the options selected at the bottom of the dialog box. The button does not display the dialog box you are creating.

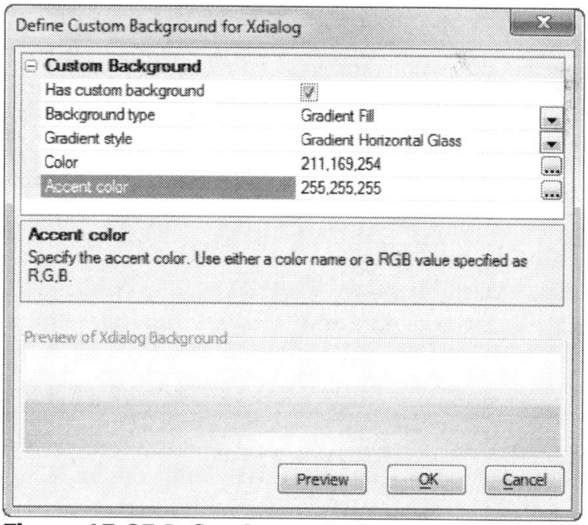

Figure 15-25 Define Custom Background for Xdialog box

1. Click the Customize Xdialog Background button, then select the Has custom background option.

2. Select a background type or color that you like.

3. Click OK, then click Next on the Script Genie screen.

Variable Options

The options shown in Figure 15-26 are used to confirm the Result Variable Name, which you can usually accept the default name that Alpha Five creates.

VARIABLE SCOPE This option is used to select where the variable can be used. **SHARED, GLOBAL** and **LOCAL** are the options. They are explained in the drop-down list on the dialog box.

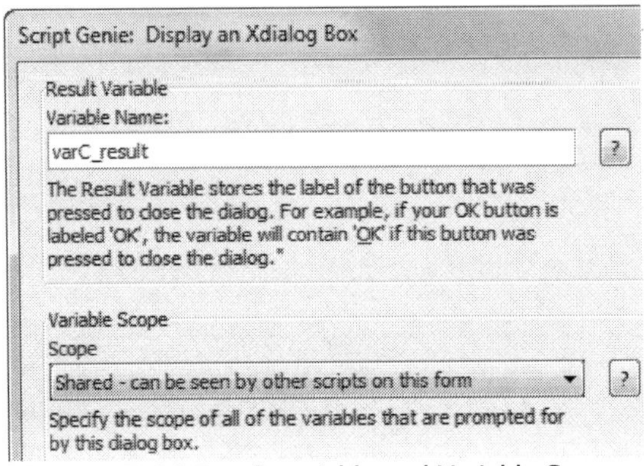

Figure 15-26 Result variable and Variable Scope options screen

The **QUESTION MARK BUTTONS** open a help file that provides more information about the option.

1. Accept the Shared default variable scope option, then click Next.

Add A Comment

The screen shown in Figure 15-27 is used to add a comment to the action that you are creating. Doing this is optional.

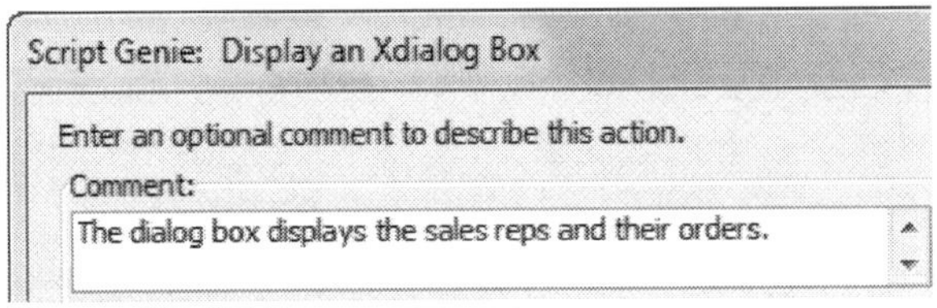

Figure 15-27 Comment screen

1. Type a comment, then click Finish.

   You should see the dialog box shown in Figure 15-28.

   Notice that the comment is displayed at the bottom of the Code Editor.

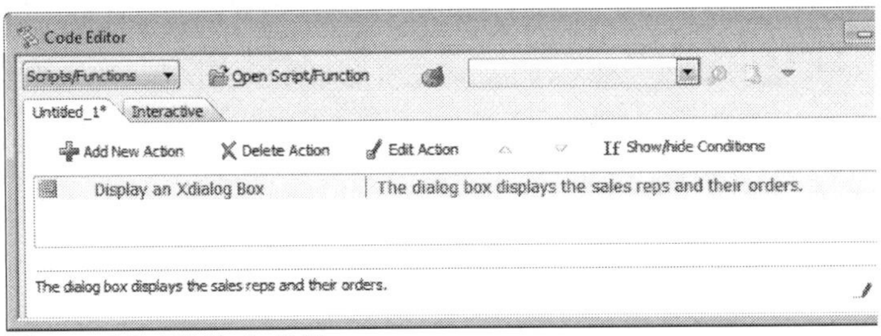

Figure 15-28 Code Editor

2. On the toolbar, click the Save button. Type `aXdialogBox` as the action script name.

Create The Sales Rep Drop-Down List

In this part of the exercise you will create a drop-down list that displays the sales reps names. This variable will be used to select the orders that will be displayed in the Order ID list control that you created earlier in this chapter.

1. On the Code Editor, click the **EDIT ACTION** button.

2. On the Script Genie, click the Add New Variable button, then click the Up arrow to move the new variable to the top of the list.

3. Select the following options.
   Variable name - `vSalesRepID`
   Prompt - `Select the sales rep to see orders for`
   Width - `20`
   Control - Combo Box

Combo Box Dialog Box

The options shown in Figure 15-29 are used to configure the Combo Box control. The options are explained below.

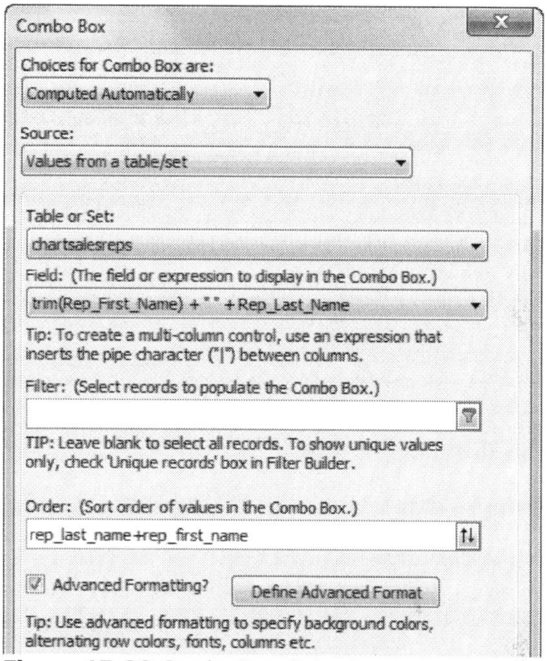

Figure 15-29 Combo Box dialog box

① **CHOICES FOR COMBO BOX ARE** Is used to select how the combo box will get data. The options are **USER DEFINED**, which is used to type in the options for the combo box, as shown in Figure 15-30. **COMPUTED AUTOMATICALLY** is used to select a source for the values displayed in the combo box. This option is used to select the values from a table. It also enables the options shown above in Figure 15-29.

② **SOURCE** Is used to select where to get the data for the control from. For example, the source can be a browse, expression or operation.

③ **TABLE OR SET** Is used to select the table or set that has the values that will be displayed in the combo box.

④ **FIELD** Is used to select a field(s) from the table or set that will be displayed in the combo box. An expression can be created to display the data in the combo box.

⑤ **FILTER** Is used to create an expression to filter the data that will be displayed in the combo box.

⑥ **ORDER** Is used to select the sort order for the values in the combo box.

⑦ **ADVANCED FORMATTING** If checked, the Define Advanced Format button is enabled. This button opens the Advanced Formatting dialog box, which is used to apply background color, select fonts and number rows.

The Define Advanced Format button opens the dialog box shown in Figures 15-31 to 15-34.

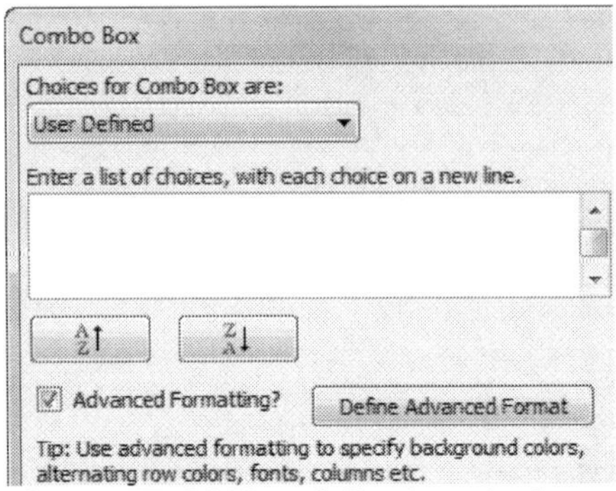

Figure 15-30 User defined combo box options

Configure The Combo Box For The vSalesRepID Variable

1. Click the Define Combo Box button on the Script Genie.

2. Select the following options.
   Choices for Combo Box are - Computed automatically
   Source - Values from a table/set
   Table or Set - ChartSalesReps (table)
   Field - Full Name
   Order - Rep last name, then by Rep first name

3. Check the Advanced Formatting option, then click the Define Advanced Format button.

   Select the options shown in Figure 15-31.

   Both of the Background Color of Selected Rows options are set to Light Yellow.

   Figure 15-32 shows the Columns tab options.

   Figure 15-33 shows the Fonts tab options.

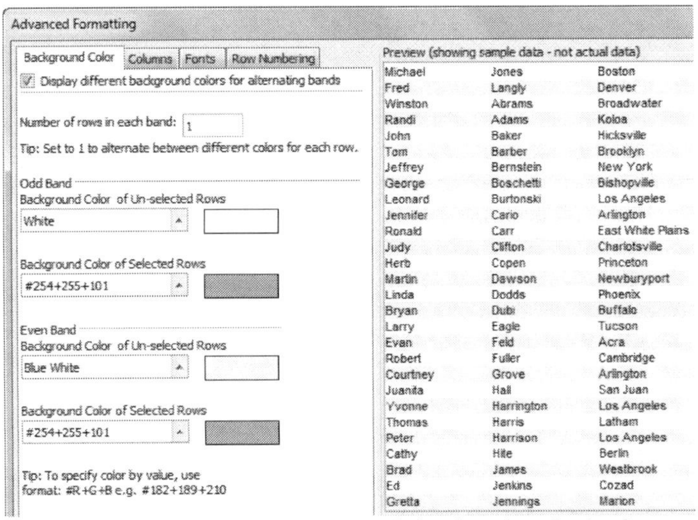

Figure 15-31 Advanced Formatting dialog box (combo box)

Figure 15-34 shows the Row Numbering tab option.

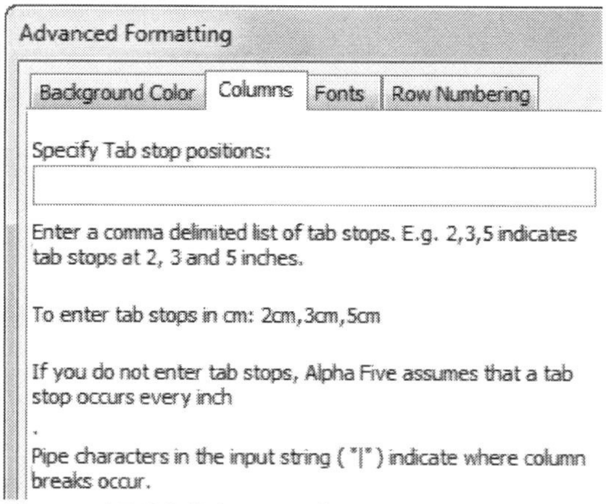

Figure 15-32 Columns tab options

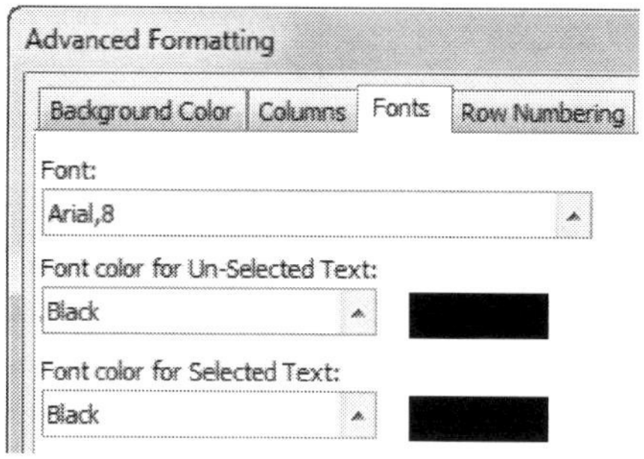

Figure 15-33 Fonts tab options

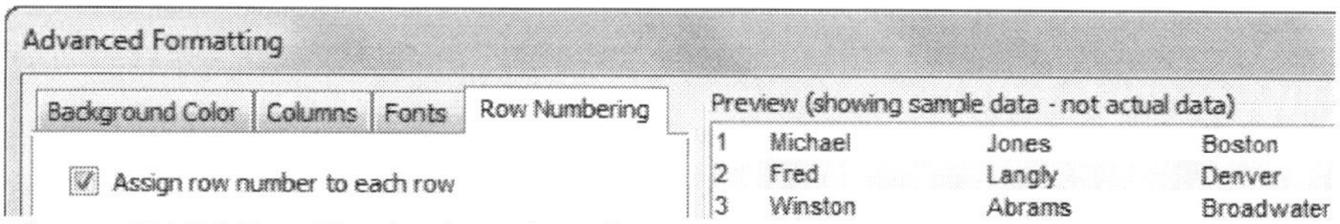

Figure 15-34 Row Numbering tab options

If checked, the **ASSIGN ROW NUMBER TO EACH ROW** option shown above in Figure 15-34 displays a number next to each row of data, as shown on the right side of the figure.

4. On the Fonts tab, change the Font color for Selected Text option to Black.

5. Click OK to close the Combo Box dialog box. Click Next three times, then click Finish. Save the changes.

Link The Drop-Down List To The Order ID List

In this part of the exercise you will link the Sales Rep drop-down list to the Order ID list. This will cause the Order list to be filtered to only display orders for the sales rep that is selected. To do this, an argument has to be created for the Order ID variable to get the value from the Sales Rep variable.

1. On the Code Editor, click the Edit Action button.

2. Select the vOrderID variable, then click the Define List View Control button.

Create The Argument

1. Click the Arguments button, then click the Insert New Argument button. Select the following options.
   Argument name - `aGetSalesRepID`
   Data type - Character

2. Click the Variable button, then select the vSalesRepID variable, as shown in Figure 15-35.

   You should have the options shown in Figure 15-36. Notice that a new variable can be created from this dialog box.

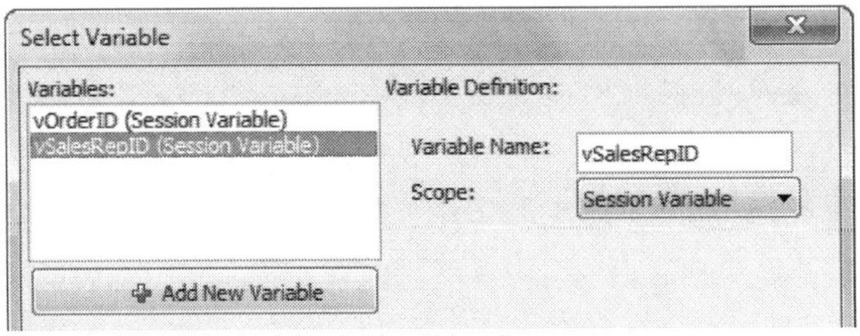

Figure 15-35 Select Variable dialog box

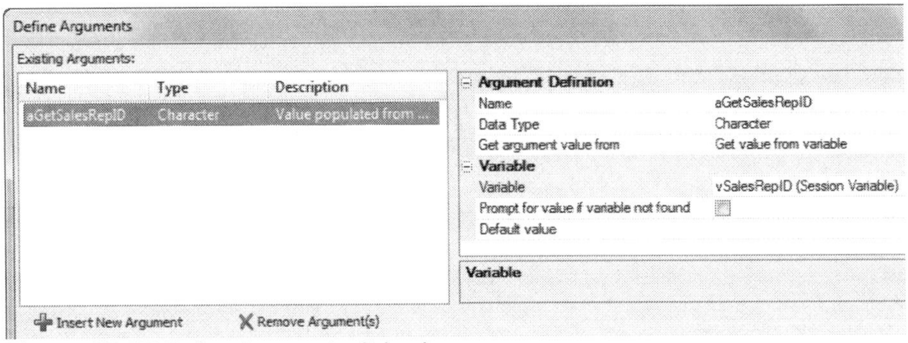

Figure 15-36 Define Arguments dialog box

Create The Filter/Where Clause For The vOrderID Variable

In this part of the exercise you will create the filter for the Order ID list to only display orders for the Sales Rep that is selected.

1. Click the Filter/Where Clause field button, then type this expression.
   `Rep_Full_Name=:aGetSalesRepID`

2. On the Script Genie screen, preview the dialog box. Open the drop-down list and select a Sales Rep. You should see the orders for the rep that you selected.

3. Click Next three times, then click Finish. Save the changes.

Create The Order Detail Variable And List

In this part of the exercise you will create a list that displays the items for the order that is selected.

1. Add a new variable. Make sure that it is the last variable in the list.

2. Select the following options.
   Variable name - `vOrderDetails`
   Prompt - `Items for selected order`
   Width - `40`
   Control - List View Control
   Height - `10`

3. Click the Define List View Control button, then select the following options. When finished, leave the dialog box open to complete the next part of the exercise.
   Populate method - Prepopulate from Data Source
   Data Source - DBF Table
   Table name - ChartOrderDetail
   Field List - Add all of the fields. Change the Column Title. Change the Column Sizing to Auto-size to column header.
   Field to Return - Order ID

Create The Argument And Filter/Where Clause For The vOrderDetails Variable

1. On the List View Genie dialog box for the vOrderDetails variable, click the Arguments button, then click the Insert New Argument button.

2. Type `aGetOrderID` as the Argument name, then click OK.

3. Click the Variable button. Select the vOrderID variable, then click OK.

4. On the List View Genie, click the Filter/Where Clause button, then type this expression.
   `Order_ID=:aGetOrderID`

5. On the Script Genie dialog box, click Next three times, then click Finish. Save the changes.

6. Code ⇒ Run.

   You should be able to select a sales rep from the drop-down list, then double-click on an order to see the detail records for the order, as shown in Figure 15-37.

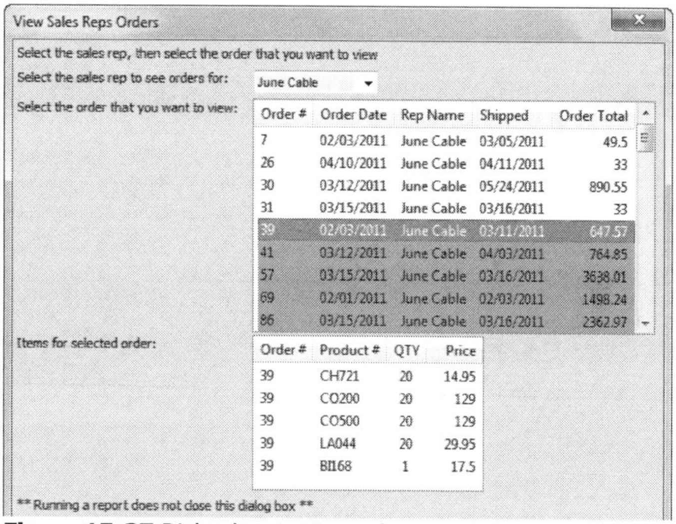

Figure 15-37 Dialog box to view sales reps orders

Create The Action Script To Run A Report

In this part of the exercise you will create an action script to run the aPromptDateRange report.

1. Control Panel ⇒ Code tab ⇒ New button ⇒ Script (Using Action Scripting). On the Code Editor, click the Add New Action button. Select the Reports category, then select the Preview a Layout action.

2. On the Script Genie: Preview a Layout Screen, select the aPromptDateRange report.
   Click Next twice.

3. Click Finish, then click Save. Type `aXdialogRunReport` as the file name. Close the Code Editor.

Add A Button To Run The Report

1. Open the aXdialogBox script in Design mode. Display the Xdialog box action.

2. Add a variable, with the following options.
   Variable name - `vReportButton`
   Prompt - `Click to run the report`
   Width - `40`
   Control - Button

3. Click the Define Button button. (For me, this button did not enable itself without clicking the Preview Xdialog button first).

   Select the following options on the Define Button dialog box.

   Button Style - Picture followed by text
   Image Name - Select an image that you like
   Button Text - `Run the Date Range report`
   Button Action - Play Script
   Script - XdialogRunReport

   When done, you should have the options shown in Figure 15-38.

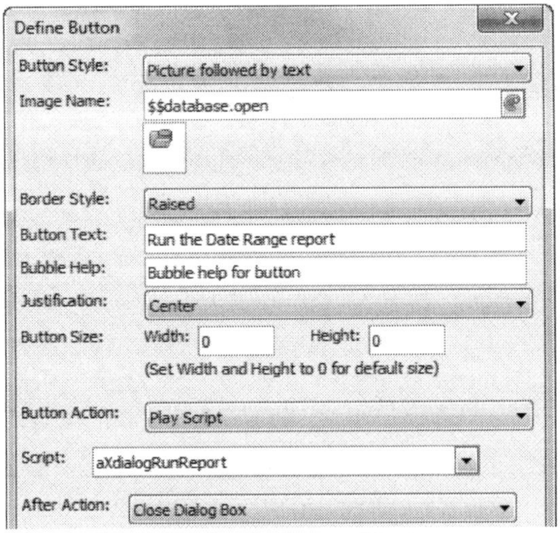

Figure 15-38 Define button options

4. Click OK. Click Next three times. Click Finish. Save the changes.

5. Run the action script.

   The dialog box should look like the one shown in Figure 15-39.

   If you click the button that you just added to the dialog box, you will see the prompts for the report.

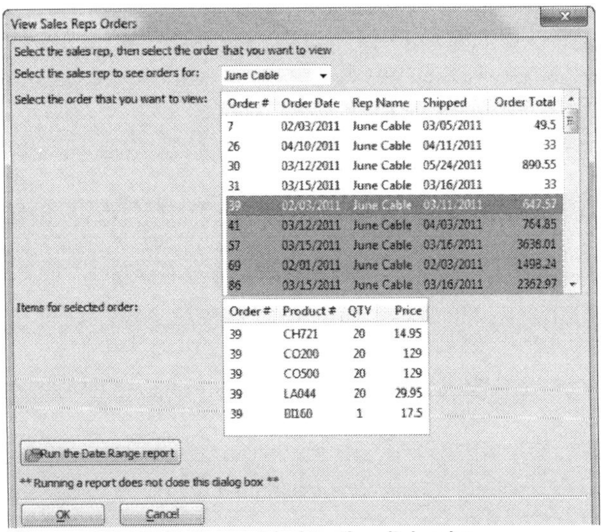

Figure 15-39 Button added to the dialog box

CUSTOM MENUS AND TOOLBARS

In this chapter you will learn how to modify the menu and toolbars that are displayed when viewing forms, browses and reports. You will also learn how to create a menu and toolbar from scratch.

CHAPTER 16

Overview

So far this book has covered items to enhance layouts. If you are gong to build an application that is going into production (aka will be used by other people), you may have the need to customize the menus and toolbars that are displayed when viewing a layout. There may be items on the default layout menus and toolbars that you do not want users to have access to, so you can remove them from the menu or toolbar. You may also want to create a menu that has the 10 most used reports. The topics covered in this chapter will show you how to accomplish these tasks.

Each menu that you save has its own file name and is stored on the Code tab. Even though menu files that you create are stored on the Code tab, they cannot be run without being connected to a layout. Custom menus and toolbars have to be added to each form, browse or report that you want them used on. That means that each form can have a different menu. The good thing is that the default menus and toolbars are not changed.

New Menu Dialog Box

The dialog box shown in Figure 16-1 is used to select the menu that you want to modify or to create a new menu.

When you want to modify an existing menu, you should save it with a new name.

When you select a menu type, you will see where it is displayed at the bottom of the dialog box.

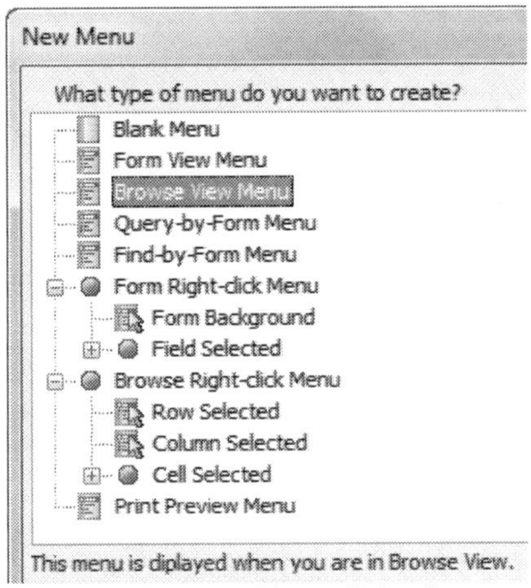

Figure 16-1 New Menu dialog box

Menu Maker

The dialog box shown in Figure 16-2 is displayed when you select a menu on the New Menu dialog box and click OK.

The Menu Maker is used to modify the menu that you selected on the New Menu dialog box or to create a new menu.

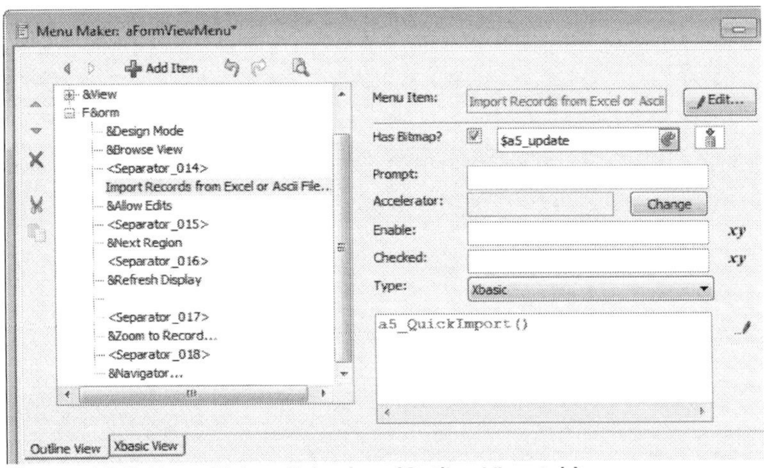

Figure 16-2 Menu Maker dialog box (Outline View tab)

The buttons down the left side of the dialog box are used to change the order of the menu items, delete, copy and paste menu items. The Up and Down buttons only move an item within the menu section that its in.

The **PASTE BUTTON** (below the scissors button) displays the dialog box shown in Figure 16-3, which is used to select where to paste the menu item that you selected to copy.

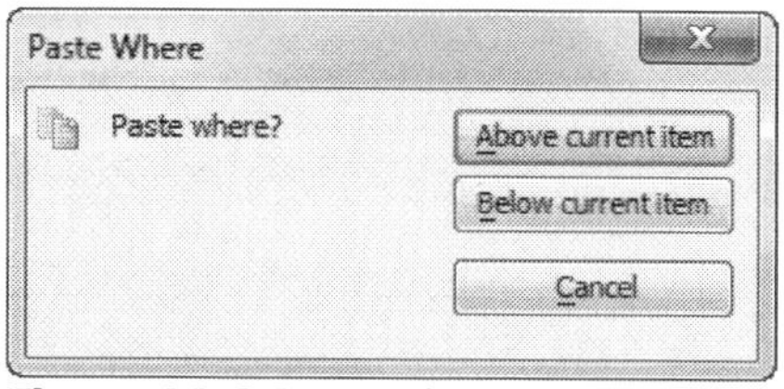

Figure 16-3 Paste Where dialog box

The **ADD ITEM BUTTON** opens the Add New Item dialog box shown later in Figure 16-23.

Menu Item Customization Options

The options on the right side of Figure 16-2 are used to customize the menu item that is selected. The options are explained below.

① The **MENU ITEM** field contains text that will be displayed on the menu. The **EDIT BUTTON** displays the dialog box shown in Figure 16-4. The options are used to change the menu item name.

② **HAS BITMAP** If checked, an image will be displayed before the item name on the menu. Clicking the first button at the end of the field opens the Insert Image dialog box, which is used to select an image file. The last button displays the bitmap image that you selected.

③ **PROMPT** Is used to enter bubble help for the menu item.

④ **ACCELERATOR** Is used to set up a shortcut key for the menu item. Click the **CHANGE** button to display the dialog box shown in Figure 16-5 to create the shortcut key.

⑤ **ENABLE** Is used to create an expression that determines when the item will be displayed on the menu. The expression must evaluate to TRUE or FALSE. The button at the end of the field displays the dialog box shown in Figure 16-6. After selecting a table or set, the dialog box is used to create the expression.

⑥ **CHECKED** Is used to create an expression to determine when the item will have a check mark. The expression must evaluate to TRUE. Clicking the button at the end of the field displays the dialog box shown in Figure 16-7. After selecting a table or set, the dialog box looks like the one shown in Figure 16-8.

⑦ **TYPE** Is used to select the type of action to run when the menu item is clicked on. The options are **BUILT-IN ACTION**, which displays the options shown in Figure 16-9. **RUN A SAVED SCRIPT**, which displays the options shown in Figure 16-10. **XBASIC**, which displays the options shown earlier in Figure 16-2. Clicking the pencil icon opens the dialog box shown in Figure 16-11.

This is the same as changing the Item name field on the Add New Item dialog box.

MENU MACROS button [See Add A Menu Macro Item]

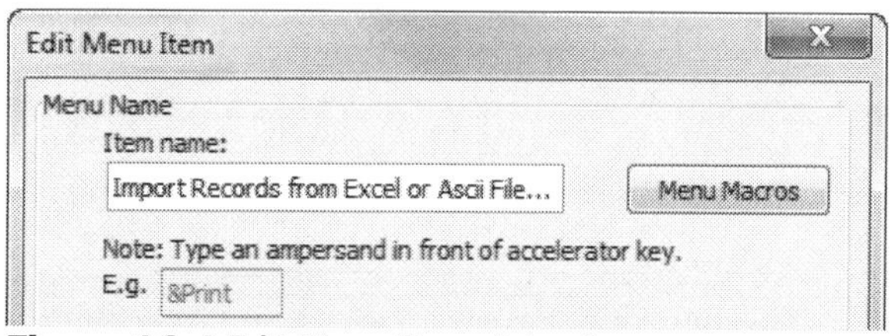

Figure 16-4 Edit Menu Item dialog box

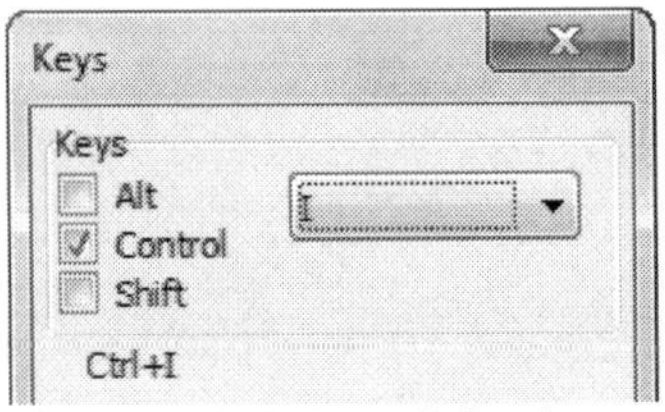

Figure 16-5 Keys dialog box

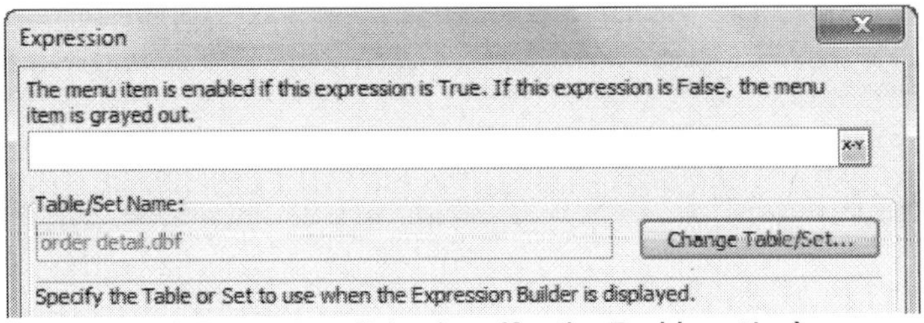

Figure 16-6 Expression dialog box (for the Enable option)

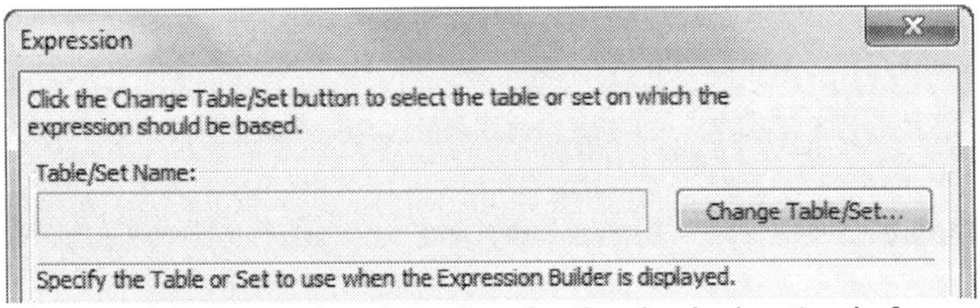

Figure 16-7 Expression dialog box for the checked option before a table or set is selected

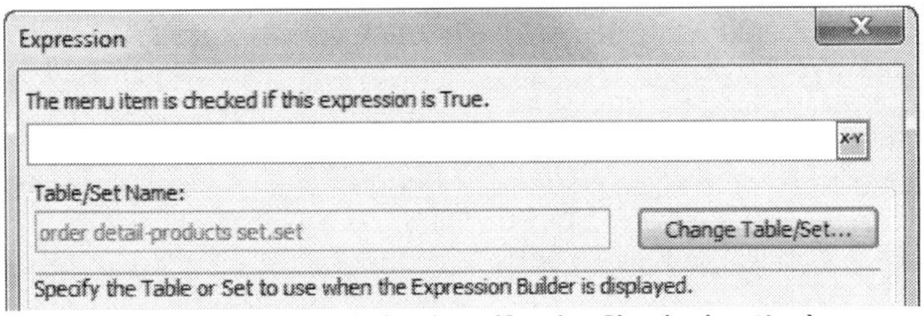

Figure 16-8 Expression dialog box (for the Checked option)

Figure 16-9 Built-in action type options

Figure 16-10 Run a Saved Script options

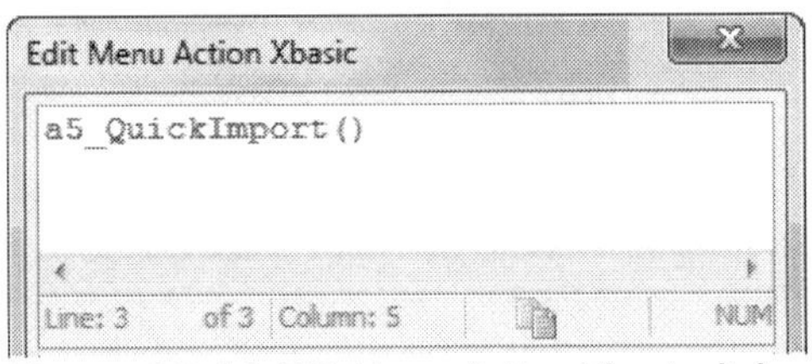

Figure 16-11 Edit Menu Action Xbasic dialog box

Built In Actions

Alpha Five comes with built-in actions that you can use. The built-in actions are the options that are available on menus, when you view a form, browse or report. To access them, click the Select button shown earlier in Figure 16-9. You will see the dialog box shown in Figure 16-12. Click the **SET CONTEXT BUTTON** to select the view that the menu will be applied to.

The dialog box changes to the one shown in Figure 16-13. Depending on the view that you select, the options that the Select Action button displays change.

Figure 16-14 shows the actions if the Form View context is selected.
Figure 16-15 shows the actions if the Browse View context is selected.
Figure 16-16 shows the actions if the Print View context is selected.

Select the action on the menu that you want to add.

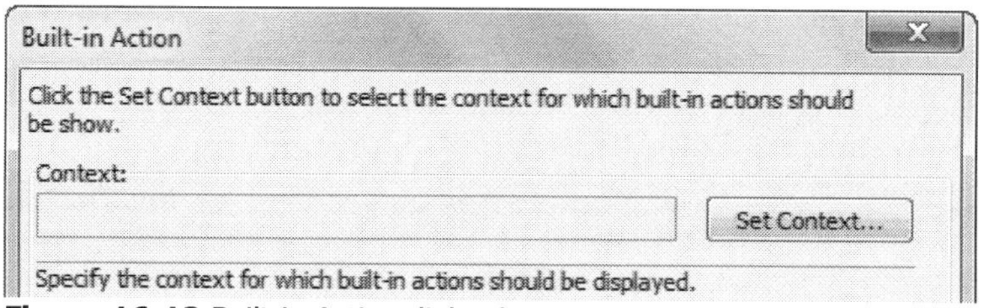

Figure 16-12 Built-in Action dialog box

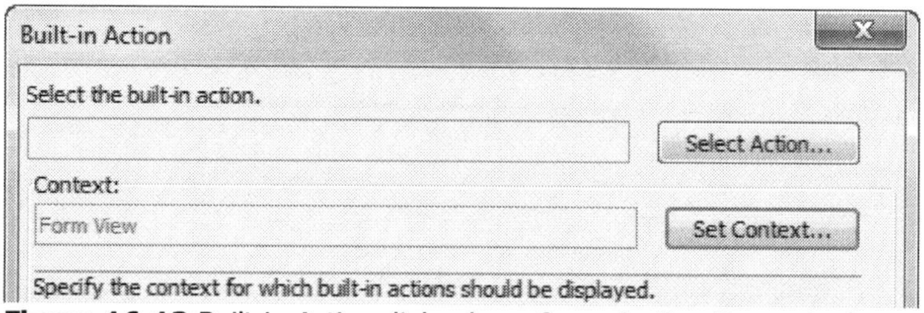

Figure 16-13 Built-in Action dialog box after selecting the context

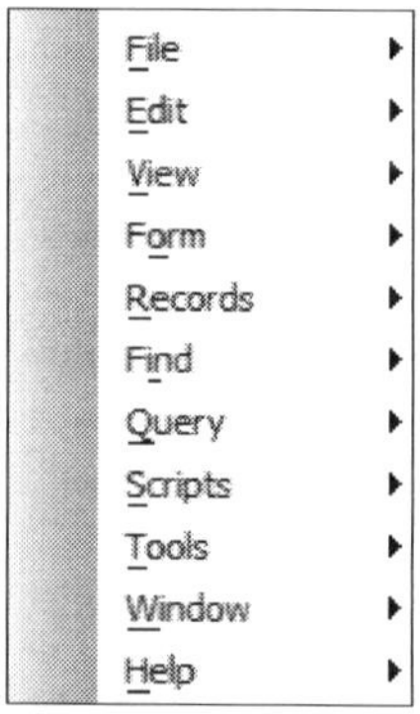

Figure 16-14 Form View built-in actions

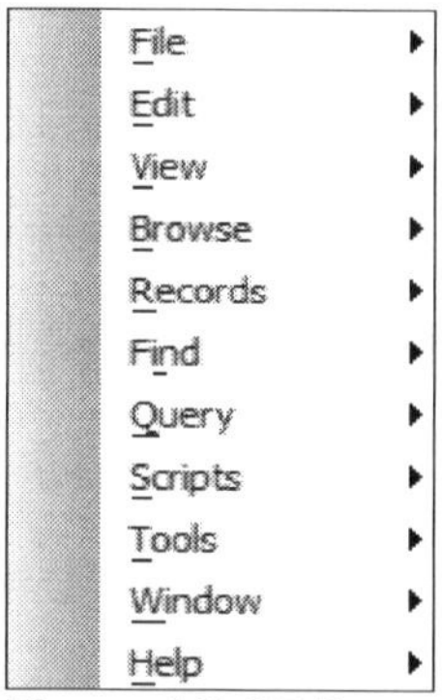

Figure 16-15 Browse View built-in actions

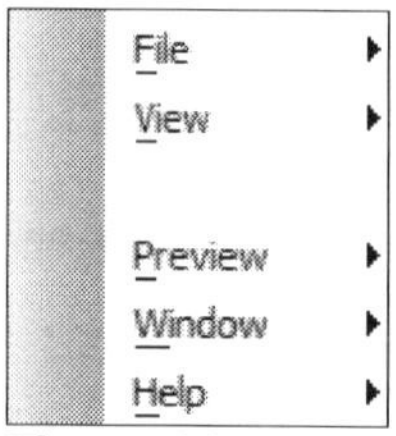

Figure 16-16 Print Preview (Report) built-in actions

Xbasic View Tab

Figure 16-17 shows the Xbasic code that is automatically generated, based on the options selected on the Outline View tab.

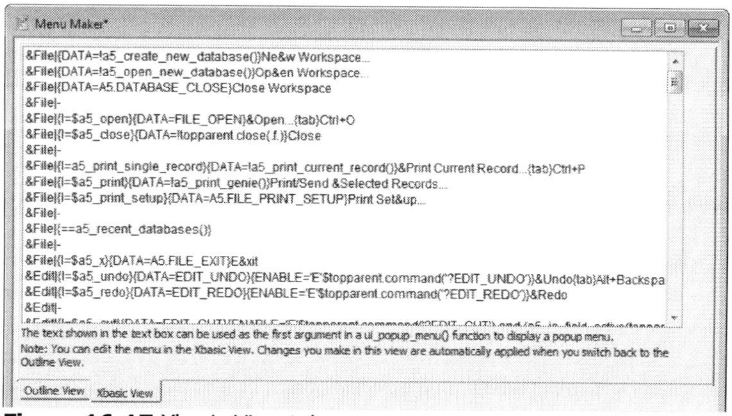

Figure 16-17 Xbasic View tab

Exercise 16.1: Modify The Existing Form View Menu

In this exercise you will modify the Form view menu shown in Figure 16-18 and add items to the Form menu shown in Figure 16-19, by completing the following tasks.

- ☑ Deleting the Records, Find, Query, Scripts, Tools, Window and Help menus shown in Figure 16-18.
- ☑ Adding the Import Records Pre-defined menu item to the Form menu.
- ☑ Add the RTF Memo menu to the Form menu.

Figure 16-18 Form View menu

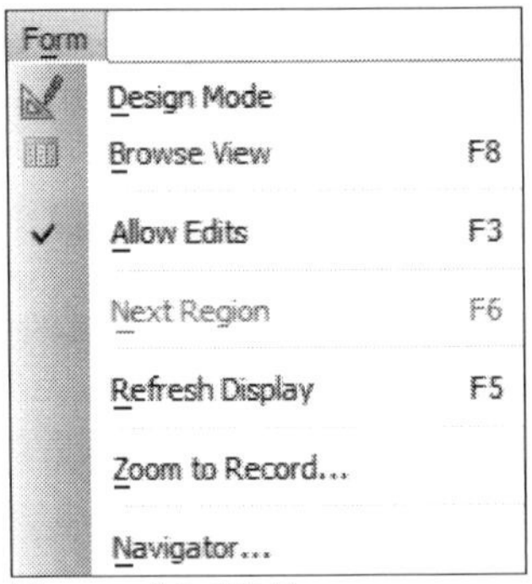

Figure 16-19 Form menu

Delete Menu Items To Create A Custom Menu

1. Control Panel ⇒ Code tab ⇒ New button ⇒ Menu.
2. Select the Form View menu item, then click OK.
3. Click on the Records menu item, then click the Delete button (the red x). When prompted to delete the item and **CHILD ITEMS**, click Yes.
4. Repeat step 3 to delete the following menu items: Find, Query, Scripts, Tools, Window and Help.
5. Click the Save Menu button on the toolbar. Type `aFormViewMenu` as the menu name.

Add A Pre-Defined Item To The Menu

In this part of the exercise you will learn how to add an existing item to a menu. It is a good idea to select the item on the menu above or below where you want to add the new item. I prefer to select the item above where the new item will go. Doing that is optional.

1. Display the Form menu, then select the first <Separator> item. Click the Add Item button. The **BELOW CURRENT ITEM** and **MENU ENTRY** options should be selected on the Add New Item dialog box.

2. Click the **PRE-DEFINED MENU ITEM** button. You will see the error message shown in Figure 16-20.

   Click OK.

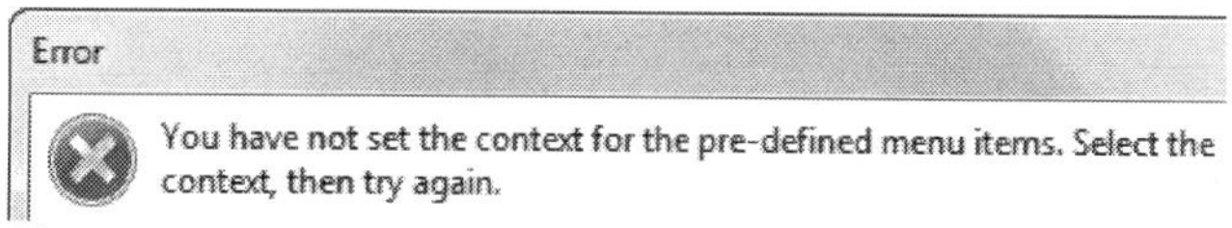

Figure 16-20 Context error message

I don't know why this error message appears, because you haven't gotten to the Pre-Defined Menu Item dialog box, which is where you select the context. When you see this error message in the future, click OK.

3. Click the Set Context button, then select the Form View option, as shown on the dialog box in Figure 16-21, then click OK.

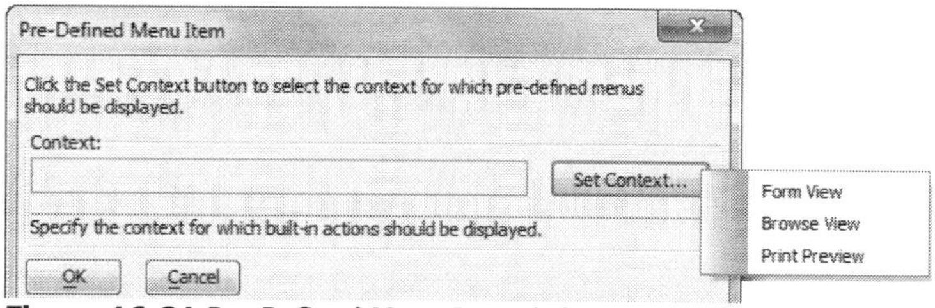

Figure 16-21 Pre-Defined Menu Item dialog box

4. Click the Pre-Defined Menu Item button again.

   Scroll down the list and open the Records menu.

   Select the Import Records option shown in Figure 16-22, then click OK.

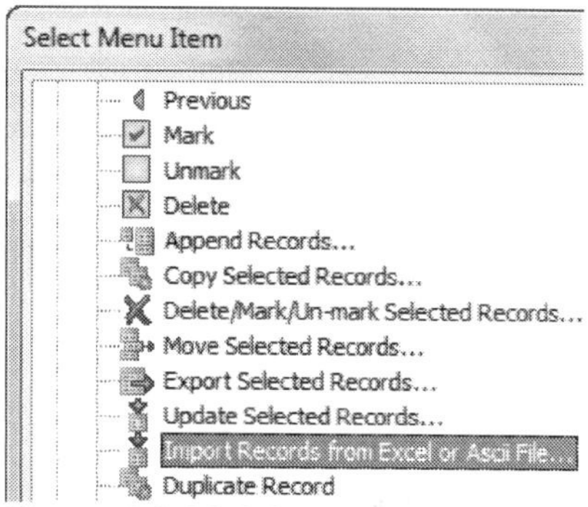

Figure 16-22 Select Menu Item dialog box

5. You should have the options shown in Figure 16-23.

   Click OK.

   On the Menu Maker dialog box you should see the Import Records item below the first separator, as shown earlier in Figure 16-2.

   Save the changes.

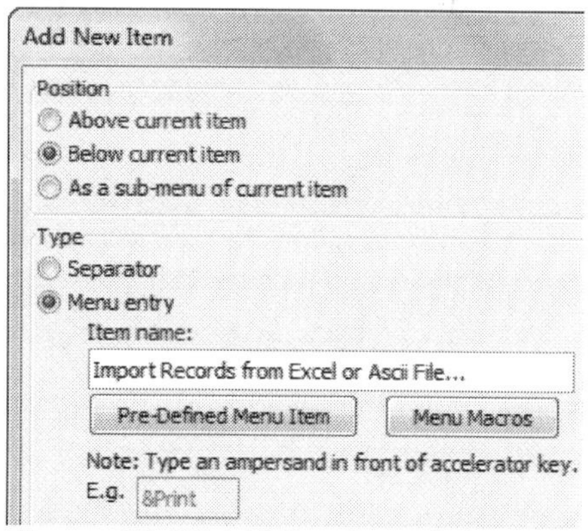

Figure 16-23 Add New Item dialog box

Add A Menu Macro Item

Menu macros are other items that can be added to a menu. In this part of the exercise you will add the RTF Memo macro item to the Form menu below the Import Records item.

1. On the Menu Maker, click on the Import Records item that you just created, then click the Add Item button.

2. Click the **MENU MACROS** button.

   On the list shown in Figure 16-24, select the <RTF Memo Import/Export Menus> option.

   Remove the brackets from the entry in the Item name field, then click OK.

Figure 16-24 Menu Macros

3. Check the Has Bitmap option, then select an image. Save the changes.

Add A Separator To The Menu

In this part of the exercise you will add a separator below the two items that you added to the Form menu.

1. Click on the RTF Memo item on the menu, then click the Add Item button.

2. Select the **SEPARATOR** option, then click OK.

   The top of the Form menu should look like the one shown in Figure 16-25.

   Save the changes, then close the Menu Maker.

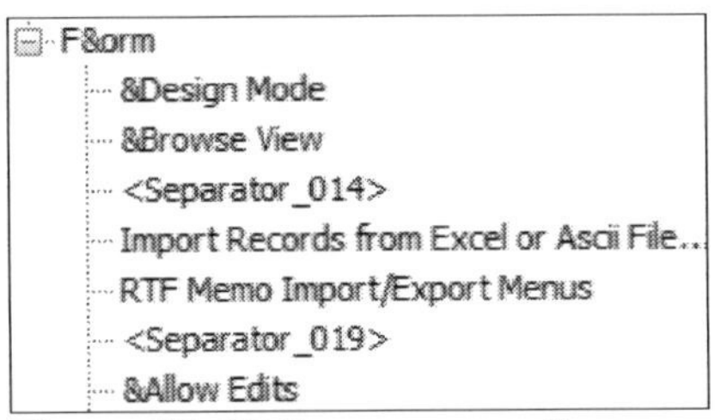

Figure 16-25 Form menu options

Attach The Menu To The Display Customer Form

In this part of the exercise you will learn how to attach the menu to the View menu option for forms. This is how the menu that you created will be available when the form is viewed.

1. Open the Display Customer Name form in Design mode, then open the properties dialog box and select the Menus/Toolbars tab.

2. Open the Menus View drop-down list and select aFormViewMenu, as illustrated in Figure 16-26.

   The options on this tab are the menus and toolbars that you can change.

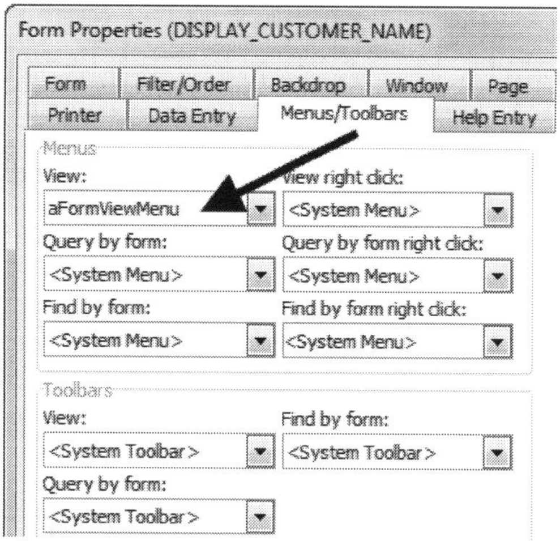

Figure 16-26 Form Menus/Toolbars tab options

3. Save the form as `aCustomFormViewMenu`.

   When you view the form, you should see the menu shown in Figure 16-27.

   The third and fourth options on the Form menu are the two that you added.

   Compare this menu to the ones shown earlier in Figure 16-18 and 16-19.

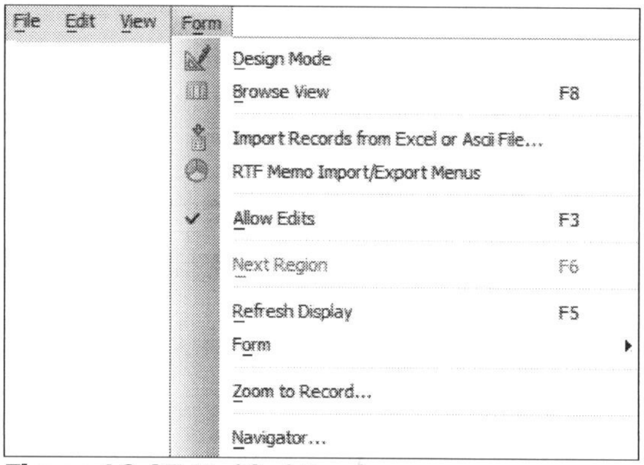

Figure 16-27 Modified Form menu

Exercise 16.2: Modify The Right-Click Menu For A Browse

As shown earlier in Figure 16-26, there are right-click menus that you can change. In this exercise you will create a menu for the right-click menu of a browse.

1. Code tab ⇒ New button ⇒ Menu.
2. On the New Menu dialog box, click on the Column Selected menu in the Browse right-click Menu section, then click OK.
3. Click the Add Item button. Select the Above current item option, then click the Pre-Defined Menu Item button. Click OK. Click the Set Context button, then select the Browse View option. Click OK.

4. Click the Pre-Defined Menu Item button.

   Open the Tools menu, select the Export to Excel option.

   You should see the Export to Excel option at the top of the menu on the Menu Maker, as shown in Figure 16-28.

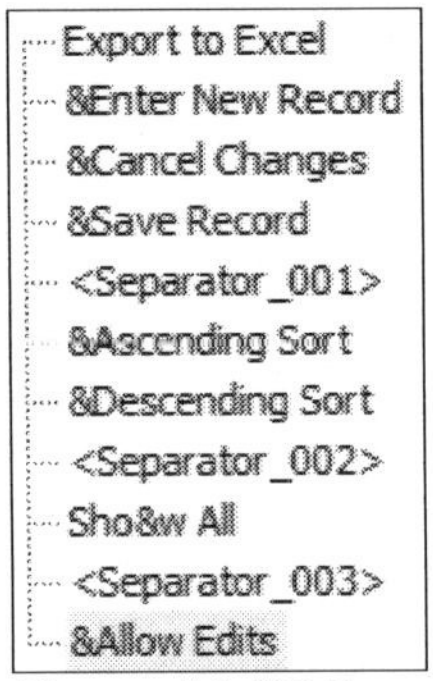

Figure 16-28 Export option added to the top of the Browse menu

5. Save the menu as `aBrowseViewRightClick`.

Attach The Menu To The Browse

1. Open the Orders Multi Table set browse in Design mode, then open the properties dialog box.

2. On the Menus/Toolbars tab, open the View right click drop-down list and select aBrowseViewRightClick, as shown in Figure 16-29.

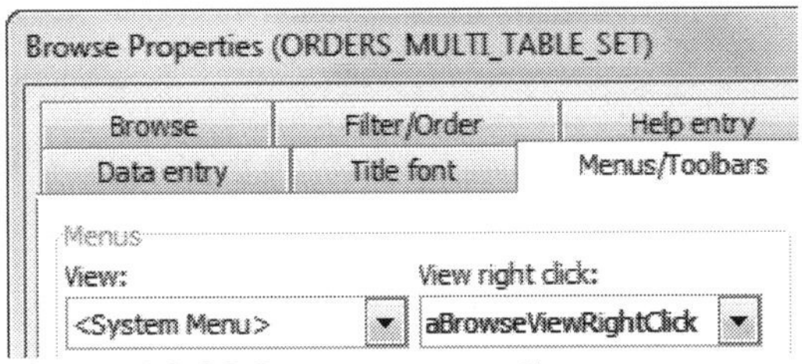

Figure 16-29 Browse menu options

3. Save the browse as `aCustomBrowseViewMenu`.

4. View the browse, then right-click on a column. You should see the menu shown in Figure 16-30 with the Export option at the top.

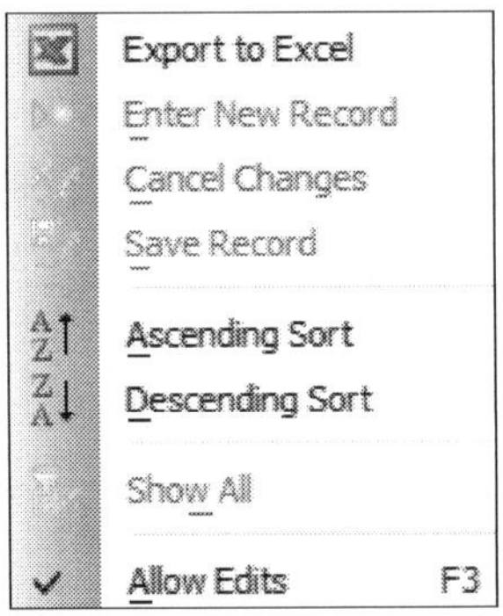

Figure 16-30 Browse column right-click menu

> **Using The Export To Excel Option**
> If you select multiple columns, then select the Export to Excel option, all of the selected columns will be exported.

Exercise 16.3: Create A New Menu

In this exercise you will learn how to create a menu from scratch. This menu will contain submenus.

Create A Script

To display forms or run reports from a menu, a script needs to be created to attach the form or report to the menu.

1. Code tab ⇒ New button ⇒ **SCRIPT (USING ACTION SCRIPTING)**. Click the Add New Action button.
2. Click on the Reports category, then select the Preview a Layout action. Scroll down the Layout Name list and select the report aOrdersGroupedByMonth, then click Next twice.
3. Click Finish. Save the script as `aPreviewMonthlyOrdersRpt`.

Create The Menu

1. Code tab ⇒ New button ⇒ Menu.
2. On the New Menu dialog box select the **BLANK MENU** option, then click OK. Click the Add Item button.
3. Select the Below Current Item option. In the Item name field type `Forms`, then click OK.
4. Click the Add Item button. In the Item name field type `Reports`, then click OK.

Create The Submenus

In this part of the exercise you will add the submenu items. You will add one form and two reports.

1. Click on the Forms item, then click the Add Item button. Select the **AS A SUB-MENU OF CURRENT ITEM** option. In the Item name field type `View Orders By Sales Rep`, then click OK.
2. On the Menu Maker, open the Type drop-down list and select **RUN A SAVED SCRIPT**. Open the Script drop-down list and select aXdialogBox.
3. Add a bitmap of your choice to the item.

   Save the menu as `aFormCustomMenu`.

   You should have the options shown in Figure 16-31.

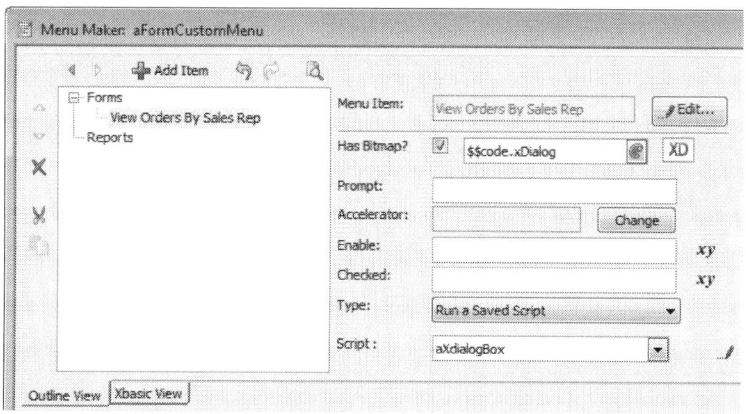

Figure 16-31 Form menu options

4. Click on the Reports item, then click the Add Item button. Select the As a sub-menu of current item option. In the Item name field type `Run Date Range Report`, then click OK.

5. Open the Type drop-down list and select Run a Saved Script. Open the Script drop-down list and select aXdialogRunReport.

6. Click on the Reports item, then click the Add Item button. Select the As a sub-menu of current item option. In the Item name field type `Run Monthly Orders Report`, then click OK.

7. Open the Type drop-down list and select Run a Saved Script.

   Open the Script drop-down list and select aPreviewMonthlyOrdersRpt.

   Save the changes. Your menu should look like the one shown in Figure 16-32.

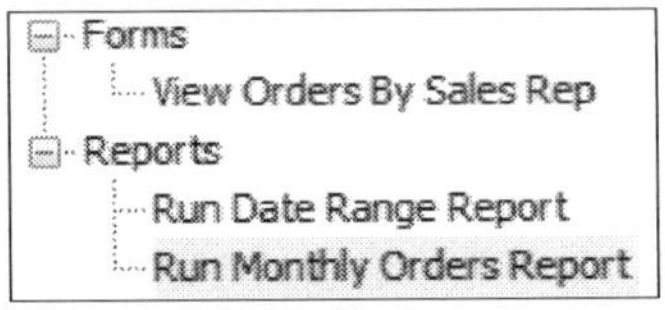

Figure 16-32 Custom menu

Attach The Menu To A Form

1. Open the Display Customer Name form in Design mode, then open the properties dialog box.

2. On the Menus/Toobars tab, open the Menus View drop-down list and select aFormCustomMenu.

3. Save the form as `aCustomViewMenu`. View the form. The Forms menu should look like the one shown in Figure 16-33. The Reports menu should look like the one shown in Figure 16-34.

Figure 16-33 Forms menu

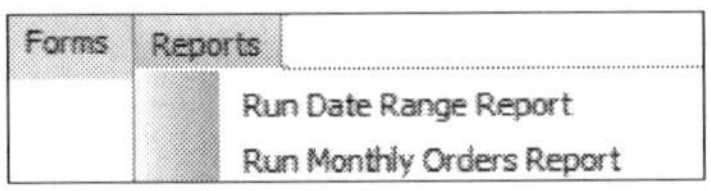

Figure 16-34 Reports menu

Toolbars

In addition to creating a toolbar from scratch, the default toolbars shown in Figure 16-35 can be modified.

The buttons on toolbars are shortcuts to selecting the same option on a menu. Usually, the buttons on a toolbar are the most used menu options. Sometimes, toolbar buttons are for options that are not on a menu.

Like menus, all of the buttons on a toolbar may not be needed for the application that you are creating.

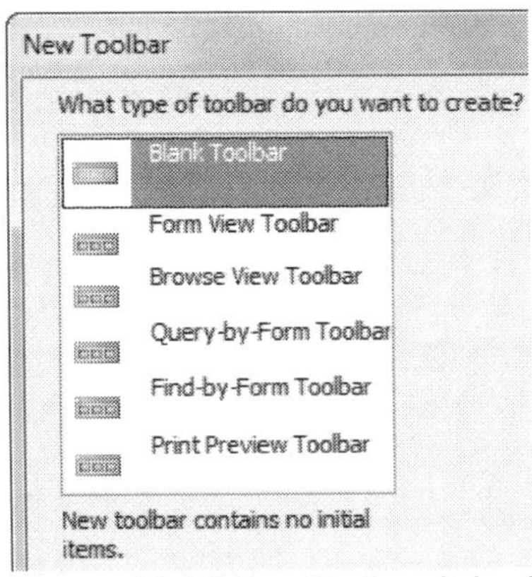

Figure 16-35 New Toolbar dialog box

Toolbar Editor

The dialog box shown in Figure 16-36 is used to create and edit toolbars.

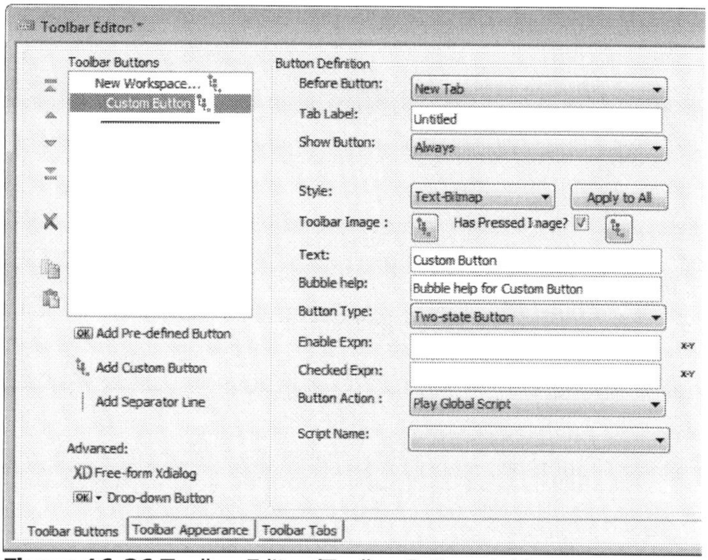

Figure 16-36 Toolbar Editor (Toolbar Buttons tab)

Toolbar Buttons Tab

The options shown above in Figure 16-36 on the right, change depending on the type of button that is selected. The options are explained below.

Button Types

The four types of buttons that can be added to a toolbar are explained below.

① **ADD PRE-DEFINED BUTTON** Opens the dialog box shown in Figure 16-37. It is used to select the item (menu command) that you want to add to the toolbar.

② **ADD CUSTOM BUTTON** Adds a button to the Toolbar Buttons list. This option is used to create a button that has different functionality then the items on the menus, like open a specific report.

③ **FREE-FORM XDIALOG** Adds a button that is used to type in or paste code that will display an Xdialog box.

④ **DROP-DOWN BUTTON** Is used to add a drop-down list to the button.

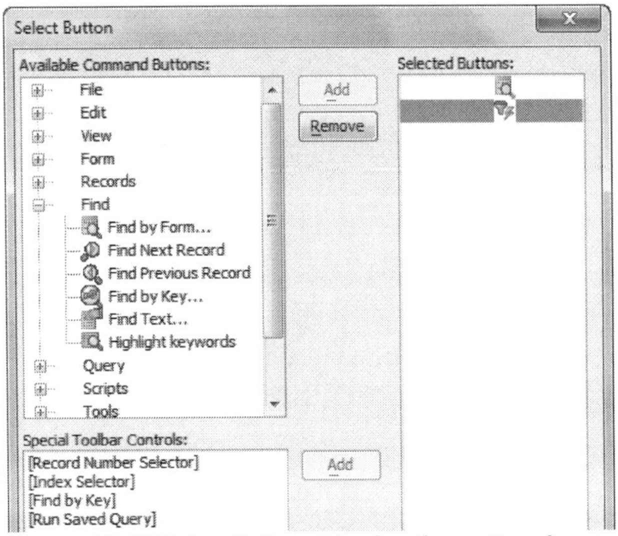

Figure 16-37 Select Button dialog box (menu items)

Button Definition Options

The options on the right side of the Toolbar Editor are used to customize the button. The options discussed below are for Pre-defined custom buttons. The Free-form Xdialog and Drop-down buttons have different options which are covered later in this chapter.

① **BEFORE BUTTON** The options are used to select where to place the button. The options are explained in Table 16-1.
② **TAB LABEL** Enter a name for the tab on the toolbar. The option is only available when the New Tab or Conditional tab Before Button option is selected.
③ **SHOW BUTTON** The options are used to select when the button will be displayed.
④ **STYLE** Select what will be displayed on the button. Clicking the **APPLY TO ALL** button applies the style to all buttons on the toolbar.
⑤ **TOOLBAR IMAGE** Select an image for the button. (1)
⑥ **HAS PRESSED IMAGE** If checked, the button can display a different image when it is clicked on. To select the image for the button, click the button to the right of the check box. (1)
⑦ **TEXT** Is used to change the text that will appear on the button. This option is only available when a Text style option is selected.
⑧ **BUBBLE HELP** Enter the help message that will appear when the mouse pointer is hovered over the toolbar button.
⑨ **BUTTON TYPE** Select the type of button. The **TWO-STATE** option enables the **CHECKED EXPN** option, which is used to create an expression to select when the button is checked.
⑩ **ENABLE EXPN** Is used to create an expression to enable the button.
⑪ **BUTTON ACTION** Is used to select if a script, Xbasic code or internal action will be connected to the button.

(1) This option is only available when a bitmap style is selected.

Option	Description
No Break	This is the default option. Selecting this option places the button to the right of the previous object on the same tab.
Break	Places the button below the previous object.
Conditional Break	When the toolbar is undocked, the object is placed on the same tab below the previous object.
New Tab	The object is placed on a new tab. (2)
Conditional Tab	When the toolbar is undocked, the object is placed on a new tab. (2)
Unbreakable Space	Places the object to the right of the previous object on the same tab and cannot be separated from the previous object.

Table 16-1 Before Button options explained

(2) Select the appropriate options on the Toolbar Tabs tab.

Toolbar Appearance Tab

The options shown in Figure 16-38 are used to select docking, color, font and border style options for the toolbar.

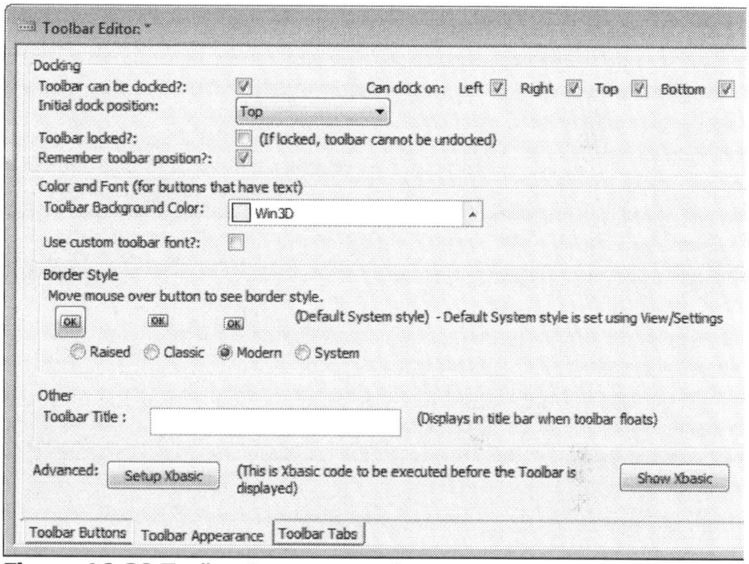

Figure 16-38 Toolbar Appearance tab

Toolbar Tabs Tab

The options shown in Figure 16-39 are used when the toolbar has tabs.

The options are used to select where the tabs are placed and whether or not the tabs are labeled.

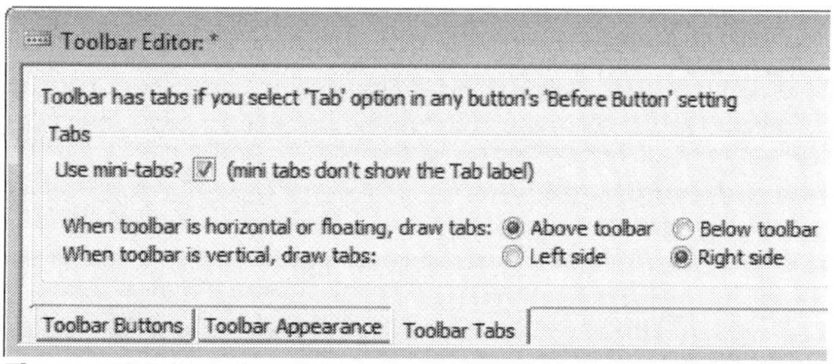

Figure 16-39 Toolbar Tabs tab

Exercise 16.4: Modify A Toolbar

In this exercise you will modify the Form View toolbar, then add the toolbar to a form.

1. Code tab ⇒ New button ⇒ Toolbar. Select the Form View Toolbar option, then click OK.
2. In the Toolbar Buttons list, delete the first two buttons, then click on the [Record Number Selector] button in the list.
3. Click the Add Pre-defined Button option. Open the Query menu and add the Query Genie option.
4. Check the Has Pressed Image option. Click the button to the right and select an image.
5. Save the toolbar as `aFormViewToolbar`.
6. Open the Customers tabbed form in Design mode, then open the properties dialog box.
7. On the Menus/Toolbars tab, open the Toolbars View drop-down list and select aFormViewToolbar, as shown in Figure 16-40.

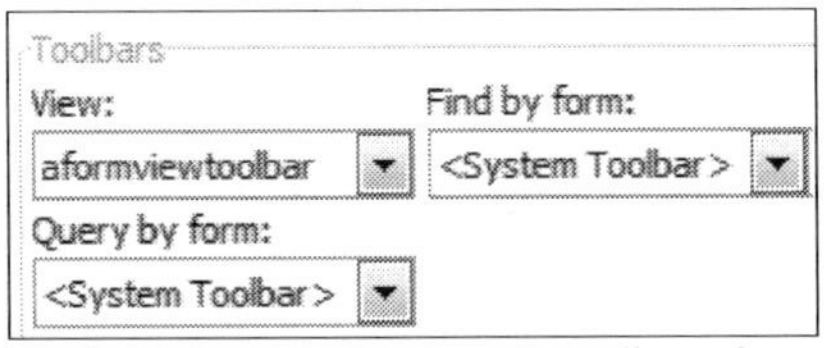

Figure 16-40 Form view toolbar changed

8. Save the form as `aFormToolbar`. When you view the form you should see the toolbar shown in Figure 16-41.

Figure 16-41 Modified form view toolbar (all buttons not shown)

To the right of the Record Number Selector, you should see the button for the Query Genie, which you added to the toolbar. When you click the Query Genie button, you should see the image change.

Exercise 16.5: Create A New Toolbar

In this exercise you will create a new toolbar that uses the Advanced button options.

Create A Drop-Down Button

In this part of the exercise you will create a button that displays three options.

1. Code tab ⇒ New button ⇒ Toolbar ⇒ Blank Toolbar ⇒ Click OK. Click the Drop-down button option. On the right side of the dialog box you should see the **DROP-DOWN CHOICES** list box.
2. Click the **EDIT CHOICE** button.

   Click the **SELECT BUILT-IN ACTION** button.

   Click OK on the dialog box shown in Figure 16-42.

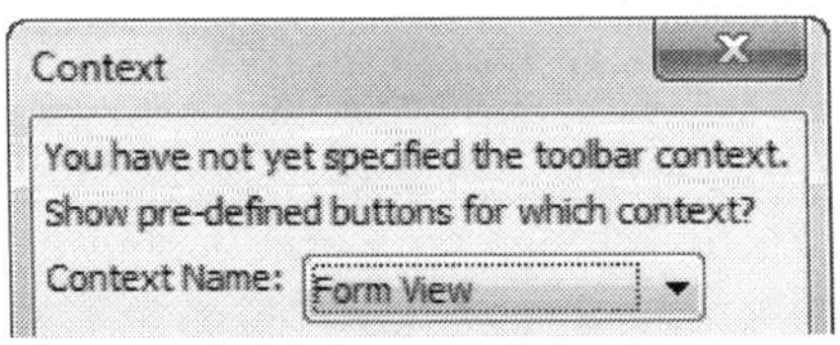

Figure 16-42 Context dialog box

3. On the dialog box shown in Figure 16-43, open the Form menu and select Zoom to Record. You should have the options shown in Figure 16-44. Click OK.

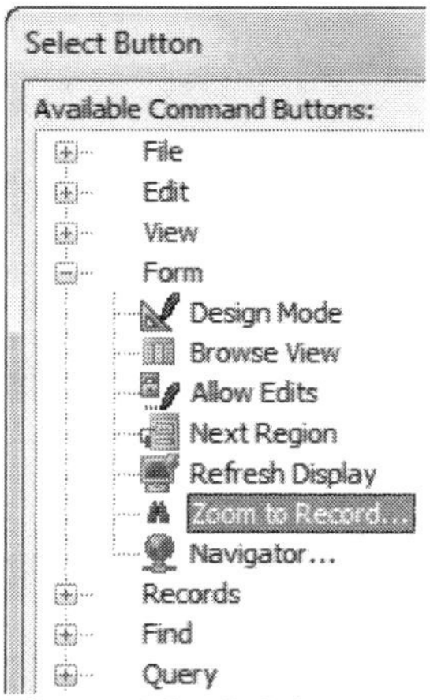

Figure 16-43 Select Button dialog box (toolbar buttons)

Figure 16-44 Edit Drop-down Menu Item dialog box

4. Click the **ADD CHOICE** button, then click the Edit Choice button. On the dialog box shown above in Figure 16-43, select the Browse View button that is on the Form menu.

5. On the Edit Drop-down Menu Item dialog box, change the **MENU TEXT** to `View data in browse`.

6. Add another choice. Select the Query Genie action.

   Delete Ctrl+Q from the Menu text field.
   Click OK. You should have the drop-down choices shown in Figure 16-45 on the toolbar.

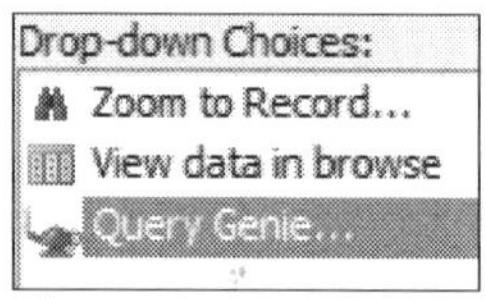

Figure 16-45 Drop-down choices

7. Add a Separator line to the toolbar.

8. Add a custom button that runs the aXdialogBox script.

9. Save the toolbar as `aCustomFormToolbar`.

Add Tabs To The Toolbar

In this part of exercise you will add two tabs to the toolbar.

1. On the Toolbar Editor, click on the first button in the Toolbar Buttons list, then click the Add Custom Button option. Move the new button to the top of the list.

2. Open the **BEFORE BUTTON** drop-down list and select New Tab. In the Tab Label field type `Pre-defined Buttons`.

3. Change the Style text.

   Delete the content in the Text field.

   Figure 16-46 shows the Button Definition options for the tab that you just created.

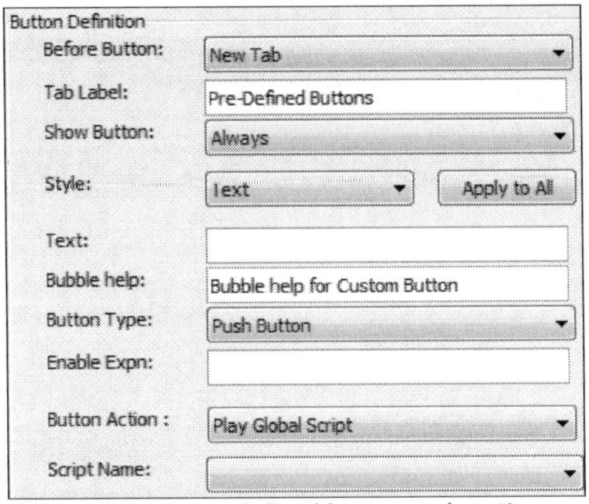

Figure 16-46 Pre-defined buttons tab options

4. Click on the last button in the Toolbar Buttons list, then click the Add Custom Button option. Select New Tab in the Before Button list.

5. In the Tab Label field type `Reports`.

6. Change the Style to text. Delete the content in the Text field.

Add Buttons To The Second Tab

1. Add a custom button to the second tab that runs the aXdialogRunReport script.

2. Change the Style to Bitmap-Text, then select an image. Type `Date Range Report` in the Text field.

3. Add another custom button to the second tab. It should run the aPreviewMonthlyOrdersReport script.

4. Change the Style to Bitmap-Text, then select an image.

   Type `Monthly Orders Report` in the Text field.

   Figure 16-47 shows the Button Definition options for the Monthly Orders report.

   Make sure that both report buttons that you just created are below the Reports tab, in the Toolbar Buttons list.

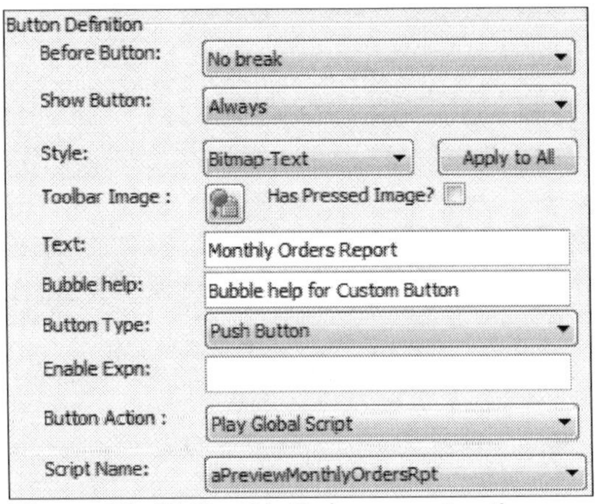

Figure 16-47 Monthly Orders report options

Finish The Toolbar

1. On the Toolbar Tabs tab, clear the **USE MINI-TABS?** option, then save the changes.
2. Display the Customers tabbed form in Design mode. Open the properties dialog box.
3. On the Menus/Toolbars tab, open the Toolbars View drop-down list and select aCustomFormToolbar. Save the form as `aCustomToolbar`.
4. View the form. The first tab on the toolbar should look like the one shown in Figure 16-48. The second tab should look like the one shown in Figure 16-49.

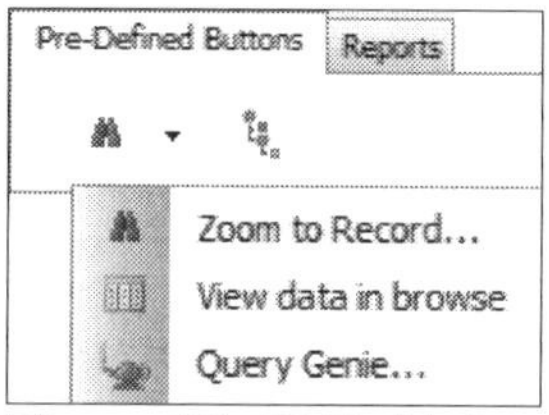

Figure 16-48 First tab on the toolbar

Figure 16-49 Second tab on the toolbar

CUSTOMIZING AN APPLICATION

In this chapter you will learn about the topics listed below that can be used to customize an application.

☑ Security
☑ Startup forms
☑ Desktop shortcut
☑ Hiding the Control Panel

CHAPTER 17

Overview

You have covered a lot of topics in this book. The focus of this chapter is on what I call "the finishing touches" of an application.

Securing The Database

Alpha Five provides the security options shown in Figure 17-1 on the Tools menu. The options are explained below.

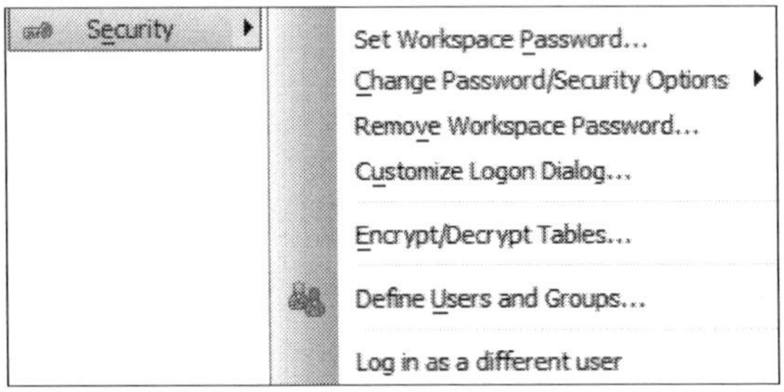

Figure 17-1 Security options

Set Workspace Password

This option displays the dialog box shown in Figure 17-2.

The options are used to create a master password, set up user accounts, login attempts and more. The options are explained below.

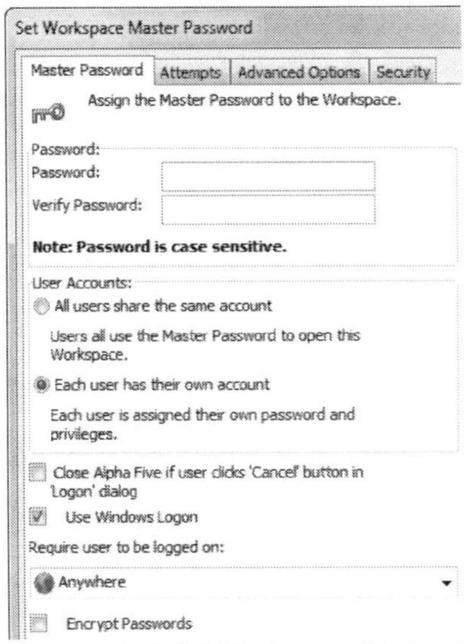

Figure 17-2 Set Workspace Master Password dialog box

① The **PASSWORD** and **VERIFY PASSWORD** fields are used to create the master password, which is like an administrator password. Setting up a master password encrypts the database (.dbf) files. This means that they can be opened inside of Alpha Five, but the files cannot be opened outside of Alpha Five.

② **USER ACCOUNTS** Select whether everyone that will use the database will use the same login account or if every user will have their own login account. Selecting the **EACH USER HAS THEIR OWN ACCOUNT** option enables the Use Windows Logon option and the Security tab, (not shown) above in Figure 17-2.

③ **USE WINDOWS LOGON** If checked, the users Windows logon will be checked against the logon accounts for the database. If there is a match, the user will be logged in automatically. The options in the **REQUIRE USER TO BE LOGGED ON** drop-down list are used to select where the Windows logon must originate from. (1)

④ **ENCRYPT PASSWORDS** If checked, Alpha Five will apply a one way encryption scheme on passwords. In this case, encryption prevents you from seeing the passwords. This will prevent the workspace from being opened in previous version of Alpha Five. (1)

(1) If needed, you can click on this option to read more information about how the option may be helpful.

Attempts Tab

The options shown in Figure 17-3 are used to select the maximum number of times someone can attempt to login and a script to run if the maximum number of login attempts has been reached.

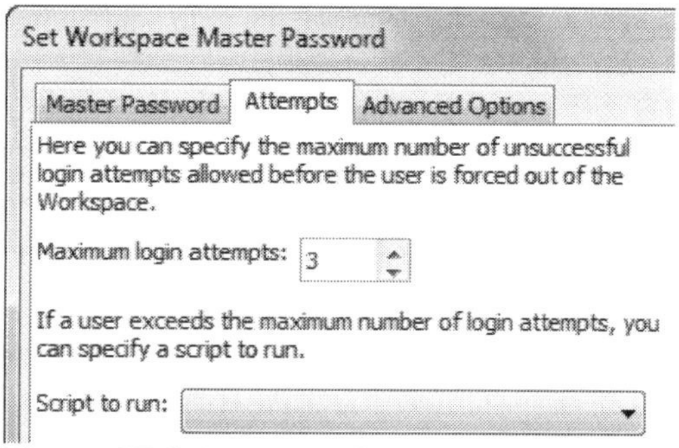

Figure 17-3 Attempts tab

Advanced Options Tab

The options shown in Figure 17-4 are available if the Each user has their own account option on the Master Password tab is selected.

The options are used to select if the user accounts are specific to the current database or if the user accounts will be shared with at least one other database.

The Define Users and Groups option shown earlier in Figure 17-1 is used to create a user account file.

The **ENABLE AUDITING OF SECURITY INFORMATION** option is used to keep a log of when the database was accessed.

Figure 17-4 Advanced Options tab

Security Tab

The options shown in Figure 17-5 are used to select the permission for objects in the database that do not have any security permissions applied.

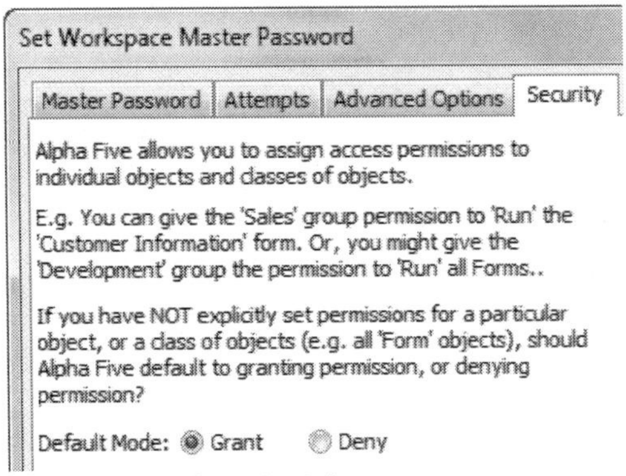

Figure 17-5 Security tab

Exercise 17.1: Add A Master Password To The Database

In this exercise you will create a master password and select that each user should have their own login account.

1. Open the a5beyond database if it is not already open.

2. Tools ⇒ Security ⇒ Set Workspace Password. On the Master Password tab, type in a password, then verify the password.

3. Select the Each user has their own account option.

4. On the Advanced Options tab, check the Enable auditing option. Click OK.

   You will see the dialog box shown in Figure 17-6, which shows the progress of security being added to the tables. Click OK on the note that says that the master password has been set.

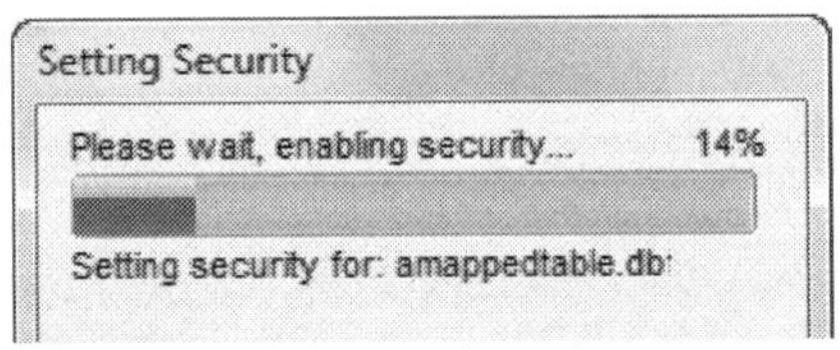

Figure 17-6 Setting Security progress dialog box

5. Close the database and reopen it.

   You will see the dialog box shown in Figure 17-7.

   Type in the password that you created, then click the **LOGIN** button.

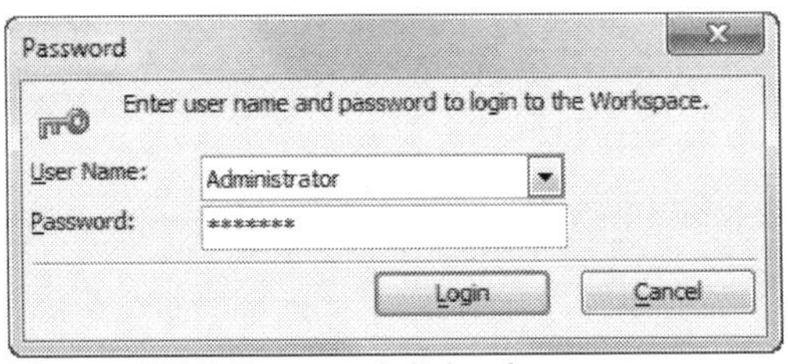

Figure 17-7 Password dialog box

Change Password/Security Options

In the previous exercise you set up some security for the database.
If you need to change the master password, security settings or logon password, select the option shown in Figure 17-8.

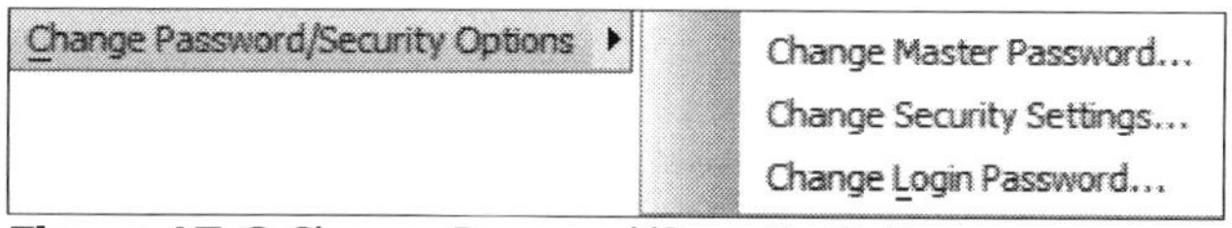

Figure 17-8 Change Password/Security Options

The **CHANGE MASTER PASSWORD** option opens the dialog box shown in Figure 17-9, which is used to change the master password.

Figure 17-9 Change Database Master Password dialog box

The **CHANGE SECURITY SETTINGS** option opens the dialog box shown in Figure 17-10.

These are the same options minus the master password fields that are on the Set Workspace Master Password dialog box, shown earlier in Figures 17-2 to 17-5.

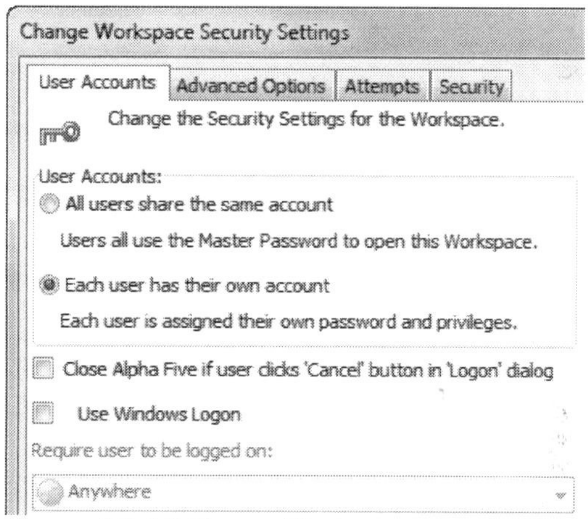

Figure 17-10 Change Workspace Security Settings dialog box

The **CHANGE LOGIN PASSWORD** option is enabled when a user is signed on.

This option opens the dialog box shown in Figure 17-11.

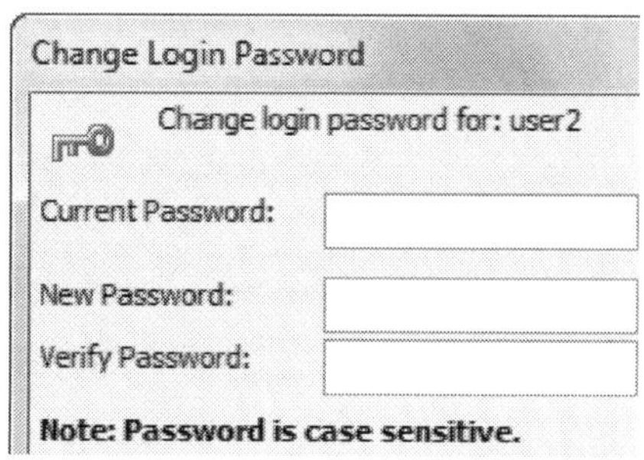

Figure 17-11 Change Login Password dialog box

Remove Workspace Password

The option opens the dialog box shown in Figure 17-12. It is used to remove the master password from the database.

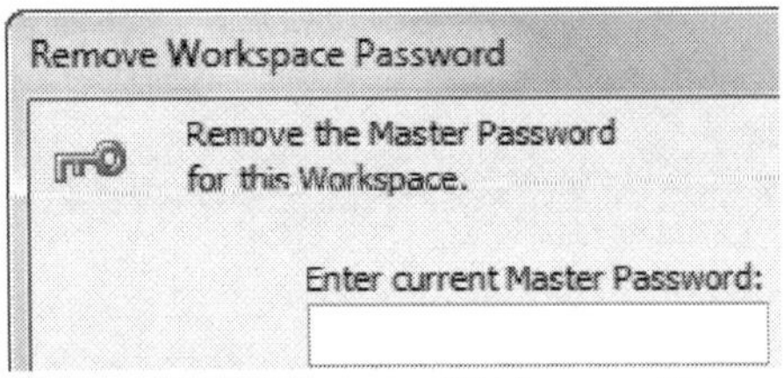

Figure 17-12 Remove Workspace Password dialog box

Customize Logon Dialog

This option opens the dialog box shown in Figures 17-13 to 2-15.

The options are used to change the appearance of the Password dialog box shown earlier in Figure 17-7.

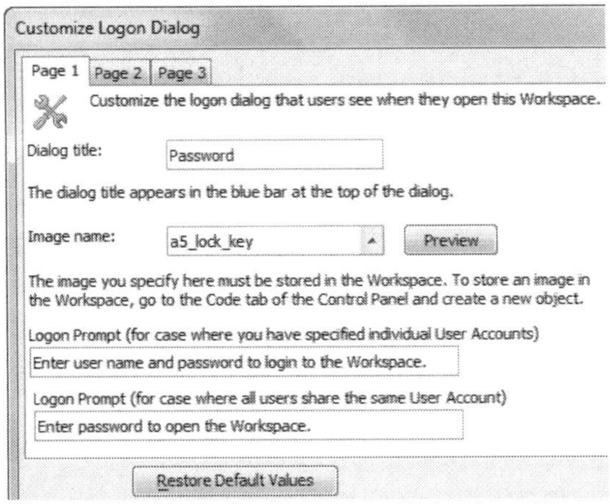

Figure 17-13 Customize Logon Dialog box (Page 1 tab)

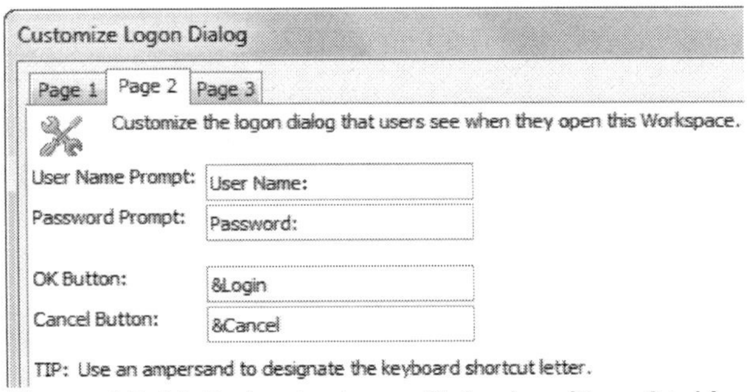

Figure 17-14 Customize Logon Dialog box (Page 2 tab)

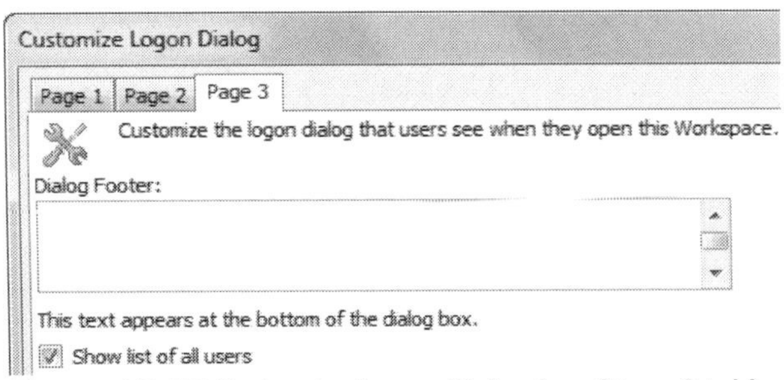

Figure 17-15 Customize Logon Dialog box (Page 3 tab)

Encrypt/Decrypt Tables

This option opens the dialog box shown in Figure 17-16.

Select the tables that you want to encrypt (meaning that the table can only be used in the database) or decrypt (clear the check mark from a table that you want to allow to be used outside of the database).

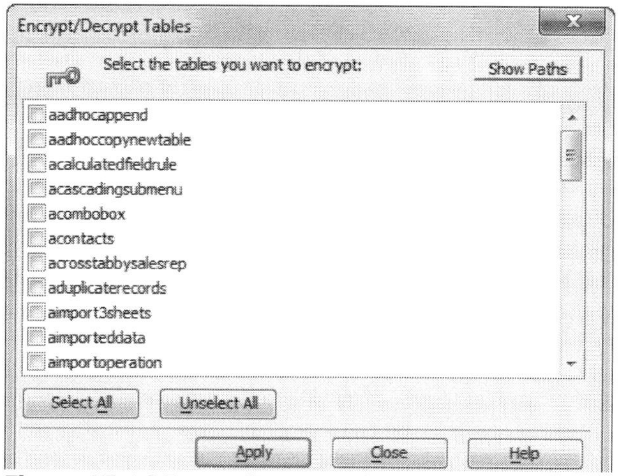

Figure 17-16 Encrypt/Decrypt Tables dialog box

Define Users And Groups

This option opens the dialog box shown in Figure 17-17. This dialog box is used to create users and groups for the database.

The **IMPORT/EXPORT BUTTON** opens the dialog box shown in Figure 17-18.

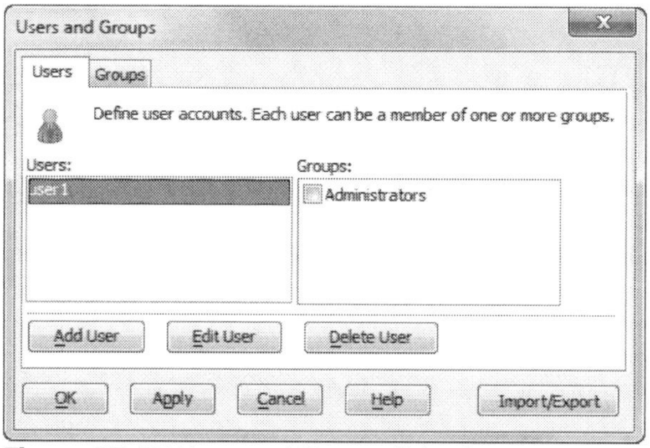

Figure 17-17 Users and Groups dialog box

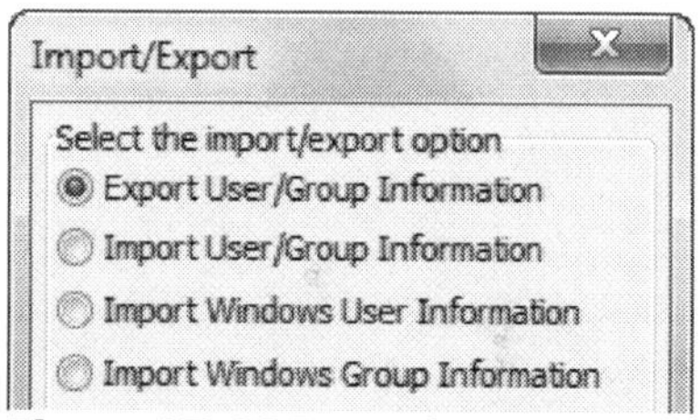

Figure 17-18 Import/Export dialog box

Exercise 17.2: Create Users And Groups

In this exercise you will learn how to create users and groups for the database.

Create User Accounts

1. Tools ⇒ Security ⇒ Define Users and Groups.

2. Click the **ADD USER** button.

   Type `user1` (all lowercase) in the User Name, Password and Confirm Password fields, as shown in Figure 17-19.

   Click OK.

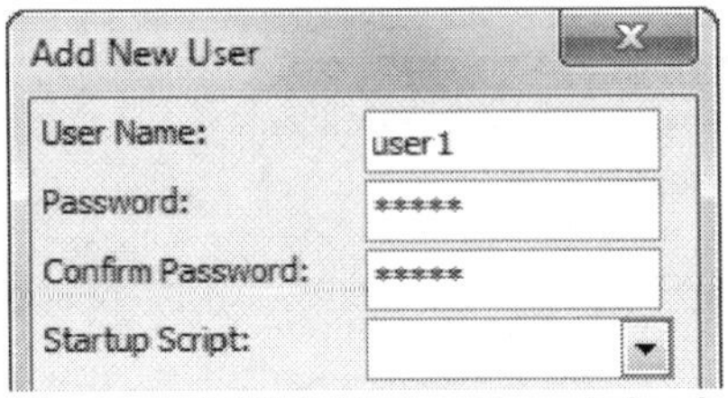

Figure 17-19 Add New User dialog box

3. Follow step 2 to create two more user accounts with the user name user2 and user3.

Create Groups

1. On the Groups tab, click the **ADD GROUP** button.

2. Type `GroupA` on the dialog box shown in Figure 17-20, then click OK.

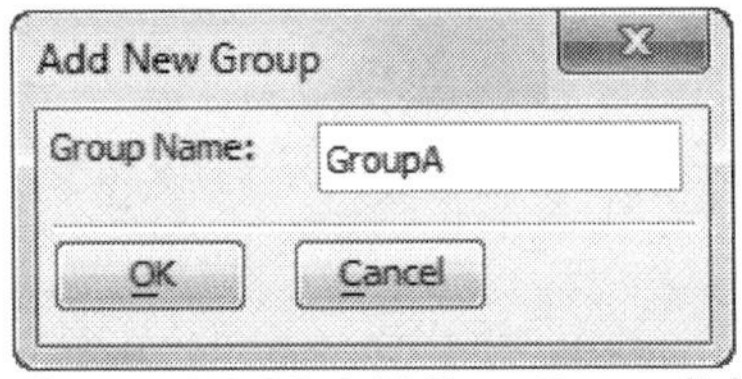

Figure 17-20 Add New Group dialog box

3. Create a group named GroupE.

Add Users To A Group

All users do not have to be a member of a group.

1. On the Users tab, click on user1.

   Check the Administrators and GroupE groups shown in Figure 17-21, then click the **APPLY** button.

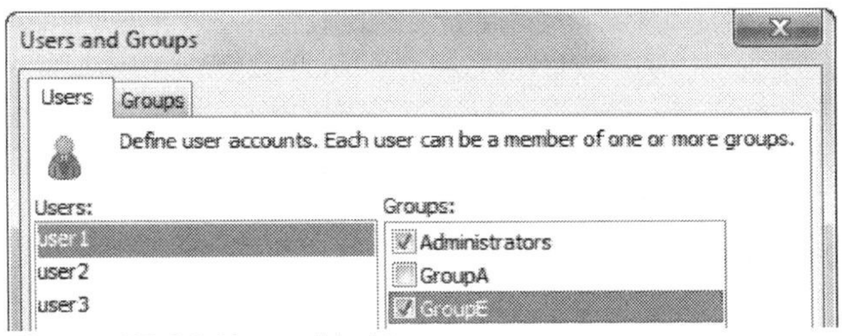

Figure 17-21 User added to groups

2. Add user2 to GroupA and GroupE.

3. On the Groups tab, click on each group to see which users are a member of the group, as shown in Figure 17-22.

   Click OK to close the dialog box.

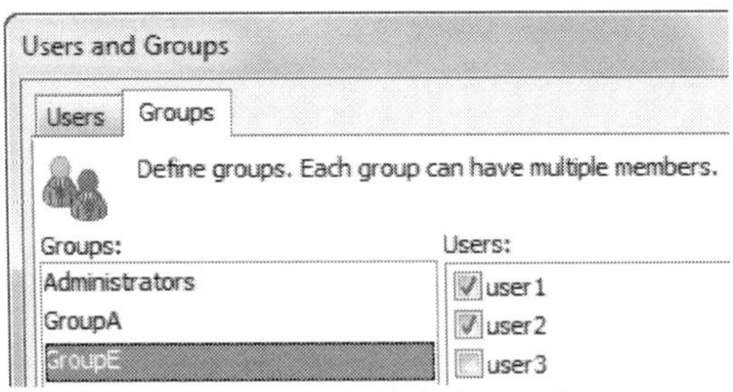

Figure 17-22 Groups and their members

Log In As A Different User

This option displays the message shown in Figure 17-23. Clicking Yes, displays the Password dialog box shown earlier in Figure 17-7.

Now, when you open the User Name drop-down list, the names of the users that have access to the database are displayed.

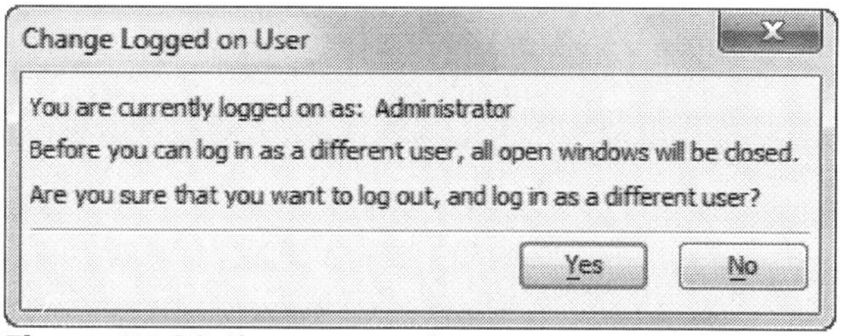

Figure 17-23 Change Logged on User dialog box

The user would select their name, type in their password and click the Login button. If you want, you can remove the master password from the a5beyond database, as well as the users and groups because they are not needed to complete any other exercises in this book.

Startup Form

This form is different from the other types of forms that you have created because it is not used to enter or view data. A startup form is automatically displayed when the database is opened. This form is often referred to as the **MAIN MENU**. This form contains options to open other forms, reports or objects that you want the user to have access to. The Startup form can be basic or as intricate as needed.

For example, the main menu form may have buttons for data entry forms, reports and importing data. Each of these buttons would open another form. For example, the Reports button opens a form that displays reports in drop-down lists by category, like invoice reports, customer reports and sales reps reports.

As you know, forms are based on a table or set. The main menu form does not need any data from a table. The best practice is to create a table with one field that does not have any data and base the main menu form on this table. Most of the time, startup forms are used to also hide the Control Panel.

Exercise 17.3: Create A Startup Form

None of the tables in the database are appropriate for a main menu startup form. In the first part of this exercise you will create a table that the main menu form will be based on. You will also create a main menu form that will display access to forms and reports that the user can select from to open.

Create The Table

1. Create a table named `MainMenu` with a field named `NoData` that has the character data type.

Create The Main Menu Form

Keep in mind that this form will not have all of the functionality that is need to be put into production, but it will give you an idea of what is needed.

1. Create a new blank form based on the Main Menu table. If you want, you can apply a style sheet to the form.

2. Change the following form properties, then save the form as `MainMenu`.
   Caption - `MAIN MENU`
   Menus View - aFormCustomMenu
   Toolbars View - aCustomFormToolbar

3. Add a Text control to the top of the form that displays the words `Main Menu`.

4. Add a Button control to the form below the text object. Select the following options on the Define Button dialog box.
   Label - `View Customers`
   Create an action script that opens the aCustomViewMenu form.

5. Add a Button control to the form across from the View Customers button. Select the following options.
   Label - `Run Date Range Report`
   Select the options to run the aXdialogRunReport script.

6. Add a Button control to the bottom of the form. Select the following options.
   Pre-defined Button option - Exit (on the File menu)
   Style - Picture followed by text
   Label - `Close Application`

7. Save the changes. The form should look similar to the one shown in Figure 17-24.

   Above the form, you should see the custom menu that you created.

   You can click on the buttons on the main menu form to make sure that they work.

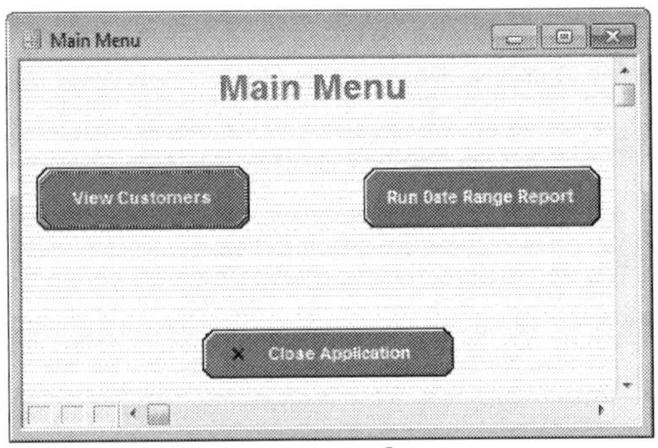

Figure 17-24 Main Menu form

Set Up The Startup Form And Hide The Control Panel

In the previous part of this exercise you created the startup main menu form. In this part of the exercise you will learn how to complete the following tasks:

- ☑ Add a hidden button to the main menu form that will let you view the Control Panel.
- ☑ Setup the main menu form to open when the database is first opened.
- ☑ Hide the Control Panel when the database is opened.

Add A Hidden Button To The Main Menu Form

This button will be used to allow you (the developer) to still have access to the Control Panel once it is hidden to keep the users from gaining access to it. This button has to be invisible and some place where users are not likely to click. The location of the hidden button will depend on the layout of your main menu form. When this button is clicked on, the Control Panel will be displayed. There is another way to gain access to the Control Panel when it is hidden on startup, which is covered in the next section.

1. Open the Main Menu form in Design mode, then add a button (make it small) to the form. In this exercise, I added it to the upper left corner of the form, across from the title. Who clicks there? <smile>. With decades of development experience, I know that many developers hide things in the lower right corner, so I avoid that section.

2. Select the following options, then click Next.
   Label - Delete the content in the field
   Select the Use Action Scripting option

3. Add a new action. Select the Control Panel category, then select the **CONTROL PANEL SHOW** action. Click OK, then click Finish.

4. Remove all of the formatting, borders, fill color etc from the button so that the button is not visible.

Another Way To Open A Hidden Control Panel

This work around is helpful if the main menu form does not have a hidden button or if you cannot remember where the button is. Do not select these options now.

1. Open another Alpha Five database that you have access to. If one does not exist, create a new database.

2. View ⇒ Settings ⇒ System ⇒ Preferences ⇒ Startup form.

   Change the **DISPLAY STARTUP FORM** Value to No, as shown at the bottom of Figure 17-25.

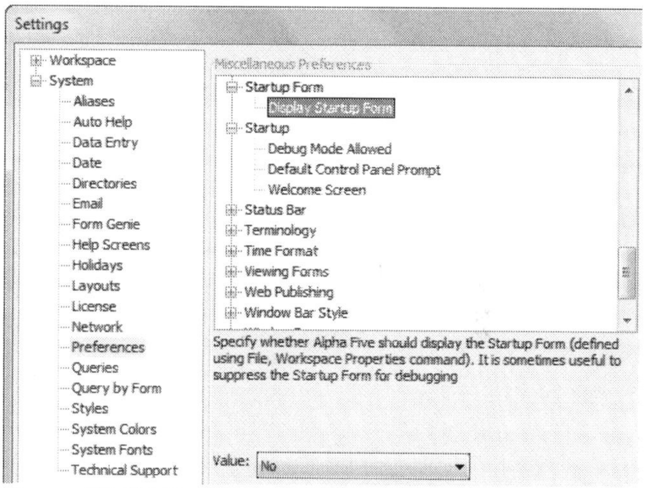

Figure 17-25 Display Startup Form option

3. Open the database that you cannot get into. File ⇒ Workspace/Database Properties ⇒ Startup tab. Clear the check mark for the When this Workspace/Database is opened and **HIDE THE CONTROL PANEL** options.

Set Up The Main Menu Form To Open When The Database Is Opened

1. View ⇒ Settings ⇒ System ⇒ Preferences ⇒ Startup form. Change the Display Startup Form Value to Yes.

2. File ⇒ Workspace/Database Properties ⇒ Startup tab.

3. Check the When this Workspace/Database is opened, open a Startup Form option, then select the Main Menu form.

   Check the Hide the Control Panel option shown in Figure 17-26, then click OK.

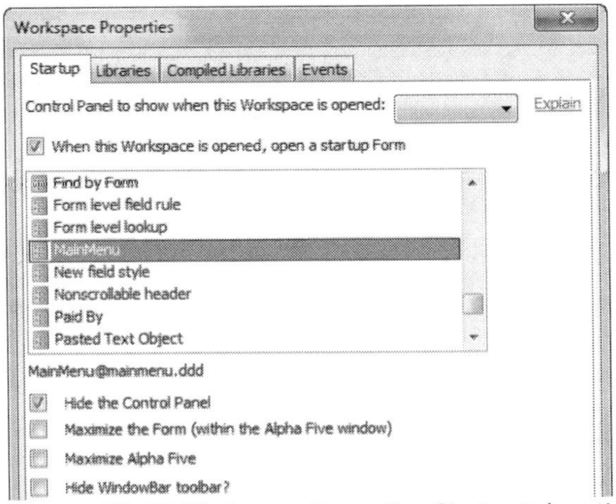

Figure 17-26 Workspace Properties Startup tab options

4. Close the database and reopen it. You should see the Main Menu form. The three buttons on the form will work. You should see the toolbars and menus that you created. The hidden button to display the Control Panel should work. You may want to disable the Main Menu form from opening to complete the rest of this book.

Leaving The Button To Display The Control Panel Visible

If you are a bit nervous about hiding the button to display the Control Panel, there is another option. You can display the button on the form and add a password to it. The steps below show you how to add a password to a button.

1. Open the properties dialog box for the hidden button on the main menu form.

2. On the Setup tab, check the **ENABLE PASSWORD** option, then click the Set Password button.

3. On the dialog box shown in Figure 17-27, type in a password in the New Password and Re-Enter New Password fields, then click OK.

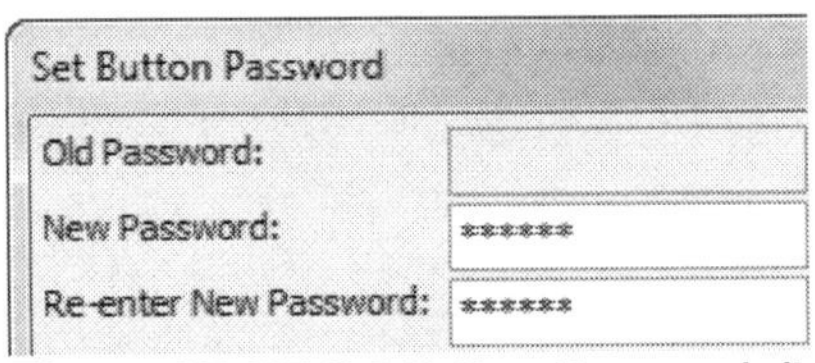

Figure 17-27 Set Button Password dialog box

4. If you want the button to display text, enter it in the Label field on the properties dialog box.

5. When the Main Menu form is viewed and you click on the button, you will see the dialog box shown in Figure 17-28.

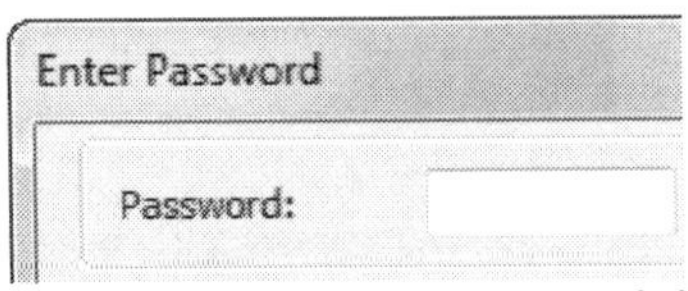

Figure 17-28 Enter Password dialog box

Create A Shortcut Icon

When you install software, there is usually an option to place a shortcut to the software on the desktop. Alpha Five provides this functionality.

Exercise 17.4: Use The Create Shortcut Genie

In this exercise you will create a shortcut for the A5Beyond application and place it on the desktop. This will allow the users to open the application without having to open Alpha Five first.

1. Control Panel ⇒ Tools ⇒ Create Shortcut.

2. In the Shortcut name field type `My A5 App`.

   Select the **ON DESKTOP** option shown in Figure 17-29, if it is not already selected.

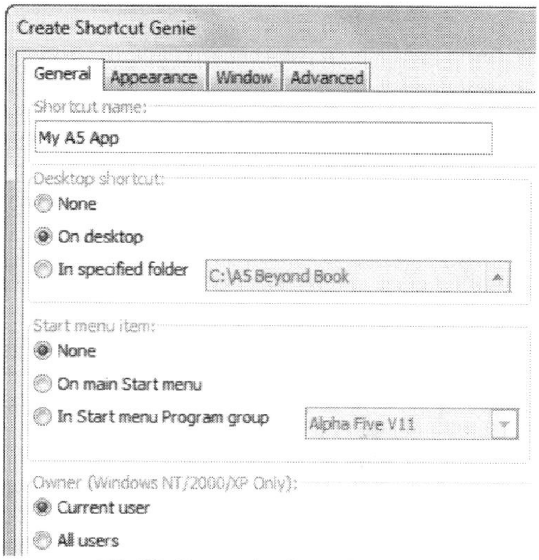

Figure 17-29 General tab options

Appearance Tab

The options shown in Figure 17-30 are used to customize the shortcut and what happens when the application is first opened. All of the options on this tab are optional.

Figure 17-30 Appearance tab options

The **TITLE OF MAIN ALPHA FIVE WINDOW** options are used to change what is displayed in the upper left corner of the Workspace.

The **SPLASH SCREEN** options are used to display a splash screen (in the form of a bitmap image) when Alpha Five is loading.

The **ICON** options are used to select a custom icon for the application.

1. Select the **USE CUSTOM TITLE** option, then type `My A5 Application` in the field next to the option.

2. Select the **CUSTOM BITMAP** Splash screen option, then select a bmp file. In this exercise, select the splash.bmp file. On your own, you can create a bmp file that also has text on it, if necessary. You should have the options shown above in Figure 17-30.

Window Tab

The options shown in Figure 17-31 are used to customize the size of the Alpha Five Workspace window, select if the minimize or maximize options are displayed and if the system menu is displayed.

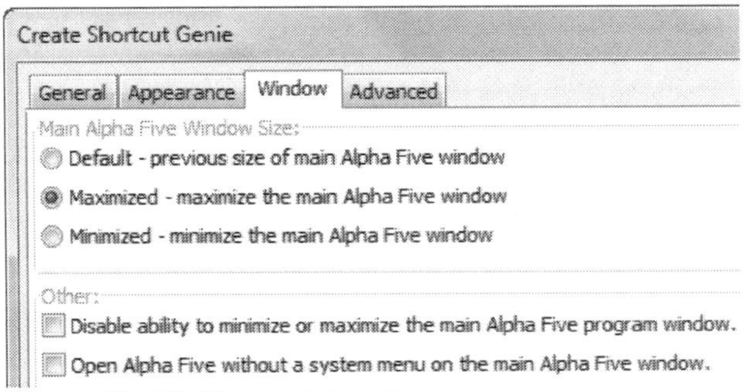

Figure 17-31 Window tab options

Advanced Tab

The tab shown in Figure 17-32 is used to create or paste in Xbasic code that needs to run when Alpha Five is first opened.

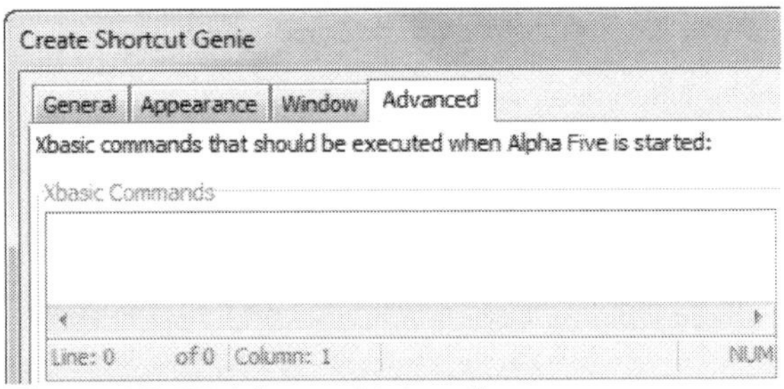

Figure 17-32 Advanced tab options

View The Shortcut

1. Click OK to close the Create Shortcut Genie. You will see a message saying that the shortcut was created. Click OK.

2. Close the database. On your desktop, you should see the icon shown in Figure 17-33.

Figure 17-33 Application shortcut icon

3. Double-click on the icon for the application. You will see the .bmp image file that you selected as the splash screen, appear. If you still have the main menu selected to open at startup, you will see it. Notice the text in the upper left corner of the workspace. It is what you entered on the Appearance tab in the Use custom title field.

INDEX

A

B

C

D

E

F

G

H

I

J

K

L

M

N

O

P

Q

R

S

T

U

V

W

X

Y

Z

59020883R00201

Made in the USA
Lexington, KY
21 December 2016